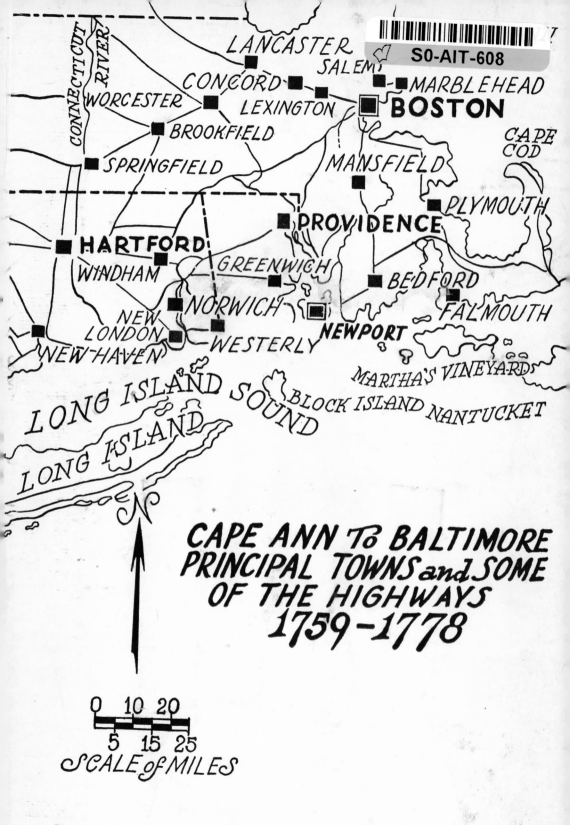

CAPE ANN To BALTIMORE
PRINCIPAL TOWNS and SOME
OF THE HIGHWAYS
1759–1778

0 10 20
5 15 25
SCALE of MILES

JOHN DRAPER

GEORGE WASHINGTON

Date Due

Demco 293-5

BOOKS BY DOUGLAS SOUTHALL FREEMAN

George Washington
Lee's Lieutenants
The South to Posterity
R. E. Lee

Charles Scribner's Sons

GEORGE WASHINGTON

A BIOGRAPHY

By

Douglas Southall Freeman

VOLUME THREE

PLANTER AND PATRIOT

NEW YORK
CHARLES SCRIBNER'S SONS
1951

WASHINGTON AT 45, IN THE DARKEST DAYS OF THE REVOLUTION
After a miniature by Charles Willson Peale, perhaps made at Valley Forge in the Winter of 1777–78.
(Courtesy of the Mount Vernon Ladies' Association)

CONTENTS

CHAPTER | PAGE

I. HAPPY RETURN TO A "RUN-DOWN" PLANTATION — 1

II. AN ENLARGED MOUNT VERNON MUST GROW THE BEST — 19

III. THE CARDS ARE STACKED AGAINST THE PLANTER — 42

IV. CHANGE AND DEBT AT MOUNT VERNON — 54

V. BUILDING ON THE COMMONPLACE — 71

VI. SPECULATIVE LIFE BECOMES COMPLICATED — 87

VII. THE MASTER OF MOUNT VERNON MISCALCULATES — 107

VIII. THE STAMP ACT STIRS A STUDY OF RIGHTS — 125

IX. SCANDAL IN THE RULING CLASS MARS REPEAL — 152

X. A LAND HUNTER WRITES A GRIM WORD — 179

XI. ASSOCIATION AGAINST TAXES AND DEBT — 212

XII. TRAINING SCHOOL ON THE POTOMAC — 228

XIII. THE COLONEL GETS NEW HOLDINGS IN THE WEST — 264

XIV. DEATH AND BOUNTY LANDS MAY CLEAR DEBT — 305

XV. "AN INNATE SPIRIT OF FREEDOM" — 339

XVI. A DELEGATE GLIMPSES A CONTINENT — 373

XVII. PREPARATION FOR A BRIEF ABSENCE IF . . . — 394

v

XVIII. "NOT THINK MYSELF EQUAL TO THE COMMAND" 418

  XIX. FIRST TRAIN AN ARMY AND BOTTLE A FOE   460

   XX. PREPARATION DISCLOSES A SHORTAGE   483

  XXI. BALANCE OF OFFENSIVE AND DEFENSIVE   510

 XXII. DECEMBER BRINGS A DARK CRISIS   542

APPENDICES

III–1 THE MOUNT VERNON COMMUNITY IN 1759   587

III–2 WASHINGTON'S "BURGESS ROUTE"   590

III–3 ORIGINAL FORM OF HENRY'S RESOLUTIONS
       ON STAMP ACT   592

III–4 MARY WASHINGTON'S MOVE TO
       FREDERICKSBURG   595

III–5 MAPS AND ELEVATIONS OF THE BOSTON
       AREA (1775–76)   599

ILLUSTRATIONS

Miniature of Washington   *Frontispiece*

BETWEEN PAGES

George Washington Becomes a Vestryman   137 and 138

Washington's Account with His Mother   137 and 138

Martha Washington—Without a Head-dress   263 and 264

John Parke Custis Knew One Art Thoroughly   263 and 264

The Poll that Started Washington on His Way   373 and 374

A Mount Vernon Guest Who Later Plagued His Host   373 and 374

"George Washington Esq: Was Unanimously Elected"   435 and 436

Birth Certificate of the United States Army   435 and 436

"Old Put"—How Good Would He Be in New Campaigns?   473 and 474

Is Gates's Face that of an Ambitious Rival?   473 and 474

Artemas Ward Who Might Have Had Washington's Task   495 and 496

John Sullivan Whose Zeal Could Not Win Good Luck   495 and 496

A Strange Cryptogram that Smelled of Treason   541 and 542

Doctor Church's Messenger Has Become Anxious   541 and 542

MAPS

Cape Ann to Baltimore—Principal Towns and Some of the
     Highways, 1759–1778   *Cover lining*

PAGE

Region of the "Bounty Land of 1754"   259

Outline Sketch of the Boston Area, 1775–76   479

The Quadrilateral of the Northern Campaigns of 1775–76   531

The Mount Vernon Neighborhood in 1759   589

Washington's "Burgess Route"   591

INTRODUCTION

As HE PLANS and labors, rides and writes, the George Washington portrayed in the first fifteen chapters of this volume appears to be essentially the man who hurried home from Fort DuQuesne at the end of 1758. Because of his marriage to a rich widow whose first husband died intestate, his fortune is ample. He still is resolved to hold the good opinion of Virginians and to keep the reputation he has won, but his ambition no longer soars. The soldier has become a planter. Instead of continuing to seek a royal military commission, he will be content to live as a gentleman and to raise the finest tobacco in the Potomac Valley. When he fails in this, on soil unsuited to that staple, he turns to wheat growing and tries to enlarge his profit by operating mills and by marketing his own brand of flour.

Most of the customary honors of a self-esteeming rural society come to him. On "court days," if he is not too busy with guests or crops, he sits as one of the bench of justices; the Sabbath usually finds him in church, as vestryman and then as warden; at intervals—some of them too short for his convenience and some too long for his wife's full pleasure—he journeys with her to Williamsburg, the colonial capital, where he serves as a Burgess. Himself unready in debate, he is politely attentive and free from "the disease of not listening, the malady of not marking." With the trained observation of an "old soldier," he soon perceives that deferential siege tactics are more effective than artifice or clamorous assault on the dignity of the law's defenders. He learns much by fifteen years of service in the General Assembly.

His undramatic life during 1759–73 differed from that of other planters of like possession in two respects only. He had in the first place the zeal of his father's generation for the acquisition of western lands, and he enjoyed a special advantage in seeking them, because of his rights under a Virginia proclamation of 1754, for the encouragement of volunteers, and under a like royal document of 1763 that rewarded veterans. Washington devoted weeks to validating his claims, to choosing fat meadows, and to having every acre surveyed and patented. He practiced diligently what he earnestly preached to his improvident neighbor, John Posey—that "the greatest estates . . . were made . . . by taking up and purchasing at very low rates the rich back lands." As a result, the real estate of Washington increased largely while the plantations of some of his neighbors shrank in size through division and waned in value as fields were worn out. Washington, in the second place, went far beyond the obligation most gentlemen of station discharged in counselling their ignorant tenants and in helping to execute the wills of their dead friends. Washington did this so admirably that he was overwhelmed. "I can solemnly declare to you," he wrote an ailing associate, in some confusion of phrase, "that for this year or two past, there has been scarce a moment that I can properly call my own: For what with my own business, my present wards, my mother's . . . Colonel Colville's, Mrs. Savage's, Colonel Fairfax's, Colonel Mercer's . . . and the little assistance I have undertaken to give in the management of my brother's Augustine's affairs . . . keeps me, together with the share I take in public affairs, constantly engaged in writing letters, settling accounts, and negotiating one piece of business or another in behalf of one or other of these concerns, by which means I have been deprived of every kind of enjoyment, and had almost fully resolved to engage in no fresh matter till I had entirely wound up the old." After saying this, he characteristically promised, should other recourse fail, that he would qualify as guardian for his correspondent's son.

This was in January, 1775, at a time of rapid rise in the heat of the quarrel with England which Washington had watched from the first with a troubled but not with a doubtful mind. He had gone to Philadelphia the previous September as an inconspicuous member of the Virginia delegation to the First Continental Congress, and in courteous silence he had heard all the arguments for united petition and remonstrance as loyal subjects. No committee assignment had been given him in the Congress. When its Journal was printed, his name appeared only in the roster of members and in the credentials of the representatives of the Old Dominion. He probably had learned more by listening than some of his colleagues had by declaiming and he had returned to Mount Vernon confirmed in his opinion of the course the Colonies should follow unflinchingly.

There had been no emotional conflict in shaping that opinion. He had on occasion the counsel of his neighbor George Mason of Gunston

Hall, one of the wisest of American political philosophers, and on his own account he possessed what he termed an "innate spirit of freedom." He did not believe that separation from England was desirable or would be necessary, but he maintained, without argument or misgiving, that if English Colonials were denied their political inheritance, they should take up arms to defend it. This, he said, should be the last resort, but a resort it might be. The right to defend right could not be wrong. In this convinced, realistic spirit he journeyed to the little town of Richmond during the third week of March, 1775, to attend a convention that had been called because the royal Governor refused to issue a proclamation for a meeting of the General Assembly. The day this convention elected him one of the Delegates to a second Congress in Philadelphia, the ears of members were ringing with the echo of Patrick Henry's thunderous warning, "we must fight." Washington heard, but in his meagre little Diary, he did not mention the speech, nor did he refer to it when he answered a letter Meriwether Smith, one of the members of the convention, had delivered him from his brother "Jack" who was organizing a volunteer Company. "I have promised," the former Colonel wrote John Augustine, "to review the Independent Company of Richmond [County] sometime this summer, they having made me a tender of the command of it; at the same time I could review yours and shall very cheerfully accept the honor of commanding it, if occasion requires it to be drawn out, as it is my full intention to devote my life and fortune in the cause we are engaged in, if need be . . ."

George Washington disclosed completely his resolution when he employed awkwardly that casual relative clause to announce what he intended to do—as if the avowal of it was a superfluous statement of something that was to be taken for granted. Should not the surviving senior officer of Virginia troops in the French and Indian War be ready, as a matter of course, to resume command of his Colony's forces if this were asked of him in event the young men had to take the field?

Less than three months later, some of the New England Delegates to the Continental Congress realized that they stood less in danger of the gallows from defeat in the field than from dissolution in the camp. They concluded that if the troops besieging Boston were to be held together, a commanding General should be sent there to act in the name of the United Colonies. Among others whom the Delegates considered as a possible choice was the tall planter of Mount Vernon who by that time was wearing a military uniform in his daily attendance on the Congress. What qualifications had he? The aim has been to answer that question on page 443ff of this volume as if the inquiry had been put to some member of the Virginia delegation who knew Washington and tried to judge the man honestly, with no foreshadow of events and no anticipation of the judgment of posterity. The conclusion of such a companion most certainly would have been undramatic and scarcely convincing—that Washington had some experience, both as a soldier and as a man of affairs and that his character was above challenge. More than this could not have been said. In comparison with some of the officers already in the service of the Eastern States, his advantage appeared to be that of availability. He personified the continental union and assistance needed to convince the ill-organized troops in front of Boston that they would not be left alone to perish when the British were ready to attack. Washington himself would have acquiesced in the most restrained judgment passed on him. He neither desired nor sought a position he considered out of scale to his ability. His experience was far better suited, he thought, to the direction of the Virginia forces. More personally, he told Patrick Henry, with tears in his eyes, "From the day I enter upon the command of the American Armies, I date my fall, and the ruin of my reputation."

Washington's election as Commander-in-Chief was on June 15, 1775. As soon as he became the American leader, members of Congress praised him more warmly. This was natural. They had selected him and they wished to rally the continent with the assurance that he had the qualifications of a victor. Besides, no General ever appears quite so full of promise as when he first puts on his new insignia of rank. Washington gained consequently in prestige between the time he received his commission and the time he opened his headquarters at Cambridge, Massachusetts, on the 3rd of July; but there was nothing in his equipment or in his known abilities to justify anyone in forecasting the quick establishment of his fame at a level from which it declined little at any time during the war.

If the first great surprise offered in his life was the winning of distinction by the time he was 22 years of age, the second surprise is represented by this language in an address the lawmakers of the Bay Colony presented him at the end of the siege of Boston: ". . . may future generations, in the peaceful enjoyment of that freedom, the exercise of which your sword shall have established, raise the richest and most lasting monuments to the name of Washington." Although this was written in an age of extravagant compliment, it was approved by legislators who had observed Washington closely for more than eight months and had marvelled that he had kept the frail vehicle of revolution from collapse. The authors of the encomium were, moreover, the grandsons of plain-spoken Puritans and they had not departed so far from their uprearing that they would flatter a soldier when their own lives and property might depend on his keeping his soul from vanity and his acts from folly. Still again, if it has to be remembered that nearness mars measurement, it likewise is true that men who have plodded after their captain on a rough new trail are to be credited, usually, with a reasonable knowledge of him and with a remembrance of the bogs and stony passages he had to cross.

Whether or not the circumstances then justified the judgment of the grateful Bay Colony, the fact is indisputable: After less than a year's military service, the retired Virginia Colonel was credited with the possession of varied abilities of which there is little or no trace in the records of his career prior to 1775. It would be the grossest distortion of the evidence to portray him as a man whose career had been one of ordered and adequate preparation for the part he was to play. The best of his previous performance never had excelled the day-by-day superiority of leadership to which New Englanders testified. Unless they were wholly mistaken, either the fire of Washington's devotion to a cause quickly recast his metal in a larger mold, or else the small neighborly acts he performed at Mount Vernon were spiritual exercises that gave him the patience, the resolution and the understanding needed to supplement his known diligence and integrity in the shining discharge of complicated duties. If the second of these theories of the swift, incredible enlargement of the man be challenged as an oversimplification of a mystery, it may be asked whether history has not vindicated in Washington the doctrine that "whosoever would be first among you, shall be the servant of all."

Once the transformation of the quiet Virginia planter into the revered continental commander is admitted to be beyond documentary explanation, the next essential is to recall that Washington shared the belief that the campaign of 1775 around Boston would end hostilities. The severity or the moderation of the settlement would be determined by relative advantage when winter halted field operations. With so short a war in prospect, there was no need to formulate a strategical plan that covered anything beyond bottling the enemy in Boston and making a bid for the adherence of Canada to the revolutionary cause. After King George's speech of Oct. 27, 1775, was received in America at the beginning of 1776, the prospect of a long and vigorously prosecuted war called for a definite strategical policy. British seapower and the feebleness of America's unorganized resources forced Washington to make this a consistent, though active defensive. No matter how cruelly he was prodded by politicians or goaded by rash subordinates, he could not afford to risk an engagement with the whole of the British army elsewhere than in a strong position of a sort he was not apt to occupy in circumstances that would tempt the enemy to assail him. Through the arduous, disillusioning period from June, 1775, to May, 1778, Washington had to adhere to the methods Nathanael Greene defined in March, 1777, when he said: "General Howe has invariably pursued the maxims of an invader, this campaign, endeavoring to bring us to a general engagement and avoid skirmishing. General Washington, as every defender ought, has followed directly the contrary conduct by endeavoring to skirmish with the enemy at all times and avoid a general engagement."

When Washington willingly or of necessity met the British, he had to employ simple strategical principles because he knew no other and did not command officers sufficiently trained to execute an elaborate plan had he been equipped to formulate it. The campaign against Boston was one of communications and later of a surprise lodgment on Dorchester Neck in rough application of the French siege device, half tactical and half strategical, of opening new parallels. Trenton and Princeton were surprise operations of a different character. Long Island (Brooklyn Heights) and Brandywine were examples of carelessness in guarding against flank movements. Washington's one attempt at a difficult strategic combination, the simultaneous convergence of columns on Germantown, was not a complete success.

The defensive strategy of Washington's few active campaigns in the Revolution had an interesting relation to his intelligence service. The memory of Braddock's defeat and his own disaster on Long Island in

August, 1776, kept the American commander daily conscious of the danger of unanticipated attack. Successful continuance of his defensive with untrained troops depended in part on early and accurate information of the enemy's movements. These were two of the reasons Washington devoted much time to the upbuilding of a sound intelligence system, and he succeeded to an extent that might have shamed some of his remote successors in command of the American Army. The most economical of Generals, he repeatedly told his subordinates to spare no expense in procuring and rewarding good spies. A reading of the plan of 1777 for espionage in New York, as published in Appendix 2 of Volume IV, may surprise some by its bold thoroughness. Counterespionage was not neglected. In at least one instance, Washington had some puzzling experiences with a double spy.

Maintenance of a defensive and the use of uninvolved strategy limits the place, if not the importance, of active combat in the story of Washington's years as revolutionary commander. This does not mean that his maneuvers, his clashes with the enemy, and the larger military developments of the Revolution lacked exciting incident or high climax. On the contrary, something of a dramatic pattern was developed: an express was forever bringing Washington news, usually bad—that Sullivan's left had been turned on the Jamaica Road, that Howe had landed at Throg's Point, that Fort Lee was about to fall to the troops who had captured Fort Washington, that the enemy had reached the Raritan and was pressing toward the Delaware, that something had happened to Charles Lee, that Ticonderoga had been evacuated mysteriously, that dust was rising beyond Birmingham Meeting House near the Brandywine, or that the men who had pushed gallantly forward across the buckwheat fields of Germantown were running to the rear in wild panic. Occasionally, too, the burdened Commander-in-Chief had experiences that made even his steady pulse beat fast and his lustreless eyes light up: Howe had abandoned the effort to trap him and had marched ingloriously from White Plains; the "Durham" boats were across the Delaware in spite of the ice; a few days later, as the Army was closing on Princeton, the wintry sun was rising symbolically. A year and more after that amazing campaign, there was compensation for much anguish of soul in the incident with which Volume IV closes, the arrival of Simeon Deane at headquarters on the 30th of

April, 1778, and his confidential disclosure to Washington of news he was bringing to Congress in one of the five packets entrusted to him by the American commissioners in Paris.

Mistakes and defeat had varied elements of drama and many a lesson for Washington and for those who received from his hands the steward-ship of the nation's safety. The timing of Arnold's march on Quebec in 1775 was dangerously optimistic in its failure to allow for contin-gencies, such as the worthlessness of the hastily constructed batteaux. Again, Washington misread the signs of the enemy's movements imme-diately in advance of the landing on Long Island in August, 1776, though he soon had troops enough around Brooklyn to cover the ex-posed left flank had the forces been employed prudently. During the early days of November that same year, Washington's military judgment was that of a mind in eclipse, and he was the victim of an indecision he could not shake off. If circumstances had been even a little more difficult during December he might have completed with the fatal word the unfinished proverb that heads Chapter IX of Volume IV— "He Who Hesitates Is . . ." After the Miracle of the Delaware the next month, Washington made no major mistake until the Battle of the Brandywine. That day, he failed for once to interpret correctly his intelligence reports, and narrowly escaped calamity. In the maneu-vers that followed on the Schuylkill, his concern for his base at Reading made it quite easy for Howe and Cornwallis to outwit him and, with no further loss, to enter Philadelphia. One phase of the British feint on the Schuylkill at that time has large military interest because it illustrates how, sometimes, a small defect in equipment—in this in-stance the flap of a cartridge box—may cause disaster or rob an army of opportunity.

As it was that torrential September day, when all the ammunition in the cartridge boxes was ruined, so it nearly always was throughout the war. Soon after the Generals and their staffs reached the Boston lines in 1775, Charles Lee barked: "We found everything exactly the reverse of what had been represented. We were assured at Philadel-phia that the Army was stocked with engineers. We found not one. We were assured that we should find an expert train of artillery. We have not a single gunner—and so on." For weeks the shortage of powder was so great that Washington had to deny every proposal for attack—and had to pray that the British would not assault his lines till his stock of explosive was replenished. That autumn and winter, when the term of many of the troops expired, Washington had to direct that where the private firelocks brought by the men to the camp were serviceable, they should be taken and paid for: without these pieces, he could not arm his new recruits.

On these and a hundred other subjects, Washington's official correspondence was burdensome even after he had a staff large enough to draft most of his letters. His sword might rust, but his pen was never dry. Because the continental government had no executive, Washington had to communicate with the President of Congress, with several of its committees, with influential members, and with the Board of War. He did this with much of his old awkwardness of expression but in the fullest understanding of the mind of the lawmaker. His tact and his consideration for the individual Delegates were unfailing. Instinctive courtesy and deep-ribbed respect for authority made him equally deferential—on occasion too much so—in his dealings with Governors and other public men in the States.

Had all these exactions and perplexities, the daily burdens and the passing annoyances been piled together at their worst and weightiest, they would not have been nearly so back-breaking as the load represented at every stage and stumble of the Revolution by Washington's two supreme administrative tasks. These were the recruitment of the Army and the maintenance of a competent corps of officers.

Early in the war, the calls for volunteers almost exhausted the supply of men who would sign for a long term of service through love of country or of adventure. The only possible means of procuring troops thereafter was by bounty or by draft. Congress could offer the bounty; it could not institute a draft. That was a prerogative of the States, and of the States only. Delegates generally were willing to approve requisitions for men, but never would a majority of the members of Congress officially ask the States to put even the young, able-bodied youth into the ranks for more than a year. Usually there was political maneuver, bargaining and compromise over the term of service: One Delegate would inquire, Could not the call be delayed until the late winter? Another would ask, Might not the soldiers be released at the beginning of December so that they could get home by Christmas? A third member would insist that a draft for nine months was adequate.

In answer to all questions and objections, Washington maintained that the one guarantee of victory was the creation of an Army enlisted for the entire war, in numbers twice the estimated effective strength of any force the British might employ in America—a margin of superiority required, Washington said, to compensate for the inexperience and poor equipment of the Continentals. When he found that the enlistment of any considerable number for the duration of hostilities was altogether beyond attainment, he proposed that Congress appeal to the States to make an annual draft in October and to send forward the men in January, so that recruits could be trained before open campaigning began. Among them would be some who learned to like a soldier's life and might agree later, in consideration of a liberal bounty, to enlist for the war. The others would remain with the Army until replaced by a new draft.

Reluctantly, almost sullenly, Congress accepted the principle Washington laid down, but a considerable number, if not actually more than half the members, held that the continental Army need not be large because it could be augmented in times of emergency by militia who could return home and raise their crops or tend their sheep and their bullocks when the danger was past. The success of the Minute Men of Massachusetts during the first stages of the Revolution was responsible, in large part, for this reliance on militia; the rally to Washington's call in March, 1776, for the operations on Dorchester Neck, was held to be a confirmation of faith in citizen soldiers. Washington's experience after the Battle of Long Island should have induced legislators to renounce their mistaken faith in temporary, untrained troops, but neither the General's warnings nor his complaints of the wastefulness and excessive cost of militia quite destroyed the reliance of Delegates on that reenforcement of the Army.

Congress had, in addition, a body of Delegates who so vastly esteemed the rights of their constituents that they insisted on putting an option into the call for troops. If a State preferred some other method to a draft, what difference did it make to the Continent so long as the recruits were forthcoming? Such was the argument. The result was that State bounties and schemes of substitution were proposed in some of the Assemblies and were debated for days. If the favored plan subsequently failed, as it usually did, the State simply did not meet its quota. It might, indeed, dispute the requisition and insist that artificers, wagon drivers and armorers be counted among the men it furnished. Recruitment of State Regiments was presented as another reason why the thinning ranks of the continental Army could not be filled. Again, though Congress asked for the able-bodied only, it did not provide for the physical examination of the draft. Some Counties therefore sent old men, idle free Negroes, puny fellows and young, weak boys. In Washington's own State, to his wrath and dismay, recruiting officers for continental Light Horse subsequently outdid the worst subterfuge: convict servants were enlisted in that part of the Army from which it was easiest to desert with a horse and accoutrements for which the British would pay in shining, hard money.

Difficult as it was to get recruits, good or bad, for long service or for short, Washington found before the end of 1775 that it was flatly impossible to keep the greater part of his soldiers a single day beyond the time they had contracted to serve. He probably had suffered no more disillusioning experience in his life than that described in the closing chapter of Volume III when hundreds of men whose liberty was at stake calmly stuffed their packs, turned in their small arms, and started home on the 31st of December, 1775, without so much as a glance at the enemy who was plainly visible and almost within cannon shot on Bunker Hill and Boston Neck.

That dreadful day of the death of the first continental Army was repeated in December, 1776, when a bold stir by a liberating foe might have brought the Revolution to collapse and its leaders to the noose. Figures are difficult to collect on so precise a point, but there probably is small risk in saying that at no time during the period surveyed in these pages could Washington count on more than 8000 men for longer than the six months immediately ahead. Again and again, it seemed that Gen. Sir William Howe was pursuing the course of economy in not spending the King's guineas and grenadiers in destroying the feeble American Army. It was being demolished for him by the indifference of the soldiers, the timidity of Congress and the selfish refusal of the States to supply men enough to win battles. The haunting dread of Washington's days and the nightmare of his uneasy sleep was the dissolution of his forces at a time when the British would be in position to seize the coastal cities, to cut off New England by forcing the line of the Hudson, and then to crush the Revolution. Had all the perplexing

anxieties of supply and transport been resolved, the frightful uncertainty of the Army's existence would have made the life of Washington
wretched.

Precisely that could have been said of his endless difficulty in creating a qualified command. As soon as he handed Israel Putnam a commission as Major General, on arrival in Cambridge, he found unconcealed dissatisfaction over the seniority Congress had established when
it elected the general officers. Artemas Ward was suspected of resenting
the failure of Congress to name him Commander-in-Chief; John
Thomas had been subordinated painfully; Joseph Spencer counte-
nanced if he did not inspire a protest against being ranked below Putnam; another Brigadier, Seth Pomeroy, simply went home and had
nothing further to do with the Army or its Commander-in-Chief.
Colonels often were guilty of sulking or back-biting; and if field
officers were not contending for seniority, Captains and Lieutenants
were disputing who ranked whom. So frequent was this that Washington developed a regular procedure for dealing with it. When General
Orders announced the appointment of a board on the "arrangement"
of a Regiment, this was synonymous with the purpose implied in the
term sometimes used, a board "to settle the rank" of officers. From
the decision of such a tribunal, appeal might be made to Congress, but
in most instances, willingly or otherwise, holders of commissions accepted the verdict that made this Captain, not that one, the man who
was to act as Major when the junior field officer was sick or absent.
Quite often, these time-consuming disputes seemed the senseless assertion of a principle of "honor" that did not deserve the name; but Washington had to be patient and not unsympathetic in dealing with these
officers, because he, when young, had ridden all the way from Virginia
to Boston and back again in the winter of 1755–56 to establish his own
seniority to Captain Dagworthy. This did not make less irksome the
task of determining the facts and then of reconciling those officers who
desired not justice but preference.

Seniority was not often in dispute, after the first weeks at Boston,
among the senior Generals whom Washington had to vest with large
responsibility. A vehement, contentious Brigadier named Benedict
Arnold was perpetually dissatisfied with his rank and his treatment at
the hands of his senior in the Northern Department; during the winter
of 1777–78 an inexcusable controversy among the Virginia Brigadiers

ended in bitterness, if not in hate. This was a scandal that probably irritated and humiliated the Commander-in-Chief more than ever he admitted.

Most of the troubles Washington encountered in his efforts to develop competent, cooperative command had their origin in the peculiarities of certain of his subordinates. Had it been possible at the time to view them with detachment, these men would have stirred both admiration and amusement, for some were as devoted as others were diverting. When Washington was dealing with their alleged grievances and affronts, in the dangerous uncertainties of war, he could not smile at the foibles of one and the blusterous evasions of another, though he daily showed his gratitude to the able, the diligent and the dependable. Such as these men were, he had to employ them, and had to make the best of any talents they possessed, until death or courtmartial or resignation disposed of them.

A stranger company never fought for a common cause. All the characters in the novels of Fielding and of Sterne did not present more contrasts than were written on the faces of the men whom the Commander-in-Chief would summon to a council of war. Putnam had reputation as a fighter and, for a time, seemed to Washington to be a good executive officer, but in the course of a single year he showed himself more intent on preserving the laurels he had won than in winning more. Nothing could have added a touch to his self-revelation in the Brooklyn defences, during the Battle of Long Island, when he stalked heavily up and down and repeated the command that had brought him fame at Bunker Hill, "Don't fire, boys, until you can see the whites of their eyes." He was already looking backward when Washington took command. David Wooster, likewise, was at the reminiscent age of command; Artemas Ward, militarily "correct" in every act, showed himself reserved and uncommunicative and, it was said, never doubted that the Almighty was partial to New England; Joseph Spencer's philosophy appeared to be, the less a man did, the less he would be called upon to do; William Heath's taste was for the pomp and routine of command; John Sullivan had energy and the heart of a soldier, but was so avid of praise, so anxious to have the good opinion of his comrades, that he was disposed to be all things to all men; Horatio Gates, an old associate of Washington's, was well schooled in army practices and useful in many ways, though the sort of man who creates, somehow, a coterie of his own and, without involving himself, makes partisans of his followers. Philip Schuyler possessed vastly larger wealth than most of the American officers, and had so much wider a knowledge of affairs that he was proud, impatient of opposition and quick to take offense, at the same time that he had a soundness of judgment which won for him the hearty respect of Washington, whom he admired, understood and supported.

Most of these men were in front of Boston when Washington assumed command. Still others were to receive commission as general officers between the summer of 1776 and the spring of 1778. Adam Stephen was to reappear with his old fondness for the bottle and an even stronger penchant for unannounced adventures he always proclaimed complete successes. Lord Stirling was to prove intelligent, friendly and courageous and, at the same time, never quite capable of finished military performance. A Pennsylvanian whom Washington did not come to know until the spring of 1777, Anthony Wayne by name, disclosed some captivating social qualities and much restless energy. Alexander McDougall, bringing troops from the Hudson to the main Army in September, 1777, proved to be an observant, intelligent Scot, of diversified experience, an officer whose usefulness was impaired to a slight degree only by ill health and long-winded correspondence. Benedict Arnold, in spite of his quarrelsomeness, had earned respect as a fighter by the time he received an incapacitating wound in the Saratoga campaign.

After the start of the Quebec expedition, Arnold did not have field command under Washington during the period covered by Volume IV. Gates and Schuyler usually were on detached service upstate in New York. The three general officers closest to Washington were Charles Lee, Nathanael Greene and Henry Knox, a most remarkable trio. Had Washington been free to choose his intimates on the basis of kindred habits and interests, it is not likely he would have included Charles Lee. Even as it was, after a brief time together in quarters at Cambridge, the two separated and seldom afterward resided under the same roof. Lee, son of a British army officer, was one year older than Washington and, like his chief, had served in the French and Indian War. After the disbanding of his Regiment, he had become a military wanderer, what now would be termed a soldier of fortune, and he had contrived to pick up odd acquaintances and strange theories. He pro-

fessed to love dogs more than men; his thin figure seemed to set off all
the more conspicuously his enormous nose. Untidy in dress, he was
loose and obscene of speech and was possessed of incredible self-impor-
tance. What was much more unusual, he had the ability to make
others believe he was as great a man as he proclaimed himself to be.
He knew, or pretended to know, everyone of exalted rank in the British
Army, and he probably would not have admitted there was a single
aspect of arms, weapons, tactics or strategy he had not mastered. In
their unconcealed and unpretending ignorance of many of these subjects, American officers, including the modest Commander-in-Chief,
listened deferentially to Lee; but it was not long before Washington
found him inconstant or, as the Virginian put it, "fickle." Washington
continued to avail himself of Lee's knowledge, but in the whole of his
biography to the date of the "accident" to Lee in December, 1776,
Washington presented nothing more fascinating than his attitude
toward his unpredictable senior lieutenant. Along with the candor of
a comrade, who credited a brother-officer with absolute good faith,
Washington habitually displayed a certain wariness. The drama of this
strange, suspicious confidence was heightened daily in the late autumn
of 1776 until it came to the strange climax described in Chapter X of
Volume IV.

Nathanael Greene was one of the most interesting personalities in
Washington's revolutionary council because of a question that arises
in almost every war: To what extent does the military "right arm" of
a Commander-in-Chief control the brain of the man formally responsible for the conduct of operations? As first observed in these pages,
Greene is a continental Brigadier from Rhode Island, 32 years of age,
well read and vigorous and hampered only by a stiff knee that made
him walk with a hobble and display a certain sensitiveness. A little
more than a year after Greene was introduced to his new commander,
those who could not quite bring themselves to blame Washington for
the disasters of November, 1776, were saying that Greene's bad counsel
and dominating influence over "the General" had carried the Army
to the abyss. The reality was not so much that Greene urged him
to do the wrong thing as it was that the Commander-in-Chief could
not come to any firm decision; but fork-tongued jealousy did not
withhold its sting. Greene received credit or criticism for perhaps a
larger part than he actually had in Washington's planning, and he

sometimes aggravated suspicions by his readiness to pass quick judgment as if he knew it would prevail. An interesting man he was, of active and courageous mind, destined to be engulfed later in a fog not unlike that which confused Washington in the autumn of the second year of the war.

Henry Knox still was under 25 years of age when Washington met him in July, 1775, on the road between Cambridge and Roxbury. The business of selling books in Boston had given the young native an opportunity of tasting his own wares, and as he read more and more of military matters, he began to practice his precepts as Lieutenant in a proudly labelled "Grenadier Corps." He manifestly had brains as well as bulk, and ability to lead men as readily as he could shout commands in a voice audible above the rumble of artillery wheels. Washington observed him favorably from the first. Himself never disposed to boast, the General in a famous letter of February, 1778, begged "leave to assume the privilege of being a tolerable judge" of the heart of a man, and he soon felt sure that Knox had qualifications of head as well as of heart. Advancement was swift. By the time Simeon Deane was ushered into Washington's quarters at Valley Forge to announce a new stage of the Revolution, Henry Knox was approaching his twenty-eighth birthday and might with absolute justice have received this commendation: he was the one officer of station in the entire Army whose organization and handling of his troops and equipment had never given Washington an hour's concern.

Slow-handed as the General always was in pouring out the wine of praise that might go to the heads of ambitious men, he would have said in the spring of 1778 that such officers as Henry Knox, Nathanael Greene and perhaps half a dozen more had eased the constant pain of effort to make stubborn-minded individualists work together as a unified corps of command. If, further, Washington ever had said in plain words that the impermanence of the Army and the idiosyncrasies of his Generals were the supreme trial of his spirit, he undoubtedly would have added that the most vexatious of all the problems of command were presented by foreign officers. When years had smoothed the scars of old wounds of the spirit, Americans spoke gratefully of such men as Pulaski and Kalb, and they forgot Conway, du Coudray, Fermoy and others of less repute. It was different in 1777. During the months covered by the later chapters of Volume IV, French visitors took so much of Washington's time by soliciting high commissions or unwarranted promotion that he seemed entirely justified in declaring he gladly would rid himself of the whole roster of them except, first, the Marquis de Lafayette—who was in an exalted category, all his own—and, second, the engineers who had come with Duportail.

In retrospect, the devices that several of the adventurers employed and the calm effrontery of some of their demands appear ludicrous; but at least one of the foreigners, Thomas Conway, was responsible in part for a threatened estrangement between Washington and Congress. The Commander-in-Chief's former membership in that body, his acquaintance with the most influential Delegates, and his experienced skill in dealing with legislators assured him support during the first year on almost every proposal he advanced. In the autumn of 1777 this was changed by the election of numerous Delegates who did not know Washington personally and did not understand why he had sustained defeats at Brandywine and at Germantown, while Gates had been winning an easy and overwhelming victory at Saratoga. To these new Delegates and to some of the admirers of Gates it appeared that Washington had worn out his Army in futile, bewildered marches between the Hackensack and the head of Chesapeake Bay. At the time when members of Congress could not or would not see how tremendously Washington was disadvantaged by British seapower, General Conway kept telling all who would listen to him that where Washington's military achievements ever rose above the mediocrity of an overcautious beginner, success was due entirely to the indolence or awkwardness of the British. Conway probably concluded, also, that Gates's star was ascendant and that he had a far better chance of profitable advancement under that officer than under Washington. The censer of Conway's oblation consequently was swung to the North. Gates was so flattered by the praise he received from the Frenchman and from many others that he took on some of the airs of a conqueror, though he continued to act in a manner that would permit of swift retreat and instant disavowal of any pretensions to supersede Washington. In short, Gates was as independent as he dared to be, and no more. Against this background developed the "Conway Cabal." It was frustrated easily by Washington with the loyal assistance of his subordinates, but it was associated always in the General's mind with French officers who, be it said again, represented in 1777–78 the most complicated and exasperating of all the puzzles of personality he had to attempt to solve in his endeavor to build up the Army command.

Strangely, the most beloved of the foreigners, the Marquis de Lafayette, was responsible, after many years, for the romantic illusion with which these events still are viewed. When the "Young Marquis" came back to America in 1824, on the invitation of President Monroe, he stirred the imagination of the entire country. At 67 years of age, he remembered individuals perfectly but he threw about the marches and battles of the Revolution a glamour that was reflected in the narratives, histories and memorials his visit inspired. New monuments to Washington thereafter represented the soldier as often as the President. School children were taught the dates and the details of the victories over the British. Washington was painted in the prow of such a boat as seldom was used on the Delaware in 1776. His place in the Revolution was presented as if he always were on the grand parade, astride a noble steed, while rank after rank of well-equipped troops passed in review to the scream of jubilant fife and the roll of defiant drum. Again, he was pictured on some lofty, smoke-swept ridge, whence he could see his Continentals in victorious pursuit of frantic redcoats.

The difference between this highly colored tradition and the earth-stained reality may be the third of the surprises some readers will find in the biography of Washington. At his headquarters, the Revolution was not a soul-stirring adventure in battle but a hard, ugly struggle with a maddening, paralyzing routine far too extensive and entangled to be handled by the assistants Washington had. For the staff departments, men of the desired stamp were almost unprocurable. The service of the States or the disorder of their own affairs commanded after 1776 the energies of competent individuals needed in the continental offices. Weeks might be spent in finding an honest, industrious person qualified to barter for shoes; it was exceedingly difficult, Washington discovered, to get even a wagonmaster who, in the later words of the General, was not "himself above his business" and "apt to indulge fantastical notions of rank and importance." When character and capacity were possessed by men willing to work hard, to bargain wisely and to buy economically on public account, these officials often were discouraged by the inclination of Delegates to suspect them of frauds perpetrated by the worst men of their vocation. Congress, in fact, attributed the rise in prices and the scarcity of goods to the defects of the purchasing system and to the venality of quartermasters and commissaries. Change of organization and rumors of still further change demoralized men on whose diligence and success the very life of the Army depended. Such matters should have been the care of able Delegates in a full Congress, and of the strongest Board of War that could be organized; but the Board lacked prestige and personnel, and Congress declined both in numbers and in the calibre of the members. Events were larger than the men who grappled with them.

Supplies of many sorts dwindled progressively. In the early days of abundance, before the war spread widely, or greed stirred, or the continental currency depreciated, the ration was so ample that an effort was made to prevail on British soldiers to desert by throwing to their outposts a printed list of the fine provisions the Americans enjoyed. Fresh milk and beer were served daily. A little more than two years later, provisions were so scarce that Washington could not supply food for troops to combat a hostile raid; and even if he could have issued bread and meat to a light force sent out for this task, he scarcely could have found a sufficient number of men with shoes that could be trusted to hold together for even one long march. This was at Valley Forge, but Valley Forge was not an exception; it was an example. As politics developed, hope waned and reserves approached exhaustion in 1777–78, it became a question whether a distant and bewildered Congress could provide enough to keep the Army from disbanding.

Washington it was who had to supply the initiative and make up the deficiencies of other men, in the discharge of a multitude of duties that should not have been imposed on him. Perhaps the sole item of a day's military news might be a belated report, via Long Island and the Connecticut shore, that British troops were embarking at New York for some unascertained port. The first task of the day for the General might be the slow drafting with a protesting pen of a long letter to the Commissary, in the hope he might induce that functionary to remove foul-smelling hides to Lancaster, Pennsylvania, where the cobblers would turn them into shoes. A second letter might inform the Clothier General that some troops could not leave their quarters because they were almost naked. Another communication might be fashioned deferentially to acquaint the President of Congress with a disgraceful fraud: some of the blankets in the bales from France had been skimped in size with so much rascality that three or four of them, stitched together, scarcely would cover a soldier. Perhaps Clement Biddle had to be thanked for what he had done to collect fodder for the horses but had to be told that the corn had been taken from the feed-troughs and ground into meal to keep the troops from starving. An uninvited French visitor must be allowed an interview and must be informed through John Laurens or Alexander Hamilton as interpreter that he doubtless had been a skillful Captain of his Most Christian Majesty's army but that it was not possible to commission him Colonel and to assign him a Regiment. Then, as likely as not, Washington had to smooth down an aggrieved Brigadier who insisted vehemently that his "honor" forbade a continuance in the Army, at dark financial sacrifice, when another man, his junior in colonial service, had been promoted over him to command a Division.

Substantially that was the daily round of duty. Those who looked at the scene without the warp of envy or ambition knew that Washington had to be a conciliator in his own camp before he could hope to be a conqueror on the field of battle. He was one-tenth field commander and nine-tenths administrator. His prime duty was not to kill the British but to keep the American Army alive. Except in rare communities, patriotism during the Revolution was the virtue of the few, rather than the impulse of the mass: Washington had to find and to hold firmly those who possessed the spirit of resistance. The States were falling apart: he was the moral cement of the loose union.

The Washington of the French and Indian War would have resigned after a few months of such maddening labor as the Washington of this phase of the Revolution had to perform every day of every week. He would have said in 1755 that he could not continue when he had such unreliable support. A double marvel thus is presented—that he endured and that he did so without threatening even once to quit. Some of the reasons for his continued bowing to the yoke are plain from his own words. He meant everything he said to his brother concerning his "full intention to devote [his] life and fortune in the cause we are engaged in . . ." From that decision there was no turning back, no wavering even. When, in June, 1775, he accepted the command, he told Congress, "I will enter upon the momentous duty and exert every power I possess in their service for the glorious cause . . ." That was a pledge to himself as well as to America, a pledge he kept with a proud fidelity: "There is one reward that nothing can deprive me of, and

that is the consciousness of having done my duty with the strictest rectitude and most scrupulous exactness, and the certain knowledge, that
if we should, ultimately, fail in the present contest, it is not owing to
the want of exertion in me, or the application of every means that Congress and the United States, or the States individually, have put into
my hands"—so he wrote in May, 1780, after nearly five years of the
woeful, wearing struggle.

Religion was yoked with devotion, pride and patience in carrying
him through the dark morasses of disappointment and defeat. It was
not creedal religion, but faith born of his own experience. He who had
been a fatalist in his twenties witnessed as American commander many
escapes from enveloping danger, and many deliverances from what
seemed to be certain doom. Washington could not explain these things
in terms of reason, and he concluded that Providence had intervened
to save America. In a subsequent desperate hour he wrote Joseph
Reed: "Providence having so often taken us up when bereft of every
other hope, I trust we shall not fail even in this." He may have had an
echo of Holy Writ in his mind as he chose his verb—"When my father
and my mother forsake me, then the Lord will take me up."

Restraint of style seems to be demanded in this presentation of Washington, the revolutionary officer, as he wrestles with the indifference,
the perversity, the vain ambitions and the blind incompetence of many
of his compatriots. The great part of the story is not rhetorical; the
presentation of it ought not to be. Where the monochrome of administrative labor is spread continuously over the calendar, often for months,
the canvas cannot be colored otherwise than with irrelevancies; where
the event itself lights the scene, "purple patches" are apt to be blotches.
With disavowel in advance of any pretense to comparable clarity, it
may be said that there appears to be no more excuse for decorating
verbally the hard, heroic life of George Washington during the Revolution than for strewing adjectives along the way of the Pilgrim whose
Progress John Bunyan set down in matchless simplicity. The style of
these two volumes consequently is unadorned and, one may hope,
unobtrusive: it is Washington and not his humble biographer who
should have the whole attention of every reader.

While words of the twentieth century have not been excluded, an
effort has been made to avoid manifest and irritating anachronisms.

Military parlance of Washington's day has been respected, because the use of later terms might suggest deceptive tactical analogies. As in earlier volumes, this has necessitated the employment of some expressions bunglesome in themselves and longer than those of present-day military dictionaries; but this has not been too heavy a price to pay for a continuing differentiation between the tactics of 1775 and those of 1950. No difficulties of definition have attended the treatment of the simple strategy of the campaigns. Other aspects of presentation have involved nothing more serious than the necessity of vigilance in the employment of names and pronouns. Where three or four men stalk through the clauses of a single sentence, they have to be tagged if the reader is not to be confused by an unidentified "he" or puzzled by a "his." The unavoidable result is that some pages are full of capital letters, and the long name of the central figure of the story has to be used hundreds of times. Quotation follows the rule laid down in Volume I: capitalization, spelling and punctuation have been conformed to current usage wherever this could be done without risk that the meaning would be put in doubt. This has seemed almost a necessity to save the reader from the distraction of odd phonetics and loosely sprinkled commas; but historic utterances have been cited verbatim, and in those instances where revision of the punctuation has been drastic, a note to that effect has been appended. For ease of identification, the numbers designating American and French military organizations have been spelled out, and those of British and German commands have been put in Arabic numerals. The main continental Army, under Washington, is the only one printed with a capital "A"—not from pride, but for convenience.

If the reader was not to be drowned in detail, a distinction manifestly had to be made between a Life of Washington and a History of the war in which his country was engaged. This requirement, which applies in varying degree to the writing of all military biography, is particularly severe in the case of Washington. Circumstances bring the hall of Congress very close to headquarters and often fuse the deliberations of that body with military planning. The nature and scope of Washington's administrative duties make it necessary to discuss questions of supply that would not be representative of their place in Washington's thought and labor if, in the most literal sense, they were not detailed, specific in background, and ipso facto, dull. To accept this unescapable reality and at the same time to keep this biography from becoming an encyclopedia of the American Revolution, these rules have been laid down: Military operations in which Washington had no direct part are described summarily, if at all—witness Montgomery's Canadian expedition and Gates's campaign against Burgoyne. Enterprises undertaken by Washington and subsequently passed on to others have not been reviewed at length beyond the date his direction of these affairs terminated or became routine. This applies, for example, to the exchange of prisoners and, regrettably, to naval affairs, of which, during 1775-76 Washington displayed understanding. The larger issues of continental policy represented by finance and foreign alliance are anticipated to a limited extent only, until they influence materially the work Washington had to perform. Finally, wherever it has seemed permissible to do so, the minutiae of the General's administrative labors in the essential if uninteresting realm of supply have been put in the footnotes rather than in the text. It seemed better to burden the page than the reader. The same unprotesting foundation has been used, also, for a considerable number of references, in odd and seldom-explored sources, to phases of the Revolution which it is hoped other students will develop. There must be several score doctoral dissertations and half a dozen fascinating biographies in the Revolutionary period. Contrary to what appears to be general opinion in universities, it is a field that should be replowed and tilled for nearly the whole of its wide area. A few interesting episodes and the events of the first year of the Revolution, but only of that year, seem to have been described with some adequacy on the basis of the materials made available during the last half century.

As they relate to Washington, those sources are of unequal value and extent for different periods of his life. Until the year 1774 is reached, substantially everything that has been uncovered in this research may reasonably be included. Apportionment of space has permitted the treatment, in addition, of a few illustrative episodes, such as the Robinson scandal that shook the walls of the society in which Washington lived, though he was not involved in it except as a creditor of some of Robinson's debtors. From the time Peyton Randolph took the chair as President of the First Continental Congress, Sept. 5, 1775, materials for most aspects of Washington's career are ample and, on some matters, overabundant. A note entered on page 339, at the beginning of Chapter

XV of Volume III, informs the reader that from that date onward, many incidents of minor importance are omitted, lest they obscure the main events. In writing of this period, a student has a right to a certain pride in the scholarship of the Americans who have edited the great collections now in print. It has been customary in recent years to discredit Peter Force and his *American Archives* because of errors of date and of attribution. Such errors there are, and often in unexpected places, but they are trifles when set against the resourceful skill of Force in gathering papers and in publishing them. The nine volumes of *Archives* issued before he had to abandon the undertaking include close to 10,000,000 words of documentary material, much of which undoubtedly would have been lost had not he salvaged it. Force's indexes of these historical stores are much more nearly adequate than they are supposed to be. As for Jared Sparks, his swift diligence and sense of historical values were not completely cancelled by his astounding disregard of veracious editing. The magnitude of his service is evidenced by the frequency of reference to his works, even though publication of his *Writings of Washington* was completed in 1837. Sparks's *Correspondence of the Revolution,* endlessly quoted in these pages as *LTW—Letters to Washington*—bears date of 1853 and still has large value. Worthington C. Ford's fourteen volumes of *The Writings of George Washington* appeared in 1889–93 and owed more to Sparks than was realized or acknowledged until the controversy between Ford and Herbert B. Adams, who himself leaned too far on the side of Sparks. If on the whole, it has to be said that Ford did not fulfil all that was expected of him as an editor of Washington, the well-known scholar who presided for seven years over the Manuscripts Division of the Library of Congress launched and commanded with magnificent success the larger venture of the *Journals of the Continental Congress.* He steered through the Government Printing Office in 1904–09 fifteen of the thirty-four volumes of the invaluable work that Gaillard Hunt, John C. Fitzpatrick and Roscoe R. Hill successively brought towards its final berth. A glance at two folios of the original manuscript *Journal,* reproduced between pages 435 and 436 of Volume III, will give a vague idea only of the problems that had to be overcome in editing these documents. Except for the surprising inadequacies of the index, completion of the enterprise in 1937 was a superb achievement.

By that date, Edmund C. Burnett's *Letters of Members of the Con-*

tinental Congress had been issued in seven volumes (1921–36). This work, financed by the Carnegie Institution of Washington, probably lighted more dark passages of the Revolution than any collection of documents ever published, with the exceptions already mentioned. Doctor Burnett's scholarship was as precise as it was inclusive. The more a student uses these *Letters,* the more respect will he have for the man who pursued the last trail to the most remote garret, where the memorabilia of the least conspicuous member of the Continental Congress might be mouldering.

Among the reasons the present study was undertaken in 1944 was the belief of Raymond B. Fosdick and others that someone should analyze the extent to which existing knowledge of Washington had been enlarged or changed in essential values by the publication of John C. Fitzpatrick's edition of the *Writings,* completed in thirty-seven volumes only four years previously. Fitzpatrick and his associates performed one of the great editorial labors of this generation and did it admirably in every particular. If notes occasionally are missing where one could wish for them, it should be remembered that full annotation of so vast and varied a correspondence would have prolonged publication far beyond the date the Washington Bicentennial Commission wished the editor to observe as the climax of the celebration. Fitzpatrick's editing bears no marks of haste; the collection of material from archives and private depositories was so thorough that the number of Washington letters remaining unpublished at the present time must be quite small. Those printed by Fitzpatrick are made doubly useful by the two-volume index prepared by that devoted scholar David M. Matteson and put in print just as ground was being broken, so to say, for this book. Some of Matteson's entries appear at first glance to be of forbidding length and complexity, but his cross references are numerous and consistent. His supplementary arrangement of letters chronologically under the names of addressees is of great convenience to students. If a special heaven is reserved for faithful indexers—as there should be—Matteson deserves a seat with the most venerated of them.

These major sources—Force's *Archives,* Sparks's *Correspondence of the Revolution,* the new edition of the *Journals of the Continental Congress,* Burnett's *Letters of Members* of that body, and Fitzpatrick's *Writings of Washington*—suffice in themselves to give an accurate and almost complete narrative of Washington's life. The figure of the Revolutionary commander can be rounded in the crosslight of many memoirs and collections of letters. Numerous biographies of lesser figures include correspondence and documents of worth. It has seemed proper to cite source material of this sort from the books in which it first was located, though subsequent search uncovered the original. When some quiet student probably had no other reward for his labor than credit for his findings, he should not be deprived of suitable acknowledgment, especially as there usually is a chance that one might not find a particular paper without the guidance of the earlier writer's footnote. For that reason, these volumes include scores of references to documents and letters, "as cited" in secondary authorities there named.

Manuscript sources dealing with Washington's part in the Revolution range geographically from the Tilghman Papers in Yass, Australia, to British, French and German reports in the respective national archives. Thence the trail comes back to America and extends from Boston to San Marino. Incomparably the most important materials are where one would expect to find them in the Papers of Washington and the Papers of the Continental Congress, Library of Congress. Anyone who turns these thousands of folios is distressed to observe how scant the use of them has been. The most serious gaps are in the returns of the strength of the Army, the reports of the courts martial, and the records of the Board of War. No returns are to be found in the Library of Congress or in the National Archives for several months of important preparation and maneuver. Loss or destruction of courtmartial minutes has left a fog around several happenings of large interest and of some strategical instruction. Study of the proceedings in the courtmartial of Charles Lee and of the court of inquiry into the loss of Forts Clinton and Montgomery will show, for example, how much knowledge of the Battle of Germantown must have been contained in the papers on the trial of Adam Stephen, papers that have eluded search if, indeed, they have not been destroyed.

The other principal manuscript materials of this period are those of Horatio Gates, Nathanael Greene, Henry Knox, Alexander McDougall, Joseph Reed, Joseph Trumbull, Jeremiah Wadsworth, Anthony Wayne and George Weedon. The Clinton Papers at the University of Michigan, needless to say, are the largest British collection in the United

States and, for that matter, the most extensive British personal papers of this era anywhere that have been neither printed nor calendared. Several of these storehouses present surprises. The letters to Gates are, if anything, more interesting than those from his pen; the McDougall Papers, though often verbose, are notably rich on Hudson River operations, and scarcely have been tapped. Those of George Weedon's letters in the Chicago Historical Society archives are of extraordinary interest and are surprisingly well written. Greene's Papers, though widely scattered, are of high value. For some reason, the quality of Henry Knox's excellent letters of 1775–76 declined as the war progressed. Joseph Reed had numerous well-informed confidants whose important communications he generally preserved. Many smaller batches of letters contain a few items that reward search, but, in the main, they disappoint hopes. The same thing has to be said of the manuscript Diaries that have survived generations of handling by the careless and the curious. William Smith's Journal in the New York Public Library is an extraordinary document that should be published in part. Among the best Diaries, bulk considered, is Isaac Beers's, a copy of which is in Force Transcripts, Library of Congress. Some of the contemporary newspapers are so rare they are almost equivalent to manuscripts, but while they are an indispensable source on the Revolution itself, articles of 1775–78 that refer to Washington usually are inaccurate in detail.

Contemporary maps have been a constant vexation. The British had some good topographical engineers, many of whose original sketches, maps and charts are preserved with the other Clinton Papers in the Clements Library at Ann Arbor. Chance, circumstance and haste have so ordered it that some of the most unsatisfactory and contradictory of these British drafts depict areas concerning which other geographical information is meagre or non-existent. English commercial maps of the seventeen-seventies are of varying reliability and are apt to deceive by the confident excellence of the engraving. Those of Boston, described briefly in the fifth appendix of Volume III, are typical in their errors but, with one exception, are below the artistic quality of several published in London during and after 1777 for other parts of the United States. In using even Faden's beautiful maps, the student needs constantly to confirm mileage and compass bearing where a mistake of a few miles in distance or of as many as 20 degrees in direction would invalidate his tactical or strategical argument.

For manifest reasons, the maps used by the Americans before the coming of the French in 1780 are inferior. Duportail and his subordinates made some sketches that are sufficiently accurate to serve their purpose, though they seldom show finished draftmanship. Robert Erskine, who died in October, 1780, displayed commendable accuracy in delineating a district he personally inspected, but in his first map of New Jersey he made some lamentable blunders concerning locations reported to him but not verified by him. One of the sketches in Volume IV is based on Erskine's "army map" of the theatre of Washington's operations in the autumn of 1776. The more serious of the cartographer's mistakes in measurement have been preserved deliberately, with suitable warning in the legend, because the limitations on the geographical knowledge then available at headquarters should be kept in mind. Like pains have been taken to be inaccurate in the map of the area of White Plains and Croton River, New York. Howe's report and other British sources are so vague that no positive conclusions can be framed, but the possibility exists that the British General's abandonment of the operation was due, in part, to miscalculation of the distances he had to cover in throwing Washington back to the Croton River. This entire subject of maps of the Revolutionary War probably deserves closer study by some interested person with professional knowledge of engineering.

The difficulties an investigator has to overcome in a detailed survey of Washington's part in the American Revolution must not be overemphasized. Materials are enormous in bulk and sometimes are deceptively unequal in quality; but no person who examines them ever will groan as he turns the folios, or will regret the investment of his hours. It would be an impertinence to say that a biographer is to be judged by the company he keeps, because the lives of the worst of mortals sometimes have large historical importance; but it is a fact that a student is twice rewarded when he is privileged to write of such a man as Washington. In youth and during his years of service in the French and Indian War, he was interesting and was to be respected for his absolute honesty, his industry and his careful planning to advance himself. He had personally attractive qualities, also; otherwise he would not have earned the good opinions he undoubtedly possessed. To say this and everything else that can be adduced in his favor is not to affirm that, on calm, historical analysis, he is likable. He does not laugh enough, and when he smiles, it seems more in courtesy than in kindness. Always, in looking at him, one has to ask: Is the core of that young man hard; is his undeniable integrity calculated rather than instinctive?

Had he remained at 42 what he was at 27, he would have met austerity with cold dignity in the summer of 1775, and he would have measured it out to Ward and Spencer as they meted it to him. Letters to the President of Congress would on occasion have equalled in complaint some of those he had written Governor Dinwiddie. As it is, when one rides behind the new Commander-in-Chief to Cambridge and sits silently against the wall while Washington converses with officers and members of the Massachusetts Provincial Congress, one has first to rub one's eyes and ask: Is this the same man who argued with Forbes and Bouquet in 1758? After observing Washington at work for a few months around Boston, one feels as if one should apologize for misgivings that were little better than suspicions. Then, stage by stage, day by day, respect rises to admiration. How can Washington preserve unruffled patience in listening to those sensitive, self-seeking and shortsighted officers who plague him? That industry with which he solves what so frequently appears insoluble—is it inexhaustible? His judgment—how can he keep it unfailingly just to every individual?

The siege of Boston ends successfully; the unhappy experiences of Long Island somehow cease to be a humiliation; the startling dispersion of force in November, 1776, and the hesitation that contributed to the loss of Fort Washington create uneasiness in one's mind. Evidently the troubled Commander-in-Chief is passing through a night of mental confusion. Admiration is rekindled when he courageously breaks contact with the enemy and accepts the odium of a deep retreat through a rich country, all the way to the Delaware. Congress has fled to Baltimore; the loyalists of Philadelphia are smiling cheerfully; the Army is no more than the ghost of itself; Washington has to write his brother, "if every nerve is not strained to recruit the new Army with all possible expedition, I think the game is pretty near up." By the time Charles Lee has finished bedeviling him by inexcusable delay, and the few reenforcements who can be expected from any quarter are shivering on the right bank of the ice-laden river, readers have seen enough of the General to know that his patience is no pose, his justice no screen of self-protection, his resolution no springtime mood, his integrity no frail-walled citadel that will capitulate to guile or force or bribe. One pities Washington in those merciless December days, at the same time that one feels reverence for his virtues. Then he issues the amazing order for the Army to recross the Delaware Christmas night and to attack Trenton. After that, observers hold their breath and doubt and fear and marvel, until the swift campaign is over and the British are pulling back to New Brunswick and the proud Continentals are established at Morristown. Then, when the Army is saved and the American cause is given new life, even the most critical of readers is apt to exclaim: This man Washington has the seeds of greatness in him!

DOUGLAS SOUTHALL FREEMAN

Westbourne,
Richmond, Virginia,
April 30, 1951.

GEORGE WASHINGTON

CHAPTER I

HAPPY RETURN TO A "RUN-DOWN" PLANTATION
(January–April, 1759)

No REGRET was in the heart of Col. George Washington as he resigned his military commission at the end of 1758 and turned his horse's head from Williamsburg toward the plantation on the Pamunkey River where Martha Dandridge Custis was waiting for him. Lack of recognition by the British government "at home" had destroyed his military ambition but it had not lessened his conviction that he had done his part, and more than his part, in defending both "the country," as he termed Virginia, and the other American domain of Great Britain. In the memory of service he was willing to put neglect behind him. Besides, there was no bleakness on the road that led to the estate of the woman of 27 who was to be his bride. Muddy stretches ran down to pine-bordered brooks; the hostile wind of an unfriendly New Year swept across the fields where the maples and the oaks were bare; but fires would be burning and wedding garments would be ready at the White House. Beyond spread the tobacco plantations and the prospect of opulent years.

Every expectation was realized. The marriage ceremony was performed Jan. 6, 1759, at the White House by Rev. David Mossom, rector of Martha's church, Saint Peter's, New Kent County,[1] in the presence

[1] Mossom, born in London in 1690, had come to Virginia from St. Michael's Church, Marblehead, Mass., where he had served for ten years as missionary of the Society for the Propagation of the Gospel in Foreign Parts. See Goodwin, *Colonial Church in Virginia*, v. 2, p. 295; Brydon, *Mother Church*, 219. His introduction to the Virginia parish was through a letter from Robert Carter to the vestry of St. Peter's, June 13, 1727, entered in *St. Peter's Vestry Book*, 207. For four reasons the marriage ceremony is believed to have been performed at the home of the bride, rather than at the church: First, it would have been inconvenient and uncomfortable to have the nuptials solemnized in midwinter at a church to which participants and guests would have been compelled to ride or to drive over at least three miles of heavy roads. Second, on the death in 1882 of Mrs. Margaret Anderson Young, aged 95, it was stated (*Richmond Dispatch*, June 2, 1882, p. 1) that she had been married in 1806 at the White House in the very room where Martha Custis had become the bride of Washington. As Margaret Anderson's father was employed at Mount Vernon before becoming manager of the White House property, this tradition of Washington's marriage on the Pamunkey estate dates probably from the lifetime of Washington himself. Third, Mrs. Hartwell Macon, who resided near the White House and

of kinsmen and neighbors. Feasting and festivity doubtless attended the nuptials, after which a happy honeymoon was spent at the well-furnished Custis home on the bank of the Pamunkey. George had seen little of the company of women for five years, except on his occasional visits to Belvoir, but he now found easy and cheerful companionship in a young woman, who, though not brilliant, had her full share of good nature. She had ample common sense, also, except where her two children were involved. The son, John Parke Custis, called "Jackie" by the family, was now 4 and a healthy, normal boy.[2] His sister "Patsy"—christened Martha Parke Custis—was less vigorous at 2, but was an attractive child. When either of them was absent or sick, their mother yielded almost frantically to concern. At the same time, she was ready and glad to pass on to her new husband the responsibility of managing her children's financial affairs along with her own. This could be undertaken formally in April, but not sooner, because the General Court did not sit in chancery until that month. Meantime, nothing of magnitude had to be settled. Even before the marriage, Martha had gone over her affairs with Washington and had recalled only one possible account she owed—a matter of perhaps £100 [3]—in addition to those of current purchases.

The bridegroom, as a good man of business, made his first inquiries concerning the details of the new duties he was to assume as a fiduciary, and then he had to go to Williamsburg where he began on February 22 —his twenty-seventh birthday—his service as one of the members from Frederick County in the House of Burgesses.[4] He probably took his

---

lived to great age, often told her grandchildren that she remembered an aunt who had attended the wedding at the White House (42 *V* 233; 46 *ibid.*, 42). Fourth, Mrs. Clarence G. Burton, of Belona, Powhatan County, Virginia, direct descendant of "Parson" Mossom, stated in 1948 that her family tradition always was that the ceremony had been at the home of the bride. No suggestion that the church was the scene of the marriage has been found prior to 1865. In that year, Gen. R. E. Lee wrote Miss Virginia Ritchie of Brandon, that he had interest in the preservation of St. Peter's Church, among several, because of "its association with the recollections of Washington, his marriage and early history" (42 *V* 231). The vagueness of Lee's language is of itself an indication that he knew little about Washington's connections with St. Peter's, but a remark by one of his sons (R. E. Lee, *Recollections and Letters of General Lee;* 364) shows that the family believed the ceremony was at St. Peter's. The earlier and more probable tradition of nuptials at the White House may be accepted as almost certainly correct.

[2] Dates assigned in the "Custis Bible" (5 *W* (1) p. 35) for the birth of "Jackie" and of "Patsy" must be late guesses. Washington wrote (3 *G. W.*, 51) that the boy would be 17 in November, 1771. "Patsy" may have been born late in 1755 or, more probably, in 1756. See *infra,* p. 325, n. 108. The tradition that she was born three weeks before her father's death does not square with references in family correspondence.

[3] See *infra,* p. 192.

[4] The composition, prerogatives and functions of this lower branch of the General Assembly are sketched in Vol. I, p. 173 ff.

bride and some of her servants with him and established temporary domicile in the former residence of John Custis,[5] within walking distance of the Capitol where Burgesses and Council sat.

In the General Assembly, which then had been in existence for 140 years, Washington found several friends and numerous acquaintances of approximately his own age. Thomas Bryan Martin, aged 28, was Washington's colleague from Frederick. Gabriel Jones represented Hampshire along with Thomas Walker, who served as commissary most of the time Washington guarded the frontier. Fairfax, Washington's County, had as its Burgesses George Mason of Gunston Hall, and George Johnston, another neighbor and a legal counsellor of the master of Mount Vernon. The County of Washington's birth, Westmoreland, had elected two of the Lees to voice the wishes of voters. One of these Burgesses, Richard Henry Lee, was of the same age as Colonel Washington and was of manifest ability, but, as a new member,[6] he was not yet trying the wings of his eloquence. Richard Henry's brother Francis Lightfoot Lee—retiring, scholarly, and of soundly reasoning mind [7]—was Burgess from Loudoun, though only 25 years old.

The control and management of the House, as usual, were in the hands of a small number of powerful seniors. In the chair still sat John Robinson, Treasurer and Speaker and Washington's consistent friend during the sternest days of the struggle for the Ohio. "Mr. Speaker" was now 55 years of age and unchallenged in his position. With him in the House worked Richard Bland, Edmund Pendleton, the Carters

[5] "Probably" has to be the word because there is no positive evidence that Martha was with him in the colonial capital or that he occupied the Custis residence. The house was furnished; no credits on account of any sales of John Custis's Williamsburg personalty were entered in the Custis accounts until Oct. 20, 1759 (*Custis Papers*, VHS). Property listed then would indicate that nothing of importance had been removed from the house prior to that date. No record has been found of any lease of the house prior to 1762 when it was rented at £40 per annum to William Byrd III. As late as January, 1765, Washington charged against Byrd £30 for "sundry repairs and alterations to the house according to your desires" (*Ledger A*, folio 135; cf. *ibid.*, folio 178). Further, there are no entries in *Ledger A* to indicate that Washington sojourned, though he probably did some entertaining, at any of the taverns of Williamsburg during the session. The largest item of expense while there was 31s 3d at Hubbard's (*Ledger A*, folio 55). It stands to reason that if the Custis house was furnished and not occupied by tenants in the winter of 1758–59, Washington would not have paid good money for less comfortable shelter elsewhere. Neither is it probable that he would have left his bride of five weeks on the White House plantation, alone with her children, when it would have been easy for her to enjoy the pleasant gaiety of the town while the General Assembly was meeting.

[6] The House had been chosen in the summer of 1758 and had been convened for its first session September 14. Richard Henry Lee took the oaths then. Washington, elected July 24, 1758 (see Vol. II, p. 320), would have qualified at the same time had he not been busy with preparations for the advance on Fort DuQuesne.

[7] See John Adams to Richard Bland Lee, Aug. 11, 1819; C. F. Adams, ed., *The Life and Works of John Adams* (cited hereafter as *John Adams*), v. 10, p. 382.

and the Randolphs. These men did not always agree among themselves but whatever a majority of them advocated, the House customarily approved. An awkward man in debate, the forty-nine-year-old Bland was tough and tenacious of mind, logical and consistent. His reputation in the House had been established by the part he had played in contesting Governor Dinwiddie's demand for the fee of one pistole before an order for a land-grant could be sealed. After that first battle, Bland was conspicuous in almost every contest on the floor.

Edmund Pendleton, 38, tall and thin, had not been born to the fortune of a great planter. Instead, because of the early death of his father and the remarriage of his mother, he had been apprenticed to a court clerk. At 20 he had won admission to the bar and after that had risen to a high place among the none-too-numerous good lawyers of the Colony. His instincts being conservative, his attitude toward government was defensive. On his feet, in court or before the Burgesses, he was a dangerous adversary. He overlooked no point of law and could shift the line of argument with so much skill that he could outwit and confound a less dexterous opponent. At the time Washington entered the House, Edmund Pendleton had advocated no great cause but he had a hand in shaping and passing many a bill. A careful member, fathering a disputable measure, did well to gain Pendleton's support in advance.

The Carters in the House numbered four—Landon of Richmond County, his brother Charles "of Cleve," this Charles's son of the same name, usually known as Charles "of Ludlow," and still another Charles, "of Corotoman," a son of "Secretary" John Carter, who had been a brother of Landon and of Charles "of Cleve." [8] The most conspicuous of the four was Landon Carter, owner of Sabine Hall. He was born in 1709, had entered the House of Burgesses in 1748, and had retained his seat in each succeeding Assembly. Because he operated an excellent plantation and had many farms besides, his voice and his point of view were essentially those of the great land and slave owners; but he was an individualist as well, a diarist and an independent thinker. Until age made him crotchety, he led many planters and himself paid homage to no master. Charles Carter "of Cleve" was a son of "King" Carter and was Chairman of the Committee of Propositions and Grievances, a body of much usefulness and hard work.

In interesting contrast to most of these men was Peyton Randolph,

[8] For Landon, see 13 *W* (1) p. 45, and for Charles "of Cleve," consult 31 *V* 39.

Burgess from Williamsburg[9] and Attorney General of the Colony. "Mr. Attorney" was 38 and had the prestige of study at the Middle Temple, where he had been called to the bar in 1744. He had been the man whom the Burgesses had sent to England to present the Colony's side of the controversy with Governor Dinwiddie over the "pistole-fee," a mission he had discharged with so much vigor that Dinwiddie had suspended him as Attorney General. The Burgesses had sustained him, had forced the Governor to reinstate him, and thereafter had regarded him as no less their advocate than the King's. In his first contact with strangers, Peyton Randolph was cold and perhaps suspicious. Closer acquaintance brought out his natural affability. His methods nearly always were those of conciliation and reason; his chief weakness was a certain slothfulness in pursuing his argument, as if it burdened his heavy body to follow his case beyond the requirements of the hour. He was not a wrestler with abstractions, an analyst of principles. Peyton Randolph's brother John was Clerk of the House, and in that position had both the confidence of the members and the political power, on occasion, to tip the beam of doubtful decision.

The leading Burgesses usually worked together in complete, almost instinctive understanding, and they carefully apportioned among themselves the chairmanships of all the important committees. Not antagonistic to these men but developing steadily in thought and in knowledge of the law were several young members whom Washington probably met for the first time. One of the ablest of these was the Burgess for the College of William and Mary in the City of Williamsburg, George Wythe, personal adviser of the resident Governor, Francis Fauquier, whose title was officially that of Lieutenant Governor. Quite frequently Wythe voiced the views of "His Honor," though never to the detriment of the Colony or to the impairment of the prerogatives of the House. Several other young Burgesses scarcely were inferior to Wythe in ability and diligence; from the counties still other youthful Virginians were looking toward Williamsburg and were hoping soon to be sitting among the members.

If Washington surveyed with polite curiosity those leading Burgesses whom he did not know already, they were interested in him as the most conspicuous of the younger soldiers of America. One of these lawmakers said of Washington:

---

[9] He had represented the College of William and Mary in 1752–58.

. . . He may be described as being straight as an Indian, measuring 6 feet 2 inches in his stockings, and weighing 175 lbs when he took his seat in the House of Burgesses in 1759. His frame is padded with well developed muscles, indicating great strength. His bones and joints are large as are his hands and feet. He is wide shouldered but has not a deep or round chest; is neat waisted, but is broad across the hips, and has rather long legs and arms. His head is well shaped, though not large, but is gracefully poised on a superb neck. A large and straight rather than a prominent nose; blue-grey penetrating eyes which are widely separated and overhung by a heavy brow. His face is long rather than broad, with high round cheek bones, and terminates in a good firm chin. He has a clear tho rather colorless pale skin which burns with the sun. A pleasing and benevolent tho a command-ing countenance, dark brown hair which he wears in a cue. His mouth is large and generally firmly closed, but which from time to time discloses some defective teeth. His features are regular and placid with all the muscles of his face under perfect control, tho flexible and expressive of deep feeling when moved by emotions. In conversation he looks you full in the face, is deliberate, deferential and engaging. His demeanor at all times composed and dignified. His movements and gestures are graceful, his walk majestic, and he is a splendid horseman.[10]

The young soldier, thus described, had been in the House only four days, among old friends and new, when on Monday, February 26, he listened to Landon Carter report on certain expiring laws which, in the judgment of the Committee on Courts of Justice, the General Assembly should renew. There followed some discussion and the reading of vari-ous petitions, among which were two from soldiers who had been captured by the French. Then, during a lull, an admirer rose, cried "Mr. Speaker," gained recognition and offered this resolution: ". . . that the thanks of the House be given to George Washington, Esq; a member of this House, late Colonel of the First Virginia Regiment, for his faithful Services to his Majesty, and this Colony, and for his brave and steady behavior, from the first Encroachments and hostilities of the French and their Indians, to his Resignation, after the happy Reduction of Fort DuQuesne."

The resolution was passed immediately with a roar of "Ayes"; Mr.

[10] Letter of George Mercer, 1760, quoted in many places, and, conveniently in J. M. Toner, *Washington as an Inventor and Promoter of the Useful Arts*, 20 n. While the description is almost "too good to be true," probability seems to be on the side of authenticity, with allow-ance for the strong chance that the document has been "touched up." G. W. P. Custis, *op. cit.*, 527, quoted Washington as saying his weight in his "best days" was 210 to 220. His eyes a "light greyish blue," and his hair "a hazel brown."

Speaker leaned forward in his chair to voice the thanks of the House; instinctively Washington arose, listened, blushed and sat down again, amid more applause.[11]

Ambitious as Washington had been for public approval and "honor," he could not have coveted a more flattering reception or, for that matter, a better committee assignment than the leaders gave him. On the opening day of the session he had been named to the Committee on Propositions and Grievances,[12] one of the four principal instruments of the House,[13] the one that passed on affairs of business and of government, on boundaries, on new parishes, on tobacco inspection and the like. Under the chairmanship of Charles Carter "of Cleve" it was a busy but not an overworked committee.

The new member from Frederick found much that was instructive in the "propositions and grievances" presented, but he had time to listen, also, to the reports of other committees and to the discussion of the subject for which, primarily, the General Assembly had been convened.

[11] *Journ. H. B.*, 1758–61, p. 66–67. The name of the author of the resolution is not known. Regrettably, too, a place in the text has to be denied the traditional account of this incident, which reads as follows: "As soon as Colonel Washington took his seat [as a member], Mr. Robinson, in obedience to this order [of the house], and following the impulse of his own generous and grateful heart, discharged the duty, with great dignity; but with such warmth of coloring and strength of expression, as entirely confounded the young hero. He rose to express his acknowledgments for the honor; but such was his trepidation and confusion, that he could not give distinct utterance to a single syllable. He blushed, stammered, and trembled, for a second; when the speaker relieved him by a stroke of address that would have done honor to Louis XIV, in his proudest and happiest moment. 'Sit down, Mr. Washington,' said he with a conciliating smile, 'your modesty is equal to your valor, and that surpasses the power of any language that I possess.'" This was published for the first time in William Wirt's *Sketches of the Life and Character of Patrick Henry*, p. 45, and was reprinted conveniently in 2 *Ford*, 126 n. Wirt's famous biography of Henry was published in 1817, more than half a century after the event described. The authority cited by Wirt was Edmund Randolph, who was in his sixth year at the time the resolution was passed. Edmund Randolph's father was John Randolph, already mentioned as Clerk of the House of Burgesses in 1752–68 (*Journ H. B.*, 1752–58, p. 3; *ibid.*, 1766–69, p. 141) and Attorney General in 1766–75. John Randolph probably was present when Robinson addressed Washington, and as Randolph resided in Virginia until 1775, he could have described the scene to Edmund at a time when the son was old enough to appreciate it. The same thing may be said of Edmund's uncle, Peyton Randolph, who lived until 1775, in which year his nephew was 22. It therefore is altogether probable that Edmund Randolph received from his father or from his uncle or from both of them a first-hand account of the episode; but as Wirt probably had moved to Richmond when he made the acquaintance of Randolph, the story scarcely could have been related to Wirt before 1800, and probably not until later. Wirt was highly imaginative, as *The Letters of a British Spy* demonstrated, and he was particularly interested in oratorical performance. It consequently goes beyond historical probability to credit fully an account he wrote in 1816, or about that year, on the basis of what Edmund Randolph communicated subsequent to 1800, from recollection of what John or Peyton Randolph had related prior to 1775. Some fabric of fact doubtless remains in Wirt's narrative but the color of truth was washed out by repeated telling of the tale.

[12] *Journ. H. B.*, 1758–61, p. 57.

[13] The others were Privileges and Elections, Courts of Justice, and Public Claims. At this session there was, also, a standing committee on Trade. Small special committees were named frequently.

As Francis Fauquier, the Lieutenant Governor, explained in his address to the two houses on the opening day, General Amherst had written to ask that, for a final offensive on the Great Lakes against the French, Virginia supply him in 1759 with as many troops as the Colony had paid during the campaign of 1758. The Governor went on: "Here I find myself at a loss. I well know the great debt this Colony has contracted; I well know the cheerfulness with which you have undertaken everything recommended to you; The first deters me from using any arguments; the last renders all needless, and I can only say that by employing your efforts this year, it is probable we may, by following the repeated blows already given, be able to drive the enemy from our frontiers, and so it may become the last of this burdensome and expensive war." [14] He added that he had supplied the half-naked troops with coats made of blanket, but, he said, if the men were continued in service, they must be reclothed. All Virginia forces in arms had been dismissed, Fauquier reported, except the First Regiment and four Companies of rangers. A detachment had been retained at Fort DuQuesne by General Forbes's orders; the other men had been posted along the frontier to protect it against attack. [15]

The House responded promptly and tactfully that if the Colony fell short of General Amherst's expectations in 1759, it would be because of "poverty alone, which has often obstructed many a noble and honest intention." [16] This was meant to be polite notice that troops would not be supplied for an expedition on the Lakes, [17] but it was not final. When the Committee of the Whole [18] began to deliberate on a bill to raise the strength of the Regiment to 1000 men and to continue it in service until Dec. 1, 1759, [19] the advocates of a strong war policy proposed that an additional 500 be raised to guard the frontiers and that the Regiment be placed at the disposal of Amherst for such use as the military situation required. Debate on this continued for days. [20]

In the intervals of the discussion, Washington had his first experience with embarrassing local bills and measures that affected Counties in which he had special interest—a plea of Augusta for better protection of the frontiers, [21] petitions for the extension of the corporate bounds of Winchester, [22] various appeals for changes in the tobacco-inspection

14 *Journ. H. B.*, 1758–61, p. 55.
15 *Ibid.*, 56.
16 *Ibid.*, 65.
17 Cf. *ibid.*, 77–79.
18 It was styled (*ibid.*, 67), "a committee upon the said speech and letters."
19 *Ibid.*
20 *Ibid.*, 88, 93, 97, 104, 105, 109, 110.
21 *Ibid.*, 59.
22 *Ibid.*, 68, 71.

laws,[23] and a measure to remove the Court House of Spotsylvania from Fredericksburg.[24] Definitely in the line of business was an appeal from the merchants of Winchester, influential constituents of Washington's, for protection against Pennsylvania pedlars in skins and furs.[25] This protest seemed to have so much justice that it prompted a revision of the law on itinerant traders.[26] The parliamentary course of these bills was not of a sort to call for great display of the art of government, but, taken together, the enactment of these measures was, for a beginner, an informative lesson in the processes of legislation.

More personal were petitions and charges that involved Washington's old Regiment and some of his officers and friends. At the previous session of the General Assembly, in the autumn of 1758, Washington's remote cousin, the fifth William Ball of Millenbeck, had been expelled because he had been presented by the grand jury of Lancaster County "for uttering forged and counterfeit treasury notes, knowing them to be so";[27] but as Washington probably had no acquaintance with the accused man, and scarcely could have traced the degree of kinship, there was no smart, no bruise of pride.[28] It was a somewhat different matter when Washington's former comrade, Major Andrew Lewis, was charged with aiding Commissary Thomas Walker in the fraudulent supply of meat to officers and rangers in Augusta County. The committee acquitted Walker of dishonesty but condemned Lewis for being party to the contract, though it was stated that no "oppression" of the soldiers or hardships to them had resulted from the transaction between the two veterans.[29]

This was not a pleasant experience, and it was followed by a worse. Burgess Thomas Johnson of Louisa, author of the charge against Walker, indignantly asserted that in the House "one holds the lamb while another skins" and that as a result "the country's money is squandered away." Specifically Johnson charged "that when the Clerk's salary was proposed to be settled, [John] Randolph, the Clerk, got up,

[23] *Ibid.*, 91–98.   [24] *Ibid.*, 109.   [25] *Ibid.*, 81.

[26] *Ibid.*, 92, 99, 110, 125, 128. This measure was not considered by Washington's committee. The act is in 7 H 283 ff.

[27] *Journ. H. B.*, 1758–61, p. 50. For the issuance of a proclamation and the offer of a reward of £50 for the arrest of Ball, who had been a member of the Court of Lancaster County, see E. J., Nov. 2, 1758, MS, VSL.

[28] Washington's great-grandfather, the first William Ball of Millenbeck, was the great-great-grandfather of this fifth William Ball of Millenbeck. The expelled member had married Lettice Lee, daughter of Henry Lee of Lee's Hall and consequently an aunt of the boy later known as "Light Horse" Harry Lee.

[29] *Journ. H.B.*, 1758–61, p. 59, 90.

and walking through the Burgesses, gave a nod to his creatures on each side, who all followed him out of the House, and promised to be for the largest sum proposed." Investigation was promptly made; witnesses were heard; "Mr. Attorney" himself reported for the committee, though his own brother was under accusation. The plain-spoken Burgess from Louisa was denounced officially for words condemned as "false, scandalous, and malicious," but the resolution against him was carried by a majority of five only—thirty-seven to thirty-two.[30] This was a most instructive if disagreeable lesson in the political education of George Washington, Gent.

Opportunities of a pleasant sort came with the petitions some of his former soldiers presented: Capt. Robert Stewart promptly received compensation for the extra service he rendered as temporary Brigade Major; [31] Adam Stephen asked that the survivors of the Virginia contingent of Grant's command be reimbursed for the shirts and blankets they had been forced to leave in their retreat from the vicinity of Fort DuQuesne.[32] Doubtless it was largely on Washington's recommendation that a special committee urged and the House approved within four days the payment of £175 to the petitioners.[33] Other appeals were to be made, some of them by humble men who had small claims. In reviewing these, Colonel Washington occasionally served on special committees.

Committee hearings and silent participation in the work of the House did not occupy all of Washington's time during the long debate over the troops Virginia was to pay during 1759. The evenings were free for social affairs, and for conversation with Burgesses and other officials who had a surprising variety of information. Tablemates were teachers; the lobby was a law school. Minutes could be snatched now and then, too, for the writing of letters on private affairs; there always was delight in quiet conversation with Martha. Some of this concerned the furnishings of Mount Vernon, which had been left bare, or worse, from the time Anne Fairfax Washington, widow of George's brother Lawrence, had departed after her marriage to George Lee.[34] First of all, the chamber to be occupied by the master and his bride had to be supplied with a bed and had to be decorated according to an acceptable color scheme. This was a subject not to be settled, of course, until Martha

30 *Journ. H.B.*, 1758–61, p. 90, 114.   31 *Ibid.*, 84, 86.
32 *Ibid.*, 97; see Vol. II, p. 346.   33 *Journ. H.B.*, 1758–61, p. 102.
34 See Vol. I, p. 264; Vol. II, p. 299–300.

reached Mount Vernon, which she never had visited; but even before she saw the wallpaper and the paint there could be preliminary discussion, eager and exciting. Invoices for dress had also to be considered, but, so far as Martha was concerned, these items were not pressing. She had ordered numerous garments from London after she decided to marry George and she had sent back for re-dyeing a bedroom gown she probably meant to wear at the time of her marriage.[35] These articles had not arrived in time for the nuptials, but if her orders were filled correctly, she could look forward to getting enough yellow, brocaded, grosgrain silk for a full costume. Martha was to receive, also, some pink lutestring and Persian silk for the lining.[36] These fabrics were to be made up in the Colony. With them were to come from London a number of fans, a white and a garnet egret, a long white necklace and other furnishings.[37] More hats and jewelry and an enlarged wardrobe would be wanted later; but the bride would be adorned for her husband as soon as the *Cornwall,* Capt. Thomas Hooper, delivered the chests that were being sent from the great English market. Already one diverting consignment was at hand in March—a collection of children's toys that Martha had ordered for "Jackie" and for "Patsy" after their father's death. There was a tiny coach-and-six, with a little stable that sheltered six additional horses. A toy whip was included for the boy and, for "Patsy," a corner cupboard and a walnut bureau.[38] Observing the children with these new treasures, Washington had in the first months of marriage one of the delights a parent does not usually enjoy until he has agonized over the ills of his infants and has seen them stumble and weep and get up again and toddle on.

The end of March approached while the Washingtons enjoyed the company of the children, the planning for the future, and the social life of the town. No action had been taken on the bill concerning the supply of the Regiment, but there were indications that even the most prolix orators were exhausting their arguments. Washington was anxious to get home and to prepare his farms for the spring planting, but he was not willing to leave the House until the bill to continue his old Regiment in service had been brought to a vote. He resolved his dilemma in his usual direct fashion: he would remain in Williamsburg for the passage

[35] This was mentioned on the same invoice with the "genteel suite of clothes for myself," that was "to be grave but not extravagant nor mourning." See Vol. II., p. 302.

[36] The invoice did not state that the "Persian" was for this purpose, but the material was so used in the eighteenth century.

[37] 385 *Papers of G. W.,* LC.

[38] 2 *G. W.,* 335 n.

of the measure and then he would apply immediately for leave of absence for the remainder of the session.

At last, on Monday, the 2nd of April, the engrossed bill was put on its passage. It bore the title, "An act for granting an Aid to his Majesty for the better Protection and Defence of this Colony, and for other purposes therein mentioned," and it presented a patriotic compromise. The Regiment was to be recruited to 1000 men who were to serve until December 1, 1759, as originally proposed. These troops, on the Governor's order, might be dispatched beyond the borders of Virginia "and employed as the Commander-in-Chief of his Majesty's forces on this continent shall appoint and direct." For this purpose, £28,000 were appropriated. In addition, at a cost not to exceed £16,000, a force of 500 was to be raised for the protection of the frontiers; but this body was not to be "incorporated with the Regiment aforesaid, joined with the King's forces, employed to garrison Pittsburgh, or sent out of this Colony upon any pretence whatsoever." The earlier proposal for covering the cost by future taxation was embodied in the measure.[39] On motion, the blanks in the bill were duly filled. Passage by an unrecorded vote followed; Charles Carter was designated to carry the paper to the Council for the concurrence of the body. The very next business of the House, the last action of the day, was the grant of a leave of absence to Mr. Washington for the remainder of the session.[40]

As soon after that as Martha, the children, the servants and the luggage were ready, the journey to Mount Vernon began. The Colonel never before had been called upon to provide for the movement of so unusual a combination of humans and trunks and chests and boxes; but a man who almost literally had shoved the expedition of 1754 over the Allegheny mountains could hope to get his wife, "Jackie," "Patsy," the attendants and the baggage across the Pamunkey, the Rappahannock, the creeks and the Occoquan. During the journey, the inexperience of the new husband came embarrassingly to light along with proof that a good soldier can keep his column closed and in motion. Returning home alone, Washington could have slept in whatever bed was avail-

---

[39] 7 H 255. See *ibid.*, 279, for an act of the same session, passed after Washington left Williamsburg. This measure provided that 200 of the supplementary force of 500 should be "artificers" who might be attached to the Regiment, with an increased bounty of £5 for each man so enlisted. While the act did not so state, these craftsmen, most of them carpenters, were needed urgently for work on the fort at Pittsburgh. See *Journ. H.B.,* 1758–61, p. 129.

[40] *Journ. H.B.,* 1758–61, p. 113. Final adjournment of the session was on April 14 (*ibid.,* 129).

able, or he could have ridden over to Belvoir and could have spent the
night there. As it was, he had displayed the forethought of leaving the
house key at the Fairfaxes, and he knew John Alton was in general
command; but he realized, about the time he reached Fredericksburg,
that he had failed to make any more advance preparation for the coming
of Martha and the children than he would have made if he had been
alone. So, in humiliating contrast to his usual early regard for the detail
of future occurrences, he had to sit down on the 5th of April and write:[41]

Jno: I have sent Miles on today, to let you know that I expect to be up
tomorrow, and to get the key from Colonel Fairfax's, which I desire you will
take care of. You must have the house very well cleaned, and were you to
make fires in the rooms below it would air them. You must get two of the
best bedsteads put up, one in the hall room, and the other in the little dining
room that used to be, and have beds made on them against we come. You
must also get out the chairs and tables, and have them very well rubbed and
cleaned; the staircase ought also to be polished in order to make it look well.
Enquire about in the neighborhood, and get some eggs and chickens, and
prepare in the best manner you can for our coming: you need not, however,
take out any more of the furniture than the beds and tables and chairs in
order that they may be well rubbed and cleaned.

Doubtless when Miles rode up, via Belvoir, with this letter and the
house key, John Alton beat "the general" call to quarters, so to say, and
had all able-bodied domestics start to work to get Mount Vernon in
order. John's allotment of time and his knowledge of the ways of
fastidious gentlewomen may not have equalled his zeal. When the
Colonel arrived the next day [42] with his bride, she may have been
excused if she tactfully showed more enthusiasm for the view of the
Potomac than for the building and its contents—no matter how diligently John had polished the staircase.

The plantation to which Washington brought his new wife that
April day was close to the centre of an interesting neighborhood framed

41 The text in 2 *G. W.*, 318 is headed "Thursday" with the editor's bracketed addition
"[April 1, 1759]." Thursday was the 5th, not the 1st. In the version printed here, abbreviated
words have been spelled out, capitalization has been modernized, and a few changes in punctuation made to facilitate reading.

42 *Ledger A*, folio 55 includes an entry of "expenses in my journey from Williamsburg to
Fairfax," dated April 7. Other items (folio 53) show Washington conducting business at home
on the 8th. It is likely, therefore, that he arrived on the 6th, and methodically charged up his
expenses the next morning, but there is a possibility that the party did not reach the house until
the 7th.

by the main stream and its affluents. From the vicinity of Alexandria to the point where the Potomac received the waters of the Occoquan, twenty miles sufficed for the noble river to twist from South to Southwest and then to South and again to Southwest. Socially and agriculturally, the Potomac did not bound or divide. It was little used by the Virginians in visiting friends at any considerable distance, but its ferries made the Maryland homes on the left bank a part of the neighborhood. Back from the river on the Virginia side, to the West and Northwest, the "Mount Vernon neighborhood" did not extend far beyond the roads that ran from Four Mile Creek to the Occoquan, for the reason that most of the wealthier planters built close to the Potomac or on one of its estuaries.[43]

Two small streams formed the natural boundaries of the tract on which Mount Vernon itself was built. These were Dogue Run to the westward[44] and Little Hunting Creek on the East and Northeast. Rising close together, these watercourses ran parallel to each other for some distance and then separated on crude arcs until they gave the land between them the outline of a frying-pan with the handle to the North. The fields within these watered boundaries were slightly more than five miles in length on the meridian[45] and spread at maximum about two miles and a quarter from East to West. Most of the ground was about fifty feet above sea level. Approximately 400 yards inland from the house site was a scarcely perceptible rise to an elevation of 100 feet.

Whether cleared or untouched by the axe, the Mount Vernon estate would have been merely a large Virginia plantation, typical of scores, had not the Potomac given it a setting of dignity, charm and ever-changing color. The front of the house faced Southeast, at right angles to and at a distance of 225 yards from the right bank of the "River of Swans" which at that point was a mile and a quarter in width. Eight and a half miles upstream, about eight miles by road, was Alexandria.

[43] The present line of the Richmond-Washington railroad is approximately that of the western boundary of the neighborhood, though some friends of the Mount Vernon household resided beyond the road, or South of the Occoquan, or North of Alexandria, and up the valley of Four Mile Creek. This stream, marked "Fourmile Run" on recent maps, rises in the vicinity of East Falls Church, flows Southeast and then East and empties into the Potomac at a point nearly opposite the mouth of Anacostia River on the Maryland shore.

[44] Now styled Dogue Creek on official maps. It surprises a visitor to discover that Dogue Run is on the western side of the property because, as one comes downstream from Alexandria to Mount Vernon, Little Hunting Creek is reached before Dogue Run is.

[45] This distance includes the "handle."

Southwest of the residence, at a distance of near a mile and a half was the long, V-shaped estuary at the mouth of Dogue Run. On the south side of this, pleasantly crowning a hill that overlooked the river, was the Belvoir mansion, dear to Washington through a hundred associations and second only to Mount Vernon itself in his affections.[46] Below Belvoir, another mile and a half of the river led to the little bay that received the waters of Accotink and Pohick Creeks. On that promontory stood a recently completed residence, Gunston Hall, which could be reached from Mount Vernon by riding over approximately eleven miles of indifferent road.

These three, Mount Vernon, Belvoir and Gunston Hall, were, so to say, the inner neighborhood of large estates. Their owners were friends who exchanged ideas as readily as they lent sugar or borrowed shingles, though visits were less frequent as muddy miles lengthened. If Colonel Washington had business with Colonel Fairfax, he could ride over to Belvoir and transact it in not much more time than would be required to draft and copy a letter. The reverse was true of Gunston Hall. Communication with George Mason, except at church, usually was in writing.[47]

The masters of both these neighboring plantations were living at home when Washington came back to Mount Vernon with his bride in the spring of 1759. Fairfax was growing tobacco and the usual "feed crops" at Belvoir. Life was opulent, but his accounts were falling into some confusion,[48] and he was suffering concern over the state of his property in England.[49] He and Sally still were without children after nearly eleven years of married life and they had a smaller household than resided at Belvoir during the lifetime of Col. William Fairfax. His son "Billy" was with the army that was being trained at Louisburg for an attack on Quebec; Bryan was establishing himself at Towlston, North of Alexandria.[50] These changes at Belvoir had not cramped the good nature of Sally Cary Fairfax. In a short time, Martha was on the friendliest footing with her and was exchanging news and notes almost

---

[46] The ruins of Belvoir, within the area of the present Fort Belvoir (formerly Fort Humphreys) were excavated and carefully mapped in November, 1931, under the direction of Col. Edward H. Schultz, Corps of Engineers, U. S. Army.

[47] To this circumstance, doubtless, America owes some of George Mason's papers which otherwise might have been lost conversations with Washington.

[48] See 3 G. W., 223.

[49] Va. Land Grants, 166.

[50] Mrs. William Fairfax, last wife of Washington's mentor, had died in 1747.

as often as the gentlemen passed tools or supplies from one plantation to the other.[51]

The household of Gunston Hall was interesting in a different way. Ann Thomson Mason, widow of the George Mason who had been drowned in crossing the Potomac, was still alive and had discharged admirably her task of making provision for her younger children.[52] Her eldest, George, had read widely and thoroughly in the library of his uncle by marriage, the well-known attorney, John Mercer of Marlborough, but he had not adopted the law as a vocation. His heart was in his plantation on Dogue's Neck which he managed in person.[53] He had married "across the river" in 1750 and now, at 34, was moving into his new home, Gunston Hall.[54] Probably because he was suffering from "gout of the stomach," [55] he shunned the excitement of public life but he was Burgess from Fairfax,[56] a Trustee of the town of Alexandria, and a justice of the County Court of Fairfax, and already he was recognized as a developing master of public law. Nothing pleased him better, when the condition of his farm and of his stomach permitted, than to pursue some theory to the last lair of objection and to destroy it or to make it his own.

Washington had other neighbors back of Belvoir; downstream was Westmoreland County, Washington's birthplace and the home of the Lees; [57] but the largest interest was up the river at Alexandria where, in 1754, the Court House of Fairfax County had been established.[58] Business as well as litigation was revolving around the new town. A visitor to Alexandria in the year of Washington's marriage pronounced it "in one of the finest situations imaginable." He elaborated: "The Potomac

[51] For examples of this barter and borrowing, see *Ledger A*, folio 105. Washington did not fail to note that some white lead sold him by Fairfax was reported by the artisans of Mount Vernon to be very old and scarcely fit for use. See also Washington to George William Fairfax, July 20, 1763: "I have not a lath in the world of any kind, seasoned or unseasoned, or you should be heartily welcome to them" (*Boston Public Library MS*).

[52] See Vol. I, p. 205.

[53] Kate Mason Rowland, *The Life of George Mason* (cited hereafter as *Rowland, Mason*) v. 1, p. 53, 56; Helen Hill, *George Mason*, 11–12.

[54] His wife was Ann Eilbeck of Mattawoman, Charles County, Maryland.

[55] This was the malady that was supposed to have been responsible for the death of George Washington's father. See Vol. I, p. 72, n. 157.

[56] Bailey (*Ohio Company of Virginia*, 189) stated that Mason was Treasurer of the Ohio Company. The first observed mention of Mason in that capacity in the *Virginia Gazette* was May 29, 1773.

[57] For mention of some of these neighbors and for a brief sketch of the Stratford Lees of this period, see Appendix III-1.

[58] See *Proceedings of Trustees Alexandria*, 24, for an order of Dec. 19, 1754, that the Court House lot be paled in with posts and rails. The various Court Houses of Fairfax are described in *Landmarks*, 321.

above and below the town is not more than a mile broad, but it here opens into a large circular bay of at least twice that diameter. The town is built upon an arc of this bay, at one extremity of which is a wharf; at the other a dock for building ships; with water sufficient to launch a vessel of any rate or magnitude." [59] Development of Alexandria had been the care of resolute and active trustees who continued to represent the best citizenship of the Potomac. Purchasers failing to build on their lots had lost title to them,[60] but those who had bought on the waterfront were to be confirmed ere long in their right to extend construction into the river as far as they saw fit.[61] Wooden chimneys had been prohibited; [62] owners of hogs had been ordered to confine them or kill them; [63] plans were under way for a new and commodious ship landing; [64] the day was not distant when the town was to have its Mayor, its Recorder, its Aldermen and its Common Council; [65] annexation, too, was in prospect to relieve the shortage of quarters that had been acute and distressful in 1755, when Braddock's camp followers had established themselves there.[66]

The social boundary now was not that of the town but, in effect, that of the little stream above Alexandria known as Four Mile Creek, not far from the falls of the Potomac. A fixed agricultural economy prevailed below the falls. West of them, the impulse of the speculating planters, as in earlier years, was to maintain the same system on their new land,[67] but conditions were beginning to change. Ownership might be vested in rich Virginians; development might depend on those Pennsylvania Germans who ten years previously had disgusted young Washington.[68]

The Colonel and his lady belonged, distinctly, to the society that lived below the falls. While Washington never forgot that more money could be made by patenting and holding land beyond the mountains than in almost any other way, he had at hand a task that would absorb for a long time all his energy and, as he soon discovered, the greater part of the capital he would get from Martha. The unhappy fact—not to be evaded, blinked, minimized or quickly ended—was this: Mount Vernon

---

[59] *Burnaby*, 50. The punctuation is somewhat modified for clarity. Smyth, *op. cit.*, v. 2, p. 201, was to state, c. 1775, "Alexandria is most delightfully situated in a most healthy and beautiful spot."

[60] *Proceedings of Trustees Alexandria*, 21.

[61] *Ibid.*, 34; Sept. 1, 1760.

[62] *Ibid.*, 28; Sept. 30, 1755.

[63] *Ibid.*, 31; Oct. 13, 1758.

[64] *Ibid.*, 32; July 18, 1759.

[65] *Md. Gazette*, Dec. 1, 1761.

[66] Mrs. Browne's quest of quarters is set forth in her journal, 32 *V* 306 ff. For the annexation of November, 1762, see 7 *H* 605.

[67] See Vol. I, Appendix I-1, p. 512.

[68] Vol. I, p. 221.

had been mismanaged dismally during the later years of service in the army. In the Colonel's absence, after the property was leased to him, "Jack" Washington had been the only person who really had made an effort to take care of the estate, and the younger brother had not been there all the time, or, apparently, successful when there. Buildings had collapsed; stock had disappeared. Almost everything needed for good management was worn out or lacking altogether. Corn crops had been so meagre and hogs had been bred so carelessly—or had been stolen and devoured in such numbers when bred—that Washington would have to buy provisions and feed to carry his family and his livestock through the winter, a situation intolerably humiliating to any good farmer.[69] Washington saw immediately that he had much to do; he was not equally quick to perceive that he lacked part of the experience he needed in order to do it well.

[69] 2 *G. W.,* 397.

CHAPTER II

AN ENLARGED MOUNT VERNON MUST GROW THE BEST

(April 1759–May 1760)

ASIDE FROM the problems a relatively inexperienced farm manager faced in restoring a "rundown" plantation, Washington had the pleasant task of transforming a bachelor's retreat into a family home. Among the first decisions—and not a small one for a bride—was that concerning the decoration of the bed-chamber, which doubtless had been discussed in Williamsburg. After Martha saw the room wallpaper, which Washington had ordered in August, 1757,[1] she concluded that furnishings and draperies should be blue or blue and white. A new tester bed would be necessary, too. Although the pitch of the room was eight feet only, she and her husband concluded that the bed should stand seven and a half feet from the floor, tester included. Bed curtains and canopy, the draperies for the two windows and the seats of the four chairs all were to match in the chosen color. A cornice of papier-mâché, or one covered with blue or blue and white cloth, would be required for each window.[2] Elsewhere in the house, the imperative needs were for two carpets, fire screens for two rooms, and a large couch for the empty hall. Glasses and dishes in small number were wanted. The proper adornment of the new marble mantle in the parlor[3] could wait on further reflection. Outside, the neglected lawn had to be reseeded.[4]

Washington carefully made notes of all these articles and duly ordered them when he went to Williamsburg late in April to qualify for the administration of the Custis estate.[5] Probably on the 28th, he appeared with Martha's attorney, John Mercer, before the General Court which

---

[1] 2 *G. W.*, 23.

[2] Apparently this "cornish," as Washington spelled it, was to correspond to a valance. He did not specify the color of the cornice in event it were papier-mâché. Perhaps Martha planned to have it painted to blend with the curtains.

[3] 2 *G. W.*, 23.

[4] 2 *G. W.*, 320.

[5] An invoice attached to a letter from Williamsburg, May 1, 1759, supplies these details of the furnishing of Mount Vernon. See 2 *G. W.*, 320-21.

was sitting in chancery,[6] and asked that he be named to administer the two-thirds interest of the Custis estate vested in "Jackie" and "Patsy," along with the third he already controlled as husband of Martha. He did not request the court to name him instead of Mr. Speaker Robinson as guardian of the children.[7]

As this was in accordance with Martha's wishes and doubtless was agreeable to the guardian, the court entered the appropriate order.[8] Simultaneously, John Mercer and Washington recommended to the court a division of the property of the estate. Under the common law, the bridegroom took the wife's real estate *jure uxoris* and could control it precisely as if it were his own, except that he could not alienate or encumber her lands to the prejudice of her ultimate rights or those of her heirs.[9] Consequently, the plantations were to be apportioned between Washington and young Custis. As large a part as possible of the bonds and like securities of the estate went to "Patsy." One-third of the Negroes, two-thirds of the cattle, one-third of the hogs and one-third of the sheep were assigned Mrs. Washington. The remainder became "Jackie's" for use on the plantations he inherited.[10] Another asset to be divided was Daniel Parke Custis's collection of books, which doubtless included those of John Custis, and numbered slightly more than 450 volumes. Most of these were set aside for "Jackie," but in his wife's name Washington took the works on business and agriculture and some of those on history.[11]

[6] Papers relating to the settlement (*Custis Papers,* VHS) bear date of Apr. 26–28, 1759. It is possible, of course, though scarcely probable, that the proceedings for a settlement of the estate were opened in court by Mercer before the arrival of Washington. The court normally considered chancery cases on April 10 and for four days afterwards (6 *H* 328). Washington consequently had started from Williamsburg for Mount Vernon with his bride and her children only a week, or approximately that long, before the court opened. The reason for what thus appears to have been an almost useless journey to the Potomac and back again is not known. One obvious possibility is the need of Washington's presence, however brief, to direct affairs at Mount Vernon. Another is that the condition of the docket, the preoccupation of Mercer, or delay in completing the accounts of the court fixed a later date for the hearing.

[7] This is established by the fact that "John P. Custis, an infant represented by his guardian, John Robinson" entered suit against a debtor as late as Aug. 18, 1761 (*York Orders,* 1759–61, p. 172).

[8] 2 *G. W.,* 319. The order itself is lost, but the wills of the testators and the bonds are in the records of the Prerogative Court, Canterbury, England. Copies have been given VSL.

[9] This is the language of an interesting analysis of the common law prevailing in 1759, as prepared for this work, Nov. 13, 1947, by William F. Hazen, counsel for the Richmond Newspapers, Inc.

[10] Division of the estate of D. P. Custis, a MS in the autograph of John Mercer, n.d., but bearing endorsements of Apr. 26–28, 1759; *Custis Papers,* VHS.

[11] 17 *V* 404 ff. Apparently the division was not completed. In the list here printed, less than 100 of the titles are marked "G. W." or "J. P. C." All the books and pamphlets probably were moved to Mount Vernon.

As finally apportioned, the estate was handsome and, for Virginia, notable in the amount of securities held. The real estate consisted of 17,438 acres.[12] Without inclusion or appraisal of this, the sum credited to each of the three heirs was £1617 sterling and £7618, currency of the country, in slaves, live stock, notes and bonds and accounts receivable[13]—an aggregate in personalty of almost £20,000 sterling.[14] No less than £8958 of these personal assets in the currency of the country were represented by slaves.[15]

The size of the personal estate was due in part to the one large potential liability—the chance, if no more than a chance, of a final adverse judgment in the Dunbar case. Daniel Parke Custis's fear that he would have to pay his maternal grandfather's debts in the Leeward Islands had led him to economize and had held him firmly to his resolution to leave his British credits intact.[16] At the time Washington and Mercer made the division of the funds Mrs. Washington's first husband had accumulated, there were indications that Custis's prudence might have been necessary for the protection of his widow and children: The Dunbar suit was being renewed.[17]

Whether the descendants of Col. Daniel Parke's illegitimate daughter wrecked the Virginia property, or merely put the lawful heirs to expense, Washington was resolved that his accounts of the estate should be accurate to a penny at the same time that he insisted on getting all that was due him as husband of the former Mrs. Custis. As soon as he received the court's approval of the division and administration of the real estate and personalty, he wrote formally from Williamsburg to the London merchants, Robert Cary & Co., who had handled the greater part of Custis business: "Gentlemen: The enclosed is the minister's certificate of my marriage with Mrs. Martha Custis, properly as I am told, authenticated. You will therefore for the future please to address all your letters which relate to the affairs of the late Daniel Parke Custis, Esqr. to me, as by marriage I am entitled to a third part of that estate, and invested likewise with the care of the other two-thirds by a decree of

---

12 Quit-rents of 1757, receipted May 8, 1758; *Custis Papers*, VHS.

13 Division as cited, *supra*; *Custis Papers*, VHS.

14 On the assumption that the current premium on sterling exchange was 35 per cent.

15 *Ibid*. At an average of £30—not too low a figure where children and the old were included—this would indicate that the estate owned about 300 slaves. Subsequent entries for "tithables," chiefly Negroes over 16 years of age, confirm these figures.

16 See Vol. II, p. 298.

17 It may, indeed, have been reopened at the April term of the General Court. Washington wrote, June 12, 1759: "Dunbar's lawsuit is again brought to Virginia" (2 *G. W.*, 324).

our General Court which I obtained in order to strengthen the power I before had in consequence of my wife's administration." That said, he proceeded, planter-like, to discuss tobacco prices and prospects, and on the reverse of his letter he wrote an invoice that included, among other items, the goods he and Martha had chosen by that time for the adornment of Mount Vernon.[18] The other merchants who had been handling Custis tobacco in the British Isles were sent similar notice of Washington's newly acquired interest in the estate. "Duty to the charge which I am entrusted as well as self-interest," he told the powerful firm of Hanbury, "will induce me to abide by the merchants who shews the greatest exertion in the sales of my own and the estate's tobacco, which will be made under the same direction, and without altering the kind or manner of treating unless you can advise a better method of making it sell well." [19]

In this state of mind, he took up his new tasks on returning to Mount Vernon.[20] One thing he had to do forthwith was to muster and to organize the household in order to assure comfortable management and to conform to his own custom of doing everything with system. "I have quit a military life," he said, "and shortly shall be fixed at this place with an agreeable partner, and then shall be able to conduct my own business with more punctuality than heretofore as it will pass under my own immediate instruction, a thing impracticable while I discharged my duty in the public service of the country." [21] He disregarded in one way—if in one only—the methods that became a veteran commander: he did not observe economy of force, doubtless because he did not need to do so. With Martha's personal domestics added, there were more servants than there was work to be done. For the household, he and Martha allowed eleven; [22] Breechy, the waiter,[23] had an immediate assistant, when needed, in the person of Mulatto Jack, who officially was the "jobber." [24] The cook, Doll, commanded Beck as a scullion. Jenny was to do the washing, and Mima the ironing. Besides Sally, her

---

[18] 2 *G. W.,* 319–20.
[19] Letter of June 12, 1759; 2 *G. W.,* 325. See also *ibid.,* 325, and a letter of May 7, 1759 (*ibid.,* p. 321), to the merchant who had been disposing of the tobacco from Mount Vernon.
[20] He was back home by May 7, 1759. See 2 *G. W.,* 321.
[21] 2 *G. W.,* 322.
[22] It is fair to add that this number of house servants was not excessive by the indulgent standards prevailing on large plantations where bondsmen could not be made to do anything like the work free servants performed.
[23] In modern establishments, of course, he would be termed the butler.
[24] This term for the modern "handy man" accorded with good eighteenth-century usage.

maid, Mrs. Washington used Betty as a seamstress. The boy Julius was chosen to wait on "Jackie"; the juvenile maid for "Patsy" bore the name Rose. To keep an eye on these youngsters, black and white, and to do their sewing was the exclusive assignment of Moll.[25]

For two reasons Washington did not attempt a similar immediate reorganization of his farms and of those belonging to the estate: Most of his own tenants had yearly agreements that had been renewed for 1759 before he resigned from the Regiment; second, the Custis plantations on the York and its tributaries were under the care of a competent and reliable steward, Joseph Valentine, whom Washington's business judgment bade him leave alone. The tobacco crop of 1758 had been small in Virginia;[26] scarcity considered, prices in London had been low.[27] Washington was not discouraged. He had ordered the best books on agriculture and farm management,[28] and as the tobacco crop of 1759 promised a handsome return,[29] he became almost enthusiastic over the future of the staple on his own lands. In September he somewhat naively wrote one of the merchants: "I am possessed of several plantations on this river (Potomack) and the fine lands of Shenandoah, and should be glad if you would ingenuously tell me what prices I might expect you to render for tobaccos made thereon of the same seed of that of the estate's and managed in every respect in the same manner as the best tobaccos on James or York rivers. I ask this question for my own private information, and my shipping of these crops will be governed in a great measure by the answer you may give; therefore you will excuse me I hope, if I again desire the favor of you to take some pains to inform yourselves exactly, because should the prices differ from those of the estate I might possibly think myself deceived and be disgusted of course."[30] Not a word was there in any of this concerning possible

[25] The total of eleven does not include the weaver, the five carpenters, their boy helper and the four tanners on Washington's roster of "Servants in and about the house." This list in the *Custis Papers*, VHS, is undated but, to judge from the age of the little Negroes assigned to "wait on" and to play with "Jackie" and "Patsy," it was prepared as soon after the Custises came to Mount Vernon as suitable selections could be made. No doubt, most of these house-servants had been employed similarly at the White House. The carpenters specifically are mentioned as "tradesmen belonging to estate."

[26] 2 *G. W.*, 319, 322, 325.　　　　　　[27] *Ibid.*, 326.

[28] *Ibid.*, 321, 323. He wanted "the newest and most approved Treatise on Agriculture," which he subsequently heard from some authority was Thomas Hale's *Compleat Body of Husbandry*. "If this is known to be the best," he wrote one of his merchants, "pray send it but not if any other is in higher esteem" (*ibid.*, 323). Washington ordered also "A New System of Agriculture, or a Speedy Way to Grow Rich," and with this, "Langley's Book of Gardening" and "Gibson upon Horses, the latest edition in quarto" (*ibid.*, 321).

[29] *Ibid.*, 329.　　　　　　[30] To Robert Cary & Co., 2 *G. W.*, 330.

differences between the soil of the Potomac region and that of the York. The seed, the culture and the handling of the leaf would be identical: ought not the quality and the price to be the same? It was a new if earnest amateur who asked.

Along with hope and the happiness of new love, despite the wretched condition of the estate, the summer brought a cargo of good news about the war. After the failure of the attack on Fort Ticonderoga in 1758, most of the British commanders in the Northern Colonies had despaired of success on the Great Lakes that year and had begun to plan for 1759; but Lt. Col. John Bradstreet, who possessed wizard-like skill in building and employing batteaux, went steadfastly on with plans he previously had made for a descent on Fort Frontenac, at the northeast corner of Lake Ontario where the St. Lawrence starts on its way to the sea. With great fortitude he and his men reached and seized on Aug. 27, 1758, the feebly manned fort.[31] It proved to be a prize astonishingly rich, almost a general base, where sixty cannon, sixteen mortars, and a great supply of provisions, ships' stores and Indian goods had been accumulated. Nine armed vessels, constituting nearly the whole French naval force on Lake Ontario, fell into British hands.[32] More important still, loss of the fort severed French communications between the Great Lakes and the Ohio and thereby brightened the prospect in Pennsylvania to an extent the commanders there may not have appreciated. If Fort Frontenac had not been captured, the evacuation of the Ohio by the French on the approach of the British in November, 1758, would scarcely have been necessary. Instead of the smoking debris at the junction of the Allegheny and the Monongahela, Forbes and his Highlanders and colonials might have found fuming cannon and a reenforced garrison.

The destruction of Fort Frontenac, moreover, had renewed hopes that stronger British armies, courageously led, would be able in 1759 to execute a revised plan of operations the resolute William Pitt had formulated. Gen. James Wolfe, who had distinguished himself by energy and daring in the final operations against Louisburg, was directed to prepare for an attack by land and water against Quebec. While Wolfe assailed that citadel of the St. Lawrence, Gen. Jeffrey Amherst was to proceed up the Hudson and was to do everything he could to create a

---

[31] Needless to say, this fort was on the site of the modern Kingston, Ontario.
[32] Parkman, *Montcalm and Wolfe*, v. 2, p. 133–34, 7 *Gipson*, 237–45.

diversion that would help the British army farther North. If all went well, Ticonderoga and Crown Point could be captured, and Amherst's troops united with Wolfe's to complete the ruin of French power in Canada. Should Amherst's task be beyond the resources allowed him, his threatening advance at least would lead the French to strengthen the troops opposing him and thereby to reduce the forces that would confront Wolfe. Large discretion was given Amherst to organize other operations, provided they did not weaken his main advance up the Hudson to the forts that guarded the southern end of Lake Champlain.[33]

Amherst wisely decided that while he made his thrust at Ticonderoga and Crown Point, he would undertake simultaneously an advance on Fort Niagara, located on the southern shore of Lake Ontario and at the mouth of the river which pours into the Lake from the South the water that has plunged over Niagara Falls.[34] This secondary thrust succeeded beyond all calculation and with results of particular personal interest to the retired young Virginia Colonel who read of them at Mount Vernon. It developed that French irregulars and Indians had been assembling on the southern shore of Lake Erie for an expedition to recover Fort DuQuesne, now Fort Pitt. They were more intent on profit and loot than on planting once again the fleur-de-lis of His Most Christian Majesty on the Ohio; but they were desperate, forest-toughened men, and if they got to the forks of the "Beautiful River" and took the fort then being constructed, the chance was small that any Englishman there would survive to tell the tale. As soon as the commander at Fort Niagara learned that a British attack was to be made on his position, he ordered to his assistance these forces that had been preparing to move from Presque Isle toward Fort Pitt. They came, but before they could form a junction with the French garrison, they encountered part of the British column that already had begun the siege of Niagara. In a brief

[33] Parkman, *Montcalm and Wolfe*, v. 2, p. 245. Pitt's instructions to Amherst will be found in 2 *Pitt,* 12, 64. They are admirable examples of the manner in which the civilian head of a government should set forth the objective of a campaign and should leave to his military subordinate the choice of means to achieve that objective. Pitt wrote Amherst: "I am to signify to you the King's pleasure that you do attempt, with the utmost vigor, the reduction of Canada: At the same time, His Majesty, placing great confidence in your judgment and capacity, is pleased to leave it entirely to your discretion, by what avenues you will penetrate into the same. . . . As, an irruption once effectually made, in whatever part it be, Canada must necessarily fall; and, with it, the French power in North America" (letter of Mch. 10, 1759, *op. cit.,* v. 2, p. 65). When Pitt wrote this he already, and in some particularity, had given Amherst information on the extent of the force that would be at the disposal of the General.

[34] A good sketch map for quick understanding of these operations is Plate 44 in *Atlas of American History.*

action, the French and Indian reenforcements were driven back in panic, and most of their surviving officers were captured.[35] Fort Niagara was surrendered immediately, July 25, 1759; the fugitives who had undertaken to relieve it returned to their starting-point, burned all the French defences there—Presque Isle, Fort Le Boeuf and Venango—and retreated to Detroit.[36] By dramatic concurrence, the day after Fort Niagara fell, the French at the lower end of Lake Champlain set fire to Fort Ticonderoga on the approach of Amherst's troops, and abandoned the place. On the 1st of August, Amherst heard that Crown Point, too, had been evacuated.[37] He promptly occupied the site but, having done this, he suddenly became cautious and seemed to forget his instructions to pursue his diversion in behalf of Wolfe, who had encountered stubborn and skillful resistance on the approaches to Quebec.

Washington at Mount Vernon had no specific knowledge of the reasons for Amherst's delay after the advance to Crown Point; but the Virginia provincial who had penetrated to Venango and to Fort Le Boeuf almost six years previously understood what it meant to have the French quit those outposts along with Fort Frontenac, Fort DuQuesne, Fort Niagara, Ticonderoga, and Crown Point: Except for what might be happening in the unknown region of Detroit, the enemy now had been driven back to the Great Lakes and the St. Lawrence and was being held, in the main, to the line of the river, Northeast of Lake Ontario. The only strong positions still in French hands were Montreal, Quebec, and the 150 miles of country between them in the region South of Quebec.

Much had been endured, much suffered and much lost since young Colonel Washington had stepped into the open at Jumonville's hiding place and had invited that May morning, 1754, the first shot of a war that had challenged colonial empire. Now, five years after that historic little engagement, Washington's life did not induce reflection on the strategy of imperial conflict; but he had been an officer ambitious for honor and he saw the long-awaited successes of the British through the eyes of the men who had won what he had craved for his country. This point of view, in language far from original, he expressed in a letter to a British merchant: "The scale of Fortune in America is turned greatly in our favor, and success is become the boon companion of our fortunate Generals. 'Twould be folly in me to attempt particularizing

[35] 2 Parkman, *op. cit.*, 256–58.   [36] *Ibid.*, 258.   [37] *Ibid.*, 250.

their actions, since you receive accounts in a channel so much more direct than from hence." Then, as if that were quite enough to say, he dropped down a line on the page and changed the subject without transition or addition: "I am now, I believe, fixed at this seat with an agreeable consort for life and hope to find more happiness in retirement than I ever experienced amidst a wide and bustling world . . ." [38]

Three days before Washington wrote this, Quebec had surrendered after a siege that had cost the lives of General Wolfe and the Marquis de Montcalm. Many of the details, when read by Washington, must have stirred all his soldierly pride, because they covered some of the most magnificent achievements in the entire history of the British army, but they found no place in any of his letters.[39] The cost of the struggle included an unhappy and direct charge on Washington's near neighbors: "Billy" Fairfax, younger brother of George William and son of Col. William Fairfax, lost his life in the contest.[40] Washington had written the previous autumn that he was "extremely glad" young Fairfax had survived the dangers of the siege of Louisburg.[41] Now his expression of his sympathy must have been directly to George William and Sally and Bryan.[42]

Quebec, its graves and its glory, were far off; Washington's prime interest now was in restoring the buildings, the livestock and the implements of Mount Vernon. Interest of a different sort prompted him to continue his efforts to adorn his house and his bride. He consulted her and doubtless deferred to her in all that concerned the "upstairs," but when he turned from the beautification of the bed-chamber to the decoration of the parlor, his military taste asserted itself once more. In the large downstairs room, there were places for eight ornaments of chimney piece and wall. Four of these could be busts, approximately fifteen inches in height, provided they were not wider than ten inches each. Washington decided that two of the four should be of soldiers of ancient time whom he much admired, Alexander the Great and

[38] To Richard Washington, Sept. 20, 1759; 2 *G. W.*, 337.

[39] Neither the index of *Ford* nor that of *G. W.* shows a single reference by Washington to Wolfe or to Montcalm.

[40] Sparks, *op. cit.*, v. 2, p. 53, recorded the tradition that Wolfe came upon "Billy" near the bank of the St. Lawrence, touched him on the shoulder, and said "young man, when we come to action, remember your name."

[41] 2 *G. W.*, 293.

[42] There is no record of any such condolence but it must of course have been voiced to his neighbors. Washington's voluntary advance of £50 to William in April, 1758 (see 2 *G. W.*, 182), was assumed, as noted in Vol. II, p. 390, by Bryan Fairfax.

Julius Caesar. One of the other busts must be of Charles XII of Sweden, a great commander who had died at 34, just fourteen years before Washington himself had been born. The other head was to be that of the Prussian, Frederick II, whose troops then were fighting against a "continent in arms" and already had won, among others, the shining victories of Rossbach and of Leuthen. Caesar had conducted his greatest campaigns when he was in his forties, but the busts of him pictured in the books seen by Washington were those of an older man. Frederick at this time was 47. The others were young captains—Alexander dead at 33, Charles XII renowned at 18. All four would be inspiring companions. Washington included the busts in the next London invoices.[43] Martha, for her part, was content to order some hose and shoes—these "of smallest fives"—a black mask, perfume, six pairs of kid gloves and six of mittens, and a multitude of small articles. Her particular want was of a negligee gown and coat of salmon-colored tabby with satin flowers and a cap, handkerchief, tucker and ruffles to match or blend. These were to be of Brussels or point lace at the stiff price of £20.[44]

The invoices began their voyage across the Atlantic; the tobacco was ripened in the warm August sun and was cut before the frost came; the autumn colored the leaves as if a curtain of red and of gold had fallen on the happiest summer George Washington had spent after he had become a man. About that time, the Colonel became surveyor again and undertook to "find out," in his own words, "the true bounds of my Mount Vernon tract of land," but as he did not know where the original line between the Washington and the Spencer parts of the first grant left the river, he had to reverse the old survey. Then, plotting his courses, he determined where the vanished landmarks must have stood.[45] It was an interesting task and, for so young a country, a verification of an "ancient" record. The original survey for Nicholas Spencer and for Washington's great-grandfather, John Washington, had been

[43] 2 *G. W.*, 333. In due time Washington was notified that no busts of these four soldiers were available in the size he desired. They would be expensive if separately modeled. Fifteen-inch busts of numerous poets, philosophers and men of letters were to be had, if wanted, at 15s. Washington did not choose their company (*ibid.*, 334 n).

[44] 2 *G. W.*, 331. Tabby was originally a striped silk taffeta, but the name subsequently was applied to any waved or watered taffeta even if of a solid color. Moiré of the present day corresponds to it. The word "tucker," as applied to women's dresses, survives now in the phrase "best bib and tucker." It was originally, perhaps, a neck frill, but in the eighteenth century it was a piece of lace worn around the top or inside the upper edge of a bodice. The bill for the negligee and accessories is in the *Custis Papers*, VHS. It shows that the tabby and the lace cost £11 each.

[45] *Survey Notes* of Oct. 1–2, 1759; Mount Vernon MSS.

made by John Alexander in April, 1669, where the earliest known grants bore date of 1657.[46]

On October 22, he took the road to Williamsburg: The personal property in the Custis residence there was to be sold at public sale on October 25;[47] the House of Burgesses was to meet November 1.[48] As administrator of the Custis estate Washington had to check the returns of the sale;[49] as a comparatively new Burgess, he could not afford to absent himself from the Assembly.

It was not a hard or a hurried journey and it probably was broken by a halt at Ferry Farm.[50] His mother was living there, much as she had since Washington's youth, and she had shown unwonted contentment of mind the previous summer in a letter to her brother. She had heard, she said, that the health of Joseph Ball and his family was so good that they might return to Virginia. Continuing, she told Ball: "I should be proud to see you. I have known a great deal of trouble since I see you: thear was no end to my Troble while george was in the army butt he has now given it up; pray give my kind Love to my Sister & Coz. Dowman & I am Dear Brother your Loving and Affectionate Sister." [51] The improvement in her spirits, shown in this letter, was pleasing, of course, to her son, but it made no material difference in their relations. Mother and son were as far apart as ever.

From Fredericksburg, Washington continued southward and, by the 26th of October, was in Williamsburg.[52] As business did not press, he was able to enjoy such festivities as the town offered before the Burgesses assembled and the House opened its sessions. Cards were one pastime; but either because he was out of practice, or else because he encountered some adversary of uncommon skill, he had much the worse of the bouts. One evening he lost 28 shillings—a considerable sum for a frugal player who previously never let the stakes run high.[53] He paid

---

[46] See Vol. I, p. 20–21.   [47] *Supra*, p. 3.

[48] It had been prorogued until Aug. 2, 1759 (*Journ. H.B.*, 1758–61, p. 129), and subsequently had been notified it need not gather until November 1.

[49] He usually termed such an affair a "sale," though "auction" and "vendue" both were familiar eighteenth-century words. In rural Virginia, "vendue" was a current word, everywhere understood, until about 1900.

[50] The probability is strong but there is no positive evidence.

[51] Letter of July 26, 1759; original MS, Penn. H.S. This letter often has been quoted in part to show how meagre the schooling of Mary Washington had been; but, if the entire paper be read, it will be found no worse in its spelling than, for example, Martha's missives.

[52] *Ledger A,* folio 62.

[53] *Ibid.* This entry is for October 28, but there is another item of 10*s* lost that day. The instance may be one of many in which Washington failed to set down the date, though he did not forget the sum.

homage to Fortune also, by contributing £1 to the purse for the Williamsburg race.[54]

The legislative session was not particularly interesting. Governor Fauquier's principal concern, as set forth in his opening address, was that the Colony's old Indian allies, the Cherokees, had become turbulent. Their discontent had so alarmed Gov. William Henry Lyttleton of South Carolina and Gov. Arthur Dobbs of North Carolina that those executives were asking Virginia to prepare jointly with them an expedition that would subdue the red men permanently. Lyttleton already had taken the field and had compelled the Indians to accept a peace of a sort. Fauquier hoped this would prevent hostilities, and, of course, he recognized that the French defeats had rendered England's white adversary less dangerous, but, he warned, "we are not yet in that state of tranquility and security which we could wish." [55] He consequently urged that the Virginia Regiment be kept in service. There was a hint of gathering trouble of another sort in this announcement: ". . . I have received an instruction from his Majesty, to recommend to you the providing for the security of the merchants of Great Britain, in the recovery of sterling debts due to them from this Colony from any loss they may sustain from our unavoidable emissions of paper money." The Governor added: ". . . As I am fully persuaded it is your intentions that no man shall suffer by any act of yours, I recommend . . . you . . . reconsider this affair, and if [the merchants'] property is not already fully secured, to provide for the security thereof in the fullest and amplest manner." [56]

With somewhat less prolonged debate than at the previous session, the House agreed to continue the pay of the Regiment from December 1, the anticipated date of dismissal, to May 1, 1760, but it stipulated that not more than 400 of these men should be employed outside Virginia. The remainder of the Regiment were to be held within the Colony for its defence. Of the 500 additional soldiers who had been authorized at the spring session, 200 were to be released from the service of the Old Dominion immediately after the passage of the new law, and 300 were to be mustered out in February, 1760.[57] Washington doubtless approved what was done and probably wished that more

---

54 *Ibid.*
56 *Ibid.,* 134.
55 *Journ. H.B.,* 1758–61, p. 133.
57 7 H 331 ff; Fauquier to Lords Comm'ers. of Trade, Dec. 1, 1759; *Journ. H.B.,* 1758–61, p. 281–82.

men could be provided, but he took no conspicuous part in framing the legislation.

Nor was he distinguished in the brief half-negative action of the House on the Governor's request for a review of the Virginia statute against which the London merchants had protested. An act "concerning executions and the relief of insolvent debtors" had been passed in May, 1755,[58] and had been designed, in part, to protect creditors who were to be paid in sterling. Previously such a debt could be discharged by a tender of other money at 25 per cent above par. Under the act of 1755, if sterling exchange was at a premium in excess of 25 per cent, the court that entered judgment had power to prescribe the figure at which the debt could be paid. In theory, at least, if prevailing exchange was at 35 per cent, the court would direct that the creditor pay that premium when he tendered "currency of the country."[59] London merchants had not suffered on this account but they had become alarmed and particularly so because every law for the emission of treasury notes, from that of May, 1755,[60] onward, had contained a provision that this paper money should be legal tender for all debts, except the King's quit rents, during the period between issue and redemption. The merchants asserted that this legal-tender provision might supersede the act for paying sterling bills at the prevailing rate of exchange. Because of the merchants' protests, the Ministry had told the Governor to warn the Assembly that further laws for new paper money must allow the creditor the explicit option of payment in sterling or in the currency of the country.

Washington's colleagues in the House of Burgesses saw no occasion for any new guarantee. They contented themselves with declaring that under the existing act of 1755, "the security of the merchants of Great Britain in the recovery of sterling debts due to them from this Colony is provided for, and their property secured in the fullest and amplest manner, and that they have not any just cause of complaint on that head."[61] The Governor was disappointed;[62] but the only formal recorded opposition to any part of the legislation on fiscal affairs came from within the Council. Two members of that body

---

[58] 6 H 478.

[59] See the argument of the Virginia Committee of Correspondence, letter of Dec. 12, 1759, to Edward Montague, the Colony's Agent in London (11 V 2 ff; cf. 10 ibid., 345 ff).

[60] 6 H 461. This was distinct from the act "concerning executions and for the relief of insolvent debtors" but was passed at the same session.

[61] Journ. H.B., 1758–61, p. 141.   [62] Cf. ibid., 153.

insisted that among the faults of a supply bill was the fact that its terms, in effect, contradicted the royal command for allowing an option to the creditor on sterling debts. No less serious was the objection of these Councillors that the law did not require the destruction of notes returned to the Treasury on maturity.[63] The Burgesses gave no heed.

Besides this complicated argument, the House had for its consideration a number of petitions in which, as at the session in February, Washington heard the echo of his own service on the frontier.[64] The central figure in all this was Capt. Robert Stobo, whom Washington had delivered to the French, along with Jacob van Braam, at Fort Necessity, July, 1754, as hostages for the return of the French prisoners captured in the Jumonville affair.[65] As Governor Dinwiddie and the Council of Virginia had refused to recognize Washington's right to bargain for the release of prisoners over whom he then had no control, Jumonville's men had not been sent back to Fort DuQuesne. Stobo and van Braam consequently had remained in the hands of the French. They were treated with consideration and were given virtual freedom of movement until the French got wind of reports that a captive at Fort DuQuesne had been communicating with the British. Stobo was suspected but was not confined.

Then came an extraordinary occurrence for which no less a person than the dead Braddock was in part to blame. After the General's arrival in Virginia, early in 1755, some official gave him the two letters Stobo had smuggled out of Fort DuQuesne soon after he had arrived there as a hostage. The originals of these papers, including the one in which Stobo drew a sketch of the defences, were duly placed in Braddock's headquarters records. Nobody took the precaution of making a copy, and of using that, instead of Stobo's autograph, on the chance that the French might get the original and punish the writer.

Precisely that happened. Stobo's letters were found in Braddock's captured baggage and were taken to Quebec. The Captain was confronted with them, was put on trial and, on Nov. 8, 1755, was condemned to death for "treason." As the order for his execution was subject to confirmation by the government in Paris, Stobo was held in prison. At length, after failing in several attempts, he escaped in the

63 *L.J.*, 1227; entry of Nov. 19, 1759. The two Councillors who had their dissent recorded in the Journal were Philip Ludwell and Philip Ludwell Lee, eldest brother of Richard Henry Lee and oldest surviving son of Thomas Lee.
64 *Journ. H.B.*, 1758–61, p. 141, 142.   65 See Vol. II, p. 366, 407.

spring of 1759. With several other Britishers, he accomplished what appeared to be the impossible feat of descending the St. Lawrence and of reaching Louisburg without detection or, at least, without capture. He was, of course, as welcome a visitor as could have come to the headquarters of Gen. James Wolfe, because he knew the geography of the region which the British commander was about ready to invade. Later, Stobo cheerfully attended Wolfe across the Gulf of St. Lawrence and up the river and gave him information the General scarcely could have procured otherwise. On Sept. 7, 1759, Wolfe sent Stobo across country with dispatches to Amherst,[66] from whose headquarters, as soon as he might, Stobo proceeded to Williamsburg. He found that the news of his escape had been received in the Virginia capital with much gratification and had been the basis of legislative action. The Assembly had voted thanks to Col. Peter Schuyler "of the Jerseys" for the "unparalleled tenderness and humanity" shown Stobo and the men who had escaped with him. Speaker Robinson had been directed to communicate these thanks to Schuyler, whom the Treasurer was instructed to reimburse, with interest, for the full cost of the assistance to the escaped officer.[67] Now that Stobo himself was back in Virginia, he was given a hero's welcome. The Assembly voted him £1000 in addition to his pay for the entire period of his imprisonment; the Governor was asked to promote him; Robert Carter Nicholas, Richard Bland, and Colonel Washington were directed to convey to Stobo the thanks and congratulations of the House.[68] Stobo's reply was felicitous and dignified.[69]

The day after Chairman Nicholas delivered the answer of Captain Stobo to the House, the General Assembly adjourned.[70] Washington lingered long enough to see that the tobacco already prized on the nearby Custis plantations was inspected and delivered at the ship's side,[71] and then he started for Mount Vernon in contentment of spirit. The tobacco crop along York River had been large; the market seemed favorable. When Washington rode into the stableyard at home, two

---

[66] *Stobo*, 71.

[67] *Journ. H.B.*, 1758–61, p. 112. The *Schuyler Papers*, NYPL, mention the efforts of Colonel Schuyler to secure the release of Stobo.

[68] *Ibid.*, 150.   [69] *Ibid.*, 152; *Va. Gazette*, Nov. 30, 1759.

[70] Nov. 21, 1759; *Journ. H.B.*, 1758–61, p. 151–53.

[71] 2 *G. W.*, 339. As the word "prized" was used in this connection, it was an interesting example of specialized and almost of reversed meaning. Strictly speaking, to "prize" was to apply leverage to move, to lift or to open; but in the tobacco regions of the South it meant to employ leverage to compress into a hogshead. The word still is heard daily in autumn on tobacco farms.

resolutions were firm in his mind—to increase his production of tobacco, which he was resolved to raise to the highest quality and cure, and, second, to acquire more land on which to employ idle servants in growing that staple.

After the Christmas holiday of 1759, the first he had spent with his wife and her children, Washington expanded these plans and, meantime, he directed the winter activities at Mount Vernon. Hogs had to be killed and the meat cured; timber was sawed; a house was moved; fencing was repaired; such grubbing was undertaken as the ground permitted; hundreds of bottles of good cider were filled; before the end of February, it was possible to begin some of the plowing for oats and clover; [72] March brought more plowing for clover and some for lucerne, [73] along with several experiments in sowing grass seed, and considerable activity in grafting cherry and nut trees. [74]

All these were the preliminaries of the "planting season" of 1760 and they were attended by many vexations of a sort to mar Washington's content. Martha developed measles the very first day of the year [75] and had a troublesome sickness; [76] Daniel French outraged his neighbor by demanding two-and-six more per hundredweight than he previously had agreed to take for pork Washington had to buy; [77] an oysterman noisily occupied the Mount Vernon landing and would not leave otherwise than on stern orders; [78] John Ballendine, delivering 3556 lbs. of bar-iron under a contract to supply two long tons, [79] opened a controversy that went on for months; [80] the tobacco from Washington's plantations in Frederick was left under an exposed shed at Alexandria, with the ends of the hogsheads open and the leaf in bad order; [81] four

---

[72] 1 *Diaries*, 112 ff, 122, 123, 124, 131, 133, 134. Where diaries exist, they list routine work at Mount Vernon and for some years they include brief entries of "Where and how my time is spent" (e.g., 1 *Diaries*, 251). The paucity of these records has been for three generations the subject of jest and regretful comment, but actually, if combed patiently, they yield many facts of much interest. The same thing may be said of Washington's letters, though these are comparatively few for this period. Fitzpatrick found eleven only for 1760, thirteen for 1761, eleven for 1762, fourteen for 1763, and for the three years 1764–66, a total of no more than twenty-one. Their story of the life of Washington in 1759–73 may be extended easily from his ledgers and account books.

[73] 1 *Diaries*, 135. The first use of "alfalfa" in place of "lucerne" is dated 1845 in the *New English Dictionary*. Older agricultural books often wrote it "la lucerne."

[74] 1 *Diaries*, 145.   [75] 1 *Diaries*, 107.

[76] Cf. Robert Stewart, May 14, 1760; 3 *Hamilton*, 182.

[77] 1 *Diaries*, 107.   [78] *Ibid.*, 108.

[79] 10 *Papers of G. W.*, 66, LC.

[80] George Johnston to Washington, Jan. 8, 1760, 10 *Papers of G. W.*, 64, LC; statement of John Linton, Jan. 10, 1760, *ibid.*, 65; John Ballendine to Washington, Jan. 24, 1760, *ibid.*, 67; Joseph Stevens to Washington, Nov. 15, 1760, *ibid.*, 84; John Ballendine to Washington, Nov. 18, 1760, *ibid.*, 65, LC.   [81] 1 *Diaries*, 117.

Negroes belonging to Washington died during the winter;[82] a heavy rain on the 15th of March, 1760, broke the tumbling dam at the mill on Dogue Run and so injured the mill itself that the owner had to hasten the execution of plans he already had shaped for rebuilding the structure;[83] an attempt to make a plow after a new model of Washington's own design yielded nothing more satisfactory than an implement so heavy that two horses could not pull it on moist ground.[84] In addition, the death of a long-time tenant, William Nations, prompted the Colonel, as a creditor, to go into court and to distrain the estate, which was appraised at £21. The most valuable asset, a horse, was sold for £5 to satisfy the debt.[85]

Bad luck attended even Washington's travel. In January, 1760, he escorted his sister-in-law, Mrs. Burwell Bassett, to Port Royal, where she was to be the guest of friends on her way home; but the weather was execrable and the company thin at the homes where he was entertained after turning over Mrs. Bassett to her husband. Washington's travel homeward included an evening with his mother and a ride from Ferry Farm to Mount Vernon through a sleet and a thaw.[86] His next journey should have been to Williamsburg to attend a session of the General Assembly that Governor Fauquier called on the 4th of March to make provision for the troops whose pay expired May 1;[87] but this time Washington excused himself. He did not think he should interrupt his farm work for what he probably expected to be a brief gathering to comply with the Governor's request.[88]

This merely delayed another long, dull journey through familiar woods and over troublesome ferries. On April 19, Washington had to start for the York River, in order to attend in Williamsburg the "spring settlement" of merchants' accounts and to inspect the Custis plantations. Almost at the outset Washington encountered an ill omen. To avoid Chopawamsic Swamp, he crossed the Potomac to Maryland and proceeded in his chair[89] down the left bank with the intention of

---

[82] *Ibid.,* 118.   [83] *Ibid.,* 136–37, 139, 142, 150.   [84] *Ibid.,* 140, 142, 149, 152.

[85] *Ibid.,* 127, 133, 162. For Nations' accounts and his rental of 1000 lbs. of tobacco per annum, see *Ledger A,* folio 69. The balance turned over to Nations' widow consisted of 112 lbs. of tobacco and £1, 11s 11d.

[86] 1 *Diaries,* 112–15. The dates were January 12–17, 1760.

[87] *Journ. H.B.,* 1758–61, p. 157–58.

[88] The session was from March 4 through March 11. Funds were voted to keep the Regiment in service to Nov. 1, 1760, and the three detached Companies on duty until Apr. 1, 1761, if the Governor thought this necessary (*Journ. H.B.,* 1758–61, p. 157–58). The supply act will be found in 7 H 347 ff.

[89] For use of this conveyance, see Vol. I, p. 152.

passing over the river again at Hooe's Ferry, which linked Cedar Point with King George County, Virginia. His chair or his team did not like this change, or else the Maryland roads were hostile to strangers. A breakdown occurred two hours after he began his passage through Maryland. As there was no smithy at hand, Washington had to walk to Port Tobacco and had to sacrifice a full day while repairs were being made to the vehicle.[90] By the 22nd he was in New Kent, but the overseers seemed to the impatient young planter to be far behind the season. At Claiborne's, which Washington visited on the 24th, work was progressing, though he did not think sufficient ground had been prepared for planting. Conditions around Williamsburg were better. The overseers, as Washington saw it, had the ground in "pretty good forwardness."[91] There was no hesitancy on Washington's part in passing judgment and in demanding that the maximum use be made of the lands and of the slaves. The quarters that were not the estate's, he spoke of as his own. When he referred to Colonel Custis's residence, it was "my house in town."[92]

The inspection of "my" quarters and of the Custis plantations was being completed when, on April 26, Washington repeated an old experience in a new form: Letters containing bad news arrived once again from Winchester, but instead of a tale of Indian murder, they announced that smallpox had broken out among the Negroes on Washington's farm in Frederick County. His impulse was to do the same thing he had done when the faithful William Jenkins or some other express had brought report of raids on the South Branch or on Patterson's Creek. He would ride to the Valley and see for himself; but, as it was Saturday, he decided to wait until the first of the week, and he did this the more cheerfully because there was a prospect he might be able on Monday to close a lease for the Custis house in Williamsburg. Church attendance on Sunday was followed by some rain and much lightning, but by nothing socially out of the ordinary. Monday morning, April 28, Washington completed arrangements for the rental of the Custis residence at £45 per annum, with the understanding that he would have it painted.[93] Then he collected his pay as Burgess and an old account due him by the Colony, to add to £790 he had received

[90] 1 *Diaries*, 156.   [91] 1 *Diaries*, 156–57.
[92] *Ibid.*, 157. The Custis place, two miles from town, was the "Queen's Creek Plantation."
[93] The tenant was to be one of Martha's brothers, for whom either Thomas or Bernard Moore acted. Occupancy was to begin in the autumn (1 *Diaries*, 157).

for the estate when debts and interest, either or both, were paid at the
meeting of merchants. Thus strengthened in purse, he set out for the
Shenandoah Valley by way of Mount Vernon.[94]

It was the 5th of May when he reached Frederick—just in time
to attend the funeral of one of his overseers. Washington heard, also,
that two of his Negroes had died of smallpox, the fifth and sixth slaves
he had lost that winter.[95] In contrast, there was a measure of diversion
and of cheer in hurrying on to Winchester where, on the 6th, he enjoyed the company of Col. William Byrd and of other officers of the
Regiment. It was the first time Washington had seen them together
since he had bidden some of them farewell at Fort DuQuesne more
than sixteen months previously. A pleasant reunion it must have been,
but Washington wasted no words when he wrote in his diary of it:
"Visited my brother's quarter and just called at my own in my way to
Winchester, where I spent the day and evening with Colonel Byrd,
etca." [96]

When he went to his farm the following day, May 7, armed with
the doctor's instructions for dealing with the victims of smallpox, he
found what he described as the "utmost confusion, disorder and back-
wardness." The overseer had suffered a broken leg and had lain flat on
his back while smallpox had done its worst among the Negroes. Farm
work had lagged; not half the ground required for a full crop had
been prepared. As a man who had overcome the disease himself,
Washington could move freely among the frightened Negroes, and he
quickly made provision for their care in event any others were stricken
at either of his quarters. In complete accordance with the assumption
of Virginia law that an owner could be expected to care for his own
property,[97] he gave orders that if any of the slaves at the upper quarter
went down with smallpox, a nurse was to be summoned, and the
stricken Negroes were to be lodged in the master's own room at the
quarter.[98]

Washington now made ready to start homeward, but as on previous
visits to the rich country of the Shenandoah, he had both eyes open for
a bargain or for a business opportunity. His basic and continuing plan
of operations, in military metaphor, covered two simultaneous undertakings—one to make the most of what he had, and the other to in-

94 *Ibid*. and n.
96 1 *Diaries*, 159.
98 1 *Diaries*, 160.
95 1 *Diaries*, 159, and *supra*, p. 35.
97 See Vol. I., p. 88.

crease his holdings. He had large land purchases in contemplation and, before he had left for Williamsburg, he had shared in some eager discussion of plans for the establishment of ironworks on some of George William Fairfax's Shenandoah holdings. Fairfax and John Carlyle were interested; they had agreed to send to the proposed site the senior Augustine Washington's old-time partner, Nathaniel Chapman. Washington himself participated in the discussion but thus far he had put up little, if any, money.[99] Now that he was so close to the place where water and ore both were supposed to be abundant, he decided to look over the property with William Crawford, a resident who knew the countryside well. Washington found that one good fall could be had by running a canal from the river, and that still more water power could be developed cheaply on a mountain stream. He examined the ground carefully, but his surveyor's caution asserted itself. In his diary he wrote: " . . . of the constancy of this stream I know nothing, nor could Crawford tell me. I saw none of the ore, but all people agree that there is an inexhaustible fund of that that is rich. But wood seems an obstacle; not but that there is enough of it, but the ground is so hilly and rugged as not to admit of making [char]coal or transporting it. I did not examine the place so accurately myself as to be a competent judge of this matter, and Mr. Crawford says there will be no difficulty in the case." [100] That was not a convincing report to bring back to George William Fairfax and to John Carlyle, but it covered all that Washington saw and heard.

He felt more confidence in his judgment of farm land. The previous summer he had decided that he would undertake as soon as he could to patent on the Ohio his share of the 200,000 acres Governor Dinwiddie and the Council of Virginia had promised to those who volunteered for military duty in 1754.[101] George Mercer, who had seemed a good partner in seeking this land, had proven enthusiastic. The terms of the Governor's proclamation, Mercer had written, were such "that we can't possibly lose by it . . ." [102] By February 1760, it looked as if Thomas Bullitt, with the support of Adam Stephen, was to be pitted against George Mercer, backed by Washington, for commission as surveyor of

99 *Ibid.*, 138. The doubt arises because *Ledger A,* folio 8 contains a charge of £5 against Fielding Lewis on account of the ironworks. While the entry is dated September, it may cover "prospecting" done in the spring, for part of which Washington might have paid.
100 1 *Diaries,* 160–61.
101 See Vol. I, p. 333–34, and 7 H 661.
102 Letter of Sept. 16, 1759; 3 *Hamilton,* 159.

the Ohio lands, a position that would give the incumbent the largest opportunity of picking the best meadows for himself and his friends.[103] Mercer was ready to make an issue of this, but Washington would not have it so. If Bullitt had power to select good lands for his friends, then the thing to do was to use him, not antagonize him. The next time Captain Bullitt was in Alexandria, Washington had him come to Mount Vernon, where he was welcomed and was dined, not one day but two. When he went away, he had engaged to procure tracts on the Ohio for his host and former commander.[104]

A warning came to the door of Mount Vernon the day Captain Bullitt rode off. In December, 1757, Washington had purchased 500 acres of land on Dogue Run for £350 and had given the seller, Sampson Darrell, his note for £90 along with £260 cash.[105] Darrell had been willing to let the note remain outstanding, but early in 1760 he had to assign it to a business house whose agent now presented it for payment. With much chagrin Washington was forced to admit that he did not have the cash to discharge the debt and he had to ask indulgence for payment, with interest, at the April court.[106] As that was the time of general settlement of accounts, Washington was not violating any part of the code of colonial finance, but it was the first time he had been compelled to have recourse to usage. Previously, every man who had called at Mount Vernon with an honest bill had the money in his pocket when he turned his horse's head from the house.

Washington already owned or held on lease 4715 acres in Fairfax[107] and he was overextending himself to put Mount Vernon in order; but he felt as strongly as ever that he must have more of good farm land if he was to employ fully the labor of all his slaves. Need and wish combined when land of quality was located near at hand, and where it would round out the boundaries of the property. He had been named one of the commissioners to settle the tangled affairs of a neighbor, William Clifton, and he had not been blind to the excellencies of Clifton's farm on the "Neck" directly across Little Hunting Creek from Mount Vernon.[108] As early as 1755, Clifton had been of a mind to sell part of his holdings,[109] which included a ferry across the Potomac[110]

103 *Ibid.*, 172–75.
104 1 *Diaries*, 130.
105 *Ledger A*, folio 49, 89.
106 1 *Diaries*, 130.
107 *Ledger A*, folio 99.
108 It was the "River Farm" on Washington's map of Mount Vernon, 1793; *George Washington Atlas*, Plate 2.
109 *Md. Gazette*, Aug. 14, 1755.
110 5 H 364.

and a place of entertainment; [111] but now Clifton, though badly in debt, wanted to reserve his home and 500 acres around it. Washington was willing to purchase the remaining tract of some 1300 acres, provided he could acquire an adjoining 300 acres that his friend John Carlyle previously had offered at half a pistole per acre.[112]

Subject to the conclusion of a bargain with Carlyle at that figure, Washington offered Clifton £1600 Virginia currency for all except the home farm of 500 acres,[113] but the Colonel reckoned without the merchant. When Carlyle was asked to sell at the price he previously had set for the 300 acres, he professed great indifference. This somewhat nettled Washington and, at the same time, increased his interest in Clifton's tract. A ride over the property so aroused the enthusiasm of the Colonel that he told Clifton he would give £1700 for the entire 1800 acres. The owner expressed complete willingness to part with the land at that price, if his wife would consent; [114] but when the time came to close the transaction, Clifton demanded £1150 sterling and the use for a year and a half of the house and the 500-acre farm.

Again Washington assented [115]—only to be told on the 2nd of March that Mrs. Clifton would not agree.[116] ". . . [Clifton's] shuffling behavior," Washington wrote in some disgust, "convinced me of his being the trifling body represented." [117] About ten days later, on a visit to Belvoir, Washington heard that Clifton had made still another bargain and had sold the property to Thomson Mason for £1200. This angered the land-hungry master of Mount Vernon. Clifton, he told himself, was a "thorough paced rascal" who would regard no bargain unless a penalty was attached; [118] but the rebuff merely aroused his determination to have the property in spite of owner and favored buyer. As it chanced, the commissioners on Clifton's affairs were soon to meet. Washington painstakingly went to Alexandria at the designated time, and had a long discussion with the embarrassed landholder. The upshot was a new offer of £1250, for which sum the troubled neighbor agreed to sell the property to Washington, if he could get out of his bargain with Mason. "I did not think myself restrained by any rules of honor, conscience or etca. from making him this offer," Washington wrote in

111 *Md. Gazette*, Aug. 6, 1746; *Snowden, Historic Landmarks*, 36.
112 I *Diaries*, 126, 128.
113 *Ibid.*, 126.   114 *Ibid.*, 128.
115 *Ibid.*, 132.   116 *Ibid.*, 135.
117 *Ibid.*   118 *Ibid.*, 137.

his diary, "as his lands were first engaged to me by the most solemn assurances that any man could give." [119]

New objections were made; prospects of litigation over the affair increased. At length it developed that Clifton's lands had to be sold at auction, anyway, to satisfy the mortgage-holders. At the sale, Washington bought the entire property for £1210 and felt that his patience had been rewarded. In his diary he wrote: ". . . under many threats and disadvantages [I] paid the money into the Commissioners' hands and returned home at night with Col. Fairfax and family" Then, without so much as the grace of a period to end that transaction and sentence, he went on to other affairs: "Captn. Dalton's Dun Mare again coverd." [120]

[119] Mch. 18, 1760; 1 *Diaries*, 140.
[120] 1 *Diaries*, 163. The subsequent distribution of the money transferred to Clifton's commissioners is shown in *Ledger A*, folio 67, 101, and is summarized partially in 1 *Diaries*, 163–64 n., after *Ford*, v. 2, p. 164. Washington's account of smith's work done for Clifton and of loans made that neighbor appears in *Ledger A*, folio 65. The inventory of Clifton's estate of £233 is entered in *Fairfax Records*, C, 1421. It is undated but apparently is of 1771. Another property acquired by Washington in 1760 was a tract of 183 acres patented April 7 in Frederick County. The only description of it is that it adjoined lands of "Col. Lee, Wormley [and] Alexander" (*Washington MSS*, Huntington Library). See also *Rind's Gazette*, Aug. 5, 1773.

CHAPTER III

THE CARDS ARE STACKED AGAINST THE PLANTER
(June–October, 1760)

TOBACCO GROWING of the sort Washington now undertook on an extensive scale was of the same pattern as that on most of the large Virginia plantations. The owner in person or through one or more overseers would divide the able-bodied slaves into groups responsible for different tracts. Quite frequently these "gangs" or "sharers" lived at separate "quarters," which were groups of small, one-room log cabins. In addition, if landless white men were available, they were hired as tenants either for a flat annual rental of tobacco, or else for specified pork and flour and a part of the crop they raised.

When the ripe tobacco had been cut, it was hung in barns, and, at the right state between dampness and brittle dryness, was put in hogsheads. Occasionally it was stemmed before it was packed; usually the leaf was left unstemmed and was part of a bundle tied at the end with another leaf. When inspected and stamped at the public warehouse,[1] the hogsheads, weighing from 660 to 1110 lbs., were ready for sale in the Colony or for shipment to England. If the planter chose to sell in Virginia he could get from 2.4*d* to 3.5*d* per pound, Virginia currency,[2] according to the quality of his offerings and the size of the crop in the Colony as a whole. The tobacco grower who sent his leaf to England or to Scotland gambled for larger profits and often took greater risks. If a favorable season rewarded his industry, he might be able to get his tobacco on a ship that left the Virginia Capes before winter increased the hazards of the turbulent Atlantic. Failing in this, he kept his tobacco for the spring sailings. In the best of circumstances it would be time to harvest another crop before he received from his merchant a statement of the sale of tobacco sent in the spring. During wartime, the vessel carrying a planter's hogsheads might have to wait in Hampton Roads

---

[1] For the history and methods of inspection, see Vol. I, p. 140–42.
[2] Cf. 2 *G. W.*, 378, 380; *Ledger A*, folio 276.

for a convoy to assemble,[3] unless the owner of a well-armed ship ventured alone across the ocean. On a heavily gunned single vessel, with an alert captain, insurance was of course lower than on the average unescorted merchantman, which might so readily be captured by the French that the cost of protection against loss was impossibly high.[4] Insurance seldom was taken on tobacco aboard a vessel in a convoy. If occasion justified, a planter could withhold his decision about insurance until the time a ship sailed, and then he could send a letter to New York and have it forwarded by the swift packet. If his instructions [5] were received and acted upon before the cargo reached England, or before any report of the capture of the ship was received, the insurance would be issued. It was not necessary that a policy be taken out prior to the beginning of the voyage.[6]

Freight on tobacco was heavy. In a normal year it was £8 a ton but when vessels were few because of the activity of the French fleet, or because of a demand for transports, the charge might be as high as £10.[7] Sometimes there was complaint that a shipmaster who had filled most of his hold with tobacco at a high rate per ton would lower the price for late consignments in order to complete his cargo and to sail early.[8]

Far heavier than the freight were the accumulated duties, imposts and "subsidies" in the United Kingdom.[9] The "old subsidy" of $1d$ per pound was in force, subject to a deduction of 25 per cent. Additional duties and imposts aggregated the formidable sum of $7.3d$ per pound, less a discount of 15 per cent—in other words about £5, 10s per hundred weight.[10]

---

[3] Cf. 2 *G. W.*, 375.   [4] 2 *G. W.*, 356, 368.

[5] Washington does not appear to have used the more modern term, "application for insurance."

[6] Washington to Robert Cary and Co.; Washington to John Gildart and to Capel and Osgood Hanbury, Sept. 11, 1762; 385 *Papers of G. W.*, LC.

[7] Cf. 3 *G. W.*, 89.

[8] 2 *G. W.*, 434. Apparently, tonnage sometimes was calculated on the basis of space theoretically occupied by the tobacco rather than on the basis of actual weight. For fifteen hogsheads of tobacco that probably weighed about 1000 lbs. each, the Custis estate was charged £7, 10s, 3d, or approximately £1 per ton of weight (*Ledger A*, folio 57). In 1775, the same estate was charged freight at "£8 per tunn," but 12,600 lbs. of tobacco were counted as three tons only. The freight bill was £24 (*Custis Papers*, VHS).

[9] As of 1760, the word "subsidy" often was used in a sense precisely the reverse of that current at present. A "subsidy" was not what Parliament paid the subject but what he contributed to government. The modern use of the term "subsidy" was familiar, also, in such matters as the subsidy on hemp mentioned *infra*.

[10] In an invoice of 1775 of approximately 12,600 lbs. of tobacco, the total involved was £555, of which taxes of various sorts accounted for £384, or 69 per cent. The grower's share was £142 or 25 per cent, out of which he had to pay all his costs of production (*Custis Papers*, VHS).

Besides taxes and freight, there were handling charges in England of approximately 14*s* per thousand pounds. The tobacco then was sold by weight, all imposts included, but from the gross weight, ten pounds a hogshead were subtracted to get the "suttle," [11] and twelve were charged off per hogshead for the "sample." After that, in accounting to the shipper, one twenty-sixth part, or four pounds in 104, were charged off as "trett." Finally, the merchant deducted a commission of 3 per cent gross on taxes, sales price and everything else that entered into the transaction. In terms of the money actually received by the planter, this commission of the merchant averaged about 10 per cent. [12]

As Virginia planters were inured to commissions and to the high costs of getting their tobacco to market, their great concern was the price their consignments brought in England or in Scotland, the only countries to which they were allowed to ship leaf. The figure varied not only according to the rate of taxation in England and the size of the crop in the Colonies, but also, of course, according to the quality of the leaf and the care taken to ship it in proper condition. During the sixteen-year period 1744–59, the Custis tobacco had brought as much as £42 gross per hogshead and as little as £11. [13] When the crop in Virginia and Maryland was of moderate size, and the leaf was of acceptable texture and smell, the gross price per pound in the United Kingdom, including the taxes, was 11, 11½ or 12*d*. [14] Quite often the apparent difference between profit and loss to the producer was the difference between 11 and 12*d,* or even between 11½ and 12*d* gross, roughly, 2.5*d* to 2.8*d* net. [15] At Mount Vernon, no records had been kept, apparently, during Lawrence Washington's time, to show what the crop had returned in net cash per pound. After Lawrence's death, John Carlyle had reported annually to the court the number of hogsheads shipped from

[11] That is, the net or "subtle" weight, after deduction of "trett" and "tare," for which a second, separate subtraction was made.

[12] A most informative detailed statement of Robert Cary & Co., showing all these charges, as of June 1775, will be found in the *Custis Papers,* VHS.

[13] *Custis Papers,* VHS. The highest figure was for the crop of 1747, sold prior to the imposition of the supplementary taxes. It was the crop of 1759 that brought £11 only. The net return per hogshead ranged from £4 to more than twice that sum.

[14] Cf. 2 *G. W.,* 257, 491; 37 *ibid.,* 492.

[15] Cf. Washington to Robert Cary & Co., Aug. 20, 1770: "That 11½*d* a lb. is such a price as a planter (in a tolerable good year) may afford to make tobacco for, I shall not deny . . ." (37 *G. W.,* 492). The present study has brought to light no records in which any planter calculated actual costs of production in terms of the cost of labor and of the investment in land. Extant evidence makes it questionable, in fact, whether tobacco was anything more than the colonial tender in an expensive barter for English manufactured goods. (Cf. Washington to C. and O. Hanbury, July 25, 1769: ". . . I only grow tobacco to supply my family with goods . . ." 2 *G. W.,* 515).

the different plantations, and as executor he had accounted for the proceeds; but his books did not demonstrate whether the growing of the leaf was profitable. The same condition had prevailed under George Lee's management and during the years young "Jack" Washington cared for the farm while Colonel Washington was absent.

The crop of 1759 had been grown on two plantations by Washington's own slaves, and on nine tracts by tenants.[16] The Colonel, in all the circumstances, had not been able to prepare for it and scarcely regarded it as a test of his management. It would be different now. In planning for the crop of 1760, Washington doubled the number of his lessees and he assigned to most of them 100 to 150 acres, only a part of which was cleared. Some of the tenants had paid an annual rent of 550 pounds of tobacco prior to 1760;[17] Washington raised this minimum to 750 pounds,[18] and either because he preferred workers who operated on a small scale, or else because he could get no others, he held, in general, to narrow allotments.[19] In his shop, he did the blacksmith work of these tobacco-growers and he charged it against them.[20] He found, also, that those who used his land regarded him as their banker and that sometimes they appealed to him to meet court judgments or to advance money to cover their county levies.[21] Several of the renters always borrowed anything they could and seldom returned it, but the vexations of this relationship developed gradually. In 1760, it had not become apparent that the tenant who was without capital and slaves of his own was helpless to advance himself on rented land of average fertility unless he was extraordinarily resourceful and hardworking.

For good or for ill, then, Washington had the tenants sign the new contracts. If none of these men quit before the tobacco was cut in 1760, they together would pay 10,000 lbs. or more in rent. The distribution of land and of slaves on the plantations under his own direct care, Washington studied carefully. He wrote down the names of the Negroes assigned the different quarters and he undertook to allot to each overseer the "sharers" required for the number of tobacco "hills" laid out on each farm.[22] "Chris." Hardwicke, who was overseer on the Bullskin

---

[16] *Ledger A*, folio 104.   [17] *Ibid.*, folio 70.

[18] *Ibid.*, folio 75, 82, 86, 115, 134, 136, 225.

[19] He was to have only six tenants who were, at any time before 1775, to pay more than 1000 lbs. of tobacco yearly. See *Ledger A*, folio 69, 70, 77, 127, 134, 137, 354.

[20] *Ibid.*, folio 185, 312, and many accounts besides.

[21] Cf. *ibid.*, folio 115, 220.

[22] Some of his rosters, etc., appear in 1 *Diaries*, 165–67, 171–72.

property, in Frederick County, had fourteen field hands for his crop. On Muddy Creek Farm, North of the Mount Vernon residence and directly West of Little Hunting Creek,[23] Richard Stephens as overseer had the labor of eight hands and a half worker.[24] With six Negroes, Washington himself undertook to supervise the crop planted on the Williamson tract.[25] All the Custis properties, save one, were farmed by Joseph Valentine, the "steward" who managed the crops and livestock of the estate. The exception was a tract in King William County over which John Roan presided, with eighteen Negroes.[26]

As far as organization could assure success, the retired Colonel proceeded in what seemed to be the soundest military manner: The detached forces, so to say, were under good captains of husbandry in Frederick, in King William and on the York; the companies of slaves in the main "army" of Fairfax County were divided appropriately: the Commander-in-Chief carried direct responsibility in one field of operations. As good a planter as Charles Carter "of Cleve" would have found it difficult to employ a like number of men more advantageously in what appeared, at least on paper, to be an economical plan.

"The greater pains imaginable," Washington wrote subsequently, "[were] used in the management of this tobacco";[27] but before it was primed, there were reminders that other considerations than those under the grower's control might affect the return. The *Deliverance,* which was carrying some Washington and Custis tobacco to the British Isles, was lost on the coast of France. At least one merchantman with tobacco belonging to the same owners was taken by a French man-of-war.[28] Heavy and continued rains threatened to ruin the crop of 1760. Reports on the sale of the leaf of 1759 were worse than depressing. The London merchant, Richard Washington, whom the proprietor of

---

[23] This property later was known as Muddy Hole Farm. See *George Washington Atlas,* Plate 2.

[24] It is not plain from the entry (*Ledger A,* folio 120), whether the half-worker was a boy or a man who labored there half his time.

[25] *Ibid.*

[26] Washington so spelled the name. The usual form is Roane.

[27] 2 *G. W.,* 357.

[28] The dates and names of all the captured ships cannot be ascertained because of gaps in Washington's correspondence and accounts. *Deliverance* carried twenty hogsheads, insured for £200 (*Ledger A,* folio 66; 2 *G. W.,* 344); Fauquier to Board of Trade, July 11, 1760, (*Journ. H.B.,* 1758–61, p. 286); *Anna,* with seventeen hogsheads, was taken by the enemy but was recovered (*Ledger A,* folio 66); *Supply* had the same fate as *Anna* (*ibid.*); on an unidentified ship, probably the *Cary,* fifty hogsheads of insured leaf were lost (*ibid.,* folio 67; 2 *G. W.,* 352), though some of this may have been of the crop of 1759. Washington apparently was puzzled over the proper entry-form for these items in his Ledger. He kept no separate insurance or risk account.

Mount Vernon regarded as a cousin, transmitted a disheartening statement of the sale of tobacco sent him: The price was below £12 per
hogshead. Washington had heard of no sales of the crop of 1759 at so
bad a figure, and, as he wrote in protest, "few, very few indeed, that did
not average [£]14 and from that to £15 and £16 per hhd: mine being
all sweetscented and neatly managed, left me no room to suspect coming in at the fall of the market."²⁹ In addition, eight hogsheads
of Washington's tobacco of 1759 had been discharged at Bristol,
England, which he had found an unsatisfactory market. He held so
little hope for a good price there that he feared the consignment might
not suffice to pay a balance of £51 odd money he owed in the town on
the Severn.³⁰ All in all, the market in England was so poor in 1760 that
Washington decided to sell in Virginia the remainder of the crop of
the previous year³¹—an ill omen for a planter who produced tobacco
enough to command the consideration of any English merchant if the
leaf was of average quality.

Nor was it encouraging to an ambitious young proprietor to note the
figures at which the invoices previously sent to England for clothing and
supplies had been filled. Washington was so shocked at the charges
made on his account that he wrote this elaborate protest to the merchants who had been supplying the Custis estate: "I cannot forbear
ushering in a complaint of the exorbitant prices of my goods this
year . . . For many years I have imported goods . . . and can truly
say I never had such a penny worth before. It would be a needless task
to enumerate every article that I have cause to except against. Let it
suffice to say that woolens, linens, nails &c are mean in quality but not
in price, for in this they excel indeed, far above any I have ever had. It
has always been a custom with me when I make out my invoices to
estimate the charge of them. This I do for my own satisfaction, to know
whether I am too fast or not, and I seldom vary much from the real
prices, doing it from old notes, etc.; but the amount of your invoices
exceeds my calculations above 25 per cent, and many articles not sent
that were wrote for."³² Truth was, larger orders at higher prices were

²⁹ 2 *G. W.*, 344.

³⁰ 2 *G. W.*, 343. "Odd money" seems to have been the standard term for fractional sums
of lower denomination. The briefer, more familiar "odd" does not appear to antedate the nineteenth century.

³¹ *Ibid.*, 344.

³² Letter to Robert Cary and Co., Aug. 10, 1760; 2 *G. W.*, 347–48, with considerable revision
of punctuation that slightly confused the meaning of the original.

eating up an expanded income and a part of the money Martha had brought him. If Washington observed that fact in the summer of 1760, he did nothing to correct it.

Through a growing season that seemed in retrospect to be one of "incessant rains," [33] Washington spent most of his time at Mount Vernon with his wife and his stepchildren, and after mid-August had to forgo even the pleasure of visiting Belvoir. George William and Sally Fairfax had sailed for England, to settle part of the estate of Col. William Fairfax [34]—an absence that involved more than the temporary loss of nearest and dearest neighbors. Because George William might remain a long time on the other side of the Atlantic, Lord Fairfax removed the Land Office of the proprietary to Greenway Court. This was a convenience to those residents of the Shenandoah region who desired to patent land,[35] but it meant that fewer visitors would come to Mount Vernon on their way to or from Belvoir.

When September opened, it was manifest, to Washington's relief, that the tobacco crop, which had been spotting badly,[36] would be short but would be better than had been anticipated.[37] Preliminary estimates led him to believe that the yield at Bullskin and on the Potomac would be as much as forty or fifty hogsheads.[38] It consequently was with some eagerness that Washington looked forward to October, when he would go to Williamsburg for the session of the General Assembly and, while there, could visit the plantations on the York and see what had been produced by Valentine.[39] As Martha naturally wished to make the journey with him at so beautiful a season in Eastern Virginia, the Colonel decided to travel in style, with the chariot and six—the first time he ever had set out for the colonial capital with the equipage that was the unchallengeable emblem of a planter of the highest affluence.[40]

The session was opened on October 6 [41] in a balance of cheer and of gloom. Intelligence that made every English face shine with satisfaction was the confirmed, official report of the complete surrender at

[33] 2 G. W., 380.
[34] Md. Gazette, Aug. 28, 1760.
[35] E. D. Neill, The Fairfaxes in England and in America, 126.
[36] 2 G. W., 349.
[37] Ibid., 351, 356.
[38] Ibid., 351.
[39] Ibid.
[40] Ledger A, folio 122. It is interesting to note that the nature of Washington's travel to Williamsburg for sessions of the General Assembly is determinable in several instances by his ledger entries of ferriage, the full expense of which was borne by the Colony, regardless of the type of conveyance. Allowance of 10s was made also for each "travel day" on the road to Williamsburg and back home.
[41] Washington's attendance that day is not of record, but is probable. He certainly was in Williamsburg on the 8th. See 2 G. W., 352, and Journ. H.B., 1758–61, p. 188.

Montreal, September 8, of the last organized French force in Canada [42] —a surrender that extended the British royal domain and removed the one white adversary who had incited and bribed the Indians to attack the English settlements. Every Virginian rejoiced with Governor Fauquier when he proclaimed in his speech to the General Assembly: ". . . the war is gloriously brought to a happy end . . ." [43]

The unhappy news, communicated in the same address, was that all the hopes of avoiding war with the Cherokees had been blasted by a succession of grisly events. When Gov. William Henry Lyttleton of South Carolina had arranged his uncertain peace with the powerful Indians on the western frontier of the Colony,[44] he had insisted that the savages leave at Fort Prince George on the Keowee River [45] twenty-two hostages for the return of a like number of white men then in the hands of the natives. Afterward, when the South Carolinians had withdrawn from the frontier because smallpox had broken out among them, a strong force of Cherokees attacked Fort Prince George in an effort to liberate their hostages. The assault was repulsed, but it cost the lives of several men in the fort and so enraged the defenders that they fell on the Indian hostages and slew every one of the twenty-two.

This of course shattered the truce and brought a call for an immediate offensive on a considerable scale. At Fort Loudoun, beyond the mountains,[46] was an isolated garrison of 200 British troops, the rescue of whom was the first obligation in the new conflict. General Amherst promptly directed that two relief expeditions be organized. One force under Col. Archibald Montgomery—a fellow-commander of Washington's in the campaign of 1758 under General Forbes—was to march on Fort Loudoun from the Southeast; another and smaller column, to be provided by Virginia, was to cross the mountains from the nearest settlements of the Old Dominion.

Obediently, at the session which Washington had not attended,[47] the

---

[42] See Parkman, *Montcalm and Wolfe*, v. 2, p. 388.

[43] *Journ. H.B.*, 1758–61, p. 183.   [44] See *supra*, p. 30.

[45] Now the boundary between Oconee and Pickens County in the extreme Northwest of South Carolina.

[46] It is stated often that this was the Fort Loudoun erected by Andrew Lewis and commonly called the "Cherokee Fort" in Virginia correspondence (See *supra*, Vol. II, p. 256), but Samuel C. Williams asserted in his *Dawn of Tennessee Valley and Tennessee History*, p. 176–77, that Lewis's Fort Loudoun was "on the north side of the Little Tennessee about opposite and a mile from the town of Chota, the capital and city of refuge of the Overhill Cherokees." The later Fort Loudoun, designed by J. W. Gerard De Brahm, was "in the fork of the Little Tennessee and Tellico Rivers . . ." (*ibid.*, 193), twenty-seven miles SSW of Knoxville.

[47] Cf. 3 *Hamilton*, 184, and *supra*, p. 35.

General Assembly in May, 1760, had approved the use for this purpose of the 300 men guarding the southwestern frontier and had authorized the enlistment of an additional 700 to serve until Dec. 1, 1760.[48] The command had been entrusted to Col. William Byrd, who had encountered the usual delays in finding recruits. It had become apparent early in the summer that Montgomery would set out for Fort Loudoun earlier than Byrd could. Thereafter, Washington at Mount Vernon followed as best he might the reports of Montgomery's preparations and advance. "It seems he has made a prosperous beginning," Washington wrote, "having penetrated into the heart of the country, and he is now advancing his troops in high health and spirits to the relief of Fort Loudoun." The Virginian hastened to add: "But let him be wary, he has a crafty, subtle enemy to deal with that may give him most trouble when he least expects it." [49]

Montgomery pushed on to the banks of the Keowee and relieved Fort Prince George. In an engagement with a Cherokee contingent, he defeated it thoroughly. More than that he did not think he could do with the 2000 men at his command,[50] so he halted—fatally. Virginians concluded that if Montgomery could not penetrate to Fort Loudoun with the number of troops he had at his disposal Byrd certainly could not hope to do so with less than half that strength. The fort was left to its fate. On the 7th of August, 1760—three days before Washington wrote his warning—the half-starved garrison signed a capitulation under which they were to be allowed to march, unmolested, to Fort Prince George or to Virginia.[51] They had proceeded about fifteen miles when, August 10, the Indians opened fire, killed atrociously at least twenty-seven men and three women, and carried most of the others away to be held captive in their villages until ransomed.[52]

News of this disaster reached Williamsburg on the 16th of September [53] and created confusion of mind and of counsel. Nothing manifestly could be done by Virginia alone to avenge the massacre near

---

[48] 7 H 357 ff. See also Fauquier to the Lords of Trade, June 2, 1760, in *Journ. H.B.,* 1758–61, p. 285. In that communication, Fauquier remarked on the extravagance of disbanding experienced Virginia troops "upon the least relaxation from . . . fears of an enemy, and as immediately raising fresh raw men at a great bounty as soon as their passions are again alarmed." He added: "I am confident the Assembly could have kept two Regiments in constant pay since my arrival in the Colony at a much less expense than the methods they have occasioned."

[49] 2 *G. W.,* 345.

[50] Fauquier to the Lords of Trade, Sept. 17, 1760; *Journ. H.B.,* 1758–61, p. 289.

[51] Text in *Journ. H.B.,* 1758–61, p. 287.

[52] *Ibid.,* 183; S. C. Williams, *op. cit.,* 250–51.

[53] *Journ. H.B.,* 1758–61, p. 289.

Fort Loudoun. In fact, the prompt appearance in Virginia of a friendly Cherokee chieftain, known as the Little Carpenter, made men think he came to seek peace and not, as he professed, to escort an officer he had ransomed after the massacre.[54] Along with doubt concerning the necessity of another campaign against the cunning Cherokees, there was positive relief in Williamsburg that Byrd had not attempted to march, unaided, to succor the troops at Fort Loudoun. Governor Fauquier echoed this feeling when he told the General Assembly on its opening day, "Several unforeseen difficulties and obstacles delayed the march of our men, and here the hand of Providence seems remarkably to have protected us; for it was impossible for our little army to have reached the fort before the capitulation was signed; and, had no delays obstructed their march, they would have been in the heart of the enemy's country before we had heard of Colonel Montgomery's retreat from the lower towns, by which the whole force of the Cherokee nation might, and probably would have been, employed to intercept our convoy, the consequence of which is obvious to us all." [55]

In this situation, the Governor had no suggestion to make. He merely asked whether, "for the sake of the pay of a few men for a few months Virginia should retire from the service at the last." [56] The Burgesses responded by voting to raise the Regiment to its full strength of 1000 men and to continue its pay and subsistence until April 1, 1761, with the proviso that the men should not be employed outside the Colony.[57] Costs were to be paid from the £52,000 that represented Virginia's part of two funds voted the Colonies by Parliament.[58]

In making these arrangements for the Regiment, the Burgesses probably availed themselves again of Washington's experience, but he was not conspicuous in debate, nor were there many calls on the committees to which he belonged.[59] He had one satisfaction in being named to carry to the Council the text of a proposed joint address to the Governor. This paper urged that the Virginians captured in Grant's expedi-

---

[54] The Little Carpenter's Indian name was Attakullaculla. For minutes of the Council of Virginia containing the chief's reference to peace negotiations, see 16 V 134 n.

[55] *Journ. H.B.*, 1758–61, p. 183, with the punctuation much revised.

[56] *Ibid.*, 1758–61, p. 183.

[57] 7 *H* 369 ff. It is not set forth in the statute, but the circumstance suggests that informal agreement was reached to tide the Regiment over the season of inactive operations and, in the spring of 1761, to make such provision as might be required under a plan that might be adopted at that time, if one was necessary, for defeating the Cherokees.

[58] *Ibid.*, 371; *Journ. H.B.*, 1758–61, p. 184.

[59] The Assembly at the session in October passed four acts only.

tion of 1758 be paid all they would have received if they had remained on active military duty [60]—a measure of relief that Washington doubtless had supported actively. Other services of the Colonel were routine and were discharged without effort. Most of the discussion on the floor interested lawyers more than it did planters, with the result that when the House adjourned on the 20th of October,[61] Burgess Washington could become immediately the diligent proprietor and trustee who was eager to know what the weight and quality of the tobacco crop of the adverse, wet season would be. The showing was not good. Some tobacco on low grounds literally had been drowned, and some on the uplands had "fired." [62] Much of the leaf was poor; the total was below the average in weight and bulk as well as in quality.[63] Washington ordered it culled with the greatest care because, as he reported to his principal merchants, he was "determined never to ship any but the very best sorts." [64]

When the bad leaf had been removed and the sound tobacco had been inspected and packed, the Custis plantation yielded thirty hogsheads for Washington and fifty-four for "Jackie," [65] a total considerably below that of the average year on young Custis's property but not bad for the lands assigned the Colonel.[66] After the chariot and six had made their way back to Mount Vernon, and Washington had collected figures on his own tobacco crop, he found that at Bullskin, "Chris." Hardwicke and fourteen hands had made 12,862 lbs. Richard Stephens, credited with eight and a half workers, weighed his crop at 6711 lbs. On Dogue Run, John Foster and five laborers accounted for 6370 lbs. Washington's own endeavors on the Williamson tract, with six Negroes, had been the least successful of all in poundage—5167. The fourteen tenants had put 13,363 lbs. in their hogsheads. John Roan on the King William tract had 18,884 to show for the work of his eighteen hands.[67] Thus, on the

---

[60] *Journ. H.B.*, 1758–61, p. 188.

[61] To meet again on Dec. 11, 1760, though actually the two houses did not assemble until Mch. 5, 1761 (*Journ. H.B.*, 1758–61, p. 197). Had Washington remained in Williamsburg until the first week in November, he would have met his former captain, Jacob van Braam, who came to the capital to report and to claim the £828 voted him at the March session (*ibid.*, p. 166) as pay and allowances during his captivity. Van Braam stated that provisions had been exceedingly scarce in Canada prior to its surrender, and that his own rations had been reduced to a pound of bread and a pound of horse flesh a day. The meat was so bad, said van Braam, that for four months he had lived on bread and water (*Md. Gazette*, Nov. 20, 1760; see *infra*, p. 59).

[62] That is, had dried before it had matured (2 *G. W.*, 351).

[63] *Ibid.*, 353.   [64] *Ibid.*

[65] "Patsy," it will be remembered, had received no tobacco lands.

[66] For the crops under Valentine's care, the prime source is a tabulation for 1760–70 among the *Custis Papers*, VHS.

[67] *Ledger A*, folio 120.

Potomac and on Bullskin, Washington with his overseers, his tenants and his slaves had raised 44,473 lbs. Added to John Roan's 18,884, this made 63,357.[68] If the thirty hogsheads prepared by Valentine as Washington's share of the Custis lands averaged 1000 lbs. each, the aggregate of Washington's various crops would be 93,357 pounds; and if "Jackie's" 54,000 were included,[69] Washington and the estate had 147,357 in spite of the bad year. It looked as if Washington was achieving rapidly and profitably his ambition to grow superlatively good tobacco in volume sufficient to crowd the hold of a proud merchantman.

[68] The total is 1680 pounds below the figure on folio 120, but the difference was represented by the carryover from the crop of 1759.

[69] An average of 1000 pounds per hogshead for the Valentine tobacco is a safe figure. In Northern Virginia, the tenants' hogsheads would not average that much.

CHAPTER IV

Change and Debt at Mount Vernon
(1761)

The first ships to leave Virginia in the autumn of 1760 with tobacco grown that year doubtless passed westward-bound vessels that carried announcements of the death of George II. He had succumbed to a rupture of the right ventricle of the heart on the morning of October 25 when, in apparent good health, he was about to start for a walk in the gardens of Kensington. George was then approaching his seventy-seventh birthday and had reigned since June, 1727. He had been on the throne almost five years when Washington was born—the only King to whom the Virginian ever had sworn allegiance. News of the demise of the old monarch reached the Colonies at the end of December, 1760,[1] but it was the 4th of February, 1761, when Governor Fauquier received instructions to proclaim the new King, George III, then 22, and son of Frederick Louis, Prince of Wales, who had died in March, 1751. Even distant colonials had heard of the angry alienation of George II and Fredrick Louis; they knew little of the old King's grandson, who now was their sovereign. Satisfaction was expressed when he said of himself in his speech at the opening of Parliament, "Born and educated in this country, I glory in the name of Britain," but some felt that he displayed poor taste in referring by indirection to the German uprearing of his predecessors. Other subjects grumbled because, as they thought, Lord Bute's love of Scotland had led him to put "Britain" instead of "England," in the King's mouth.[2]

So loyal a Governor as Francis Fauquier neither anticipated gossip nor echoed partisanship. "I immediately summoned the gentlemen of His Majesty's Council," he wrote, "to meet on the 11th [of February,

[1] The *Md. Gazette,* Jan. 1, 1761, announced the death of George II and the accession the next day, Oct. 26, 1760, of George III. In the *Va. Gazette,* Jan. 16, 1761, the only known copy for this period, was the statement that Governor Fauquier would go into mourning for George II the following Sunday.

[2] George maintained in 1804 that the sentence was his own and was interpolated by him in Lord Chancellor Hardwicke's text without suggestion by anyone.

54

1761] to consult on the proper measures for proclaiming His Majesty in the most solemn manner." Then, half apologetically, he continued in his report to the Board of Trade: "But by the inclemency of the season and the great rivers my messengers had to cross in their way up, and the gentlemen to come here, only four who live pretty near, attended: however, I proceeded to proclaim His Majesty here on the 12th, attended by the scholars and masters of the college, the corporation of this city, as many gentlemen of the Colony and of the House of Burgesses as I could collect, and the gentlemen of the Council present. The procession was closed by the militia of the city under arms, and the proclamations of His Majesty's right to the crown of these realms, and for continuing the officers in their places till His Majesty's further pleasure is made known, were read, amidst the joyful acclamations of the people, at the capitol, the market place, and the college, each proclamation followed by a discharge of small arms." [3]

Washington was not present, but he had a somewhat unpleasant reminder that a change of Kings forecast an early dissolution of the House of Burgesses and that this would necessitate an active canvass for votes if he wished to continue to represent Frederick County. His colleague, Thomas Bryan Martin, had decided not to stand for reelection.[4] George Mercer consequently had declared himself for the vacancy and had become in a sense Washington's associate precisely as Martin had been in 1758. Washington had not then learned that he fared best when he ran alone; he and Mercer consequently made common cause, but, it now developed, were to be challenged vigorously by Adam Stephen who had both ambition and forehanded zeal. Sometime after the middle of February, 1761, Washington received from his loyal admirer, Capt. Robert Stewart, notice that Stephen already was afield, though the House of Burgesses had not even assembled for what probably would be its last session prior to dissolution. "Stephen, . . . I'm certainly informed," wrote Stewart, "is ceaselessly employed in traversing this County and with indefatigable pains practices every method of making interest with its inhabitants . . . his claims to disinterestedness, public spirit and genuine patriotism are trumpeted in the most turgid manner; it's said he will reduce these shining virtues to practice (for it's undeniable that if his pretensions to them had ever an existence it must have been in idea) by introducing various commercial schemes,

[3] Dispatch of Feb. 17, 1761; *Journ H.B.,* 1758–61, p. 293.
[4] 22 *W* (2) p. 221.

which are to diffuse gold and opulency through Frederick . . ." Stewart had to confess that Stephen's promises had won some following for the Lieutenant Colonel, but he gave assurance that "the leaders and all the patrician families" were loyal to Washington. Even so, said Stewart, "I conceive your own presence, as soon as you can conveniently come, would highly conduce to fix [the outcome of the election] beyond the most distant doubt." [5]

Whatever else the year 1761 held, then, it probably would involve a dissolution of the House of Burgesses, a journey to Frederick, a series of visits to the more influential citizens and, after that, a polling of free-holders. It was not a pleasant prospect for a man who desired most of all to remain at home and to attend to his own affairs; but if it had to be done, Washington would do it. Membership in the House of Bur-gesses was at once the duty and the avocation of a gentleman. He could not discharge the duty if he shunned the contest.

Pending a further call from friends in the Valley, or a meeting and actual dissolution of the House, Washington had to busy himself with farm affairs and, in particular, with preparations for the crops of 1761. He decided to limit his tobacco to three varieties and even then, as he found later, the men who sowed the plant beds made a mistake and planted a narrow-leaf type of doubtful excellence.[6] Along with changes in tobacco were some new men among the overseers who were to direct the cultivation of it.[7] A number of tenants, as usual, went to greener fields or wanted more for less labor. Eleven only who were worth trial could be found, compared with fourteen the previous year.[8]

In all other respects, save one, the passing of winter and the approach of spring at Mount Vernon were full of delight. The exception was the non-arrival of a child. Martha was in good health; by her previ-ous husband she had four offspring. Now the second anniversary of her marriage passed without any indication that she had conceived or ever would.[9] "Jackie" was in his seventh year, and "Patsy" was five,

[5] Letter of Feb. 13, 1761; 3 Hamilton, 200 ff.   [6] 2 G. W., 377, 393-94.
[7] Ledger A, folio 148, 149.   [8] Ibid., folio 148.
[9] Among the MSS of the Penn. His. Soc., Dreer Coll., is a letter of Martha's to her sister, Mrs. Burwell Bassett, June 1, 1760. In this is a passage that sometimes has been interpreted to mean that Mrs. Washington thought herself pregnant at that time. The pertinent sentences read: ". . . and here I must do myself the pleasure of congratulating you very sincerely on your happy delivery of I wish I could say boy as I know how much one of that sex was desired by you all . . . The children are now very well and I think myself in a better state of health that [sic] I have been in for a long time and don't dout but I shall present you a fine healthy girl again when I come down in the fall, which is as soon as Mr. W-ns business will allow him to leave home." This last admittedly is a puzzling sentence, but of the several constructions that may be

but there was no son or daughter to carry the name of Washington. Mount Vernon seemed fatal to the children of its owners and lessees. Lawrence during his lifetime had lost three children; a fourth, born on the plantation, had died later; George apparently could beget none. It was a gloomy reflection in an age of large families and ample succession, but it did not destroy the happiness of life with Martha, who had disclosed no weakness to add to her worry over her children, unless, indeed, one puritanically branded as serious defects her love of dress and her dependence on others for entertainment.

From home and her company the Colonel had at length to pull himself away and to go tardily to Williamsburg, where the General Assembly had convened with manifest reluctance. There had been no formal prorogation the previous October. The Governor simply had adjourned the Assembly to the 11th of December and, when few members had met then, he again had adjourned the session to the 5th of March.[10] Burgesses had been slow in reaching Williamsburg over roads deep with the mud of late winter, and they had been welcomed considerately by the Governor with the assurance that he would not have called them together had it not been necessary for him to announce officially "the great loss we have sustained by the decease of our late Sovereign, of happy and glorious memory." With another verbal flourish the Governor had continued: "Deplorable indeed would our loss have been had we not the greatest reason to form the most sanguine expectations of enjoying the blessing of freedom, in the same full latitude we experienced under the grandfather, in the person of his successor, his present Majesty." Thereupon Fauquier had sounded an elaborate encomium on the virtues of young George III.[11]

Washington did not hear this, because he had been detained in Fairfax by a development that changed his status. On the 14th of March,[12] Anne Fairfax Lee had died—the widow of Lawrence Washington and later the wife of George Lee. Her only surviving child by Lawrence had

---

put on it, the least probable is that Martha intended to predict she soon would have a girl baby. She may have been referring to herself in the sense that she was a "girl" who soon would be in fine health. It is possible, too, that she had shifted her thinking in the middle of her sentence and was writing of "Patsy."

10 *Journ. H.B.*, 1758–61, p. 197.

11 *Journ. H.B.*, 1758–61, p. 198. There is no record of Washington's presence in the House of Burgesses before March 21, when he was added to the Committee on Propositions and Grievances, a formality that usually occurred shortly after a former member of a committee reported for service.

12 *Lee of Virginia*, 140.

been her little daughter Sarah, who had expired in 1754.[13] Anne therefore had no issue within the terms of Lawrence Washington's will. The estate consequently passed to its lessee, George Washington himself.[14] In the six years of his tenancy, which had been for the duration of Anne Lee's life-interest, Washington had come to look on Mount Vernon as so completely his own that actual inheritance could produce no substantial change in his state of mind. From the time of Sarah's death he had known the property was to be his if he outlived Anne, and after he had signed the lease in December, 1754, he had assurance that he could not be evicted unless he failed to pay annually the promised 15,000 pounds of tobacco or its cash equivalent. The difference now was that of direct proprietorship—and the annual saving of those fifteen or sixteen hogsheads of standard leaf.[15] That would count substantially with a man who was running in debt by undertaking speedily to restore and to equip the estate.[16]

When Washington arrived in Williamsburg, after Anne Lee's death, he found the House of Burgesses and the Council confronted with a mass of petitions and with several applications for laws of local scope that either had been delayed by the war or had been made necessary because of it. Washington had his share of these measures to sponsor— a bill for the establishment of a town of Woodstock,[17] and another, an exceedingly realistic one, "to preserve the water for the use of the inhabitants of the town of Winchester and the limits thereof, by preventing hogs from running at large therein." From Oct. 1, 1761, no person was to raise or keep hogs in the town; if a hog was found at large there, it might be killed by any person; the meat of animals so slain was to be given to the poor. Nothing in the bill was to forbid the driving of swine into the town for sale or through the town in transfer from one plantation to another. The operation of the measure, when it became a law, was to be suspended until the King's approval was

---

13 See Vol. II, p. 2.

14 Vol. I, p. 264. For Lawrence's will, see 14 *Ford*, 423. The original is in *Fairfax Wills*, Book A, 539.

15 George Lee did not long survive his wife. His will, dated Sept. 13, 1761 and probated Jan. 26, 1762, will be found in 14 *Westmoreland Wills and Deeds*, 91.

16 It is almost certain that Washington's late appearance at the session was due to Anne Lee's death, the date of which is established; but there is a possibility that he went to Frederick early in March, to ascertain the need of the legislation he subsequently introduced. Although *Ledger A*, folio 142, contains an entry of traveling expense, "To Frederick in March, 8s, 9d," the amount is so small that it suggests a mistaken reference to some expenditure during Washington's known visit in May, presently to be mentioned.

17 *Journ. H.B.*, 1758–61, p. 227, 233, 240, 241, 257; 7 *H* 406.

given;[18] but if the townsmen really wished to be rid of hogs that stretched themselves out in springs or befouled the ground around wells, Burgess Washington's bill would do it.

There were some proposals, also, for the relief of soldiers,[19] though the Assembly was disposed to pass these on to the next House of Burgesses.[20] Jacob van Braam fared better. He was voted £500 in addition to his pay and allowances "as a compensation for his sufferings during a long and painful confinement as a hostage in the enemy's country," [21] and he was recommended to the Governor, who was asked to seek the Dutchman's promotion.[22] This doubtless was a relief to some of the officers of the Virginia Regiment, because they had feared that van Braam might return to their station and take rank as senior Captain.[23]

The Regiment itself was to go through a new recruiting campaign in another effort to raise its enlisted strength to 1000 men, and it was to continue in service till Dec. 1, 1761. Fauquier was given authority to send it where it best could carry out the plans of the commanding General for the defeat of the Cherokees. Expenses were to be paid from the funds granted the Colonies by the Crown.[24] A special plea by Colonel Byrd in the closing days of the session for an additional 700 men was met immediately with a resolution "that we have done the utmost for the defence of the country that our circumstances will admit of." [25] The Governor did not protest. On the contrary, when Fauquier signed the last bill and delivered his final address, April 10, 1761, he told the Burgesses: "I can never expect, or even desire, to meet an Assembly composed of Gentlemen more acceptable to myself, who have happily found the means of joining your duty to His Majesty to your care for the interest of the Colony, which can never be separated but to the disadvantage of both." [26] With that he made the expected [27] announcement of a dissolution [28] and sent the Burgesses home to seek reelection or to participate in the choice of their successors.

Washington had not been so engrossed in the work of the session that he had neglected opportunities of discussing public affairs and, in par-

[18] *Journ. H.B.*, 1758–61, p. 241, 248, 251, 257; 7 *H* 411–12.
[19] Cf. *Journ. H.B.*, 1758–61, p. 205.   [20] *Ibid.*, 205, 209, 211, 255.
[21] *Ibid.*, 227, 232, 258.   [22] *Ibid.*, 238, 246.
[23] 3 *Hamilton*, 212.   [24] 7 *H* 382.
[25] *Journ. H.B.*, 1758–61, p. 255.   [26] *Ibid.*, 258.
[27] See Fauquier to the Board of Trade, May 12, 1761: ". . . it was known a dissolution was to take place . . ." (*ibid.*, 294).
[28] *Ibid.*, 258.

ticular, of procuring all the information he could concerning the tobacco market. Some of the news directly affecting his own crop of 1760 was most unpleasant: James Gildart, a Liverpool merchant who had a small consignment of the tobacco, reported the sale of a hogshead at £8, 4s, when other Custis and Washington leaf was bringing £17 and £18 in London. Gildart had been complaining for two or three years of the quality of the product sent him. Washington recalled this, expressed his astonishment at the low figure, and assured Gildart that the tobacco entrusted to him was exactly the same as that which Cary was marketing at almost twice the figure Gildart reported. " 'Tis unreasonable, therefore," George concluded, "to expect I can continue a correspondence under such obvious disadvantages," [29] which was Washington's polite way of saying that he would send no more of his offerings to Gildart.

If Washington praised Cary to Gildart, he protested in a separate letter to Cary that he was being discriminated against. "I am at a loss," he said, "to conceive the reason why Mr. Wormeley's, and indeed some other gentlemen's tobaccos, should sell at 12s last year and mine . . . only fetch 11½ (and that I am certain of for no more than a part, having accounts of only four hogsheads)." Then he added: "Certain I am no person in Virginia takes more pains to make their tobacco fine than I do and 'tis hard then I should not be as well rewarded for it." [30] The old ambition to excel still burned: only the course of the flame had changed.

In the end, disappointed, he decided to withhold from the market part of his unsold crop of 1760. The amount left in America was not large—only some 8300 lbs.[31] or less than 6 per cent of the whole; but the retention even of that much, coupled with slow and confused reporting, probably discouraged careful book-keeping. Washington did not even attempt to draw up a full statement of his tobacco account. He was resolved to go on and to see what gain there was, if any, in putting quality above quantity,[32] but to a worse extent than he realized, he was keeping his books in so superficial a way that they could not supply the answer. Ledger accounts might be opened by him for some of those

29 2 G. W., 358.   30 Letter of Apr. 3, 1761; ibid., 357.
31 Ledger A, folio 120.
32 Cf. Letter of Oct. 12, 1761, to Robert Cary & Co.: "I am more anxious about the quality than quantity of what I ship . . ." (2 G. W., 368).

from whom he bought land or slaves on credit, but he was satisfied to balance these with a "contra" entry of the bond he gave or the bills of exchange he drew in settlement. He did not maintain a general account of bills payable.

Within about three weeks of the time Washington returned to Mount Vernon after the adjournment of the General Assembly, he felt that he should go to Frederick to counteract the electioneering of Adam Stephen. In March, Robert Stewart had reported that Stephen "continues indefatigable" but he said that nothing could create belief that Washington was in danger.[33] Burgess Washington took no chances. He had not been in Frederick when the election of 1758 had been held;[34] it would be neither proper nor prudent to have the voters of the County regard him as indifferent. So, over the mountains he went once more, and found a situation distinctly unpleasant. Colonel Stephen had been in some sort of trouble in the streets of Winchester while the Sheriff had been present, but Stephen now was going about the County and was writing letters in which he said he had acquitted himself of what had been charged against him.

In Washington's eyes, Stephen's "principles"—if they deserved the name—were of an alien sort. It was distressing to reach that conclusion regarding a man with whom Washington had stood at Jumonville's camp and at Fort Necessity; but if a break was to come on a question of "principles," Washington would not compromise. He visited most parts of the County, renewed old acquaintances, attended a cockfight and then a wedding, and at length openly assailed his rival. ". . . his conduct throughout the whole," wrote Washington, "is very obvious to all who will be convinced, but I find there are some that do not choose to have their eyes opened." He went on: "I hope my interest in your neighborhood"—he was addressing Sheriff van Swearingen—"still stands good; and as I have the greatest reason to believe you can be no friend to a person of Colonel Stephen's principles, I hope, and indeed make no doubt that you will contribute your aid toward shutting him out of the public trust he is seeking . . ." Then, practical in politics as in everything else, Washington suggested that if "Mercer's friends and mine [could be] hurried in at the first of the poll, it might be an advan-

<hr>

[33] Stewart's language was, ". . . nothing can raise the most remote suspicion of your interest's being immutably established," but his meaning was exactly the reverse (3 *Hamilton*, 204).
[34] See Vol. II, Chapter XIX.

tage," though the Sheriff should not do anything that could "give so designing a man as Colonel Stephen" any ground for making trouble.[35]

This was the first instance in which Washington had challenged on such personal grounds any of his officers of 1754–59. While at the head of the Regiment, he had been compelled to discipline some of the company commanders and several of their Lieutenants. In all probability he had little or nothing to do with George Muse after the Major had confessed cowardice at Fort Necessity. Where Stephen, a man of reputation, was involved, Washington had to be certain that the shortcoming was serious and the proof convincing. He had satisfied himself on both scores and then he had hit hard. His courage and his candor were rewarded. Doubtless he would have been reelected decisively in any event, but he could not have been given a much stronger vote of confidence than the poll of May 18 showed: Washington, 505; George Mercer, 399; Stephen, 294; scattering, three.[36] The experience reflected the man and perhaps it framed in thinking a rule he came to apply almost instinctively: when justice had been done and patience had been tried, then strike for your cause and for yourself.

It was victory at a price. George Mercer, canvassing actively, had spent approximately £50 on account of his fellow-candidate. Washington repaid him in cash the day after the election,[37] but he soon found he had a much heavier bill to settle in a severe cold he caught while visiting among his constituents. This cold persisted and stirred up old maladies.[38] Fever produced a lassitude that Washington in some humility of spirit attributed to indolence.[39] He probably was denied for this reason his full enjoyment on May 28 of the Alexandria Race which he, John Carlyle and Charles Digges were managing.[40] In intervals of fever, Washington was able to attend the June fair in Fredericksburg [41] and, in August, he was strong enough to travel to Marlborough plantation to consult John Mercer.[42] Most of the conferences of a hard, tedious

35 Letter of May 15, 1761; 2 *G. W.*, 359. Washington's own vague references cover all that is known of "what was charged to [Colonel Stephen] in the streets of Winchester." Court records of Frederick County shed no light on it.

36 Poll by Thomas Wood; 10 *Papers of G. W.*, 96-99 LC, cited in 2 *G. W.*, 359 n.

37 *Ledger A*, folio 40.

38 Washington to Archdeacon Andrew Burnaby, July 27, 1761; 22 *W* (2) p. 221.

39 Cf. letter to Richard Washington, July 14, 1761; 2 *G. W.*, 361.

40 *Md. Gazette*, Apr. 23, 1761. John Carlyle's wife, Sarah, sister of Anne Fairfax Lee, had died Jan. 22, 1761 (*Md. Gazette*, Feb. 12, 1761).

41 *Ledger A*, folio 142.

42 *Ibid.* He probably made this journey to be counselled on some point of law that concerned the Custis estate, or the inheritance of Mount Vernon, but no direct evidence of this has been found.

summer were with physicians. Doctor Craik and Doctor Laurie [43] came often but they could not beat off the adversary. [44] Washington had to keep Mount Vernon, so to say, in a state of siege that was aggravated by the illness of "Patsy." The girl was not thriving and required frequent visits from the doctors. [45]

Financially, the summer of 1761 brought a shock: Robert Cary & Co. reported that the Custis estate had a credit of upwards of £2000 on their books and that Washington himself was in their debt for approximately a like amount. It was plain from Washington's own ledger that several items had been placed on his account that should have been charged against the Custis estate and vice versa. An invoice of £151 had been debited twice. Even with proper deductions and adjustment, the estate had a credit of £2038 and Washington found that he had an accumulation of bills to a total of £1871. This was far more money than he ever had owed at one time but it did not destroy the confidence he had been acquiring in financial matters ever since his marriage. He was quick to point out to the merchants that the net combined balance against himself and the estate was only £18, and he was not deterred by the magnitude of his obligation from completing the purchase of slaves to a total of £259 sterling. After he had analyzed the accounts, he added to the letter he addressed the merchants a postscript in which he announced that he was drawing on them for the cost of the Negroes. "I hope," he concluded, "the bill will meet with due acceptance and I am as before, Gentlemen, etc."—as if an increase of his indebtedness to £2130 on the books of a single merchant was a casual matter for a planter whose prosperity depended largely on the price his tobacco would fetch on the uncertain London market.

Truth was, the master of Mount Vernon still had to improve the estate and he rightly was expending on it sufficient money to make it as good a property as its land would permit. In the end, he

[43] This was Dr. James Laurie, who for some years attended the Mount Vernon slaves and occasionally treated members of the family. See *Ledger A*, folio 93.

[44] Washington's account of his symptoms is too vague to serve as a basis of diagnosis. His trouble began, as stated, with a cold of unusual severity. Subsequent reference by him to his health as "in a very declining way" (22 *W* (2) p. 221) suggests pulmonary trouble, because "decline" was the word commonly used in Virginia to describe the wasting of the body from a "consumption." On the other hand, Washington's mention of severe fluctuating fever and of being "very near my last gasp," (2 *G. W.*, 371) might indicate another and prolonged attack of bloody flux. This view is somewhat strengthened by the fact that his reference to the abatement of his fever and the continuance of his pain (e.g., 2 *ibid.*, 365) is quite similar to his accounts of his waning intestinal disorders in 1755 and in 1757–58.

[45] Her bill in 1761 was £19; Washington's was £128 (*Ledger A*, folio 141).

would gain, but for a time he faced the danger of being caught in the chain that had ruined many planters. He wanted to enlarge the estate and to round out its boundaries; he believed there was profit in the labor and breeding of slaves if there was regular work for them to do; to provide the work, he bought more land; to till the land he purchased more slaves—and so it might go dangerously on. During the year, besides the Negroes mentioned in the letter to Cary, he bought slaves to the value of £130 from Thomson Mason. Similarly, Washington promised to deliver £150 for a farm of William Ashford's; and at two sales of stock—one of them by "Jack" Washington—he added thirty-one head of cattle for £141.[46]

All these had to be paid for and principally with Martha's assets and with the money tobacco brought. Fortunately, prospects for the crop of 1761 appeared to be good, even though Washington remained too ill to apportion farm work to the best advantage. He made one experiment, in planting tobacco as late as July 11 while replanting simultaneously, in order to ascertain whether late tobacco would mature before frost;[47] but in most particulars that concerned the crop, he had to trust the judgment and the diligence of the men who directed the work of field hands divided among the farms much as they had been in 1760. As for the tenants, he could do little with them even when he was well. They grew their tobacco in the traditional manner and did not relish instruction, even by so well known a gentleman as "the Colonel"; but they could be counted on to look to him whenever they wanted a plow repaired, a broken hoe heated and rehammered, or the Sheriff held off in levying for a debt they could not pay.

As Washington continued to charge this service against ignorant men who had practically no capital and no credit elsewhere, there developed between owner and tenants an inclusive system of barter concerning which, in sickness as in health, Washington had to make many ledger entries. A man with a sense of humor would have found them diverting, if troublesome and, at the same time, an index to the resourcefulness, or lack of it, that poor farmers and their wives possessed.[48]

Nor was barter confined to men who admittedly had none of the rare coin of His Majesty, and scarcely any of the paper money that had

---

46 *Ledger A,* folio 143.   47 1 *Diaries,* 177.

48 Incidentally, these accounts of the tenants of Mount Vernon, meagre though they are in detail, are among the few records that show anything of the economic life of tenants and small farmers in Virginia during the years that preceded the American Revolution.

been printed, perhaps too freely, in Williamsburg. Some of Washington's well-to-do neighbors and even Lord Fairfax himself found barter more convenient, on occasion, than the dispatch of cash by a messenger who might run away. Washington undertook to oblige them all, rich and poor, with smith's work and with anything else he had that they needed and could pay for. In return, he accepted whatever they offered that he could use.[49] Mrs. Sarah Lewis, for example, required the service of the blacksmith to a total of 13s; she paid in part with butter;[50] Isaac Gates used another familiar medium of exchange—eggs and chickens, the fowls being valued at 3s per dozen;[51] Hanson Marshall paid his bill with old iron[52] and William Crump with a brown cow.[53] Peter Wise desired wagonage and tendered leather to balance the charge.[54] Thomas Fleming ran out of pork and settled for 1536 lbs. from Mount Vernon by transferring a boat and painting it besides.[55] When a wide-awake drover saw that one of Washington's hogs had been crippled while being led over the mountains, he traded the "felled" animal to Israel Thompson, for timothy seed.[56] John Vestal emulously exchanged his hempseed for some of Washington's imported salt.[57]

The gentry, of course, had a larger variety of products and services to offer in barter. Daniel McCarty, for instance, negligently let his blacksmith's bill accumulate for several years at Mount Vernon but he cut £3 from the accounts by having his stallion cover four of Washington's mares at 15s each. Robert Alexander, on the other hand, bought Washington's English stallion[58] and, after seven years, settled by paying £40 Maryland currency and giving title to a large tract in Charles County, Maryland.[59] Lord Fairfax did not feel himself out-traded or pinched in purse when he cancelled a bill of £12 for smith's service and grain by sending Washington nine head of cattle.[60] William Digges, residing on the other side of the Potomac, borrowed brick, salt, steel, wheat and sea coal and duly reduced his adverse balance by sending across the river no less a treasure than a quarter-cask of port wine.[61] Rev. Charles Green, who had procured butter and molasses as well as blacksmith's

[49] The examples that follow in the text must not be understood to have been chosen from the accounts of 1761 only. On the contrary, they are selected from entries as late as 1775. More of them belong to the 'seventies than to the 'sixties because, as is explained *infra*, p. 243, the shop later operated extensively under a more skillful blacksmith.

[50] *Ledger A*, folio 116.
[51] *Ibid.*, folio 87.
[52] *Ibid.*, folio 139.
[53] *Ibid.*, folio 80.
[54] *Ibid.*, folio 346.
[55] *Ibid.*, folio 135.
[56] *Ibid.*, folio 128.
[57] *Ibid.*, folio 153.
[58] See *infra*, p. 78.
[59] *Ledger A*, folio 96.
[60] *Ibid.*, folio 119.
[61] *Ibid.*, folio 156.

labor from his former patient and parishioner, had the good fortune to pick up one of Washington's runaway Negroes and thereby won a credit entry of £2.[62]

None of this barter approached in versatility that of Samuel Braselton, who sent his broken implements to the Mount Vernon shop with some frequency and had, on occasion, to borrow a little money, corn, and salt from his well-stocked neighbor. The return, first and last was: (1) the dressing of several skins and the tailoring or altering of sundry trousers, (2) the knitting of a pair of socks, (3) the repayment of corn, in kind, (4) the delivery of six head of cattle and a flock of turkeys and (5) finally and professionally, the service of Mrs. Braselton as midwife to two Mount Vernon slaves, one of whom was given a bottle of rum.[63]

Even the most unusual barter scarcely could amuse a man who was suffering through the heat of summer from a malady that defied his doctors and weakened him day by day. Not unnaturally Washington took a dark view of his Colony's affairs as well as of his own health. General Amherst and several of the provincial Governors had reasoned that the Cherokees' extreme need of goods would induce the redmen to come to terms with England. Nothing could be procured by the savages from the French at any post closer than Mobile; it was not thought the commanders and traders there could supply all that so large a "nation" as the Cherokees required.[64] At the same time, it was expensive and wasteful for the British to maintain forces in idleness until the Indians saw fit to lay down the war-hatchet in order to get hunting ammunition and blankets.

The safest, most economical course appeared to be that of attacking the Cherokees and of compelling them to sue for peace. Accordingly the plan of 1760 was readopted. A column of British and Carolinians was to advance along substantially the route that Lyttleton and later Montgomery had followed. From Virginia, a smaller column was to converge. The only substantial difference was that of command: In place of Montgomery was to be Col. James Grant, the same Grant who had been made prisoner after the failure of his wretchedly mismanaged reconnaissance against Fort DuQuesne in September, 1758.[65] As the southern column slowly got under way, Washington scarcely had energy to array the arguments for and against its probable success. "What may be the event of these expeditions," he wrote wearily, "is

[62] *Ibid.*, folio 118.   [63] *Ibid.*, folio 81, 158.
[64] Cf. 2 *G. W.*, 361.   [65] See Vol. II, p. 339 ff.

difficult, and perhaps may be improper to conjecture; but they afford matter of speculation, and while some think the Indians will make the most abject submissions rather than come to blows, there are others of very different opinions and fearful of the consequences; but so it is with all doubtful matters of importance." [66]

An ex-soldier who could say no more than that manifestly needed "a change of air." Washington's physicians so concluded; he himself confided: "I have found so little benefit from any advice yet received that I am more than half of the mind to take a trip to England for the recovery of that invaluable blessing, Health." [67] Another suggestion was that he consult Philadelphia physicians.[68] The final decision was to try what had failed to help Washington's half-brother Lawrence—the waters of the Berkeley Baths. George had no faith whatever in "the air," which he believed unwholesome,[69] but he was willing to test the effect of the mineral water, and he accordingly set out on the 22nd of August [70] with Martha and the children in the chariot. The Colonel himself was so weak that the easiest part of the journey was an ordeal; adverse weather made the later stages torture. After the family and the attendants crossed the Opequon, the vehicle scarcely could proceed because of the large number of trees that had fallen across a road that was not itself impassably steep or out of repair.

When the crude resort finally was reached, August 25, Washington had the servants put up immediately a tent and marquee he had procured in Winchester as a temporary abode. For himself, he had to confess that he was "much overcome with the fatigue of the ride and weather together." A disturbed night's sleep did not refresh him, but he had promised to write Rev. Charles Green about conditions at the springs and he sat down the day after his arrival to describe for the parson the primitive spa that had not changed materially since his visits there with his beloved Lawrence. Food was more readily procured in greater variety; the assembled company was larger, though the season was nearing its close; the absence of acceptable habitations was as serious as ever. In telling Doctor Green something of this, Washington said: "lodgings can be had on no terms but building for them; and I am of

[66] Letter of July 27, 1761, to Archdeacon Andrew Burnaby; 22 *W* (2) p. 221.
[67] *Ibid.*   [68] 3 *Hamilton*, 225.
[69] 2 *G. W.*, 365.
[70] The date is nowhere given, but the itinerary Washington prepared for Rev. Charles Green covered four days. As stated in the text, Washington's known arrival was on the 25th (*ibid.*, 364).

opinion that numbers get more hurt by their manner of lying than the waters can do them good." [71] While this bespoke no great faith in the place or in its minerals, Washington purposed, in his own words, "to stay here a fortnight and longer if benefitted." [72]

The water, the weather, his state of mind or the vigor of his body— one or more than one of these—soon brought improvement and made the eastward journey less taxing. When he reached Mount Vernon about the 18th of September,[73] he was in a mood to pick up business matters that had been neglected.[74] A month later he was able to say: "Thank God I have now got the better of my disorder and shall soon be restored, I hope, to perfect health again." [75] One indication of recovering health was his increased hopefulness concerning the outcome of the Cherokee war,[76] in which Colonel Grant on the 10th of June had administered a bloody defeat to the savages near the scene of Montgomery's battle of the previous year.[77]

While his own financial war seemed now to face defeat and now to promise victory, Washington never ceased buying and planning for the future, even though he had thought at one time that he would lose the fight for his own life.[78] Now that stimulating autumn weather had come to Virginia, he felt able to make the journey to Williamsburg for the first meeting of the newly elected General Assembly. After arrival in the colonial capital on the evening of the 2nd of November, he was able, also, to transact some private business and to write with cheer not only of the prospect of peace with the Cherokees but also of a settlement of the larger struggle of empire between Britain and France. He explained to his London merchants, Robert Cary & Co., that the Assembly had been convened to grant supplies for the Indian war should the Cherokees pursue it, "but this," said Washington, "I am persuaded [the Indians] are by no means inclined to do, nor are they prepared for it, as they have been soliciting peace for sometime past." Then he added: "I wish the powers of Europe were as well disposed to an accommodation as these poor wretches are. A stop would soon be put to the effusion of human blood, and peace and plenty would resume its empire again, to the joy and content (I believe) of most ranks and degrees of people." [79]

[71] *Ibid.*, 365.   [72] *Ibid.*   [73] Cf. 2 *G. W.*, 367.
[74] See his letter of Sept. 23, 1761 to John Moorey; 385 *Papers of G. W.*, LC.
[75] Letter of Oct. 20, 1761 to Richard Washington; 2 *G. W.*, 371.
[76] *Ibid.*   [77] S. C. Williams, *op. cit.*, 261.
[78] 2 *G. W.*, 371.   [79] Letter of Nov. 3, 1761; 2 *G. W.*, 373.

Governor Fauquier was of much the same mind concerning the Cherokees, but for months he had heard nothing from the Southern expedition, and he had no information of any advance beyond Big Island on the Holston River by the Virginia Regiment, which now was under command of Adam Stephen.[80] These troops, in the judgment of General Amherst, should be continued in service until a firm peace had been concluded. Fauquier loyally seconded this recommendation, though he displayed no enthusiasm for it. Costs, he thought, probably could be covered from the funds voted the Colonies by the home government.[81]

In the main, then, lawmakers talked of troops and of peace. Argument was clouded by a report that Amherst had informed Fauquier he had no further need of the Virginia Regiment and that the Governor had suppressed the letter. Fauquier met this falsehood by sending the House the full file of his correspondence with the General.[82] Satisfied, the House voted to continue the Regiment in service until May, 1762, with the proviso that if peace with the Cherokees were concluded before that date, the Regiment would be marched to Fort Lewis, Augusta County, where it would be disbanded forthwith.[83] Fauquier accepted the proviso and formally promised to conform to it.[84]

As always, there were private bills for docking entails. These were ominously more numerous than usual and had to do with the lands of several prominent planters. Among them was Bernard Moore, who was heavily in debt to the Custis estate on interest-bearing loans made him before Washington took over the management of the property.[85] Along with these petitions were others in large number and of much diversity. Washington's particular charge was a request by Peter Stover that some of that pioneer's Shenandoah land be incorporated as the town of Strasburg. Washington succeeded in having this made part of a bill for establishing two other towns, Staunton and New London, that had numerous supporters in the House.[86] At one time, circumstance compelled Washington to turn over the management of this bill to Israel Christian, one of the Burgesses from Augusta,[87] but this did not hamper. The measure duly was passed;[88] the Shenandoah Valley was to have its third and fourth towns. With the founding of two of them,

[80] *Journ. H.B.*, 1761–65, p. 6.
[81] *Ibid.*
[82] *Ibid.*, 27.
[83] 7 H 463–65.
[84] *Journ. H.B.*, 1761–65, p. 27.
[85] See *infra*, p. 172.
[86] Cf. *Journ. H.B.*, 1761–65, p. 17, 21, 23, 25, 26.
[87] 2 *G. W.*, 373–74.
[88] 7 H 473.

Woodstock and Strasburg, Washington was directly connected. No longer was he Conotocarios, "devourer of villages," as the redmen had called him: he now was a creator of towns.

Illness was the circumstance that kept Washington from the House during the time the bill for Strasburg was nearing passage.[89] The malady probably was a recurrence of the one that had afflicted him during the summer, but if so, it was another instance of ex malo bonum. Washington consulted the best of the Williamsburg doctors, Peter Hay and William Small,[90] precisely as he had gone in desperation to the town's ablest practitioner in 1758.[91] This time the fees were high, particularly those of Doctor Small, but the counsel and treatment were worth what they cost, or else time itself worked a speedy cure.[92] Washington had no further trouble.

Able now to travel and to give his tobacco crop the attention he could not bestow during his illness, Washington doubtless visited the plantations in New Kent and on the York. He found that Valentine had enjoyed a more favorable season than in 1760. The yield was larger—thirty-four hogsheads on Washington's property as compared with thirty the previous year, and seventy-seven on "Jackie's" land as against fifty-four in 1760. On the two accounts, the total was 111 hogsheads, an increase of twenty-seven. The tenants on the Potomac and in Frederick County had not done quite so well—10,116 lbs. compared with 13,363 in 1760, but the yield on some of the plantations was larger.[93] Other farmers of course had shared the same favorable weather. The merchants' returns in 1762 should demonstrate whether Washington was winning or losing—whether his special care for the quality of his leaf was a profitable expenditure.

---

[89] 2 G. W., 373–74.   [90] For these worthies, see Blanton, 75, 204.

[91] See Vol. II, p. 277.

[92] See Ledger A, folio 141, for the payment of £15 to "Dr. Hay" and of £20 to "Dr. Small." These entries are undated and are without the initials of the two individuals; but the Williamsburg physicians of those names doubtless were the men Washington consulted. For Dr. Small, who was one of Jefferson's teachers, see 1 Jefferson, 3; 5 ibid., ii, 14 ibid., 231.

[93] Unfortunately, a change by Washington in his system of keeping his tobacco-account makes it difficult to say precisely what this increase was. Apparently, the plantation crops, as distinguished from the tenants' 10,116 lbs., ran to a total of 53,000 lbs., to which should be added the 18,000 lbs. grown by John Roan in King William, an aggregate of 81,000 lbs. On the ledger appear two other accounts, equalling 14,000 lbs., but these may have been included in Valentine's report. Roan's also may have been a duplicate entry in 1761. The most that can be said, then, is that the plantations under the care of the overseers personally directed by Washington yielded 53,000 lbs., or with the tenants' tobacco, a total of 63,000.

CHAPTER V

BUILDING ON THE COMMONPLACE
(1762)

THE GENERAL ASSEMBLY met on Jan. 14, 1762, without the senior Burgess from Frederick. Washington doubtless knew that the session was to be brief and was to be devoted to one question, the continuance or disbandment of the Virginia Regiment. He probably anticipated what the decision of the lawmakers would be, and he did not feel that members from the more remote Counties were so badly needed that they should be called upon to make the long journey in the bitter weather of midwinter. His decision to stay at home was an odd anticlimax and at the same time a dramatic evidence of the extent to which he had separated himself from the career that once had held his heart: The Virginia Regiment, his own command, his own creation, might be broken up when he was not there to say "No," or, if he acquiesced, to seek proper compensation for faithful officers and men who had obeyed his orders.[1]

His colleagues were neither forgetful nor ungrateful. After listening to the Governor's statement of the preliminary arrangements for carrying out the act to disband the Regiment, they read letters from Amherst and Stephen, who urged delay.[2] The Burgesses were not convinced of the need of retaining an armed force in the service of the Colony, but they were unwilling to disband it until they had positive assurance, not then forthcoming, that the war with the Cherokees had been ended under a firm, dependable treaty of peace. That view shaped the law.[3] The long-contested statute "for preventing mutiny and desertion," the one that had been strengthened after so many exhortations by Washington, was revived for the period that ended on the 1st of May,[4] but no

---

[1] The *Journal* itself has no record of his presence; his books show no absence from home in January. Although his ledger account (*folio* 122), shows that he drew pay for the preceding and the next subsequent session, it contains no entry for the meeting in January, 1762.

[2] *Journ. H.B.*, 1761–65, p. 33.   [3] *Ibid.*, 36, 37.

[4] It had expired May 24, 1761; 7 H 491–92.

further provision was made for the pay of the troops. Officers fared better. Each of those in service at the time was allowed a full year's compensation beyond that due him on the date the Regiment was disbanded.[5] This seemed reasonable, generous indeed, but Robert Stewart wrote Washington, "it was vastly short of our expectations." He added, politely rather than reproachfully, "we missed your friendly offices excessively." [6] A favorable reception was given the petition of the tireless express, the honest William Jenkins. He admitted that he had agreed to furnish his own mounts but he reported that he had lost eleven horses and mares in the public service. The Burgesses voted him £100.[7] Then, on the 21st of January, the General Assembly adjourned.[8]

Washington read and doubtless approved the brief proceedings. He kept up his correspondence with his old comrades, and with Robert Stewart in particular; but he now had the normal operations of his plantations in full swing and he was busying himself with an interesting routine. In January, of course, little could be done on the farms except to see that the stock were comfortable, the fires were kept bright, and the indoor labor performed. By the 9th of February, the forehanded master of Mount Vernon began plowing for oats.[9] This labor usually lasted more than a month in the prevailing uncertain weather. Sowing and harrowing followed.[10] Simultaneously, about March 24, the tobacco plant beds were burned over and then were seeded.[11]

Washington himself took a hand during March in grafting cherry and apricot trees.[12] He had a large number of fruit trees and he normally had apples enough for cider and for brandy, but of eating apples he produced few that satisfied him. Perhaps the worthies who were making plans for the advancement of Virginia agricultural arts [13] would not have been pleased to learn that the gentleman who was trimming and pruning and crossing was to order three barrels of apples from New York that autumn.[14]

[5] 7 H 492–93. The act lists the forty officers by name. Perhaps it was significant of the domination of the proprietor class that nothing whatever was done for the men in the ranks.
[6] Letter of Jan. 25, 1762; 3 Hamilton, 232. These officers had memorialized the General Assembly Mch. 7, 1760. See Journ. H.B., 1758–61, p. 162–63.
[7] Journ. H.B., 1761–65, p. 36, 37, 38, 42.   [8] Ibid., 42.
[9] These entries are from a diary of Jan. 27-Dec. 3, 1762, which Washington kept on the blank pages of the Virginia Almanac for that year. The Diary was deposited in the Library of Congress by J. K. Paulding and consequently is known as the Paulding Diary. Permission to quote from it was granted most generously by the owner.
[10] In 1762, the plowing was finished on the 20th of March; sowing and harrowing were completed by the 29th.
[11] Paulding Diary.   [12] Ibid.   [13] Cf. 7 H 563 ff.
[14] Letter of Sept. 27, 1762, to Beverley Robinson; 2 G. W., 383.

While the plows were turning the earth where corn rows soon were to stretch, Washington had grim news from Westmoreland: His brother Augustine—"Austin" to all the family—had succumbed to an illness that had pursued him for years. As long previously as the summer of 1759, "Austin" had been to England, presumably for treatment, but he gained little or nothing in health and had suffered much unhappiness besides.[15] His end had come at Wakefield, where he had lived amply and with furnishings and servants not much inferior, if at all, to those of Mount Vernon.[16] Down the banks of the Potomac, and across country, therefore, Washington journeyed as quickly as he could to the home of the dead brother who never quite had succeeded to Lawrence's place in the affection of George but always had counselled him wisely and with patience. Especially had "Austin" been helpful at the time of the publication of the "Virginia Centinel's" tenth article in which the officers of the Virginia Regiment had been denounced as "drunken debauchees." [17] George could do nothing now to show his appreciation except to stand by his brother's grave. "Austin's" affairs were in order, though he referred gloomily in his will to his debts. His personal property was appraised at £1694, his seventy slaves at close to £2900, and his total estate, exclusive of his large holdings of real estate, at £4617.[18] His family was not apt to need monetary help from George, who had to decline, regretfully but positively, to serve as one of the executors.[19] The reason doubtless was compassed by one word—distance.

Perhaps directly from Westmoreland and certainly in a short time after his visit to his birthplace, Washington had to travel to Williamsburg for a reason that was becoming monotonous—another session of the House of Burgesses, the second in two and a half months. Governor Fauquier, indeed, was in a fair way of establishing a record for consultation with the General Assembly. He had arrived in Virginia

---

[15] 2 G. W., 336–37.

[16] The date of his death has not been determined but it was subsequent to Feb. 16, 1762, when he signed a codicil to his will of Sept. 18, 1758. That document was probated May 25, 1762. George Washington's items of expense for his journey to Westmoreland appear in his ledger immediately ahead of entries during the session of the General Assembly that began March 30. See Ledger A, folio 146. "Austin's" last testament is in Westmoreland Records, Deeds and Wills, No. 14, p. 126 ff. His inventory, which shows clearly his scale and standard of living, was dated Nov. 30, 1762. See Westmoreland Records, No. 4, 1756–67, p. 178 ff. Ford, op. cit., v. 14, p. 427 made the strange mistake of assigning the death date of the father, Augustine, to the son of the same name.

[17] See Vol. II, p. 212, 221.

[18] In the original, the numerals look as if the figures were 4017, but the addition shows the larger digits, £4617, 7s 6d.

[19] 3 G. W., 262.

during June, 1758,[20] and in three years and nine months he now had held eleven sessions.[21] This time, at a meeting begun on March 30, the Governor had to report that he had disbanded the Virginia Regiment as soon as he had received formal news of peace with the Cherokees and even before he had learned the details of the treaty. He had wished, he confessed, that he had been authorized to continue the Regiment in service until His Majesty's pleasure had been known, but he had obeyed the instructions of the Assembly. Later he had received notice that the King desired a Regiment to "be kept in the pay of the Colony." In addition, His Majesty demanded that a quota be raised to aid in filling the Regiments under General Amherst.[22] This was not all. The day before the General Assembly met, the Governor had received notice that Spain had joined France in the war on Britain.[23] If, therefore, peace had been made with the Cherokees, a new adversary had to be accepted in their stead.

Somewhat to the surprise of Fauquier,[24] the General Assembly voted to raise 1000 men for a new Regiment and to recruit the 268 designated as Virginia's quota for Amherst's depleted forces.[25] For the discipline and control of its soldiery the Assembly passed a new mutiny and desertion act, effective for a period of eight months.[26] This legislation was a tribute to the leadership of Fauquier as well as to the loyalty of the Burgesses and was the more remarkable because the vote in the House was sixty-six to three and in the Council five to four, though traditionally the lower branch was the champion of popular right and the Council the defender of royal prerogative.[27] The House deserved the parting praise given by the Governor on April 7 when he said: "The cheerfulness and alacrity with which you have so generously provided

[20] Journ. H.B., 1752–58, p. xxix.

[21] Strictly speaking, perhaps, the sessions of October, 1760–March, 1761, might be regarded as one, because the House merely was adjourned on Oct. 20, 1760, and was not prorogued. As pointed out supra, 57, the adjournment was to Dec. 11, 1760, and then was to Mch. 5, 1761. If this be counted as a single session, the total would be ten, not eleven.

[22] Journ. H.B., 1761–65, p. 47–48.

[23] Ibid., p. 48. France had called on Spain for this assistance under the Third Family Compact of the Bourbon dynasties.

[24] See his letter to the Board of Trade, Apr. 8, 1762: "This almost unexpected conduct of His Majesty's most loyal and dutiful subjects of the Colony and Dominion of Virginia . . ." (Journ. H.B., 1761–65, p. xvi).

[25] The cost was to be met by a poll-tax of 1s per tithable, for each of the years 1764–69 inclusive. Notes in the sum of £30,000 were to be issued meantime, but to the redemption of this currency the Colony was to apply all funds received from the Crown for provisions. See Journ. H.B., 1761–65, p. 50, 51. The act itself is in 7 H 495.

[26] 7 H 502.

[27] Cf. Fauquier to the Board of Trade, Apr. 8, 1762; Journ, H,B., 1761–65, p. xvi.

for the raising another Regiment for His Majesty's service, immediately after the disbanding the old one, and entered into every measure recommended to you, must at once convince the world of your judgment and spirit, confirm the character Virginians have long borne of being loyal, faithful and dutiful subjects, and render you dear to your royal Sovereign." [28]

Whether or not the new Regiment actually was raised, Washington's old command was disbanded. That was a matter of record and was a sharp distress to some of the officers who had learned to love a soldier's life on the frontier.[29] In Washington's eyes, doubtless, the action of Governor and Assembly closed the book of adventure to which he had written "Finis" in December, 1758. For the future, there would be memories only, continuing general interest in military matters, perhaps occasional aid for the petitions needy veterans submitted to the General Assembly, and some day the patenting of the land the Governor and Council had promised in 1754 to those who enlisted in the Regiment for the first advance to the Ohio.

More immediately, in the spring of 1762, there was interesting work and, as Washington still hoped, the prospect of a comforting profit from good management of the land to which he returned when the brief session ended. It was time to be preparing for corn-planting and for the mild weather when hoes in strong, dark hands would shape the "hills" where tobacco plants would be set. As it chanced, the herring began to run in the Potomac on the 24th of April, just two days before the Negroes started to plant corn—a labor that lasted until May 4.[30] Orderly work was upset somewhat, also, by the fact that John Foster, overseer of Dogue Run Plantation,[31] decamped on the 15th of April; but Colonel Washington was too experienced an officer not to have a faithful substitute for a deserter. He sent John Alton to take charge of the plantation,[32] and he could do this without undue personal inconvenience because Thomas Bishop, who was almost as useful as John, was now back at Mount Vernon after a brief renewal of service as a soldier in the ranks.[33] Attachments of the effects of Foster soon were in Washington's hands [34] and of course were troublesome, but the dislocation caused by the flight of the overseer soon was corrected. By May 10, no less than

---

[28] *Journ. H.B.*, 1761–65, p. 58.
[29] Cf. Robert Stewart to Washington, Feb. 26 and Mch. 19, 1762; 3 *Hamilton*, 234, 236.
[30] *Paulding Diary*, May 4, 1762.   [31] Cf. *Ledger A*, folio 120.
[32] *Paulding Diary*, Apr. 21, 1762.   [33] *Ledger A*, folio 124; 1 *Diaries*, 117, 144.
[34] *Paulding Diary*, April 22. Presumably, Foster had fled his creditors.

97,000 "hills" were ready for tobacco. On the 28th, planting began.[35]

All went well except for the essential—good weather. A drought began at the very time the tender tobacco plants and the germinating corn most needed moisture.[36] As late as June 29, Washington had to replant tobacco and corn, also. On some of the fields, the discouraged green stems of the corn were just then breaking the ground.[37] There was every prospect, of course, that if the tobacco crop was small, prices would be high [38]—but even that hope was eclipsed by reports that the Mount Vernon product had not been sold at a good figure by the Hanbury merchants in London.[39]

While buyers withheld shillings and Nature begrudged rain on the banks of the Potomac, Washington busied himself in the summer of 1762 with some of the many improvements he had projected. In spite of debt and doubt concerning the tobacco crop, Washington continued steadily to restore and to improve the plantation. He bought more slaves at a cost of £415; [40] title was acquired to 314 additional acres of land,[41] which raised his total to 8505 acres.[42] Much of this ground was unimproved and of small value, but for a man who had started out with little more than a farm of modest acres, the holdings evidenced achievement over which even an habitual land speculator need not have hung his head. The record was the more creditable because Washington had not reached his thirtieth birthday till February, 1762.

New slaves and more land meant heavier calls on the Mount Vernon blacksmiths and carpenters. The smithy was an old one, which Washington had repaired soon after he leased Mount Vernon. He now examined the account of the shop, and concluded that his receipts for the previous year had been something in excess of £9.[43] Apparently he did not carry his calculations far enough to determine whether this revenue covered costs.[44] As for carpenters, several of the slaves had acquired some skill. The difficult construction had been entrusted to hired white

---

[35] *Paulding Diary*, May 10.   [36] 2 *G. W.*, 379.
[37] *Paulding Diary*, June 29.   [38] 2 *G. W.*, 379.
[39] Cf. Washington to C. and O. Hanbury, May 28, 1762; 385 *Papers of G. W.*, LC.
[40] *Ledger A*, folio 143.
[41] This language has to be employed because the form of entry in Washington's ledger (*ibid.*) may indicate that he settled in 1762 for the Ashford farm which he purchased in 1761. The alternative interpretation is that he purchased two properties of the same size from Ashford in successive years. That is not probable.
[42] *Ibid.*, folio 99, 143.   [43] *Ibid.*, folio 145.
[44] In the absence of any reference in 1762 to an employed blacksmith, it may be assumed that the work in the shop was by slaves.

men, the most recent of whom was a young [45] joiner, Turner Crump. He had been working at a wage of £30 per annum [46] and he agreed now [47] to take charge of the Negro carpenters for one-sixth of what he could get from their labor. In event anything was done for Washington himself, it was to be charged at regular prices, with due credit to Crump. Work for other persons was to be by contract, with the overseer's 16⅔ per cent deducted from the gross.[48]

In Washington's agreements with carpenters, the man who used the tools made a promise "to work duly from sunrise to sunset, allowing proper time only for eating; and if he shall lose any time at his said work, either by negligence, sickness or private business of his own, the days and hours so lost is [sic] to be made up . . . at the year's end." [49] Sundays had been included in at least one of these all-the-year agreements, but later the seventh day had been eliminated with a proportionate decrease in pay.[50] The risk of unpleasant disputes over the time carpenter-overseers absented themselves from their work probably was one reason Washington changed from a regular salary to a commission basis. He soon found this unsatisfactory, also, and he returned to an agreement at an annual wage from which deduction of 2s 6d was made for each day's absence.[51] In the end, this experiment with the carpenters' overseer "on shares" was to cost Washington £27 and more.[52] Arrangements for bricklayers were not quite so troublesome. Washington had no slaves who knew enough about this art to be acceptable workmen, so he hired a skilled man from Mrs. Daingerfield [53] and later in the year, when he needed brick and tile and a mason to work on a mill race, he employed a white artisan, Philip Fletcher by name.[54]

Still another change of 1762 in the management of the farm indus-

[45] That is, young enough to have a father alive in July, 1763. See 2 G. W., 400.
[46] Ledger A, folio 121.   [47] As of Mch. 18, 1762.
[48] Paulding Diary, Mch. 18, 1762; Ledger A, folio 169. Earlier overseer carpenters had been employed on a salary that had ranged from £2 a month (John Summers, 1759; Ledger A, folio 60) to £25 or £30 a year with house and food. John Askew received £25 per annum under a contract made in 1761, but for temporary work he got £4 monthly (Ledger A, folio 60, 182). He later contracted at £35 annually (ibid).
[49] Agreement of Sept. 1, 1759, with John Askew; 10 Papers of G. W., 50, LC. See also ibid., 106, entry of Oct. 22, 1761.
[50] Ledger A, folio 182.
[51] The date of a new contract with Turner Crump has not been found, but in July, 1763, he was being "docked" for absence (Ledger A, folio 169). By 1765, Washington was again completely on the basis of an annual wage for the overseer of his carpenters (Ledger A, folio 60).
[52] Ledger A, folio 169.   [53] Paulding Diary, May 3, 1762.
[54] Ledger A, folio 130.

tries was Washington's decision to sell his English stallion.[55] He had stood the horse at 10*s* 10*d*,[56] but apparently he did not find many customers. Some of his own best mares he had bred to Brent's stallion at the stout price of 2 guineas each.[57] Although Washington was beginning to have new interest in improving the stock of his hunting dogs, he concluded to close the account of his English stallion and to make the sale to Robert Alexander that remained so long unsettled.[58]

Business always was interesting to the master of Mount Vernon, especially if there was profit in it; but the bargain in land had to be a promising one that absorbed him as completely as did provision for new equipage, for good wine, for the furnishings and beautification of the house, and for the pleasure of Martha and the children. His desire to select and to enjoy the best was sharpened as he increasingly became a family man. For these reasons, the year 1762 was one of much purchasing and planning.

He had ordered a new still in 1761 and he intended to put it into service in the autumn of 1762 if it arrived by that time. Use of it could eliminate numerous bills for spirits used on the plantation—for example, one for more than fifty-six gallons in 1761 at *7s 6d* a gallon.[59] Among the milder beverages, the one he most used and most frequently served was Madeira, which he imported directly from the Islands.[60] He had ventured lightly into the purchase of Rhine wine and of Canary.[61] Now he was debating a change in his Madeira merchant[62] and he was about to order a pipe of "best Lisbon wine."[63] Drink in itself made no strong appeal to him: he liked three or four glasses of Madeira at dinner, but even these were merely a part of the grace of living.

Doubtless he would have described as like accessories of beautiful life the four dozen knives and forks he soon was to order, "properly disposed of in neat mahogany cases for decorating a sideboard."[64] The entire household must have been made conscious of abundance when, on July 20,[65] the ship *Unity* discharged the goods Washington had ordered

---

[55] The circumstances in which he bought or traded for this animal are not known.
[56] *Ledger A*, folio 76. [57] *Ledger A*, folio 101. [58] See *supra*, p. 65.
[59] *Ledger A*, folio 118. [60] 2 *G. W.*, 321, 364, 378, 379.
[61] 2 *G. W.*, 332; invoice of Oct. 12, 1761; 385 *Papers of G. W.*, LC.
[62] 2 *G. W.*, 384.
[63] Letter of Aug. 6, 1762; 385 *Papers of G. W.*, LC. "Lisbon" was a white wine of Estremadura.
[64] Invoice of Nov. 15, 1762; *ibid*. Almost everything purchased for Mount Vernon was on a large scale. The previous January, 1762, Washington had ordered no less than a dozen iron pots of varied capacity from four to ten gallons (Invoice of Jan. 20, 1762, *Ibid*).
[65] *Paulding Diary*, July 20.

in the fall of 1761.[66] From salt to saddles, from spirits of lavender to diversified leather portmanteaux, from "one dozen augurs, sorted" to "three pecks almonds in the shell," from the plainest fabrics for the slaves' garments to more egrets for the headdress of Martha, the goods were brought forth and were appraised and admired or criticized and pronounced too expensive.

This cargo arrived in the year when "Jackie" became eight and "Patsy" six. The previous October, their mother had decided they were reaching the age at which they should begin to follow the fashions of the time and to dress as miniatures of their adults, and she had put into the orders from England many articles for them. She had not been altogether consistent in what she purchased for "Patsy." Along with a "persian quilted coat" and "one pair of pack thread stays" Mrs. Washington indulged "Patsy" in "one fash-dressed Doll to cost a Guinea," one "Do. a 5/" and "a Box Ginger br'd Toys and Sugr. Imags. and Comfits." The girl was to have, moreover, a "neat small Bible" and a corresponding Prayer Book, "b'd in Turkey and Martha Parke Custis wrote on the Inside in gilt Letters." For "Jackie," his mother had ordered a silver laced hat, two hair bags, silver shoe and knee buckles, two "handsome suits," an assortment of shoes, a Bible and Prayer Book similar to "Patsy's," and—convincing evidence of the rise of Master Custis to new dignity—a suit of livery for his fourteen-year-old Negro body servant. The invoice had been strict on this: "Note let the Livery be suited to the Arms of the Custis Family." [67] All these interesting belongings were to be put in two strong trunks, each of which was to be marked with the name of its youthful owner.[68] With equal care, Colonel Washington directed that the goods were to be shipped to him but were to be charged to the accounts of the young Custises.[69]

Of course, life for "Jackie" and "Patsy" was not to consist altogether of filling out inventories and then of opening trunks over which Aladdin himself had rubbed his lamp. Colonel and Mrs. Washington had resolved that the children must begin the acquisition of serious knowledge, and that "Patsy," in addition, must learn the graceful arts of a young lady of fashion. They had a tutor now in the person of

[66] 385 *Papers of G. W.,* invoice of Oct. 12, 1761. See also 2 *G. W.,* 369. Still other items subsequently were added.

[67] In the *Custis Papers,* VHS, is an entry of Apr. 10, 1762 in payment of a bill for a search in the Herald's Office to make certain this livery conformed to the Custis arms.

[68] Details are given in the invoice of Oct. 12, 1761; 2 *G. W.,* 369–70.

[69] *Ibid.,* 368.

Walter Magowan,[70] who was determined to expose "Jackie" and "Patsy" as early as possible to the cultural contagion of the classics. A challenging, perhaps forbidding list of Latin grammars, dictionaries and texts had been ordered.[71] Soon the invoices were to include Greek books with stern titles in Latin.[72] Furthermore, for exercise or for entertainment, Miss Custis now had—probably by that same argosy, the diligent *Unity*—a spinet that had been ordered for her in 1761 with superlative care. Washington then had written his merchant: ". . . it is begged as a favor that Mr. Cary would bespeak this instrument as for himself or a friend and not let it be known that it is intended for exportation."[73]

To this order for a sturdy spinet—not for one that crusty Grandfather Custis would have styled an "old shop-keeper"[74]—Washington had added a further instruction: "Send a good assortment of spare strings . . ."[75] That doubtless was intended to be protection against embarrassing muteness on the keyboard, even perhaps to C Major itself; but Washington's forethought might well have taken into account the possibility that in resentment or through juvenile delight in noise, Miss Custis might bang so hard that a string protestingly would snap.

Already, in other matters, there were indications that the gentleman who had preserved on the frontier both the discipline of his Regiment and his own amiability might not be equally successful with his wife's children at Mount Vernon. The reason would not be special perversity on the part of the children but the indulgent extremity of their mother's love for them. The oddest aspect of this was Martha's own recognition of a weakness she could not overcome. That summer of 1762, after a trip to Westmoreland County, she confided to her sister Nancy: "I carried my little Pat with me and left Jackie at home for a trial to see how well I could stay without him. Though we were gone but one fortnight, I was quite impatient to get home. If I at any time heard the dogs bark or a noise out, I thought there was a person sent for me. I often fancied he was sick or some accident had happened to him, so that I think it is impossible for me to leave him as long as Mr. Washington must stay when he comes down [to the meeting of the General Assembly]."[76]

---

[70] He first is mentioned in Washington's correspondence under date of Oct. 12, 1761 (2 G. W., 368).

[71] 2 G. W., 371.

[72] See the invoice of Nov. 15, 1762; 385 *Papers of G. W.*, LC.

[73] 2 G. W., 370.   [74] See Vol. I, p. 165–66.

[75] 2 G. W., 370.

[76] Letter of Aug. 28, 1762, Anne Wharton, *Martha Washington*, 56.

This was a serious state of mind to be encountered by a man who doubtless had grim memory of his mother's efforts to shield him from danger. He had escaped her and, having immense ambition and small means, he had made his way. "Jackie" had far greater advantages of wealth, but he might be pampered and spoiled in proportion.[77] For the moment, there was satisfaction in "Jackie's" progress as a student, and relief that "Patsy" seemed to have recovered from her illness of the previous year.[78]

While the children still were enjoying the new treasures that had been brought on the *Unity,* Colonel Washington had to prepare for cutting tobacco and for sowing wheat. John Alton was doing well as overseer of Dogue Run plantation, but more help was needed as newly purchased slaves went to work on wider acreage. Edward Violett, a diligent tenant, appeared to have the intelligence, character and industry a man should possess if he was to be a trustworthy and successful overseer of the Bullskin property, which manifestly had to be better managed. Washington accordingly drafted with care a contract whereby Violett was to have one-eighth of the tobacco raised on Bullskin and was to get an additional 1s 6d per hundredweight for it because of the "well known intention of the said George Washington to have his tobacco made and managed in the best and neatest manner which in some measure lessen the quantity." [79]   In addition, Violett was to receive shelter and the part-time service of one Negro woman as a helper of his wife. One-sixth of the butter was to be Mrs. Violett's. Allowance of pork and of livestock also was made.[80] Another contract was completed at the end of August for an overseer of Gist's and other farms closer at hand.[81]

The sowing of wheat was begun August 16 and was continued to

77 This must be read as an interpretation of the facts at the time and not as an attempt to record Washington's own reflections. It is not certain when he became concerned over Martha's extravagant anxiety in everything that affected "Jackie."

78 Martha Washington to Nancy Bassett, as cited *supra,* n. 76.

79 "Articles of agreement," Aug. 5, 1762; 10 *Papers of G. W.,* 117, LC. Taken with Violett's subsequent account (*Ledger A,* folio 131, 186), this contract gives a clear picture of what the overseer of a detached plantation was expected to do. At the same time, the contract presents a puzzle in accounting. The "two shares" promised Violett suggest that the crop was divided into sixteen parts or shares; but in neither of two instances does Violett's share work out at precisely one-eighth of the whole, though it does not vary materially from that fraction.

80 "Articles of agreement," (*loc. cit.*). Apparently, Violett in 1762 received slightly more than £26, 12s in cash, but part of this must have been for work done before he became overseer of Bullskin.

81 *Paulding Diary,* Aug. 31, 1762. This overseer is listed merely as "Nelson." No details of the contract are given in the diary; but among the Washington papers at Mount Vernon are fragments of a contract of 1763 with Nelson Kelley. Although Washington rarely used first names in such references as that in the *Paulding Diary,* it is possible that he did so in this instance, and that "Nelson" was Nelson Kelley.

September 8.[82] Cider was bottled during this time,[83] though the new still was not yet put in service.[84] Soon the tobacco was cut, and the annual argument over the probable size and price of the new crop was renewed. As always, Washington was dissatisfied with the return for so much labor on tobacco.[85] For a time, too, he was fearful that he would have few hogsheads to offer.[86] He thought that this short crop would bring a good price, but he felt disappointment that the bad season had halted his experiments with what he considered to be promising types of tobacco. ". . . I have not succeeded in any one sort . . . which . . . I . . . proposed to plant," he told his merchants, "and my whole crop falls short by at least one half, of the usual complement." [87]

The situation was not as bad as he thought it. When he had put up the hogs to be fattened,[88] he made a visit to Frederick, probably to ascertain what his political constituents were seeking and how his Valley lands were faring; [89] and then, after a rest at Mount Vernon, he set out November 10 [90] for Williamsburg, where the General Assembly had met on the 2nd of the month—for the third time that year. En route, Washington probably visited some of the Custis plantations. He found the crops on the York relatively better than those on the Potomac and he permitted himself to hope, as he phrased it, that "the tobacco, what there is of it, will prove exceedingly good this year . . ." [91] If that hope

[82] *Paulding Diary.*   [83] *Ibid.*, August 20.

[84] To this period belongs a social letter dated Aug. 28, 1762, and assumed to have been written by Washington to Burwell Bassett. This document, which of course was tendered in good faith, was published in 37 *G. W.*, 484. It stands most of the tests of internal criticism in that it was written when Washington is believed to have been at Mount Vernon, and on a date when Mrs. Washington was answering a letter her sister Nancy Dandridge Bassett had written her the day Burwell Bassett penned the letter to which Washington is supposed to be replying. The date of Bassett's letter, July 25, was a Sunday, precisely as is stated in the paper to which Washington's name is appended. It is the literary style of the paper that arouses suspicion. The bantering letter is written lightly, almost facetiously, and in a tone and spirit wholly different from that employed in Washington's authenticated letters to his friend Bassett or to anyone else. It has seemed prudent, for this reason, to regard the letter as an original so elaborated by an alien hand at some unknown date that the authentic parts cannot be disentangled from the spurious.

[85] 2 *G. W.*, 380.   [86] *Ibid.*, 381–82.

[87] Letter of Sept. 18, 1762, to Robert Cary & Co.; 2 *G. W.*, 381–82. Another letter (Nov. 10, 1762), probably to the same firm, concerning tobacco, is in *L. W. Smith Coll.*

[88] *Paulding Diary*, October 4 and 26.

[89] The only discovered record of this journey is in the entry of his expenses; *Ledger A*, folio 145.

[90] *Paulding Diary*, November 10.

[91] 2 *G. W.*, 387. The date of Washington's arrival in the colonial capital is not known, but the letter of November 15, just quoted, reads as if he had been in Williamsburg a day or two. He could not have been there for any length of time, because he was assigned to a special committee of the House of Burgesses on the 15th (*Journ. H. B.*, 1761–65, p. 92) and on the 17th was given a place on his old committee, that on Propositions and Grievances (*ibid.*, 97). As a rule, reassignment of this character was made soon after a tardy member put in his appearance.

was realized and the next season was a favorable one, then Washington might achieve as a planter the ambition that had been his since boyhood—the ambition to excel.

The legislative session was interesting to him in his rôle of planter. Governor Fauquier had explained in his opening speech that he had called the members of the General Assembly together that they might now enter upon the usual business of the country, and provide for the future safety and well-being thereof." [92] Of particular importance, said the Governor, were carefully matured action to relieve the shortage of bullion and measures of similar wisdom to regulate trade with the Cherokees. Military operations on American soil had ended, though the war against the French and Spanish continued at sea. The Virginia troops, Fauquier pointed out, were well clothed and were being victualed by the Crown. It was prudent, the Governor thought, to keep them in service for a time, and it would be cheaper to provide for their pay, which would be the only cost to the Colony, than to raise another force if assistance should be required by the King. [93]

Thus exhorted, the Burgesses drafted and enacted a new election law, [94] amended the troublesome militia legislation, [95] put on the statute books a measure for the relief of insolvents, [96] provided for the inspection of pork, beef, flour, tar, pitch and turpentine, [97] and fashioned a modified plan to encourage wine-making and silk-culture in Virginia, enterprises to which Washington, among many others, had pledged £2 per annum for eight years. [98]

Military legislation was not extensive. Members agreed promptly with officers of the Virginia Regiment who maintained that a year's pay was not a sufficient reward on dismissal from service. [99] An additional six months' pay and flat grants of £50 to £100 were voted. [100] Furthermore, an address to the King in the interest of the officers was adopted and was to be transmitted by committee to the Colony's London agent for presentation. [101] Among the petitions of officers who had suffered special hardships, Washington had the responsibility of

[92] *Journ. H.B.*, 1761–65, p. 65.
[93] *Ibid.*, 66.
[94] 7 H 517.
[95] *Ibid.*, 534.
[96] *Ibid.*, 549.
[97] *Ibid.*, 574.
[98] *Ibid.*, 563. Seven of those whose names appeared on the original list of sponsors, Oct. 30, 1760 (*ibid.*, 568), promised more than £2 yearly to supply prizes to wine growers and silk producers. The largest pledge was Governor Fauquier's, £10 yearly.
[99] *Journ. H.B.*, 1761–65, p. 124.
[100] *Ibid.*, 137, 146. Cf. Stewart's remarks in 3 *Hamilton*, 243.
[101] *Journ. H.B.*, 1761–65, p. 160.

passing on one submitted by Maj. Andrew Lewis who received a supplementary grant of £350.[102] The Burgesses resorted to a formal address on the larger question of continuing troops in service at the expense of the Colony. Protesting the loyalty of Virginia, they told the Governor they had no way of defraying the expenses of the Regiment otherwise than by a further emission of treasury notes, which could create new complaints and perhaps depreciate the currency already outstanding[103] —a verdict the Governor was not unwilling to accept.[104] The Burgesses' belief in the early return of peace was shown by a dramatic enactment: On being informed that much gunpowder was unguarded in the magazine at Williamsburg, the General Assembly requested the Governor to sell as much of it as he thought proper.[105]

The bulk and importance of this diversified legislation kept the General Assembly in session until December 23[106] but it did not detain the senior Burgess from Frederick until so close to Christmas. Probably on a report that Mrs. Washington was sick,[107] he left Williamsburg about the 29th of November[108] and reached home on the 1st of December[109] in time to see the corn crop measured and some of the hogs killed.[110] He computed the weight of the pork sold and of that shared with the overseers, and, after the necessary subtraction, he set down the total for the use of "the family" at 6632 pounds.[111]

This weight of meat, virtually three tons, was typical of the magnitude of many of the operations at Mount Vernon. Everything was expanding; some things were prospering. The estate had a credit balance of £1317 as long previously as April on the books of a single merchant,[112] and had increased that, no doubt, by late shipments of tobacco. Bernard Moore, one of the heavy borrowers from the Custis inheritance, had paid £210 interest and had reduced his bond by £250.[113] The Custis tobacco crop, in spite of another adverse season, had amounted to sixty-four hogsheads, or about midway between the fifty-four hogsheads of 1760 and the seventy-seven of 1761.[114] Washington's own crop on Martha's part of her first husband's land was twenty-nine hogsheads, as compared with thirty-four the preceding

102 *Ibid.*, 111, 117, 166.
103 *Ibid.*, 115, 124.
104 *Ibid.*, 133.
105 7 H 594.
106 *Journ. H.B.*, 1761–65, p. 166.
107 Cf. 3 *Hamilton*, 242.
108 Last mention of him in the *Journal* is of that date (*op. cit.*, 117).
109 *Paulding Diary*, November 30.
110 *Ibid.*, December 4–8.
111 *Ibid.*, December 8.
112 Robert Cary & Co.; *Custis Papers*, VHS.
113 *Ledger A*, folio 142.
114 *Custis Papers*, VHS.

year and thirty in 1760.[115] Twelve tenants turned in slightly more than
12,500 pounds, to which was to be added the total from the Bullskin,
Dogue Run, Muddy Hole plantations, and from two quarters. Washington's total was almost 60,000 pounds.[116]

That seemed a reassuring figure but, now that he was completing
his fourth year's work after his retirement from the Army, a number
of circumstances should have kept the Colonel from financial complacency. In the first place, he knew no better than when he began his
adventure with tobacco whether he could hope at Mount Vernon to
raise the superlative leaf he was ambitious to grow. Adverse weather
had defied his efforts; nothing that he had grown on any of his farms
had been any better than his neighbors' tobacco, if, on the average, it
had been as good. Second, he was engaged in a new dispute with the
executors of Col. George Lee over the terms of Lawrence Washington's
will.[117] Further, during the year Washington had been compelled to
handle £273 of protested bills. His debtors had given him exchange
which the merchants had refused to honor.[118] Washington had adjusted
his accounts accordingly and might lose nothing in the end, but the
situation was a disquieting one. Coupled with the succession of petitions to the General Assembly by wealthy planters for docking entails,
the evidences Washington had seen in 1762 of impaired credit might
have made observant men wonder if the plantation economy was not
dying, and dying fast. Washington's own debts were not diminishing,
either. That was the fourth unfavorable condition. He had done the
essential things at Mount Vernon. When he had come with his bride
in 1759, the gates sagged, some of the fences had fallen, and neglect
was visible under every shed and in every field. Even now, as on
every plantation, repair seemed endless;[119] but the place was decently
equipped in almost every requirement—teams, livestock, implements,
buildings, Negroes. All this had made the estate more valuable but it
had cost many hundred pounds and it had not demonstrated what

[115] *Ibid.*

[116] Here again it has to be noted that Washington's bookkeeping, based on information that
no accountant can recapture from the incomplete records, makes reservation necessary. The
great difficulty is in ascertaining how much of the tobacco from "York River and King William"
is duplicated on Washington's records and on those of Valentine. Similarly, the carry over was
sold from year to year in such a manner that the price obtained for it scarcely is determinable.

[117] This is all that can be said about the controversy, except that the issue could not have been
an involved one. Capt. George Johnston's fee, entered in Washington's accounts Oct. 19, 1762,
was 10s only (*Ledger A*, folio 5).

[118] *Ledger A*, folio 145.

[119] See the amusing memorandum of 1763, *infra*, p. 88.

Washington had taken for granted—that first-class tobacco could be grown at Mount Vernon in quantity and at a sufficient profit to pay off the debt and to keep up the plantation.

These were the concerns of a man who intended to remain a planter, to grow richer if he could, and to enjoy the luxury and beauty of a life he had earned for himself. In larger preparation for the uncertainties of the future, political and personal, could he have told himself that he was learning anything—that he was a better man by any standard than when he had quit military service four years previously? He was not of a nature to spend many hours exploring his own mind and gauging his impulses. Had he done so, he could have said for himself at the end of 1762 that during the forty-eight months that had elapsed since he had taken off his red-and-blue uniform he had learned more of law-making, he had gained in good will to men, and, facing the vagaries of season and of human nature, he was becoming more patient and more willing than in previous years to bear what he could not cast off. By the thorough performance of commonplace, daily duties he was building slowly the stronger structure of the spirit that men call character.

CHAPTER VI

Speculative Life Becomes Complicated

(1763)

During those four difficult years of the struggle to make Mount Vernon a profitable tobacco plantation, Washington had been drawn closer to the church and on Oct. 25, 1762, had been elected a vestryman of Truro Parish in succession to William Peake, deceased.[1] Much had happened in the parish since Washington's father had assisted in making Dr. Charles Green its rector.[2] No little scandal and resentment had been aroused by Lawrence Washington's legislative bill of 1744 for dissolving the vestry. Colonel Washington's elder half-brother had alleged then that many of the vestrymen had been chosen illegally and that several who pretended to discharge the duties of the office could neither read nor write. Lawrence had carried his point,[3] but Rev. Dr. Green had taken care to record that one vestryman only was illiterate, and that one was reelected when the new vestry was named.[4] Another scandal had been stirred in Truro parish over the appointment of William Grove as Clerk of the old "Upper" or Falls Church in 1747. Grove was recommended to the Rector as qualified to be Clerk and was given a trial. He proved incompetent and was found to be a transported convict besides. Doctor Green promptly removed him and then had to face a mandamus to restore the man. Fortunately for the peace of the parish, Grove disavowed the proceedings and renounced all claim to the clerkship.[5] Now, if like trouble arose, the amiability and just judgment of Colonel Washington could be invoked in a settlement. His first important official duty was to attend a vestry meeting at Falls Church and to consider the need of a new structure there. The old edifice, the one Richard Blackburn erected in 1733—forty by twenty-

---

[1] *Truro Parish Vestry Book*, 97.   [2] See Vol. I, p. 54.
[3] See the act in 5 *H* 274; see also Vol. II, p. 230.
[4] *Truro Parish Vestry Book*, 48. Cf. Slaughter, *History of Truro Parish*, 22 n.
[5] Subsequently, on proof of good behavior, he was made sexton of the new Falls Church. For the mandamus, etc., see *Truro Parish Vestry Book*, 56 (June 29, 1747).

two feet, with a pitch of thirteen feet—was decayed beyond repair and had to be replaced.[6]

Beyond this election as vestryman, Washington had no new public distinction. He did not shine as a Burgess, though his character and his military reputation gave him influence. As yet, he was not even a member of the County Court. More and more he was becoming a planter who had his holidays and enjoyed them but had, between them, to discharge duties that were as humdrum as they were numerous. Here, for example, was one memorandum handed him in 1763, to be deciphered and executed:

oyl will be wanting for Lether Soon the fence must be made Cloaser by the old Stable for to Keep Hoges out—the Seen mended—400 Hop poles wanting the mares & Colts must be Taken out of the Peach Orchard—a new Axeltree wanting to Tumbrill Cart the old Stable Dore wants mending up— & the Stalions Stable Dore & manger wants mending The Boats must be Corked before they Can be yoused
new wheel barrows wanting & old ones mended.[7]

These and many similar tasks had to be performed with the farm labor and with the hired "tradesmen," as most of the artisans were styled. The previous year, 1762, wages at Mount Vernon and at Bullskin had amounted to £107.[8] They still were rising, though the revenue from tobacco was not. The narrow leaf did not find favor in London, "nor do I much wonder at it," Washington manfully told his merchants, "for it was a sort planted by mistake, and altogether without my approbation, and I am so unlucky as to have some of it this year again, mixed with the others." [9] Leaving the narrow leaf out of account, Washington had troubles enough with tobacco. By no process of reasoning could he understand why his crop fetched a lower price than that of his neighbor, George William Fairfax.[10] To his distress, also, Washington learned after many months that the hogsheads lost at sea and on the coast of France numbered thirty-four and represented an account difficult to settle.[11] He perhaps was influenced by the endless annoyance and uncertainty of the sale of tobacco when he made in January a contract—

[6] *Truro Parish Vestry Book*, June 9, 1733, Oct. 25, 1762. This first "Upper Church" at Michael Reagen's crossroads, when replaced by a brick edifice, received the popular name "Falls Church."

[7] *Mount Vernon MSS*; a fragment.   [8] *Ledger A*, folio 145.

[9] Letter of Apr. 26, 1763, to Robert Cary & Co.; 2 *G. W.*, 394.

[10] *Ibid.*   [11] 2 *G. W.*, 391, 393.

more or less perfunctory at the moment—for the sale to Carlyle & Adam, the Alexandria merchants, of all his surplus wheat for a term of seven years.[12]

Good bargains seemed better and bad crops appeared not quite so intolerable when set against the joyful news of the return of peace through the Treaty of Paris, signed Feb. 10, 1763. The struggle then ended between France and England had been opened, in a sense, by Washington's own attack on Jumonville, May 30, 1754. Virtually five years of the young Virginian's life had been devoted to that contest, which, according to the computations of Frederick of Prussia, had cost the lives of 853,000 soldiers and of unreckoned hundreds of thousands of civilians.[13] England was supreme in North America and had gained enormously in India. The Earl of Granville did not exaggerate when he aroused himself from the languor of his last illness to affirm this "the most glorious war, the most honorable peace, this nation ever saw."[14] Very different were the comments of the Virginia former Colonel. "We are much rejoiced at the prospect of peace which," he wrote, " 'tis hoped will be of long continuance and introductory of mutual benefits to the merchant and planter, as the trade to this Colony will flow in a more easy and regular channel than it has done for a considerable time past."[15] That was all: peace meant easier, profitable trade. The planter of 31 seemed to bear little resemblance to the Lieutenant Colonel of 22 who had spoken ardently if clumsily of "this interesting cause that should arouse from the lethargy we have fallen into, the heroic spirit of every free-born English man to attest the rights and privileges of our king (if we don't consult the benefit of ourselves) . . ."[16]

That interjected "benefit of ourselves" would be apparent now, Washington hoped, when trade was smooth and the price of tobacco was better. Meantime, he and the more provident of his neighbors were short of cash and were being importuned to assist the landless and the prodigal. For example, Capt. Robert Stewart of the disbanded First Virginia Regiment wanted Washington to lend him £400 with which to purchase in England a commission as Captain.[17] The Colonel was

---

[12] Contract of Jan. 18, 1763; 10 *Papers of G. W.,* 122, LC.
[13] 2 Parkman, *Montcalm and Wolfe,* 424.
[14] Robert Wood, *Essay on the Original Genius of Homer,* vii.
[15] Letter of Apr. 26, 1763 to Robert Cary & Co.; 2 *G. W.,* 395. A briefer statement to the same effect will be found in a letter of that date to C. and O. Hanbury (*ibid.,* 392).
[16] Letter of Apr. 27, 1754, to Gov. Horatio Sharpe; 2 *G. W.,* 44. Cf. Vol. I, p. 356.
[17] 3 *Hamilton,* 250; cf. *ibid.,* 246.

anxious to assist Stewart, who had no estate;[18] but he now was in debt
to the Hanbury merchants as well as to Robert Cary & Co. and he did
not know whether the small balance on the books of another English
correspondent was in his favor or against him. Washington felt compelled, as a first move, to send Stewart a copy of his most recent statement from Cary & Co. and then he explained: "This, upon my soul, is
a genuine account of my affairs in England; here they are a little better
because I am not much in debt. I doubt not but you will be surprised
at the badness of their condition unless you will consider under what
terrible management and disadvantages I found my estate when I
retired from the public service of this Colony; and that besides some
purchases of lands and negroes I was necessitated to make adjoining me
(in order to support the expenses of a large family), I had provisions
of all kinds to buy for the first two or three years; and my plantation to
stock, in short with everything; buildings to make, and other matters,
which swallowed up, well before I knew where I was, all the money I
got by marriage, nay more, brought me into debt, and I believe I may
appeal to your knowledge of my circumstances before."[19]

All this was true, of course, except as Washington unconsciously
disregarded the extent to which the ambition to be a great planter
probably led him to acquire more land and more Negroes than he
could employ profitably until he had the plantation reorganized and
operating at minimum waste. It was not necessary for him to explain to
Stewart that a great part of his landholdings still were unimproved
forests of indeterminable value. That was a familiar condition, indeed
an almost universal condition, in those parts of Virginia close to the
frontier through which settlement had broken in the seventeen-forties.

The financial plight of the master of Mount Vernon was, for these
reasons, one that would have justified completely an unqualified denial
of Stewart's appeal, but "No" was not written. Washington's inherent
amiability, his regard for the comradeship of his old Regiment and his
respect for the code of gentlemen's credit made him undertake to raise
three-fourths of the amount the Captain sought. If the money could
be found, Washington wrote, he would remit directly to the discharged officer and not through the merchants, who would maintain
that if he had any funds he should reduce his obligations to them and
not create new debt by lending to friends.[20] After some days, Washing-

[18] 2 *G. W.*, 513.   [19] Letter of Apr. 27, 1763; 2 *G. W.*, 397.   [20] 2 *G. W.*, 397–98.

ton was able to borrow money with which to purchase bills of exchange
to a total of £302. These he sent forthwith to Stewart, and in doing so
had nothing to say of the time and method of repayment. He knew
he had no security other than, as he subsequently wrote, "the word of
a gentleman of no estate."[21] Experience, already accumulating, was a
warning that debtors were slow-footed. Washington's difficulty in collecting for the stallion he sold Robert Alexander[22] was to be duplicated
even in so small a matter as that of some winning lottery tickets purchased for Col. Dudley Digges.[23] All the same, as Washington saw it, a
gentleman had, on request, to lend money to another gentleman worse
circumstanced than himself.

Climbing debt and dragging repayment did not keep Washington
from ordering another pipe of a "rich, oily" Madeira at the very time
he was trying to borrow money with which to oblige Robert Stewart.[24]
Nor was Washington deterred from new expenditure by a controversy
over exchange that now threatened the amity of Virginians. To raise
the money Stewart wanted for the purchase of a commission and to
transact other business at the spring meeting of the merchants, Washington had gone to Williamsburg, and while there he had heard that
British merchants trading in the Dominion had filed in February a
protest against the volume of paper money issued by the Colony. The
injustice of the act for the relief of insolvent debtors likewise had been
challenged in the memorial, which the Lords Commissioners for Trade
and Plantations had hastened to transmit to Fauquier. The Governor,
in turn, had laid the paper before the Council on the 28th of April and
had said he thought it imperative that the Assembly be convened. A call
then had been sent out for the 19th of May.[25] Besides this summons,
Washington received from some source an intimation of the specific
currency reform the Board of Trade had told the Governor to demand
of the General Assembly. This alarmed him both as indebted planter
and as duty-bound Burgess. ". . . I suppose," he wrote, "[the board's
report and orders] will set the whole country in flames." He continued:
"This stir of the merchants seems to be ill timed and cannot be attended
with any good effects; bad I fear it will . . ." That said, he dismissed all
speculation on the subject until the Assembly met.[26]

[21] 2 G. W., 513.   [22] See supra, p. 65 and Ledger A, folio 96.
[23] Washington made the advance of £16 in 1764. He was repaid in 1771. See Ledger A,
folio 240.
[24] 2 G. W., 398.
[25] E. J., P.R.O., C.O. 5: 1435, p. 51, VSL Photostat.   [26] 2 G. W., 399–400.

When the Burgesses filed into the council chamber, May 19, to receive Francis Fauquier's view of the situation, they found the friendly and diplomatic Governor in a mood of unwonted stiffness. The Board of Trade, he said, was offended because the General Assembly had failed to obey instructions to provide better security for debts due in sterling. "I have never yet deceived you," Fauquier continued, "and I will not now attempt it; but, in plain language, inform that all endeavors to evade [the] force [of the Board's resolutions] will prove fruitless, and plunge you still deeper in His Majesty's displeasure." He reiterated: "It is absolutely necessary that something should be done to give the merchants that satisfaction for which they call upon you, and for which, in case of failure here, they will call upon a higher Power." The Governor did not undertake to suggest how the merchants were to be satisfied, but he urged the lawmakers to provide adequately for the redemption of the paper currency on maturity, and he called on them to repeal the amended act for the relief of insolvents.[27]

The Burgesses were ready for the Governor. As soon as they tramped back downstairs to their own hall and went through the traditional formality of two readings of the speech, they passed resolutions that had been prepared earlier in full knowledge of what the Board of Trade had called on the Governor to demand. Emission of treasury notes had been necessary, the Burgesses maintained, because there had been no other means of meeting the King's requisitions. The notes had been made legal tender, except for quit rents, in the conviction that this was essential justice to all. Provision for judicial determination of disputed rates of exchange was proper; sufficient funds had been provided for the redemption of the notes; "no person trading to this Colony could receive any injury"; British merchants would gain as much as they would lose in the fluctuations of exchange.

All this was set forth positively. Then the House added that it would review these matters, the insolvency act in particular, lest it might be mistaken. The general tone was one of professed surprise that the House was censured for what it had considered "acts of duty to our Sovereign."[28] To this view, the Burgesses adhered. No appeal, no persuasion, could shake them. In the formal address that embodied the

---

[27] *Journ. H.B.*, 1761–65, p. 171–72. The insolvency act is in 7 *H* 549. A careful explanation of the reasons for the passage of the measure at the session of November, 1762, will be found in a letter from the Committee of Correspondence to the Virginia agent in London, 1763, n. d.; 11 *V* 135–37.

[28] *Journ. H. B.*, 1761–65, 172–73.

resolutions, the arguments were elaborated and were aimed in part at those members of the Council who had complained [29] that matured paper money was not being withdrawn from circulation.[30] A tabulation of the "State of the Treasury Notes" was prepared in a form to convince the doubting Governor that all outstanding issues could and would be retired from existing taxes.[31] The insolvency act of the previous November was repealed.[32] More than this the Burgesses refused to do. "I think," the Governor confessed, "I brought but four gentlemen over to my opinion, to consider this matter in the light in which I consider it . . ." [33]

In this discussion, Washington had no place of prominence. As usual he was named on special committees to consider petitions for relief that some of his old comrades filed,[34] but he probably was not present when the Governor called the Burgesses to the council chamber on the 31st of May, scolded them mildly for their failure to act, and then prorogued them.[35] The absence of the senior member from Frederick was not due to unconcern over sterling debts but to a desire to increase his fortune and to discharge some of his own debts otherwise than from the uncertain returns of an unpredictable crop. Washington was convinced that land speculation of the sort he had known and had practiced since young manhood held as good a promise of profit as ever. He still was looking westward, always westward; but along with some of the planters and merchants, he now turned to an undeveloped area not far from the first watercourses up which the original English caravels timidly had turned their inquisitive prows. The Great Dismal Swamp, as it picturesquely was styled, long had defied settlers. South of Chesapeake Bay, with its eastern rim not more than twenty-five miles from the ocean, it extended through the western part of Norfolk County into Nansemond and southward across the boundary between Virginia and North Carolina. Much of the ground was so swampy that a horse would sink into it above his fetlocks. Vast stretches of tall reeds contended with cypress trees and with white cedar. In places, heavy winds had overthrown great trees, the roots of which had been insecure in the

---

[29] See *supra*, p. 32.

[30] The committee entrusted with the preparation of the address consisted of Charles Carter, Edmund Pendleton and George Wythe (*Journ. H.B.*, 1761–65, p. 173). For the text of the address, see *ibid.*, 188–92.

[31] Fauquier to the Board of Trade, June 1, 1763; *ibid.*, xxxiv.

[32] 7 H 643.   [33] *Journ. H.B.*, 1761–65, p. xxxv.

[34] *Ibid.*, 175, 179–80.   [35] *Ibid.*, 197.

damp earth. Fallen one on another, these trees were a barrier even the
trapper despaired of passing. Where the speculator could penetrate, he
found the soil of widely varying quality, but there was general belief
that if the swamp were drained, tens of thousands of acres of ideal
farming land would be the reward. Here and there, where dry strips
led inward, small planters had established themselves and, it was said,
had prospered.[36]

William and Thomas Nelson and a few of their friends had decided
to seek the patent of the unoccupied and waste land of the swamp and
to draw off the water from the best of it. These men readily interested
Washington, who agreed to visit the Great Dismal while he was in
Southern Virginia and to see for himself what it would offer of fine
timber while it was being drained, and of rich flatlands when it was
cleared. On the 25th of May he rode from Suffolk to a stream then
called the Pequamin River and thence to a narrow strip of land between
the watercourse and the swamp. From that point, the party went northward for about five miles. En route, Washington observed the character
of the soil and of the trees as carefully as when, at 16 years of age, he
first had examined Greenway Court in the Shenandoah Valley.[37]

In this part of the swamp he found little or no timber, but under the
gross reeds the ground seemed, in his own phrase, "excessive rich." [38]
Without great difficulty, the visitors led their horses through the tangle
and reached at length what the natives called "New Found Land." It
was thickly settled and "very rich." Washington was careful to write
down later: "This land was formerly esteemed part of the Dismal, but
being higher, though full of reeds, people ventured to settle upon it and
as it became more open, it became more dry and is now prodigious fine
land, but subject to wets and unhealthiness." [39]

As they made their way, Washington and his companions tried to
ascertain the number and direction of the slow, overflowing watercourses, themselves called swamps, on the edge of the Great Dismal.
After collecting such information as residents could supply, Washington concluded there was a "pretty considerable fall" to the land on the

---

[36] See E. G. Swem, ed. *A Description of the Dismal Swamp* . . . from 4 *Ruffin's Farmers Register*, 521–24 (1836) in Heartman Historical Series, No. 38. Cf. W. K. Boyd, ed. *William Byrd's Histories of the Dividing Line*, 62 ff and particularly 84–85; 2 *Smyth*, 100; Joseph B. Dunn, *The History of Nansemond County*, Virginia, 55 ff.
[37] See Vol. I, p. 213. The modern spelling of Pequamin is Perkimon.
[38] 1 *Diaries*, 192.
[39] *Ibid.*

western side of the swamp.[40] He could ascertain nothing positive about the low ground to the eastward, but, he wrote, "it is certain, I believe, that the water does drain off at the east end somewhere: in which case a common causeway through at the crossing place would most certainly lay all that arm dry." [41]

The prospect was one of undisguised and unabashed speculation, some would say of a long gamble; but if the swamp could be drained successfully, the reclaimed land might yield fabulous crops, close to the market of Norfolk and to the open sea. Washington decided he would make the venture along with the Nelsons, Robert Tucker, Robert Burwell and the others who had shown special interest in it. The first step, of course, was to ascertain what property rights already existed in the Great Dismal. If these titles were not extensive, they might be acquired. In the event patents were numerous but did not cover all the desirable land, then surveys could be made to take up as much as could be reclaimed to the financial benefit of the speculators.

This would take a long time, because lines must be drawn through parts of the swamp never previously reached by man. A petition of an unusual nature consequently was drafted for presentation to the Governor and Council: Permission was sought to make the surveys and to return them to the Secretary's Office within seven years. During that time, the "rights" granted the petitioners would hold; no other persons could attempt to take out patents and to make surveys in the region the petitioners sought to reclaim. The Council received this paper May 25, 1763, and not unnaturally deferred action of so sweeping a proposal, even though some of the most influential names in the Colony were attached to it.[42]

In this state Washington perforce left the Dismal Swamp venture [43]

---

[40] Unless conditions have changed completely since 1763, Washington was mistaken in this. At present, Cypress Swamp, its various branches and the small Moss Swamp drain into the Great Dismal and constitute mere outstretched arms. This is true, also, of Taylor Swamp and its branches, South of the Virginia-Carolina line. To the eastward, as Washington surmised, the flow of the streams is away from the Great Dismal. Northwest River flows from one of the small swamps East of the Great Dismal proper; Deep Creek courses from the northeastern corner of the wide, swampy area.

[41] 1 Diaries, 193.

[42] E. J., P.R.O., C.O. 5: 1435, p. 53, VSL Photostat.

[43] He had drawn on May 16 his Burgess' pay and travel allowance for the session of November, 1762, and he did not linger now to collect for the time given to his public duties at the session ending in May, 1763. See Ledger A, folio 122. Fitzpatrick (1 Diaries, 194 n.), mistakenly assumed the £33, odd money received by Washington on May 16 was for the current session, but the payment balances the debit entries of November, 1762, and not those of May, 1763, which were settled Oct. 26, 1763.

temporarily and started back northward to resume his everyday life as a planter, but he did not abandon his reawakened interest in speculative land enterprises. Almost immediately he became a sharer in a new Mississippi Company that had bold, ambitious designs: Fifty subscribers, and no more than that number, were to contribute funds with which to send to England an agent who was to solicit the grant directly on the Mississippi River of a domain large enough to allow each member of the company 50,000 acres. This land was to be protected from Indians by royal troops and was, if possible, to be procured free of composition money,[44] quit rents and all other expenses for twelve years. The company would promise to settle the territory by the end of that time unless Indians prevented. Each adventurer was to hold his tract in fee simple, not in joint tenancy, but he was not to dispose of his share without the consent of the company. No member was to have more than one vote, even though he purchased shares of others.[45] These terms, like the aims that shaped them, were the ideal of speculation, such an arrangement as the land-hungry dream about but never hope in waking hours to achieve. Apparently the project won numerous signatures before it came to Washington [46] and it had the highest respectability. Whether or not Washington realized the difficulties in the way of such a grant, he thought the gamble worth the stake. He signed his name to the agreement and subsequently undertook mildly to persuade George William Fairfax, now back from England, to become one of the adventurers.[47]

Later in June Washington went to Frederick County and while there had news of the sort grimly associated in his mind with that beautiful region. After the surrender of Montreal, many of the French Indians, particularly those of the region around Detroit, had refused to accept the rule of the conquering English. Within little more than a month,

[44] Current usage in England would have justified the word "composition," as the sum involved in a financial settlement of this nature, without the addition of "money."

[45] Agreement of the Mississippi Company, June 3, 1763; 10 *Papers of G. W.*, 129, LC. The place of the initial meeting is not mentioned in the paper here quoted. From the number of subscribing members of the Lee family, it may be surmised that the project originated along the lower Potomac. This would seem the more probable because the agreement stipulated that a majority of the members were to come from Virginia and Maryland.

[46] His name is the nineteenth on the list, but as this list is in two columns, he may have signed at the bottom of the first, right-hand column before any names were written to the left. The first name in the left-hand column is that of Francis Lightfoot Lee, followed by that of Washington's brother John Augustine—"Jack." On the right the leading signatures were those of Richard Henry Lee and Thomas Ludwell Lee. Among the other subscribers were Adam Stephen, Thomas Bullitt and William Fitzhugh.

[47] 37 *G. W.*, 486; the original is in the Boston Public Library.

during the spring of 1763, these Indians captured all the English out-posts North of the Potomac and the Ohio, except Niagara, Detroit and Fort Pitt.[48] No massacres had been reported from any part of Virginia when Washington reached the Shenandoah Valley, but terror once again had gripped the entire frontier. The little stockades that long had been regarded as worthless now proved havens for hundreds of anxious farm families. Although Washington heard of the murder of nine persons only, East of the Allegheny mountains, and those nine in Penn-sylvania, he knew what to expect. When he had returned home at the end of June, he wrote: ". . . it is melancholy to behold, the terror that has seized them and the fatal consequences that must follow in the loss of their harvest and crops, the whole back country being in forts or flying." [49]

There followed a brief period of calm—as often there had during the years of Washington's command—and then, roving bands of Indians carried the tomahawk and the torch to all the unprotected homes on the Greenbrier and the Kanawha.[50] "In eight years' service," wrote one of Washington's former officers from Staunton, "I never knew such gen-eral consternation." He predicted: "Should they make a second attempt, I am assured the country will be laid desolate . . ." The people, he said, were almost completely without arms and ammunition; the County Lieutenant was inactive; most of the militia officers were "unfit persons, or unwilling, not to say afraid to meet an enemy, too busy with their harvest to run a risk in the field." [51] It was an old story to Wash-ington's ears and was different only in that there now were no Virginia regimental troops on whom to rely when the militia failed.

Governor Fauquier's impulse to convene the Assembly was curbed by his knowledge that the lawmakers could raise money and provide troops in no other way than through the emission of more such Treasury notes as the Board of Trade had rebuked Virginia for issuing. He had to call out the militia, whose pay might be provided later under existing law. Washington wrote of this to Robert Stewart, almost in sarcastic strain: "Five hundred . . . are to be drafted from Hampshire,

[48] As this famous "conspiracy of Pontiac" is covered by one of Francis Parkman's best known books, and was not a campaign in which Washington was engaged, it is not here treated in any detail, though the story is a fascinating one. Randolph G. Adams has shown in *DAB* that several of the familiar traditions of Pontiac and his "war" will not bear critical scrutiny. In the light of the research of Adams, some of Parkman's conclusions must be revised and perhaps abandoned.
[49] Letter of July 5, 1763, to Burwell Bassett; 2 *G.W.*, 401.
[50] Parkman, *op. cit.*, v. 2, p. 94 ff.
[51] Letter of unidentified writer, July 26, 1763, quoted in Parkman, *op. cit.*, v. 2, p. 93 n.

etc., and [to] be under the command of Colonel Stephen whose military courage and capacity (says the Governor) is well established. The other 500 from the Southern frontier Counties are to be conducted by Major Lewis, so that you may readily conceive what an enormous expense must attend these measures. Stephen,[52] immediately upon the Indians retiring, advanced to Fort Cumberland with 200 or 250 militia in great parade and will doubtless achieve some signal advantage of which the public will soon be informed." [53]

Happily for the Colonies, some of the Highlanders who had fought in Forbes's campaign of 1758 had been left in Pennsylvania under the command of Col. Henry Bouquet. That veteran could get no troops from any of the provinces but he hurried westward from Carlisle on July 18, 1763, with approximately 460 regulars. Detaching a handful to garrison Raystown, which now had become Bedford, and another score and a half to guard Fort Ligonier, formerly Loyal Hannon, he left his wagons, loaded 400 horses with flour and essential supplies, and struck westward along the route he had followed with Forbes five years previously. On the afternoon of August 5, the Indians attacked in force on Bushy Run, an upper branch of Turtle Creek. Their tricks were those that had led to the massacre of Braddock's men; but Bouquet was not Braddock, nor were his troops untrained in the warfare of the woodlands. Bouquet had applied all he had learned and he had developed tactics that combined those of frontier tree-to-tree fighting with those of line fire and of rapid assault. He matched the Indians' worst until nightfall and, when they renewed the battle on August 6, he lured them forward by a pretended retreat, then delivered a fierce bayonet charge, and finally routed them at 1 P. M. though at heavy loss.[54] The relief of Fort Pitt followed immediately. West of that outpost, the savages still were violent, but the retired Colonel of Mount Vernon knew that the defeat administered by Bouquet would dull their zeal for war. "They have lately met with some pretty rugged treatment," he wrote one of his English merchants, "and it is hoped they will sue for terms again in a very little while." [55]

52 The text reads "Stephens."

53 Letter of Aug. 13, 1763; 2 G.W., 403–04. Stewart's remarks from Philadelphia, Sept. 3, 1763, were sharp: "The noble expedient they have fallen on in Virginia to employ the militia in order to save money and perform actual service would do honor to the most sublime military genius . . . some torgid [turgid?] accounts of the mighty achievements of S's parties have already reached this place, but his letters do not make that impression they used to do" (3 Hamilton, 257).

54 See Bouquet to Gladwin, Aug. 28, 1763; Br. Mus., Add. MS 21649, p. 313.

55 Letter of Sept. 27 1763, to Richard Washington; 2 G.W., 409.

This was all that Washington thought the situation justified him in saying at a distance from the frontier. Closer at hand he had a multitude of small vexatious duties that would have alarmed a timid planter and would have harassed a man less reconciled to detail than Washington was. His apparent prosperity and his known acquisition of wealth through his marriage made him something of a private banker in the eyes of distressed friends and, in particular, of a neighbor and comrade in arms, Capt. John Posey, owner of Ferry Farm, directly West of Mount Vernon. Strictly speaking Posey had not commanded directly under Washington, but he had been a Captain in Col. William Byrd's Second Virginia Regiment [56] and, when the force was reduced, he had agreed to accept a Lieutenant's commission.[57] He had served actively, also, as a recruiting officer for the expedition against the Cherokees in 1760,[58] in which position he had been more persuasive than discriminating. Posey had prevailed upon sixty-one men to enlist for a bounty of £10 each, but a number of these had fallen sick, some had deserted, and some had failed later to meet Andrew Lewis's requirements for a soldier. Colonel Byrd, being hard put, had accepted eight whom the stern Lewis had rejected. The result had been confusion over the amount the Colony owed Captain Posey. In ascertaining what justly was due, the General Assembly of 1761 had been as generous as ever toward the defenders of the Colony and had allowed Posey £137 for bounties and for the subsistence he had provided.[59] At the session held in December, 1762, Captain Posey was back again as a petitioner. This time he and Capt. John Field set forth that in 1758 they had used their Companies as artificers, to clear roads to Fort DuQuesne. By Forbes's order the men had been paid 30s each for this extra duty but had been told to apply to the General Assembly for the balance due them at the rate of 6d daily. Posey and Field asked to have this money turned over to them in order that they might distribute it among their former soldiers. The General Assembly held this a reasonable application and voted payment. Something over £302 had been placed in Posey's hands for the remuneration of his men.[60] Afterwards, the prompt and equitable disbursement of the money had been brought into question, whereupon, at the session in May, 1763, the two Captains were directed to render an accounting.[61]

[56] *Journ. H.B.*, 1761–65, p. 134.   [57] *Ibid.*, 101.
[58] *Journ. H.B.*, 1758–61, p. 236.   [59] *Ibid.*, 239–242.
[60] *Journ. H.B.*, 1761–65, p. 101, 109–10, 134, 141–42.
[61] *Ibid.*, 195. So far as the records show, neither of them did this in 1764 (*ibid.*, 244).

Washington was interested in these transactions both because Posey was a neighbor and friend and also because from 1755 onward, Posey had been in his debt. Whether in Winchester or at home, whenever the easy-going Captain found himself in immediate need of cash or credit, he turned to Washington, who always obliged.[62] The master of Mount Vernon also had a bill against Posey for a survey made at that gentleman's request,[63] and, year in and year out, he did the smithy work of the Captain, who included among his pursuits the operation of a ferry across the Potomac.[64] In 1762, moreover, Turner Crump and Washington's slave carpenters had built a barn on Posey's property and at his cost.[65] Few of these accounts had the Captain ever settled, and now he was in serious financial entanglement. His creditors demanded cash in place of renewed promises; interest charges threatened to drag him down. As soon as Posey could ascertain even vaguely how much he owed his creditors and what they were willing to accept, he came to Washington and sought a loan of £700, to be secured by a mortgage on all his land and slaves.[66] Washington acquiesced, generously, but rashly. This large new liability involved serious risk for the Colonel who already had assumed £300 of new debt in a year when he remained heavily on the wrong side of his merchants' books.

Final action on Posey's loan and mortgage was not taken until October 1, by which date Washington had harvested his summer crops,[67] had sown his winter wheat [68] and had cut his tobacco. He was pessimistic about his "money crop" in every particular except that he felt some satisfaction in sending to market the last of the undesired narrow leaf.[69] The yield on the York appeared to be good, "but," Washington had to write his London dealer, "my crops on the Potomac are vastly deficient; in short, a wet spring, a dry summer and early frosts have quite demolished me." [70] It was the third adverse year in succession for the growing of tobacco on the Potomac,[71] a stern discouragement for a man still ambitious to excel as a planter.

---

62 Posey's early account is in Washington's *Ledger A*, folio 14.

63 This was Mch. 6, 1760 (*Birch Cat.* 663, item 80). It is possible this was the land covered by a lease and release of 136 acres in Muddy Hole, previously assumed to be 145, that had been involved in a transaction between Posey and Daniel French, June 17, 1760 (see *ibid.*, item 34). Details are not known.

64 *Ledger A*, folio 14.   65 *Ibid.*, folio 121.   66 *Ibid.*, folio 168.

67 He cut his rye July 1, his wheat July 5–13, his hay July 14–22, and his timothy for seed July 28–29, too early a date, he concluded (1 *Diaries*, 186).

68 This was begun August 29, about a fortnight after the sowing of turnips (1 *Diaries*, 187).

69 2 *G. W.*, 404.

70 Letter of Jan. 22, 1764, to Robert Cary & Co.; 2 *G. W.*, 412.   71 *Ibid.*, 416.

When the hogsheads had been filled on all the plantations, the total was better than the Colonel had thought it could be. Half a score tenants weighed in about 12,000 pounds of tobacco in Northern Virginia; on some tracts where the plantation tobacco had almost been lost in weeds during the first days of the season, the final cutting was heavy.[72] The well-managed Custis properties yielded Washington thirty-six hogsheads and "Jackie" no less than ninety-seven—both totals the largest since Washington's marriage.[73] On the other hand, quality was so lacking in the leaf that bulk and weight were more than cancelled. Washington realized this and did not attempt to catch the opening of the market by sending off any great amount on the ships that sailed during the autumn.[74] In spite of delayed sales and his deep indebtedness in England, he continued to purchase luxuries, though not as recklessly as in the past. His largest single item in the orders that fall was for a set of chariot harness for six horses.[75] That was the utmost he allowed himself even in the equipage, which always was one of his extravagances. For everyday use he was content to have his old "chair" relined instead of buying a new one.[76]

Land was different; he could not resist that. By the end of summer he had carried his total holdings to 9381 acres,[77] and almost before the tobacco crop was housed he went to Stafford Court House to attend a meeting of the men who sought the vast grant on the Mississippi. The decision then was to assess the members £8, 15s each, probably to supply initial funds with which to ascertain whether the Crown would look with favor on the project.[78] The next month, October, Washington started again for the Great Dismal Swamp—to get still more land. Travel during the summer had been light,[79] but this journey to the North Carolina line was more serious and more arduous. With some of his fellow adventurers, Washington "went the rounds," [80] of the swamp, as he said, and visited its southern border in North Carolina, where he saw some excellent land he subsequently determined to purchase.[81] He concluded that the profitable drainage of the swamp was possible and, with the other speculators, he then returned to Williamsburg in an

---

[72] *Ledger A*, folio 164.   [73] *Custis Papers*, VHS.
[74] Twenty-one of his own and sixty of Custis's hogsheads were held for spring shipment (2 *G. W.*, 415).
[75] 2 *G. W.*, 406 n.   [76] *Ledger A*, folio 93.
[77] 11 *Papers of G. W.*, LC, 3.   [78] *Ledger A*, folio 169.
[79] It probably included a visit to the Rappahannock at the end of July (2 *G.W.*, 402).
[80] *Ledger A*, folio 194.   [81] 2 *G. W.*, 411.

effort to procure action on the petition filed the previous May for the grant of lands in the swamp.[82] It had developed earlier that the petition itself had disappeared and that the Council had done nothing about it. Thereupon a new paper had been circulated in the names of the original applicants, their kinsmen, their friends and their tenants, to a total of 148 persons. Washington doubtless was responsible for the inclusion of his brothers, his cousins, his neighbors, and even his servants.[83] On presentation of this paper, the Council was quick to make amends for delay and neglect. It resolved, Nov. 1, 1763, "that each of the petitioners have leave to take out a patent for 1000 acres of the said land upon condition of giving legal notice to the proprietors of the contiguous high lands and that they will not interfere with any entries antecedent to this day . . ." The desired seven years were allowed for the return of the surveys.[84]

With this assurance, the minute of which was filed immediately in the Auditor's office,[85] the promoters met in Williamsburg and organized their company. The first stipulation of the articles of agreement was that each member should pay his part of such funds as were necessary for draining the swamp. If he failed to meet any call for his *pro rata,* he could not continue in the enterprise, but must sell his interest or return it to the company on the repayment of the sum he previously had advanced. A share in the company could be bequeathed by its owner; no distribution of the holdings of the company could be made otherwise than by vote of a majority. When division was so ordered, the lands were to be laid off in lots, for which the individual members would draw.[86]

Agreement was reached, also, that members should be selected to ascertain what grants already were outstanding, and to make surveys accordingly. For this task, Washington volunteered along with his brother-in-law, Fielding Lewis, and his former Commissary of the French and Indian War, the indefatigable Thomas Walker. The plan was to begin drainage of the swamp as soon as rights could be established and lines run. Consequently, each of the members promised to supply ten able-bodied Negroes, with clothing, tools, etc., by July 1, 1764. For housing these slaves, it manifestly was necessary to buy a

---

[82] See *supra,* p. 95.
[83] The original, with the autographs, is in the *Papers of the Dismal Swamp Company,* LC.
[84] *Papers of the Dismal Swamp Company,* loc. cit.
[85] *Ibid.*   [86] *Ibid.,* "Articles of Agreement."

plantation and to apportion the cost among the members.[87] These members were ten in number and no more—William Nelson, Thomas Nelson, Robert Burwell, George Washington, Fielding Lewis, Robert Tucker, Thomas Walker, William Waters, John Symes and Samuel Gist.[88] Now that rights had been acquired, nothing more was heard of the remaining 138 petitioners.

To ascertain what lands had been patented in the swamp, Washington and Fielding Lewis [89] employed Gershom Nimmo of Norfolk, who reported promptly that so far as he could recollect, the total was 5800 acres of which not much more than 600 had been surveyed. Entries for 3000 acres of this total had been made in the name of Robert Tucker, one of the members of the new company, after plans for organizing the enterprise had been initiated.[90] Nimmo's information showed, in brief, that abundant land in the swamp was unpatented, but the season now was so advanced that nothing could be undertaken till spring returned to Eastern Virginia. Washington's only immediate contribution could be in pondering how the rich, wet land could be reclaimed for the plow. This was an interesting problem for reflection when winter descended on the Potomac and the road was so deep in mud that few visitors ventured to Mount Vernon.

The year 1763 was drawing to a close. For tobacco, to repeat, it had brought the third discouraging season in succession and on that account had deepened debt. Washington was losing faith in his ability to raise on Little Hunting Creek a superlative leaf that would command the admiration and the guineas of the critical London buyers. There must be new enterprises at Mount Vernon and more money from wise specu-lation in good lands. Tobacco was too uncertain, too much subject to fluctuation in price.

That stern fact meant much to Washington and, in a dramatic manner, to all Virginia Counties where the leaf was grown. In 1755, for example, when the tobacco crop was a failure and prices were high, the General Assembly had passed an act to permit citizens to pay in cash all fees, rents, judgments, bonds or levies which by law were

---

[87] *Ibid.*

[88] Treasurer John Robinson subsequently was a partner. At this meeting, Symes and Gist were not present and were represented by Thomas Walker (*Papers of the Dismal Swamp Company;* minutes of meeting of Nov. 3, 1763).

[89] Thomas Walker's name does not appear in this particular undertaking for the Company.

[90] Nimmo's report of Nov. 20, 1763; *Papers of the Dismal Swamp Company,* loc. cit. Nothing has been found in these papers to show whether Tucker was acting for the Company or on his own account.

payable normally in tobacco at an average of 16s 8d per hundred weight, or two pence a pound. Ostensibly the law had been passed because of the scarcity of tobacco; [91] actually the reason was that tobacco was expected to be so high as a result of the shortage that it was cheaper for a man to sell his leaf and to pay his taxes in cash than it was to discharge his obligation in tobacco.

The chief losers were the ministers of the established church whose annual salary was 16,000 pounds of tobacco. It was vain for the clergy to argue that as they had been compelled to accept tobacco when the leaf sold at less than two pence a pound, they were entitled to be paid in tobacco when the price was high. Planters answered that two pence was the average at which tobacco sold in Virginia and that if they used that medium of exchange when tobacco was abnormally high, they were paying one and a half times and might even pay twice what they had promised. Argument was ended by the expiration of the law, which was for ten months only.[92]

Threatened recurrence of a similar shortage of tobacco in 1758 had led the General Assembly to consider the enactment of another "two penny law," as it was termed.[93] Debate had been prolonged, and public discussion had been so violent that a minister who then was Professor of Moral Philosophy in the College of William and Mary had exclaimed, "How many of the House of Burgesses were to be hanged?" He went on to assert "that every member who should vote for settling the parsons' salaries in money would be scoundrels, and that if any member wanting to receive the sacrament, was to apply to him, he would refuse to administer it." [94] Such language hurt the cause of the ministers in a House where the influence of the tobacco-growers far outweighed theirs. After full debate, the new "two-penny bill" was passed, was accepted in amended form by the Council and, on Oct. 12, 1758, was signed by the Governor.[95]

Outraged by its terms the clergy sent to England Rev. James Camm to appeal to the throne for the disallowance of the law. He proceeded so skillfully that the Privy Council, as of Aug. 10, 1759,[96] declared the

[91] See the act in 6 H 568.   [92] Ibid., 569.

[93] Apparently, the immediate occasion was a petition of "sundry inhabitants of the County of Prince George" (Journ. H.B., 1758–61, p. 5).

[94] This was Rev. Jacob Rowe (Journ. H.B., 1758–61, p. 16). For his arrest, apology and discharge from custody, see ibid., 17–18.

[95] Journ. H.B., 1758–61, p. 7, 15, 17, 21, 29, 32, 45. The act is in 7 H 240–41.

[96] W. W. Henry, Patrick Henry, Life, Correspondence and Speeches (cited hereafter as W. W. Henry), v. 1, p. 33.

law null. It was a short-lived victory because the act expired on Oct. 12. 1759, but it raised a vehemently controversial question when, at length, official notice of the action of the Crown reached the Colony: [97] Was the law operative between the date it was signed by the Governor and the time it was disallowed? If the law was not in effect during that period of approximately ten months, the clergy were due their tobacco at the market price, but how were they to collect the money due them?

In the end the courts held, almost uniformly, that the "two-penny act" of 1758 had never been good law,[98] and that for the period covered by the measure, the parsons were entitled to be paid in tobacco or at the market price of the staple. A complaining minister of high character, Rev. James Maury of Hanover County, thereupon demanded that the extent of the damage he had sustained in being paid in money at 2d a pound should be determined. The needed evidence concerned only the price at which tobacco was selling when the minister was paid at 16s 8d per hundred weight. Proper damages then could be fixed, of course, by subtracting 16s 8d from the market price and multiplying that by 160, which represented the number of hundreds of pounds of tobacco due Maury. For hearing this suit, on Dec. 1, 1763, the sheriff drew a jury of Hanover men so humble in station that they did not satisfy counsel for the minister. Few on the list, he protested, were known in the County; none of them was conspicuous. Patrick Henry, lawyer for the defendants—the officials who had collected the tax—replied stoutly that the panel consisted of honest men against whom no charge had been made. As there was no peremptory challenge, the jury was sworn, and the essential evidence was presented. Maury's attorney, a man of some ability, argued his case and concluded with a eulogy on the clergy who were, in actual fact, none too popular in a County where dissent already had taken root.

Then Henry arose—a young man of 27, who seemed awkward and somewhat abashed. Hangers-on and persons residing near the Court House remembered him well as a fair fiddler and a capital story-teller, who had visited often in the village and on occasion had assisted his

[97] See Fauquier's letters of June 30 and Sept. 1, 1760, to the Lords of Trade, *Journ. H. B.,* 1758–61, p. 285–86, 287.

[98] *W. W. Henry,* v. 1, p. 33. Perhaps the fullest early review of the law is in Charles Campbell, *History of the Colony and Ancient Dominion of Virginia,* ed. 1860, p. 507. All previous accounts doubtless will be superseded by that in Dr. R. D. Meade's forthcoming life of Henry. For bibliographical references to the two most renowned pamphlets in this dispute, see *Journ. H.B.,* 1761–65, p. xlviii.

father-in-law, proprietor of the ordinary across the road from the public building. To lawyers and to other auditors of serious mind, Henry was familiar as a busy and promising young practitioner, son of the presiding justice of the County Court, Col. John Henry.[99] In a few minutes he warmed to his cause and boldly asserted that a just law, such as the two-penny act, could not be disallowed otherwise than by misrule and tyranny.[100] As he pictured the distress that had dictated the law, his imagination soared and his words took on sonority and splendor, but soon his style changed again.

In flaming phrase he denounced the indolence and rapacity of the clergymen who were demanding the utmost for themselves. It was a speech of such eloquence as men of the Virginia countryside never had heard, a speech pitched exactly to the reasoning, the prejudice and the self-interest of the men who were to pass on the case. Jury and spectators were stunned, overwhelmed. The twelve went out like men in a trance—to return soon with a verdict of one penny for the plaintiff. Sorrowfully, the minister wrote: "After the court adjourned [Henry] apologized to me for what he had said, alleging that his sole view in engaging in the cause, and in saying what he had, was to render himself popular. You see, then, it is so clear a point in this person's opinion that the ready road to popularity here is to trample under foot the interests of religion, the rights of the church, and the prerogatives of the Crown." [101]

These words did not come under Washington's eye. If he heard anything of the "parson's cause" at the time it was second-hand and perhaps was vague; but there was a challenge in the echo of that young lawyer's voice in Hanover. A law passed by the General Assembly was *ipso facto* a valid law; for the King to set it aside was misrule or tyranny. The people had listened to that, had applauded, had approved.

---

[99] Unfortunately for a good story, no credence can be given the tradition that young Patrick Henry was completely unknown in 1763. He had been practising for three years and had handled an extraordinary number of cases. William Wirt Henry estimated (*op. cit.,* v. 1, p. 35) that from the autumn of 1760 to the close of 1763, Patrick "charged fees in 1185 suits, besides many fees for advice and for preparing papers out of court." Exaggerated as these figures must be, Henry was already a conspicuous attorney. Had he not possessed reputation, it scarcely is probable he would have been chosen to defend the most widely discussed current suit in that part of Virginia.

[100] Here again, tradition of cries of "treason" has to be discounted, if not discarded. The only reports of Henry's speech that William Wirt Henry could collect approximately half a century afterwards were fragmentary and vague. They may have confused this address with that of May, 1765. Rev. James Maury's letter, presently to be quoted in the text, included no reference to any protest by auditors.

[101] James Maury to John Camm, Dec. 12, 1763, in Anne Maury, *Memoirs of a Huguenot Family,* 418–23. The quotation is p. 423.

CHAPTER VII

THE MASTER OF MOUNT VERNON MISCALCULATES

(1764)

SEVERAL POSSIBILITIES of making more money existed at Mount Vernon. The mill, if operating regularly, might be profitable. Distilling might yield something besides brandy for sick servants and chilled laborers. The river more than once each spring seemed almost solid with vast, marketable schools of herring and of shining shad. Hemp or flax or wheat might be a cash crop in place of tobacco.

Washington would investigate but, meantime, he must go again to Williamsburg, whither the Governor's irresistible inclination to consult with the Assembly had prompted His Honor to summon the lawmakers on the 21st of January, 1764.[1] The reason was the familiar one— a call from the British commander for Virginia troops to join in a new campaign against the Indians. Beaten the previous year, the redmen still were halting the advance of English settlement and were threatening to bring the torch and the scalping knife to the frontier again. Amherst had gone home, as Governor Fauquier told the Burgesses, "to receive those honors which his conduct here had merited."[2] In his place, Thomas Gage, who had served as Lieutenant Colonel of the 44th Regiment in Braddock's campaign, was now Major General and American Commander-in-Chief. Both Gage and Amherst had urged that Virginia supply 500 men for a western offensive designed to relieve Detroit and either to annihilate the resisting Indians or to force them to make peace.

Obedient to this requisition, Fauquier asked that the lawmakers consider whether it was not better, as Amherst and Gage urged, "to march into the enemies country than by waiting at home to revenge yourselves

[1] The *Journal* contains no reference to Washington, but *Ledger A,* folio 122, includes pay for the entire session. Moreover, in 2 *G. W.,* 412, appears a letter written from Williamsburg, Jan. 22, 1764, while the Assembly was there.

[2] *Journ. H. B.,* 1761–65, p. 203. Amherst already had been made a Knight of the Bath and had been appointed titular Governor of Virginia. He was not raised to the peerage until 1776.

107

when they think proper to enter yours and commit all kinds of outrages and murders." [3] He had been employing the militia, Fauquier
said, and had found it expensive. The force had been reduced to 500
men and would have been diminished still further had not the call for
the Assembly been sent out. As the lawmakers were soon to meet, the
Governor tactfully explained, "I thought it highly proper you should
determine for yourselves what measures you would for the future pursue
in times of such danger and distress." [4] Then followed in Fauquier's
speech a paragraph that must have had a strange sound to the senior
member from Frederick County: "I cannot quit this subject without
doing justice both to the officers and private men of the militia, by thus
publicly testifying my great approbation of their conduct and courage,
and recommending them to you for payment in the most speedy manner
the laws and constitution of your country will admit of, in recompense
of their services, by which they have done credit to the Colony in general, and great honor to themselves in particular." [5] Washington never
could forget his own repeated disappointment with the militia, and, as
he listened to the Governor, he may have wondered whether a miracle
had occurred or whether, in a metaphor at the opposite pole of human
conduct, Adam Stephen had been pulling the wool over Fauquier's eyes
as he and Robert Stewart had suspected. [6]

The General Assembly did not share that suspicion. At least, it preferred using the militia to raising troops by extravagant bounties, and
it promptly named a commission, with Washington as chairman, to
examine the accounts of the militia and to certify them for payment.
The same act provided a small bounty for militia called into service. [7]
In arguing against the proposal of Gage and the Governor, the Burgesses
asserted once more that the only way they could raise money for bounty
and for pay would be through the emission of more treasury notes,
against which the London merchants already had protested. [8] The
Governor scarcely could resist an argument that echoed almost the
very language of the Board of Trade. He had to find such comfort as
he could in the willingness of the Assembly to entrust the use of the
militia to him. [9]

All in all, the session was dull but it was different in one respect: For

---

[3] Ibid.
[5] Ibid., 204.
[7] 8 H 9.
[9] Ibid., 222.

[4] Ibid., 203–04.
[6] See supra, p. 98.
[8] Journ. H.B., 1761–65, p. 206, 212, 217.

the first time, the Burgesses showed impatience with some of those who thought they could get public money by exhibiting their wounds or telling of the massacre of their families. Even so established a favorite as Robert Stobo knocked once too often at the door of the House of Burgesses. He had gone home for a year in 1760 to look after his private affairs and on his return to Virginia had sought his pay as Major for the period of his absence. The Governor had referred him to the General Assembly, before which he duly laid his petition. Burgesses would not even put the paper in the hands of a committee: they rejected it, viva voce, on the first reading.[10]

Washington fared better. He had nothing to ask as a veteran, but he and his fellow adventurers of the Dismal Swamp Company had run into a difficulty. If they were to succeed in draining the swamp, they must dig long ditches in some localities across property patented by individuals who were not members of the company. It was necessary to get legislative approval of this. Leave consequently was sought and was granted without protest for bringing in a bill that authorized the company to enter or pass through any property and to make canals or causeways anywhere in the swamp "without being subject to the action or suit" of any person for doing so. In event a proprietor considered himself damaged, he and the agent of the company were to agree on proper compensation or, failing to reach terms, were to call in a third person to decide. This measure passed quickly;[11] Washington and his companions could plan now to follow an economical straight line through the swamp.

After the close of the short session, which was prorogued on the 21st of January, 1764, Washington remained in Williamsburg long enough to arrange for the shipment of fifty-two hogsheads of his and "Jackie" Custis's tobacco. The Colonel examined, also, the possibilities of investing some of the surplus funds of the estate.[12] Then, with a brief halt to enjoy the hospitality of Mann Page, Jr.,[13] he went back to the Potomac, the beauty of which no storm could lessen or winter mar. Time sufficed in February for renewed study of the drainage of Dismal

---

10 *Ibid.*, 212.

11 *Journ. H. B.*, 1761–65, p. 214, 215, 217, 218, 222; 8 *H* 18.

12 2 *G. W.*, 412.

13 This may not have been at Rosewell, Gloucester County, but at Mann Page's excellent plantation, later known as Mansfield, near Fredericksburg. Evidence of Washington's presence "at Mann Page's," Jan. 24, 1764, is offered in an entry of that date in *Ledger A*, folio 8, to the effect that Washington there lent Fielding Lewis £12.

Swamp. Washington had leisure, too, for some careful reading on improved agriculture.

What especially appealed to him was a published description of a new "engine" with which, it was said, six men in a day could pull up 200 or 300 large trees by the roots. Washington was incredulous and at the same time unpleasantly conscious of the fact that he did not yet own a sufficient number of slaves, or at least did not find time for them, to clear new ground so that he could enlarge the scale of his operations and change crops frequently on land long used.[14] Where few farm laborers could be hired, his own hands were available in considerable number for opening new fields during no longer a period than that between the killing of hogs in the late autumn and preparations late in February or in March for the new crops. It would be an immense boon if a machine could pull up the trees and, as Washington understood the report, could put an acre of forest land in condition for plowing in a single day of work.[15]

Besides, if the "engine" really operated, it might open the way for experiments of a sort that Washington had not pursued. He had done nothing further about the plow that had proved too heavy for a two-horse team,[16] but he had undertaken to discover whether mud from the small streams and swamps on the estate had any value as a manure.[17] It proved worthless. He had tried new seed consistently and had planted standard seed under unusual conditions but without learning any lesson of value.[18] Grafting small fruits had become a seasonal amusement.[19] These things represented the extent of his experimentation. Now, if there was a profit from new ground, by the use of a different method of getting rid of trees and stumps, he was willing to buy the advertised "engine." [20]

He was, in fact, buying about as freely as ever and was not stinting the luxuries he, Martha, and their guests enjoyed. Madeira, for example, was becoming more and more his favorite wine. In January, 1764, he

[14] Washington did not use at this period the familiar term "crop-rotation." The earliest quotation in the *New English Dictionary* of the words in that sense dates from 1778.

[15] Cf. 2 *G. W.*, 413.

[16] March, 1760; 1 *Diaries*, 140; cf. *supra*, p. 35.

[17] *Paulding Diary*, Apr. 8, 1762. The word "fertilizer," in the familiar agricultural sense, dated from 1661 or earlier in England but apparently was not in general use in Virginia when Washington wrote. As late as 1786 (3 *Diaries*, 42) he spoke of "manuring" in the sense of "fertilizing."

[18] Cf. 1 *Diaries*, 141; *Paulding Diary*, July 26, 1762.   [19] Cf. 1 *Diaries*, 199.

[20] Needless to say, if he subsequently received a report from England concerning this tree-puller, it did not encourage him to buy the machine.

had sent for another pipe of it. In the spirit of a developing connoisseur he had written the dealer in the islands that a pipe ordered the previous year still was untasted, but, he had continued, "from your recommendation of it [I] shall suppose it good and therefore desire you will send me such another pipe . . ."[21] It was much the same with other acquisitions, even slaves. Washington had sold only one—an able-bodied man named Fortune who had brought £70[22]—and he had been on the alert for the purchase of others, particularly those who belonged to estates that were being settled. It was better, he reasoned, to pay a good price for Negroes who had some knowledge of Virginia plantation life than to buy at a lower figure those a slave ship had just brought from Africa.

Washington, indeed, was becoming a bit reckless, not to say extravagant. He was not deterred from the purchase of luxuries or of Negroes by the size of the debt he owed Cary & Co.; he scarcely was restrained by the fact that money was scarcer than ever, that many planters were in difficulty, and that several more bills of exchange given him in repayment of loans proved worthless at the time. Col. Bernard Moore, the largest debtor of the Custis estate, was in such straits that one of his bills of exchange for as little as £100 was protested by his London merchant.[23] Another bill, for £194, drawn in Washington's favor by the estate of William Armistead, had the same inhospitable reception, though the executors were among the most distinguished planters.[24] These and other protested bills of course were charged against Washington who in most instances had drawn for their face value soon after he had forwarded them for collection. Extravagant living was the vice of a class which neither could pay what it owed nor could collect what was owing it. That same year, 1764, Col. John Baylor had to confess to his London correspondents that while he had £3000 due him, he had to draw on the merchants for £140 he needed imperatively. Said Baylor: ". . . there is no getting cash here for anything else but bills of exchange. Poor Virginia, what art thou come to?" She was "held in derision," Baylor insisted, by merchants and factors, and he added: "surely this will open the eyes of my dear countrymen and make them more frugal for the future."[25]

[21] 2 *G. W.*, 412–13.
[22] He was sold in 1765 to Richard Stephenson of Frederick County (*Ledger A*, folio 3).
[23] *Ledger A*, folio 151. The protest was dated Apr. 30, 1763.
[24] Thomas Nelson, Ralph Wormeley, Warner Lewis and Dudley Digges. See *Ledger A*, folio 150, 192. This account was not settled till Dec. 8, 1772 (*Ledger B*, folio 14).
[25] Letter of July 18, 1764, to John Backhouse; 21 *V* 91.

Washington's eyes were opened to reality, if not to frugality, by a letter he received shortly before the 1st of May from his chief London agents, Robert Cary & Co. The merchants informed him that "Jackie" Custis's balance had shrunk to £1407 and that Washington was in their debt for no less than £1811, or almost as much as the balance of £1871 charged against him in the summer of 1761.[26] They would be pleased to have him reduce that obligation and, meantime, to pay interest on it.[27] Washington could not believe it! The figures must be wrong. "Jackie's" true balance must be higher; his own debit balance must be less. He had completed his settlement with the General Court of the assets and liabilities of the Custis estate, and he had set up separate accounts for each of the children. As far as he knew, he was keeping these accounts entirely distinct from his own,[28] but he told himself that Cary must have confused the credits. Without argument and as a matter of right, Cary should be told to charge interest. The merchant might be reminded, also, that poor crops and bad debtors explained the magnitude of a debt Washington scarcely had reduced at all in three years' operations. There the matter must rest until the corrected accounts were received. Buying need not be stopped. A dozen chairs were wanted at Mount Vernon; let them be sent from England, along with two casks of bottled ale, carefully packed.[29] Four Negroes had been bought in 1763 and were to be paid for at the end of June, 1764. The necessary £131 would be found.[30] When Col. Samuel Buckner's slaves had been auctioned the previous year, Washington had been successful bidder on three able-bodied men, Robin, Charles and Jerry. The time was close at hand for paying the Buckner estate £204: that sum, too, must and would be forthcoming.[31] Besides, Mrs. Sarah Alexander had a useful Negro, Lewis, who could be bought for £76: Washington would purchase him;[32] Mount Vernon must be manned. Robert Cary & Co. could wait for their money from a customer who that very spring

---

[26] See 2 *G. W.*, 362–63, Letter of Aug. 1, 1761, and *supra*, p. 63.

[27] This part of the letter of Feb. 13, 1764, is reconstructed easily from Washington's reply of May 1 in 2 *G. W.*, 414–15.

[28] One good example was a debt of £194 due on Custis funds that later were assigned to Mrs. Washington's dower. Washington took pains to note, in effect, that the original investment had been for the estate and that he had an account for the whole of it. In the event of loss, one-third only was to be charged against him. The other two-thirds would be the liability of "Jackie" and of "Patsy" (*Ledger A*, folio 150). A similar entry was made concerning a debt of £28 (*Ibid.*).

[29] Letter of June 5, 1764, to James Gildart, Liverpool; 385 *Papers of G. W.*, LC.

[30] *Ledger A*, folio 173.   [31] *Ibid.*, folio 173.

[32] *Ibid.*

was sending them fifty-two hogsheads of tobacco, with more to follow.[33]

While some of that tobacco still was at sea, America received unwelcome word of new taxes that might be levied by Parliament. In the long war with France from 1754 to 1763, Britain had increased her national debt to £130,000,000. Her interest charge alone was £4,500,-000; new and continuing expense must be assumed for the protection of the American frontier. All these and a multitude of other gloomy aspects of public finance had been presented complainingly by George Grenville, Chancellor of the Exchequer, in a long speech to the House of Commons on the 9th of March, 1764. He had raised then the question of colonial contribution to the cost of defending the English settlements. The next day he had proposed a change in the tax on molasses and had called for an impost on Madeira wine shipped to the Colonies in return for the grain and timber sent to the islands. He asserted and the Commons promptly agreed that "it may be proper to charge certain stamp duties in the said Colonies and plantations."[34] No action to this end was taken at the time, but this was because Grenville said he wished to consult the agents of the Colonies regarding the form the duties should take. Parliament seemed ready to act whenever the Ministry brought in the bills.

Reports of this new policy reached Virginia and Maryland about the middle of May[35] and met with instant challenge. The Colonies were familiar with taxes on commerce and were reconciled to them as a part of the economy of the empire. Every exporter and every shipper knew where and why he could and could not trade. In Virginia, for example, planters had become so accustomed to the law requiring them to send all their tobacco to Great Britain that they never thought of protesting. Direct taxation of the colonials by act of Parliament never had been attempted. Such general levies as had been imposed in any Colony had been by laws of its own Assembly, chosen by the people who were to pay the taxes. This had been so unvarying a practice that only constitutional lawyers of inquisitive mind had taken the pains to analyze taxation in terms of inherent political right. Nobody else ever felt called upon to justify what never had been disputed. Colonials had now to unlock the forgotten armory of their rights to get weapons for their

[33] 2 G. W., 415.
[34] Journ. House of Commons, v. 29, p. 935.
[35] Md. Gazette, May 17–24, 1764.

defence against parliamentary taxation. Practice had to be vindicated by principle. The colonials rediscovered their inheritance in protecting their interests. Had not their forefathers possessed all the rights of British subjects, including the right of taxation through representatives of their own choice, when they came to America? What had they done that deprived them of any guarantee they possessed under the English constitution? The first rumors of direct taxation of Americans by the Parliament of Westminster prompted every colonial who knew anything of the history of his country to think again of Runnymede and of the long struggle of Parliament itself to establish taxation as the right of the taxpayer. Even before the precise form of contemplated British action was known, Washington's fellow-Burgess, Richard Henry Lee, put the question that shaped endless protests: "Can it be supposed," he asked a correspondent in London, "that those brave adventurous Britons, who originally conquered and settled these countries . . . meant thereby to deprive themselves of that free government of which they were members, and to which they had an unquestionable right?" [36] Benjamin Franklin's racy observation was fashioned in practical terms of British profit and loss: ". . . what you get from us in taxes you must lose in trade. The cat can yield but her skin. And as you must have the whole hide, if you first cut thongs out of it, 'tis at your own expense." [37]

Washington, like most Virginians, was concerned, and instinctively disposed to resist, but, as usual, was not inclined to anticipate events. That applied to taxation and, more immediately, and more personally, to his debts. Summer brought him from Cary & Co. a letter which confirmed the accounts previously summarized. This was followed by one its recipient somewhat indignantly regarded as a dun. Washington undertook to answer it with a statement that "mischances rather than misconduct" had been responsible for his financial ills. He had been afflicted with three bad crop years in succession; bills of exchange given in payment of debts due him had been protested. It was "unlucky likewise," he admitted, that he had bought land and slaves for which he had paid with current funds. Even at that, if crops had sold well, "the balance, I think could never have been against me."

---

[36] Letter to unidentified correspondent, May 31, 1764; J. C. Ballagh, ed., *The Letters of Richard Henry Lee* (cited hereafter as *Ballagh, Lee Letters*), v. 1, p. 5.

[37] Letter of Apr. 30, 1764; A. H. Smyth, ed., *The Writings of Benjamin Franklin*, (cited hereafter as *Smyth's Franklin*), v. 4, p. 243.

Having made this confession none too graciously, the disappointed and humiliated master of Mount Vernon renewed his expression of willingness to pay interest, and in the same long, involved sentence proceeded: "I shall now in consequence of your other letter . . . beg leave to inform you, in terms equally sincere and direct, that it is not in my power I should add in a manner convenient and agreeable to myself, to make remittances faster than my crops (and perhaps some few occasional sums which may fall in my way) will furnish me with the means; but if notwithstanding, you cannot be content with this mode of payments you have only to advise me of it and I shall hit upon a method (tho' I would choose to avoid it) that will at once discharge the debt, and effectually remove me from all further mention of it; For I must confess, I did not expect that a correspondent so steady, and constant as I have proved, and was willing to have continued to your house while the advantages were in any degree reciprocal would be reminded in the instant it was discovered how necessary it was for him to be expeditious in his payments."

Not satisfied with this protest, he elaborated: "Reason and prudence naturally dictates to every man of common sense the thing that is right and you might have rested assured, that so fast as I could make remittances without distressing myself too much my inclinations would have prompted me to it: because in the first place it is but an irksome thing to a free mind to be any ways hampered in debt; and in the next place, I think I have discovered no intentions, since I have found how the balance was likely to turn, of increasing that debt (unless it should appear in the amount of my invoices last year which greatly indeed exceeded my expectations but will be balanced I hope by the contracted one of this year): but on the contrary all the willingness I could, under the accidents that have happened, of decreasing it to the utmost of my power; but I have already run into much greater prolixity on this head than I promised or intended. Your answer will determine my measures, and upon this issue it must rest." [38]

He was chagrined but not chastened. The invoices of 1763 to which he referred with implied, parenthetical apology, had been high; those of February, 1764, had not contained any single item of extravagant nature, except perhaps one for 187 yards of Irish linen, but the total had run to £474. Moreover, the very day he wrote Cary, he ordered an

[38] Letter of Aug. 10, 1764; 2 *G. W.*, 417–18. The punctuation is preserved.

expensive livery from a London merchant whose charges had been, as he complained, "most exorbitantly high," [39] and he allowed himself a subscription to the *County Magazine*.[40] Whether this was defiant or casual or was considered so small a matter as not to involve any principle of frugal living, it was his last fling. Orders from England must be reduced. Luxuries for the time being were banned. If stout-muscled young Negroes were to be had at reasonable prices, or if any imported article were required for comfort or for good appearance, Washington would make the expenditure. He would defer other purchases in order to reduce his invoices and thereby to reduce his debt.

That was one measure of relief. His other and more acceptable recourse obviously was an increase of income by one or another of three methods open to him. The first, of course, was to buy land ahead of settlement; but in this Washington was hampered, without being aware of it, because he could not bring himself as yet to get ready capital for new investment by selling any of his holdings at the price they would command. He held tenaciously to what he had. His second expedient, manifestly of limited possibilities, was to make the plantation industries more profitable. Washington now had the still he had ordered from England,[41] and when fruit was available, he operated it at capacity. Every day that 144 gallons of cider could be fed to the still, it delivered thirty gallons of brandy. When the peaches from the farms had been reduced to mobey,[42] sixty gallons would yield twenty-two gallons of brandy and sometimes a little more than that.[43] Much of this was consumed on the estate, especially during the wheat harvest, but if the volume were larger, some of the brandy might be sold.[44] Perhaps two or three of the other industries at Mount Vernon might be developed profitably also, though in a small way.

By elimination, then, substantial increase in farm income at Mount Vernon might be, perhaps must be, through the last of the three possibilities open to Washington, the substitution of some other large crop for

---

[39] 2 *G. W.*, 420; for the invoices of February, 1764, see 385 *Papers of G. W.*, 32, LC.

[40] 385 *Papers of G. W.*, LC.

[41] *Ibid.* The order, it will be remembered, had been sent Robert Cary & Co. in October, 1761.

[42] Doctor Green in his *Virginia Word-Book* used the spelling *mobby* for the juicy pulp of fruit made ready for distillation.

[43] The "run" of peach brandy Sept. 27, 1764, was twenty-four gallons. See MS fragments, Mount Vernon, evidently intended for entry in some lost account book.

[44] *Ibid.* All surviving entries of 1764 are for brandy delivered to Thomas Nicholas or Nicols, who apparently was in charge of the "harvest hands" that year. Washington spelled the name Nicholas in his account with the man in *Ledger A* (folio 179), but the signature on receipts for brandy, June–July, 1764, is Thomas Nicols.

tobacco. Culture of the troublesome and exacting tobacco-plant would continue of necessity until a profitable staple could be grown in its stead. Perhaps it would be wise on the lower Custis farms to make no change; but at Mount Vernon the coveted leaf could not be matured and marketed in condition or of a quality to make it yield anything more than cost, if even cost, on the London market. Although neighboring plantations might produce thousands of pounds that made buyers open purses in London, the land between Little Hunting Creek and Dogue Run simply would not. The young master of those stubborn acres had done his utmost to achieve his ambition and to grow leaf of superlative savor and texture. Steadily, through the years that had passed since Washington had come home from the war, merchants' letters from England had reiterated the discouraging fact it was foolish to attempt to evade: Mount Vernon tobacco was second rate.[45] If the new crop, which was of large proportions,[46] brought no more than formerly, then Washington must try something else—wheat, hemp, flax, anything that was profitable. Carlyle & Adam were seeking more and more vigorously each year to encourage the growing of wheat and they complied readily with the seven-year contract they had made in 1763 to buy all that grain produced at Mount Vernon in excess of farm requirements. The total for 1764 was not great—257 bushels only—but the possibility was manifest, the market was only a few miles up the river, and the financial settlement at 3s 6d per bushel would be with friends.[47] Washington was sufficiently encouraged to increase the acreage he normally devoted to wheat.

This wheat was in the ground and some at least of the tobacco of 1764 was ready for shipment when, about the 28th or 29th of October, Washington completed another journey to Williamsburg for what promised to be a long session of the General Assembly. The Governor had given abundant notice to the lawmakers that they would be brought together,

[45] G. W. Patteson, an authority on Virginia soils, explains this by saying that Mount Vernon has a sandy surface and below that a heavy soil. At a depth of eighteen inches to two feet, approximately, is the clay pan. This accentuates both wetness and dryness. Precisely the "right year" is required for good growing conditions. This is not soil for wheat and is still worse for tobacco—a statement that applies equally to Upper Marlboro, Maryland, and to a part of nearby Southern Maryland. Farmers now abstain from planting tobacco there. Because of the Potomac the growing season at Mount Vernon is about as long as it is around Richmond. Rainfall is abundant.

[46] Ten of the men who had rented Washington's land turned in 10,700 lbs. of the crop of 1764. The Custis plantations reported thirty-two hogsheads for the new master and eighty-seven for the son of the old owner (Ledger A, folio 206, 207; Custis Papers; VHS).

[47] 10 Papers of G. W., 122, LC.

and, when he welcomed them on the opening day, October 30, he urged them "to consider of and go through the business of the country." He felt that "many matters of importance will come under your consideration"; but for his own part he had three subjects only to put before them—legislation to make sterling debts payable in sterling, a measure for the extension of the post, and provision for meeting the costs of defence.[48] The Burgesses responded cordially [49] but they gave short shrift to complaints about sterling debts and other alleged weaknesses in the execution of judgments. Existing statutes were declared forthwith to be the best that could be devised, unless the Colony abandoned the principle that Virginia currency was legal tender for all debts—a course that could not be followed without injustice to those who had accepted that currency in good faith.[50] As for the post, the laws seemed to be adequate, but if specific changes were recommended they would be considered.[51] The Governor was of one mind with the Assembly on the second of these matters and, on the first, he had to acquiesce in the Burgesses' request that he forward their polite "No" to the Lords of Trade and Plantations. If their Lordships were displeased, Fauquier told the lawmakers, "you can blame no one but yourselves for any consequences which may follow the reception you have given the matters recommended to you from that right honorable board." [52]

One reason for haste on the part of the Assembly in dealing with sterling debts was belief that time need not be spent on a subject concerning which members were of a single mind. In larger degree, perhaps, the Burgesses wished to clear the way for consideration of pressing bills and, in particular, of the subject that had alarmed the Colony in the spring. According to a letter from a committee of the Massachusetts Assembly, passage of a direct tax on the Colonies might be near, perhaps as close as the next session of Parliament.[53] Virginia lawmakers must decide what they would do about it. On the 14th of November, just two days after the Governor had expressed himself on sterling debts, the Burgesses reached their main conclusion. It was the traditional one— to address the throne and to protest to the Lords and to the Commons. It was normal procedure for the House to decide upon a policy, to pass

[48] *Journ. H.B.*, 1761–65, p. 227–28.   [49] *Ibid.*, 229.
[50] *Ibid.*, 233–34, 241, 249.   [51] *Ibid.*
[52] *Journ. H.B.*, 1761–65, p. 252.
[53] 10 *V* 2 ff. Virginia's exact information at this time concerning parliamentary plans for imposing direct taxes on the American Colonies became a matter of dispute in 1766. The reference cited here is to that controversy.

a summary resolution, and to instruct a committee to find the fitting phrases in which to dress a formal declaration. The only difference now was in the gravity of the subject and in the distinction between what loyal subjects should say to their King and what they might with propriety assert in appealing to a Parliament one branch of which was an elected body similar to their own.[54] So delicate a task naturally was assigned those members of the House best skilled in letters and in the lore of the British constitution. Peyton Randolph, who was still "Mr. Attorney," was appointed chairman. With him were associated Richard Henry Lee, Landon Carter, George Wythe, Edmund Pendleton, Benjamin Harrison, Archibald Cary, and John Fleming.

Washington was not a member of this committee because words and arguments were not his forte; but he had during the session a vexatious task of a different sort. He and the other commissioners named under the act of January, 1764 [55] for examining the militia accounts prepared a report which he presented to the House on November 9.[56] It was not a pleasant document to offer or to defend because justice to taxpayers required that Washington and his colleagues deny applications it would have been a satisfaction to grant. Adam Stephen, for instance, had served as County Lieutenant both in Hampshire and in Frederick during the time he had commanded the militia who were guarding the frontier. In spite of Stephen's growing inclination to magnify his service and to glorify himself, it would have been gratifying to recommend that he be granted pay, as he requested, for each of the Counties; but the law did not take into account the possibility of double service. It merely provided that the pay of a County Lieutenant on active duty should be 10s per diem. That must be the compensation, and all the compensation, proposed for Stephen in the commissioners' report. Harder still was the case of John Field, a militia Captain of Culpeper, who had been accepted as a private volunteer but had been employed by Stephen to discharge the duties of a Major. Field "had been extremely active, brave and zealous," Washington and his colleagues told the Burgesses, and had been "constantly exposed to the greatest dangers"; but as he had not been "lawfully appointed," the commissioners could do no more than commend him to the "favor of the House" and could

---

[54] 10 V 7–8. [55] 8 H 9 and *supra*, p. 108.

[56] Submission of the report eleven days after the opening of the session of course suggests that the claims were not reviewed until the commissioners came to Williamsburg for the meeting of the General Assembly, but no evidence on this point, one way or the other, has been discovered.

not approve pay for him at the rank of Major, though they thought him entitled to it. So it was with a number of other cases of varying merit.[57]

The report was referred to the Committee on Propositions and Grievances,[58] which soon ran into an ugly series of charges against Adam Stephen. He was accused of sending militia out of the Colony to guard provisions and he was alleged to have hauled his own flour a long distance for the use of the militia, who could have been supplied as cheaply with good flour nearer at hand. In the end, the House condemned him for two derelictions, limited his pay of 10s a day to the time he was in active service, and then voted that in other respects he had discharged his duty "as a brave, active and skillful officer." [59] To Washington, who was a member of the investigating committee as well as one of the signers of the report to the House, the experience must have been disagreeable and, as concerned Adam Stephen, embarrassing.[60]

The session witnessed another investigation that involved a kinsman of Martha Washington's and had additional interest of a dramatic sort. In Hanover County, the resignation of Nathaniel West Dandridge from the House of Burgesses had been necessitated by his acceptance of appointment as Coroner. James Littlepage decided to offer for the vacancy, as did Samuel Overton who had been a candidate in a previous election. Both of them proceeded to solicit votes. Littlepage, in particular, wrote a number of letters in which he sought support by promising to have an objectionable feature of the tobacco law repealed. He offered "treats" also, to a number of freeholders, not omitting some citizens who had no vote, and he invited to his home several whom ordinarily he scarcely would have welcomed. Most of this entertaining was prior to the receipt of the writ of election but some of it was alleged to have been done after that time and in violation of the election law of 1762. This measure provided specifically that no candidate should either himself or through some other person, directly or indirectly, "except in his usual and ordinary course of hospitality in his own house," give any voter "any money, meat, drink, entertainment,

[57] *Journ. H.B.,* 1761–65, p. 248.

[58] That is to say, this committee filed the report on the cases, as set forth in the text, though the Journal, *loc. cit.,* stated that Washington's paper was referred to the Committee on Claims. There is no entry in the Journal concerning any transfer of the paper from one committee to the other.

[59] *Journ. H.B.,* 1761–65, p. 251, 296–98. The charges against Stephen were preferred by Thomas Rutherford, Burgess from Hampshire.

[60] Settlement of the claims of the other officers was prompt and generous (*ibid.,* 253).

or provisions, or make any present, gift, reward, or entertainment, or any promise, agreement, obligation or engagement." Violation of the statute was declared to be bribery and corruption that disqualified a man from sitting in the House to which he had been elected.[61] As the canvass progressed, Littlepage and Overton struck a bargain by which Overton retired from the contest in return for £75 paid him by Littlepage to cover his expenses in that contest and in the previous polling.

The day after the session opened,[62] all this was alleged formally against Littlepage by Nathaniel West Dandridge and was referred to the Committee on Privileges and Elections, at whose instance a time limit for filing charges was set.[63] The hearing itself was of a sort to create talk because "treating" was involved, but the real sensation promised to be the appearance of Patrick Henry, the lawyer who had participated during the previous winter in the hearing of the "parsons' cause." [64] This bold and imaginative young man, who came as counsel for Dandridge, was known in person to few, if any of the Burgesses except those of the Counties in which he had been practicing, but, of course, he was stared at, talked about and appraised by all those who previously had heard of his remarkable success in limiting Parson Maury's damages to one penny.[65] Washington probably saw Henry but did not hear him examine witnesses and argue that Littlepage had violated the election law.[66] Henry, for his part, impressed his auditors by the sweep of his eloquence and his penetrating discussion of the principles involved in elections,[67] but he had a weak case at law. Littlepage's

[61] 7 H 526. Apparently, this disqualification did not extend to membership in any House subsequently chosen.

[62] *Journ. H.B.*, 1761–65, p. 232.   [63] *Ibid.*, 235.

[64] Oddly, W. W. Henry asserted (*op. cit.*, v. 1, p. 46) that it was doubtful whether Henry ever had visited the colonial capital previously though, on p. 20, the author had described Henry's experiences in procuring there a license for the practice of law.

[65] Stories of the uncouth appearance of Henry in "country dress" and of his walking unrecognized through the halls of the capitol probably should be regarded as part of the unfounded traditions of Henry's early years as a lawyer. He almost certainly was accompanied to Williamsburg by Dandridge who, as Burgess from 1757 through 1763, of course knew most of the senior lawmakers. As Dandridge's purpose was to have Littlepage expelled from the House by vote of the members, he doubtless introduced to them the man who was to present the charges.

[66] It often may be noticed in the chapters on events of 1764–1775 that no record exists of Washington's observations on scenes or actors in the drama then opening. The explanation is twofold. Washington at this period apparently did not possess large interest in legislative affairs, except as they concerned liberty and property. His lack of facility in debate and in writing denied him leadership when words were weapons. Second, his diary, when kept at all, was designed to be merely a brief reminder of where he had been on a particular day. When Henry came to Williamsburg, Washington probably was interested in seeing the orator, but he did not have the zest for legal issues that would incline him to sit and listen to the examination of witnesses in a dispute over an election in a County with which he had no direct association.

[67] John Tyler, quoted in Wirt, *op. cit.*, 40, but, once again, perhaps with tradition infused. See also L. G. Tyler, *Letters and Times of the Tylers,* v. 1, p. 26.

bargain to eliminate Overton from the contest was not covered by the statute; the other allegations of Dandridge's witnesses were trivial. After the hearings, the Committee on Privileges and Elections reported, November 26, that Littlepage was duly elected, that the petition against him was "frivolous and vexatious," and that Dandridge must pay Little-page's costs of defence as determined by the Committee on Claims.[68] Littlepage emerged completely victorious except for what appeared to be a trifle—his indirect admission in bargaining with Overton that if Patrick Henry had been a candidate against him in the election of 1763 his chance of winning would have been reduced.[69] That might have meaning for the future. Strange things might happen in the House— that decorous body dominated by the great planters and their lawyers— if Henry became a member and delivered there any such speech as the one that had swept Hanover jurors off their feet. At the moment, although members disapproved Dandridge's plea, they may have been grateful to him, in a sense, for filing his petition because he and Henry between them gave color and drama to a session that dragged inter-minably on while the House debated uninteresting bills, and the special committee weighed words and sanded phrases in perfecting the address to the King and the appeals to the House of Parliament.

Relief broke tedium on the 10th of December, when the Governor forwarded a letter he had received from Col. Henry Bouquet, who was able to report that he had pressed on from Pittsburgh into the Ohio country and had forced the Indians there to make peace. Col. John Bradstreet had made a treaty in August at Detroit with savages who from the outset showed little intention of respecting it; but Virginia Burgesses were so confident Bouquet's peace would be enforced [70] that they advised the Governor, the day after the submission of Bouquet's letter, to disband the militia who still were guarding the frontier.[71] Bouquet was to be "recommended to His Majesty's favor for the spirit, activity and zeal" he had displayed. To some who voted for this resolu-tion in a knowledge of the hazards and hardships of Indian warfare, the comradeship of the frontier may have appeared in ironic contrast to the contention over the threat of direct parliamentary taxes on America.

---

68 *Journ. H.B.,* 1761–65, p. 272.

69 *Ibid.,* 271. His bargain was that if Henry entered and won the contest, Overton was to be paid £50, instead of £75 for withdrawing.

70 *Journ. H.B.,* 1761–65, p. 287; H. H. Peckham, *Pontiac and the Indian Uprising.* Peace was not confirmed and completed until Sir William Johnson procured final action at Oswego, July, 1766.

71 *Journ. H.B.,* 1761–65, p. 289–90.

At last, on December 13, 1764, the address and the memorials to the Lords and the remonstrance to the Commons were ready for consideration in Committee of the Whole.[72] Then, after two conferences with the Council and various amendments,[73] the papers were in a form acceptable to both branches of the General Assembly.[74] The "whole study" of some members of the drafting committee, they told Fauquier, had been an "endeavor to mollify" the original terms of the documents, and they had satisfied themselves there was nothing in the final drafts that would "give the least offense."[75] The core of the address to the King was a plea that he would protect the people of Virginia "in the enjoyment of their ancient and inestimable right of being governed by such laws respecting their internal polity and taxation as are derived from their own consent, with the approbation of their sovereign or his substitute."[76] In the memorial to the Lords, the central argument was that the settlers of Virginia had all the rights and privileges of British subjects, and that the descendants of the first comers had done nothing to deprive them of this inheritance. One sentence read: "Your memorialists conceive it to be a fundamental principle of the British constitution, without which freedom can no where exist, that the people are not subject to any taxes but such as are laid on them by their own consent, or by those who are legally appointed to represent them."[77] As the Colonies—the plural must have been deliberate—could not be represented in the British Parliament, taxation by that body "must necessarily establish this melancholy truth, that the inhabitants of the Colonies are slaves of Britons from whom they are descended . . ." Virginians had been invested with the right of taxing themselves from "the first establishment of a regular government in the Colony"; requisitions had been made on them by their Sovereign when their assistance had been considered necessary for the preservation of British interest in America, "whence," the memorial maintained, "they must conclude they cannot now be deprived of a right they have so long enjoyed, and which they have never forfeited."[78]

The arguments in the remonstrance to the House of Commons were the same with the added protest that if taxation were justified, it would be unwise because it would be intolerable to a people already burdened

---

[72] *Ibid.*, 293.
[73] *Ibid.*, 294, 300.
[74] *Ibid.*, 302.
[75] Fauquier to the Lords of Trade, Dec. 24, 1764, *ibid.*, lviii.
[76] *Ibid.*, 302.
[77] *Ibid.*
[78] *Ibid.*, 303.

by the costs of the war with the French. Virginians who had helped to build up British fleets and trade no longer would be able to buy British goods and, "reduced to extreme poverty, would be compelled to manufacture those articles" they formerly had imported from Britain.[79]

Together the three documents included about 2000 words, and they meant much more than their authors realized or Fauquier epitomized when he said, "the subject matter of them is praying to be permitted to tax themselves." [80] The Virginians were not asking a favor: they were asserting a right. It was done politely and with restraint, but with conviction and resolution. They had gone into the armory of their inheritance and they had faith in the weapons they found there. Right, rediscovered, was reenforced. That which pride and self-interest prompted, the constitution vindicated. Burgesses had satisfied themselves that their resistance to the principle of direct parliamentary taxation not only was justified but also was demanded of them as free men. In that spirit the session [81] and the year came to a close. It might not be easy to get the address of Virginia before the King, but the papers could be printed and circulated.[82] If that were done, then the Parliament would admit the validity of colonial right and would not attempt to tax the Americans. Surely, surely that would be the outcome!

79 *Ibid.*, 304. One tradition is that the address to the King and the memorial to the Lords were written by Richard Henry Lee (see *DAB*), but no proof of this has been found. Jefferson (*op. cit.*, v. 14, p. 168), stated in 1814 that Peyton Randolph wrote the address and George Wythe the remonstrance but that he did not know who was the author of the memorial.

80 Letter of Dec. 24, 1764, to the Lords of Trade; *Journ. H.B.*, 1761–65, p. lviii.

81 Adjournment was on Dec. 21, 1764 (*Journ. H.B.*, 1761–65, p. 309). For a futile proposal to make a grant of funds to persons who had volunteered for service with Colonel Bouquet, and for controversy over an alleged attempt by Adam Stephen to prevent enlistment of those volunteers in Bouquet's command, see *ibid.*, 292, 296, 297.

82 Fauquier's letter of Dec. 24, 1764, *loc. cit.*, Address to his Majesty, *ibid.*, liv. See, also, the Committee of Correspondence to the Agent in England, Dec. 20, 1764; 9 *V* 354.

CHAPTER VIII

THE STAMP ACT STIRS A STUDY OF RIGHTS
(1765)

WHATEVER BURDEN of taxation 1765 might or might not bring His Majesty's Colony and Ancient Dominion of Virginia, the year called for no less than seven things at Mount Vernon: Invoices from England must be drafted to include nothing beyond the articles indispensable in the operation of the farms; no more slaves should be bought; no additional lands should be acquired. These were the economies. Income must be increased by the planting of more wheat, by an effort to produce and market hemp profitably, by a larger use of the mill, and by making greater hauls of the river's fish.[1]

This was not an impossible plan for reducing the debt to Cary & Co. Large as that obligation was, good crops and sound management of a property which now was well stocked, assuredly would clear in time the account with the London merchant. Washington was sure of that, though the "bonds" given in 1764 for the Negroes purchased then had to be counted among the bills payable in 1765. For this and other purposes, Washington had £290 in cash, almost all of it Virginia currency.[2] In addition, the servants were now apportioned and nearly sufficient in number—eleven in the house, seven on the home plantation, eleven working at trades, nine at Muddy Hole, ten at Dogue Run and seven at the mill—a total of fifty-four.[3] For directing this labor more carefully and for undertaking the new and larger farm activities, the owner employed his remote cousin, Lund Washington, a descendant of Lawrence, the immigrant brother of George Washington's great-grandfather, John. As a member of the "Chotank" branch of the family,

---

[1] These facts are plain from Washington's financial accounts of 1765; but it is not certain, though by no means improbable, that he laid down this explicit program at the beginning of the year.
[2] *Ledger A*, folio 203.
[3] On the tax-list of Fairfax County, he was charged with seventy-four tithables, that is, white males and Negro males and females above sixteen years of age (*Ledger A*, folio 159; 11 *Papers of G. W.*, 58, LC).

Lund had been reared where George had spent happy days. Twenty-eight years of age, industrious and well-informed on agricultural methods, Lund had served as estate manager at Ravensworth and could discharge many of the irksome duties that had crowded the Colonel's days.[4]

Under this arrangement, the winter months passed quietly. Washington did little traveling; Lund could act for him in visiting the Bullskin plantation;[5] both "Jackie" and "Patsy" were at home under the tutelage of Walter Magowan, who was developing aspirations for the ministry. Young "Master Custis," having far more money than his step-father to spend, was being outfitted at the instance of Mrs. Washington with numerous articles of fine apparel and furnishings from England.[6] The proud mother, incidentally, was wiser about her daughter than about her son, who was only two years older. While "Jackie" was to have hats with narrow silver lace, a white cock feather and the like, "Patsy's" clothes from London were to be more modest. If they could be "more genteel and proper," Mrs. Washington wrote, there would be no objection, "provided it is done with frugality for as she is only 9 years old a superfluity or extravagance in dress would be wholly unnecessary."[7]

The first month of spring brought much grafting of trees[8] and a long, contentious argument over the standard weight of the wheat that was to be delivered under the contract with Carlyle & Adam. That, in turn, was followed by an election in which Washington was a candidate for an old office in a new creation—the office of vestryman in a freshly established parish. At the previous session of the General Assembly, the Burgesses from Fairfax County had represented that the parish of Truro had become so populous it should be divided.[9] Obligingly, Burgesses and Council had agreed to make two parishes of one, along a line

4 Lund was the son of Townsend and Elizabeth Lund Washington (3 G. W., 103 n). It has been asserted often that Lund came to Mount Vernon as Washington's manager in 1767, but the correspondence of 1765 and Lund's account in Ledger A, folio 190, show him employed in the earlier year. Apparently, his compensation at this period was the use of a farm and a percentage of the crops grown on all the plantations he supervised.
5 Cf. 2 G. W., 422.
6 Invoice of Feb. 13, 1765; Custis Papers, VHS. This invoice ran to the impressive total of more than £45.
7 Letter of Aug. 10, 1764; 385 Papers of G. W., LC.
8 Including an attempted crossing of the native and the English mulberry. See 1 Diaries, 209–10.
9 Part of Cameron Parish had been added to Truro under an act of November, 1762. See 7 H 612.

extended from Dogue Run and Washington's mill; [10] and they had provided that a vestry of twelve be chosen for the old parish, which kept the name Truro, and a separate vestry for the new parish, which was to be styled Fairfax. In the election, Mch. 28, 1765, of the "most able and discreet persons" to serve Fairfax Parish, Washington's name of course was put forward, because Mount Vernon was in the new parish, and his poll was exceeded by that of four men only.[11]

The vote had been counted, the talk about it had ended, and the hands were preparing to sow oats, hemp and lucerne [12] when Washington once again set out for Williamsburg to attend what might be another difficult session of the General Assembly. No word had been received of action by the British Parliament to impose a stamp tax on the American Colonies. There was hope, doubt, gloom, according to the temperament of the individual. Amid varying predictions, the average Burgess probably recoiled slightly from the position taken in the memorial and in the remonstrance of the previous year. Conservatives argued that if a tax were levied by Parliament, injustice would be done, but injustice that loyal subjects would have to endure until they could prevail on Parliament to repeal the act.[13] Washington himself probably held to his usual practice of not attempting to anticipate what time would make plain.

The session was not one of prorogation but of adjournment. Consequently, there was no formal opening, no speech by the Governor, and no address by the House. Members simply met on May 1, 1765, and prepared to start debate on the subject for which the session primarily had been arranged. This was the revision of the tobacco law, a measure so often and sometimes so clumsily amended that it was in great confusion.[14] Aside from this, all indications were for so dull a session that

[10] 8 H 43.

[11] Ahead of him, in order, were Col. John West, Charles Alexander, William Payne and Capt. John Dalton. Below him were Maj. Charles Broadwater, Capt. George Johnston, Townsend Dade, Richard Sanford, William Adams, Capt. John Posey and Daniel French. Nine others received votes. See 11 Papers of G. W., 17, LC.

[12] The sowing of oats was completed May 12, hemp was sown May 12–18, and lucerne (alfalfa) May 20 (1 Diaries, 211).

[13] Reservation has to be made here. The absence of files of the Virginia Gazette for the greater part of this period and the paucity of private correspondence reduce almost to nothingness the extant evidence concerning the state of mind of Virginians between November, 1764, and May, 1765.

[14] See the preamble of the revised act, 8 H 69. Through misunderstanding of the fact that this was an adjourned session, the laws passed at the session of May, 1765, were printed by Hening under the date October, 1765, in spite of the continued enumeration of the "chapters" from the last number of the session of Oct. 30–Dec. 21, 1764.

attendance was below average. Four vacancies were reported—one each in Chesterfield, Amelia, Lunenburg and Louisa. The last of these was due to the appointment of William Johnston as Coroner. Writs for new elections were requested of the Governor; the session got under way and rumbled slowly along.

As Colonel Washington was reducing his production of tobacco on the Potomac, he had somewhat less interest in the tobacco bill than formerly, though, of course, a better law or a worse would affect the profits from the leaf grown on the Custis estates. In any event, the subject was one for sharper debaters than himself. The bill that most concerned him personally was one for which he as Burgess from Frederick had no special responsibility, even though he might be involved as a vestryman of Fairfax County. Churchmen of that County had disapproved the act passed at the previous session for the division of Truro Parish. Many of George's neighbors contended that the line had been wrongly drawn and that nearly twice as many tithables had been alloted the new parish of Fairfax as remained in Truro. Demand was made for the repeal of the law passed the previous winter and for the apportionment of a larger part of the population to Truro. The measure duly passed with speed;[15] Mount Vernon went back into Truro Parish; ecclesiastical peace was restored.

Anticipated dull days of routine followed so drearily that members procured leave to go home for the remainder of the session or left without permission. Then, about May 20, sensations began to develop. Louisa County duly reported that she had complied with the writ of election to fill the vacancy caused by the retirement of William Johnston and in his place she had chosen Patrick Henry of Hanover. Although it was unusual to name a man from another County when he owned no property in the County that chose him, there was nothing in the election law to prohibit it. Without argument or contest, the oath was administered to the man who had made so powerful a speech to the Committee on Courts of Justice.[16] The return of his writ, along

15 *Journ. H.B.*, 1761–65, p. 346, 347, 348, 350, 363; 8 *H* 157.
16 Committee assignment was on May 20; Henry had subscribed to the oath that day or on the 18th. Strangely, the Clerk habitually omitted from the Journal the names of all those individuals who came to the House, presented their writs and offered to take the oath as member, unless there was immediate challenge of them. The normal entry was, "A member returned on a new writ, having taken the oaths . . . was admitted to his place in the House." (Cf. *Journ. H.B.*, 1761–65, p. 343.) If the procedure in Henry's case was normal, as there is every reason to assume it was, he had not been in the House more than a day or two when he received his committee assignment.

with those of other new Burgesses, was referred to the Committee on Privileges and Elections.

Henry himself did not wait on committeemen or defer to the dignity of ruling members. On the 17th, there had appeared in one of the rival Gazettes an argument in advocacy of a Virginia loan in England that would permit the Colony to retire its outstanding currency and to advance funds to individuals on the security of their lands.[17] The immediate reason for this proposal, which sounded as if it had been written by a debtor,[18] became apparent on the 23rd, when the leaders of the House moved that the body go into Committee of the Whole immediately "to take into . . . consideration the state of the Colony." [19] Then Washington, the new member from Louisa, and all the others who had ears for it heard some of the revered seniors of the House explain the details of the plan, even to the rate of interest Virginia was to pay for a loan of £250,000 in London, and the form of the tax she was to impose until 1795 in order to meet the debt. As Washington himself was among the planters whose balances were on the wrong side of the merchants' ledger he of course had interest in the subject, but, so far as is known, he had no part in the debate, which was not prolonged. Those Burgesses sufficiently versed in matters of finance to understand the meaning of the resolutions doubtless had been lined up in advance; those who did not comprehend could not oppose. The Committee of the Whole reported the resolutions that same day.

On the 24th, the measure came up for action by the House.[20] Washington probably was present when the fledgling Burgess from Louisa arose to challenge the measure. Henry had no schooling in public finance, but he sensed that one aim of the proposal was to permit rich debtors to mortgage their lands to pay for luxuries and he skillfully brought down the complicated "resolves" to language the least-tutored member from the newest frontier County could understand. The gentle-

---

17 *Jefferson*, v. 14, p. 163, with a reference to Royle's *Gazette*. From 1761 to 1766, the *Virginia Gazette* was published by Joseph Royle in succession to his brother-in-law, William Hunter. The paper then passed to Alexander Purdie who soon associated John Dixon with him. Their partnership continued to 1774. From 1775 to 1780, Purdie alone was responsible. For the years 1766–1774, the rival *Gazette* was issued by William Rind and John Pinkney. As no copy of *Royle's Gazette* for May 17, 1765 is known to be in existence, the scope of the argument has to be surmised from Jefferson's brief references and from the terms of the resolution itself.

18 *Jefferson*, loc. cit.

19 *Journ. H.B.*, 1761–65, p. 350. It will be remembered that a scheme for a "loan office," presumably analogous, had been put forward in 1755. See *Journ. H.B.*, 1752–58, p. xxiv, 328–32, and Vol. II, p. 140.

20 *Ibid.*, 349, 350.

man from Louisa scorned the argument that such loans as were contemplated by the scheme would enable debtors to discharge their obligations. "What, sir," he demanded, "is it proposed then to reclaim the
spendthrift from his dissipation and extravagance, by filling his pockets
with money?" Most vehemently, he exposed what he declared to be the
favoritism of the plan and the abuses to which it certainly would lead.[21]
The leaders had the votes, if not the answer, and they proceeded to pass
the resolves; but they were as doubtful of their handiwork as they were
suspicious of the outcry from Henry, and they appointed a conference
committee at the time they sent the resolutions to the Council for concurrence. This they seldom did except when they knew that opposition
was to be encountered in the upper branch of the Assembly.[22]

If Washington anticipated action by the Council, he waited in vain
for it. Either because the unwisdom of the resolutions led a majority
to say "No," or else because the patrons took alarm at Henry's attack,
there came back no message from the council chamber that concurrence had been voted. On the contrary, "Mr. Attorney," on behalf of
the House managers of the conference committee, had to report "that
the Council had considered the resolutions . . . and could not agree
to them, and directed that the same should be returned" to the House.[23]
This was most unusual. Council amended often; it rarely rejected out-
right a measure the lower branch of the Assembly had passed.

The whole affair had about it an urgency and a mystery that few
understood. All that was certain was that the recognized leaders of the
House—men who had not admitted Colonel Washington into their
inner circle—had favored the resolutions with an earnestness that was
almost nervous, and that the young Burgess from Hanover had opposed
the scheme with a violence his elders regarded as disconcerting if not
actually impertinent.

More startling things came quickly. On the 26th of May, House and
Council compromised their differences over the tobacco legislation.[24]
Only the business of passing a few minor measures and of witnessing
the signature of bills remained. Most of the members had started
home. Of a total of 116 Burgesses, thirty-nine and no more, besides
the Speaker, were in their seats when, after the bulk of the day's
work had been done, George Johnston of Fairfax moved that the

[21] 14 Jefferson, 164.
[23] Ibid., 356.
[22] Journ. H.B., 1761–65, p. 350.
[24] Cf. ibid., 354.

House go into Committee of the Whole to consider the "steps neces-sary to be taken in consequence of the resolutions of the House of Commons of Great Britain relative to the charging certain Stamp duties in the Colonies and Plantations in America." [25]

The motion itself announced what had not been published officially—that the House of Commons had set in operation the parliamentary procedure for passing the Stamp Act Grenville had threatened the previous year. A copy of the pending or completed bill [26] had "crept into the House," as Governor Fauquier later expressed it,[27] and had convinced members that the new tax was to be stiff and inclusive. For example, a copy of a simple judgment of court had to carry a four-shilling stamp or the equivalent; a pair of dice were taxed ten shillings; on each full sheet newspaper, there had to be a penny stamp.[28] Some of these details probably were known at the time Johnston made his motion. When Henry seconded it, Burgesses must have told themselves they were about to witness as vigorous an assault as the young Hanover lawyer had made on the speciously mysterious "loan office bill." The motion was put and carried; the Speaker left the chair and sat as com-mittee chairman; the thin House looked to Johnston; he deferred to Henry. From his place, the junior Burgess of Louisa County rose, took out a paper and submitted a series of resolutions, which read substan-tially as follows: [29]

Resolved—

That the first Adventurers and settlers of this his Majesty's Colony and Dominion brought with them and transmitted to their Posterity and all other his Majesty's Subjects since inhabiting in this his Majesty's said Colony, all the Privileges, Franchises and Immunities that have at any Time been held, enjoyed, and possessed by the People of Great Britain.

That by two royal Charters, granted by King James the first the Colonists

25 *Journ. H.B.*, 1761–65, p. 358.
26 The Stamp Act passed the House of Commons Feb. 27, 1765 (*Journ. House of Commons*, v. 30, p. 192–93) and the House of Lords March 8 (*Journ. House of Lords*, v. 31, p. 303). Royal assent was given by commission, the King then being insane, March 22. (See the text in Pickering, ed., *British Statutes at Large*, v. 26, p. 179). It would have been possible for a ship leaving the Thames promptly after that date to have anchored in Hampton Roads in time for its dispatches to have reached Williamsburg by May 29, but it seems more reasonable to assume that only the action of the Commons would have been known with certainty in Virginia by the date of Henry's appeal.
27 Fauquier to the Lords of Trade, Nov. 3, 1765; *Journ. H.B.*, 1761–65, p. lxxxiii.
28 *Statutes at Large*, v. 26, p. 181, 186.
29 The interesting historical puzzle of the original form of the "Stamp Act Resolutions" cannot be solved completely on the basis of surviving evidence, but it is reviewed briefly in Appendix III – 2.

aforesaid are declared entitled to all the Privileges, Liberties and Immunities of Denizens and natural-born Subjects, to all Intents and Purposes as if they had been abiding and born within the Realm of England.

Resolved—

That the Taxation of the People by themselves or by Persons chosen by themselves to represent them, who can only know what Taxes the People are able to bear, and the easiest Mode of raising them, and are equally affected by such Taxes themselves, is the distinguishing Characteristic of British Freedom and without which the ancient Constitution cannot subsist.

Resolved—

That his Majesty's liege People of this most ancient Colony have uninterruptedly enjoyed the Right of being thus governed by their own Assembly in the article of their Taxes and internal Police, and that the same hath never been forfeited or in any other way given up, but hath been constantly recognized by the Kings and People of Great Britain.

Resolved—

Therefore, That the General Assembly of this Colony have the only and sole exclusive Right and Power to lay Taxes and Impositions upon the Inhabitants of this Colony and that every Attempt to vest such Power in any Person or Persons whatsoever, other than the General Assembly aforesaid, has a manifest Tendency to destroy British as well as American Freedom.

A majority of the Burgesses manifestly favored a protest of some sort against a Stamp Act, though they certainly would differ over content and phrasing,[30] but some of the older leaders of the Assembly frowned and shook their heads as they listened to Henry's paper. As soon as they could get the floor, one after another of them assailed the resolutions.[31] Their argument must have been that in so far as the reso-

---

[30] Diary of unidentified French visitor, who heard the debate, printed in 26 *AHR*, 745–46 and cited hereafter as *French Visitor's Diary*.

[31] It must be noted that, as usual, no Journal of the Committee of the Whole was kept. Nor, if there had been one that conformed to the style of the Journal of the House, would it have shown the order of the speeches or the text of amendments, whether accepted or rejected. Information of this character, be it ever so desirable for a narrative, is not to be had of any Virginia public bodies prior to the convention of 1788, the deliberations of which were reported stenographically. Reports of Council's proceedings, if they survive at all, are not stripped down to the bare bones of decision; but the only supplement to the meagre, begrudging entries in the Journal of the House is in the *Virginia Gazette*, the files of which are broken, in diary entries and in personal reminiscences, which often were not written until many years after the event. In this particular case, the natural order of the debate would have been for Henry or Johnston to have opened, for the opposition to follow, and for one or the other of the movers to close, if permitted to do so by more numerous adversaries. This course may have been the actual one; but, young as Henry was, he had the sure instinct of actor and orator and he scarcely would have undertaken in his opening speech to make his full emotional appeal.

lutions were proper, they duplicated the address, memorial, and remonstrance of 1764,[32] and that where the resolutions went beyond the action of the previous year, colonial threats and defiance might assure passage of the Stamp Act or prevent repeal if it already had been signed. Conciliation, not denunciation, should be the weapon of the Colonies. Justice in the end would prevail.[33] When the utmost had been made of this general objection, a motion was put and passed to consider Henry's resolution *seriatim*.[34] The first paragraph of Henry's paper was read:

"Resolved, that the first Adventurers and settlers of this his Majesty's Colony and Dominion brought with them and transmitted to their posterity, and all other his Majesty's Subjects since inhabiting in this his Majesty's said Colony, all the Privileges, Franchises and Immunities that have at any Time been held, enjoyed and possessed by the People of Great Britain." [35]

That was incontestable. It could not be opposed by supporters of the royal prerogative on any other ground than the one already taken— that it was a needless repetition of what had been said in 1764. In fact, if there was amendment it was from Henry's own side. Where reference was made to "the privileges, franchises and immunities" the "first adventurers and settlers" brought with them from Great Britain, the word "liberties" was inserted ahead of the other nouns. As thus amended, the first resolution was adopted.[36]

Henry had written all the resolutions, as he afterwards recorded, on a blank page of an old lawbook, and he had done this "unadvised and unassisted." [37] He probably had no objection to the strengthening of the first resolution, and he certainly could not fail to thank the Burgess who suggested how the language of the second resolution could be

[32] See *supra*, p. 123.

[33] This is another case where reliance has to be placed on inference from the known facts. Some of the early reviews of what is supposed to have been said on the floor, including Jefferson's, in Wirt, *op. cit.*, 60, assume mistakenly that "no reply" to the appeals of 1764 had been received—as if the parliamentary introduction and basic terms of the Stamp Act had not then been reported in Virginia. The probability that the news had reached the Colony was discussed in n. 26 *supra*, but a general caveat is in order: Perhaps four-fifths of what has been written about the proceedings of May 29–31, 1765, in the House of Burgesses is guesswork.

[34] This is demonstrated by Fauquier's reference, *loc. cit.*, to the different majorities for the various resolutions.

[35] The text is that of the copy Henry himself preserved. See endorsement in *W. W. Henry*, v. 1, p. 81–82.

[36] It is to be noted that the amendments indicated by the variations of the first and final texts are here assumed to have been made in Committee of the Whole on the 29th and not in the House on the 30th. This may not have been true of all amendments, though the only difference that would make probably would be in one day of chronology.

[37] Endorsement cited *supra*, n 35.

improved somewhat without any change of meaning. The same thing happened to the third resolution, which set forth the right of the people to be taxed by their own action "or by persons chosen by themselves to represent them." After this had been debated, it emerged in form stronger than that of Henry's own text. Then the committee took up the fourth resolution:

"Resolved, that his Majesty's liege People of this most ancient Colony have uninterruptedly enjoyed the Right of being governed by their own Assembly in the article of their Taxes and internal police, and that the same hath never been forfeited or in any other way given up, but hath been constantly recognized by the Kings and People of Great Britain."

That did not suit the conservatives or the lawyers who prided themselves on their knowledge of the British constitution. They maintained that the Assembly did not alone govern Virginia. Its authority was derived from the consent of the people, but behind that was the approbation of the Sovereign, or of men acting for him, as they were at that very time because of the "illness" of the King—it was not good manners to speak of him as insane. Further, as respected the King, the lawyers pointed out that he, as well as the people of Britain through their Parliament had recognized the Colonies' right of self-government. This was important, the seniors insisted, because it meant that without the consent of the King, Parliament could not of itself abridge or destroy the rights of the Colonies. These points doubtless were labored and, in the end, were accepted. The older men who had controlled the House for a generation continued to protest the whole procedure was unnecessary and unwise; but the younger members—"the young, hot and giddy members" as Fauquier was to call them—stood squarely with Henry.[38] Robert Munford and John Fleming spoke with special vigor.[39] In those parts of the argument where Henry's knowledge did not extend, George Johnston dealt with the heavy artillery of the House—Peyton Randolph, George Wythe, Edmund Pendleton, Richard Bland and Robert Carter Nicholas.[40] On every resolution, the leaders demanded a division— and in each case lost narrowly. None of the resolutions commanded a larger majority than twenty to seventeen.[41]

[38] Fauquier to the Lords of Trade, June 5, 1765, *loc. cit.*
[39] *W. W. Henry*, v. 1, p. 82 n.
[40] Jefferson in Wirt, *op. cit.*, 60.
[41] Fauquier to the Lords of Trade, June 3, 1765, *loc. cit.*

The firmest of all the declarations, the fifth, now was up for approval or rejection. It read in this wise:

"Resolved, therefore, that the General Assembly of this Colony have the only and exclusive [42] Right and Power to lay Taxes and Impositions upon the Inhabitants of this Colony, and that every Attempt to vest such Power in any Person or Persons whatsoever, other than the General Assembly aforesaid, has a manifest Tendency to destroy British as well as American Freedom."

To some, the mild conclusion may have seemed anti-climactic; but as the conservatives interpreted the fifth resolution, they felt that it went beyond the assertion of the right of self-taxation and laid down the dictum that neither King nor Parliament had any right to impose or to supplement taxes of any sort on the Colonies. A few members would admit the principle of royal and parliamentary taxation, but would deplore the application; others still were willing to say as they had earlier, that no right to tax Virginians inhered in any other body than the General Assembly, but that if a tax were imposed, it had to be endured by loyal subjects until it was repealed. Henry did not trim to the shifting winds. The fifth resolution was the one to which all the others led up. That was why he had put "therefore" after that particular "resolved" and not after any of the others. There was no power outside the General Assembly that had any right to tax Virginians. Were that power usurped, it would be tyranny. So Henry reasoned.

An undertone of threat had prevailed in the debate and had angered him. Abuse by his adversaries was a goad. Knowing that the conservatives would do their utmost to prevent the passage of this resolution, and thereby to blunt the others, Henry took the floor. He was thoroughly aroused now. His garments fittingly were as plain as those of a prophet; his voice was proclaiming what men had been thinking behind the handles of a plow that was furrowing new ground. As Henry asserted that self-taxation was the rock and the fortress of freedom, his words took on the nobility of his theme. Listeners were carried up to new heights of thought. Their breath came faster, as if they were on a mountain-peak. Young Thomas Jefferson, standing at the door, was

[42] In Henry's original copy, the words "only and exclusive" are underlined, and "sole" is scrawled in the space above them. See the reproduction *Journ. H.B.*, 1761–65, frontispiece.

swept back to Troy by the rhythmic eloquence of Henry. "He appeared to me," said Jefferson long afterwards, "to speak as Homer wrote." The air became wine. Every auditor was possessed of a nobler self. A tax was lost in a principle. Williamsburg became Runnymede. The walls of the chamber melted into the deep background of the Englishman's struggle to shape his own destiny. Henry's imagery took bolder and still bolder form. Presently he began to describe the consequences for Britain as for America, if the power to tax were exercised otherwise than by the elected representatives of the people. The Stamp Act itself was tyrannical—the work of Parliament and of King, not of the people of Virginia. With a sweeping, defiant gesture and a voice that impaled his hearers, Henry shouted: "Tarquin and Caesar each had his Brutus, Charles the First his Cromwell, and George the Third—

"Treason," ruled the outraged Speaker.

Henry lifted his shoulders still higher as he paused for an instant only—"and George the Third may profit by their example! If *this* be treason make the most of it!"

Skillful as this was, the Speaker did not intend to permit the utterance or the apparent acquiescence of the House to go unrebuked. Robinson again ruled Henry's words treasonable, and he expressed surprise that no member of the House had been loyal enough to stop the orator before the gentleman from Louisa had gone so far. Henry had made his point; he had no intention of having prejudice aroused against his resolutions because of a ruling that the author of them had uttered treasonable words. He promptly apologized to the Speaker and to the House and avowed his loyalty to the King, even to the last drop of his blood.[43] Some of his colleagues sustained him; the matter was dismissed; division was demanded. When the members who opposed the fifth resolution stood to be counted, they appeared as numerous as the "Ayes" who had just taken their seats, but the count showed the declaration to have been carried by twenty to nineteen.[44]

There may have been motions, after that, for the inclusion of other resolutions, more positive even than Henry's, but none of these was approved, if offered.[45] The Committee of the Whole rose; Peyton

[43] The author of the *French Visitor's Diary* is the only authority for this incident, but as Henry had apologized for the extremes of his speech in the parsons' cause, it was entirely "in character" for him to make a similar statement to the House.

[44] Fauquier to the Lords of Trade, June 5, 1765, *loc. cit.*

[45] For the involved question of the scope of the resolutions submitted to the Committee and to the House, see Appendix III–2.

Randolph reported to the House that certain resolutions had been adopted and that he was ready to deliver them. As the hour was late, the House voted to receive the report the next day.[46] Randolph then waddled angrily out. "By God," he said as he passed the door where young Jefferson was standing, "I would have given 500 guineas for a single vote!" The student who overheard him understood precisely what he meant: "one vote would have divided the House, and [John] Robinson was in the chair, who he knew would have negatived the resolution." [47]

The next day, May 30, it may have been honest if belated chance, or it may have been the cunning of old parliamentary leaders that suddenly brought into question the right of young Henry to speak on the floor. Just before the House prepared to take up his resolutions, the Committee on Privileges and Elections reported on a contest and on the return of the writs in the Counties that had named Burgesses to fill the vacancies reported at the beginning of the adjourned session. One writ was passed as in proper form, several others could be amended at the table, but the one from Louisa certifying Henry's election was in such order that the House voted to send for the Sheriff of the County "in custody to amend his said return." [48] If this was designed to discredit the "sitting member," it failed of its purpose. When the seniors undertook forthwith to defeat Henry's resolutions, his lines held without the loss of a vote. All five resolutions were adopted with some slight amendments, by exactly the same vote that had been recorded in Committee of the Whole.[49] The House disapproved a further motion by some member to the effect that anyone who maintained the right of Parliament to levy direct taxes on America was an enemy of his country.[50]

In the belief that the declaration of the Colony was now firmly a matter of record, Henry mounted his horse that evening and started back to Hanover to deal with law cases that had been postponed during

---

[46] *Journ. H.B.,* 1761–65, p. 358.

[47] Jefferson in Wirt, *op. cit.,* 61. Strictly speaking, of course, Robinson was not "in the chair" as Speaker during the deliberations of the Committee of the Whole, but was presiding on motion, as chairman only. Any other member might have been named to sit as Chairman of the Committee of the Whole. It was not the Speaker's prerogative.

[48] *Journ. H.B.,* 1761–65, p. 359.

[49] *Journ. H.B.,* 1761–65, p. 359–60; Fauquier to the Lords of Trade, June 5, 1765, *op. cit.,* lxvii. The French visitor misdated these occurrences and gave May 30, not May 29, as the date of Henry's speech.

[50] *French Visitor's Diary,* loc. cit., 746.

GEORGE WASHINGTON BECOMES A VESTRYMAN

The "declaration" reproduced on the facing page was signed by the men elected to the vestry after the old parish of Truro was divided (p. 126–27) and approximately half of it was constituted Fairfax Parish. This arrangement put Mount Vernon in the new parish, where Washington stood fifth among those elected, Mch. 28, 1765, to the vestry. Later in the year, when it was found that the division of the original parish had been uneven, the lines were redrawn, and Mount Vernon was restored to Truro Parish. In a new election held July 25 (p. 142), Washington became a vestryman of his old parish. The record printed here is part of the first page of the register of Pohick Church, which Washington attended with some regularity. Among the signers, besides Washington, were George Mason and John Posey.

It will be noticed that this paper was not an oath. Vestrymen did not "swear"; they "declared," in accordance with a law of the Colony adopted in March, 1661–62. This act, printed in Hening's *Statutes at Large,* v. 2, p. 44, provided that "twelve of the most able men of each parish be by the major part of the said parish chosen to be vestrymen . . ." Stipulation was made "that none shall be admitted to be of the vestry that do not take the oath of allegiance and supremacy to his Majesty and subscribe to be conformable to the doctrine and discipline of the Church of England."

Philip Alexander Bruce once wrote that a vestry was composed of the foremost men residing in the parish represented by it, whether from the point of view of intelligence, wealth or social position. Perhaps it would be more nearly accurate to say that a vestry always included such men but did not consist entirely of them. The desire of the small farmer to be represented in the affairs of the church frequently resulted in the choice of some men of humble estate. One of the vestry of Truro Parish at the time it was dissolved in 1744, on Lawrence Washington's motion (Vol. I, p. 230), was an illiterate. He was reelected when a new vestry was chosen.

(After the Original in the Records of the New-York Historical Society)

I A B do declare that I will be conformable to the Doctrine & Disciplne

of the Church of England as by law established. et vac...

Tho* Withers Officer   16 Ab 1760

Tho: Ford

John Ford

19 August

G Washington

Daniel McCarty

Edw* Payne

Tho* Withers Officer

Mc: Ford

Ed: Dulin

John Dalton

Dan* French

Rich* Sanford

Tho* Shaw

Tho* Moor

20 Aug 1765

Cha* Broadwater

W Payne

William Adams

20 Aug 1765

G W Fairfax

John West

William Linton

The State of [Virginia] to Mrs. Mary Washington Dr.

Mrs. Mary Washington [her] acct. Dr.

1782			£	s	d
Novr 1	To Cash brought from ledger A	47	4	12	6
Feby 4	To Cash paid		5	—	
	To Ditto paid for my brother of my books	60	30	—	
	To Ditto	62	15	—	
Decr 9	To Ditto paid to B.o Geo. & Lewis	62	10	—	
	To sundry expenses of Washington				
	To cash paid for the Car: ? ...		5	10	—
1783					
	To cash paid for ...		13	5	0
May	To cash paid for ...		10	—	
Octr	To Ditto paid for provisions		15	—	
Dec.	To Ditto Washington advance of		30	—	
1784					
April	To Ditto ...		25	—	
Sept.	To Ditto ... on my acct.		10	—	
Augt	To Ditto for do. on my acct.		23	—	
24	To Ditto ...				
27	To Ditto ...	40			
			60	2	1
	Balance 25 p Ct.		10	5	
		144	2035	9	2

Folio 45 of Washington's "Ledger B" covers part of his carefully preserved account with his mother. Years later, he was to write of her: "She has had a great deal of money from me at times, as can be made appear by my books . . . and over and above this had not only had all that was ever made from the plantation but got her provisions and everything else she thought proper from thence. In short, to the best of my recollection I have never in my life received a copper from the estate, and have paid many hundred pounds (first and last) to her in cash. However, I want no retribution; I conceived it to be a duty, whenever she asked for money, and I had it, to furnish her, notwithstanding she got all the crops, or the amount of them, and took everything she wanted from the plantation for the support of her family, horses, &c. besides" (30 *G.W.*, 401).

It manifestly seemed unreasonable to him that he never "received a copper" from the farm his father bequeathed him; but he meant the "however" in the quoted letter to be all-inclusive: whether or not his mother's calls on him measured her actual necessities and took his financial condition into account, he would supply her when he could. On one future occasion, recorded on a later folio of his Ledger, it was to be by a hard pinch that he sent what she sought—but he did it.

She lived comfortably after she removed to Fredericksburg, and she used for years a riding "chair," he bought for her in 1774 while he was attending the First Continental Congress. Apparently she retained to the last her love of horses. The tradition of this is positive and probably authentic, but of other aspects of her life in the lovely town at the falls of the Rappahannock, little is known. After her son became renowned, she received numerous visits from travelers and foreign dignitaries who wished to pay homage to "the mother of Washington." These men usually made brief references only in their diaries to her appearance, her conversation and her style of living. As will be recorded in a later volume, her dress was an embarrassing subject to her son at Mount Vernon.

(After a Microfilm in the Virginia State Library of the Original in the Library of Congress)

his absence. The following morning, May 31,[51] Henry's absence was noted in a House perceptibly thinner than it had been even during the debate on the Stamp Act. Randolph and the other leaders proceeded immediately to move that the resolutions be expunged, but, as the five parts of the paper had been adopted one by one, protesting Burgesses insisted, or else the chair ruled, that the expunging vote be put separately on each resolution. Weakened though Henry's supporters were by the absence of their leader, they held together and beat down the motion to efface from the record the first, the second, the third and the fourth resolutions. The fifth, the resolution carrying the climactic "therefore," they lost. It was stricken from the Journal without the entry of a line to indicate that it or any of the other resolutions had so much as been challenged. In the official text of the Journal, under date of May 30, the four stand in this form as if they, and they only, had been adopted when Henry was crying out of Tarquin and Caesar and Charles I:

Resolved, That the first Adventurers and Settlers of this his Majesty's Colony and Dominion of Virginia brought with them, and transmitted to their Posterity, and all other his Majesty's Subjects since inhabiting in this his Majesty's said Colony, all the Liberties, Privileges, Franchises, and Immunities, that have at any Time been held, enjoyed, and posessed, by the people of Great Britain.

Resolved, That by two royal Charters, granted by King James the First, the Colonists aforesaid are declared entitled to all Liberties, Privileges, and Immunities of Denizens and natural Subjects, to all Intents and Purposes, as if they had been abiding and born within the Realm of England.

Resolved, That the Taxation of the People by themselves, or by Persons chosen by themselves to represent them, who can only know what Taxes the People are able to bear, or the easiest Method of raising them, and must themselves be affected by every Tax laid on the People, is the only Security against a burthensome Taxation, and the distinguishing Characteristic of British Freedom, without which the ancient Constitution cannot exist.

Resolved, That his Majesty's liege People of this his most ancient and loyal Colony have without Interruption enjoyed the inestimable Right of being governed by such Laws, respecting their internal Polity and Taxation, as are

---

[51] Jefferson was one day "off" in the account he gave Wirt of this incident. He thought the resolutions were accepted by the House the day they were approved in Committee of the Whole (see Wirt, *op. cit.,* 61) and that the episode about to be related in the text was on the 30th. The *Journal* itself (p. 358, 359–60) corrects part of this error. Fauquier's letter of June 5, *loc. cit.,* gives the chronology with precision.

derived from their own Consent, with the Approbation of their Sovereign, or his Substitute; and that the same hath never been forfeited or yielded up, but hath been constantly recognized by the Kings and People of Great Britain.

Mild as were these resolutions, when Governor Fauquier came to report them to the Lords of Trade, he felt he should apologize for them and consequently he wrote: "I hope I am authorized in saying there is cause at least to doubt whether this would be the sense of the Colony if more of their representatives had done their duty by attending to the end of the session." [52] The Governor was not sure that even this statement would satisfy their Lordships or excuse the Burgesses; so, on June 1, the day after the expunging resolutions were submitted and four days before he reported to the Board of Trade, he summoned the Burgesses to the council chamber, signed the completed bills and joint resolutions and then, without a word either of thanks or of reproach, dissolved the House. The King must appeal from the Burgesses to his people in new elections. [53] Appeal he might, but Henry had not penned his resolutions

[52] Letter of June 5, 1765, *loc. cit.*

[53] It seems improbable that Washington witnessed these scenes and heard Henry's historic speech. His *Ledger* (folio 191) shows that he received pay for twenty-eight days' attendance during the session, which extended from May 1 through June 1. Sundays excluded, twenty-eight "working days" lay between the dates of the opening and of the closing of the session. If, then, the Burgesses were paid for the week days only, Washington drew pay for the entire session and presumably was in attendance throughout. Was this the practice? Were the Burgesses paid for Sundays as well as for week days in Williamsburg, or for week days only? The terms of the act of 1730 (4 H 278) specifically included pay for Sundays and would have applied, of course, unless the law was changed or, improbably, the practice was abandoned. There is no evidence of amendment or of disuse. Washington's own accounts demonstrate that for those sessions during which he is known to have been present from the opening day to that of final adjournment, he was paid for "elapsed time" and not merely for week days. Specifically, this was true for the session of Nov. 6-Dec. 16, 1766 (forty-one "elapsed days"), for the session of May 8-17, 1769 (ten such days) and for the session of Nov. 7-Dec. 21, 1769 (forty-five calendar days). For the session of Oct. 30-Dec. 21, 1764, he drew pay for fifty-four days, one more than actual "elapsed time." It is manifest, therefore, that pay was allowed for Sundays and that in the spring session of 1765 Washington was absent four days during a session of thirty-two days. Was this at the beginning of the session, in the course of it, or at the end? His name is not mentional in the Journal. Consequently there can be no official proof that he was in attendance on any particular day; but the date of convocation, May 1, was such that if he were apprehensive he might not be able to remain for the duration of the session, it would be better, so far as his plantation was concerned, for him to come early and to leave early than to arrive late and to remain to the end. The possibility that he absented himself during the session cannot be excluded, though no evidence has been discovered, one way or the other, to show whether a Burgess was "docked" for the days he did not occupy his seat during the course of a session. The probability is strong that if he were away from home and were sustaining expense, he would be paid even if he were not on the floor every day. It was on this very ground of expense that every Burgess was allowed "travel days" at 10s each en route to Williamsburg and on his way home. All these considerations indicate, though they do not prove positively, that Washington's four days of absence were at the end of the session. The likelihood of this is increased by the course of legislation. After Council and House agreed, May 26, on

in vain. The British commander in North America had later to inform his government that the Virginia resolves "gave the signal for a general outcry over the continent."[54]

These were serious matters for Colonel Washington to consider on his return to Mount Vernon. To his own financial distress was added concern for the future of the Colony. At a time when he was changing crops, relations with Britain were changing also. A new uncertainty was creeping into life when defeat of the French had given promise of stability. Even the power of the leaders in the General Assembly was being challenged, and not by rivals of like station but by Burgesses of the upcountry. In pounds and shillings, the wealthy planters might suffer most from the Stamp Act, because they patented the land and transacted the business and employed the processes of law to which the new statute most heavily applied. When the small farmer's lack of money was considered, he might be the worst victim of the Stamp Act because he would have to pay for a new stamp every time he renewed the loans he never seemed able to discharge. At least, the legislative opponents of the new law so contended.

At home Washington found the family well,[55] but conditions on the farms were bad. About the 1st of May heavy rains had wet the ground thoroughly. After that, the top soil hardened. June brought one shower that freshened the corn and gave a start to the hemp with which Washington was experimenting.[56] Again the skies cleared. The wind blew steadily from the West and Southwest and, as usual, brought fair weather. No thunderstorms roared down from the Northwest; there was not even one of the familiar three-day downpours that usually attended an east wind or a steady blow from the Southeast. Drought settled on the Hunting Creek estate. It was all the more depressing

---

amendments to the revised Tobacco bill, no important legislation remained, so far as anyone except Henry, George Johnston and perhaps one or two of their followers knew. On the plantations, the time was at hand for planting tobacco, and for arranging the wheat harvest. These circumstances prompted many Burgesses to start home, on and after May 26. The chances are that Washington was of this number, that he left on the 28th, and that he was not present to hear Henry, or to cast his vote for or against the resolutions. As will appear in the text, nothing definite is known concerning Washington's opinion of the Stamp Act prior to Sept. 20, 1765.

[54] Thomas Gage to Secretary Conway, Sept. 25, 1765, in C. F. Carter, ed., *The Correspondence of General Gage with the Secretaries of State, 1763–1775* (cited hereafter as *Gage*), v. 1, p. 67.

[55] No medical bills for this period appear in the Ledger, though the usual "ague" (malaria) doubtless appeared a little later in the summer.

[56] This language is almost precisely that of Washington's letter of Aug. 2, 1765, to Burwell Bassett; 2 *G. W.*, 424.

because Nature seemed to be discriminating against the planters on the river. Inland, the farmers enjoyed a good season.[57]

Besides drought, there was rust on the wheat crop from which Washington was hoping to get cash to offset the decline in returns from the Potomac tobacco. The flax and the hemp, too, had been planted as part of the shift from bondage to the leaf, but the dry weather was hard on these new plants of odd and unfamiliar habits of life.[58] Other crops scarcely were better. By the middle of July, Washington was at the doubtful mercy of persistent drought. He had to find such comfort as he might in the reflection that if he were compelled to purchase corn the next winter he would not have to haul it farther than from the nearby farms that had been blessed with rain.[59]

The hard summer was not without its satisfactions and its honors. Writs of election went out in June for the new House of Burgesses. In Fairfax, where the poll was to be opened July 16, there was to be a vacancy. Patrick Henry's associate in advocating the Stamp Act Resolutions, George Johnston, decided because of declining health that he would not be a candidate for the seat he had held since 1758. The other Burgess from Fairfax, Col. John West, would stand again. It obviously was far easier for Washington to make a canvass among his own neighbors than over the mountains in Frederick, and it was simpler, also, to carry out the wishes and to do the legislative business of constituents he saw frequently—at church, on the road, at court. Washington accordingly declined in Frederick County and declared himself a candidate in Fairfax. It would have been gratifying, of course, if his announcement had led all other aspirants to stand aside in the knowledge that none of them could defeat him and did not wish to compete with him. Most of the leading planters were of this mind, but Washington's neighbor and debtor, Capt. John Posey, had ambitions of his own. He did not plan or even wish to beat Washington but he thought he had a chance of getting a larger poll than John West. In this, the Captain did not miss his mark by a humiliating margin. The result of a light vote on July 16 was: Washington, 201; John West, 148; John Posey, 131.[60] It was not a costly canvass, either. Under the act of 1762, which had been invoked in the case of Littlepage, voters no longer could be "treated" with all

---

[57] *Ibid.* These remarks on prevailing winds and weather at Mount Vernon are based on the observations made in recent years by Superintendent C. C. Wall.

[58] Letter of Sept. 20, 1765, to Robert Cary & Co.; *ibid.*, 431.

[59] *Ibid.*, 424.   [60] 816 *Papers of G. W.*, LC, Toner Transcripts.

the liquor they would drink—as in the Frederick polling of 1758—but it was permissible, after the election had been completed, to offer refreshment. In this instance, Washington provided cake, not spirits, and at a cost of £7, 11s 1d.[61] In addition, he placed £2 in Captain Dalton's hand for contingencies.[62] Washington was entirely satisfied. It was, he confessed, "an easy and a creditable poll," [63] and it was followed by another honor. The amended act on the parish lines of Fairfax County, which had placed Mount Vernon once again in Truro Parish, had provided also for the election of a new vestry there as well as in Fairfax Parish. In the poll of July 25, Washington shared third place with his neighbor, Capt. John Posey.[64]

This vestry service was frequent but seldom was pressing; attendance on the new Assembly seemed immediately in prospect. Washington was preparing to start for the colonial capital when word came on July 28 that the session had been prorogued. "I am convinced . . ." said Washington somewhat grimly, "that the Governor had no inclination to meet an Assembly at this juncture." [65] That was the belief not in Fairfax only, but also and equally in every part of Virginia. The lawmakers of Massachusetts had sent out on the 8th of June, 1765, a call for a meeting in New York on October 7 of representatives of all the Colonies: [66] Governor Fauquier did not want the Houses of Burgesses to meet because he feared it would approve participation in this enterprise which he regarded as seditious.

Opposition to the Stamp Act was shifting now from argument to resistance and was spreading in Virginia from the "giddy fellows" to the leading planters and to most of the merchants long resident in Virginia. The stamps themselves had been printed by this time in England and were being sent to each of the Colonies for allotment by agents who, in some instances, had been commissioned on nomination by the London representatives of the colonial governments. For Virginia, the designated "Distributor" was a son of the lawyer John Mercer, no less a person, in fact than Col. George Mercer—Washington's former aide,

---

61 *Ledger A,* folio 211.
62 *Ibid.,* folio 203. For the law, see section xix in 7 *H* 526.
63 Letter of Aug. 2, 1765, to Burwell Bassett; 2 *G. W.,* 424.
64 Ahead of him were Col. George Mason and Capt. Edward Payne. Behind Washington and Posey were Capt. Daniel French, Daniel McCarty, Col. George William Fairfax, Alexander Henderson, Thomason Ellzey, T. W. Coffer, William Lynton and Thomas Ford. Seven others received votes. See 817 *Papers of G. W.,* 17, LC.
65 2 *G. W.,* 424. This prorogation is not mentioned in Kennedy's edition of *Journ. H.B.*
66 Cf. *Proceedings of the Stamp Act Congress,* printed by Jonas Green.

Burgess from Frederick, and one of the most highly esteemed veterans of the French and Indian War. The recommendation of the Virginia Council and George Mercer's own active effort in England had yielded him no office at the hands of the Ministry until this appointment was made, presumably in the belief that Mercer's popularity and influential connections in Virginia would reduce antagonism to the law. Instead, Mercer's known acceptance of the office had cost him already his place in the affection of many of his own people. On the Northern Neck, he had been burned in effigy.[67] At least one of Mercer's old companions-in-arms believed the voluntary exile first had taken and then in better understanding, had relinquished a position that made him, in the eyes of Virginians, a tool of tyranny.[68] Regardless of his action, thousands of the colonials were resolved they would not use the tax-paper in any circumstance or share any transaction in which the application of stamps was a matter of law. Some members of County Courts were saying already that they would not serve a single day after legal processes had to be stamped. Whispers soon were to be passed also, that if an attempt were made to execute the law, men would come from the upcountry to Williamsburg and would seize and destroy the stamps.[69]

Washington heard and pondered. He was not excited and in his own mind he had not made common cause with those who were advocating an extreme course. On some of the possible results of the law he did not attempt to pass advance judgment. Regarding other consequences of the new British policy, his mind was clear. When he acquainted English correspondents with the response of Virginians to the Stamp Act, he displayed a measure of political restraint that might have seemed to be positive detachment. Almost four months after the adoption of Henry's resolutions, Washington wrote: "The Stamp Act imposed on the Colonies by the Parliament of Great Britain engrosses the conversation of the speculative part of the Colonists, who look upon this unconstitutional method of taxation as a direful attack upon their liberties, and loudly exclaim against the violation; what may be the result of this and some other (I think I may add) ill judged measures, I will not undertake to determine . . ." His correspondent, pausing here in the middle of a sentence, might note that Washington said "their," not "our" liberties, when he spoke of the opinion the "speculative part of

[67] See *infra*, p. 169.
[68] Robert Stewart to Washington, Aug. 18, 1765; 3 *Hamilton*, 277.
[69] Fauquier to the Lords of Trade, Nov. 3, 1765; *Journ, H, B.,* 1761–65, p. lxviii–lxix.

the Colonists" had of the "violation." At the same time, was it not
apparent that when he wrote of "this unconstitutional method of taxation," he meant that adjective "unconstitutional" to express his own idea ·
as well as that of the "speculative part" of society in Virginia?

Washington proceeded: "but this I may venture to affirm" and he
then maintained that the gain to Britain from the Stamp Act would be
far less than the Ministry anticipated, because the colonials were beginning to realize they could dispense with many of the luxuries they were
buying in Britain. Most of the "necessaries of life" were to be had in
America. "This," said he, "consequently will introduce frugality and
be a necessary stimulation to [colonial] industry." As for the operation
of the new tax measure, the people did not have the money to buy the
stamps, even if they were willing to do so. He concluded: ". . . if a
stop be put to our judicial proceedings, I fancy the merchants of Great
Britain trading to the Colonies will not be among the last to wish for a
repeal of it." [70]

Washington's own experience that very year with English merchants
was so disappointing that he needed the fulness of his innate sense of
justice to keep him from wishing that they should pay for the worst
follies of their government, which, on the 10th of July, 1765, had passed
into the hands of a coalition Ministry headed by Lord Rockingham.
Whether or not the new ministers ended the calamity of the Stamp Act,
the year in Virginia was certain to be a disastrous one on the plantations. While the drought did not prove as nearly ruinous as Washington had expected, the yield of his greatly enlarged acreage of wheat was
not more than 1112 bushels.[71] Tobacco rents from a dwindling eight
tenants were 9300 pounds.[72] The Custis farms produced only seventeen
hogsheads for Washington under his reduced planting. "Jackie's" crop
was seventy-one hogsheads, compared with eighty-seven the previous
year and ninety-seven in 1763.[73] The wheat crop on the Pamunkey and
the York never had been large and now it was a complete failure.[74]
Returns from English sales of earlier crops were discouraging—"pitifully low" was Washington's word for them.[75] Cary & Co. got even less
for plantation crops in London than a Liverpool firm reported for light

[70] Letter to Francis Dandridge, Sept. 20, 1765; 2 *G. W.*, 425–26. The substance of this was
repeated in a letter of the same date to Robert Cary & Co. See *ibid.*, 431.
[71] *Ledger A*, folio 180.   [72] *Ibid.*, folio 233.
[73] *Custis Papers*, VHS.
[74] *Ibid.* Washington had thirty-eight bushels and Custis ninety-three.
[75] 2 *G. W.*, 427.

"rent tobacco." Washington's Potomac leaf sold below that of some of his neighbors, and—what he could not understand—his hogsheads from the Custis lands found less favor than the offerings on "Jackie's" account, though the two crops seemed indistinguishable and were grown and cured under the same competent direction of Joseph Valentine on farms almost identical.

Some of the goods bought for him with the proceeds of this tobacco seemed very high to Washington. This, he protested, was "another thing I cannot easily account for, unless it is on a presumption that they are bought at very long credits," but how could that justify extortion? He argued: "Where a person has money in a merchant's hands he should doubtless have all the benefits that can result from that money, and in like manner where he pays interest for the use of the merchant's, should he [not] be entitled to the same advantages, otherwise it might well be asked, for what purpose is it that interest is paid?" [76] On this basis he again gave warning that if he did not procure needed goods on the best terms, and did not get a reasonable price for his tobacco, he would have to change merchants.[77]

Finally, the experiments with flax and hemp bore out Washington's earlier fears of partial failure that season. On the 9th of August, he began to rot his hemp.[78] Breaking it was a hard task, clumsily done [79] but, in the end, Washington had 7585 pounds of it.[80] Quality was low and the market was undeveloped, though the prospect was not altogether disheartening. Washington wrote some of his merchants for advice on culture and selling and on the bounty Parliament had offered for American hemp and flax. He did not believe that much of the Virginia land was suited to the plants, but if the trade was not hedged about with too many harassing restrictions, he might make further effort to determine whether flax and hemp were among the profitable substitutes for that enslaver, tobacco.[81] There might be other "money-crops," too, or larger use of resources already at hand—the river, for example. Washington had concluded that he could catch many more fish if he had a new schooner to replace a craft that probably had been swinging at the landing for many years. During the summer a number of his "tradesmen," as he termed them, had been at work on a stout frame.[82]

[76] Letter of Sept. 20, 1765, to Robert Cary & Co.; 2 G. W., 427–29.
[77] Ibid., 429.   [78] 1 Diaries, 213.
[79] 3 Hamilton, 280–81.   [80] Ledger A, folio 297.
[81] 2 G. W., 430–31, 432–33.
[82] Ledger A, folio 145, 222; 1 Diaries, 214–15.

The vessel would be ready by the time the shad and the herring began to run in the spring of 1766; all the seine must be mended meantime.[83] Regular reaping, plowing and sowing went on. Wheat-planting began in mid-August[84] and continued at intervals till November 13.[85] Turnip seed were broadcast August 3, September 5 to 9, and October 26;[86] fodder was pulled after September 25.[87]

The difficult crop year was ending when Washington read the details of the meeting in New York during October of the "Stamp Act Congress" in which Virginia was not represented because her Assembly had been prorogued so that it had not been able to name delegates. New Hampshire, North Carolina and Georgia likewise had no spokesmen at the gathering, but twenty-seven from nine Colonies had conferred for about a fortnight and had formulated a "Declaration of Rights and Grievances" to which most Virginians would have subscribed.

Following his survey of this document, Washington heard that a startling new scene in the drama of the Stamp Act had been staged in Williamsburg. It developed that Col. George Mercer had not resigned the appointment of Stamp Distributor for Virginia. Mercer, instead, had crossed the Atlantic with a full stock of stamps and had arrived in Hampton Roads at a time when the Colony's anger over the tax measure was rising to new resentment with the approach of November 1, the date on which a stamp would be required to validate almost any act of business or of law. Rumors multiplied of the threatened descent on the capital by men from the upcountry to seize and to destroy the hated paper. The story next ran that a march on Williamsburg was impending. Justices of two Counties had filed petitions for the appointment of their successors because they had resolved not to act officially in any way after stamps were required for legal process. These left-handed resignations had been laid on the table by the Council, in order to compel the Justices to administer the law till a new bench was named, but the example of these Counties was ominous and alarming. Justices, clerks, lawyers and debtors—all might revolt passively. Business might be brought to stop and stagnation by a paralysis of the courts. Every autumn day seemed the forerunner of calamity. Little besides the Stamp Act was discussed in Williamsburg as October was closing and attorneys, merchants and planters gathered for the usual settlement of

[83] For the repair bill, see *Ledger A*, folio 196.
[84] 1 *Diaries*, 213.
[85] *Ibid.*, 213–14, 215–16.
[86] *Ibid.*
[87] *Ibid.*, 214.

accounts at the meeting of the General Court, scheduled for the same fateful Friday, November 1.

On the 30th of October, when the throng was close to its crest, Colonel Mercer arrived in York River on the ship *Leeds,* rode to Williamsburg,[88] and went forthwith to private lodgings,[89] but he brought none of the detested stamps with him from the vessel. Word of his presence quickly reached the Governor who decided immediately to go to Mrs. Campbell's Virginia Coffee House,[90] ostensibly to see what was happening but actually to be at hand in event of disorder. Before long, about mid-afternoon, while the Governor was observing, someone shouted "One and all!" Others took it up and began to move toward the building where Mercer was supposed to be. "This concourse of people," the Governor said afterwards, "I should call a mob, did I not know that it was chiefly if not altogether composed of gentlemen of property . . ."

The crowd came upon Colonel Mercer at the Capitol, while he was on his way from his lodgings to the coffee house. He had shown abundant courage during the French and Indian War and he did not cringe now. The question was shot straight at him: he saw how the people felt about the stamps; was he going to distribute them or would he stand with his own people and resign the office? Mercer kept his head. The issue meant a great deal to him, he said. He could not attempt to answer the question immediately. Thought had to be given it. Friday, the day the stamps had to be used, he would make his answer there—in front of the Capitol—at 10 o'clock in the morning.

With that he started again toward the coffee house. The crowd was not satisfied. Men hung around him, changed their pace to his, argued, protested, exhorted. Mercer kept on, afoot. When he reached the coffee house, there on the porch, seated together, were the Governor and most of the members of the Council, with Speaker Robinson between them and loiterers.

Mercer, of course, went straight to the Governor, whom he had not seen since his arrival. Fauquier and the Council had smiles and hearty handshakes and "received him," as the Governor said later, "with the greatest marks of welcome." The crowd did not like this. There were scowls and black looks but no outcries. Mercer joined the group on the

[88] *Penn Gazette,* Nov. 21, 1765.
[89] Their location is not determinable from surviving records.
[90] Located, Dr. L. J. Cappon stated in a letter of Aug. 12, 1948, "behind the Capitol on Waller Street, just South of the second colonial theatre."

porch; the throng kept below the stairs that led from the street. Presently old-time friends in the crowd began to send messages that urged Mercer to reconsider and to declare for the people. He answered steadfastly that he had stated when he would announce his decision. Threats would wring no more from him. By this time, cries were rising from the street: "Friday is too late," "The law goes into effect then," "Promise to give your answer tomorrow." Mercer did not yield. He would stand by what he had said.

"Let us rush in!" a voice called. Thereupon, the whole crowd seemed to move toward the steps as if those nearest the porch were to be pushed up to seize Mercer. Instinctively Fauquier and the members of the Council rose and took position at the head of the stairs to resist attack.

"See the Governor," someone shouted; "take care of him." At that, the leaders hesitated, halted and, a moment later, backed down the steps. Then the whole throng retired a short distance and left neutral ground between themselves and the elderly men around Mercer on the porch. A parley followed. After various messages and appeals, Mercer reluctantly agreed to give his answer at 5 o'clock Thursday afternoon instead of at 10 A.M., Friday. Even that did not induce the crowd to scatter. In gathering autumn twilight, the angry planters and townsmen persistently hung around the coffee house until Fauquier became fearful of harm to Mercer if he left the agent there or permitted the loathed official to return to lodgings. For a while Fauquier debated what to do. Making up his mind, he walked again to the top of the steps and observed audibly that he did not believe anyone would do him hurt. With that he went back to Mercer and said quietly that if the agent would walk with him through the crowd he believed they could go in safety to the Governor's house.

Mercer was willing. They came down the steps side by side and started up the street toward the Palace. It was the moment of moments when, in the deepening night, a push, a press and a shout would start a fight in which Mercer would be torn to pieces and the Governor injured, if not killed. Something restrained the throng—a sense of fairplay, respect for the Governor, or a belief that Mercer would refuse to execute his hateful commission. There was muttering but no violence. Fauquier and Mercer completed the walk, entered the Palace, and closed the door behind them without having to lift a hand to ward off a blow.[91]

[91] This is little more than a paraphrase of Fauquier's letter of Nov. 3, 1765, *Journ. H.B.*, 1761–65, p. lxviii–lxx, a model report in every particular.

By the next afternoon at 5 o'clock, the crowd was larger than ever and was collected in the Capitol, where Mercer had promised to appear.[92] In a few minutes he arrived from his lodgings, faced the throng and read this letter:

Gentlemen, I now have met you agreeable to yesterday's promise to give my country some assurance which I would have been glad to do so with any propriety sooner. I flatter myself no judicious man could blame me for accepting an office under an authority that was never disputed by any one from whom I could have been advised of the propriety or right of the objections. I do acknowledge that some little time before[,] I heard of and saw some resolves which were said to be made by the House of Burgesses of Virginia, but as the authority of them was disputed, they never appearing but in private hands, and so often and differently reported to me, I determined to know the real sentiments of my countrymen from themselves and I am compelled to say that those sentiments were so suddenly and unexpectedly communicated to me that I was altogether unable to give an immediate answer upon so important a point; for in however an unpopular light I may lately have been viewed, and notwithstanding the many insults I have from this day's conversation been informed have been offered me in effigy in many parts of this Colony, yet I still flatter myself that time will justify me and that my conduct may not be condemned after having been cooly inquired into.

The commission so very disagreeable to my countrymen, was obtained by the genteel recommendation of their representatives in the General Assembly, unasked for, and though this is contrary to public report, which I am told charges me with assisting in the passage of the Stamp Act upon the promise of a Commission in this Colony, yet I hope it will meet with credit when I assure you I was so far from assisting it or having any previous promise from the Ministry that I did not know of my appointment until some time after my return from Ireland where I was at the commencement of the session of Parliament and for a long time after the Act had been passed.

Thus, Gentlemen, am I circumstanced. I should be glad to act now in such a manner as would justify me to my friends and countrymen here and the authority which appointed me but the time you have all allotted me is so very short that I have not yet been able to discover that happy medium and therefore must entreat you to be referred to my future conduct with this assurance in the meantime that I will not directly or indirectly by my deputies or myself proceed further with the Act until I receive further orders from England and not then without the assent of the General Assembly of this Colony and that no man can more ardently or sincerely wish the prosperity of than myself . . . Your sincere friend and humble servant[93] . . .

92 *Ibid.*, lxx.   93 *Penn Gazette*, Nov. 21, 1765.

That was enough! Those who had seemed willing to kill him on Wednesday now made a hero of him and carried him out of the Capitol in triumph and to the coffee house where lavish entertainment was tendered him.[94]

The General Court met the next day, but not a litigant appeared and not a lawyer, except the Attorney General. Fauquier subsequently reported: "I waited sometime and then ordered proclamation to be made again, once in the cryer's place, and once at the door; and upon no suitors appearing I called for Colonel Mercer and asked him in open court whether he could supply the Court with proper stamps that the business might be carried on, according to law. He replied he could not, and gave the substance of the answer he had given the evening before. I then asked the Clerk whether he could carry on the business without them. He said he could not, without subjecting himself to such penalties as he would not expose himself to. I then took the opinions of my brother judges on the bench, seriatim, whether we might not legally adjourn to the 10th of April next, as there was no business before us. I was asked by one of the gentlemen whether I had received any particular instructions or directions how to act on this occasion. I replied I had not. Then the Court was unanimous that we might adjourn to the next court in course, which was accordingly done." [95]

There was more in the scene—an effort by Mercer to tender his resignation to the Governor who refused to accept it,[96] and the transfer of all the stamped papers to a war vessel as the sole depository safe from possible plundering by the colonials [97]—but that tableau in the General Court, and not later incident, was the ominous climax. "The first and most obvious consequences of all this," Fauquier reported, "must be the shutting up all the ports and stopping all proceedings in the courts of justice.[98] A few days later the optimistic Governor was wondering whether the colonials would stand fast: ". . . I am not without hopes that the distress the country will feel on a total stagnation of business will open their eyes and pave the way for the act's executing itself. For I am very credibly informed that some of the busy men in opposing the reception of the stamps are already alarmed at the consequences of the imprudent steps they have taken." [99]

[94] See also Fauquier's Report, *loc. cit.*, and cf. 17 V 325.
[95] Fauquier's Report, *op. cit.*, lxx.   [96] *Ibid.*, lxii.
[97] Fauquier to the Lords of Trade, Nov. 8, 1765; *Journ. H.B.*, 1761–65, p. lxxii.
[98] *Ibid.*, lxx.   [99] Letter of Nov. 8, 1765, *loc. cit.*

"Credibly informed," the Governor said he was. He might be concerning a few of the merchants, but not concerning the man who read of this at Mount Vernon, nor Patrick Henry whose imagination still flamed, nor that young student Jefferson whose heart had beaten high as he had listened to Henry cry, "Caesar had his Brutus . . ."

CHAPTER IX

Scandal in the Ruling Class Mars Repeal

(1766)

THE TEMPER displayed toward George Mercer and his stamps was warning that 1766 might prove a year of grim and stubborn contest in Virginia. As far as Washington could gauge the feeling of the people across the Potomac, it was no less fiery in Maryland. All he knew about conditions in other Colonies was what he read in the Gazettes. Plans for the year's crops at Mount Vernon and on the other farms had to be based on the possibility that no ships would be cleared, no debts would be collected, and no legal business of any sort transacted because no stamps would be purchased or used. To prevent the rusting of all the wheels of trade, the Stamp Act must be repealed. Every colonial must labor to that end. England must be brought to realize that the measure was as unenforceable as it was unjust. Should this effort prove vain, then Mount Vernon and every like plantation must produce the articles necessary for self-support. More cloth must be woven; the blacksmith shop must mend every broken tool and must hammer new implements from old iron. If nothing could be exported for sale unless the manifest carried stamps, then nothing would be imported. Master "Jackie" Custis's idolizing mother could order no more shining apparel for him; Miss "Patsy" could not have her long-delayed adornment; Messrs. Robert Cary & Co. must wait for their money, precisely as all Virginia creditors had to do.

In accordance with resolutions already formed, Colonel Washington did not undertake to grow any tobacco in 1766 on the Potomac, though he did not forbid his tenants doing so. He determined, instead, to increase his wheat and, at least experimentally, to continue with flax and hemp. In addition, as Capt. David Kennedy offered to rent the Bullskin plantation for £28 per annum, that gentleman should have it.[1] This would end all bother concerning hemp-breaking and tobacco-growing

---

1 *Ledger A*, folio 248; *Ledger B*, folio 22.

there. Still again, the schooner was finished and rigged and could be used during the spring for fishing and, later, for bringing needed plank from the Occoquan sawmill.[2] All in all, though the economy of the plantation, of Virginia and of most of the other Colonies had to be changed in event the Stamp Act were not repealed, the outlook was not hopeless. Unfavorable conditions would correct themselves if Parliament would abandon all direct taxes in frank realization that the Colonies would not yield, could not be made to do so, and would be quick and violent in dealing with any attempt by any of their own people to comply with the law.[3]

This was the view of most of Washington's neighbors and it found logical justification in a pamphlet Richard Bland issued in Williamsburg, an "Inquiry into the Rights of the British Colonies." Hot blood on the Rappahannock did not wait on Bland's fine distinctions. A merchant and shipowner of Hobbs Hole, Archibald Ritchie by name, boldly declared at the court in Richmond County during February that he intended to clear his wheat-laden [4] vessels on "stamped paper" and that he knew where he could get the stamps. The countryside was aghast and then enraged at the merchant's declaration. Everywhere along the Rappahannock the comment was the same: If merchants yielded, the Stamp Act could be enforced in part at least, and the right of exclusive colonial self-taxation would be destroyed. On the 27th of the month a number of prominent planters met at Leedstown to decide what they should do about Ritchie's defiance. They proceeded, Englishman-like, to formulate the principles on which they would act and they drew up these articles of association:

Roused by danger, and alarmed at attempts, foreign and domestic, to reduce the people of this country to a state of abject and detestable slavery, by destroying that free and happy constitution of government under which they

---

[2] 1 *Diaries*, 227.

[3] Washington's account books make it a relatively easy task to explain his activities in 1766. The one difficulty is in making plain his stand on the great event of the year, the repeal of the Stamp Act. Eight only of his letters of 1766 survive. With the single exception of the one of July 21 to Robert Cary & Co. (2 *G. W.*, 439), these letters do not concern public affairs. There consequently is danger of assuming too much or too little regarding his part in events. Nothing indicates conspicuous leadership by Washington, so long as the issue was one of debate and pamphlet writing, but it would be equally erroneous to suppose that he remained silent and irresolute at Mount Vernon, absorbed in his own affairs. He must be credited with conviction and with active participation but not with any preeminent part in resistance to the Stamp Act.

[4] The account in *Rind's Gazette* of May 16, 1766, does not state that the cargoes were of grain, but that information was added in the defence of Ritchie published in *ibid.*, May 30, 1766.

have hitherto lived,—We, who subscribe this paper, have associated, and do bind ourselves to each other, to God, and to our country, by the firmest ties that religion and virtue can frame, most sacredly and punctually to stand by, and with our lives and fortunes to support, maintain, defend each other in the observance and execution of these following articles.

First.—We declare all due allegiance and obedience to our lawful Sovereign, George the Third, King of Great Britain. And we determine to the utmost of our power to preserve the laws, the peace and good order of this Colony, as far as is consistent with the preservation of our constitutional rights and liberty.

Secondly.—As we know it to be the birthright privilege of every British subject, (and of the people of Virginia as being such,) founded on reason, law, and compact, that he cannot be legally tried, but by his peers, and that he cannot be taxed, but by the consent of a Parliament, in which he is represented by persons chosen by the people, and who themselves pay a part of the tax they impose on others. If therefore any person or persons shall attempt, by any action or proceeding, to deprive this Colony of those fundamental rights, we will immediately regard him or them as the most dangerous enemy of the community; and we will go to any extremity, not only to prevent the success of such attempts, but to stigmatize and punish the offender.

Thirdly.—As the Stamp Act does absolutely direct the property of the people to be taken from them without their consent expressed by their representatives, and as in many cases it deprives the British American subject of his right to trial by jury; we do determine, at every hazard, and, paying no regard to danger or to death, we will exert every faculty to prevent the execution of the said Stamp Act in any instance whatsoever within this Colony. And every abandoned wretch, who shall be so lost to virtue and public good, as wickedly to contribute to the introduction or fixture of the Stamp Act in this Colony, by using stamp paper, or by any other means, we will, with the utmost expedition, convince all such profligates that immediate danger and disgrace shall attend their prostitute purposes.

Fourthly.—That the last article may most surely and effectually be executed, we engage to each other, that whenever it shall be known to any of this association, that any person is so conducting himself as to favour the introduction of the Stamp Act, that immediate notice shall be given to as many of the association as possible; and that every individual so informed shall, with expedition, repair to a place of meeting to be appointed as near the scene of action as may be.

Fifthly.—Each associator shall do his true endeavour to obtain as many signers to this association as he possibly can.

Sixthly.—If any attempt shall be made on the liberty, or property of any associator for any action or thing done in consequence of this agreement, we do most solemnly bind ourselves by the sacred engagements above entered into, at the utmost risk of our lives and fortunes, to restore such associate to his liberty, and to protect him in the enjoyment of his property.

In testimony of the good faith with which we resolve to execute this association, we have this 27th day of February, 1766, in Virginia, put our hands and seals hereto.[5]

Then the new "associators" decided to make Ritchie sign a declaration that was duly drafted and approved. If he refused to subscribe, he was to be seized, stripped to the waist, and put in the pillory for an hour. In event that failed to convince him that he had sinned against his fellow-citizens, he was to be brought before the whole body of his outraged neighbors and customers for such further chastisement as they thought he deserved.

The next day, no less than 400 men assembled at Hobbs Hole—"Sons of Liberty" they called themselves in proud acceptation of the name Col. Isaac Barré had applied to the colonials during the original debate in the House of Commons on the stamp bill. While most of these wrathful Virginians waited in line on either side of the street in a little town, a committee went to Ritchie's house to demand that he sign the paper drawn up the previous day. At first Ritchie protested: Would not the gentlemen name a Committee to "reason with him on the subject?" No! His case had been passed upon, his punishment fixed. It was for him to say whether he would go willingly to the street where the other Sons of Liberty were waiting for him. Ritchie could not hesitate otherwise than at the risk of worse things to come. He went out, listened as the declaration was read to him, admitted on inquiry that it was just, and then, with his hat off, signed and swore to this paper:

Sensible now of the high insult I offered this County by my declaration at Richmond Court lately of my determination to make use of stamped paper for clearing out vessels; and having been convinced such proceedings will establish a precedent by which the hateful Stamp Act might be introduced into this Colony to the utter destruction of the Public Liberty, I do most submissively in the presence of the public sign the Paper meaning to show my remorse for having formed so execrable a Declaration and I do hereby solemnly promise and swear on the Holy Evangelist that no vessel of mine shall

[5] 2 *Meade*, 434–35. The original is in VHS.

clear on stamped paper; that I never will on any Pretence make use of Stamped Paper unless that use be authorized by the General Assembly of this Colony.

Archibald Ritchie.[6]

The most that anyone dared to say thereafter in Ritchie's defence was that, though not born in Virginia, he would go to as great lengths to serve the Colony as anyone reasonably could require, but that it was too much to expect him, with a wife and five tender children, to sacrifice £2800 sterling. If any gentlemen, said the apologist, would take the grain Ritchie had intended to ship, at the price he had paid for it, he would forego all profits and allow his vessels to rot at the wharf.[7]

This affair on the Rappahannock occurred at a time when the weather on the Potomac was abominably wet and disagreeable. Scarcely two fair days came together. Neither hoe nor plow could be put into the ground otherwise than to stir up mud.[8] It was a question whether public or private affairs had the gloomier cast. At Norfolk, Virginia, the Sons of Liberty resolved to use "all lawful ways and means" that Providence had put in their hands for preserving the right "of being taxed by none but representatives of their own choosing, and of being tried only by a jury of their own peers";[9] in London, the agents of the Colonies and some of the merchants were pleading before Committees of Commons for the repeal of the Stamp Act. Benjamin Franklin underwent examination at great length, by friends and by adversaries, before the House in Committee of the Whole and he won great praise by his answers. The prime distinction he drew in his argument was between a tax on commerce, imposed and accepted in the interest of the empire, and a direct internal tax on the American Colonies, levied without their consent. His climax had been full of warning so deftly phrased that it could not be resented.

"What," asked a friendly member, "used to be the pride of the Americans?"

"To indulge in the fashions and manufactures of Great Britain."

"What is now their pride?"

---

[6] *Rind's Gazette*, May 16, 1766.

[7] *Ibid.*, May 30, 1766. Ritchie either regained a measure of good will or else held a financially strong position in spite of this affair. In the autumn of 1772, he and John Tayloe had power of attorney for a firm of British merchants that had failed. See *Rind's Gazette*, Oct. 15, 1772.

[8] 1 *Diaries*, 223.

[9] This was Mch. 31, 1766; *Va. Gazette*, Apr. 4, 1766.

"To wear their old clothes over again, till they can make new ones." [10]

Other colonial agents and a number of merchants gave depositions, also, before a Committee of the Privy Council. Capel Hanbury, with whom Washington did some business, was pessimistic on the future of British trade in the Colonies his house served. He told the committee he did not see how Virginia and Maryland could pay the stamp tax with so small an amount of specie as was at their command. The act, he said, could not be enforced without troops. Even then, everything would be thrown into confusion. Normally, he went on, the colonials paid well enough to permit his house to carry on a large trade, but if the Stamp Act remained in force, he would be willing to sell his American accounts for half their face value.

"How could the people in Virginia and in Maryland pay if the Stamp Act was in execution?" a member inquired.

"I don't see it can be carried into execution," said Hanbury, and added grimly: "The collectors might turn merchants and sell the tobacco."

Again, he was asked: "If the act was to continue, in expectation of the distresses, would you execute the orders you have received?"

"Not if any part of it existed," answered Hanbury stoutly.

"What will be the remedy of these evils you have described?"

"First, a repeal of the Act. Anything short of a total repeal will be inadequate. A modification would not answer."

"Why?" the parliamentary inquisitor demanded.

"On account of the uneasiness of the inhabitants, [which]is so great that if force were used, they would repel force by force."

Presently the question was, "Would they act against the forces of Great Britain assisting the civil officers in execution of the law?"

Hanbury replied, "In the Stamp Act, I believe they would."

James Balfour—probably the same "Mr. Balfour" who had helped provide specie for General Braddock in 1755 [11]—testified on the basis of

[10] As reproduced fully in John Bigelow, ed., *The Works of Benjamin Franklin* (cited hereafter as *Bigelow's Franklin*) v. 4, 173–214, Franklin's testimony is probably the clearest and most persuasive of all the arguments against the Stamp Act, and likewise is the fullest summary of what the Colonies could do and were planning to do in order to free their industry of dependence on British imports. If the American cause in 1765 had to be rested on a single document, Franklin's testimony well might be that "Exhibit A." For the record of his appearance, see *Journ. House of Commons,* v. 30, p. 512, 513, 532.

[11] See Vol. II, p. 42 n. The *Va. Gazette* of Apr. 14, 1775, reported the death at Little England, near Hampton, of James Balfour, "an agent for the house of Mess. Hanbury & Co., of London."

long Virginia residence. In reply to an inquiry concerning the probable yield of the stamp tax in Virginia, he quoted estimates of £25,000 to £30,000 per annum.

"On whom would [the tax] fall?"

"Greatly," said Balfour, "on the lower class of people for they can neither buy nor sell but [that they are] affected by it, nor proceed in law proceedings [sic]. I, as executor, have obligations on bonds from 2 shillings upwards."

Someone wished to know whether the colonials' complaint over the Stamp Act was their first.

"I have been twenty-five years in America," Balfour answered, "and never heard of a more loyal, affectionate people." He remembered: "They before complained of acts made in 1763, but did nothing but complain, then submitted to the authority of the British Parliament, ever before held sacred."

"Should you continue any trade during the continuance of the Stamp Act?"

"I don't know how to answer," said the merchant, "for all is at stake, and I have large concerns there which I would not give 50 shillings for if the Act is not repealed."

"Will you carry back a freight of British merchandise if the Act is not repealed?"

"Not a farthing!" Balfour answered, "it would appear madness to do it as the people are in such confusion, but [I] will if the Stamp Act is repealed."

A member came back to a reply Balfour already had made: "Why do you think several thousand pounds in Virginia not worth fifty shillings?"

"Only on supposition of the present violence now going on." [Sic]

George Mercer was still another witness before the Committee. Like Balfour, he thought the burden of the stamp tax would fall most heavily on the poor because the great part of the taxes were "very trifling" in amount and would mean little to persons of wealth.

"Of what description of people?" a member pressed.

"From debtors of 3s to £5."

"Is there specie," he was asked, "to pay the tax in the Colony?"

Mercer answered that merchants had told him Virginia did not have specie to pay even a tenth part of what the Stamp Act would take every year.

Had Virginians ever thought of opposing any other tax or of coming to any such resolutions as those adopted against the Stamp Act?

"I never heard."

After being questioned concerning the probable yield of the Stamp Act, Mercer was subjected to inquiries distinctly personal. "Do you think yourself safe if you go back to Virginia and have given evidence in favor of the Stamp Act?"

"I should never think myself in danger in any part of the world from speaking the truth; then I should never be afraid anywhere."

Objection being raised, the question was rephrased: "Would you not be liable to danger on your return to Virginia if you gave evidence of favor of the Stamp Act there, or favor of continuance of any part of the Stamp Act?"

"I think I know the people there too [so?] well that they would not hurt me for speaking the truth. [I] certainly [am] not liable to damage for speaking the truth."

"Did you think yourself liable to damage for obeying the Act of Parliament when you accepted your office of stamp deliverer?"

"I did not then," Mercer replied, "but I find myself mistaken."

"Would you give [your giving?] evidence to a matter of fact here be equal to the same objection as acting as stamp officer?"

"Certainly."

"Were any officers insulted for carrying an act into execution?"

"Never."

"Do you think any modification of the Stamp Act will quiet the minds of the people?"

"From the humor I found and left them in," Mercer answered, "I think no moderation will do."

"What will be the result of enforcing the Stamp Act?"

"God knows!"

"What will be the consequence of repealing it?"

"I should think they would be totally satisfied and well pleased."

"Do you think the repeal would reduce them to their allegiance?"

"Indeed I think so," Mercer answered.

"If the Stamp Act is repealed," some member objected, "will they submit to any tax?"

"I never heard of any objection to any other act than this," Mercer replied, and then added cautiously, "but I can't look forward as to say what may happen."

"If any other tax, however light, would be laid, would they be contented?"

Mercer promptly made the distinction on which Benjamin Franklin already had laid much emphasis: "The grand objection was to any *internal* tax, and this is the only institution to which the Legislature has been opposed." [12]

The examination then shifted to the effect of the Stamp Act on prices and exchange. Mercer's answer on one aspect of this was impressive. The question has to do with the price of slaves. "I have given £80 for a working slave," the witness explained.

"When you came away, what was the price?"

"I saw some sold at £40 and £50, and I am told the lands are fallen in proportion."

Other witnesses were equally firm in saying that attempted enforcement of the Stamp Act would be calamitous and that nothing less than complete repeal would satisfy the Colonials or save the merchants. [13] Perhaps the most vehement cry of all was in a petition of the London merchants, who described the markets that had been created in the Colonies for British goods and the benefits that had been Britain's from commodities the Colonies had shipped in part payment for the products sent them. ". . . this commerce," the merchants told the Commons, "so beneficial to the State and so necessary for the support of multitudes, now lies under such difficulties and discouragements that nothing less than utter ruin is apprehended without the immediate interposition of Parliament." Several million pounds sterling were due the merchants by colonials who could not pay or make remittance. At the end, the merchants repeated the ugly word "ruin" that represented the superlative of disaster: "Your petitioners are by these unhappy events reduced to the necessity of applying to this Honorable House in order to secure

[12] Franklin's detailed replies concerning acceptance of "duties to regulate commerce" and objection to an internal tax appear in 4 *Bigelow's Franklin,* 183–84.

[13] 345 *Newcastle Papers,* Br. Mus. Add. MSS 33030. Apparently these interesting documents which are in bad physical condition, are notes of testimony or deposition, written by two distinct hands, as part of an effort to assemble the views of merchants who traded in one or more of all the Colonies. It may be that after the action of March 18, presently to be described, it was not thought worth while to make "clear copies" and to complete the record for publication. The papers, some of which are represented by *LC Transcripts,* are to be commended to those who wish to study the effects of the Stamp Act in the different Colonies.

themselves and their families from impending ruin, [and] to prevent a multitude of manufacturers from becoming a burden to the community or else seeking their bread in other countries . . ." [14]

Washington and the other Virginians did not hear promptly of any of this, but they learned that the Rockingham Ministry still held office and that friends of the Colonies were urging the repeal of the Stamp Act. There was hope but along with it was uncertainty. Commerce remained at a standstill in a manner different from anything the Virginians previously had known. During the French and Indian War, when idle ships had ridden with the shifting tides in Hampton Roads, even the most restive master knew that before many months a day would come when a gathering convoy could count gun muzzles in sufficient number to justify a start across the Atlantic even though French men-of-war lurked off the Virginia capes. Now the west wind might blow, the favoring tide might seem to wait on the skipper's word, above and below decks every hand might be steady, every head sober and every heart hungry for home. It was not enough. The boatswain might not blow his whistle. No hatch might be battened down, and no sail raised so long as a stamp had to be attached to the manifest.

Analogous conditions prevailed in the administration of the law. Planters assembled at the Court House, as usual, when the Justices were due to mount the bench; but if the members of the Court themselves attended, it usually was to protest to all comers that they would not hear a case or enter an order that required a stamp. Where Justices felt themselves obligated by their commissions and oaths to hold court, the answer to the crier's "Oyez, oyez" was not the tramp of waiting feet on the courtroom floor, but silence or sneers or defiant laughter. Woe then to the Scottish merchant who might venture to seek a judgment against even a notorious slippery debtor: The crowd would mutter, the Justices would look the plaintiff through, the Clerk would sputter that he had no stamps and dared not act without them.

Conversation was changed, too. When men of station were not talking of repeal of the act, their speech was of how to carry on the business of plantations in spite of it. Ladies of fashion had pride no longer in what they were importing from England but in what they were doing without. Refusal to send any orders whatsoever to Britain now was as sure a distinction as the ostentatious length and high cost of an invoice

14 *Ibid.*, folio 210.

of fine dress previously had been. On a large estate, the humble weaving hut became the most interesting place around the "great house." Farmers' wives who had learned how to finish a decent homespun suddenly found their counsel desired by wealthy planters who previously had done no more than bow a proud head condescendingly when meeting them at church. In range and depth of change, it was almost as if England had ceased to be "home" or even to exist. The enforced self-dependence of the frontier had become the voluntary law of life in Tidewater.[15]

In the midst of this period of protest and uncertainty, Washington had to make a journey in April to the Dismal Swamp with his brother-in-law, Fielding Lewis. Their ride from Fredericksburg southward carried them past some of the older estates at the very time the maples were leafing. Everywhere the questions must have been the same— Will the Stamp Act be repealed; what can we do to make the Ministry see that we will resist to the utmost? Although most of the planters repeated identical arguments, each man was educating himself by explaining to others his conception of the rights of freeborn Englishmen. The experience of 1764–65 was being duplicated. Again it could be said: Before the Stamp Act few of the Virginians ever had occasion to define rights that had been exercised so long that they were taken for granted; now those rights were proclaimed and extolled in order to justify the resistance on which the colonials already were resolved.

Washington and Lewis, listening and answering, passed through Williamsburg[16] and probably crossed the James to Hog Island and followed the road that led to Suffolk.[17] They found the Negroes apparently making sufficient progress to renew faith in the success and profit of the undertaking in the Great Dismal. So hopeful were the visitors, in fact, that they decided to purchase on their own account approximately 1100 acres of Marmaduke Norfleet's land on the southern side of the swamp, partly in Virginia and partly in North Carolina, for

---

[15] The meagreness of records for the period between May, 1765 and May, 1766, makes it difficult to describe with accuracy the extent of the revolt against the Stamp Act, but the few newspapers and resolutions that survive after almost 200 years suggest more of determination, anger and effort to build up colonial industry than has been assumed for any year prior to the "Associations." Everything indicates that 1765–66 was preparation for 1771 in Virginia as surely as 1771 was rehearsal of the Revolution.

[16] This is established by Washington's entry of the sum he paid for Lewis's expenses "from Fredericksbg to Wmsbg." (*Ledger A,* folio 193).

[17] The crossing to Hog Island doubtless was by Burwell's Ferry, sometimes known as Kingsmill Ferry. For the road to Suffolk, see Vol. I, p. 150.

£1200 Virginia currency.[18] It was another dangerously large obligation to be assumed at a time of perplexity by a man already in debt to his London merchant for a considerable sum; but Washington believed in the future of the swamp. When he believed in anything, he would stake his money on his judgment.

The early days of May brought developments that seemed to justify his and every man's faith in the future.[19] As if she were proud to be the messenger, the ship *Lady Baltimore* arrived in York River on the 2nd of the month with the news for which the entire Colony had been hoping: the Stamp Act had been repealed! After a resounding debate in which William Pitt was the strategist of all the argument against the measure, the House of Commons had voted to erase the offending tax from the statute books. Two hundred members were said to have carried the repeal bill to the Lords for their concurrence.[20] That had been on March 5. The Lords had followed with a furious discussion in which the logic of Lord Mansfield was overthrown and the bitterness of the Earl of Sandwich and of the Duke of Bedford was offset by the friendliness of Lord Shelburne, Lord Camden and the Duke of Grafton. It was a close contest. On the first division, the Lords voted fifty-nine to fifty-four for the execution of the Stamp Act, but in the end they accepted the repeal bill.[21] Royal assent was given March 18.[22] Merchants had been so confident this would be the action of Parliament that some of them already had started cargoes on the way to America.[23] The fulfilment of these hopes was celebrated by many of those who manu-

---

[18] Gates County, N. C., *Register's Office,* Book 64, p. 49.

[19] Unfortunately, it has not been possible to ascertain with absolute certainty where Washington was at the beginning of May. His Ledger entries (folio B 193) show the expenditure on his and Fielding Lewis's account of £3, 17s for "our expenses in Dismal Swamp," a sum sufficient to cover a stay of considerable duration. There is, also, an item of £47, 19s paid Lewis in cash on May 1. This suggests strongly though it does not prove positively that Washington still was in Lewis's company on that date and, therefore, presumably not North of Fredericksburg. Washington's diary is of no help on the question. Entries for April indicate that he was at Mount Vernon through the 13th. Thereafter, nothing appears until June 16; but this does not mean necessarily that he was absent during the whole of the interval. The gaps simply may indicate that he was neglecting his diary, as he frequently did. During June, for example, notes were made on three days only (1 *Diaries,* 226). If a guess were necessary, it might be that on May 1, Washington was leaving Lewis in Fredericksburg and was preparing to start home; but this could be no more than a guess.

[20] *Rind's Gazette,* May 16, 1766.

[21] This is a paraphrase of C. H. Van Tyne, *The Causes of the War of Independence,* p. 189–91. See *Journ. House of Commons,* v. 30, p. 609, 621; *Journ. House of Lords,* v. 31, p. 627.

[22] A convenient reprint of the repeal act appears in *Journ. H.B.,* 1761–65, p. lxxv. The King's speech on the repeal was published in *Rind's Gazette,* Sept. 5, 1766.

[23] Boston dispatch in *Rind's Gazette,* May 16, 1766.

factured, sold or carried goods. Pitt himself declared he "never had greater satisfaction than in the repeal of this Act."[24] Commercial England's gratification was as nothing compared with the jubilation of America.[25] Resistance had justified itself, one element proclaimed; faith in King and in Parliament, said others, had been vindicated. One of the Williamsburg papers reported: ". . . the rejoicing on occasion of the repeal of the Stamp Act—General illuminations, bells, bonfires, guns, fireworks—will be in duty and loyalty to the King and in respect and gratitude to Mr. Pitt and of [sic] the Illustrious Five who brought about the repeal."[26] In their praise of Parliament, the Virginians boxed the compass. The lawmakers of Westminster, denounced in 1765 as the destroyers of American liberty, now were accepted gratefully as the champions of colonial rights. Prediction was made that even the law of 1764, limiting the issue of paper money on the western side of the Atlantic, might be repealed.[27]

So completely were Washington's fellow-planters convinced of the sympathy of Parliament with the Colonies' interpretation of constitutional principles that scarcely any attention was paid in Virginia to a "Declaratory Act" that had been responsible, in part, for the willingness of the Lords to reverse their vote against repeal. The new measure, which was passed almost simultaneously with the repeal bill, referred to the assertion by the American Colonies of the exclusive right of taxing themselves. Then, in plain words, the Colonies were told they did not possess that right without qualification. Specifically, the Declaratory Act set forth that Crown and Parliament "had, hath and of right ought to have the full power and authority to make laws and statutes of sufficient force and validity to bind the Colonies and people of America, subjects of the Crown of Great Britain, in all cases whatsoever." Further, colonial proceedings of every sort that challenged or

[24] Basil Williams, *William Pitt*, v. 2, p. 200–01, quoted in Van Tyne, *op. cit.*, 191.

[25] The account in the *North Briton*, Apr. 19, 1766, of workmen's satisfaction over repeal was quoted in a supplement to *Va. Gazette*, Aug. 15, 1766. By that date, it was reported in Virginia that the Colonial Governors had been instructed to send back the stamped paper (*ibid.*). William Nelson wrote sagely: ". . . repeal of the Stamp Act hath put us into a good humor; it hath taken away the hateful cause of disgust and ill blood between the Mother Country and the Colonies which might have brought on the ruin of both; for believe me we are so connected in interest and mutual dependence on each other that we should have fallen together. So much justice, such moderation and tenderness shewn on the part of our most Great Sovereign, his Parliament and Ministers, cannot fail to procure the warmest returns of duty, gratitude and obedience" (Letter of July 26, 1766, to John Norton; *Nelson Letter Book*, 1).

[26] *Rind's Gazette*, May 16, 1766.

[27] *Ibid.* For the act, see *Penn Gazette*, July 12, 1764. It became effective Sept. 1, 1764.

disputed the powers of King and Parliament were "utterly null and void to all intents and purposes whatsoever."

This declaration might well have been interpreted as a warning by Commons and Lords to the American Colonies that the repeal of the Stamp Act was not to be regarded as an admission that the law itself was unconstitutional or that the provisions of it were arbitrary and tyrannical. Parliament, in fact, did more than assert full authority to do again what it voluntarily had undone: it served notice that it could and, if need be, would declare colonial laws of no effect—a power that previously had been exclusively the prerogative of the Crown. According to the theories of some Virginia lawyers, even the royal prerogative was limited to the extent that if a statute were put on the books by a colonial Assembly and were allowed by the Crown, it could not thereafter be nullified even by the King, otherwise than with the consent of the Assembly that had enacted it. Now Parliament declared itself empowered to put a colonial law aside without any restriction of time or circumstance.[28] This was minimized, if not ignored [29] by the leaders of the General Assembly who felt that everything they had said about the undoubted love of the King for his oldest dominion was borne out by the repeal of the Stamp Act. It mattered little, as they saw it, that powers had been declared that never would be exercised by Parliament.

It was tragic for the leaders of the General Assembly, and shocking to Washington that the news of the repeal should be followed on May 11 by the death of Speaker Robinson, who for so many years had seemed to exemplify good will. Death was not his worst fate. At the time of the attempt to pass a bill for the borrowing of £250,000 and for establishment of a loan office, there had been intimation that in his rôle of Treasurer, Mr. Speaker was in trouble of some sort. If its exact nature was known to any Burgesses, they were few. Others subsequently recalled that in December, 1764, when Richard Henry Lee had proposed that a committee be named to examine the Treasurer's accounts,[30] the

---

[28] Involved here but not clearly set forth in Virginia was what Jefferson later regarded as the sound principle modestly but logically expounded by his law teacher, George Wythe—that Britain and all the American Colonies were distinct and legislatively independent in government under the same King. See Jefferson to William Wirt, Aug. 14, 1814; 14 *Jefferson*, 168.

[29] Again it must be pointed out that the lack of a file of the *Virginia Gazette* of this period makes precise statement impossible. Perhaps significantly, the issue of July 11, 1766, contained a "computation of the number of inhabitants in each Colony and a proportion of duties which might be raised in each, in lieu of the Stamp Act." Virginia was credited with a population of 180,000 and was "charged" with £6000.

[30] *Journ. H.B.*, 1761–65, p. 305.

Speaker-Treasurer had appeared to be offended. His close friends manifestly had been disturbed,[31] too, but the resolution for the appointment of the committee had been passed in spite of this somewhat suspicious opposition. At the session of May, 1765, on the very day that Henry had introduced his resolutions on the Stamp Act, the special committee had reported briefly, "It appears that the said accounts are truly stated," and then the committee summarized in a few words the various balances. The approving action of the House was in seven words—"Resolved, that the said Accounts do pass." [32] In this the Council concurred [33] and thereby ended action without silencing tongues. Hints of heavy loans by Robinson were met with the question: Was he not rich enough in his own right to repay anything he borrowed or lent? He so completely personified wealth, station, benevolence and uprightness that corruption on his part was unthinkable.

Robinson was buried with honor and lament; Robert Carter Nicholas was named in his place as Treasurer.[34] In a short time the new official reported that Robinson was delinquent in some vast, undetermined sum, which enemies styled defalcation and apologists declared to be loans made to protect the estates of friends. In the general shortage of specie, they said, numerous planters of the very first station, Robinson's companions and fellow Burgesses, had found themselves unable to pay their debts and had appealed to him at a time when he had in his custody a balance of current funds that included valid paper money and, along with it, old issues called in but not yet burned as the law required. In return for their notes, duly secured, Robinson had permitted hard-pressed debtors to take this currency, which he expected them to be able to replace before the committee of Assembly came to count the balance and to destroy the retired paper. Virginia's favored panacea of a loan office probably had been invoked, in the bill Henry had defeated, to help debtors in general and Robinson and his friends in particular.

The dead Treasurer's friends stood squarely by him, some of them perhaps in self-defence, and they did not disclose the identity of those who had borrowed public funds. It was realized, of course, that at least

---

[31] See R. H. Lee, *Memoir of Richard Henry Lee*, v. 2, p. 21–23, quoted in *Journ. H.B.*, 1766–69, p. xii.

[32] *Journ. H.B.*, 1761–65, p. 357.

[33] *Ibid.*, 359. The accounts were referred in Council May 29, 1765, to Thomas Nelson and Robert Burwell who reported the next day that they had examined the Treasurer's accounts "and found them truly stated." (3 *L.J.*, 1347).

[34] Appointment was May 21. *Rind's Gazette*, May 30, 1766.

a part of the truth would be brought to light when the General Assembly convened. Meantime, the utmost possible was done to keep dark the details of so humiliating a fall by the topmost figure in the political structure of Virginia.[35] To Washington, the discovery of Robinson's shortage must have been particularly distressful. The Colonel had ceased to have intimate correspondence with "Mr. Speaker" after he left the military service of the Colony—indeed after the disbursement of the funds for the troops was vested in the Governor [36]—but he could not forget the kindness and encouragement Robinson had shown him when he was an inexperienced young officer. It seemed unbelievable that Robinson, the all-powerful, was dead and discredited!

The full measure of the former Treasurer's "debt to the public" was not known when, on June 6, 1766, Governor Fauquier formally proclaimed the repeal of the Stamp Act [37] and thereby gave justices and lawyers, merchants and planters the signal to go back to work and, if possible, to forget the Stamp Act. Washington was not sure to what influences the repeal was due, but he was convinced that difficult, even dangerous times had been escaped both for Britain and for the Colonies. He wrote his merchants: "The repeal of the Stamp Act, to whatsoever causes owing, ought much to be rejoiced at, for had the Parliament of Great Britain resolved upon enforcing it, the consequences I conceive would have been more direful than is generally apprehended both to the Mother Country and her Colonies. All therefore who were instrumental in procuring the repeal are entitled to the thanks of every British subject and have mine cordially." [38]

It was gratifying, on principle, to get rid of so provocative an issue, and doubly so because conditions at Mount Vernon called for the undiverted attention of the owner. The transfer from tobacco to wheat-growing was not easy. A controversy was brewing with Carlyle & Adam over the proper weight of wheat per bushel. That firm, moreover, was far from prompt in paying for the grain Washington already had delivered. Some acceptable lots in Alexandria, for instance, had

[35] The leaders of the time were so successful in keeping the Robinson affair from the public that there is, after almost two centuries, no adequate account of it. A few of the related documents and contemporary newspaper letters are given in the introduction to *Journ. H.B.*, 1766–69, p. xi-xxvi. Many of the essential papers are in the possession of David J. Mays, who will use them in his forthcoming study of Edmund Pendleton and probably in a later book on the Robinson defalcation.

[36] See Vol. II, p. 245.   [37] *Journ. H.B.*, 1761–65, p. lxxv.

[38] Letter of July 21, 1766, to Robert Cary & Co.; 2 *G. W.*, 440. The substance of this was repeated by Washington a year later in a communication to the Hanbury firm (*ibid.*, 466).

been his return in September, 1764, for the wheat crop of 1763.[89] Still again, information was discouragingly meagre concerning the growing and shipment of flax and hemp [40] and the collection of the bounty that had been offered by Parliament.[41] Goods from England were high in price and, sometimes, poor in quality or shipped without regard to specifications.[42]

Washington was having trouble, also, with some of his servants. He always had been exacting of men hired on yearly wage. If any of them lost time through illness or absence, it had to be made up,[43] a stern but perhaps a necessary provision of contract with those who, at the end of twelve months, could go elsewhere if they would. Tasks assigned bondsmen by Washington probably were no heavier than those fixed for the average slave, but either the Negro or the indentured servant was apt to find himself assigned to remote Bullskin or to gloomy Dismal Swamp. Valuable slaves were lost, too, by death or by running away.[44] As long previously as August, 1761, four slaves had disappeared simultaneously, and, as Washington had written in his advertisement, had done so "without the least suspicion, provocation or difficulty with anyone or the least angry word or abuse from their overseer." [45] Now there was trouble of an irritating sort with a field hand named Tom. He was strong, skillful with his hoe and sufficiently intelligent to serve as foreman, but he was a rogue and, in addition, had become addicted to the bad habit of slipping away at intervals. He would be caught and brought home but would again be an absconder. Washington decided that plantation discipline would be better if Tom were sold to the West Indies whither, of all places, Virginia Negroes most disliked to go. Tom accordingly was entrusted to Capt. Josiah Thompson of the schooner *Swift,* with instructions to transport him to the islands and "to sell him for whatever he will fetch," the proceeds to be devoted to specified quantities of rum, molasses, limes and other fruits and the balance in "good old spirits." Thompson was given Tom's record and

---

[39] 2 *G. W.,* 448 ff.

[40] *Ibid.,* 438.

[41] *Ibid.,* 439.

[42] *Ibid.,* 436, 440.

[43] Cf., as typical, the account of Jonathan Palmer; *Ledger A,* folio 294; *Ledger B,* folio 28. See, also, the transactions with Turner Crump, *supra,* p. 77.

[44] Cf. Washington to Carlyle & Adam, Feb. 15, 1767: ". . . God knows I have losses enough in Negroes . . ." (2 *G. W.,* 446).

[45] *Md. Gazette,* Aug. 20, 1761. The description of these Negroes shows how close Virginia slavery then was to Africa. One Negro had "a small face with cuts down each cheek, being his country marks." The teeth of another were "filed sharp." Two were "bought from an African ship in August, 1759, and talk very broken and unintelligible English."

was admonished to "keep him handcuffed till you get to sea, or in the Bay, after which I doubt not but you may make him very useful to you." The Negro, Washington said, should bring a good price "if kept clean and trimmed up a little when offered for sale." [46]

Within less than two months after Tom was on his way to be exchanged for molasses, rum and spirits, there was another disagreeable affair, this time with a ship captain, Joshua Pollard by name, who put five hogsheads of Washington's tobacco on a barge in the bottom of which twelve to fifteen inches of rainwater accumulated while the tobacco was aboard. Instead of having the extent of the damage determined immediately, the master loaded the tobacco on the ship from the barge and then put the hogsheads in the hold. Washington did not learn of the incident until it was too late to get the tobacco out of the vessel for re-inspection. As the captain refused to make a reasonable settlement, Washington could do no more than report the matter to the merchant in the hope of being repaid for the damage.[47]

The unpleasantness of these incidents found its place in letters and ledger-entries; the happiness of domestic life left no record except in the heart. Private life was better, not worse—even though another scandal in the ruling class was added to that of Speaker Robinson. It was not so great a scandal but it affected the distinguished Northern Neck name of Lee. In Rind's *Virginia Gazette* of July 18, 1766, appeared an anonymous article signed "Enemy to Hypocricy." This reminded the public that George Mercer had gone to England in July, 1763, after having served Virginia for ten years, and that he had taken with him the formal recommendation of the General Assembly, who instructed the Colony's agent to assist him. Mercer, the article continued, had polite reception and generous entertainment. He was preparing to return home when, after the passage of the Stamp Act, he received without solicitation what appeared to be the "genteel appointment" of Stamp Distributor for Virginia. Because he accepted, he was burned in effigy in the Old Dominion. The man most responsible for this, the first man to cry "Rogue" at Mercer was himself the "greatest rogue of all": Col. Richard Henry Lee, who assailed Mercer for taking the post of Distributor of Stamps, had himself solicited the office in October, 1764, with the plea that he had a large family and a small

[46] Letter of July 2, 1766; 2 *G. W.*, 437.
[47] 2 *G. W.*, 441–42, 443–44.

fortune. Councillor Richard Corbin had offered at that time to secure the place for Lee.[48]

That was a shock to the Sons of Liberty! If the charge was true, it meant that Lee had sought a lucrative office he had tried to persuade Parliament not to create. At the time he shared in drafting an address to the King and like appeals to Lords and to Commons, his application for the hateful post of stamp act publican may have been before the Board of Trade. His participation in the burning of an effigy of Mercer was spiteful as well as hypocritical. So said surprised and unfriendly critics.

Fortunately for his future good name, Lee met this accusation with candor. He wrote the editor of the *Gazette*: "Early in November 1764, I was for the first time informed by a gentleman of the intention of Parliament to lay a stamp duty in America, with a friendly proposition on his part to use his interest for procuring me the office of Collector. I call it friendly, because I believe the gentleman, no more than myself, or perhaps a single person in this country had at that time reflected in the least on the nature and tendency of such an act. Considering this only in the light of a beneficial employment, I agreed the gentleman should write, and did also write myself, enclosing my letter to a gentleman now in this country. It was but a few days after my letters were sent away that reflecting seriously on the nature of the application I had made, the impropriety of an American being concerned in such an affair struck me in the strongest manner and produced a fixed determination to exert every faculty I possessed both in public and private life to prevent the success of a measure I now discovered to be in the highest degree pernicious to my country. I considered that to err is certainly the portion of humanity, but that it was the business of an honest man to recede from error as soon as he discovered it, and that the strongest principle of duty called upon every citizen to prevent the ruin of his country, without being restrained by any consideration that should interrupt this primary obligation." [49]

This satisfied Richard Henry Lee's friends but not his adversaries and certainly not John and James Mercer, the father and brother of the man who had been abused for accepting the position that Lee, however briefly, had sought. The two of them pounced on Lee's statement that

---

[48] *Rind's Gazette*, July 18, 1766; *Va. Gazette*, July 18, 1766.

[49] Letter of July 25, 1766, to the editor, printed in *Rind's Gazette* of Aug. 8, 1766 and republished in *Ballagh, Lee Letters*, v. 1, p. 16 ff.

at the time he applied for the collectorship no person in Virginia had understood the "nature and tendency" of a prospective Stamp Act. They undertook to demonstrate that when Lee attempted to get the office, Virginians had been put on notice by a letter from a committee of the Massachusetts Assembly that the American Colonies were about to be subjected to internal taxation of a specified character by the British Parliament. As brevity was not among the virtues of the Mercer family, a long controversy began.[50] It soon was lost in distinctions and abstrusities of a sort in which Colonel Washington had little interest, but it was an unhappy indication of differences of opinion within a dominant class that previously had few rivalries other than those of ostentation and of land patenting.[51]

Some of the discussion of the Robinson case was of like purport. "A Prophecy from the East," printed in Rind's *Virginia Gazette* parodied the form of Scripture and told of those who extolled benevolence: "And they shall write about it and they shall call peculation Benevolence, and they shall say it is a very great virtue and of great service to the public. And they shall say, let us write about Patriotism—And they shall write about Patriotism and they shall praise it and they shall say it is a very fine thing and that it will make a man guilty of Malversation and ruin his Country." [52]

"Ruin" did not seem the appropriate word for a time when America had been delivered from the certain confusion and the possible chaos the Stamp Act might have created; but there could be no denying the acute distress that Robinson's defalcation had brought to some of the planters who had been piling up debt because they insisted on living beyond their means. While details had not yet been made public, it might be that the sureties as well as the heirs of the dead Treasurer would be compelled to part with thousands of acres and hundreds of slaves to make good the difference between the amount of his deficiency and the value of his estate. Still again, if it were true, as generally reported, that Robinson had lent the Colony's money to hard-pressed planters, then, of course, the administrators of his estate would collect

[50] See an interesting note on this in 10 *V* 1 ff. W. G. Stanard there pointed out that the dispute of 1766 brought to light some obscure facts concerning the adoption in 1764 of the address to the King, the memorial to the Lords, etc.

[51] This statement concerning the political solidarity of the governing class in Virginia seems entirely justified, but it may have been that unity prevailed chiefly because the years before 1763 had developed few issues over which the lawyers and the leading planters and merchants could disagree. Perhaps the times were amicable rather than the men amiable.

[52] *Rind's Gazette*, Aug. 15, 1766, supplement. The erratic capitalization is preserved.

as much as they possibly could on these accounts. That might involve still more bankruptcies and more appeals to the General Assembly for special acts to dock entails.

Washington had at least two of these entrapments of great planters recorded on his own books. Thomas Moore, a borrower from the Custis estate prior to Washington's marriage, had become more and more involved, but Speaker Robinson had come to his help and, in June, 1760, had written Washington that he would be responsible for the debt, which Moore hoped to discharge within six months.[53] Actually ten times six months had passed without a settlement. Now that Robinson was dead and his estate overwhelmingly involved, his security for Thomas Moore was valueless. Both Thomas and his brother Bernard, in fact, were ruinously in debt to Robinson. At a later date, Thomas's obligation to the Robinson estate was put at £3442 and Bernard's at £8500.[54]

On behalf of the Custis estate, Washington had either to sue Thomas, get judgment and have it executed, or else extend the loan and let the unpaid interest be added to the debt. Where the lack of specie was almost universal, Washington had no assurance that buyers could be found for a part of Moore's estate otherwise than at the sacrifice of property worth several times the sum of £1400 and accumulated interest. Although Moore professed himself ashamed to ask for further leniency, Washington regarded forbearance as one of the prices of survival in a day of financial woe, and he extended the loan of Thomas Moore. The account of Bernard Moore, which had given Washington concern for a number of years, now became even more of a risk to the Custis estate. After 1761, this member of the Moore family was chronically delinquent in his interest on his debt of £1400,[55] and he showed in more ways than one that an extension of time would not of itself enable him to clear his obligation. Pressed by many creditors and unable to collect any considerable part of the large sums due him, Bernard Moore had to face the possibility of selling out.[56]

---

[53] 3 *Hamilton*, 187.

[54] These figures are supplied most courteously by David J. Mays from the *Pendleton Papers*.

[55] 3 *Hamilton*, 287, 288; *Ledger A*, folio 142, 151, 204.

[56] 3 *Hamilton*, 291–92. Financial records left by the Moores are so meagre that it is impossible to state the reasons for their distress. It may have been due to speculation or, on the other hand, to nothing more than the chronic overspending of large families that undertook to support English living on Virginia tobacco. Each of the Moores had borrowed £1400 of Custis money.

In this atmosphere of public relief and of private distress—of satisfaction over the repeal of the Stamp Act and of dismay over the spread of individual misfortune—the new Burgess from Fairfax received the usual summons to Williamsburg: Governor Fauquier had set a date for a session of the General Assembly in March, then in May, then in July, and once again in September, but he postponed it until November,[57] when farmwork would be over, except for hog-killing, and planters would have time for the leisured discussion of the diversified laws a disturbed but growing Colony required.

Washington went in style this time, with coach-and-six [58] and no doubt with Martha and the children.[59] He found himself immediately on the scene of a vigorous contest for the office of Speaker, vacated by the death of Robinson. As the Governor months previously had named a Treasurer who had his hands full without presiding over the House, an oft-discussed separation of the two offices was almost automatic; but the potentates were divided over a choice between Peyton Randolph and Richard Bland. "Mr. Attorney" was nominated by Archibald Cary. The qualifications of Richard Bland were extolled by Richard Henry Lee, who apparently had resolved that he would not permit the criticism of the Mercers to deter him from seeking leadership on the floor of the House. While sponsorship by Lee made Bland in some measure the candidate of the younger members,[60] the line that had been drawn in the contest over the Stamp Act was not renewed. Both Randolph and Bland were of the same dominant type of Burgess—Randolph 45 and Bland 56—and both had opposed Henry's resolutions the previous year. The majority were for Randolph,[61] who proceeded at once to take the chair and to organize the House. First action of all was a unanimous vote for the appointment of a committee of eleven to examine the state of the Treasury and, in particular, to scrutinize all receipts and to check all issues of Virginia paper money after 1754. Bland was named chairman with ten associates, including Patrick Henry, from among the ablest members of the House. Pendleton alone of the leaders was not

[57] *Va. Gazette*, Aug. 15, 1766; *Journ. H.B.*, 1766–69, p. 5–10.
[58] *Ledger A*, folio 191.
[59] As the Custis House in Williamsburg had been leased, the probability is that Martha stopped at Eltham to visit her sister, Mrs. Burwell Bassett, and went to crowded Williamsburg for the principal social affairs only; but there is nothing in Washington's accounts to show where the family stayed.
[60] Lee was only one month older than Washington.
[61] *Journ. H. B.*, 1766–69, p. 11. Unfortunately, the vote is not given.

selected because he was one of the administrators of Robinson's estate. Washington was not a member either, but he was not counted as yet among the most influential Burgesses.

The committee soon ascertained that representatives of Robinson's heirs were seeking to find out substantially what the House wished to know and, consequently, the committee stood aside until the agents of the estate had completed their work. It developed that the settlement submitted by Robinson in December, 1764, was not current but was of October 10 and was erroneous besides. The committee had to go back in Robinson's accounts to April, 1755, from which date it followed all the issues of treasury notes, all the collections and all the major disbursements—a long and troublesome task. Without attempting to pass on the Treasurer's right to certain commissions he had charged against the Colony, the committee concluded that the balance due by Robinson was £100,761. Time would be required, the committee reported, to ascertain how errors in the accounts were to be corrected, how justice was to be done, and how satisfaction was to be given the defrauded public. The committee asked therefore that it be allowed to proceed during the recess of the Assembly.

Immediately after the filing of the committee's report, Edmund Pendleton presented a memorial on behalf of the administrators of Robinson's estate. The substance of this was that the £100,761 due by Robinson as Treasurer for taxes received by him "was re-emitted and lent out to sundry persons, from whom the same is now due." Robinson, at death, was creditor to a total of £105,000, of which £12,000 could not be recovered. On his private account, Robinson owed at the time of his death about £3500 and was surety for others in the sum of approximately £20,000. His lands were estimated to be worth £11,000; his interest in a number of mines, including two of copper, was reckoned—most extravagantly—at £8000. In addition, he had a share in the Dismal Swamp enterprise and he owned about 400 slaves.[62] His security for the faithful discharge of his duties was £190,000. The public, therefore, ultimately would recover the amount of the deficiency, Pendleton said, but when money was as scarce as it was at the time, rigorous measures for the quick sale of the estates of persons in debt to Robinson might ruin many families and might defeat their own end.

[62] Although the committee did not so state, these slaves could be considered as worth £30 per capita, young and old, able-bodied and children; so that the gross was roughly £12,000, or more than the assumed value of the lands owned by Robinson.

For these reasons, the administrators asked three years in which to settle, and they requested further that they be authorized by law to sell such parts of Robinson's real and personal estate as they thought proper.[63]

The Assembly was loath to prolong the period during which the Colony might be crippled by the defalcation. After discussion in Committee of the Whole, the decision was, first, to request the Governor to institute suits against Robinson's estate, and, second, to instruct the Attorney General, after obtaining judgment against Robinson's securities, not to issue executions in a larger sum than was necessary to make good the difference between what Robinson owed and what his estate would yield.[64] An act granting substantially everything requested by the administrators was passed, except that the sale of Robinson's mining lands was assigned to trustees of the public.[65] Still another statute required the new Treasurer to collect taxes and balances that were due the Colony [66] but had been allowed by Robinson to remain in the hands of negligent county Sheriffs. These measures were thought to compass all that could be done at the moment to recover the £100,000 of which the people had been defrauded.[67] The initial legislation appeared to be prompt and uncompromising, but the humiliation persisted: through Robinson, the integrity of the ruling class had been assailed.

Washington bore his part of responsibility for the decisions in the Robinson case but he took advantage of his proximity to the Dismal Swamp to procure leave of absence during the session and to visit the new enterprise for a week.[68] He felt no compunction about quitting Williamsburg temporarily, because he went November 20–26, while the House was transacting routine business and was awaiting the report on Robinson.[69] Even in the swamp, Washington had proof of the wide reach of Robinson's liability. In the outworking of plans for the shareholders to supply slaves for draining the swamp, the Negroes sent to the Great Dismal by Robinson had proved less valuable, in terms of market price, than those of Washington and perhaps of other members

---

[63] *Journ. H. B.,* 1766–69, p. 65–67.   [64] *Ibid.,* 70, 72.
[65] 8 *H* 270–71.   [66] *Ibid.,* 211–12.
[67] By April, 1768, the debt of Robinson, including interest, was £109,335, odd money. (*Journ. H.B.,* 1766–69, p. 154–55.)
[68] *Ibid.,* 33.
[69] Washington served during this session on the Committee on Privileges and Elections and also on the Committee on Propositions and Grievances, *ibid.,* 14, and, on motion, delivered to the Governor the Burgesses' address for two special writs of election (*ibid.,* 22). He likewise was one of several to whom was entrusted a measure concerning certain entailed lands of Ralph Wormeley (*ibid.,* 54).

of the company. Consequently Robinson had paid the master of Mount Vernon nearly £53 to cover the difference.[70] There had now to be adjustments and preparations for the purchase of Robinson's interest, by the remaining partners in the undertaking.[71] In addition, many details had to be arranged in the settlement of accounts with Marmaduke Norfleet, from whom Washington and Fielding Lewis had bought the land near the Virginia-North Carolina line.[72] Washington was not discouraged by any of this. He continued to believe that drainage would make the swampland prodigiously fertile. All money devoted to the work would prove an investment of high value.

It was pleasant to look forward to the development of new, rich farms because some of those on the Potomac still seemed to rebel against anything that was planted after the plow had passed over. Washington now owned 9581 acres of land on which he was paying quit rents of 2s 6d per hundred acres—a total that did not include any of the plantations acquired through Martha.[73] On those Custis farms along the York and the Pamunkey, Joseph Valentine that year had grown sufficient tobacco to fill seventeen hogsheads for Washington and fifty-one for "Jackie" Custis [74]—distinctly a "short" crop. From the Potomac, Washington received none of the staple other than the "rent tobacco" which eight tenants had raised.[75] This leaf continued so poor in quality and sold so much below the market that Washington was considering a transfer of tenants' contracts to a cash basis, even though the failure of the new lessee of Bullskin to forward his rent [76] was a warning that annual monetary payments were more readily pledged than made. The wheat crop of 1766 had been good, but neither the yield nor the weight had been exceptional.[77] Nor were relations with the purchasers, Carlyle & Adam, marked by any closer approach to the spirit of full

[70] *Ledger A,* folio 194. This appears to have been in 1764 but the contra entry is not clear. The entire episode, indeed, is obscure. The explanation may be that Washington and Robinson, as owners of large numbers of slaves, agreed for a consideration to supply jointly all the Negroes needed in the swamp.

[71] *Ledger A,* folio 194.

[72] Norfleet had supplied wheat, sows, beef and corn for the Negro hands sent to work at or close to Norfleet property. See settlement of Nov. 22, 1766, covering £90, 10s; *Washington MSS,* Huntington Library.

[73] A table of these quit rent lands is reproduced in 2 *G. W.,* 436.

[74] *Custis Papers,* VHS.

[75] *Ledger A,* folio 250. Cf. 2 *G. W.,* 442, 454.

[76] *Ledger A,* folio 248.

[77] The figures are missing from Washington's accounts, which cover most of the years of his contract with Carlyle & Adam, but there is nothing in Washington's correspondence to indicate that the crop was unusual. Landon Carter had complained that the grass was late in his neighborhood because of the "prodigious dry years" prior to 1766. His Diary for the year was written into the printed *Virginia Almanac.*

friendliness that Washington desired.[78] Once again, if Washington had sought or had needed consolation, he would have found it in the delights of home life and in the knowledge that Mount Vernon was better equipped every year. If money could be made at any time, through any crop, on the thin land of the area adjacent to Hunting Creek, Washington now had the slaves and the implements to make it as soon as he could determine over a period of normal years, which crops did best there. At the moment, wheat seemed much the most promising, despite the light weight of the grain.

He was becoming more and more rooted into the life of the Potomac. Seven years of almost constant residence on the river had increased his love of his land and waterfront and also his interest in the advancement of the simple institutions of Fairfax County and of Alexandria. On the death of George Johnston,[79] who was one of the trustees of the town, Washington was named in his place. At first, he hesitated to accept[80] but in the end he decided to do so and in that manner strengthened associations that went back to the days when, as a youthful surveyor, he had run the lines of the lots. He had not lost that old interest in surveying. If a new farm was purchased, or a check on the area of a given field was needed, he took out his compass and his Jacob's staff and returned for a day to his first vocation. A little later he undertook in person the survey of a road that was to be opened from Dogue Run to Colchester.[81]

Another continuing, perhaps increasing, interest was in the affairs of Truro Parish. Now that he was a vestryman, he had duties which, as always, he discharged with care and diligence. Dr. Charles Green having died in 1765, Rev. Lee Massey became minister[82] and proceeded to appeal for the erection of a new church. As the vestry concurred, the decision was to erect the structure "on the middle ridge near the Ox Road, the ground to be laid off by Mr. Edward Payne et al,[83] on land belonging to Mr. Thomazen Ellzey, who being present, consents to the

---

[78] This will be more apparent in the next chapter.

[79] He died Aug. 31, 1766 (*Md. Gazette*, Sept. 14; *Va. Gazette*, Sept. 19, 1766). For his testament, with an unhappy echo of family discord, see *Fairfax Wills*, B, 1, p. 432.

[80] Cf. 2 *G. W.*, 444 n.

[81] *Ledger A*, folio 262. This was in 1767. No details are available other than that of "expense in surveying" the road.

[82] *Truro Parish Vestry Book*, Feb. 3–4, 1766.

[83] This is the reason the structure often was styled "Payne's Church," though the more familiar, if confusing name, until the erection of the edifice at Pohick in 1772, was "the upper church." Washington's brother Samuel at this same period was engaged with the other warden of St. Paul's Parish, King George County, in procuring bids for a new church there (See *Rind's Gazette*, July 18, 1766).

same." [84] Edward Payne agreed to build the church for £579 Virginia
currency; Washington was one of five named to "view and examine"
the structure at intervals.[85] The master of Mount Vernon was designated also to handle the parish collection [86] and, with George William
Fairfax, to sell the parish tobacco for the payment of the minister and
for the erection of the new place of prayer.[87] Theirs, too, was responsibility for auctioning the glebe and the plate of the old parish.[88] In sign-
ing these accounts, Washington soon was authorized to write "Warden"
after his name. That honor came to him and to his neighbor, Col.
George William Fairfax, in 1766, when Washington was approaching
his thirty-fifth birthday, the half-way mark to three score and ten. Life
was ordered, life seemed full.

[84] *Truro Parish Vestry Book*, Feb. 3–4, 1766. The donor's correct name was Tomison
Elzey.
[85] *Ibid.*   [86] *Ledger A*, folio 224.
[87] *Truro Parish Vestry Book; Ledger A*, folio 259.
[88] The glebe included approximately 400 acres. (*Va. Gazette*, Mch. 19, 1767).

CHAPTER X

A Land Hunter Writes a Grim Word
(January, 1767–April, 1769)

PLANS FOR 1767 at Mount Vernon were explicit. No tobacco was to be grown by Washington on any of his Potomac farms, though eight or ten of the "renters" would continue to pay, for the time being, in leaf. The main crop was to be wheat. Under the contract with Carlyle & Adam, all that grain grown by Washington would be delivered to that firm; but as the mill on Dogue Run was now operating smoothly on a moderate scale, it could grind the wheat of other planters from whom Washington might buy flour as well as take toll.[1] A flour business, in fact, might develop profitably from enlarged wheat growing. Besides, more corn would be planted on land where it flourished better than tobacco or wheat did. Experiments with hemp and flax would be continued for another year.[2] The finished schooner could be used in fishing and, when not needed for other purposes, might be chartered by planters or shipmasters.

Weaving would be the farm industry Washington would develop most vigorously, because the shortage of specie with which to purchase English cloth had increased the demand for every sort of homespun. Washington had hired a weaver, Thomas Davis, to begin work on the 1st of January, 1767. Like every other free tradesman employed at Mount Vernon, he must be made to earn his pay.[3] The same was true of Mrs. Lettice Corbin's Negro bricklayer who had been hired in 1766 at £25 per annum.[4] So much work had to be done in this trade that if a bricklayer could be picked up at a reasonable figure from some cargo of indentured servants, or if a handy slave of that craft were offered at a sale, he might be a good investment.[5] The carpenters would be sawing

---

[1] Washington credited himself (*Ledger A*, folio 249), with £200 on account of flour in 1767.
[2] 1 *Diaries*, 236.   [3] Weaving Book; 390 *Papers of G. W.*, LC.   [4] *Ledger A*, folio 205.
[5] Such a purchase was made July 25, 1768 (1 *Diaries*, 278). Needless to say, Washington was by no means unique in looking on human flesh as a marketable commodity to be judged and appraised as any other would be.

and hammering daily, and if time could be found, they might erect a
barn on the Neck Plantation, where one was needed.[6] Timbers for it
were ready, though somewhat warped from long exposure to the elements.[7] Along with all these enterprises, there would of course be vigorous prosecution of the bold venture of draining Dismal Swamp; and,
needless to say, if fine western land could be found at a low figure, it
must be purchased, even though Robert Cary & Co. had to wait a little
longer for the balance due them. These plans were followed in 1767
with few disappointments. To be sure, when the time came to sift the
Dogue Run wheat that had been in the barn since the harvest of 1766,
Lund was distressed to find how much dirt there was in it and how few
bushels it yielded;[8] but, in general, everything went as well during the
late winter and spring as the average experienced planter, being inherently cautious, could expect during a normal year.

In February, Washington went to Williamsburg on business of the
Custis estate,[9] and in mid-March he had to attend another session of the
House of Burgesses. It did not prove exciting. Perhaps the report that
created most talk was another on the state of Treasurer Robinson's
accounts, which showed a payment to the Colony of only £553 by his
administrators. His outstanding delinquency, recomputed, was set
down as slightly over £102,000.[10] On this debt to the public, the Assembly resolved that his estate must pay interest at 5 per cent.[11] By a separate
measure, his administrators received the desired authorization to dispose
simultaneously of some of Robinson's lands and of a part of his slaves,
instead of auctioning all the bondsmen before offering any of his real
estate. This substitute policy was pursued in order that there might be a
sufficient number of Negroes left to till such lands as remained unsold
for any length of time.[12]

The familiar, the almost unendurable shortage of money that made
the sale of Robinson's property slow and expensive was the subject of
an attempt at elaborate relief legislation. This followed the main lines
of the two earlier proposals for a loan office, though the patrons undertook to simplify the scheme and to remove some of the previous objec-

---

[6] It was built that year. See Lund Washington to George Washington, Aug. 17, 1767;
Mount Vernon MSS. Lund's occasional letters of this period are the most illuminating of all
accounts of operations on the home plantations.

[7] *Ibid.*

[8] Lund Washington to George Washington, Mch. 22, 1767; *Mount Vernon MSS.*

[9] Cf. 2 *G. W.*, 444.   [10] *Journ. H.B.*, 1766–69, p. 120.

[11] *Ibid.*, 108.   [12] *Ibid.*, 112, 123, 130; 8 *H* 272.

tions. The House passed the measure with less protest than might have been expected [13] and named immediately a conference committee to explain it to the upper branch of the General Assembly. Washington was one of the six managers for the House—the first time in nine years of service that he had been named to a conference committee on any important bill. He and his colleagues found the Council willing to name managers and to confer, but not to approve.[14] Perhaps the Councillors disagreed with less compunction because the issuance of paper money depended not only on success in procuring a loan in England but also on the highly improbable grant of royal permission to print additional currency which Parliament had forbidden the Colonies to issue as legal tender.[15] Fundamentally, the objection was the one Henry had urged two years previously—that public loans to private individuals might encourage extravagance and aggravate the very condition they were designed to correct.[16] The day the Council said "No" to these proposals, April 11, the Governor signed the remaining bills of the session and prorogued the Assembly.[17]

Washington again found proximity a good occasion for another visit to Dismal Swamp,[18] and he arranged, also, for advertising a lease of the Custis plantation near Williamsburg.[19] Then Washington went home and, among other things, renewed a controversy with Carlyle & Adam. While in Williamsburg in February he had written at great length to the partners concerning the interpretation of his wheat contract with them. The issue was that of weight per bushel or, specifically, whether deduction in price was to be made if the wheat fell below an arbitrary weight, which had not been specified in the original agreement. Contention was sharpened because the merchants had written Washington bluntly that they "had rather be £1000 in any other gentleman's debt than the trifling sum of £100" in debt to him.[20] This reference to his close col-

---

[13] *Journ. H.B.*, 1766–69, p. 115–16, 125–28.

[14] 3 *L.J.*, 1376.

[15] Strictly speaking the act of 1764 (*Statutes at Large*, v. 26, p. 103) accomplished its purpose by forbidding colonial assemblies (1) to make future issues of paper money legal tender and (2) to extend the life of outstanding note issues.

[16] One is tempted to compare the various "loan office" proposals, as far as they are known, but the matter is more a part of the economic history of Virginia than of the biography of George Washington.

[17] *Journ. H.B.*, 1766–69, p. 131.   [18] *Ledger A*, folio 194.

[19] *Va. Gazette*, Apr. 2 and 16, 1767. This advertisement contained a somewhat detailed account of the property. In *Rind's Gazette*, Jan. 5, 1769, appeared an offer of Custis lands adjoining the Governor's pasture and the property of John Coke.

[20] The language is Washington's quotation from the merchants' letter which seems to have disappeared. See 2 *G. W.*, 451.

lecting did not, said Washington "POSITIVELY give me a moment's concern," and he carefully shaped the word in capitals. He explained: "I have asked you for nothing but my due, for nothing that I do not need, nay for nothing that I have not suffered for want of . . ." As for his own settlements with them, "to pay a just debt never fails to fill me with as much pleasure as to receive one." [21] He had concluded his Williamsburg letter with an offer to "let sensible and honest men, concerned with neither party, take the contract and judge from thence the payments and plain stubborn facts such as can be incontestably proved on both sides." On this he now stood.[22]

Next began a singular controversy involving the estate of Rev. Charles Green. Late in life, that gentleman had signed a careful deed of trust for the benefit of his wife, but on his death in the summer of 1765 [23] had left a singular loosely-drawn holographic will from which he had stricken three sections with a pen. His principal bequests were to his elderly wife, Margaret. Should she remarry, she was to make provision for her sister. In every other particular, the widow was the legatee of all his property in America. The deed of trust previously made for her was continued in force. Any property that might have been left Green in Ireland was to go to his sisters. It was so strange a testament that its validity was questionable, but John Mercer considered it "on the whole" a sound instrument,[24] and the court of Fairfax admitted it to record and certified it for probate.[25] In due time, Washington and Bryan Fairfax were named temporary trustees for Mrs. Green [26] and were placed under bond.

They soon found that their direct trusteeship would be of brief duration, because Dr. William Savage, who lived at or near Dumfries,[27] laid siege to the lady's heart and fortune and won both. At some date prior to Apr. 25, 1767, Mrs. Green became Mrs. William Savage. The doctor

---

[21] Ibid., 451–52.

[22] Ibid., 452. No record of arbitration has been found. As Washington continued to deliver wheat until the termination of the contract and thereafter sold the firm some flour, it is to be supposed that an amicable settlement was reached. Students who may wish to follow Washington's activities as a grain-grower and miller should perhaps be warned concerning the firm names. Carlyle & Adam, the shipping firm, ultimately (1771) became Robert Adam & Co., which apparently had a parent concern styled Adam & Co. The affiliated retail establishment, from which Washington made some purchases, was Carlyle & Dalton.

[23] His will was probated Aug. 17, 1765.   [24] 2 G. W., 453.

[25] Fairfax Wills, B, 1, p. 398.

[26] Existing records do not show whether they became substitute trustees under the original deed of trust, though this is the natural assumption.

[27] Thus far, he has defied identification. He is not mentioned in Blanton and he could not have been any of the men of that name indexed in Swem.

assumed promptly the position of co-executor and instituted with her a succession of suits to recover debts due Charles Green's estate. Some of these were for considerable sums, due by leading gentry. John Carlyle and George William Fairfax, for example, were alleged to owe Green's heirs £184. The two denied liability but lost the suit.[28] Every one of these actions entered by "William Savage and Margaret his wife, executors of Charles Green" was pressed mercilessly, and every one of them was successful.[29] Washington himself was indebted to the estate in the sum of £278, on account of a bond of Capt. John Posey's for which he had made himself responsible; but he was able to discharge this through Adam & Co., who owed him money and took over the bond from Savage.[30]

As Washington and Fairfax had no reason to question the integrity of Doctor Savage, they naturally wished to transfer their trusteeship to him, the manager of all the other property of the former Mrs. Green. They encountered one obstacle in the possibility that trouble might be created by some of the Irish kin of Charles Green, who had been making inquiry concerning his estate and his will.[31] In addition, Doctor Savage had been talking of departure from the Colony. Washington and Fairfax consequently wished to be protected in the event Green's will was invalidated and the trustees were held liable for payments made under it to a man who might be beyond the jurisdiction of the court.[32] Further, under the deed of trust given by Green to his wife, Washington and Fairfax had been remitting to her £100 a year, which was the net income from the fund, and they required security that the assets they transferred to Savage be used to pay her that amount annually, unless the court, on review or appeal, decided to terminate the trust. For a time it appeared that Savage's "counter-bond," as Washington styled it, would be forthcoming as a matter of course. The doctor professed himself very busy but ready to go into court and to present acceptable security;[33] Washington was equally considerate of the other man's engagements.[34] Somehow repeated delays occurred, delays that might have been regarded as an effort on Savage's part to avoid posting the

---

[28] *Fairfax Orders*, 1768–70, p. 311. Washington sat as one of the justices when this case was heard, Feb. 22, 1770.

[29] *Ibid.*, 175, 205, 311, 312; *Fairfax Orders*, 1770–72, p. 9, 20, 198.

[30] *Ledger A*, folio 180, 213.   [31] 2 *G. W.*, 453.

[32] *Ibid.*

[33] See his letter of May 25, 1767; 3 *Hamilton*, 293.

[34] 2 *G. W.*, 453, 455.

bond, but Washington and Fairfax persisted. At length, with Thomson Mason as security, Savage gave the bond to pay his wife £100 a year.[35] This paper was entrusted to Bryan Fairfax, and was not examined or even seen by Washington.[36]

Both he and Fairfax were glad to be relieved of a troublesome duty, but in Washington's case, one bother for a neighbor seemed always to preface another. On the very day the wheat harvest began on his plantations, June 24,[37] the private banker of Mount Vernon had to sit down and write at length to his friend John Posey. The Captain was deeper than ever in debt. He had paid nothing of principal or of interest on his debt of £700 to Washington and now he was seeking an additional loan of £300 on assets which he hopefully overvalued. Washington scolded him politely and warned: ". . . you will find that many things which you perhaps have lavished large sums in the purchase of, in order to gratify your own tastes, will neither suit nor probably please others. . ."[38] Washington went on to say he could not make any further loan to Posey, and then, half-apologetically, he explained the reason: He found it "next to impossible" to collect any of the money due him; for two years he had been trying, and without success, to raise £400 or £500 "to lend a very particular friend of mine, who I know must sell part of his estate without it."[39] Besides, when he wrote, Washington had not discharged the bond of Posey's he had assumed with Charles Green. "How absurd and idle would it be then," Washington wrote, "under these circumstances, to enter myself security for the payment of your debts unless I foresaw some prospect of raising the money."[40]

His counsel was direct. He would be as lenient as he could afford to be regarding the payment of the money already due.[41] If Posey could not hold his estate together three or four years till debtors as a class found some relief, then the Captain should sell enough of his property to cancel his obligations and, if he had anything left, to buy frontier lands, which would be certain to increase greatly in value. In elaborating this, Washington renewed his profession of faith in the development of the West: ". . . look to Frederick, and see what fortunes were made

35 2 *G. W.*, 523.   36 *Ibid.*
37 1 *Diaries*, 238. A typographical error makes this entry appear as one of May.
38 2 *G. W.*, 456–57.
39 The absence of reference to this in Washington's correspondence and failure to find any hint of it in his accounts suggest that the would-be borrower was a near neighbor or some other person Washington saw so frequently that letter writing was unnecessary.
40 2 *G. W.*, 457.   41 *Ibid.*, 458.

by the Hites and first takers up of those lands: [42] Nay, how the greatest estates we have in this Colony were made. Was it not by taking up and purchasing at very low rates the rich back lands which were thought nothing of in those days, but are now the most valuable lands that we possess?" [43] It was one of the oldest and most exciting questions men had asked in Virginia. When Washington had been a child of three, Richard Blackburn had written William Fairfax about a land patent. He was an entire stranger, Blackburn had said, to both the quantity and the quality of land, but he had been advised to take out patents because he had a "stock of children" and was anxious to do the best possible for them. [44] At that time, Blackburn had been in the country three years only, but had he been a native and had been as successful as Robert Carter, he could not more accurately have set forth the code of the land speculator.

John Posey was not a man to be satisfied with a paper when he wanted pounds. Margaret Savage's account was to be blurred by her tears and importunities and was to be written in with many a strange "contra" entry. As were these two, so many were to be—debt-distraught friends whom Washington's code of noblesse oblige would not permit him to turn away, perplexed farmers of humble station who valued his judgment above the advice of lawyers and the more so because it cost them nothing, old soldiers who seemed to think their Colonel must remain their counsellor, aging planters of wealth who wanted a prudent executor of their will, or a careful guardian of their sons. All these were beginning now to call on Washington. To hear them took hours; to solve their problems or to relieve their distress sometimes called for days of writing and of riding. It was costly but it was not shunned. Instead, Washington's service for his neighbors daily increased his sense of obligation to them and, at the same time, gave him longer patience and new understanding of men. Contact with human woe subtly slackened his acquisitive impulse and tightened his self-discipline. He had to be more diligent and orderly than ever in looking after his own business, because he had to give so much of his time to the affairs of others. All this service was training, though he probably did not so regard it and certainly did not ask himself for what purpose this training would be used.

As soon as Washington had done what he could to help his friend

[42] See Vol. I, p. 212 ff.
[43] 2 *G. W.*, 459. This quotation was anticipated in Vol. I, p. 14.
[44] Letter of **Aug. 22, 1735**; *Fairfax MSS*, Huntington Library.

Posey once more, he returned to his supervision of the wheat harvest, which continued until the 14th of July.[45] It was a formidable farm enterprise and one that called for careful planning. To make certain, for example, that the whole of the crop did not ripen and shatter before the cradlers possibly could cut all the fields, Washington every year planted a number of varieties of wheat from the earliest to the latest. In 1767, within less than a fortnight after the slowest-growing of the late wheat had been put in shocks, the skilled "hands" were afield again to sow the white wheat that would be reaped eleven months later.[46] Even with the harvest season extended in this manner to the utmost, the hands at Mount Vernon and on the other plantations who were able to swing a cradle and to sharpen its blade did not suffice to cut so large a crop as spread its golden heads across the fields in July. Cradlers had to be hired—as many as could be had—at 5s per day with pay for two days' travel both coming and going back home. Five such men had been found for an average of about eight days' work, at a total cost in excess of £15,[47] but the harvest was worth it. When all the grain was threshed, including Washington's share of tenants' crops, the total was at least 2778 bushels.[48] It was marketable, too, without troublesome packing and haggling over freights, on the wharf and at a guaranteed price for the whole of it, even if there was controversy with Carlyle & Adam at recurring intervals.

While the crop still was being stored in the driest barns on the plantations, Washington went with Martha and the children over the mountains to the Berkeley Springs, where he had spent anxious days of youth with his beloved Lawrence. The journey, which was for pleasure and for health, began about the 3rd of August [49] and carried the Washingtons and the Custises to the resort by the 8th. "Jackie" was now approaching the advanced age of 14 and, as circumstances might shape the day, was easily bored or no less easily entertained. He was a good-natured boy, in spite of the spoiling to which he was subjected by his

---

45 1 *Diaries*, 239.   46 *Ibid.*

47 *Ledger A*, folio 252. In 1769, Washington—or more probably Lund—hired nine cradlers at 5s daily each, with a flat allowance of three dollars per man for travel (*ibid.*, folio 292).

48 Here again, Washington's accounts are confusing. An item of 3625 bushels for 1767 appears on folio 180 of *Ledger A*, but on folio 271 the "crop of wheat in 1767" is put down at 2778. The assumption in the text is that the larger figure represents the wheat delivered during the calendar year and that the smaller digits refer to the wheat actually grown that year. Carlyle & Adam paid the same price per bushel for the whole of it, 3s 9d per bushel.

49 First entries of expense are for "corn and other provisions," but the initial road charge was August 3 at "the Glade," which evidently was between Mount Vernon and Leesburg (11 *Papers of G. W.*, 52, LC).

mother, but he was lazy and disposed to make the most of the good things lavished on him. "Patsy," now about 12, was old enough to have expensive music lessons from John Stedlar,[50] but young enough to enjoy a toy tea canister, purchased for and charged against her at the price of 1s.[51]

Neither she nor her brother could have found life exciting at the Springs after the first few days, because there was almost nothing for young people to do. The family resided in a cottage that belonged to the Mercers, and did not have to camp in such a tent and marquee as Washington had used in 1761.[52] Food was abundant. With a baker at hand, bread could be had without smoke and bother. The meat supplied by a resident butcher was chiefly veal, mutton, young pig and a little venison. No fowl except chicken was offered, but eggs and a wide range of vegetables were to be had almost daily.[53] As the cook had been brought along from Mount Vernon, food could be prepared acceptably. If Washington drank his usual Madeira about the hour the sun disappeared behind the mountains and the early chill spread through the Valley, it had to be from a stock he had transported. The demand for fine beverages did not justify the cost, the trouble and the breakage involved in hauling them over the heights. Pasturage and oats were available for the carriage horses, together with a man to see that the animals were fed. The only material discomfort in enjoying whatever virtues the waters possessed, internally or as a bath, was that of cramped quarters.

Along with the cripples and the feeble, Washington met at the Springs an old comrade of the French and Indian War—Col. John Armstrong, senior officer of the Pennsylvania contingent in Forbes's campaign of 1758. Armstrong, Irish-born and, like Washington, a surveyor, had come to the Springs with his wife, who was suffering from chronic rheumatism.[54] Washington did not have much of the Pennsylvanian's company at the resort but he learned that Armstrong was residing at Carlisle and he got the impression that his companion on the march to Fort DuQuesne now was managing, or had some

[50] Not otherwise identified. The name does not occur in *Swem,* but the man may have been the same individual mentioned in *Fithian* as Stedley.

[51] *Custis Papers*, VHS. Stedlar's bill for £12, 18s, covering an unspecified period, is among the Washington MSS at Mount Vernon.

[52] 2 *G. W.*, 365; 3 *ibid.*, 53.

[53] 11 *Papers of G. W.*, 51, LC.

[54] 3 *Hamilton*, 306; Washington to Armstrong, Aug. 24, 1769, a most interesting letter, loaned by Alfred Young of Northwestern University.

connection with, a public land office in Pennsylvania. It was pleasant, in any event, to see Armstrong who had borne arms in Pontiac's War and knew in detail of some operations concerning which Washington probably had received vague reports only.

By the middle of the second week in September,[55] these associations were memories. Washington was back at Mount Vernon but with his appetite for Western lands whetted by developments in the two controversies over the boundary lines of Pennsylvania. One of these disputes had to do with the line between Maryland and Pennsylvania. According to the view of the Maryland Proprietors, Philadelphia actually was in Maryland. If the argument of the Penns was accepted, Baltimore was in Pennsylvania. When a compromise on this was reached, the next question was, where would the stone be set for the Western boundary of Maryland? From that point a line drawn southward to the Potomac would be the eastern boundary of territory Virginia asserted to be hers. In the related matter of the Virginia-Pennsylvania boundary, Washington's fellow-Burgesses insisted that where the King had not specifically set aside land for other provinces or proprietaries, the charter of 1609 left to Virginia the whole of the Northwest as far as the domain of his Majesty might run.[56] The charter of the Penns provided that their Colony extend westward five degrees from the Delaware River. Men disputed whether this meant five degrees from some fixed point on the Delaware or on an irregular line precisely corresponding to the curves of the river. In either event, all territory more than five degrees beyond the western boundary of Pennsylvania was affirmed by Virginia to be hers and subject to her patent, under such restrictions and within such limits as the King imposed. If, then, the survey of the Maryland-Pennsylvania line was continued westward till it was five degrees from the eastern boundary of Pennsylvania, this, said the Virginians, would follow necessarily: a line drawn from that point northward would be the western boundary of Pennsylvania, subject to minor changes, perhaps, that would correspond to the course of the Delaware. Nothing East of that line would be subject to patent by Virginia; all lands West of that north-and-south line could be granted by Virginia.

55 On or about Sept. 9, 1767; 11 *Papers of G. W.*, 51, LC.

56 The charter had provided that Virginia extended 200 miles northward and southward from "Cape or Point Comfort" and thence from sea to sea, North and Northwest. Virginia always maintained that the northwestern projection was from the northern and not from the southern end of the eastern line. Had the line been projected northwestward from the southern end of the eastern boundary, and the western line been drawn from the northern end, the area of Virginia would of course have been a relatively small triangle.

To ascertain the Maryland-Pennsylvania boundary, two British surveyors, Charles Mason and Jeremiah Dixon, had started work in 1764. Their survey had been suspended in November, 1766, on the Allegheny Mountains, but now was being extended westward. Washington received information that certain highly valuable lands, previously unpatented because of the boundary dispute, were to be declared within Pennsylvania and might be procured under grants of that Colony. He began immediately a campaign to get 1500 or 2000 or even more acres of the best of this land. Capt. William Crawford, another old comrade of Forbes's march to the Ohio, resided on the Youghiogheny, in the very country toward which Washington was looking. Two letters went promptly to the Captain to enlist his services. Crawford must find out whether and how patents could be had; Colonel Armstrong would help him; if Crawford succeeded, Washington would compensate him and, in the spring of 1768, would visit him on the Youghiogheny to explain the whole matter and another of even greater importance, which he proceeded to sketch.

This was the patenting of a very large tract West of the Pennsylvania boundary and West, also, of the "Proclamation Line" set over the royal seal, Oct. 2, 1763. That frontier separated the eastern settlements of all Colonies from the lands left to the Indians for their hunting and occupancy. As the proclamation read: ". . . for the present, and until our further pleasure be known," English subjects were not to settle "beyond the heads or sources of any of the rivers which fall into the Atlantic Ocean from the West and Northwest." Persons who already had gone west of that watershed were commanded "forthwith to remove themselves." Washington now confided to Crawford: ". . . I can never look upon that proclamation in any other light (but this I say between ourselves) than as a temporary expedient to quiet the minds of the Indians and must fall of course in a few years especially when those Indians are consenting to our occupying their lands. Any person therefore who neglects the present opportunity of hunting out good lands and in some measure marking and distinguishing them for their own (in order to keep others from settling them) will never regain it . . ."

A loose partnership was to be formed: Crawford must locate the lands in the closed area and must mark them; Washington would pay all the costs of surveys and patents and would engage to procure the lands as soon as it was possible. A "reasonable proportion of the whole"

was to go by agreement to Crawford, but the enterprise must be kept
secret or at most be confided only to those who could assist. ". . . I
might be censured," Washington went on, with all his old-time regard
for public criticism, "for the opinion I have given in respect to the
King's proclamation." Besides, were the plan known, rivalries might
wreck the execution of it. "All this must be prevented," Washington
told Crawford, "by silent management and the [scheme] snugly carried
on by you under the pretence of hunting other game, which you may, I
presume, effectually do at the same time you are in pursuit of land . . ."
Crawford was to proceed and was to notify Washington of results.
". . . if there appears but a bare possibility of succeeding any time hence
I will have the lands immediately surveyed to keep others off, and leave
the rest to time and my own assiduity to accomplish." [57]

A letter of inquiry was dispatched simultaneously to Colonel Armstrong: would he please advise concerning the procedure for patenting
lands in Pennsylvania? [58] Armstrong's answer was not encouraging.
Lands could be had but they were not cheap; he gladly would do all he
could to assist in every possible manner. [59] Crawford, in his prompt
reply, was entirely at Washington's command. He knew of a fine tract
on Chartier's Creek [60] and he gladly would have Washington join him
in acquiring it, if he could get to it before someone else patented it.
The other offer, the one for joint acquisition of lands farther westward,
Crawford embraced heartily on Washington's terms. He already had
considered such a plan, he said, but he had not found anyone in whom
he could confide. He would keep the matter secret, search out the land
as soon as possible, and report to Washington. [61]

The tall master of Mount Vernon could read this letter, cast up his
present holdings, and look forward to the day the inventory of his lands
would run to a dazzling total—more than 9500 acres under Fairfax
quit rents, Martha's part of the Custis estate, a share in the Dismal
Swamp, perhaps some new acquisitions on Chartier's Creek, and, when
the proclamation of 1763 was nullified, some vast tracts lower down
the Ohio, the very first pick of the choicest bottoms! Ultimately, too,
Washington and his veterans of Fort Necessity should get the 200,000
acres Governor Dinwiddie promised them in 1754. Meantime there

---

[57] Letter of Sept. 21, 1767; 2 *G. W.*, 467–71.
[58] 2 *G. W.*, 473.   [59] Letter of Nov. 3, 1767; 3 *Hamilton*, 302.
[60] He used the familiar spelling Shurtees.
[61] Letter of Sept. 29, 1767; 3 *Hamilton*, 295–301. Crawford's spelling was almost unique.

seemed to be a chance of sucessful land speculation at Augusta Springs, with the resounding Thomas Bullitt.[62]

Washington was practising what he had preached to John Posey, who now was back with two letters that told a new story of financial need. In a manner that scarcely could be considered peculiar to himself, Posey was an optimist when trying to borrow money. He still required £300, he said, and required it more urgently than ever, in order to pay certain bills, but he had security, ample, overabundant security. Six acres purchased not long previously were very valuable. Land bought from one of Washington's brothers was worth, with its improvements, almost £700. Thus circumstanced, Posey could get £300 from George Mason, but that gentleman stipulated that he was seeking to acquire a piece of property and, if he succeeded, he would have to recall within three or four months the loan to Posey. Besides, Colonel Mason wanted surety for the loan. Would Colonel Washington . . . ?

Washington began his reply with something less than his usual patience. Posey's security for his outstanding loan to Washington was worth no more than the principal, £750[63] and the interest already accumulated. The new assets, Washington wrote, had far less value than Posey thought. Besides, eight of the slaves included in the security for Washington's loan had disappeared from the list of the Captain's possessions. If, in this situation, Posey borrowed £300 from George Mason on the terms candidly set forth, Posey might be compelled, in the midst of a growing season, to sell field hands in order to repay the owner of Gunston Hall. It was far better for Posey to reduce his holdings, to rid himself of interest, and then to make a fresh start. All this Washington explained again, logically and in detail, and then, when he made out an irrefragable case, he proceeded to say that if Posey *insisted* on borrowing the £300 from Mason, he would become surety, provided Posey would make further assets available for immediate sale by him in event Mason suddenly demanded that the loan be discharged.[64]

Washington had written this out, carefully and fully in his own hand, and was about to dispatch the letter, when Posey's affairs were mentioned in conversation with someone at Mount Vernon. This person

---

[62] This did not develop, according to *Ledger A*, folio 262, 264. For an obscure transaction with the Strother family, involving £20, odd money, see *Ledger A*, folio 241.

[63] *Ledger A*, folio 256.

[64] Letter of Sept. 27, 1767 to John Posey; 2 *G. W.*, 473–77.

quoted the Captain as saying that he had paid the whole of his debt to Washington with the exception of about £20. The Colonel added this report in a postscript and inquired: ". . . does such disingenuity as this deserve any favor at my hands? I think anybody might readily answer for you, No." [65] In the face of his own question, Washington sent the letter to Posey, and adhered to his promise to become the Captain's surety for the £300 after demonstrating that his neighbor ought not to borrow another shilling.

It usually worked that way. The times were out of joint. Everyone seemed to owe everyone else and, on occasion, forgot even bills receivable. In October, for example, Washington received a letter from William Neale of King William County, who was acting for Bernard Moore. It developed that in the account of Speaker Robinson against the hopelessly indebted Bernard Moore, one item read: "To Mrs. Washington, October, 1758, being what she agreed to lay out in the Chamberlayne Estate, £100." Moore had not known why this was charged to him, but in the settlement with Robinson's administrators he had acknowledged liability. Neale wrote now to say that Moore had the claim which, with interest from 1758, he was holding against Washington.[66] This was disconcerting. Before her marriage, when Martha had talked with Washington about her financial affairs, she had remarked that through Speaker Robinson she had agreed to purchase articles offered at the Chamberlayne sale to a total of £100,[67] but she had received no goods and no call for the money. Washington subsequently had asked Robinson for details, but the Speaker had replied that he "could not well tell what to say about it," or words to that effect. Because of this vagueness, Washington had concluded that the original promise on Martha's part had been connected with some general, neighborly tender of security for the success of the sale. After nine years he certainly expected no call for the money. How the item ever came to be charged to Moore, it was impossible for Washington to imagine, and why Moore should undertake to charge him interest on the alleged debt, he could not understand. Neale was requested to inform Moore that Washington would "strictly comply with whatever honor and justice" might demand regarding Martha's engagement; but, Washing-

[65] *Ibid.*, 476–77.
[66] Neale to Washington, Sept. 15, 1767; 11 *Papers of G. W.*, 59, LC.
[67] See *supra*, p. 2.

ton added, he could not conceive himself bound to pay more than the original amount.[68]

It was a strange episode. Robinson's administrators, Moore, Martha, Washington—none of them knew how or where the debt originated or what it actually represented, but there it was, typical of the confusion of the times! Most of the Virginia planters were more deeply in debt than ever. Their economy appeared to be collapsing. It had been based for a century and a half on a staple apparently well-suited to slave labor but viciously destructive of the land. This tobacco could be delivered to one market only, where it was handled by merchants who lent money and sold manufactured goods to the producers. All the evils of this were aggravated by ostentation and extravagance by planters who suffered from a chronic shortage of specie and an adverse exchange. Unless there was early and general relief of some sort for creditors, bankruptcy was ahead not of an occasional Robinson or Moore but of a large class of agrarian society. As the planters faced recurring threats of new taxation, some of them were becoming desperate: nothing could be worse than what they had to endure; any resistance that reduced their purchases in England would reduce likewise their debts.[69]

Washington was far better off than most men of his station as respected debt, ready cash and marketable staples. If the economic order survived, he could hope to prosper; if it failed, he might save his estate from the wreckage. The tobacco crop of 1767 was short—he had seventeen hogsheads only and "Jackie" thirty-six [70] on the York and Pamunkey—which forecast better prices.[71] Corn fields yielded a full 4000 bushels for sale on the Potomac [72] in addition to all used on the plantations. The gross corn crop "below" was about 2800 bushels, of which almost four-fifths grew on "Jackie's" lands.[73] On other accounts, "Jackie" was doing quite well. Washington maintained for him a balance of £1300 to £1500 in the hands of Robert Cary & Co.,[74] and

---

68 2 *G. W.*, 477–78. Washington paid the claim, without interest, charged it against Mrs. Wilhelmina Chamberlayne Byrd and, on Jan. 1, 1772, marked it off as a loss (*Ledger B*, folio 33).   69 Cf. Vol. I, p. 167 ff.

70 *Custis Papers*, VHS.   71 2 *G. W.*, 466.

72 *Ledger A*, folio 280. The account actually is 4304 bushels delivered between May 31 and Nov. 24, 1768 to Robert Adam, but 4000 of this were marketed before June 26 and consequently were of the crop of 1767. The 300 bushels turned over to Adam on Nov. 24, 1768, probably were of the crop of 1768.   73 *Custis Papers*, VHS.

74 *Ledger A*, folio 198. This was the general account with Cary, covering all transactions without distinction of the Custis credits from Washington's own; but Washington's letter of July 20, 1767 to Robert Cary & Co. makes it plain that Custis had a credit and Washington still a debit balance, which probably had been reduced little, if at all (2 *G. W.*, 461).

through this eased the merchants of concern over his own debt to them. In an emergency, he could borrow from the estate account. More immediately, therefore, unless the wheat crop of 1768 was a failure and heavy calls for cash were made on Washington for someone whose surety he was, he could endure the cruel shortage of specie in the Colony.

The close of 1767 would have been peaceful and the beginning of 1768 cheerful but for the action of the British Parliament. Instead of the accord and forbearance expected by most of the colonials, there was insistent exercise of the right of taxation asserted in the Declaratory Act. Import duties were fixed on paints and their ingredients, on glass, on many kinds of paper, and on all tea. Proceeds of these taxes were to be used to pay for a centrally controlled customs system and then for the compensation of Governors, judges and other officials of the Crown. These Townshend Acts, so styled after the name of the Chancellor of the Exchequer, were passed between June 15 and July 2, 1767.

When known in America, these tax laws were denounced as violations of the fundamental rights of Englishmen in America. Everywhere, public men renewed the argument that it was tyrannical to have taxes levied without the consent of the people who were to pay them; and they added gloomily that it would be ruinous to have Governors and other appointees of the Crown no longer dependent upon colonial lawmakers for salaries. In Virginia, had not the wise William Byrd the Second more than thirty years previously said of the King's chief representatives, "Our government is so happily constituted that a Governor must first outwit us before he can oppress us, and if he ever squeeze money out of us, he must first take care to deserve it"? [75] How would it be when the Governor had no favors to ask? Whose will would he then regard, that of the colonial Assembly or that of the British Ministry and that of the new Board of Customs Commissioners who were to set themselves up in Boston, whence they would send their agents to every inlet and wharf? [76]

The future of all the colonial legislative bodies might be forecast by the punishment imposed on the New York Assembly under the very first of the Townshend Acts. Because the greater part of the British

[75] See Vol. I, p. 172.
[76] It should be remembered that distilling was a plantation rather than a commercial industry in Virginia. The prospect of the stern pursuit of smugglers consequently meant far less than in Massachusetts and Rhode Island.

troops in America had been billeted on New York, the Assembly had declined to vote salt, vinegar and cider or beer, on the ground that these were not allowed His Majesty's troops in European barracks, though the Assembly did not withhold the grant it previously had made under the Quartering Act of 1765.[77] When General Gage reported this to the home government, Charles Townshend had Parliament pass a stern act: The New York Assembly was suspended from the exercise of its functions until it complied with all the requirements the British commander set for the billetting of his troops. No law of any sort could be passed, no resolution adopted, and no supply voted unless every single thing that Gage demanded for the subsistence and the comfort of his soldiers was provided.

Alarm over this "Suspending Act" spread throughout the Colonies. Previously, without exception, the assemblies had been convened, prorogued and dissolved by the Governor, as the representative of the Crown. Now it appeared that Parliament had usurped royal authority at the behest of an irritated politician. Parliamentary control of colonial lawmakers, taxation without representation, without consultation even, a royal rein on Governors and judges because they had to look to the King for their pay, the denial to the assemblies of all control over customs—these provisions of the Townshend Acts, taken together, were regarded as a threat to the most cherished, most essential rights of America. If these rights were lost, what remained?

That was a grim question for Colonel Washington, as for every colonial, but in the knowledge time and time only would give the answer, he adhered as usual to the first law of equanimity and did not try to anticipate. One secret of his balance was his deliberate refusal to be the *avant-coureur* of calamity. Besides, there was full occupation of mind at Mount Vernon when 1768 began, occupation and hope, too, because he could see some of the benefits of the shift from tobacco growing to wheat. The change meant vast saving in labor, for the reason that no Virginia crop was quite so demanding of time and of backbreaking toil as tobacco was. Every leaf had sweat on it. From the time the plant bed was prepared in late winter until the last hogshead was put on the flatboat, King Tobacco cracked the whip over the grower's back. Even when the tobacco ship had sailed, it had to be followed with

[77] See Gov. Sir Henry Moore to Secretary Conway, June 20, 1766; 7 *Col. Docs. N. Y.*, 831; Gage to Conway, June 24, 1766; 1 *Gage*, 95 ff, with numerous editorial citations.

letter after letter. Wheat was different. As Washington had found already, sale was simple even if collection was not always easy. The ground was plowed; the grain was planted; after that, nothing need be done or could be done, except to keep livestock away, until harvest. New tasks now could be undertaken—the development of farm-fisheries, the improvement of the mill, the expansion of weaving, the construction of a new barn [78] and the enlargement of the residence at Mount Vernon.

In his favored situation, Washington had more time for hunting and could look forward, if all went well, to visiting in summer Martha's kinsfolk and his own, of whom he had seen far less than he had desired during the preceding ten years of hard work.[79] Bryan Fairfax was an ardent foxhunter; Captain Posey had ample hours for the chase and apparently for anything else not connected with paying his debts; when Dr. William Rumney came to treat the sick at Mount Vernon, he frequently would stay in order to study the habits of Muddy Hole foxes— doubtless in a spirit that befitted a scientist. Washington entered zestfully into all this. Six days were given to fox hunting in January, 1768; one day was devoted to shooting, and one to card-playing. Directions were given that paths be cut through the tangle of Muddy Hole so that reynard might be pursued.[80]

In February, the carpenters who had completed work on the smiths' shop [81] turned to the building of an overseer's house.[82] New ground was cleared and drained; wheat was threshed:[83] Washington had seven days of fox hunting, two days of ducking, and one day in the fields with a gun for any game that might take wing or might scamper off through the broom sedge.[84] March called for more farm activities and left only five days for hunting—not to mention five during which the Colonel

---

[78] Cf. 1 *Diaries*, 275.

[79] As respects hunting, it has to be noted that for most of the years from 1759 through 1767, Washington's diaries are thin or are no longer in existence if, indeed, any daily records were kept. Those that have survived the years contain no references to hunting, but this does not mean necessarily that Washington devoted no time to field sports. In 1768 he began more elaborate diaries and made two sets, for a while three sets of entries—one of "observations," in reality the dates of his principal farm activities, another of the weather, and a third, which he headed, "where and how my time is spent." It was in the third of these that he entered the memoranda of his hunts. The possibility cannot be excluded that if he had earlier diaries of this type, they would show Washington chasing foxes. On the other hand, not until 1768 and after that year are occasional references to hunting found in Washington's correspondence. The conclusion in the text consequently seems entirely justified—that circumstances gave him more time for hunting.

[80] 1 *Diaries*, 245–47.   [81] *Ibid.*, 251.
[82] *Ibid.*, 254.   [83] *Ibid.*, 250. This was begun in January.
[84] 1 *Diaries*, 253.

had to contend with a rebellious stomach and a defiant indigestion for the first illness of any consequence in several years.[85] When he added three more days of fox hunting in April,[86] spent one night at a ball in Alexandria [87] and then set out on the 26th for Eltham with his family and young Billy Bassett, stay-at-home critics might have shaken their heads and might have asked, "What has come over Colonel Washington?" Somewhat the same question might have been asked also, in more polite form, when he reached Williamsburg, because a session of Assembly had been opened the last day of March and had been prorogued on the 16th of April, without so much as a single day's attendance by the junior Burgess from Fairfax.[88]

It had been a session of some distinction. To the general grief of the Colony, Governor Fauquier had lost on the 3rd of March a long struggle with illness. He was all that the *Virginia Gazette* represented him to be, "a gentleman of a most amiable disposition—generous, just and mild, and possessed in an eminent degree of all the social virtues." [89] Burial in the Williamsburg church was with every honor the people of the capital could give him.[90] His temporary successor, under existing colonial practice, could be none other than the President of the Council. John Blair, who still held that office, was eighty-one years of age, but was alert, acceptable, and able, though somewhat reluctant to assume the duties of Governor, precisely as he had been after Dinwiddie went to England in 1758. On assuming the post, "Mr. President" had believed that Fauquier's call for a session of Assembly at the end of March should stand, because the reason for it remained. Encroachment by white settlers on Indian lands along Red Stone Creek and Cheat River had aroused the redmen to threats of reprisal that still were alarming the frontier. Blair's opening address to the Burgesses had called for

---

[85] 1 *Ibid.*, 256. [86] 1 *Ibid.*, 264–65.
[87] 1 *Ibid.*, 264.
[88] *Journ. H.B.*, 1766–69, p. 141, 171. Fitzpatrick evidently had misread the dates or had not checked them when he noted (1, *Diaries*, 266 n), that Washington left Mount Vernon, April 26, to attend a session of Burgesses who had started home ten days previously. No reason for Washington's absence from the Assembly is known. As his diary shows no occurrence at Mount Vernon that might have necessitated his presence there, the natural assumption is that he did not think the session of sufficient importance to require his presence. Plans may already have been formulated for the family to visit the Bassetts late in April. Attendance on the General Assembly would have necessitated two long journeys to the York within a month of each other. Originally this session of Assembly had been prorogued from Nov. 26, 1767, to May 5, 1768. See *Journ. H.B.*, 1766–69, p. 138.
[89] *Va. Gazette*, Mch. 3, 1768. Lady Fauquier and her son Francis had left the Colony in May, 1766 (*ibid.*, May 30, 1766).
[90] *Ibid.*, Mch. 10, 1768. Interment was on March 8.

action against these white men who had defied the King's proclamation and had refused to leave the bottom lands they unlawfully had occupied.[91] At the same time, "Mr. President" had pointed to a favorable report of collections by the new Treasurer: might not this justify the Assembly in lightening the load of taxation?

The Assembly, in turn, had resolved politely to urge Indians and frontiersmen to avoid hostilities.[92] Action had been taken, also, to cancel the land tax and the poll tax for 1768 and 1769;[93] but the most serious deliberations had been on the subject of alarmed public discussion, the Townshend Acts. Freeholders of half a dozen Counties had sent in protests against these measures and in support of the appeal the Massachusetts General Court had made in a "Circular Letter" of Feb. 11, 1768, for united action of the Colonies against measures that deprived them of their rights.[94] In Committee of the Whole, the Virginia Burgesses then had drafted another address to the King, a memorial to the House of Lords, and a remonstrance to the House of Commons.[95]

These papers were marked by a change of temper in that they were more argumentatively explicit and somewhat less rhetorical than those adopted prior to the passage of the Stamp Act. Colonials had learned more about their rights in four years of discussion among themselves, and they now had their case logically organized. The address implored the display by the King of "fatherly goodness and protection" to the people of Virginia and of the other American Colonies "in the enjoyment of their ancient and inestimable right of being governed by such laws only, respecting their internal polity and taxation, as are derived from their own consent with the approbation of their Sovereign."[96] In the memorial and the remonstrance, the Virginians maintained more vigorously than ever that the fundamental principle of British government was, "No power on earth has a right to impose taxes upon the people or to take the smallest portion of their property without their consent, given by their representatives in Parliament." As the Colonies were not and could not be represented in the House of Commons, the right of self-taxation must rest exclusively in the colonial legis-

---

[91] *Journ. H.B.*, 1766–69, p. 141–42.   [92] *Ibid.*, 148–49.

[93] *Ibid.*, 158, 159, 164; 8 *H* 295. For Treasurer Nicholas's activity in collecting taxes, see *Rind's Gazette*, Dec. 25, 1766, Feb. 10, 1767.

[94] *Journ. H.B.*, 1766–69, p. 145–46, 148. The Massachusetts letter was printed in *Va. Gazette*, Apr. 14, 1768.

[95] *Ibid.*, 149, 150, 153, 157, 161, 165 ff, 173.

[96] *Ibid.*, p. 165.

lative bodies. Parliament properly might make laws to regulate the trade of the Colonies. "Sometimes duties have been imposed to restrain the commerce of one part of the Empire that was likely to prove injurious to another, and by this means the general welfare of the whole may have been promoted." The Virginia Assembly added in stout antithesis: "But a tax imposed upon such of the British exports, as are necessities of life, to be paid by the Colonists upon importation, and this not with the most distant view to the interests of commerce, but merely to raise a revenue, or in plainer words to compel the Colonists to part with their money against their inclinations, your memorialists conceive to be a tax internal to all intents and purposes." [97]

The "Suspending Act" aimed at the New York Assembly presented the Virginians with possibilities they had not canvassed in any of their previous declarations, but in their appeal to Parliament they branded the statute as even "more alarming" than the other measures "to the Colonies in general, though it has that single Province in view as its immediate object." Parliamentary orders to a colonial Assembly to supply any single article implied the power to order everything. On that ground the Virginians asked, ". . . what advantage could the people of the Colonies derive from their right of choosing their own representatives, if those representatives, when chosen, not permitted to exercise their own judgments, were under a necessity, (on pain of being deprived of their legislative authority) of enforcing the mandates of a British Parliament, though ever so injurious to the interests of the Colony they represented." [98]

The heart of the memorial to the Lords was an earnest request for the repeal of the Townshend Acts and for the security and "full enjoyment of all our natural and constitutional rights and privileges." [99] In the last paragraph of the remonstrance, the language of the General Assembly was an expression of hope that the Commons would not regard the colonials as exiles who had forfeited their rights, and "that British patriots [would] never consent to the exercise of anticonstitutional powers, which, even in these remote quarters, may in time prove dangerous in their example to the interior parts of the British Empire." The final sentence was: "Should the remonstrants be disappointed in these hopes the necessary result will be that the Colonists, reduced to

[97] *Ibid.* The punctuation of the original is preserved.
[98] *Ibid.*, 168, with the original punctuation.
[99] *Ibid.*

extreme poverty, will be compelled to contract themselves within their little spheres and obliged to content themselves with their homespun manufacturers."[100]   In this, of course, was an imitative echo of Benjamin Franklin's parting shot in his testimony before the House of Commons on the repeal of the Stamp Act;[101] but the threat to suspend the importation of British cloth was not so important as the fact that the Burgesses had not been divided sharply, as in 1764. On the contrary, they had been unanimous in approving all three papers.[102] The Council had concurred, also, and had agreed that its representative in England would join the regular agent of the Colony in supporting address, memorial and remonstrance.[103] Finally, and again with unanimity, Speaker Randolph was given two instructions: First, he was to reply to the "Circular Letter" of the Massachusetts House and was to inform the body "that we could not but applaud them for their attention to American liberty and that the steps we had taken thereon would convince them of our opinion of the fatal tendency of the acts of Parliament complained of and of our fixed resolution to concur with the other Colonies in their application for redress." Second, Peyton Randolph was "to write to the respective Speakers of the Assemblies and Representatives on this continent to make known to them our proceedings on this subject and to intimate how necessary we think it is that the Colonies should unite in a firm but decent opposition to every measure which may affect the rights and liberties of the British Colonies in America."[104]

The arguments on rights thus had crystalized in the four exciting years after the adoption of the first protest of 1764 against the taxation of the Colonies by the British Parliament. Virginians, to repeat, had found the firm ground on which they could justify resistance; they were of one mind concerning the valid arguments they could employ. Further, they had become conscious of some of the results that might be achieved by joint action. Previously, more often than not, the Governors had declined on behalf of "His Majesty's Ancient Dominion" to participate in meetings with representatives of other Colonies on the ground that no good could be accomplished where provincial interests were diverse. Now the Burgesses, not the Governor, decided. Common danger created common cause.

100 *Ibid.*, 171.
102 *Journ. H.B.*, 1766–69, p. 171.
104 *Journ. H.B.*, 1766–69, p. 174.

101 See *supra*, p. 156–57.
103 *Ibid.*, 173–76; 3 *L.J.*, 1384–85.

Colonel Washington's absence had denied him the right of voting "Aye" on the adoption of these papers at the spring session of the Assembly of 1768. Had he been present he would not have hesitated for an instant. Dissent, amendment, or insistence on some legalistic distinction never would have occurred to him. Once the issue had become that of the rights of Virginians, it no longer was in the realm of debate with him. Like most of his contemporaries outside the legal profession, he may not have formulated opinion till fundamentals of the inherited rights of the colonial subject had become clear. Thereafter his course of duty was plain.[105]

He probably would have sat silent, though not of doubtful mind, during the debate on the Townshend Acts, but he might have shared usefully, had he been present, in considering once again the enigma of the settlement of John Robinson's "debt" to the Colony. The committee had revised its figures and had reported that the amount due the Colony, with interest, was £109,000 as of May, 1768, the second anniversary of the death of the Treasurer. Of taxes and licenses due in Robinson's later years, and negligently uncollected by him, some £60,000 remained unpaid. While some of this money would be lost, much could be recovered. Continuance for two years of existing taxes on tobacco, carriages, writs, and ordinaries would supplement past-due accounts in a sum sufficient to retire the remaining Treasury notes, which represented a maximum of £170,000.[106]

After considering this report in Committee of the Whole, the House had agreed by a narrow margin [107] that funds would be available to retire the outstanding currency by the date set in the law, but it had insisted at the same time that for "better securing the redemption of the paper money, the most effectual methods ought to be taken against the estate of John Robinson, Esq.," with the concession that interest should not begin until two years after his death.[108] Legislation to this end was delayed so long [109] that the Council refused to give the measure hurried, last-minute approval.[110] Whether the council in this was moved by a desire to perfect the bill at a later session, or by a wish to protect

---

[105] This will be abundantly evident from his letter of June 5, 1769, quoted at the end of this chapter.

[106] The total issues from 1754 through 1762 had been £539,000 of which £369,000 had been called in and burned (*Journ. H.B.*, 1766–69, p. 155).

[107] The House on this point reversed its vote in committee (*ibid.*, 163).

[108] *Ibid.*, 163.   [109] *Ibid.*, 171, 172, 175.

[110] 3 *L. J.*, 1384.

the sureties and the heirs of Robinson, each informed colonial was free
to judge for himself. Everywhere in the proceedings, of course, the
hand of Edmund Pendleton, one of the administrators of the Robinson
estate, had been deftly employed; but, whatever the shrewd attorney's
aim, the effect of the Council's disagreement was to continue the earlier
act that allowed three years for the settlement of Robinson's obligation
to the Colony.

Washington heard, of course, all that was to be said on both sides of
this question during his visit to the York, a visit fashioned for pleasure,
not for politics. With Martha and the children, he made Eltham his
headquarters in a succession of forays against foxes and sturgeon, to say
nothing of a descent on Williamsburg for a theatrical performance.[111]
On the return journey, which began May 20, the family drove through
part of Westmoreland and through Chotank to visit Washington kinsfolk.[112] Not until May 31 did the travelers reach home again by way
of Hooe's Ferry and the Maryland road past Port Tobacco.[113]

Holiday was preparation. That spring, the children's tutor, Walter
Magowan, had decided to proceed to England and to seek admission to
holy orders. He intended to remain in Britain for a brief time only,
though he did not purpose to resume his instruction at Mount Vernon.
Washington did what he could to facilitate the young man's introduction in London, entrusted one or two small commissions to Magowan,[114]
and, of course, undertook to make new arrangements for the instruction of the children. He went about this conscientiously, in a businesslike
manner, and without reflecting, probably, that he was acquiring some
knowledge of the way of thinking of a boy younger than most of his
soldiers had been in the French and Indian War. Washington had been
away from home during the years his own younger brothers had been
growing up; now, in educating a youth, he was to extend his education
in youth. Mrs. Washington might provide instruction for "Patsy" at
Mount Vernon or in the neighborhood, but the stepfather had to find
a new teacher for "Jackie." It did not prove difficult. Perhaps while on
the way from the York, Washington had heard of the well-attended
school for boys that Jonathan Boucher, a clergyman of the established
church, and rector of St. Mary's, Caroline County, was conducting on
the minister's glebe, twelve miles from the church. The Colonel wrote

111 1 *Diaries*, 267–68.   112 *Ibid.*, 269–70.
113 *Ibid.*, 270.   114 2 *G. W.*, 482–84.

forthwith to Boucher but by some strange lapse of judgment and of taste, made a bad start for the wise training of his wife's son. "He is," Washington wrote of "Jackie," "a boy of good genius, about 14 years of age, untainted in his morals, and of innocent manners." Then, in describing "Jackie's" preparation, Washington admitted casually to the minister that young Custis had received no instruction since Christmas, 1767, though Magowan had not left until March, 1768. Washington went on: "If he comes [to your school 'Jackie'] will have a boy (well acquainted with house business, which may be made as useful as possible in your family to keep him out of idleness) and two horses, to furnish him with the means of getting to church and elsewhere as you may permit; for he will be put entirely and absolutely under your tuition and direction, to manage as you think proper in all respects." This flourish was indulged next: ". . . as to his board and schooling (provender for his horses he may lay in himself) I do not think it necessary to enquire into and will cheerfully pay £10 or £12 a year extraordinary to engage your peculiar care of and a watchful eye to him, as he is a promising boy, the last of his family and, will possess a very large fortune; add to this my anxiety to make him fit for more useful purposes than a horse racer." [115] In this, the pen may have been Washington's but the concern was Martha's. Had the Colonel displayed the judgment that usually was his in dealing with the frailties of human nature, he scarcely would have put anything more into his letter than that he wished to enter "Jackie" in Boucher's school if terms and conditions were acceptable to both parties.

Boucher's replies contained first a doubt because the school might be moved to Maryland, and then an eagerness to have "Master Custis." In elaborating this, Boucher said regretfully that he had been teaching for seven years and could not boast of "having had the honor to bring up one Scholar." No sooner did promising pupils reach the proper age of successful application to study than they either married or quit school. Boucher went on: "You, sir, however, seem so justly sensible of the vast importance of a good education that I cannot doubt of your heartily concurring in every plan that might be proposed for the advantage of your ward: And what I am more particularly pleased with is the ardent desire you express for the cultivation of his moral as well as

---

[115] Letter of May 30, 1768; 2 *G. W.*, 487–88. The punctuation is revised somewhat drastically to make Washington's reasoning plain.

his intellectual powers, I mean that he may be a good as well as learned and a sensible man." [116]

These professions must have lightened somewhat the grief of Martha at the prospect of having her son taken from under her wing, though nothing could reconcile her to it.[117] About the 1st of July, "Jackie" was escorted by Washington to Caroline County along with his body servant, his two horses, his portmanteaux and his luggage but, accidentally or otherwise, without sundry Latin texts he soon was to need. First reports from Boucher were to the effect that the young gentleman had enjoyed perfect health except for two or three days of stomach-ache. This, the reverend dominie somewhat incautiously wrote, "I at first took for the colic but since think it more likely that it might be owing to worms." [118]

It was almost cruel for Boucher to mention the possibility that "Jackie" might have worms, because that would trouble Mrs. Washington at a time when something had happened to "Patsy" that had created justifiable anxiety. On the 13th of June, Washington and Martha had ridden over to Belvoir, where Colonel and Mrs. Fairfax were entertaining the Seldons and other friends.[119] On their return home, the Washingtons found that Bryan Fairfax had arrived during their absence. They proceeded to make him welcome, of course, and they prepared, also, to entertain the Belvoir family and guests on the 15th. There was nothing unusually exciting about any of this, but for some reason, "Patsy" suddenly became ill and had what unmistakably was a fit. Doctor Rumney was summoned and, on arrival, was able to relieve the twelve-year-old girl. She recovered to such an extent that the physician felt justified in leaving the next morning. The party on the 15th went off according to arrangement; but the child's illness was alarming. Fits might recur.[120] The solicitous mother could do nothing more than the doctor suggested, except to give "Patsy" the pleasure of pretty possessions. In the new invoices prepared while she was still convalescing, a

---

[116] 3 *Hamilton,* 314–18.

[117] The absence of other letters from Washington to Boucher prior to "Jackie's" departure suggests the possibility that Mrs. Washington may have written the final instructions and requests concerning the care of "Jackie."

[118] Letter of July 15, 1768; 3 *Hamilton,* 320. The reason for saying Washington accompanied "Jackie" is the remark of Boucher (*ibid.*) that the boy had been in good health "ever since you left him" except for the "stomach ache."

[119] 1 *Diaries,* 272. Washington did not state that Martha went with him, but that was almost certain. As Belvoir was crowded with guests, "Patsy" probably stayed at home.

[120] It is possible, of course, that the child had suffered previously from some obscure malady, but no earlier references have been found to convulsions of any sort. Besides, Washington in July, 1770 (3 *G. W.,* 20–21) wrote that "her complaint [had] been of two years' standing."

"very handsome and fashionable" saddle ... "with bridle and everything complete" was included for "Patsy," along with gloves and satin pumps and much besides.[121] September invoices were to list for her a "neat pocket looking glass" and a lady's black furred riding hat with a white feather.[122]

Along with the task of easing Martha's concern over her daughter, to whom he was himself devoted, Washington had in the summer of 1768, and on into the autumn, a succession of calls to relieve the distress of neighbors. More and more he was becoming counsellor, executor, surety, and private banker. In the average Virginia neighborhood, few planters had both the experience and the willingness to advise less-favored men in matters of business. Governor Fauquier, in fact, once had observed "that in few Counties" were there "gentlemen enough properly educated and qualified" to be Justices.[123] In the same way, if a man of station and of friendly impulse died, the survivors of like position and conscience usually were burdened and sometimes overloaded because they, and not new public servants, had to perform the duties he laid down. Washington increasingly was approaching that plight because he had business ability and diligence along with a sense of obligation.[124]

Mrs. Savage's bond proved a nuisance to him. Doctor Savage changed tactics, somewhat mysteriously, and prevailed upon his new wife, the former Mrs. Green, to petition for the release of the bond given by him for payments to her. Washington and Bryan Fairfax declined in open court to do this on the avowed ground that they doubted whether the trust could be revoked. Privately, they believed Mrs. Savage had yielded under pressure from her husband or through fear of him. Soon they discovered from an unsigned letter of Mrs. Savage's to Washington that she wished them to hold the bond even though she continued to pretend to Doctor Savage that she was willing to release it. Washington patiently exhorted her to be candid concerning her insistence on her rights. For his own part, said Washington, if he were questioned, he would have to say why he retained the bond, in order, as he wrote her, "that my conduct may not stand the reproach of insincerity or want of candor."[125] He and Bryan Fairfax scarcely knew whether to be glad

---

[121] 1 *Diaries*, 273 n.

[122] Invoices of Sept. 26–28, 1768; *Custis Papers*, VHS.

[123] Fauquier to Board of Trade, Nov. 3, 1765; *Journ. H.B.*, 1761–65, p. lxix.

[124] See *supra*, p. 185.

[125] 2 *G. W.*, 497–98. Cf. *ibid.*, 495 and 3 *Hamilton*, 318–19, 321.

or sorry when Mrs. Savage changed her mind once more, announced her intention of going to Ireland, and again called on them to surrender the bond.[126] They prudently concluded that duty to her demanded they wait and see whether she changed her mind still again.

Another troublesome trust was that of Col. Thomas Colville, who left Washington £100 and placed on him and on John West, Jr., responsibility for the sale of the Colville slaves and for the distribution of some of the property among unknown heirs.[127] A third, less vexing obligation, apparently shared with Fielding Lewis, was that of serving as executor for the estate of George Carter, who held more than 5000 acres of land.[128] Little time but some embarrassment was involved in the arbitration of a controversy between George West and Charles Alexander.[129] Help had to be given, also, to an effort for the repair of the road to Fort Pitt and the improvement of the post between the Ohio and the East.[130] In the same line of duty, when James Gibson appealed for assistance in selling Warm Springs lottery tickets, Washington was at his command; and when Mrs. Dawson, widow of the college President, undertook to raffle her coach, Washington was manager.[131]

All these matters—of continuing education on the hard road of patience and in the ways of humankind—were Washington's in a year when he had business enough on his own farms to occupy many hours, even if pressure was less than in 1759 and immediately thereafter. The breaking of a dam during the heavy rains of April had called for much labor;[132] so had the construction of the new barn at Mount Vernon.[133] An attempt had to be made, with small result, to collect for the damage done the tobacco put aboard Captain Pollard's ship;[134] a settlement was reached after some correspondence, concerning a defect in the title to some of the Rappahannock land purchased from the Strothers.[135] Much more serious, with a threat of heavy loss to the Custis estate, was the fast-multiplying evidence that the Moore brothers were making no

[126] 3 *Hamilton*, 323. Savage himself announced in the spring of 1768 that he intended "to leave the Colony soon," (*Rind's Gazette*, May 12, 13, 1768). In October, Thomas Montgomerie of Dumfries advertised that Doctor Savage "on his going home, has left the management of his affairs to me." Savage's slaves, "about twenty" in number, were offered for sale by Montgomerie (*ibid.*, Oct. 13, 1768). For Savage's power of attorney to Montgomerie, see *Prince William Deeds*, 1768–71. Savage was back in America in 1773. See *infra*, p. 337.

[127] *Ledger A*, folio 246; *Ledger B*, folio 21; 2 *G. W.*, 483. John West's share in this is established by an advertisement in *Va. Gazette*, Dec. 12, 1767. See, also, *infra*, p. 588.

[128] *Ledger A*, folio 265, 283.   [129] 1 *Diaries*, 273.

[130] 37 *G. W.*, 487.   [131] *Ledger A*, folio 274.

[132] 1 *Diaries*, 267, 271.   [133] *Ibid.*, 275.

[134] 2 *G. W.*, 481. See *supra*, p. 169.

[135] This was done amicably (3 *Hamilton*, 312, 313–14).

progress in their efforts to discharge their debts without having to sell their land and slaves. Bernard Moore was planning a lottery, with Washington as one of the twenty managers.[136] The best that Thomas Moore could promise, in his desperation, was that if his debtors met their obligations in October, he would pay at least a part of what he owed the Custis estate.[137]

Tobacco once again had a bad season. Four years in five Washington had received less money, net, for the leaf he had sent to England than he could have commanded for it at Dumfries.[138] This year he sold 53,000 lbs. at 22s 6d per hundredweight, Virginia currency,[139] to Hector Ross of Colchester. The crops of 1768 from the York were twenty hogsheads of Washington's and thirty-six of "Jackie's."[140] These probably would go to England. The debt to Robert Cary & Co. had not yet been discharged,[141] but Washington's credits were accumulating. Carlyle & Adam owed him £528, on which he could count, and now they would take the fine wheat crop of 1768, which yielded more than 4900 bushels.[142] Furthermore, Robert Stewart, who had been made Comptroller of Customs at Kingston, Jamaica, sent word that he was ready to repay the £300 his former Colonel had lent him in 1763. Washington accepted no interest, though he received the principal gladly, and he forthwith proceeded to use the money in a manner that demonstrated his belief he was at the end of the financial distress caused by the restoration of Mount Vernon and by the failure of his efforts to grow high-quality tobacco: Instead of applying the bills of exchange to a reduction of his debt to Cary, he ordered a new chariot, the specifications of which he drew with much care.[143] Circumstances seemed, also, to justify expenditure for handsome clothing and for more of the special luxuries which Washington had been ordering in lessened quantity, though he had not dispensed with them.[144]

As always, he tried to sow again if he harvested and feasted. During the spring and summer he had attended two meetings of the company that sought vast acreage on the Mississippi,[145] and in October he set out

136 *Va. Gazette*, Apr 14, Sept. 8, 1768.   137 3 *Hamilton*, 311–12, 313.
138 2 *G. W.*, 491.   139 *Ledger A*, folio 276.
140 *Custis Papers*, VHS.
141 For evidence that the debt remained, see *infra*, p. 284, 326.
142 *Ledger A*, folio 271, 280.
143 2 *G. W.*, 488–92; 3 *Hamilton*, 307–311, 335. Through no fault of Stewart's, difficulty was experienced later in having Washington's draft on him honored (2 *G. W.*, 513).
144 2 *G. W.*, 492–93; 1 *Diaries*, 273 n.
145 *Va. Gazette*, Feb. 11, 1768; 1 *Diaries*, 270 n, 275.

again for the Dismal Swamp where he spent three days.[146] Since his previous visits, nothing had happened there to hasten greatly the day when thousands of drained acres would yield barn-bursting crops, but neither had any obstacle of magnitude been encountered. Immediately, some excellent cypress shingles were being made available. Washington's schooner almost at that very time was on her way home with a cargo of them.[147]

From the Great Dismal, Washington went back to Williamsburg to make an inspection of the Custis farms and to attend the usual settlement of accounts at the autumn session of the General Court. As soon as he reached the capital, Washington learned that a proclamation had been issued on the 27th of October for the dissolution of the General Assembly.[148] This was the act of the new Governor, Norborne Berkeley, Baron de Botetourt, who had arrived ceremoniously the day before he signed the paper.[149] Lest the Virginians assume that his proclamation indicated a suspension of the General Assembly, the Governor announced in the document that he intended "shortly to issue writs for the election of Burgesses to serve in the new Assembly at such time as by the advice of his Majesty's Council shall be judged most fit and convenient."[150] The attitude of the new Governor was conciliatory. He said nothing of any secret instructions designed to curb the resentful Colonials. No word came that dissolution was punishment for the papers of protest adopted in April.[151] To most of the Burgesses, the proclamation meant only that if they wanted to retain their seats, they had to undergo the expense and annoyance of an election in the late autumn.

[146] He left home October 19, and was in the swamp October 26–28 (1 *Diaries*, 295, 296–97).

[147] 1 *Diaries*, 293.   [148] *Journ. H.B.*, 1766–69, p. 185.

[149] Some colorful details will be found in *Rind's Gazette*, Oct. 27, 1768. Other comment on his record and on the impression he made on arrival will be found in *ibid.*, Oct. 6, 1768, and in William Nelson to John Norton, Nov. 14, 1768 (*Nelson Letter Book*, 99).

[150] *Journ. H.B.*, 1766–69, loc. cit.

[151] Actually, Botetourt was instructed to reason with the Councillors and the other Virginia leaders, after dissolving the Assembly, and to prevail on them, if he could, to accept the principle of the supremacy of Parliament. In event a new Assembly persisted in its denial, it was again to be dissolved, and Councillors who sided with the Burgesses were to be suspended. No election was to be held thereafter until further instructions were received by the Governor. A grim addendum to Botetourt's instructions was to this effect: If commotion was stirred among the people, the Governor was at liberty to call for help from the General commanding in North America (Botetourt's instructions, Chalmers Cols., *Virginia Papers*, v. 2, unpaged, NYPH, cited in C. R. Lingley, *The Transition in Virginia from Colony to Commonwealth*, 52). The Governor's desire to win good will, regardless of embarrassing instructions, was evidenced in many ways and not least by his entertainment of Williamsburg residents at Christmas time. See *Va. Gazette*, Dec. 28, 1768.

Washington had no thought of declining the contest. He felt the responsibility and he enjoyed the distinction. Besides, he just now had attained to the full honors of a gentleman of the County and he did not wish to forgo any of them. In addition to holding the office of Burgess and that of Warden of Truro Parish, he was appointed in September a Justice of the County Court of Fairfax and a member of the Court of Oyer and Terminer of the County,[152] to sit with George Mason, John Carlyle, Bryan Fairfax and others of the same station.[153] This duty was to be somewhat exacting for a man as busy as Washington had become, but it was part of the pattern of life that society had established for him and he had set for himself. When he left Williamsburg, then, on the 6th of November, 1768, it was to go home to be Justice as well as virtually everything else in the County, except Sheriff and Coroner.

He lost no time on the last leg of the journey. In weather that made even Chopawamsic Swamp appear friendly, he rode from Fredericksburg to Mount Vernon in seven and a half hours—such time as never he had been able to record before.[154] Arriving, he found everything in order. The 490 bushels of wheat that had been planted for the crop of 1769 were thriving,[155] the hogs had been "put up" to fatten,[156] beeves and wethers were receiving the same flattering attention.[157] There was ample leisure for fox-hunting, and as Lord Fairfax was in the neighborhood,[158] gentlemen in ample number were glad to ride with a peer if not after the hounds. Dinners followed hunts; the pheasant as well as the fox was sought.[159] In anticipation of success in the election, which was set for December 1, Washington arranged a ball to which his adherents were invited. The poll justified both the plan and the expense, which, with the usual cakes to voters, reached the stout sum of £25, 12s.[160] Washington and John West were re-elected—Washington by a somewhat smaller lead than in the previous poll. Captain Posey again was the third man in the field and the loser.[161] When the vote had been

---

[152] The honors usually went together but were by separate appointment.

[153] *Fairfax Orders,* 1768–70, p. 36, 53. Washington was present as a justice during this period on the following dates: Nov. 21, 1768; Feb. 20, 21, 22; Apr. 17, 18; July 17, 18, 19; Sept. 18, 19; Oct. 16, 17, 1769; Feb. 19, 20, 21, 22; Mch. 20, 1770.

[154] 1 *Diaries,* 298. This was November 9.

[155] *Ibid.,* 297.   [156] *Ibid.,* 301.

[157] *Ibid.,* 301.

[158] Presumably at Belvoir but nowhere so stated; cf. 1 *Diaries,* 298.

[159] 1 *Diaries,* 303.   [160] *Ledger A,* folio 281.

[161] The poll was: Washington, 205; John West, 175; John Posey, 132. See 816 *Papers of G. W.,* LC. This is a Toner transcript—the only poll in Washington's candidacy that is not represented by a copy in his autograph.

counted and proclaimed, well-wishers danced till the night was gone.[162]

After that came Christmas, the long holidays and, in the New Year, 1769, new plans and commitments. At home, the slaves worked on the opening of an avenue to the house;[163] from Pennsylvania, William Crawford wrote of the land he had procured in his own name for Washington, though the Captain had to admit the prospect of getting large tracts on the Kanawha did not appear to be bright at the moment.[164] In the green upcountry, Washington had bought 2682 acres of Loudoun and Fauquier land from the estate of George Carter, and in March he went there to survey it and to divide it into small tracts. It was a task that taxed muscles, but it showed Washington to be physically sound. Although he tramped for nearly two weeks through the woods and across the fields, and then rode back over the mountains, he still was so vigorous when he got home that the very next day he went fox-hunting.[165]

He did not find the usual cheer at Mount Vernon. "Patsy" had suffered more fits and apparently had to face that recurring affliction, in relief of which the regular physicians had been able to achieve nothing. There was a tradition that when all else failed, an iron ring could draw the spasm from the body. In desperation, the family had such a ring applied to "Patsy" by Joshua Evans on the 16th of February. Evans's charge was £1, 10s;[166] the effect, of course, was solely to raise false hopes that were shattered almost immediately. Doctor Rumney continued to come frequently and to charge heavily,[167] but the patient grew worse, rather than better. Once, when the family was driving to Captain McCarty's for a visit, "Patsy" had a seizure in the carriage, with the result, of course, that the journey had to be abandoned.[168]

Washington grieved with Martha and with the girl, of course, but he did not let sorrow in his own household blind him to opportunity in other homes. Having no son of his own, he was interested in the promising boys of his neighbors, and as his means increased, so did his beneficence. The old acquisitiveness remained: it was dignified by a new philanthropy. He found it inconvenient at the moment to comply with

[162] 1 *Diaries*, 301.   [163] Jan. 9–Feb. 25, 1769.
[164] Letter of Jan. 7, 1769; 3 *Hamilton*, 329–332. Washington had paid Crawford £8 in 1768 for land purchased for him (*Ledger A*, folio 277).
[165] 1 *Diaries*, 316, 317.   [166] 1 *Diaries*, 313; *Ledger A*, folio 287.
[167] His bill in the spring of 1769 was £19, odd money (*Ledger A*, folio 287).
[168] This was in April, shortly after the events about to be described in the text (1 *Diaries*, 321).

the request his friend William Ramsay of Alexandria made for a loan, but he had heard Ramsay speak in praise of New Jersey College as if it were the wish of the father to have young William Ramsay attend that school. If expense were the only obstacle, Washington wanted the boy to have the benefit of college. He accordingly wrote his friend that he would make £25 a year available for the education of the youth. In what was the most generous sentence that ever had come from his pen, Washington wrote: "No other return is expected or wished for this offer than that you will accept it with the same freedom and good will with which it is made, and that you may not even consider it in the light of an obligation, or mention it as such; for be assured that from me it will never be known." [169]

These were the channels in which life was moving—now over shoals, now over rocks and now through pleasant pastures when, early in April, Washington received from Dr. David Ross of Bladensburg, Maryland, papers in which proposals were made for "associations" of merchants and citizens who would agree not to import or to buy non-essential British goods so long as Parliament undertook to impose direct taxes or to suppress colonial assemblies.[170] The argument was knotty and by no means new. Washington, who already had some familiarity with the subject, read the papers Ross sent him and then he forwarded them to George Mason for that wise man's reflection. Vigorously, that 5th of April, 1769, Washington wrote: "At a time when our lordly Masters in Great Britain will be satisfied with nothing less than the deprication [171] of American freedom, it seems highly necessary that something should be done to avert the stroke and maintain the liberty which we had derived from our ancestors; but the manner of doing it to answer the purpose effectually is the point in question."

He dropped a line and continued as if what he was about to say was almost too obvious to labor: "That no man should scruple, or hesitate a moment to use a-ms in defence of so valuable a blessing, on which all the good and evil of life depends, is clearly my opinion; yet A-ms, I would beg leave to add, should be the last resource, the denier resort." [172]

Arms! He had not spoken of them before. Arms!

[169] Letter of Jan. 29, 1769; 2 *G. W.*, 500.
[170] The definitive treatment of this subject is in A. M. Schlesinger, *The Colonial Merchants.* As any paraphrase of Schlesinger's findings would carry this paragraph into the wider ranges of the history of the period, it has seemed permissible to make this general reference and to refer the student of the associations to that work.
[171] It is impossible to say whether he mean deprivation or depreciation.
[172] 2 *G. W.*, 501. The misspelling of *dernier ressort* is preserved.

CHAPTER XI

Association Against Taxes and Debt
(April–June, 1769)

"Addresses to the throne and remonstrances to Parliament we have already, it is said, proved the inefficacy of; how far their attention to our rights and privileges is to be awakened or alarmed by starving their trade and manufactures, remains to be tried."

Thus Washington continued in his letter to George Mason after he had spoken grimly but without hesitation of an appeal to arms as the last resort of the colonials. The Northern provinces, Washington went on, were using this weapon. It might be effective if generally employed. Clashing interests and selfish, designing men would make difficult everywhere the task of cutting off the importation of British goods. This would be particularly true in the tobacco Colonies, Washington reasoned, because trade there was diffused and was conducted not by native merchants but by factors acting for principals "at home." Even so, he maintained, the enterprise would not be hopeless if gentlemen would stop importation and purchase and would "explain matters to the people." This would stimulate the public "to a cordial agreement to purchase none but certain enumerated articles out of any of the stores after such a period . . ." In the face of a general agreement of this nature, factors might be prompted to stop importing goods; they would at least be cautious in doing so. Prohibited articles would be sold only to the man who would not subscribe to an association or to the pretended patriot who would join and then disregard his promise. Both these classes, Washington added, "ought to be stigmatized and made the objects of public reproach."

If gentlemen could not assure repeal of the offending Townshend Acts by this and other devices, they at least might save some members of their own class who were drowning in debt and extravagance. A spendthrift who was too proud to reduce a ruinous style of living in normal times might be willing to do so if thrift became fashionable.

Washington explained to Mason: ". . . I see but one set of people (the merchants excepted) who will not or ought not to wish well of the scheme, and that is those who live genteely and hospitably on clear estates . . . Were these [men] not to consider the valuable object in view and the good of others, [they] might think it hard to be curtailed in their living and enjoyments."[1] He might have included himself among those who lived opulently on properties not threatened with ruin, but he would not be content with their life, or share their indifference.

"The more I consider a scheme of this sort," Washington wrote Mason, warming as he progressed, "the more ardently I wish success to it . . ." Public gain might be uncertain, because if Parliament could tax, it could prohibit manufactures in the Colonies, but private gain would be so positive that the scheme should be tried in Virginia. Methods had to be considered. It might be well for gentlemen to do no more than to correspond on the subject and to delay action until the General Court and the Assembly met in May and agreed on a plan that could be put in operation simultaneously in all the Counties.[2] There scarcely was a clause in any of this to show that Washington realized he was entering what was for him the new field of political leadership. As a Burgess since 1759 he had transacted his constituents' public business, had presented their petitions, had voted according to his judgment and convictions, and had learned much about the mind and methods of lawmaking bodies. He had not essayed to be a leader in a House that had counted Pendleton and Henry and Wythe among its debaters. Now it was different in this important respect: The struggle to stop the arbitrary exercise of power by the British Parliament was one that depended for success on the action of all the people. It was therefore the duty of gentlemen to explain the principle of non-importation to persons who otherwise might not understand what was involved.

[1] 2 G. W., 502–03. The original of these sentences reads: "And I can see but one set of people (the merchants excepted) who will not, or ought not, to wish well of the scheme; and that is those who live genteely and hospitably, on clear estates. Such as these think it hard to be curtailed in their living and enjoyment; for as to the penurious man, he saves his money, and he saves his credit, having the best plea for doing that, which before perhaps he had the most violent struggles to refrain from doing."

[2] 2 G. W., 500–04. This is one of the worst written of Washington's letters, though on a subject to which he manifestly had devoted much thought. The effort in the text has been to break up the sentences and to simplify the argument even if this has necessitated the use in the paraphrase of words not in the original. If a closer approximation of Washington's own words is desired, the text in G. W. should be consulted.

George Mason already had concluded that Virginia should follow the Northern Colonies in organizing firm associations for the non-importation of British goods, though he believed the tobacco Colonies had to use certain British goods the Northern provinces could do without because New England, New York and Pennsylvania had some manufactures of their own. As Mason wrote in a prompt reply to Washington, it might be necessary "to publish something preparatory to [the adoption of a non-importation agreement] in our Gazettes, to warn the people at least of the impending danger and induce them the more readily and cheerfully to concur in the proper measures to avert it." He had started an article of this sort but because of illness had not completed the appeal. Now, with his usual readiness to perform the hard task, he prepared a list of the articles he thought Virginia could refuse to buy in Britain. Neither he nor Washington had ever looked at exports and imports from the viewpoint of the plain farmer. Their experience with foreign trade, moreover, did not include that of the merchant or factor. Consequently they drafted the terms of the proposed association according to the requirements of plantation management. Cloth with which to provide garments for slaves must be imported. Spices and sewing silk likewise might be brought into the country or purchased from merchants. All luxuries of food and of dress, all alcoholic beverages, virtually all manufactured articles, ought to be excluded. Mason sent Washington the first text of this paper, and later he forwarded a few amendments that seemed in the public interest.[3] All the while, the view of both men was that if this association led British merchants and manufacturers to procure a repeal of the Townshend Acts, a full resumption of trade across the Atlantic was to be desired, because it was beneficial both to the mother country and to the daughters in America. Should Parliament be unwilling to erase the statutes, then, said Mason, Virginia should stop exports to England, particularly of tobacco, "by which the revenue would lose fifty times more than all their oppressions could raise here."[4]

When Washington was ready to set out for Williamsburg on the 30th of April, 1769, he had with him the final text of Mason's paper on the terms of association and that gentleman's hearty wishes for an "agreeable session" which, the master of Gunston Hall had to confess, "I fear

[3] 3 *Hamilton*, 345–49; 1 *Rowland*, Mason, 141 ff.
[4] Letter of Apr. 5, 1769; 3 *Hamilton*, 343–44.

you will not have." [5] The journey, which took four days, was made uneventfully in Washington's "chair" and with three horses,[6] but the long drive across reawakened fields and through forests newly dressed in green probably was not given over entirely to the contemplation of the beauties of Nature and to reflection on the grievances of his Majesty's subjects in America. Washington had a new, a nearer and a more personal interest. The Treaty of Fort Stanwix with the Iroquois, Nov. 5, 1768,[7] and the Treaty of Hard Labour with the Cherokees, Oct. 14, 1768,[8] had done precisely what he had told William Crawford in September, 1767, he anticipated: Together the two documents had wiped out the "Proclamation Line" of 1763 and had extended much farther westward the region open to the English. The Iroquois had agreed to surrender all their claims to territory on a line from Fort Stanwix near Lake Oneida, New York, to Fort Pitt and thence along the eastern bank of the Ohio to the mouth of the Cherokee (Tennessee) River. By their treaty, the Cherokees yielded everything East and Northeast from Fort Chiswell to the mouth of the Great Kanawha.[9] While this new Cherokee line was not satisfactory and was re-negotiated almost immediately, the two pacts threw open the country to which Washington long had been looking. By prompt action with Captain Crawford, he could hope to patent some thousands of acres he could sell at great profit when settlement advanced that far to the West.

Another and perhaps a less doubtful prospect was that of having the Colony of Virginia execute a promise made so long previously that men of shorter memory or of less acquisitiveness might have forgotten it or might have despaired of having it redeemed. This was the formal pledge of Governor Dinwiddie and the Council of Virginia in February,[10] 1754, to allot 200,000 acres of land to those who would volunteer to go to the Ohio "to erect and support" the fort to be built at "The Forks." The proclamation had stated that 100,000 acres of this bounty land were to be contiguous to the fort and the other 100,000 "to be on or near the River Ohio." Further, Dinwiddie had stated in the proclama-

[5] 3 *Hamilton*, 345; 1 *Diaries*, 322.   [6] *Ledger A*, folio 191; 1 *Diaries*, 324.

[7] Text in *Journ. H.B.*, 1766–69, p. xxviii.

[8] Text in Alden, *John Stuart and the Southern Frontier*, with citations from the *Gage MSS* and P.R.O., C.O. 5: 1435 and 1437. Much of the relevant correspondence is in 13 *V* 20 ff. and in *Journ. H.B.*, 1766–69, p. xxvi ff.

[9] The lines are simply and admirably shown in the *Atlas of American History*, Plates 60 and 61. Fort Chiswell was near the site of the present-day Wytheville, Va. The site is marked by a pyramid of boulders.

[10] February 19. See Vol. I, p. 333–34.

tion: "the said lands shall be divided amongst [the volunteers] immediately after their performance of the said service, in a proportion due to their respective merit, as shall be represented to me by their officers; and held and enjoyed by them without paying any rights and also free from the payment of quitrents for the term of fifteen years." [11] The "said service" had lengthened into a war. Some of the volunteers of 1754 had perished in Braddock's defeat and some had died of sickness. Others doubtless had wandered off, none could say whither. Until the peace treaty had been signed in 1763, it had not been altogether certain that his Majesty's standard would continue to fly on the Ohio. Then, in the year that assured English rule of that great domain, the King had forbidden settlement beyond the heads of the rivers that flowed into the Atlantic. Now that the proclamation of 1763 no longer applied, Dinwiddie's of 1754 could come into effect. The promise made to Washington and to the men who had marched to meet Jumonville and had capitulated at Fort Necessity must be redeemed. Two hundred thousand acres, divided "in a proportion due to . . . respective merit"! That was a promise no government should be allowed to forget: By any arithmetic it meant some thousands of acres to be added to the holdings of George Washington, Esq., Burgess of Fairfax, who had in his pocket Colonel Mason's plan for an association, when he drove into Williamsburg the 3rd of May, 1769.

He found most of the old leaders duly returned in the December election. Edmund Pendleton, Richard Bland, Peyton Randolph, Archibald Cary and Charles Carter all were there. Patrick Henry now represented Hanover instead of Louisa. An unusual number of new members appeared, some of them the successors of elders of the same names, and some of them men who had come from new Counties where few of the "old gentry" had settled. Among these novitiates was a tall, thin young man of 26 who represented Albemarle. His tawny skin and hair were relieved from all appearance of oddity by the intelligent light of his eyes, the set of his mouth and the independent, half-tossing manner in which he carried his head. Washington perhaps had seen him as an eager auditor of the debates on the Stamp Act resolutions but he probably had never heard the young man's name—Thomas Jefferson.

Burgesses senior and junior were treated to such ceremonial as the

[11] 5 E. J., 499–500.

Colony never had known. The Governor rode from the Palace to the Capitol in a resplendent coach behind cream-white Hanoverian horses which, it was said in awed tones, the Duke of Cumberland himself had given to his Lordship. It even was whispered that the mannerisms of the Governor were those of King George in reading the speech from the throne.[12] The House itself was organized with fuller regard for all the impressive formalities than any earlier Clerk had recorded—even to such matters as a silent pointing of the Clerk's finger at the man who nominated the Speaker, and the solemn removal of the mace from beneath the table to a place on it.[13]

The Governor's speech was ingratiating. After the usual references to the King's love of his subjects, Botetourt said: "I have nothing to ask, but that you consider well, and follow exactly, without passion or prejudice, the real interests of those you have the honor to represent; they are most certainly consistent with the prosperity of Great Britain, and so they will forever be found, when pursued with temper and moderation." He added the flattering information that the King intended the Governor of Virginia to reside thereafter in the Colony and not to act through a Lieutenant.[14]

When Botetourt had finished and the Burgesses had trooped downstairs to their own chamber, Edmund Pendleton arranged in a fine spirit of generosity that young Jefferson, who already had some reputation as a writer, should draw up the resolution that called for an address along specified lines in answer to the Governor's speech. Jefferson did so and, when the House approved, *nem con.,* he had the honor of appointment to the committee of House leaders who were to draft the document in the spirit of the resolutions. Here again Pendleton proposed and the committee agreed that Jefferson compose the paper. The ambitious young Burgess from Albemarle a second time tried his pen, but not to the satisfaction of Robert Carter Nicholas. That Burgess from James City County, officially "Mr. Treasurer," shook his head over Jefferson's paragraphs. They adhered too closely, he insisted, to the language of the resolutions; the address should be more elaborate. He "was desired," Jefferson wrote long afterward, "to draw [an address] more in large, which he did with amplification enough, and it was accepted." Jefferson added: "Being a young man as well as a young member, it

[12] Cf. Philip Alexander Bruce's Sketch of Botetourt in *DAB*.
[13] *Journ. H.B.,* 1766–69, p. 187, 188.
[14] *Journ. H.B.,* 1766–69, p. 189.

made on me an impression proportioned to the sensibilities of that time of life." [15]

Nicholas's address was in the somewhat flamboyant style of the courtier but it was unanimously approved by the Burgesses, who voted to present it en masse to his Lordship.[16] As Botetourt received it with graciousness and modesty,[17] the session opened auspiciously.

Washington was assigned to his old Committee, that of Propositions and Grievances and, in addition, to Privileges and Elections, and later to the new Committee on Religion.[18] The three assignments represented work enough for any Burgess, but Washington found time and opportunity to acquaint the Governor—who was now "His Excellency" and not merely "His Honor" [19]—with the terms of the proclamation of February, 1754. While Washington did this in a somewhat cursory manner,[20] he had no intention of leaving so large and valuable a grant where it might or might not be remembered by Lord Botetourt. The Colonel was sowing the seed now; he would come again, to till and then to harvest.

As legislation was neither large in volume nor important in scope, Burgesses talked much of what might be accomplished by such an association as Mason had modeled after those in the Northern provinces and had sketched in the paper entrusted to Washington. There was discussion, also, of threats made in Parliament to have persons accused of treason in the Colonies sent to England for trial there. A statute of Henry VIII, authorizing this, had been unearthed and brandished over the heads of colonials.[21] This alarmed Virginians. They had begun to lose faith in the efficacy of appeals to Parliament and they felt that a blow at England's trade was a better defence than argument with Lords and Commons. In their address to the Governor, the Burgesses somewhat tactfully made reservation to this effect: "It is an indispensable duty which we owe to our constituents, and which at present is strongly enforced by your Lordship's recommendation and advice, that

15 Jefferson to William Wirt, Aug. 5, 1815; 14 *Jefferson*, 335–42.
16 *Journ. H.B.*, 1766–69, p. 199–200.   17 *Ibid.*, 202–03.
18 *Ibid.*, 190, 211.   19 *Ibid.*, 187, 211.
20 Cf. *Ibid.*, 187; 2 *G. W.*, 528–29.
21 Cf. the familiar observation of Lecky: "By virtue of an obsolete law, passed in one of the darkest periods of English history and at a time when England possessed not a single Colony, any colonist who was designated by the Governor as a traitor might be carried three thousand miles from his home, from his witnesses, from the scene of his alleged crime" (*History of England*, v. 3, p. 394–95, quoted from a different edition in G. E. Howard, *Preliminaries of the Revolution*, 199).

we should dispassionately, and with the greatest candor, consider the important business upon which we are now assembled; and we beg leave to assure your Excellency that if, in the course of our deliberations, any matters should arise, which may in any sort affect Great Britain, they shall be discussed on this ruling principle, that both our interests are inseparably the same." [22] Discussion of the threatened removal of accused colonials for treason trials in Britain seemed so clearly a matter "affecting" the home country that members wished to bring it up. The House had resolved on the day of the Governor's address to consider his remarks in Committee of the Whole [23] and after two postponements,[24] it set a new date for the discussion and it rephrased its resolution in such a manner as to give least offense to His Excellency, who already was becoming popular.[25]

On the 16th of May, the date finally agreed upon, a motion was made to refer to the Committee of the Whole the early British acts on treason trials that had been cited as justification for the threats to send offending colonials to England. Debate on these statutes and on the operation of the tax laws disclosed no difference of opinion. Inclusive resolutions were presented for reaffirmation of the principle that the sole right of taxing the inhabitants of Virginia was and always had been "legally and constitutionally vested in the House of Burgesses, lawfully convened according to the ancient and established practice, with the consent of the Council, and of his Majesty, the King of Great Britain, or his Governor for the time being." A second resolution asserted the right of petition to the throne and sharply added, "it is lawful and expedient to procure the concurrence of his Majesty's other Colonies, in dutiful addresses, praying the royal interposition in favor of the violated rights of America." Next came solemn affirmation of the right of trial in Virginia of any person charged with any crime there. Further, "the seizing any person or persons, residing in this Colony, suspected of any crime whatsoever, committed therein, and sending such person or persons, to places beyond the sea, to be tried, is highly derogatory of the rights of British subjects; as thereby the inestimable privilege of being tried by a jury from the vicinage, as well as the liberty of summoning and producing witnesses on such trial, will be taken away from the party accused." The recommendation of the Committee of the Whole

[22] *Journ. H.B.*, 1766–69, p. 199–200.
[24] *Ibid.*, 200, 207.

[23] *Journ. H.B.*, 1766–69, p. 192.
[25] *Ibid.*, 210.

was that "an humble, dutiful and loyal address" be presented the King
to assure him of the "inviolable attachment" of the Colony to his person
and government, and to beseech "his royal interposition" to quiet the
minds of his subjects in America and to avert from them the "dangers
and miseries" of arrest and removal for trial "in any other manner
than by the ancient and long established course of proceedings." [26]

Unanimously, the House approved its own action in Committee of
the Whole, resolved to continue its discussion of the state of the Colony,
and directed that the Speaker send copies of the paper to the presiding
officers of all the American provinces, with a request that the other
Assemblies concur. Finally, a committee under the direction of John
Blair was selected to prepare the address to the King. Neither Washington nor Jefferson was named to this drafting committee, but Patrick
Henry and Richard Henry Lee were. [27]

These members and their colleagues were ready the next morning
with a somewhat theatrical address. Loyalty was professed to the King,
the adequacy of colonial justice was maintained, and the horrors of
transportation and trial in England of American offenders were set
forth emotionally and with a surplus of rhetoric. The final paragraph
was to this effect: "Truly alarmed at the fatal tendency of these pernicious counsels, and with hearts filled with anguish, by such dangerous
invasions of our dearest privileges, we presume to prostrate ourselves
at the foot of your royal throne, beseeching your Majesty, as our King
and Father, to avert from your faithful and loyal subjects of America,
those miseries which must necesarily be the consequence of such
measures. After expressing our firm confidence in your royal wisdom
and goodness, permit us to assure your Majesty, that the most fervent
prayers of your people of this Colony, are daily addressed to the
Almighty, that your Majesty's reign may be long and prosperous over
Great Britain, and all your dominions; and that, after death, your
Majesty may taste the fullest fruition of eternal bliss, and that a descendant of your illustrious house may reign over the extended British empire
till time shall be no more." [28] Bombast and all, the address was adopted
unanimously without challenge or amendment. "Mr. Speaker" was

---

[26] *Journ. H.B.*, 214. The authorship of these resolutions is not known. They manifestly are
the work of an experienced lawyer, Bland perhaps, and they suggest the probability that they
were drawn by someone less interested in displaying his craftsmanship to his legislative colleagues than in explaining to the average intelligent Virginian the nature of the differences that
had arisen between the Colonies and Great Britain.

[27] *Journ. H.B.*, 1766–69, p. 215.   [28] *Ibid.*, 215–16.

directed to transmit a copy to the Virginia agent in London, who was to have it presented to his Majesty and afterwards to have it published in the English newspapers.[29]

Then the House proceeded to the business of the day—a petition of sundry Albemarle men against the spread of seines near the mouth of the "north branch of James River," a report on a proposal to dissolve the vestry of Overwharton Parish, and other matters of no larger import. At length the Clerk read a petition in which planters of Brunswick County asked larger option in the number of warehouses from which tobacco notes might be procured for the payment of taxes and public dues. This petition had just been referred to the Committee on Propositions and Grievances,[30] when, about noon,[31] the Sergeant-at-Arms called out: "Mr. Speaker, a message from the Governor!"

In accordance with the polite procedure of the House, the Speaker directed that the message be received immediately.

Nathaniel Walthoe, Clerk of the General Assembly, strode down the aisle and halted.[32] "Mr. Speaker," he said, "the Governor commands the immediate attendance of your House in the Council Chamber."

Down from his chair and out of the House Peyton Randolph walked. Behind him, in no order of seniority, the Burgesses streamed up the stairs to the council chamber. The upper branch of the Assembly was in recess,[33] but at the head of the table, in his chair of state, sat Governor Botetourt. He waited until the last members had massed around the table and along the walls. Then he said: "Mr. Speaker, and Gentlemen of the House of Burgesses, I have heard of your resolves, and augur ill of their effect: You have made it my duty to dissolve you; and you are dissolved accordingly." [34]

Dissolved! Dissolved within a little more than five months after the elections and within less than seven months after Botetourt's proclamation of Oct. 27, 1769, which had forecast those elections! If this was the spirit of a Governor, who personally was affable and manifestly well-disposed to Virginia, what was to be expected of a Parliament that already was threatening to invoke against Americans a two-hundred-year-old treason act? Burgesses asked themselves many questions as

[29] *Ibid.*, 216.   [30] *Ibid.*, 218.

[31] *Ibid.*, xxxix.

[32] To this point, the narrative of the appearance and reception of the Clerk is based on the traditional procedure of the House and not on any extant record. The journal covers the remainder.

[33] 3 *L. J.*, 1392.   [34] *Journ. H.B.*, 1766–69, p. 218.

they left the Council Chamber, went back to their own House, got their hats and papers, and then, still talking, walked out of the Capitol.

Soon, word was passed that there was to be a meeting at Anthony Hays's Raleigh Tavern. Thither most of the Burgesses flocked and into his largest room, the Apollo. Washington went, of course, and shared in the unanimous election of Peyton Randolph as moderator. The House thereupon reconvened unofficially and listened as members gave warning that the Colony soon might lose its liberties. Washington was the one man who had a definite plan in the form of Mason's project for an association, and he consequently had to take a more prominent part than ever he had in a deliberative body. He probably did not attempt any extended address, because he always spoke quite briefly and to the main issue,[35] but leadership largely was his.[36] When the discussion gravitated to the associations that had been organized in other Colonies, a motion was made that a similar association be formed and that a committee be chosen to prepare a plan. The fires of resentment burned so hotly at the moment that little or no opposition to the general idea was expressed, but the details of what should and should not be imported into Virginia were so close to the life of every Burgess that men who usually were silent in the House had views to vent. At length the motion was put and passed; the committee was named with Washington one of its members; adjournment was taken until the next day to give the committee time to draft its recommendations.[37]

The questions to be determined by the Committee were the practical ones of the articles to be excluded, the date when the association should become operative, the duration of the agreement, and the methods by which all citizens could be induced to sign. On almost all these points, Mason's draft was accepted in an effort to make non-importation hurt Virginia as little as possible, while alarming Britain by the loss of exports. To achieve this in a Colony that had a small stock of goods and almost no manufactures, the committee endorsed a highly complicated scheme: No taxed article—tea, paint, pigment, paper other than the

---

35 Cf. 1 *Jefferson*, 87.

36 This statement cannot be buttressed with any contemporary proof and is in large measure traditional, but all the circumstances, and, in particular, Washington's custody of Mason's plan, lend high probability to the tradition.

37 See the minutes, as reprinted in *Journ. H.B.*, 1766–69, p. xxxix ff. This brief record does not give the names of committeemen, but, so far as Washington himself is concerned, an entry in his diary supplies the needful information. It reads: "Was upon a committee at Hays till 10 o'clock." The committee undoubtedly was the one that agreed on the terms of the association, the most important work of the day in Virginia.

cheapest sheets—was to be imported. Of the supply in the Colony, none was to be purchased after Sept. 1, 1769, for so long a time as it was taxed by Parliament for the purpose of raising a revenue. During the continuance of the tax on those particular items, none of a long list of untaxed luxuries and articles of British manufactures was to be brought to America on new invoices or was to be purchased after September 1, no matter when landed or by whom. Prior to the repeal of the offending taxes, the association could only be dissolved at a general meeting of the subscribers after a month's prior notice of the meeting, or automatically after the taxes were terminated. Even if the association were abandoned by consent, the pledge against the importation and purchase of taxed articles would remain in force. All this was precisely as Mason had suggested. The list of prohibited articles remained exactly as he had drawn it.[38]

Committeemen next decided that the importation of slaves or the purchase of those imported by others should not be forbidden until November 1.[39] Then the committee applied to wines the general prohibition on purchase and importation after September 1, or until the repeal of the acts of Parliament that imposed duties on those beverages. Still again, the committee drafted a section that pledged members of the association not to kill or to sell for slaughter any lambs weaned before May 1 in any year—a restriction that had been incorporated in some of the northern associations in order to increase the supply of wool for winter garments. Mason's somewhat wordy preamble was endorsed, except that the Committee opened it with renewed assurance of "our inviolable and unshaken fidelity and loyalty to our most gracious Sovereign" and a little more in the same strain.[40]

The next morning, May 18, 1769, the committee presented its report. Apparently the document was discussed but was not amended. In final form it was approved and then was signed individually by the members. Chance or purpose so fixed it that when the list was printed, "Peyton Randolph" headed one column and "Patrick Henry, Jun" the other— as if the old party and the new in the House of Burgesses, the defenders of the throne and the author of the "Stamp Act resolutions," wished it

[38] "Nets" in the text in 3 *Hamilton,* 348, evidently was a misreading of "hats," which is the word used in the printed minutes.

[39] This provision, which will be shown to be subject to two interpretations, doubtless was shaped for the convenience of those who already had ordered slaves or had cargoes in transit.

[40] Text in *Journ. H.B.,* 1766–69, p. xl–xlii. Deliberations had been suspended during the evening for dinner. Washington was the guest of Treasurer Nicholas (1 *Diaries,* 325).

to be known that they stood together in this pledge of resistance to what they considered arbitrary taxation. Under Peyton Randolph's name, "Mr. Treasurer," Robert Carter Nicholas, signed the sheet. Next was Richard Bland, then Archibald Cary—these four among the veterans of the House. Richard Henry Lee followed. After him was Charles Carter. Thereupon the tall figure of Washington bent over the table as his large right hand swept across the sheet. The sixth name in the next column was that of Thomas Jefferson. By no means all the Burgesses signed. Absentees included, twenty-two members of a House of 116 failed to attach their signatures. Most conspicuous of those whose names were missing from the list was Edmund Pendleton, but he had procured leave of absence on the 14th and probably was not in Williamsburg.[41] "Mr. Attorney," the former Clerk John Randolph, did not join. George Wythe's name was absent. He now was Clerk in succession to John Randolph,[42] and no longer had a seat [43] in the House.

Even in the face of this dissent—whether born of fear, of indifference or of conviction—the majority represented three-fourths of the House and nearly all the men apt to have influence in prevailing on the people of their Counties to join the association. Virginia would stand with her northern sisters. Moreover, Washington's logic about the effect of a non-importation agreement on the finances of debt-ridden planters was in itself good reason for satisfaction that gentlemen had made a pledge. It might work out precisely as Washington had said: Even if an unfriendly Parliament stood fast, frugality might save many Virginians from deepened debt and some of them from ruin.

This conservative view was not enough for the fervent, excited men who now had completed their discussions in the Apollo room. They must celebrate and must repeat in wine the pledges they had made in ink. Glasses were called for; toasts were proposed. The first, of course, was to the King, the second to the Queen and the royal family, the next to Lord Botetourt and prosperity to Virginia. When glasses again were lifted, the toast was to "a speedy and lasting union between Great Britain and her Colonies." Then the call was by some man who knew precisely what he wanted to say: "The constitutional British liberty in America, and all true patriots, the supporters thereof." [44]

[41] *Journ. H.B.*, 1766–69, p. 209. Leave was for eight days.
[42] *Ibid.*, 141. He became Clerk at the spring session of 1768.
[43] James Wallace succeeded him as Burgess from Elizabeth City.
[44] The six subsequent toasts were principally to British friends of America. See the full list in the reprint of the minutes, *Journ. H.B.*, 1766–69, p. xlii–xliii.

After adjournment, Washington was glad enough to go to his lodgings and to be abed by 8 o'clock. The next day, May 19, he had odds and ends of business to transact, and when these were finished, he remained in town as a loyal subject to attend at the Palace the celebration of the Queen's birthday. This was held on invitation and at the expense of the Governor, who was resolved not to lose the good will of the Burgesses, even though he had dissolved their House.[45] Then on the 20th, Washington set out for Eltham at the fastest pace he could force from a team that pulled his chair across roads less bad at that season of the year than at any other. He stopped for the afternoon and spent the night with the Bassetts, but on Sunday, the 21st, he pushed as far as Port Royal, and on the 22nd resumed the journey.

With him, he carried one personal concern only: the old skeleton of the Parke-Custis family was stirring again in its coffin. The Dunbar case was being revived. After almost sixty years, the third and fourth generations of the issue of Col. Daniel Parke might be called upon to pay for his amours with Catherine Chester in the Leeward Islands.[46] Charles Dunbar now was dead, but his sons John and Joseph were interested, speculatively at least, in seeing whether they could make the descendants of Colonel Parke's legitimate children pay the debts that had accumulated against the estate he had left the daughter born out of wedlock.[47] The Dunbar brothers, acting through the London merchants, Edward and Samuel Athawes, had been well advised in their choice of representatives in Virginia. William Nelson, the most influential of native merchants, had succeeded his father Thomas Nelson as agent for the plaintiffs. Nelson was next to John Blair in seniority among members of the Council and, by marriage, was affiliated with the powerful Carters and Burwells. As counsel for the plantiffs, Nelson had selected Robert Carter Nicholas, and with that able attorney had undertaken to effect in 1766 a compromise with Washington.[48] Either because Washington felt confident of winning the case, or else because the Dunbars set too high a figure, these negotiations came to naught. Blame for this failure of compromise did not rest on William Nelson, because he frankly told John Dunbar: "If [the Parke heirs] pay your demand they will naturally expect an acquittal from every other claim-

[45] 1 Diaries, 325.   [46] See Vol. II, p. 281 ff.
[47] It is fortunate that the trail of the Dunbar case, though lost in the Custis Papers, can be taken up in Nelson Letter Book, VSL.
[48] William Nelson to John Dunbar, Sept. 11, 1766; Nelson Letter Book.

ant; besides, the sum of £3000 sterling which you compute to be costs must be vastly too high; for my father before me and I since have paid all that accrued on this side and they amount not to one third of that sum." [49]

For a time, the Dunbar brothers were discouraged. They and their friends on Antigua were slow to furnish documents essential to the prosecution of the suit in Virginia.[50] There was like delay in supplying Nelson with the indemnifying bond on which he insisted in order to protect him against the contingency of a demand by the Parke heirs for the costs of their defence in event the remanded suit was decided against the Dunbars.[51] Another complication arose in 1767 because of improper directions given Nicholas by the plaintiffs concerning the style of the suit to be entered.[52] All the while, Nelson was writing in vain for papers on file nowhere outside the Leeward Islands. ". . . I fear," the Virginia agent wrote the Athawes firm, "Mr. Dunbar will make nought of his suit here, for he seems not to have a friend in Antigua that will send us over a copy of his father's will and other necessary papers to carry on the affair." [53]

At this stage of proceedings, Robert Carter Nicholas had to abandon the practice of law in order to conserve his frail health for the discharge of his duties as colonial Treasurer. Within a few weeks after the dissolution of the House of Burgesses, Nelson was able to write: ". . . our chief dependence must be on Mr. Wythe who is second to none of the profession with us, yet we shall not be without the advice and assistance of [Nicholas] whilst his health permits." [54] Dunbar was now bestirring himself, also. He supplied ample security to protect Nelson and he started on the long voyage to Antigua to procure the essential papers.[55]

George Wythe and William Nelson were not men to conspire secretly in a corner against the descendants of Parkes and Custises and Byrds or, for that matter, against any man. As attorney and as agent, Wythe and Nelson would respect, of course, the confidence of the Dunbar brothers and would not disclose the details of their procedure, but they must have notified Washington that the suit once more was to be

[49] *Ibid.*
[50] William Nelson to Martin Goble, Sept. 11, 1766; *Nelson Letter Book,* 8.
[51] William Nelson to E. and S. Athawes, Sept. 13, 1766; *Nelson Letter Book,* 14.
[52] William Nelson to E. and S. Athawes, Aug. 12, 1767; *Nelson Letter Book,* 34.
[53] William Nelson to S. Athawes, Nov. 15, 1768; *Nelson Letter Book,* 101. The punctuation is revised slightly.
[54] William Nelson to J. Dunbar, June 12, 1769; *Nelson Letter Book,* 121.
[55] William Nelson to S. Athawes, July 5, 1769; *Nelson Letter Book,* 123.

brought before the General Court. It was not a pleasant prospect for even the stoutest of hearts. Still, Washington was not of the nature to agonize as John Custis had over the possible consequences of a loss of the action. More and more strongly, if subtly, Washington was developing ability to disregard what he could not avert. He would meet the Dunbar brothers when and as he must . . . even if George Wythe was their counsel and William Nelson their agent; he would meet them, though money never had been so scarce, and debt hung like a pall on the gateposts of many a plantation between the York and the Potomac.

It was different at Mount Vernon when he drew rein on the evening of Monday, the 22nd.[56] The house was full of guests. "Jackie" Custis was there with Rev. Jonathan Boucher, his new instructor. Walter Magowan had come to report himself back from England, duly accepted for holy orders.[57] Doctor Rumney was paying a social call. Mrs. John Bushrod and Mrs. Warner Washington, with their families, were on a visit.[58] Plans were afoot for attending a race at Cameron on Friday, the 26th, and a barbeque in Alexandria the next day. On the following Wednesday, a party was to drive to Towlston, near Difficult Run,[59] where Washington was to stand as godfather for Bryan Fairfax's third son by his wife Elizabeth Cary, younger sister of the adorable Sally. These plans were interesting, but there was one commonplace circumstance that perhaps meant far more. Coming home, Washington had seen the greenest of green fields, and when he sat down to write his diary entry for that day of return from the most fateful session of Assembly he yet had attended, there was consolation in the first entry he made: ". . . found my wheat much better in general than ever it was at this season before . . ."[60].

That was consolation; it might be augury.

[56] It will be observed that Washington made the journey from Williamsburg to Mount Vernon in three days. This time included an afternoon and night at Eltham and represented the fastest journey he ever had made over that familiar route.

[57] He promptly procured in Maryland what Washington termed "a valuable living" (2 G. W., 514).

[58] 1 Diaries, 326. Another guest was "Mr. Addison," not otherwise identified.

[59] Col. William Fairfax had styled it Towlston Grange, after his birthplace in Yorkshire (1 Diaries, 131) but the shortened name was more frequently used.

[60] He added: "being ranker, better spread over the ground, and broader in the blade than usual. It was also observable that in general the head was shot out, and in many places in blossom" (1 Diaries, 327).

CHAPTER XII

Training School on the Potomac

(July, 1769–December, 1770)

After the brief festivities of the last days of June, Washington had to take up again—as so often he had—a life that combined direction of his own farms, patient effort to solve some of the problems of his neighbors, and steadfast planning for the increase of his private estate. In the early summer of 1769 he had, also, a measure of responsibility to make it certain that planters of his County understood the association and subscribed to it. He followed closely and doubtless shared personally in what was done to acquaint the residents of Fairfax and Prince William with the Williamsburg agreement, and he hoped for hearty endorsement of it everywhere in Virginia, though he did not know at the time what fortune attended the circulation of the printed terms in remote districts.[1] Reports from the capital were not encouraging. The merchants of the town were supposed to have reached a firm understanding on non-importation, but by the middle of June they had to publish the names of eight establishments that had brought in goods from England.[2] Denunciation in heated terms attended the printing. The "baseness" of the offenders' "crime," the assurance they would be "shunned by their neighbors," the price of "blind avarice," the punishment of "guilty consciences," and even the need of forgiveness in the next world—all these were set forth; but the fact was, the association soon proved itself too rigid and too complicated.

Even an intelligent, educated man would need to have at hand the text of the association to verify its essential provisions and to reconcile, if possible, its contradictory provisions. A merchant or an individual who had ordered tea from England before May 18 could accept the shipment without criticism, but if a dealer's stock did not arrive before September 1, no member of the association was to buy any of it there-

[1] 2 G. W., 512.　　　　　　　[2] Rind's Gazette, June 15, 1769.

after. Everything else in the agreement could be changed by a general meeting of the association on thirty days' notice, but the ban on the importation of any taxed goods was to be permanent. Beer could not be imported till the tax on tea was repealed, but wine could be brought into the country and be bought and sold after the duty on wine was dropped by the British government. Whether a slave imported at any time prior to the association could be purchased by a subscriber depended on whether the introduction of a comma in the committee's revision of George Mason's language had changed his manifest intent.[3]

Washington himself became confused. In July, only a little more than two months after he had helped to organize the association, he prepared invoices of goods and wares to be purchased for him in London by Robert Cary & Co. He carefully stipulated in his covering letter: ". . . if there are any articles contained in either of the respective invoices (paper only excepted) which are taxed by acts of Parliament for the purpose of raising a revenue in America, it is my express desire and request that they may not be sent, as I have very heartily entered into an association . . . not to import any article which now or hereafter shall be taxed for this purpose until the said act or acts are repealed. I am therefore particular in mentioning this matter as I am fully determined to adhere religiously to it, and may perhaps have wrote for some things unwittingly which may be under these circumstances." His caution was more than justified. In his invoices he had listed numerous articles that a critic might have said the association excluded, chiefly trinkets, manufactured goods, hardware and equipment for the chase.[4] Hoes, for example, were excluded, but spades were not specifically banned: Washington ordered half-a-dozen. Either he drew some close distinctions or else he forgot that certain commodities were not to be imported so long as a tax remained on tea, glass, paint and pigments. Washington must have thought, also, when he drafted his invoices in July, 1769, that the ban on importation applied solely to taxed articles. If that mistake was made by a man who had helped to draw up the

[3] Mason wrote (3 *Hamilton*, 348): "That they will not import any slaves or purchase any hereafter imported until the said acts of Parliament are repealed." In this the clause "purchase any hereafter imported" was Mason's purposeful correction of his original "purchase any imported slaves." The text prepared by the committee and approved at the meeting on May 18 was "purchase any [slave] imported, after the first day of November next, until the said acts" etc. Did this mean the members would not purchase any slave imported after November, or did it mean the members after November 1 would purchase no imported slave? The member who was unfamiliar with Mason's original draft might readily have been perplexed.

[4] 2 *G. W.*, 512–513; 11 *Papers of G. W.*, 113, LC.

association, other planters, less informed, could not be expected to hold to its rigid terms.

When Washington made out these invoices, he was preparing to journey again to the Berkeley Springs in the hopes that a few weeks there would divert Martha and improve "Patsy's" health.[5] "Jackie" was permitted to come to Mount Vernon to see his mother and sister before they left.[6] Master Custis, in fact, after the manner of youth, had contrived on more than one occasion to get away from school briefly. His progress, or lack of it, was the subject of frequent report by Mr. Boucher to his patron, who replied painstakingly, even on such a matter as a choice between rival dancing teachers for the young gentleman.[7] Concerning the time and money spent on dancing, Washington was more tolerant than his friend of Sabine Hall who at a later date expressed much satisfaction that a neighborhood dancing school had closed. Landon Carter's grievance was that it had taken the boys away from their books for two days every three weeks.[8]

Regardless of added items for dancing, Boucher had not proved an inexpensive teacher. The bill submitted about the time "Jackie" came home on this visit was in the stout sum of £42.[9] Washington had some doubt concerning the fairness of the charge for the keep of young Custis's mounts, but he met it with the generous gesture he usually displayed when "Jackie's" bills were involved and particularly those for the boy's education. "I shall pay it cheerfully," he said, "as I am more anxious for his improvement than a little paltry saving." [10] As for the development of the intellectual abilities of the "hope of the house," Washington and Martha still had to content themselves with the assurance given by Boucher soon after the boy entered school—that he was "far from being a brilliant genius" but that he gave the fairest promise of being "a good and useful man." [11]

"Jackie" caused no trouble at home while his stepfather made the arrangements for the exacting journey to the Springs; but Washington's

---

[5] 2 *G. W.*, 512. It is entirely possible that Washington's own health was another reason for this journey. After he came home in September, as will appear in the text, he recorded in his Diary that he "returned with my ague [malaria] again"; but there is nothing to indicate whether he had this before he left for the springs, whether he went to avoid the disease, or whether he developed it after he again was in marshy, mosquito-infested Tidewater.

[6] *Ibid.*, 512 n.

[7] W. C. Ford, ed., *Letters of Jonathan Boucher and George Washington*, 12; 3 *Hamilton*, 324.

[8] This was in May, 1774; 14 *W* (1) p. 182.

[9] *Ledger A*, folio 292.

[10] Letter of July 27, 1769; *Parke-Bernet Galleries, Cat. 598* (1944), p. 202.

[11] Boucher to Washington, Aug. 2, 1768; 3 *Hamilton*, 326.

vexatious protégé, John Posey, was adding a new misadventure to his downward slide. The Captain had remarried about the 1st of June and boasted that he had improved his fortunes greatly by the union. His wife had landed property and, Posey affirmed, had full 300 half-joes in her possession.[12] Washington congratulated him but reminded him that much of his property was attached, that Colonel Mason wanted the sum lent Posey, that Hector Ross was suing, and that the money pledged Washington himself was long overdue. Old counsel was renewed: Posey must dispose of enough of his property to pay his debts. Especially was it desirable to sell a tract of 200 acres that had been acquired from Charles Washington.[13] If Posey would part with this at a reasonable price, Colonel Washington would buy it for immediate occupancy, standing crops included, because, as he frankly told Posey, he had a good offer to lease the Custis farms near Williamsburg but did not feel justified in doing so and in removing the slaves unless he had more land on which to employ them.[14] Posey, as always, sought to postpone a sale in the hope that he somehow could pay his debts and keep his property, too.

With the Captain's affairs uncertain, but everything else in good order, Washington, Martha and "Patsy" set off on July 31 in the chariot [15] and on the 6th of August reached Berkeley Springs about 1 P.M. By this time, Washington had learned the art of establishing the household quickly at the resort. Soldier-like, he soon had everything comfortable in the Mercer cottage, which was again at his disposal, and, by the 9th he could invite guests for dinner without risk of embarrassment.[16] Lord Fairfax and George William Fairfax were in residence; the life was as agreeable as it could be at so crude a place; but "Patsy" did not improve.[17] By the 9th of September, chill, circumstance and the calls of business led the Washingtons to start home. Although the chariot broke down before the family had covered a mile, they had the vehicle repaired and, on the 12th, stepped out on the lawn at Mount Vernon.[18] For the Colonel there were only a day and a half at home. Then he had to go to Alexandria for the election of a new House of

[12] 2 G. W., 508, 519.

[13] This land has an interesting history. It had been originally part of the Spencer half of the Epsewasson tract.

[14] 2 G. W., 509. This is one basis for the statement previously made that by 1768–69 Washington had accumulated a sufficient labor force for his Potomac plantations.

[15] 1 Diaries, 336, 344.

[16] Ibid., 340; cf. 2 G. W., 521 and 3 ibid., 53.

[17] Cf. 1 Diaries, 342.   [18] 1 Diaries, 344.

Burgesses, to succeed the one Botetourt had dissolved in May. Captain Posey was not well circumstanced to run again; nobody else wished to challenge the incumbents. As there was no occasion for opening a poll, Washington and John West were declared the County's choice.[19] It was ill luck, after so gratifying an experience, to have the ague return just at the beginning of the hunting season.[20]

The reason Captain Posey did not stand for the House of Burgesses was that the poor man was facing the black tragedy of a sale for debt. He was drunk most of the time now and, probably to escape arrest, was at the Maryland home of his new wife. She had at length to flee him. In an altercation with him at Colonel Fairfax's and again in private conversation with Sally Fairfax, she asserted that Posey was planning to take her servants and such of his own as remained on his plantation, and send all of them on a vessel to Pensacola for sale there.[21] Colonel Mason was calling for his money and was looking to Washington as surety, in the knowledge that Posey would not pay.[22] Hector Ross, another of Posey's creditors, had entered suit in chancery against Posey and Washington jointly in order to force the sale of Posey's property and, after satisfaction of Washington's prior lien, to meet various claims of approximately £375.[23]

The Captain had made and had broken so many promises that Washington had been compelled in July to ask concerning some of the pledges, "Were they intended for no other purpose than to deceive a man who has discovered by every means in his power an inclination to serve you and your family with the best advice he was capable of giving, and with his purse also?" Even then Washington had agreed to wait until October for the money with which to repay Colonel Mason.[24] Now the wreck was beyond repair. Interest included, Posey's debt to Washington had risen to £200 sterling and £977 current money. On paper, all the property of the Captain, real and personal, was under mortgage for the debt,[25] but assets continued to disappear. There might be truth to the tale about Posey's plans for a secret move to Pensacola. Besides, whether or not Washington induced Posey to sell out while something still remained, Ross could compel action by court order.

[19] 1 Diaries, 344.

[20] Ibid., 345. The first recurrence was September 23.

[21] 2 G. W., 526.　　　　　　　　[22] Ibid., 508, 517–18.

[23] Hector Ross, Neil Jameson et al. vs. John Posey and George Washington; Fairfax Orders, 1768–70, p. 243.

[24] 2 G. W., 518, 521.　　　　　　　　[25] Hector Ross's bill in chancery, supra.

Washington consequently prevailed on Posey to advertise a sale as of October 23,[26] and thereupon he promptly acquainted Ross with all the reasons for urging an auction on short notice. At the same time Washington wished to rid the merchant's mind of any possible suspicion that he was trying to ruin Posey in order to get land lying advantageously close to Mount Vernon. He wrote: "I have no sinister inducements for desiring the sale to be hastened; indeed I have no other motives for it than what I have candidly confessed and such I conceive as most of his creditors will find their advantage in. To secure my own debt is the object I have principally in view; and to effect it does in some measure (latterly) appear to be a matter of doubt when I compare one part of Posey's conduct with another and take a retrospective view of the whole." Then, when the man of business had declared himself, Washington's old sense of justice prompted this final sentence: "From a tender concern for characters you will readily perceive that [a] great part of this letter is intended for your private information only, for if Captain Posey's intentions are honest and upright, I shall be sorry even for my suspicions of him, but should be more so if anything was propagated through my means that should cast an unjust odium on his character, though I have some reasons to believe that what I have here mentioned is pretty generally talked of."[27]

Ross and his associate, Jameson, preferred to take no chances at any sale other than one under court control. They procured the necessary order but had the court set Posey's advertised date, October 23, as the one for turning Posey's effects into cash. Probably as a precaution, the creditors had Washington named to act in event Posey refused to do so.[28] Duly, on the 23rd, there began at Posey's home, Rover's Delight,[29] a sale of the sort that always drew as large a crowd as a debtor's funeral possibly could. For three days the auctioning and bargaining continued.[30] Washington bid in the 200 acres he wanted,[31] and probably collected enough from the purchases made by others to balance his account with Posey and to rid himself of the bond he had signed for Posey's improvident loan from George Mason.[32] The Captain clung

[26] *Rind's Gazette*, Oct. 19, 1769.
[27] Letter of Oct. 9, 1769; 2 *G. W.*, 525–27.
[28] Order in Hector Ross and Neil Jameson et al *vs.* John Posey and George Washington, as *supra*, n 23.
[29] Posey's advertisement made the word "Rover's," not "Rovers'."
[30] 1 *Diaries*, 349–50; *Ledger A*, folio 256.
[31] *Birch Cat. 663*, item 48. [32] *Ledger A*, folio 276.

to a few belongings; the unlucky Mrs. Posey died within a month or a little more.[33]

The familiar story of neighborhood woe ran tediously on. In the midst of his trouble over Posey's debt to him, Washington had to wrestle again with the affairs of Mrs. Savage. Her husband, the Doctor, apparently was enjoying the use of her property and was spending the income from it without paying her a shilling of the £100 due her annually, but as Washington and Fairfax had Thomson Mason's bond for Doctor Savage's regular payment of the annuity, they were not altogether helpless. In October, Washington directed that suit be instituted against the bondsman unless Savage promised to pay at the next General Court one year's annuity, which was now almost thirty-six months in arrears.[34] The reply from Savage's agent was prompt and polite but positive: ". . . it would not be prudent or safe in me to answer your demand in behalf of Mrs. Savage." [35] Although Mrs. Savage complained that she was in real distress,[36] there was nothing for the trustees to do except to follow the processes of chancery law for her relief.

This vexing service as neighborhood councillor had to be laid aside temporarily at the end of October: Lord Botetourt had called the General Assembly to open on the 7th of November [37] what might prove a long session of regular legislation. For the sake of Martha's company and of her own pleasure, Washington wished to take his wife with him at least as far as Eltham. Another reason was a desire to have one or more of the Williamsburg physicians examine "Patsy" and see if they could do anything to alleviate the girl's fits. "Jackie," by some of his mysteriously persuasive power, prevailed on his mother to let him go, too. For so many travelers, the new chariot would be needed. It had arrived early in 1769 but it had never been shown in Williamsburg, and it should be. Its carved exterior and its green leather finishings

---

[33] See Daniel McCarty to Washington, Dec. 6, 1769; 3 *Hamilton*, 366. Lund Washington bought a "large looking glass" at the sale for £3, 1s. While Captain Posey will appear again briefly in these pages, it may be permissible to note here that if existing court records sufficiently supplement the references in *G. W.* and in *Ledger A* to give a correct picture of Captain Posey's affairs, a brief monograph on his decline and fall might be an interesting exhibit of the unstable agricultural economy of Virginia at a level somewhat below that of Washington. Before Posey began drinking so heavily that he became irresponsible, his troubles seem to have been due to over-sanguine speculation in nearby lands he could not utilize at a profit.

[34] Cf. 4 *Hamilton*, 14.   [35] 2 *G. W.*, 523; 3 *Hamilton*, 363.
[36] 2 *G. W.*, 523.
[37] The first date set by Botetourt had been September 28, but on the 7th of that month he had fixed the new and later date (*Journ. H.B.*, 1766–69, p. 223).

were not altogether unworthy of appearing on the same street with Governor Botetourt's coach.[38] Seven horses must be carried along, so that there might be no delay and no humiliating spectacle for the countryside if, by evil chance, the envious mud of Caroline or of King William should attempt to grip a wheel and to have so noble a vehicle remain immovable for exasperating hours.[39] It was the last day of October when the chariot left Mount Vernon, and the 6th of November when Washington reached Williamsburg.[40] Martha and "Patsy" were to remain temporarily at Eltham, with the understanding that Washington was to ride there on Saturday and enjoy Sunday with them and the Bassetts. A little later the family would come to Williamsburg and join in the festivities there when Colonel and Mrs. Bassett opened their town house.[41] "Jackie" was to spend a few days at both places and then was to go back to school.

The day after Washington reached town he attended the opening of the General Assembly, took the oaths and, with his fellow-members, listened to a speech which showed why the Governor, Lord Botetourt, so readily enlarged goodwill already acquired. Although the membership was substantially that of the General Assembly he had sent home in May, His Excellency had not a word to say regarding the circumstances of the dissolution. Instead, the Governor told of the King's approval of a farther extension of the boundary in the Cherokee country if Virginia would bear the expense of negotiating it.[42] Then, with a few regretful words about disorders on the frontier, Botetourt hastened to repeat assurance from Lord Hillsborough "that his Majesty's present administration have at no time entertained a design to propose to Parliament to lay any further taxes upon America for the purpose of raising a revenue, and that it is their intention to propose in the next session of Parliament to take off the duties upon glass, paper and colors, upon consideration of such duties having been laid contrary to the true principles of commerce."[43]

Botetourt scarcely could have phrased it more skillfully, nor have announced more deftly what was in reality a proposal for a compromise —that the tax on tea only was to be left but that the repeal was to be

---

38 It was shipped in September, 1768, and was described fully in the invoice. The cost, freight included, was £315. Details are given in 2 *G. W.*, 489 n.

39 *Ledger A*, folio 191.   40 1 *Diaries*, 350, 352.

41 This is manifest from the entries in 1 *Diaries*, 352–53.

42 Some of the background is described in *Journ. H.B.*, 1766–69, p. viii ff.

43 *Journ. H.B.*, 1766–69, p. 227.

ostensibly in the interest of commerce and must not be regarded as an
admission that Parliament had no right to levy internal taxes on
America. The Governor hastened to anticipate the objection that a new
Ministry might reverse the action and renew the taxes. It was his "firm
opinion," Botetourt said, the existing policy would "never be departed
from." He reiterated: ". . . so determined am I to abide by it, that I
will be content to be declared infamous, if I do not, to the last hour of
my life, at all times, in all places, and upon all occasions exert every
power with which I either am or ever shall be legally invested, in order
to obtain and to maintain for the continent of America that satisfaction
which I have been authorized to promise this day, by the confidential
servants of our gracious Sovereign, who, to my certain knowledge,
rates his honor so high that he would rather part with his crown than
preserve it by deceit." [44] Those were the words of enchantment. Listening to Botetourt as he spoke, with all the charm of manner and all the
trappings of office that he commanded, Burgesses may have felt reassured, perhaps enthusiastic; but if any of them sat down in the quiet
of a bedchamber and took Botetourt's fine sentence to pieces, they could
find in it nothing but a promise to labor for Americans' "satisfaction."
That was itself a vague term.

Most of the Burgesses accepted the Governor's statement as the proclamation of a truce but they did not overlook the fact that the tax on tea
was to remain. In their address, which was from the pen of "Mr.
Treasurer" Nicholas,[45] the members of the House did not mention the
continuance of this levy. If the Governor was tactful and considerate,
they would not let him outdo them. Gratitude was expressed to the
King "for recommending to his Parliament a repeal of the act imposing
duties upon glass, paper and colors, especially as"—these clauses were
the milk in the coconut—"we cannot doubt but the same wisdom and
goodness, which have already induced his Majesty favorably to regard
the humble entreaties of his faithful subjects in America, will still
farther incline the royal breast to an exertion of his Majesty's gracious
and benign influence, toward perfecting the happiness of all his
people." [46] Not a word was there of the continuance or abandonment

[44] *Ibid.*, 227.

[45] He and Edmund Pendleton constituted the committee (*Journ. H.B.*, 1766–69, p. 227).
The style of the address is identical with that of May 10, 1769 (*ibid.*, p. 199–200), which is
known, from Jefferson's statement, to have been the work of Nicholas.

[46] *Journ. H.B.*, 1766–69, p. 233.

of the association, not an added line of protest against the revival of the acts of Henry VIII for treason trials in England. Only the one hint was dropped—of "perfecting the happiness" of all the King's subjects. That went beyond the "satisfaction" Botetourt had pledged.

Speech and answer, then, evidenced the amity and restraint alike of Governor and of Burgesses and gave the auguries of accord to what Washington found to be a busy session. Now that he had been conspicuous in organizing the association, he was named more frequently to special committees.[47] On a considerable part of the numerous bills, moreover, he could bring to bear his business judgment along with that of other large planters.[48]

The most important general measure in which he had prospective personal interest was an address to the King, accompanied by a memorial to the Governor, on the extension of the western boundary in the wide Cherokee country.[49] Determination of this line might affect the claim that veterans of the expedition of 1754 had to 200,000 acres of bounty land. Washington's eager examination of the chances of getting this land had uncovered three obstacles. The first was the multiplicity of large western grants and "orders" for land. Numerous as these were on the books of Virginia, rumor had it that companies were being organized in England for the control of vast areas beyond the Alleghenies, and that at least one of these attempts must be taken seriously—an enterprise to be associated with the names of Samuel Wharton and Thomas Walpole and to be known as the "Walpole Grant." This might lead to the establishment of a large new Colony, with its own government and with authority to make or to deny land grants in a western region Virginia always had considered indisputably hers. Second among the obstacles encountered by Washington was the occupation of so much of the land around Fort Pitt by previous patentees that it was doubtful whether the 100,000 acres promised in that region to the veterans—half of the total bounty—would be anything more than barren mountainside. Third was the question, never formally asked

---

[47] *Ibid.*, 289, 314, 332–33, 334. He served on the same three regular committees as in the previous House—Propositions and Grievances, Privileges and Elections, and Religion.

[48] The acts of Assembly at this session are hopelessly confused in 8 *H* 305–444. Because the spring meeting of 1770 was by adjournment and not by prorogation, Hening included its laws with those of the session of 1769 and numbered them to a total of eighty-nine "chapters," but in his arrangement some acts of 1770 are given early chapter-numbers as if they were enactments of 1769. Chapter I, for example, was in reality a law of 1770, not of 1769.

[49] *Journ. H.B.*, 1766–69, p. 334–36.

but often hinted: Did not the volunteers of 1755 have a right to share this bounty with the man who had gone out in 1754?

Washington first made these difficulties entirely clear in his own mind. Then he developed carefully the means of dealing with them. He and other interested persons, as an initial step, had Dinwiddie's proclamation of Feb. 18, 1754, read in the House of Burgesses and placed on the table "to be perused by the members" [50]—a familiar preliminary to the introduction of a motion for the drafting of a bill. Then, the next day, and probably at Washington's instance, the House voted an address to the Governor concerning the lands between the Allegheny Mountains and a line drawn from the western boundary of North Carolina to the confluence of the Ohio and the Mississippi. In those instances where the usual terms of "seating" grants had not been met in this area, the Burgesses wished to know whether the government of the Colony had made any pledge to confirm "orders" previously approved by Council.[51] Further, would the Governor be pleased to discourage monopolies of land in Virginia? [52] On the third day of his offensive, Washington wrote the Governor directly, outlined the history of the claim and explained, in particular, why he thought no veterans except those of 1754 had any right to share in the grant. All who enlisted after that year, he said, did so "upon a quite different and much better establishment." [53] He had completed this letter and was preparing to transmit it to the Governor, when one of his fellow-claimants, Dr. Thomas Walker, told him that the lands close to Fort Pitt had been reserved for traders. Washington mentioned this in a postscript and added that if this were the case, the former soldiers would rather have good lands laid out for them elsewhere than await a final determination in England of their rights at the forks of the Ohio in competition with those of the traders.[54]

The Governor answered the address of the House with the assurance that no commitments had been made and that no monopolies would be approved by him.[55] Then, on December 15, in formal petition the officers and men of the expedition of 1754 asked His Excellency that the land promised them be granted "in one or more surveys" on the Monongahela, New River, the Great Kanawha, Sandy Creek and adjacent

[50] *Journ. H.B.*, 1766–69, p. 317–18.
[51] For the difference between "orders" and patents, see the Hite case, Vol. I, p. 234–35.
[52] *Journ. H.B.*, 1766–69, p. 318–19.   [53] Letter of Dec. 8, 1769; 2 *G. W.*, 531.
[54] 2 *G. W.*, 532.   [55] *Journ. H.B.*, 1766–69, p. 323.

streams.[56] In this petition, another delicate matter was broached—the privilege of having the surveys for the veterans made by a representa-- tive of the claimants, and not by the County Surveyor. The signers somewhat piously pointed out that the regular procedure would swell the expense "much beyond what a poor soldier is able to bear, a purpose which your petitioners conceive could never be intended." [57] Wash- ington's aim, in this last request, was to use William Crawford, who did not have a Surveyor's commission; but in spite of polite words by the authorities of the College of William and Mary, who issued all such commissions, it became apparent that Captain Crawford would have to come to Williamsburg to qualify.[58]

The response of Governor and Council on the question of allotting the land was one of hearty acquiescence: Virginia would keep her word. As for details, if one very large area of rich land could be located, all the grants might be within it, but the words used in the petition—"one or more tracts"—meant that if exploration showed that the men could do better for themselves by searching out individual stretches of good land, they would be free to do so. "One or more" might be one hun- dred "or more." Washington's own feeling was that the fairest arrange- ment would be to designate some large unoccupied region and to permit each claimant to get the most fertile land of allotted acreage he could find there. By this means, Washington said later, "every man would stand upon his own bottom and not a few burdened with the expense of the whole." [59] Besides, if the land were in one tract of limited area, an equitable apportionment of it among the various claimants would be difficult.[60]

Governor Botetourt and the Council would not accept this reasoning. They probably concluded that if the men prowled about, seeking the richest land, the surveys would be so scattered that future occupation and patenting would be complicated hopelessly. So the Council decided that claimants could make as many as twenty surveys but no more. In these twenty areas must be contained all the 200,000 acres the vet- erans were to receive. On the lesser details, Council's action conformed to petitioners' wishes: Washington was free to urge the College of William and Mary to appoint some properly qualified person to survey

[56] 11 *Papers of G. W.*, 106, LC.   [57] *Ibid.*
[58] 3 *Hamilton*, 366–68.
[59] Letter of Nov. 7, 1771, to George Mercer; 3 *G. W.*, 67.
[60] *Ibid.*, 67, 76.

the land immediately and he was authorized to say this would be agreeable to Council. Further, Colonel Washington was directed to advertise that all claims should be attested by Oct. 10, 1770. As he knew his old soldiers individually, they were to present their claims to him. He in turn was to certify them to Council for final determination. Five years were to be allowed the veterans for surveying their lands. No person could qualify "who entered the service after the Battle of the Meadows in 1754." [61] Washington had considered the original petition "consistent with every principle of common justice," [62] and he felt chagrin and astonishment that the number of general surveys was limited to twenty, but he had no alternative to acceptance: He would come back again. At the moment, it was this arrangement or none.

A second business interest to be protected at the capital was that of the Dismal Swamp grant. William Nelson, Washington, Fielding Lewis and their associates originally had been allowed seven years in which to complete the drainage of their part of the swamp; the special privileges granted them would expire in November, 1770. As the work was far from success, more time would be required. To procure this, the partners petitioned the Council, in which Nelson was next in seniority to President Blair. The approving minute of the Council was written with the utmost courtesy, to this effect: "Satisfied that the execution of so arduous and expensive an undertaking as that of draining and rendering fit for cultivation such a large body of land hitherto esteemed of little value or rather a nuisance to the neighborhood, will be productive of general utility," an additional seven years were granted for the partners "to perfect their work and return their surveys to this office." [63]

There was still another private interest for Washington to serve—if not in procuring new land, then in recovering old debts. All other plans for the relief of Col. Bernard Moore having failed, the details of the lottery of a great part of his estate had been arranged in the names of its distinguished managers. Tickets to a total of 1840 were offered at £10 each,[64] but so many of these remained unsold that the drawing,

---

[61] E. J., Dec. 15, 1769; P.R.O., C.O. 5: 1440, p. 23; VSL Photostat. This involved the rights of Thomas Bullitt who did not receive his commission formally until after the battle. See ibid., 5:1349, p. 67, petition of Thomas Bullitt. The case of John Carlyle is mentioned infra.

[62] 3 G. W., 67.

[63] E. J., Nov. 9, 1769; P.R.O., C.O. 5: 1435, p. 54; VSL Photostat. This Executive Journal of the Council doubtless will be printed in the series of which five volumes appeared prior to 1949.

[64] Rind's Gazette, Apr. 14, 1768. This advertisement described the property included in the lottery.

which was scheduled for the early autumn,[65] had to be postponed to December when it was assumed that additional purchasers would be found in the large company that came to attend the General Assembly and the Court of Oyer and Terminer.[66] Washington bought four tickets [67] and, on the evenings of December 15 and 16, shared in the drawing [68] but apparently without winning a prize.[69] Moore's affairs continued to be entangled with those of Speaker Robinson's administrators who, in the closing hours of the session, were authorized to allow a year's credit in selling the property of the dead Treasurer.[70] Washington was not particularly alarmed over any of this because Col. John Baylor, a man of large property, now was Moore's surety for the debt to the Custis estate.[71]

So much legislation had Washington and his fellow-members to consider [72] that it was December 21 when they were able to adjourn,[73] and to talk not only of the new laws but also of a ball that was memorable among all those held at the Capitol. The affair was for the Governor, and was given by the Speaker and the Burgesses, with the wives of members and the ladies of Williamsburg in attendance. These patriotic women most diligently had prepared in advance for the occasion and had entered into a unique agreement, with which His Excellency the Governor may or may not have been made acquainted before he went on the floor. When he arrived and gallantly gave his attention to the loveliness around him, he found that the ladies, "to the number of near a hundred," were appareled in homespun. If Botetourt said more than that the feminine beauty of Virginia adorned anything it wore—or whatever the particular form of his compliment—the correspondent of the *London Chronicle* indulged in this admiring couplet:

> Not all the gems that sparkle in the mine
> Can make the Fair with so much lustre shine.[74]

[65] *Rind's Gazette*, Oct. 19, 1769.
[66] *Journ. H.B.*, 1766–69, p. 235.
[67] *Ledger A*, folio 318.
[68] *1 Diaries*, 355.
[69] As will appear in a later paragraph, Washington's bookkeeping at this period was most negligent. If he won a prize, the entry of it has not been found.
[70] *Journ. H.B.*, 1766–69, p. 351, 352, 353; *8 H* 349.
[71] The date when Baylor unwisely assumed this obligation is not known. First observed mention of Baylor in connection with Bernard Moore's debt on Washington's books was May 1, 1767.
[72] Washington received a week's leave of absence December 16 (*Journ. H.B.*, 1766–69, p. 343), but apparently he did not use the whole of it. He was in the House on the 19th, or else the Speaker blundered in naming him to carry a bill to Council (*ibid.*, 347).
[73] *Ibid.*, 355.
[74] Williamsburg letter of Jan. 3, 1770, in *London Chronicle*, Apr. 17–19, 1770, quoted in

With her great interest in dress, Martha Washington doubtless was sorry she did not see this ball, which Washington himself did not attend. He left Williamsburg the day the House adjourned, slept that night at Eltham, and on the 22nd, set out with his family for home. Christmas was spent at Fielding Lewis's in Fredericksburg; the night of the 26th was passed under the roof of Washington's mother; on the 28th, the Colonel and Martha and "Patsy" were back at Mount Vernon, where "Jackie" and Mr. Boucher joined in the festivities of the Year's End.[75]

It had been in achievement and in promise the best year of the eleven spent at Mount Vernon after Washington's return from the French and Indian War. The collection of debts had been almost impossible; the burden of counselling the luckless had been heavy; a few loans had been made to embarrassed friends when it would have been more prudent to say "No." [76] In nearly every other aspect of Washington's business affairs, there had been success. More of the tenants were paying in cash; [77] tobacco rents were still in excess of 8000 lbs., but this simply reflected increase in the number of farms leased to tenants.[78] For his own part, Washington now was convinced of the wisdom of his shift from tobacco to wheat. In July he had written Cary & Co. that he had grown no leaf on the Potomac "for two or three years and" he added "[I] believe I never again shall." [79] Another merchant was assured, "I only grow tobacco to supply my family with goods." [80] The total of 1769 on Custis plantations was only seventeen hogsheads for Washington and thirty-eight for young Custis [81]—a short crop that had suffered from early drought but had the prospect of a favorable market.[82]

Farm industries were thriving in a small way. Weaving, of course, was stimulated more than ever by the association that had kept mem-

---

Boston Port Bill, 303. The report stated that the ball was on Wednesday, which would have been Dec. 27, 1769, but such dating often is inaccurate. As the House adjourned December 21, it is entirely possible that the ball was on December 20. The report, which is quoted concerning the number of ladies in homespun, does not make plain whether all were so dressed.

[75] 1 *Diaries*, 356.

[76] Cases in point were a loan of £500 to Robert Alexander for the purchase of land in Charles County, Maryland (*Ledger A*, folio 352), and of £150 to Bryan Fairfax, (*ibid.*, folio 155). Either in 1769 or in 1770 a loan of approximately £1000 was made Carlyle & Adam, but this was on "Patsy's" account (*ibid.*, 326).

[77] These rentals varied perceptibly. Some land was leased at 9½d per acre (*Ledger A*, folio 72), and some at 1s 6d (*ibid.*, folio 266). Small tracts rented as a whole brought in from 50s (*ibid.*, folio 48), to £5 (*ibid.*, folio 328). After 1770, most of these rents were somewhat greater. Where tobacco remained the basis of rent, the highest figure was 3000 lbs. a year for the Clifton Neck Place (*ibid.*, folio 77, 134). This rent was not sustained.

[78] *Ledger A*, folio 289.   [79] 2 *G. W.*, 514.
[80] 2 *G. W.*, 515.   [81] *Custis Papers*, VHS.
[82] 2 *G. W.*, 514, 515.

bers from purchasing any expensive British goods after September 1. The year's production at Mount Vernon was 1270 yards, with cash receipts of £45. Washington had estimated in 1768 that the cloth woven on his own plantation cost him £28 less than he would have had to pay for it if he had imported it, but from this he had to deduct the cost of spinning, which had occupied the time of one white woman and of five Negro girls.[83] Home manufacture of cloth was, in other words, manifestly unprofitable but it now was necessary and patriotic. Blacksmith's work always had to be done, because on so large an estate, many tools and implements were broken and could be repaired far more cheaply than they could be replaced. Even if cost were disregarded, growing crops and contentious weeds would not wait on the delivery of new hoes by slow sailing ships. Now that no British ironwork of any sort could be purchased by members of the association, Washington needed more skill in his smithy than he had; so, as the year ended, he was searching for a white "tradesman" who knew more about metals than any of the slaves had learned. Such a man soon was to appear in the person of Domenicus Gubner. His daily pay was to be 3s, but he was shifted, before long, to a yearly wage of £32. As usual with Washington, the formal contract signed by Gubner contained a provision that all time lost on account of sickness was to be made up. Gubner was to prove a faithful but scarcely a frugal artizan: he ate up too large a part of his wage.[84]

Besides his weaving room and his smithy, Washington in 1769 developed his fisheries in the Potomac. During April there had been good "runs" of white fish and of herring, which Washington's men had caught in large number.[85] Most of the fish, salted and packed, doubtless were used on the farms, but a small consignment was available for shipment in the autumn to Antigua, where it brought £6, 12s.[86] The market seemed so promising that Washington resolved to expand his fishing in 1770.

The main development of 1769 was in milling. During the year Washington delivered to Carlyle & Adam 6241 bushels of wheat—25 per cent more than in 1768 and almost six times as much as in 1765 when he first had undertaken large scale production.[87] Influenced per-

---

[83] Mount Vernon Weaving Book, 390 *Papers of G. W.*, LC.
[84] *Ledger A*, folio 325; *Ledger B*, folio 34. In *Ledger B*, blacksmith's accounts are in the name Hovener, but the individual appears to be the same.
[85] 1 *Diaries*, 323.   [86] *Ledger A*, folio 299.   [87] 10 *Papers of G. W.*, 122, LC.

haps by the favorable condition of the crop, Washington had concluded in June that if there was a profit for Carlyle & Adam in selling his wheat to a miller, and a profit for the miller in dealing with the baker or merchant, he himself could make this money by grinding his own wheat into flour and selling it on a wisely chosen market. He intended to keep the stones at work in the old building, but he engaged a mill-wright of Fredericksburg to choose the best location for a new and larger mill, and he proceeded to buy adjoining land so that, as he explained, he would not "be incommoded" by the proximity of Charles West's property line.[88] Now, at the year's close, the site was selected, the water apparently assured, and everything in order for the beginning of work. On December 30, Washington made an agreement with John Ball to build a mill in which he was feeling already an ambitious interest.[89] There would be gain in self-dependence as a farmer and in independence as a colonial, because he would not have to rely on the British market. If to this might now be added the prospect of a new fortune in western lands, the future was brighter than ever. The name of George Washington most certainly would not appear among those of planters whose ruined estates were being offered for sale in the newspapers.[90]

One humiliation, if one only, Washington had to endure at the close of this successful year, 1769. His bookkeeping never had been as good as it should have been, perhaps never as informative as he thought it was. Debits and credits on individual account were kept; the affairs of the Custis estate doubtless were watched with vigilance;[91] but often there was confusion of cash income from crops with money repaid on capital account. Investments in slaves occasionally were entered as "expenses."[92] Worst of all was Washington's negligence when he jotted down in his pocketbook or on a bit of paper his memoranda of payments and of receipts that were to be entered subsequently in their proper place when the books were "written up." Often the date of the notes was omitted and could not be recalled when the items were transcribed. During 1769, Washington had been more remiss than ever and, perhaps because he was busy, he was guilty on occasion of failing to write so much as a line to remind him of money paid. The result

[88] 2 *G. W.*, 505–07.

[89] 1 *Diaries*, 357.

[90] Cf. letter of June 24, 1767, to John Posey; 2 *G. W.*, 459–60.

[91] This has to be an assumption because the Custis ledgers that survive among the *Lee Papers* at Washington and Lee University are in part illegible.

[92] For example, a mother and child bought in 1759 for £80 (*Ledger A*, folio 56).

was that when he tried to strike a balance on the last day of the year, he was "out" £143.

There had been a time not more than twelve or fourteen years previously when he would have carried on a correspondence all winter with Governor Dinwiddie over a sum far smaller. Now he merely wrote down, "Cash lost, stolen or paid without discharging it"—and then, closing the Ledger, proceeded with the first affairs of what promised to be the crowded year, 1770. He would be 38 years of age in February. In the days of largest opportunity that lay immediately ahead, four things must be done: The lands promised by Botetourt under Dinwiddie's proclamation of 1754 must be located, surveyed and patented; some of those rich hills and meadows of Pennsylvania and of the Ohio Valley must be added to the Washington holdings before all of them were preempted; the new mill must be completed and put in operation; more of the fat herring and shining shad that ran in the Potomac must be seined and sold. Smith and weaver and spinners and carpenters must be kept busy—and time still must be found for visiting and entertaining, for correspondence and bookkeeping, for service as justice and Burgess, warden and town trustee, for special care of Mrs. Savage's bond, Captain Posey's affairs and Colonel Colville's tangled estate,[93] and for whatever might be required in support or in revision of the non-importation agreement. It would be a busy year!

Washington's largest stake was in the lands promised the volunteers of 1754. In any equitable apportionment of the 200,000 acres, he might get 10,000 or even 15,000. There was another speculative opportunity under a royal proclamation of 1763. This authorized the Governors of the Colonies to grant "without fee or reward, to such reduced officers as have served in America during the late [French and Indian] war, and to such private soldiers as have been, or shall be disbanded in America; and are actually residing there, and shall personally apply for the same, the following quantities of lands, subject at the expiration of ten years, to the same quitrents as other lands are subject to in the province within which they are granted, as also subject to the same conditions of cultivation and improvement, viz. To every person having the rank of a field officer, five thousand acres; to every Captain three thousand acres; to every subaltern or staff officer, two thousand acres; to every non-commissioned officer, two hundred acres; to every private

---

93 Cf. 3 *G. W.*, 24; cf. *supra*, p. 206.

man fifty acres." [94] There was doubt whether this was designed for soldiers of the Colonies as well as for those of the regular establishment. In either event, the initiative rested with the individual. Each veteran of the later campaigns must make personal application for such land as he wanted. No agency existed for selecting and apportioning acreage. As a result, few veterans knew what to expect or whether they actually would get anything. Former Lieutenant Charles Mynn Thruston, for example, questioned Washington concerning this in a spirit of skepticism. The Colonel replied by exhibiting to him the inquiry of the House concerning land companies and the Governor's reply which showed, in Washington's own words, "between six and seven million of acres actually granted and petitioned for, and most of the grants made in such general and indeterminate terms that, if confirmed, no man can lay off a foot of ground and be sure of keeping it, till they are servd." [95] Thruston would be entitled to 2000 acres of land under the proclamation of 1763, but he was so much discouraged by this report that for £10 he forthwith sold his claim to Washington, who thought, for reasons of policy, that it would be well to have the transfer of the rights of Thruston made out to Lund, rather than to himself.

To Washington this was a gamble, nothing more nor less. He might draw a blank; he might get as good land as he knew how to select. "Could I purchase 12,000 or 15,000 acres upon the same terms," he said, "I would do it, considering of it as a lottery only." [96] In telling his brother Charles of his plans to acquire additional claims under the proclamation of 1763, Washington wrote on the last day of January: ". . . if you can buy any of the rights of those who continued in the service till after the Cherokee Expedition, at the rate of about five, six or seven pounds a thousand acres I shall be obliged to you, and will pay the money upon demand. I am of opinion that Chew,[97] and some of those who may be in want of a little ready cash would gladly sell." [98] Charles was asked to make inquiry, half-jestingly, about the willingness of former soldiers to sell their claims, and, Washington particularly enjoined, "in the whole of these transactions . . . do not let it be known

---

[94] Similar provision was made for naval officers. The proclamation is printed in Marshall's *Washington*, v. 1, Appendix, Note X, p. 39, and is reprinted in 7 *H* 663.

[95] 3 *G. W.*, 2. "Servd" probably is an abbreviation of "surveyed."

[96] *Ibid.*

[97] This may have been Joseph Chew on account of his brother Colby. Cf. 3 *Hamilton*, 113; 4 *ibid.*, 352.

[98] 3 *G. W.*, 2–3.

that I have any concern therein." The form of agreement in the bargain with Thruston was to be followed. Charles was to act for his brother as Lund had done in the first purchase of rights, and Charles was to retain the title, "till matters are riper than they appear to be at present." [99]

Washington thus broadened his plans for the acquisition of western lands to embrace: first, his own claims and such others as he might procure for the bounty-lands promised in 1754; second, similar personal claims and those of indifferent or necessitous veterans under the proclamation of 1763; third, such patents of desirable land as might be taken out for him in Pennsylvania by William Crawford; fourth, any further patents of large, well-watered fertile tracts that Crawford might find outside districts where grants already had been made, and finally, any rival or established claims that could be bought up at a low figure to assure a good title or single, sure ownership of wide stretches. [100] Bold plans these were, and all the bolder because they might call for large outlays of cash when, as one merchant wrote, "the scarcity of money is so great in this country [Virginia] that it is impossible for ablest men to comply with their engagements." [101]

Washington was willing to take the risk, which was less in his case than with most of his contemporaries. He knew how to live in the wilderness and how to find his way anywhere he wished to go. If he located a desirable rich bottom, he need not fear that someone else might enter claim while he waited for the Surveyor to come: he still was a commissioned Surveyor; he could draw the lines and make the plat himself. Ever since young manhood, he had been lucky on the frontier. When the virgin lands had been in the Shenandoah Valley, he had been a favorite of the Proprietor's agent and had procured everything the influence of the Fairfaxes could help him get with such funds as he had. Now that the frontier on the Ohio was about 135 miles beyond the western bounds of the proprietary, he was a major claimant under the proclamation of 1754 and he might become a holder of sub-

[99] *Ibid.,* 4.

[100] On the details of the holdings acquired in accordance with these plans, the most useful authorities are Eugene E. Prussing, *The Estate of George Washington, Deceased* (1927) and Roy Bird Cook, *Washington's Western Lands* (1930). The broad background is supplied with much care in T. P. Abernethy, *Western Lands and the American Revolution* (cited hereafter as *Abernethy*).

[101] Thomas Adams to Perkins, Buchanan & Brown of London; *Adams Papers,* VHS. Part of this was printed in 23 *V* 56. Adams went so far as to say: "At present let a man's estate be what it will and his necessities what they may, he cannot borrow one hundred pounds."

stantial claims under the proclamation of 1763. His cash in hand might not match the fullness of his opportunities, but now that he was succeeding he felt more strongly than ever that if an investment was sound, he somehow would find the money for it. Nor was he restrained by the debt to Cary or deterred by the knowledge, which he must have had in part at least, that both William Nelson and George Wythe were working vigorously on the Dunbar case.[102] Dunbar or no Dunbar, debit or credit on Cary's books in London, Washington would exploit his opportunity to the fullest and the boldest.

When he went to Williamsburg in May, 1770, he had the advancement of the claims of the veterans of 1754 as one of his principal duties.[103] He found little legislation of importance in prospect but much concern over the violence with which British troops in Boston on the 5th of March had fired on a crowd of about sixty rioters who had been engaged in a fight with a squad of soldiers. Three of the rioters had been killed, two others had been wounded fatally. New England had been outraged and the other Colonies alarmed by this "Boston Massacre." Another cause of concern in Williamsburg was the failure of the association of May 18, 1769, to scare Parliament. All news from England made that plain. Lord North, on May 1, 1769, had prevailed on the British Cabinet, by a majority of one, to keep the tax on tea, and seven months later, as First Lord of the Treasury, he took over the direction of affairs. The issue of the *Virginia Gazette* published the day after Washington's arrival in Williamsburg contained a disappointing report of the proceedings of the House of Commons on the merchants' petition for the repeal of the taxes as previously promised by Lord Hillsborough and announced in Virginia by Governor Botetourt. "I was present in the House and heard the debate," the correspondent of the Williamsburg paper reported, "and, to my great surprise, the patriots (or pretended patriots) that we expected would be strong in our favor, did little for us, except abusing the ministerial party, some of whom spoke and voted to our side of the question, particularly

---

102 Nelson was fearful that the slow delivery of papers would prevent consideration of the case at the April term of the General Court. William Nelson to John Dunbar, Feb. 24, Mch. 7, 1770; *Nelson Letter Book*, 151, 155. Nelson complained that a letter from Norfolk, addressed to him at Yorktown, was fourteen days in transit.

103 Washington left home on the 19th of May, called at his mother's, lodged at Fielding Lewis's, and reached Williamsburg in the early morning of May 22, the day after the adjourned session of the General Assembly opened (1 *Diaries*, 378–79; *Journ. H.B.*, 1770–72, p. 5).

General [Henry Seymour] Conway who was for a general repeal. On a division there were for taking off the tax on paper, painters' colors and glass, leaving it on tea, 204: for a total repeal, 142.[104] Lord North gave us some room to make us think that the duty on tea will be taken off at a future day, provided an agreement, in agitation, takes place between government and the East India Company, which at present is at a distance and will hardly be brought about, if at all, at this session." [105]

This was not encouraging. In addition, there were in Virginia some known and a larger number of suspected cases of importation and purchase of goods contrary to the terms of the association. Many planters, no doubt, had found the terms too exacting, and some had confused the provisions of the complicated document, as Washington had, but others may have professed ignorance to cover design. The treatment administered Archibald Ritchie at Hobbs Hole[106] had not deterred some merchants from importing on one pretense or another. Where one man offered goods which he professed to have ordered before the association was formed, his competitors were tempted to match him. In certain instances, as one writer affirmed, "prodigious importations" were made before the date when purchase was forbidden, and the price of all manufactured goods and of shoes in particular, was raised.[107] Another correspondent, returning from travel in other provinces, reported that complaint was made of Virginia's failure to adhere strictly to the non-importation agreement: ". . . they insisted that we ought to contribute at least equally to the re-establishment of American liberty; and if some prudent steps are not taken to regulate importation, Virginia would be remarkable only for resolving." [108] Those who had entered whole-heartedly into the association and honestly had relied on home industry could point to some proud results. Said William Nelson: "[the British] have already taught us to know we can make many things for ourselves and that we can do very well without many things we used to indulge in. I wear a good suit of clothes of my son's wool, manufactured as well as my shirts in Albemarle and Augusta Counties;

---

[104] This historic vote was Mch. 5, 1770; *Journ. House of Commons*, v. 39, p. 750.
[105] *Va. Gazette*, May 24, 1770.   [106] *Supra*, p. 155.
[107] *Va. Gazette*, Mch. 22, 1770.
[108] Supplement to *Va. Gazette*, June 14, 1770. Cf. William Nelson to John Norton, July 19, 1770: ". . . I blush on reading what you say about the Virginians, that their invoices rather increase than diminish. I wish such persons were of any other country than mine" (*Nelson Letter Book*, 159).

my shoes, hose, buckles, wig and hat of our own country and these we improve every year in quantity and quality." [109] The trouble was that few were willing to send for goods of American production. Most Virginians trod the old way.

Even the most enthusiastic had to admit, therefore, that if the non-importation agreement was to be kept alive at all, it had to be revised. On the 25th, after dining with the Governor at the Palace, Washington attended a meeting of the association, where so many divergent opinions were expressed that a committee of twenty [110] was appointed, as in 1769, to formulate a new association on which general agreement might be reached. Washington again was named to this committee, which met on the 28th but uncovered opposition of such stubborn temper that adjournment to the 31st became necessary. When the committeemen came together at the tavern on the evening of the last day of the month, dispute rose high. It was 1 A.M. when argument was suspended [111]— only to be renewed in a general meeting of the association the next day at the Capitol. Five hours of debate did not bring a meeting of minds. [112] New negotiations then proving necessary, Washington did not attend another meeting until the 15th [113] and meantime journeyed to and from Eltham and attended the long-delayed, inevitable sale of Thomas Moore, from whose bankrupt estate he bought two Negroes. [114]

The dispute on importation was dual—whether there should be any association at all, and, if so, whether it should be stern or moderate in its terms. Edmund Pendleton and others argued at least inferentially that association should be abandoned. Parliament, they said, had compromised by repealing all the taxes except that on tea; the Colonies should be equally reasonable and should accept that levy. Landon Carter recorded this proposal and gave the answering argument: "Fine language this, as if there could be any half way between slavery; certainly one link of the former preserved might be the hold to which the rest of the chain might at any time be joined when the forging smiths thought proper to add to it." [115] Differences over the terms of a new association arose, on the one hand, from the requirements of farming

---

109 Letter to John Norton, Jan. 24, 1770; *Nelson Letter Book*, 150. In a communication of Nov. 17, 1769 to Edward Hunt and Son, Nelson had noted that two suits of Virginia cloth "equal in quality to Yorkshire of 6/ or 7/ a yard" had cost only £5, 13s Virginia currency.
110 Landon Carter's Diary, May 29, 1770; 13 *W* (1) p. 50.
111 1 *Diaries*, 378, 380.   112 *Ibid.*, 382.
113 *Ibid.*, 383.   114 *Ibid.*, 383.
115 13 *W* (1) p. 50.

and the complaints of merchants, and, on the other, from the feeling of many planters that unless they were willing to endure the shortage of cloth, of implements and of other goods, association would be a failure, and the cherished liberties of all the Colonies would be lost. Washington himself was for the sternest of non-importation agreements—"I could wish it to be ten times as strict," he said later,[116] but he felt that a covenant which did not command support of the merchants and supply the minimum requirements of planters would fail.

Final agreement was reached June 22, 1770, on a more moderate compact than the one of the previous year. Instead of denouncing prospective violators, it promised support to those "truly worthy merchants, traders, and others, inhabitants of this Colony, who shall hereafter conform to the spirit of this association."[117] Committees of five were to be named in each County to publish the names of violators and to examine invoices of imported goods. If they found goods that had been imported contrary to the association, they were to urge that these be shipped back to Great Britain. In event the merchant refused to do this, an account of the transaction was to be printed. Prohibited goods were limited, in the main, to luxuries and to expensive products. Cheap cloth, shoes, stockings and horse-furnishings were to be allowed. A committtee of merchants was authorized to prepare and to report at the next meeting of the association a list of such other articles as should or should not be admitted.[118] Meantime, the Williamsburg dealers accepted the pact.

Washington signed this association, resolved to conform fully to it,[119] and did not deceive himself concerning the terms. It was, he said, "the best that the friends to the cause could obtain here, and though too much relaxed from the spirit with which a measure of this sort ought to be conducted, yet will be attended with better effects (I expect) than the last, inasmuch as it will become more general and adopted by the trade." He added: "Upon the whole I think the people of Virginia have too large latitude and wish that the inhabitants of the North may not have too little. What I would be understood by it is that their public virtue may not be put to too severe a trial to stand the test much longer if their importations are not equal to the real necessities of the people . . ."[120]

[116] 37 G. W., 494.
[117] Text in Journ. H.B., 1770–72, p. xxvii ff.
[118] Ibid., xxviii–xxix.
[119] See his instructions to his merchants in 3 G. W., 22, 23–24; 37 G. W., 494.
[120] Letter to Rev. Jonathan Boucher, July 30, 1770; 3 G. W., 21.

In the House of Burgesses that sat while the association was being revised, Washington found the local bills of small interest.[121] Nor was he able to do more in furtherance of the recognized claim of the veterans of 1754 than to arrange for a meeting of beneficiaries August 1 in Fredericksburg.[122] Governor and Council could not act until application was made for particular tracts, and they were unwilling to make grants in districts where, even if no conflicting claims existed already, the jurisdiction of Virginia might be denied by royal approval of the Walpole Grant.[123] Washington understood the reasons for this caution but he was maneuvering already either to get lands outside the probable limits of the prospective grant or to have surveys made as soon as boundaries or exceptions were known.

In the spirit of his letter of September, 1767, to William Crawford, he was willing to leave the final result to time and to his own assiduity,[124] but he did not intend to let time lag or assiduity lose its edge. At the meeting in Fredericksburg, August 2,[125] Washington met comrades whose hand he had not shaken for years and some, perhaps, whom he had not seen after he and John Mackay had left Wills Creek in July 1754, to report to Colonel Innes.[126] Doubtless the Colonel greeted his old officers with the same straightforwardness and amiability that always had won their hearts. He was less military now, of course, but not less businesslike: Reminiscence and comradeship had their place at such a meeting but that tract of promised western land was an immediate concern. How was it to be located, surveyed and patented? In what manner was it to be apportioned? Should it be according to terms recommended by Andrew Lewis, Thomas Walker and Washington? Who was to pay the cost of the surveys? Most of the survivors were known; their claims could be certified without question; but what rights had John Carlyle, the Commissary, who maintained that he should be included among the beneficiaries? Should he be admitted?

The precise acreage that would be received by each man had to be

---

[121] For his assignments to special committees, see *Journ. H.B.*, 1770–72, p. 55, 78–79. On June 20, he procured leave of absence for the remainder of a session that continued until June 28 (*ibid.*, 83, 109). He started home June 23 and arrived on the afternoon of the 26th (1 *Diaries*, 384, 385).

[122] *Va. Gazette*, June 21, 1770.

[123] Cf. Washington to Botetourt, Sept. 9, 1770; 37 *G. W.*, 494–95.

[124] 2 *G. W.*, 471.

[125] Apparently a sufficient number did not reach Fredericksburg on the 1st of August for the meeting to be held that day, as originally announced.

[126] See Vol. I, p. 420–21.

determined by the number of persons whose claims were attested before the date fixed by the Governor, Oct. 10, 1770, but agreement was reached on the percentage of the whole that would go to men of each rank. There was agreement, also, that in 1754 John Carlyle was not a volunteer within the meaning of the proclamation.[127] As for costs, all participants were called upon to make a pro rata payment for surveys and other expenses. Washington's accepted duty, under the resolution of Governor and Council, simply was to receive and certify individual claims; but he now had acquired so solid a reputation for doing well whatever he undertook that he was prevailed upon to assume the handling of this thorny business.[128] He had a busy and a pleasant round of visits with Martha and "Patsy" in the Fredericksburg district.[129] The only disappointment was that the girl gained nothing from the treatment of Dr. Hugh Mercer, whose professional reputation perhaps led the Colonel and Mrs. Washington to hope for more than any physician could accomplish.[130] The girl now had suffered for at least two years from intermittent seizures,[131] and that summer she had been under much excitement during the festivities that attended the visit to the Potomac in July of the frigate *Boston,* which had anchored off Belvoir.[132]

When Washington brought "Patsy" and her mother back to Mount Vernon on the 9th of August,[133] he had made one firm resolution on the whole question of western claims: he would go to the Ohio and Great Kanawha and make his own choice of vacant lands as soon as the dispatch of his business and the falling of the leaves favored the journey. Much had to be done in advance. First of all was the duty of having the planters and merchants in Fairfax sign the new association, printed copies of which were available with the names of the original signers attached. Under each of six of these broadsides, Washington wrote: "The Subscribers, Inhabitants of the County of Fairfax, having duly considered the above agreement and association, and being well convinced of the utility and real necessity of the measures therein recommended to the Public Attention (at this critical juncture) do sin-

[127] Cf. 3 *G. W.,* 22.   [128] Cf. 3 *G. W.,* 11; 37 *G. W.,* 495.
[129] 1 *Diaries,* 391–92.
[130] Cf. payments to Mercer, July 31–Aug. 1, 1770. The dates suggest that "Patsy" had an attack on the road or soon after her arrival.
[131] 3 *G. W.,* 21.   [132] 1 *Diaries,* 385–86.
[133] 1 *Diaries,* 392. In favorable weather, Washington by this date was making the journey between Mount Vernon and Fredericksburg regularly in one day, though apparently he had not yet duplicated his feat of completing the ride in seven hours and a half.

cerely and cordially accede thereto and do hereby voluntarily and faithfully each and every person for himself upon his word and honor agree and promise that he will strictly and firmly adhere and abide by every article and resolution therein contained according to the true intent and meaning thereof." Washington then circulated these papers among his neighbors and doubtless entrusted to other hands the copies meant for Alexandria and Dumfries.[134] Nearly everyone signed—from George Mason to five humble men who had to make their mark—until the total reached 420.[135] When this was done, the Colonel was ready to accept duty on the Fairfax Associators' Committee whenever it was formed.[136]

Next among the undertakings of the master of Mount Vernon was the building of the mill, a troublesome task that involved among other things a controversy with Thomas Marshall over encroachments on his land [137] and a dispute with Robert H. Harrison over riparian rights.[138] There were, in addition, half-a-score of lesser, time-consuming matters to settle—invoices to be made out subject to the repeal of the British tax,[139] a troublesome arbitration to be undertaken for friends,[140] more explanations to be made concerning the entangled Colville estate,[141] preparations for the shipment of a cargo of herrings to the West Indies,[142] a discussion of the possible navigation of the upper Potomac,[143] and a review of a long, earnest correspondence with Jonathan Boucher regarding "Jackie's" immediate future.

The reverend instructor had concluded that a tour of Europe, with himself as guide and mentor, would be a proper part of the education of "Jackie" who, the minister admitted, was proving himself at seventeen years of age "constitutionally too warm, indolent and voluptu-

---

[134] Cf. 1 *Diaries,* 389.

[135] Text of the agreement, as drafted by Washington, is in 3 *G. W.,* 16; the original broadsides are in 12 *Papers of G. W.,* LC.

[136] This probably was not until September. Washington's fellow-committeemen were George Mason, John West, Major Waggener and John Dalton. See *Rind's Gazette,* Oct. 11, 1770.

[137] 3 *G. W.,* 5; 3 *Hamilton,* 369. Washington later settled this with Marshall by paying him £5 (*ibid.,* 371 n).

[138] 4 *Hamilton,* 11.

[139] 3 *G. W.,* 22, 23–24; 37 *G. W.,* 497. These are the same invoices mentioned *supra,* n 119. Cf. *supra,* p. 229.

[140] 1 *Diaries,* 393.

[141] 3 *G. W.,* 24–25.

[142] 3 *G. W.,* 25; *Ledger A,* folio 310.

[143] 3 *G. W.,* 17. A subject that had been under consideration in the House of Burgesses during the session of November–December, 1769, but had been recommitted. See *Journ. H.B.* 1766–69, p. 314, 334.

ous." [144] Truth was, young Mr. Custis was now aware that he was a gentleman of superior estate and he was disposed to enjoy it with minimum concern over books. His expenses at Boucher's school, as charged up by the master, were £65 a year; [145] his, too, must have been the inspiration for the entry of the invoices of many articles of fine dress from England, for delivery if the tax on tea was repealed. [146] "Jackie" scarcely was to be blamed for extravagance or Mr. Boucher for his ambitions, after what Washington incautiously had said about the boy's future possession of "a very large fortune"; [147] but now that the minister began to talk of heavy expenditures, Washington recoiled. Boucher, shooting high, had said that their joint travel would cost £1500 or £1600 a year; [148] Washington explained that the sum exceeded the boy's annual income, that he did not wish to expose himself to censure for reckless use of "Jackie's" property [149] and, in general, that while young Custis had "what is called a good estate, it is not a profitable one." The Colonel added: "His lands are poor, consequently the crops short; and, though he has a number of slaves, slaves in such cases only add to the expense." [150] It was the first time Washington ever had made any such confession regarding the proudly held Custis plantations. [151] He did not say even now that "Jackie" could not go; he left the question in abeyance with the probabilities somewhat against his approval of the "grand tour." [152]

By this time Washington had most of these matters behind him, autumn had come and the falling leaves were giving him assurance that the range of his vision in western forests would be far enough to show where the axe might widen meadows or open new fields. William Crawford had reported as long previously as May continued uncertainty about lines and boundaries, though he had selected for Washing-

[144] 4 *Hamilton*, 24.
[145] *Custis Papers*, VHS.
[146] 3 *G. W.*, 24.
[147] 2 *G. W.*, 488; cf. *supra*, p. 203.
[148] 3 *G. W.*, 15.
[149] 3 *G. W.*, 13.
[150] 3 *G. W.*, 14.

[151] Washington, of course, may have made some such statement in letters now lost but, in general, the tone of his earlier correspondence is one of pride in the Custis estate. The question consequently rises, had Washington concluded by 1770 that tobacco growing was as unprofitable on the York as it was on the Potomac; had he merely learned more about the nature of the soil on the various farms; or had there been a perceptible decline in the yield of the Custis lands during a decade that included at least four unfavorable seasons? It is much to be regretted that sufficient data apparently do not exist for a study that would show the effect on Tidewater lands of the intensive cultivation of tobacco during the forty years after the passage of Gooch's inspection law, for which see Vol. I, p. 141.

[152] Boucher's first letters concerning the proposed tour do not appear to have survived the years. By May, 1770, the teacher was pressing for a decision. See 4 *Hamilton*, 18 ff.

ton, for Lund, and for two of George's brothers what he considered patentable tracts.[153] Washington himself had lacked information concerning the Walpole Grant and in September he had written the Governor to inquire whether it was true, as rumored, that the grant actually had been made for a separate Colony.[154] Botetourt had replied, through the Clerk of the Council, and had enclosed some extract from correspondence that showed where the proposed new Colony was to be established.[155] Before leaving for the Ohio Washington concluded that he should make formal reply of such a nature that Botetourt, if willing, could dispatch it to England, as in effect a petition to the Crown to protect the rights of the volunteers of 1754.

The Walpole Grant, he told the Governor, would devour four-fifths of the territory Virginia had voted to purchase from the Cherokees and to survey at a combined cost of £2500.[156] With this general statement as a preface, Washington argued for full recognition of the grant of the 200,000 acres. In particular he asked that the claimants be allowed to amend their application of the previous December because Sandy Creek,[157] on which was located some of the land desired by the veterans, most certainly would not be within the territory that would be opened to the English on the conclusion of the renewed negotiations with the Indians.[158] In place of this land on Sandy Creek, Washington asked that part of the acreage given the veterans be between the western boundary of Pennsylvania and the Ohio.[159]

The day Washington finished a fair copy of this letter, October 5,[160]

153 4 *Hamilton*, 15.
154 Letter of Sept. 9, 1770; 37 *G. W.*, 494.
155 The letter of Clerk Blair has not been found but this part of its contents is plain from Washington's letter of Oct. 5, 1770; 3 *G. W.*, 26.
156 It has not seemed necessary to trace here the history of the complicated Cherokee negotiations, the details of which are given with admirable clarity in *Abernethy*, 66 ff.
157 The modern Big Sandy, which divides West Virginia from Kentucky.
158 These negotiations led to the Treaty of Lochaber, for which see *Abernethy*, 71, and *Atlas of American History*, Plate 60–61. This excellent map shows also the boundaries of Vandalia, as the area of the Walpole Grant subsequently was styled.
159 That is, in the "Panhandle" or Wheeling district of the present State of West Virginia, though it is probable Washington did not realize how narrow that region is from East to West.
160 3 *G. W.*, 26–29. Fitzpatrick entered under date of April 15, 1770, a letter substantially the same as this one. He expressed the belief (3 *G. W.*, 29 n) that the letter of the earlier date was written but not sent, and that, in October, Washington rewrote it from a copy of the original that Bartholomew Dandridge meantime had transcribed in the Letter Book. No copy of the letter of October 5 is preserved; the original of it, when Fitzpatrick wrote his note, was in the hands of Dr. A. S. W. Rosenbach. In the known circumstances, it seems much more probable that the letter was written for the first time in October and was entered wrongly in the Letter Book from a preliminary draft of approximately the same date. If Washington actually had amended in October a letter written in April, he scarcely would have referred to a communication sent him by Blair in April as "just received." Besides, there is good reason to

he set out with his friend and wartime Surgeon, Dr. James Craik,[161] three servants and a packhorse. The first stage of the journey was rapid and devoid of other incident than the sickness of attendants and mounts.[162] On the 8th Washington visited Colonel Cresap, at that pioneer's familiar post, to ascertain what Cresap had learned concerning the Walpole Grant on a recent visit to England. Whether Cresap communicated much or little, it was not of a nature to make Washington turn his horse's head homeward.[163] With fresh mounts,[164] the party pressed on to Great Meadows and the site of Fort Necessity, which were reached October 13. The remainder of the day's journey was past Jumonville's Camp, and continued beyond Christopher Gist's New Settlement, where Washington had agonized and debated when news had come in June, 1754, that the French in force were moving against him. He must have seen and remembered but when he wrote of the ride he had no recorded thought for anything except good land. Positive enthusiasm echoed in his note: ". . . When we came down [Laurel] Hill to the plantation of Mr. Thomas Gist, the land appeared charming; that which lay level being as rich and black as anything could possibly be . . ."[165] Beyond Thomas Gist's, across the Youghiogheny, was Washington's first objective, the home of his land prospector and surveyor, Capt. William Crawford.[166]

That worthy was ready for his visitor. On the 15th of October, Washington went with him to examine the land that Crawford had selected for his correspondent, for Samuel Washington, for "Jack" and for Lund. The tract chosen for the Colonel delighted him. It covered about 1600 acres and, wrote Washington, "includes some as fine land

believe that the letter of October 5 was in answer to one Blair penned, on Botetourt's order, after the receipt in Williamsburg of Washington's letter of Sept. 9. The existence of this last mentioned paper (37 *G. W.*, 494–95) was not known when Fitzpatrick wrote the note in 3 *G. W.*, 29, on the letter of October 5. Washington's letter to Botetourt was forwarded to Lord Hillsborough by vote of the Council of Virginia, Oct. 19, 1770. See *E. J.*, P.R.O., C.O. 5: 1349, p. 63.

[161] One suspects that the hand of Martha was in the selection of Doctor Craik as a traveling companion. As an insistent "worrier" during the absence of those she loved, Martha probably wished her husband to have the attendance of the physician in the event of sickness.

[162] This journey is covered more fully in Washington's Diary than any other of which he kept a record. (1 *Diaries*, 400–52). Most of the details are without great interest, some are undeniably tedious. The present narrative consequently is much condensed.

[163] 1 *Diaries*, 405.   [164] *Ibid.*, 406.   [165] 1 *Diaries*, 407.

[166] It is interesting to note in this Diary how some places that had no designation when Washington first visited them in 1753–54 had received by 1770 the names they have retained ever since. The ford near which Crawford lived on the Youghiogheny, for example, was close to, if it was not the identical one Washington had used several times in his early movements. Now for the first time, he noted that it was "commonly called Stewart's Crossing." (1 *Diaries*, 407).

as ever I saw, a great deal of rich meadow, and, in general, is leveller than the country about it." Although the land chosen by Crawford for the other Washingtons was not so superlatively good, it was most distinctly worth having.[167] Washington felt that this first acquisition of new Western lands was to be confirmed heartily. It was precisely the sort of bargain he had in mind when he had voiced his speculator's creed to John Posey—"the greatest fortunes we have in this Colony were made . . . by taking up and purchasing at very low rates the rich back lands which were thought nothing of in those days . . ."[168] He was determined to prove it!

En route to the Youghiogheny, Washington had sent word to Col. Adam Stephen that he was on his way to examine lands for the volunteers of 1754.[169] Now, when Washington returned to Crawford's, he found Stephen there.[170] That former comrade and none-too-trusted friend doubtless sought and procured full information of Washington's plans but he did not elect to go along. Bidding him farewell, Washington rode on to Fort Pitt, which he reached on the 17th. He devoted a brief paragraph in his diary to the new defences, but, though he passed Turtle Creek and the scene of Braddock's disaster, he had no comment on the country other than that much of it was "exceedingly fine land."[171] One diversion of the 19th of October could not fail to turn Washington's memory to his first experiences near that meeting-place of great waters. On invitation of Col. George Croghan, the Virginia visitor went four miles up the Allegheny to Croghan's home and there found White Mingo and several other Chiefs of the Six Nations. The sachems received him ceremoniously, gave him a string of wampum, and, with White Mingo as their orator, made a formal speech of welcome and goodwill. Washington replied briefly [172] and, it may be ventured, with far less hesitation and embarrassment than he had shown when, seventeen years before, at Logstown, he had made his first answer to an Indian speech.[173]

Croghan decided to accompany Washington a short distance down the river and he courteously procured an Indian interpreter and two savages to serve as guides and hunters. With canoes, equipment and all necessary supplies from the commissary at Fort Pitt—how different

[167] 1 *Diaries*, 408.

[168] By reference to the full quotation, *supra*, p. 184–85, or 2 *G. W.*, 459, it will be observed that two sentences are here combined.

[169] 1 *Diaries*, 405.

[170] *Ibid.*, 409.

[171] *Ibid.*, 409–10.

[172] 1 *Diaries*, 411.

[173] See Vol. I, p. 295–96.

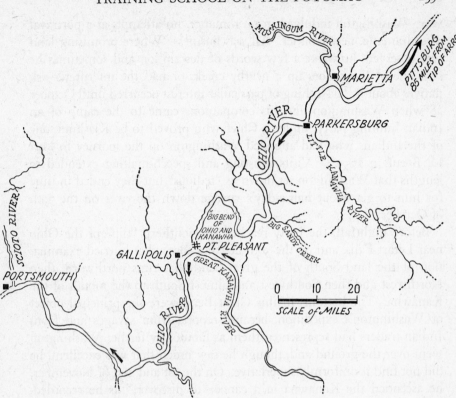

REGION OF THE "BOUNTY LAND OF 1754"

As visited by Washington in October-November, 1770. The names of some of the adjacent modern cities have been entered to facilitate identification of the "Great Bend."

from the early days!—the party set out October 20. On the left bank, above Raccoon Creek, Washington saw the land that Croghan professed to have purchased from the Indians. The tract extended fifteen miles southward, upstream as far as the Monongahela and, according to Croghan, was "a body of fine, rich, level land," for each 100 acres of which he wanted £5 sterling. Washington jotted down a memorandum on the quit-rent conditions but he entered an admonitory note: "the unsettled condition of this country renders any purchase dangerous." [174]

From the mouth of Raccoon Creek, the canoes proceeded along the river without loss or upset. On the 22nd, the expedition had a threat of danger in a report that two traders had been killed farther down the Ohio, but as this proved a mistaken rumor, the party continued on its

[174] 1 Diaries, 413.

way. Washington indulged in no romance, no attempts at a portrayal of a dramatic, new frontier. All was business. Where promising land was observed, he wrote a few words of description and sometimes he sent one of the canoes up a nearby creek, or had the interpreter ask natives about it.[175] Nothing of particular interest occurred until October 28 when Washington and his companions came to the camp of an Indian hunting party, under a Chief who proved to be Kiashuta, one of the Indians who had attended Washington on the journey to Fort Le Boeuf in 1753.[176] Visits, feasting and speech-making extended to lengths that Washington set down as "tedious" but they ended in time for him to get about half-a-day's voyage down the river on the 29th of October.[177]

Before nightfall, the party reached the southern "dip" of the Ohio near Letart Falls, and on the 30th began a somewhat hurried examination of the land South of the great bend that runs northward, then Northwest and then Southwest and almost South to the mouth of the Kanawha. The bottoms in this Great Bend were the principal object of Washington's expedition, because reports from savages and from Indian traders had represented them as fabulously fertile. Washington went over the ground and, though he saw much that was excellent, he did not find it uniformly superlative. On the 1st and 2nd of November, he ascended the Kanawha in a canoe "to discover," as he recorded, "what kind of lands lay upon" the river. Satisfied by this search that the bend and the land on nearby streams included as good acreage as he was apt to find, he devoted the 3rd to marking boundary trees and to taking the courses of the river in the bend as far as this could be done with a pocket compass and without measuring any of the distances along the bank.[178] Sunday, November 4, was devoted to rest; on the 5th, Washington started the canoes upstream around the Great Bend and walked across it himself to make his final observations.

Then came the paddle back up the river, uneventful except that bad weather and high water delayed the party.[179] When Mingo Town at length was reached on the evening of November 17, overflown creeks held Washington there two days and a half. He occupied himself in

[175] 1 *Diaries*, 415–22. Identification of streams and of campsites will be found in the footnotes of the Diaries. Supplementary details of the country are given in Roy Bird Cook, *Washington's Western Lands*, 11 ff.

[176] See Vol. I, p. 301.   [177] 1 *Diaries*, 423–24.

[178] 1 *Diaries*, 426–29.

[179] Parts of the original Diary from November 6 to 16 have been eaten by mice but enough remains to make it plain that the obstacles encountered on the return voyage were those only of the season and the stage of the water.

bringing his diary down to date and in computing distances on the Ohio [180] and, at length, when the horses arrived at Mingo Town on the afternoon of the 20th, he set out for Fort Pitt. Arriving there on the 21st, he entertained the officers of the fort and the gentlemen of the town to the tune of £26 on the 22nd.[181] Among the guests was Dr. John Connolly, a nephew of George Croghan's, who had traveled much in the country West of Fort Pitt and had great faith in its fertility and its future. Washington took Connolly to be "a very sensible, intelligent man" [182] whose opinions he thought it worth while to enter in his journal. Then, paying his interpreter and Indians,[183] he said farewell to Fort Pitt on the 23rd and started for Mount Vernon. He reached there December 1, "after an absence," as he wrote with his usual precision, "of nine weeks and one day." [184]

The journey and voyage had been expensive, in large part tedious and in main purpose not altogether satisfying. Again and again Washington had used the words "exceeding fine" to describe particular tracts, but he had seen much poor land along with the good and a great deal that was neither better nor worse than the average new ground of Eastern Virginia. The Great Bend of the Ohio to the mouth of the Great Kanawha was most certainly worth patenting. Other of the tracts nearby on the Kanawha, or up the creeks, would be desirable, but they were comparatively small. There nowhere appeared such rolling, rich, dark earth, mile on mile, as had been desired for division among the veterans of 1754. In fact, Washington had not grown as enthusiastic over any land he had seen on the lower Ohio and Kanawha as he had over the acreage William Crawford had procured for him near the Youghiogheny. Next that, the finest land Washington had seen in a single large tract was that which George Croghan was offering between Raccoon Creek and the Monongahela. Washington resolved to buy 15,000 acres of this at £50 per thousand if William Crawford could find as much as that in a single tract of quality, to which Croghan could give title. That was not all. Croghan had intimated that he would be one of the proprietors of the new Colony to be established on the Walpole Grant. Washington immediately proceeded to inquire whether Croghan would sell that interest and if so, at what figure.[185]

The patenting of the Kanawha lands for the veterans of 1754 must be pressed. Many of the best meadows lay back up the creeks and

[180] 1 *Diaries*, 439 ff, 451–52.
[181] *Ibid.*, 447, 452.
[182] *Ibid.*, 447.
[183] *Ledger A*, folio 329.
[184] 1 *Diaries*, 452.
[185] Letter to George Croghan, Nov. 24, 1770; 3 *G. W.*, 29–30.

would be difficult to locate in large connected tracts.[186] Perhaps as many as ten of the allotted twenty surveys would have to be used to provide even a third of the 200,000 acres wanted.[187] Land-hunters from Virginia and elsewhere were moving down the Ohio and were marking the best fields. These men already had reached the Little Kanawha; in another summer they would get at least as far as the Great Kanawha. Then, Washington reasoned, "a few settlements in the midst of some of the large bottoms would render it impracticable to get any large quantity." [188]

Behind these two difficulties was the great doubt concerning the new boundary line in the Cherokee country and the boundaries that would be set for the Walpole Grant if it should be perfected. During Washington's absence something had occurred that made this and all the other obstacles harder to surmount: Lord Botetourt had died on the 15th of October.[189] Although the Governor had an eye on Western lands for his own profit, he had declared himself against monopolies and he had learned something, at least, concerning the justice of the claim under Dinwiddie's proclamation of 1754. Now it might be necessary for Washington to start again under a new Governor, but it must be done. The claim was just, the opportunity was great.

Much work for Washington was closer at hand and more pressing. A fresh effort had to be made to prevail upon poor Mrs. Savage to abandon her policy of compliance in front of her husband and of pleading with Washington behind the doctor's back to make him pay her annuity.[190] Another call had to be answered for an arbitration at Colchester.[191] A further exchange had to be completed with Jonathan Boucher on "Jackie's" behavior. The boy was growing up and was interested in dogs, horses and guns: he required the most friendly aid and counsel, Washington thought, especially as Boucher was now operating his school at Annapolis, where temptation would be greater than in Caroline County. "I would beg leave to request," Washington wrote the teacher, "that he may not be suffered to sleep from under your own roof, unless it be at such places as you are sure he can have

---

[186] 1 *Diaries*, 442.   [187] See *infra*, p. 283, 298.
[188] *Ibid.*, 441.
[189] *Va. Gazette*, Oct. 18, 1770. Landon Carter probably spoke for most Virginians when he wrote in his Diary: "[Botetourt] was, anecdotes say, pitched upon to be the agent of a dirty tyrannical ministry, but his virtues resisted such employment, and he became the instrument of a dawning happiness; and had he lived we should have been so; for through his active and exemplary rule order everywhere evolved out of that confusion our own dissipation and indolence had thrown us into" (13 *W* (1) 52).
[190] 3 *G. W.*, 32; 4 *Hamilton*, 39.   [191] 1 *Diaries*, 454.

no bad examples set him; nor allow him to be rambling about of nights in company with those who do not care how debauched and vicious his conduct may be." [192] Boucher was back promptly in a long, long letter with the somewhat disconcerting central theme: "I must confess to you I never did in my life know a youth so exceedingly indolent or so surprisingly voluptuous: one would suppose Nature had intended him for some Asiatic Prince." [193]

But for that unhappy affirmation and "Patsy's" continued fits, Christmas, 1770, would have been one of the best that had been spent at Mount Vernon. Nearly everything was going well on the farms. Tobacco-renters had been reduced to five, whose rent was 7000 pounds of tobacco. The other tenants paid cash.[194] On the Custis estates, the season had been good: Twenty-two hogsheads of tobacco were credited to Washington and seventy to "Jackie"—the largest crop since that of 1764.[195] The fisheries had done well. No less than 473,000 herring at 3s per hundred, and more than 4000 shad at 1d each had been sold Carlyle & Adam.[196] Exact records had not been kept of the weaving but it had developed now to include woolen plaid, striped wool, wool and cotton, broadcloth, dimity, thread and cotton, jump stripe, calico, barricum, striped silk and cotton, and other fabrics.[197] Even of hemp, though it was not flourishing, enough had been grown to bring a bounty of almost £5.[198] Far more interesting to Washington than hemp or weaving or fisheries or tobacco was the fact that the new mercantile flour mill was nearing completion.[199] The contract for the delivery of wheat to Carlyle & Adam had expired;[200] a miller, William Roberts, had been employed at £80 per year.[201] Washington now had ground enough to grow wheat for half-a-dozen such mills—9263 acres of quitrent land [202]—and he hoped to add many other thousands. Soon he would be a planter of the very front rank.

---

[192] Letter of Dec. 16, 1770; 3 *G. W.*, 35-36.
[193] 4 *Hamilton*, 42.   [194] *Ledger A,* folio 289.
[195] *Custis Papers*, VHS.   [196] *Ledger A,* folio 326.
[197] *Ledger A,* folio 88, 200, 218, 227, 243, 263, 298, 300.
[198] *Ledger A,* folio 318.
[199] Details of construction, expenditure and mishaps, subsequent to those mentioned *supra,* will be found in 1 *Diaries*, 366, 377; *Ledger A,* folio 320, 324.
[200] It was for seven years from the crop of 1763, 10 *Papers of G. W.*, 122, LC. This doubtless explained why no figures for the wheat crop of 1770 were preserved.
[201] *Ledger A,* folio 332.
[202] Located as follows: Fairfax 2318; Frederick, 2498; King George, 1250; Hampshire, 240; Loudoun, 275; Fauquier and Loudoun, 2682 (*Ledger A,* folio 257). It is impossible to tell from surviving records when some of this land was acquired. Certain of the unexplained items probably represent lands located in parts of old Counties that were set up as separate new Counties. A few tracts, even of 1770, are identified with less trouble from Washington's will (37 *G. W.*, 295 ff), than in any other manner.

MARTHA WASHINGTON—WITHOUT A HEAD-DRESS

If Martha Washington is a picture and not a personality in American history, she has one of her three prime weaknesses to blame for it: She insisted on being fashionable and, as she lived in a day when the head-dress of women went to extremes, she seldom consented, if ever, to sit for her portrait otherwise than in a decorated cap that holds the viewer's eye at the expense of Martha's pleasant face. Had she gone to England before the Revolution and seen there some of the pictures Sir Joshua Reynolds was painting of women with natural hair and simple coiffure, she might have agreed to experiment with a first-class portrait that showed the shape of her head. She probably thought that a high cap would make her look taller; she seems never to have realized that a misstyled adornment of the sort she liked best emphasized her broadness. How she really looked "off parade" can be glimpsed from this photograph of a miniature in the Art Gallery of Yale University. The original, which is the work of Charles Willson Peale, probably served as a model for other pictures in which Mrs. Washington is more adorned. As she is in Peale's simple portrayal, so she doubtless appeared across the breakfast table—before she yielded, for another day, to her excessive fondness for caps and finery.

Her other weaknesses were the cause of much unhappiness: She worried ceaselessly over her children, and she could not bear to be alone. Her state of mind about "Jack" was exemplified perfectly by her statement that she could wish he would undergo inoculation for smallpox and recover before she knew anything about it. Her husband's pains to conceal the facts from her when her son went to Baltimore for the treatment are a remarkable index to the absurdities of her concern for a youngster who seems to have enjoyed excellent health and appetite.

She had compensating fine qualities, the most notable of which was her unfailing discretion. Even as early in Washington's career as the years described in this volume, Martha might have done her husband infinite harm by careless talk of what he was thinking and planning. There was honor and a measure of security for her in the fact that no other woman ever could excite the females around the tea table by beginning, "Guess what Mrs. Washington told me today. . . ."

JOHN PARKE CUSTIS KNEW ONE ART THOROUGHLY

Much as George and Martha Washington may have wished for children of their own, there may have been reasons why, paradoxically, they were fortunate in having no issue. A boy scarcely could have lived up to the name George Washington, Jr. If, again, Martha's ceaseless worry over her son by her first husband was typical of what her attitude toward a son by her second mate would have been, she probably would have kept at least three persons miserable—herself, her husband and the boy. In the third place, if Washington's handling of his own son had been no wiser than his method of dealing with "Jack" Custis, he who was successful in nearly everything else would have failed as a parent.

The heir to the Custis estate was not morally bad by any test. He was good-natured and well-mannered and had no known vice worse than that of laziness and love of an easy life he knew from youth he could afford. Learning was desirable, no doubt, for clerks and lawyers and parsons and school-teachers, but why should he burden himself with Latin conjugations and mysterious equations? There was more fun in horses and fine clothes. Washington was strangely proud of the wealth of his step-son and he came as near to boasting of this as he did of anything. It is difficult to realize, in particular, how a man of his sound judgment could have written such a letter as that of May 30, 1768, to Rev. Jonathan Boucher concerning "Jack's" admission to the school the clergyman was conducting (p. 203). Washington seems to have had a certain deference for "Jack" and to have made often the most frequent of parental mistakes—that of expecting much and of demanding nothing. The incident of the inoculation of Jack may give the key to the whole of Washington's attitude toward the boy: Martha's excessive tenderness for her offspring may have made fatherly firmness impossible. Be that as it may, "Jack" is amusing rather than provoking and was almost infallibly discerning in this: he knew precisely how to keep his mother always on his side.

(By the Kind Permission of E. L. R. Smith of Baltimore, Md., Owner of the Original)

CHAPTER XIII

The Colonel Gets New Holdings in the West
(1771–1772)

Besides the coming of the day when the water could be turned on the wheel of the new mill, Washington could anticipate that 1771 would bring much closer, if it did not actually witness the completion of the surveys of the land granted under the proclamation of 1754. He planned, also, to secure beyond challenge the Pennsylvania lands selected and surveyed by William Crawford. If Croghan really had a valid title to the wide and fertile area west of the Monongahela, and would sell part of it at a reasonable price, Washington might buy some thousands of acres there. The prospect would have dazzled eyes less clear: Recognition of the bounty granted in Dinwiddie's time, cheap acquisition of the rights of soldiers under the proclamation of 1763, the probable determination of the Virginia-Pennsylvania line, the westward extension of the boundary of settlement in the Cherokee country— never again could so many opportunities of making a fortune combine. Washington had to arrange his days so that he could give to those land enterprises all the time they demanded and, of course, he had to find the hours in which to perform those duties of home and neighborhood that increased with the years. This was heavily true, even though Lund Washington was proving himself entirely acceptable as manager and was discharging many irksome tasks that had eaten up the proprietor's leisure.

A long and very disagreeable arbitration consumed the greater part of a week in January, and another devoured as many additional days in February; [1] but Washington and like-minded planters gave the time because arbitration was a substitute for complicated and costly proceedings that might continue term after term in General Court. Early in 1771, there came, too, another twist to the troubles of Bernard Moore. That gentleman wrote to say that the payment of his debts would

---

[1] 2 *Diaries*, 5, 7; 3 *G. W.*, 38–39.

require the sale of his entire estate.[2] He consequently was having his nephew wait on his friends to inquire if they would lend him money without interest for a few years in order that he might buy Negroes and use them on good lands which he could get rent-free. By this arrangement he could provide support for his family: the slaves purchased with the money his friends advanced him would be security for the repayment of the loan.[3] After all the inconvenience Washington had suffered at the hands of the Moore brothers—to say nothing of the risk of Custis capital lent those gentlemen—he would have been entirely justified in refusing to put another shilling in their hands; but that did not conform to the code. It still was more embarrassing in Virginia to decline to make a loan than to seek one. So, at Colchester, where Bernard Moore's letter and messenger reached him while he was in the arbitration, Washington painstakingly wrote an apology for not being able to do more for the embarrassed debtor than several friends were doing. All he asked, Washington continued, was that he should be put on as good a footing as any other creditors, and that the debtor protect him and his brothers on a bond they had endorsed for Moore. With this letter Washington sent one that informed Moore's trustees he would be answerable for £100 a year later.[4]

The general shortage of specie had been one of several reasons why some of the veterans who had claims under the proclamation of 1754 had been slow to pay their part of the cost of the surveys of the western lands. Other claimants were discouraged by the news that the powerful interests in England, with whom Governor Botetourt was now believed to have been connected, most certainly would get the region they sought on the Ohio.[5] "Our affairs, never in a very promising way," Washington later wrote, "began to grow very alarming";[6] but that did not keep him from setting out Mch. 2, 1771, for Winchester[7] to participate in the meeting of those who, like himself, were willing to gamble for the stake of those 200,000 pledged acres.

Attendance was not large, but it included Colonel Stephen, Capt.

[2] Cf. his advertisement in *Va. Gazette*, Mch. 7, 1771.

[3] 4 *Hamilton*, 47–48.

[4] 3 *G. W.*, 37–38. In all its parts, this episode illustrated the weakness of an extravagant plantation economy which suffered from chronic shortage of money. This lack of gold and silver was due primarily to the limited output of marketable goods and to the British imperial policy that forbade the direct sale in foreign countries of tobacco, the only product of the Southern Colonies for which there was large and sustained international demand.

[5] See 3 *G. W.*, 121.   [6] *Ibid*.

[7] 2 *Diaries*, 9.

Peter Hog, Doctor Craik, who made the journey in Washington's company, and several others in person or through representatives. Washington reported on his visit to the Great Kanawha and recommended that the survey up the valley of that river be continued by Crawford. The Colonel suggested, further, that when Crawford had finished work there, he should see what was available along the Tygart River [8] branch of the Monongahela, a district which Washington probably had been told by some qualified person contained the most promising land near the forks of the Ohio. As Washington's associates were entirely agreeable to this, they promised to meet another assessment, which amounted in the case of field officers to more than £11 each, and they cheerfully gave Washington full authority over William Crawford as surveyor.[9] After the meeting adjourned, Washington devoted three days to preparing detailed instructions for Captain Crawford and then, on the 11th of March, he started home again. He continued resolute in all that related to veterans' lands under the proclamation of 1754, but, as he wrote one interested claimant, he realized that, "We have many difficulties and some uncertainties to struggle through, before our rights to these lands will be fully recognized." With more conservatism than in some of his less formal utterances, he predicted, "the land will be well worth the trouble and expense we may bestow to obtain it, notwithstanding the remote distance it is from navigation." [10]

Life now was so diversified for Washington that there no longer was such a thing as performing a task and then waiting happily at home till another call came. Instead, a new duty was awaiting him the day he discharged an old. Back from Winchester, March 13, he was eager to have news of the mill. During the last week of January, 1771, part of the wall of the new structure collapsed, but it was raised again promptly. On March 1, the day before Washington had left for the Valley, the water of Piney Run was turned on the wheel. The stones began to revolve and the flour to run, but unfortunately there was not sufficient water for continuous operation,[11] whereupon Washington gave orders that the flow of Dogue be carried to the millrace.

The work, though progressing well, was not complete when the

---

[8] The official minutes styled it "Tyger's Valley."

[9] Proceedings of the meeting, Mch. 6, 1771; 12 *Papers of G. W.*, 57, LC; *Ledger A*, folio 333; 3 *G. W.*, 121.

[10] 3 *G. W.*, 47–48. He meant, of course, navigation on the streams that flow into Chesapeake Bay.

[11] 2 *Diaries*, 12.

owner got back from the Shenandoah. To speed the labor, Washington rode almost daily to the creek and, on the 5th of April, had the satisfaction of seeing the sluice opened. There now was water enough for both mills. One or the other could be run as long as the miller and his men could stand to their tasks. Soon Washington was selling his own flour at 12s a barrel, and ere long, he was operating on a scale that made the delivery of 497 barrels more an occasion of rejoicing than it was a strain on mill and workers; [12] but much rust was found in the wheat,[13] and the quality of the product was not satisfactory. Washington was determined to make his flour the best, and, before the summer was past, he was to order a pair of French burr millstones for earliest possible delivery.[14]

The spring was as interesting on the river as at the mill. Washington spent much time at Posey's "fishing landing" and he had an immense catch at the spring "run." In addition to the herring kept for use on the plantation, 679,000 were sold to Carlyle & Adam at the former price, 3s per hundred. The shad caught and salted by Washington's men numbered 7760.[15] Some of the herring were poorly packed and were not acceptable to the buyer [16] but, on the whole, the business was well-handled and moderately profitable. In serving the fishermen, the new schooner proved so satisfactory that Washington sold the old one. Although it brought no more than £4, the low price was evidence that its owner had made the longest possible use of it.[17]

"Jackie" was not as deeply interested in fishing as in hunting, but he had been much in Washington's thought and correspondence that winter and spring. At the beginning of the year, young Custis had started back to Boucher's school and had given his "Poppa," as he termed Washington,[18] many promises of earnest study. The Colonel explained to the teacher the somewhat feeble reasons for a delay in the boy's return, and then he modestly named some of the subjects with which he hoped "Jackie" could be familiar—Greek, if it was not too late to start, French, arithmetic, other branches of mathematics and philosophy, "moral, natural, &c." These, Washington said, "I should think a very desirable knowledge for a gentleman; but as I said before, I leave the whole to your direction; with this earnest request, that in

---

[12] *Mount Vernon MSS; Ledger A,* folio 341; *2 Diaries,* 21.
[13] *2 Diaries,* 22.
[14] *3 G. W.,* 63.
[15] *Ledger A,* folio 326.
[16] *4 Hamilton,* 67.
[17] *Ledger A,* folio 337.
[18] Cf. *4 Hamilton,* 234.

whatever kind of study you think proper to engage him, he may be kept diligently to it, for he really has no time to lose." [19]

Next with "Jackie" came the exceedingly delicate matter of inoculation against smallpox, which had been discussed often in the family. Martha had expressed her wish that her son might have this protection but she never had been able to bring herself to approve the required step. She had said, in fact, that she wished "Jackie" might be inoculated and might be out of danger before she knew anything about it, so that, in Washington's words, "she might escape those tortures which suspense would throw her into, little as the cause might be for it." [20] Perhaps in a desire to spare her, "Jackie" professed to have given up all idea of inoculation, but in April, most unexpectedly, when Washington was preparing to take Martha and "Patsy" to Southern Virginia, he received a letter from Jonathan Boucher with the news that the clergyman and "Jackie" had gone to Baltimore where the boy had been inoculated successfully. [21]

Washington had never planned a military operation with greater care than he now displayed in arranging to keep from Martha the news of the inoculation until "Jackie" had recovered completely. ". . . as one step towards this," he told Boucher, "I should be obliged to you to address any letter you may write me under cover to Lund Washington, and in a hand not your own; for notwithstanding it is believed Jack was resolved to postpone this business, yet her anxiety and uneasiness is so great that I am sure she could not rest satisfied without knowing the contents of any letter to this family of your writing." If, in fact, Martha knew that "Jackie" was in Baltimore for the treatment, she certainly would not go to Williamsburg herself and might delay her husband's departure on April 26, a date to which his business required him to conform. steadfastly. On the other hand, Washington continued in his letter to Boucher, if "Jackie" showed any dangerous or even any unfavorable symptoms, he would proceed immediately to Baltimore. Barring that, would Boucher advise him before the 26th if all was well with "Jackie"; and when the patient returned to Annapolis, would Boucher perform the great kindness of sending a letter to the colonial capital by post? That, Washington concluded, would "be the first information of this affair I purpose to give if I can keep it concealed so

[19] Letter of Jan. 2, 1771; 3 G. W., 36–37.
[20] Letter of Apr. 20, 1771 to Jonathan Boucher; 3 G. W., 42.
[21] 4 Hamilton, 50–52.

long." [22] It always had to be that way in matters that concerned "Jackie." Any business of any other sort had to be deferred where his wife's son was in trouble. Her anxiety over the boy was so great that it was better to soften her concern than to try to strengthen her heart.

As "Jackie" progressed steadily, Boucher was able to report that only eight pustules [23] had developed. The clergyman faithfully gave the location of each of these, gratefully reporting that not one of them was on the face, and he so relieved the Colonel's mind that the start for Williamsburg was made April 27, within one day of the date originally set. [24] Martha and "Patsy" duly shared the journey, which was made in the chariot. As usual, Martha's plan was to stay with her sister at Eltham, to visit her friends and kinsfolk in the neighborhood, and, if special attraction offered, to go to Williamsburg for a few days. When the Bassett home was reached, Washington halted with the others to enjoy hospitality that always was superlative there, and then, on the 3rd of May, he went to the capital to meet the merchants and to transact with them his business and that of the estate. Apparently he did not attempt to do anything about the soldiers' lands under the proclamation of 1754, but he probably heard at least one thing that pleased him: On the 12th of April, the President of the Council, acting Governor, told the members he had received a letter, dated Jan. 2, 1771, in which the Earl of Hillsborough promised that attention would be given the equitable claims of bona fide settlers under the grant to the Ohio Company and to "such [claims] as were passed in consequence of the instructions from his late Majesty or Lieut. Gov. Dinwiddie's proclamation at the commencement of the late war." [25] This was not a specific promise but was the next thing to it.

The days were busy and the nights were gay during the time Washington pondered this and the other news of the town. Evenings were spent at the theatre or in conversation with friends until, on May 11, he left Williamsburg and gave another ten days to the enjoyment of Eltham, to the visitation of the Custis farms, to hunting and fishing, and to calling and dining. The stay at Williamsburg had been marked by a notable bit of horse-trading that gave Washington some of the cream-white carriage animals that Lord Botetourt had brought to Virginia.

22 3 G. W., 41–42.
23 Boucher used the contemporary word "pocks."
24 2 Diaries, 15.
25 The language is that of the Council Journal. See E. J., Apr. 12, 1771, P.R.O., C.O. 5: 1440, p. 12, VSL Photostat.

After the Governor's death, William Nelson had bought these handsome animals and probably had sold all except a pair to William Byrd who, in turn, transferred them to Washington for £130.[26]

Another matter, more personal, had been the consultation of Dr. Carter on "Patsy's" condition and the purchase from him of "fit drops" that might help the girl.[27] She was now about 16 and for nearly three years had been suffering from those heart-breaking, sudden seizures that threw her into convulsions. In spite of this affliction,[28] both she and her mother found much pleasure in the purchase of fine clothing, trinkets and whatever else might brighten her hours. Her account that year contained some strangely contrasting items of pleasure, of pain and of investment:

1771 May	7	By Mr Prentis for a piece of silk	7.	0.	0	
		By 4 boxes of fitt drops pr Mr J Carter	1.	5		
	8	By 1 Blewstrand Necklace		3	9	
	11	By curls from Geo. Lafong				
		By Jas Mercer's Bond & Mortgage	1119	11	6	
		By Mr Peale drawing her minia.	13	5		
Oct	21	By a song book, the Bullfinch		6	6	
		By a parrot bought for her	1	16		[29]

It was diverting to the entire family to start home on the 21st of May [30] with new horses at the pole, and to journey through a land where Washingtons and their kin were so numerous that visits and overnight stays multiplied. Best of all was the fact that when the chariot stopped on the 30th at Mount Vernon, there was "Jackie" Custis, recovered from his inoculation, unmarred, unperturbed and as much disposed as ever to take the best possible care of his mother's son when excessive study might hurt his appetite or shorten his leisure. Mrs. Washington rejoiced at the sight of him and perhaps secretly regarded his voluntary inoculation as a feat of heroism fully equal to Colonel

[26] Nelson Letter Book, 183, 193, 199, VSL; Ledger A, folio 337. The number of horses sold by Nelson to Byrd and by him transferred to Washington is not given. All that is known from the record is that Nelson kept two of a team that doubtless numbered at least six. As Washington sold Lewis Burwell four chariot horses for £130 almost simultaneously with this purchase (Ledger A, folio 210), the natural assumption is that Washington bought a corresponding number. The price, £130, would have been very high for two horses only. Good Virginia animals were selling for £20 each at this time.
[27] Ledger A, folio 337.
[28] Washington termed it her "unhappy situation"; 3 G. W., 52.
[29] Custis Papers, VHS.　　　　　　[30] 2 Diaries, 19.

Washington's return from Fort Le Boeuf in the winter of 1753–54. Mr. Boucher had not been in quite that adoring state of mind. He had in fact been angry with his best customer because young Custis had lingered in Baltimore to attend a wedding when he had thought the young gentleman should have hastened back to exhibit a cure.[31] After "Jackie" had returned to school, the teacher had been half-pleased and half-provoked at the pupil's appetite. ". . . We almost find [it] inconvenient," said Boucher, "at this scarce season of the year and dear markets." [32]

The question of "Jackie's" tour of Europe remained in doubt. Boucher wanted to travel in luxury but hesitated to give up his ministerial living; the boy of course was anxious to travel; friends were divided into the camps of "Go" and "Stay." Washington's inclination to let the boy spend the money for the journey was challenged by his judgment; Martha was timid about the long voyage now that "Patsy's" unhappy condition made the continuance of the Parke-Custis line depend on "Jackie." In reviewing all the arguments, Washington had come almost to the conclusion that "Jack"—as the lad now was styled was too immature to profit greatly by the tour. Young Custis had done well in his Latin but he had forgotten all the Greek he had learned under Magowan; he knew nothing of French. As for the branches of learning that Washington himself found most useful, he had to tell the teacher that "Jack" was "little or nothing acquainted with arithmetic and totally ignorant of mathematics, than which, so much of it at least as relates to surveying, nothing can be more essentially necessary to any man possessed of a large landed estate, the bounds of some part or other of which are always in controversy." [33] Boucher had in time to confess himself partly to blame for this, though, he maintained, "there are not many masters under whom ["Jack"] would have learned more than he has done under me." [34]

The boy himself came into his step-father's court with a plea of nolo contendere. When Washington carefully corrected the misspelling of one of the boy's letters and sent the paper back with a mild lecture on haste and negligence, Custis replied humbly and with thanks. He said: ". . . I was in a hurry when I wrote; and though undoubtedly I might have found time, I am obliged to own, that I am one of those who put

[31] 4 Hamilton, 58.
[33] 3 G. W., 51.
[32] Ibid., 59.
[34] 4 Hamilton, 83.

off everything to the last. And how it should or does happen, I know not, but so it is, that tho I can certainly write as good English, and spell, as well as most people yet when hurried I very seldom do either. I might perhaps account for it in a manner less reproachfully to me, but as you have attributed it to carelessness alone, and as appearances are so much against me, I suppose it is true. All therefore that I can do is to pomise to be more attentive and watchful for the future: your gentle, yet very striking observations shall have their due weight with me; they shall by no means deter me from writing to you every opportunity and I desire you would whenever you find a mistake point it out to me to the end, that by discovering my errors I may endeavour with more success to amend, and at length be capable of holding a correspondence with you, more agreeable than at present, on account of my incapability." With that Mr. "Jack" passed to a brisk, brief discussion of the price Washington might get for "stock"—presumably cattle—on the Annapolis market, and then he dwelt on the importance of making early arrangements for quarters at Annapolis if Washington intended to come to the fall races.[35]

With a boy who wrote in that manner and spirit, it was difficult to be severe, even though the promised amendment, like everything else, was "put off to the last." Washington began to ponder whether "Jack" should not be taken from Boucher and sent to college. He himself had a poor opinion of William and Mary; Boucher was most anxious that "Jack" should not go to Princeton and was favorably disposed to King's College in New York.[36] In that city, Boucher believed, "Jack" would stand "a better chance for receiving that liberality of manners, which is one of the best uses of travel, mixing occasionally with truly well-bred people." Speaking more fundamentally, Boucher was of opinion one "general fault" of young men educated in America was "that they come out into the world furnished with a kind of smattering of everything and with very few exceptions, arrant coxcombs." [37] Mr. Custis did not deserve that appellation for his behavior or pretense of knowledge, but the young gentleman was increasing still further his love of fine

[35] Letter of Aug. 18, 1771; 4 *Hamilton*, 80. "Jack's" spelling and punctuation are preserved but he is credited here with his own corrections of his letter. His lapses, which were not numerous, are noted in Hamilton's careful text.

[36] 37 *G. W.*, 497; 4 *Hamilton*, 86. Boucher thought better of William and Mary than did Washington, but he admitted in January, 1773, that the school must, as alleged, have been mismanaged (*ibid.*, 175. See also, *infra*, p. 311–12.

[37] 4 *Hamilton*, 176.

plumage. As soon as the terms of association permitted, "Jack" wanted to import a dark crimson dress suit with velvet lining, a pearl-colored half dress suit and jewelry and fittings of like quality.[38]

For many Virginians, "Jack's" contemporaries and seniors, the lifting of the ban on the importation of luxuries would mean little, if it came in 1771 or in 1772, because calamity had befallen them. The second and third weeks of May, 1771, had been bright and almost cloudless in Eastern Virginia. Planters had been able to bring to the warehouses hundreds of hogsheads of the tobacco grown in 1770; the inspectors were worked to the limit; the ships to carry the tobacco to the British market soon would arrive and clear the warehouses, but on May 26 the buildings were crowded. Then, overnight, such a flood as never had been known in Virginia swept down the valleys of the Rappahannock, the James and the Roanoke. The water rose rapidly to a height of forty feet. At some warehouses, all the tobacco was swept away or was hurled ashore, mud-covered and watersoaked. On the James alone, more than 2,300,000 pounds were lost or damaged.[39] Houses rolled down the stream; frenzied animals struggled to keep afloat; dead bodies were tossed on the foaming surface or were cast, unknown and unidentifiable, on fields perhaps a hundred miles from home. Fences, plantbeds and early crops vanished. Worse far than the loss of tobacco, of buildings and of cattle was the damage to the low grounds. In many places, these were swept clean, down to the infertile hardpan. Bottom lands that escaped this fate were covered with as much as six feet of sand. Direct loss was estimated at £2,000,000; the uncounted dead were reckoned at 150. Ships that arrived for the tobacco crop found at some landings nothing more than the piles that had supported the warehouses. Life on James River was shattered. Debt-ridden planters were bankrupted; the proprietors of many unencumbered estates had to start anew in building fences, in clearing lands and in restocking their farms. It was no comfort to these men to learn that the flood was due to ten or twelve days of "heavy and incessant rains upon the mountains" at a time when fair May weather had prevailed in Eastern Virginia.[40]

---

38 Invoices of Oct. 3 and 12, 1771; *Custis Papers,* VHS.

39 *Journ. H.B.,* 1770–72, p. 127.

40 Richard Bland to Thomas Adams, Aug. 1, 1771; *Adams Papers,* VHS. This is perhaps the best contemporary account of the flood. Another excellent report, not quite so specific in detail, is Roger Atkinson to Lyonel and Samuel Lyde, June 10, 1771; 15 V 351. See also Thomas Cary to John Norton & Sons, June 8, 1771, F. N. Mason, ed., *John Norton & Sons,* 160. The estimate of 150 dead is from Campbell, *History of Virginia,* 560.

This "grate fresh," as two warehouse inspectors styled it,[41] so manifestly was "an act of God" within the meaning of the common law that the colonial government thought itself justified in aiding the losers. William Nelson, President of Council and acting Governor, summoned the General Assembly to meet in Williamsburg on the 11th of July,[42] though he knew the time to be inconvenient for planters.[43] Washington had seen nothing of the flood, because it had not swept the Potomac Valley and had occurred while he was on the way home from Williamsburg.[44] He did not lose a shilling in the downrushing waters either on his own property or on any of the Custis farms. In realization of the magnitude of the "great calamity," he assumed it would mean higher prices for tobacco,[45] and now he prepared to see what could be done for relief of the victims; but he reasoned that the first few days of the session would be spent in marking time, so he supervised his wheat harvest through the 11th of June, and on the 12th, started for Williamsburg, which he reached on the 15th.[46] He found no disagreement in the House of Burgesses other than over the details of how the actual loss of planters' tobacco was to be determined and compensated. The conclusion was to name a commission to ascertain the damage and to certify payment at specified rates from a fund of £30,000 that would be provided by the emission of treasury notes. These were to be redeemed not later than Dec. 10, 1775, from the receipts of new taxes.[47]

No other legislation of large importance was considered; but most of the men who sat by day as Burgesses discussed by night as "associators" the future of the non-importation agreement. The compact of June 22, 1770, had been no more successful than the one approved on the 18th of May, 1769. Less than six months after the adoption of the second agreement, an effort had been made to abolish the association as unnecessary, but this had been defeated. A meeting of the signers, called for December 14, was so thinly attended that it did nothing

---

[41] Samuel and R. Price of Byrd's warehouse; *Morison Papers*, VSL. A part of this is printed in 18 *V* 275.

[42] Proclamation of June 13, 1771; *Journ. H.B.*, 1770–72, p. 118. John Blair, for the third time, would have become acting Governor on the death of Botetourt in 1770 but he immediately resigned from the Council because he did not feel himself physically able to discharge the duties. William Nelson, second in seniority, thereupon became acting Governor. Blair died Nov. 5, 1771. For his renunciation of office, see E. *J.*, P.R.O., C.O. 5: 1349, p. 61; proceedings of Oct. 15, 1770.

[43] *Journ. H.B.*, 1770–72, p. 119.   [44] 2 *Diaries*, 19.

[45] 3 *G. W.*, 60.   [46] 2 *Diaries*, 25–26.

[47] *Journ. H.B.*, 1770–72, p. 119, 122, 123, 127–29, 131, 134–36, 137–38, 140; 8 *H.* 493–503. Payment was made only for tobacco lost in public warehouses.

except to adjourn until the June session of the General Court of Oyer and Terminer.[48] "The spirit of Association which hath prevailed in this Colony for some time past," William Nelson wrote Lord Hillsborough, "seems to me from the defection of the Northern Provinces, to be cooling every day." He knew something of what was happening in the Colonies North of the Potomac and he regarded the empty seats at the meeting of December 14, as evidence of "such lukewarmness as convinces me that this engagement will soon die away and come to nought."[49]

George Mason had a slightly different estimate of the situation. With the intellectual honesty that shaped all his reasoning, he had concluded before the end of 1770 that the earlier associations, which included his own, "were drawn in a hurry and formed upon erroneous principles." Too much was expected in a short time from the stagnation of British trade by the withdrawal of American orders. "Time has pointed out our mistakes," he said, "and errors well known are more than half corrected." The better plan, he argued in clear, plain words, was to have a uniform agreement for all the Colonies to refrain from the importation of "articles of luxury and ostentation," to build up American manufactures, and to encourage industries from Europe to move to the New World. ". . . an association being formed upon these principles," Mason asserted, "would have gathered strength by execution, and however slow in its operations it would have been certain in its effects."[50]

When Mason wrote, he said that an agreement of this proper scope was "in contemplation," but his experience during the early months of 1771 duplicated that of his neighbor at Mount Vernon. Washington had served with Mason, Peter Waggener, John West and John Dalton[51] as members of the Fairfax Committee organized in accordance with the association of July, 1770. They had examined several cargoes of im-

[48] Richard Henry Lee to William Lee, Jan. 8, 1771 (1 *Ballagh, Lee Letters,* 53); William Nelson to Lord Hillsborough, Dec. 19, 1770 (*Journ. H.B.,* 1770–72, p. xxxi). It is possible that the call for the meeting in December was part of what Richard Henry Lee (*loc. cit.*) described as a "North British scheme for the abolition of the association."

[49] *Journ. H.B.,* 1770–72, p. xxxi.

[50] Letter of Dec. 6, 1770, to an unnamed young kinsman in the United Kingdom; (1 *Rowland, Mason,* 148–51). This letter includes some interesting reflections on the absence in America of any desire for separation from England: "There are not five men of sense in America who would accept of independence if it was offered." In later sentences he said: "We have always acknowledged, we are always ready to recognize, the government of Great Britain, but we will not submit to have our money taken out of our pockets without our consent . . . We owe our mother country the duty of subjects; we will not pay her the submission of slaves."

[51] See *supra,* p. 253–54.

ported goods and had found no violation of the terms of the association, other than in the trivial matter of a dozen hats that apparently had been shipped in error. The committee gave a clean bill of health to the importers, who filed a public declaration to this effect: ". . . they [the merchants] found little regard paid to the association by others, and such quantities of goods imported into different parts of the Colony diametrically opposed both to the spirit and the letter of the articles entered into, that they should think themselves obliged for the future, in justice to their constituents (however contrary to their own sentiments) to send their orders in the same manner with other importers; restraining themselves only from importing tea and other taxed articles which they were still determined to adhere to."

Washington, Mason and the others had agreed that this was not an unreasonable position, and they consequently drew up a letter to Peyton Randolph as Moderator of the association. Quoting the declaration from the merchants, they proceeded:

"We will not presume to dictate to the members of the association in general how far it may or may not be consistent with good policy to attempt keeping up a plan here which is now being dropped by all our sister Colonies,[52] except refusing to import tea and such other articles as are or may be taxed for the purpose of raising revenue in America (which we trust will never be departed from until our grievances are redressed) but we must beg leave to represent to you, sir, the real necessity there is for speedily convening a sufficient number of the associators to form such regulations as may put all the members on an equal footing, in practice as well as in theory; for at present those who faithfully adhere to their engagements have the mortification, not only of seeing their own good intentions frustrated by the negligence, the insincerity, and the malpractice of others, but many of them find themselves from the same causes greatly embarrassed in their business and their trade daily falling into the hands of men who have not acted upon the same honorable principles, and who have very little title to the countenance, or even the connivance of the public."[53]

This document Washington doubtless brought with him to Williamsburg when he came to attend the session for the relief of the victims of the flood. Probably this same paper was the basis of much of the discussion at night in the taverns and on the lawns of Williamsburg. When

---

[52] For the details of the wane of the associations, see Schlesinger, *op. cit.*, 209 ff.
[53] *Rind's Gazette*, July 18, 1771.

a decision was reached to drop the association, abandonment of the agreement was quiet, almost sheepish. In one of the *Gazettes* the only notice to the public was a single unheaded paragraph to the effect that at "a general meeting of the gentlemen of the Association at the Capitol [on July 15], it was agreed upon to dissolve the same; except as to tea, paper, glass and painters' colors of foreign manufacture upon which a duty is laid for the purpose of raising a revenue for America." [54] That was all.

Washington had said in August, 1770,[55] that he wished the association of 1769 to be ten times as strict as it was. He preferred a strong to a weak second agreement and he labored for the most effective terms that would be supported by the mass of Virginians. Now, if the association was at an end, obligation was, also, except of course for the articles directly taxed. As soon as the association was dissolved—before he left Williamsburg and on the very day the statement of the Fairfax Committee appeared in Rind's *Virginia Gazette* [56]—Washington prepared an elaborate invoice of the expensive English clothing, fittings and horse-furnishings he had been waiting to purchase.[57] He ordered eight pairs of shoes and boots for himself,[58] and for "Jack" a "very handsome and fashionable suit of clothes, made of superfine broadcloth" for dress, a thinner but similar suit for summer wear, together with sundry modish waistcoats and breeches, and "a fashionable sartout coat of best, blue beaver coating." [59] His only instruction to his merchants concerning prohibited goods was, "You will please . . . to be careful that none of the glass, paper &c., contained in my invoices are of those kinds which are subject to the duty imposed by Parliament for the purpose of raising a revenue in America." [60]

He would adhere to the agreement if there was one; he would conform to fashion if that was not forbidden, and he would look to his meadows and his mill, and to the western lands for the money with which to buy the best that London dealers would send colonials.[61] Circumstances would not, must not defeat him. There had been speck or spot on the wheat during June; the drenching rains of May had been

[54] *Va. Gazette,* July 18, 1771.
[55] 37 *G. W.,* 494 and *supra,* p. 251.
[56] Cf. 2 *Diaries,* 26.
[57] 3 *G. W.,* 61–62.
[58] *Ibid.,* 53.
[59] *Ibid.,* 54. Needless to say, Washington meant to write *surtout.*
[60] Letter of July 20, 1771, to Robert Cary & Co.; 3 *G. W.,* 60.
[61] Cf. 3 *G. W.,* 57, for an instance of the receipt of moth-eaten duffle—"Duffield" as he and most of the Virginians called it.

followed by drought; the corn crop was unpromising; but the price of
tobacco, as Washington had predicted, doubtless would be high because
so much had been lost in "the Great Fresh." [62] Besides, plantation
activities were so numerous now and so diversified at Mount Vernon
that the results of a few failures seldom were as bad in the sum as they
seemed in the parts. That was one of the numerous rewards of emanci-
pation from tobacco as the sole market crop.

Always, too, there was the hope, real if remote, of rich gains from
those western lands. At the moment, negotiations with Croghan for
large acreage between the Monongahela and Raccoon Creek were not
progressing. In fact, Washington began to doubt whether Croghan
would be confirmed in the title he asserted, though Washington was
loath to abandon all hope of patents in that fertile district of Pennsylvania.[63] Crawford had finished surveying some of the lands between
the two Kanawha rivers, though he had not completed the "drafts,"
which always were difficult for him. When he had everything in order,
Crawford was to come to Mount Vernon and lay all the papers before
Washington.[64] Manifestly, much remained to be done before the veterans of 1754 had clear titles to the lands promised them almost twenty
years previously. Washington was becoming convinced, in particular,
that the Walpole Grant was a reality but he did not know, as yet, where
the boundaries were to be run.[65] The surveys for the men who had
fought at Fort Necessity might be invalidated; perhaps it would be
necessary to find new tracts; perhaps, on the other hand, existing patents might be recognized in the new Colony. Washington weighed all
the doubts and concluded that the "lottery-tickets" of soldiers' claims
under the proclamation of 1754 and under that of 1763 were worth
holding until the final drawing.

The busy master of Mount Vernon and leader of the veteran claimants might have hoped for a quiet season between the time the corn was
"laid by" and the date of the Annapolis races, which he purposed to
attend. Some of this leisure Washington did have during the weeks
when the watermelons were at their best, but it was not for long. If he
was not wrestling with his own troubles, he had to untangle the woes

---

[62] 2 *Diaries*, 22; 4 *Hamilton*, 81; 6 *V* 130.
[63] 4 *Hamilton*, 76–77, 79; 3 *G. W.*, 65, 78.
[64] 4 *Hamilton*, 76–77.
[65] This was his view in December, 1771. It is not certain how long previously he mistakenly had become satisfied that the grant had been approved in final form. The papers were
being held up, in reality, by the Solicitor General.

of his neighbors and of his family. He was both experiencing and evidencing the truth of what he sometimes heard the parson read in the lesson of the day—that "we then that are strong ought to bear the infirmities of the weak, and not to please ourselves." Captain Posey, for example, was sinking lower and lower. Although he had several fine children by his first wife—one of them, "Milly," was a playmate of "Patsy's" [66]—he now wrote that he had been considering the possibility of marrying an elderly widow whom he thus described: "She has large sums of cash by her and a pretty good estate. She is as thick as she is high and gets drunk at least three or four times a week, which is disagreeable to me—has valiant spirit when drunk." He added: "It's been a great dispute in my mind what to do. I believe I should run all risks if my last wife had been an even-tempered woman, but her spirit has given me such a shock I am afraid to run the risk again. When I see the object before my eyes, it is disagreeable." [67] This was part of a letter soliciting a small loan; it was followed by another successful appeal for £12.[68]

Mrs. Savage was not in the same category but she and her annuity continued to harass Washington and Bryan Fairfax. The pressure of Doctor Savage had forced his wife to direct her trustees to endorse her bond as satisfied to the preceding January. With much reluctance the two trustees did so, but they recovered some hope for the vacillating lady when she sent a power of attorney to still another man, who was of a fibre to defend her interests. A way was opened, Washington thought, to get the woman's annuity from her husband, if only Mrs. Savage would stand fast. ". . . I do in behalf of Mr. Fairfax and myself beseech you," Washington wrote her, "to be steady, and no longer suffer the conflict between love and interest (which has been the source of your own disquietudes and of our perplexities) to sway you any longer." He continued: "You certainly must by this time know the ultimatum of your dependence upon the Doctor's affection and support; and as to his threats and dreadful denunciations, if you are separated from him, what have you to fear from them? A steady and resolute behavior on your part will soon put an end to his persecution and re-

[66] Washington once supplied her pocket money on "Patsy's" account (*Ledger A*, folio 319). Later, Washington paid for sending Captain Posey's son, Lawrence, to school (*Ledger B*, folio 125).

[67] Letter of May 25, 1771; 4 *Hamilton*, 66.

[68] *Ledger A*, folio 340; July 10, 1771.

lieve you from every apprehension of abuse; and though it is far, very far from me, to foment differences, or to instigate a separation of man and wife, yet under the circumstances you describe yourself to labor, it is highly eligible and much to be wished." [69]

A crisis in the affairs of Washington's mother next demanded his counsel and decision. Mary Ball Washington was now about 63 years of age. Her youngest son Charles had passed his thirty-third birthday and had established himself on his own plantation. Betty Washington Lewis resided across the Rappahannock in Fredericksburg and of course did what she could for her mother; but Mrs. Washington continued to live at Ferry Farm, which was in reality George's, and to manage it according to her way, as she did her own quarter farther down the river. Ferry Farm had declined steadily. One field was still fairly good; [70] the rest of the land, never particularly fertile, was now poor and worn. Two hundred acres only of the two tracts were cleared. From time to time Mrs. Washington had asked money from her eldest son, who always had considered it his duty to meet her calls. None of these gifts had been above £10 and the aggregate had not exceeded £30 or £40; [71] but apparently no part of this money or of the receipts from the tobacco crop had been spent on repairs or improvement. From stock to fences, everything had "run down." At Ferry Farm, though Edward Jones was an acceptable overseer, he had five slaves and two horses only for the field work. The overseer of Mrs. Washington's quarter either had quit or had proved worthless. For the employment of the five "hands" living there, Mrs. Washington had no more than four horses, at least two of which were of little use. [72]

By September, 1771, affairs had dropped to such an ebb that Washington was called to Ferry Farm to confer with his brother Charles and his brother-in-law, Fielding Lewis, on the disposition to be made of Mrs. Washington and of the property. On most of his many previous journeys, North and South, Washington had stopped for a meal and sometimes for a night at his mother's, but his longer halts had been at

---

[69] Letter of Sept. 5, 1771; 3 *G. W.*, 63–65.

[70] See the notation on Washington's survey of Sept. 13, 1771; *George Washington Atlas*, Plate 9.

[71] Observed substantial items in Washington's accounts, not recorded in the course of the narrative, are as follows: n.d., prior to June 18, 1765, £8 (*Ledger A*, folio 208). n.d., prior to Dec. 24, 1767, £10 (*ibid.*, folio 262); n.d., spring 1769, £3 (*ibid.*, folio 287); n.d., prior to Oct 9, 1771, £4, 12s 6d. (*ibid.*, folio 344). It is quite probable that additional small sums were paid and not entered.

[72] 2 *Diaries*, 36.

Fielding Lewis's home on the opposite bank. As a consequence, Washington had no intimate knowledge of the condition of the farm or of the quarter. His first act on the morning of the 12th, having arrived the previous afternoon, was to ride entirely over the farm and then over the quarter, where he promptly made a bargain with a new overseer.[73] Dinner was with Charles and Fielding at Mrs. Washington's. Then the three men went over to Lewis's where, no doubt, they talked of the difficult situation of a difficult matron. The next day, Washington surveyed his fields [74] and entered into a new contract with the overseer at Ferry Farm.

It then was decided that Mrs. Washington was to relinquish all care of the property. Her son George was to take over the management through the overseer, was to supply her with such needed food and poultry as the place yielded, and was to pay her a fixed rent for the lower quarter and the Deep Run tract. The old holding and that "above the Falls" were to remain hers. Allowance was to be made her, also, for her effects at Ferry Farm, appraised at £215; [75] she herself was to remove to Fredericksburg as soon as a proper residence could be chosen by her.[76] In restored ownership of his Ferry Farm, Washington of course had to equip it with needed animals and tools. All this was as generous an arrangement as he knew how to make for his mother.

It doubtless was a relief to Washington to put affairs in such order as was possible at Ferry Farm and, on the 15th, to go back to Mount Vernon. After a few days at home and two days on the bench of the County Court, he proceeded to Annapolis for the races and the plays staged in that season of gaiety.[77] The ten days at the Maryland capital cost him £10, 16s, but when he entered the item in his ledger, he did not use a hesitating or regretful hand.[78] He manifestly thought he got his money's worth.

Upon his return home October 1, he found Edmund Pendleton there

---

73 The terms are given *ibid.*

74 To this survey, the lines of which are reproduced in *George Washington Atlas*, Plate 9, the world owes nearly the whole of its knowledge of Ferry Farm in Washington's lifetime. The description of the place in Vol. I, p. 58–59, is based on that paper. Full details are in Survey Notes, 1770–99, *Papers of G. W.*, LC.

75 For Mrs. Washington's supplies, see 30 *G. W.*, 398 ff. Her continued ownership of the Deep Run tract is mentioned in 12 *ibid.*, 63. The appraisal of her effects by Charles Washington and Fielding Lewis was noted in *Birch Cat.* 663, item 7.

76 21 *G. W.*, 241. For the details, see Appendix III–4, *infra.*

77 2 *Diaries*, 36.

78 *Ledger A*, folio 344.

and doubtless with that gentleman he discussed the Dunbar case which presumably was to be heard by the General Court sometime between the 10th and the 15th.[79] Old Colonel Custis himself had not been more resolved than Washington was to resist to the limit the efforts of the descendants of Col. Daniel Parke's illegitimate daughter to deprive his lawful issue of their inheritance. Now as always, Washington believed in fighting cunning with skill, and he had decided to retain not only Pendleton but James Mercer and John Randolph also. Their counsel would cost £20 each, but no chance could be taken with mediocrity where the stake was so great.[80]

Washington had not expected to appear in court himself, but until the third week in October, he thought that when he went to Williamsburg for the fall meeting of the merchants he also would have to attend a session of the General Assembly, which had been prorogued to October 24. As it befell, the successor to Governor Botetourt arrived shortly before that date.[81] He was John Murray, Earl of Dunmore, who had been for eleven months Governor of New York. One of Dunmore's first acts was to dissolve the Assembly and shortly afterward to issue writs of election.[82] Washington consequently could look forward to a visit during which he could devote himself to his private affairs, to the entertainment the town offered, and to the leisured presentation of the veterans' surveys for the approval of Governor and Council.

The journey itself was not a pleasant one. Washington's horses were lost on the night of October 24th at his mother's, probably because so many of the fences were "down," [83] and they were not recovered until the 27th. He proceeded to Williamsburg, arrived before dinner and promptly indulged an appetite that had been sharpened at Annapolis the previous month: the players were performing that afternoon; he would see them! He did—and did so again the next day and the next and the next.[84] On the 30th of October he dined with Speaker Peyton Randolph, and on the 31st with the Governor. Twice the Council were his hosts and once the Treasurer was. Socially, all was gracious and

<hr />

[79] The term began, it will be remembered, October 10. Chancery cases were docketed for the first five days the Court was in session.

[80] The receipts of these men, dated Oct. 26 to Nov. 6, 1771, are in the *Custis Papers,* VHS.

[81] He took his place in Council Sept. 25, 1771; E. J., P.R.O., C.O. 5: 1350, p. 58; VSL Photostat.

[82] See Dunmore's proclamation of Oct. 12, 1771; *Journ. H.B.,* 1770–72, p. 145. This conformed to advice of Council, in accordance with precedent; E. J., P.R.O., C.O. 5: 1350, p. 59.

[83] Cf. 4 *Hamilton,* 165, in which the overseer gave assurance he did not intend to burn the rails, as if that had become a practice on the farm, to the ruin of the fences.

[84] October 29–November 1, inclusive; 2 *Diaries,* 39–40.

pleasant; but the business in hand, the business of the surveys for the proclamation lands of 1754, became snarled in this manner: At the session held Dec. 15, 1769, it will be recalled, the Council had advised the Governor that the veterans of 1754 should "have leave to take up" the 200,000 acres "in one or more surveys not exceeding twenty on the Great Canhawa and the other places particularized in their petition." [85] The ten largest tracts of desirable land found in the region had subsequently been surveyed by William Crawford, but they contained only 61,796 acres. No attempt had been made to claim or to survey any veterans' land around Fort Pitt because that district was thought to be in Pennsylvania, or at the least, to have been seized by settlers or speculators, chiefly traders, under "rights" issued by the government of that province. "It was thought to be impolitic," Washington later explained, "to engage in private disputes, whilst there appeared but a gloomy prospect of getting any land at all." [86] Washington consequently now renewed his plea that the Council fix the allotment for men of all ranks and remove the limit on the number of surveys that could be made. Each claimant then would be free to select his own farm—and so for the remainder of the argument previously presented.

The Councillors were ready enough to fix the allotments and did so generously for all those whose claims had been attested by Washington.[87] Every man's acreage was to accord with the rank he held when he entered the service of Virginia in 1754, before the action in the Great Meadows. Field officers were to have 15,000 acres each, Captains 9000, Lieutenants 6000, Cadets 2500, Sergeants 600, Corporals 500, Privates 400. Inasmuch as many men in the ranks had not filed their claims, 30,000 acres were reserved for them and—Washington was careful to stipulate—for those who bore the expense of making the surveys and of assuring their comrades' rights. The Council agreed to this suggestion but on the question of the number of surveys, Council refused to yield. If no more than 61,000 acres had been included in ten surveys, 139,000 must be covered by the remaining ten. The original action by Council had provided "not more than twenty"; that number must suffice.[88]

[85] 5 *E. J.*, 499. Colonial variants of the spelling of Kanawha were numerous.

[86] 3 *G. W.*, 68; *E. J.*, P.R.O., C.O. 5: 1350, p. 64–65.

[87] This attestation was required by Oct. 10, 1770 (see *supra*, p. 240) and doubtless was completed by that date, but a few scattered certificates only have been found among the Washington Papers.

[88] 3 *G. W.*, 69; *Rind's Gazette*, Jan. 14, 1773; *E. J.*, as cited *supra*. John Carlyle filed an appeal for inclusion in the grant, but this was rejected. *E. J.*, P.R.O., C.O. 5: 1350, p. 66.

This disappointed and angered Washington. He did not think Council should have been so rigid in its adherence to the number of surveys where the rights of the defenders of Virginia were involved. If the former soldiers searched out the best land, they should be alloted it. "What inducements have men," he asked indignantly, "to explore uninhabited wilds but the prospect of getting good lands? Would any man waste his time, expose his fortune, nay, life, in such a search if he was to share the good and the bad with those that come after him? Surely no! . . ."[89] Washington reasoned that if Crawford's ten surveys had yielded less than a third of the total acreage promised the veterans of 1754, there had to be careful exploration before the other ten surveys were undertaken, so that, in the end, a minimum of poor lands would be included with the good.[90]

Difficult and expensive as this was going to be, Washington did not intend to turn back but, on the contrary, he would increase his stake in what he still regarded as a lottery. Neither Jacob van Braam nor Robert Stobo had sent a shilling to aid in meeting the costs of exploration and survey. These two former officers—the hostages given at the surrender of Fort Necessity [91]—were in Great Britain and retained their recognized rights, but, Washington wrote, they "cannot expect much for their shares and therefore I would give a trifle in order to take a chance of gaining as well as of losing as I must carry on the work." [92] The man to whom he explained this was Robert Adam, who was about to leave for England. Adam was to wait on Stobo and van Braam, whom Washington separately notified by letter, and he was to offer each of them a sum not exceeding £100 sterling "at the utmost" for their rights.[93] Washington told Adam: "Whatever sums you agree for (and I have no doubts of your purchasing upon the best terms you can) I have desired Robt. Cary Esq. & Co. to pay." [94] Cary, in turn, was asked to advance the money on Washington's account, at interest. "If," said the gentleman who was hopeful of the capital prize in the great land lottery, "you have any unwillingness to do this, I then request that the money may be paid out of Mr. Custis's money in your hands and I shall allow him the interest for it here." [95] As Stobo and van Braam had been Captains

---

[89] 3 G. W., 68.

[90] Cf. 3 G. W., 69.

[91] Vol. I, p. 408.

[92] 3 G. W., 77.

[93] 3 G. W., 75–77.

[94] 3 G. W., 77.

[95] Ibid., 74–75. This is the first observed instance of any suggestion of direct borrowing by Washington from the Custis trust funds, though he had used his wards' balances on Cary's books more or less as collateral for his debt to the firm.

at the time of the fight in the Great Meadows, each of them was entitled to 9000 acres of the "proclamation land." [96] Washington's gamble, therefore, was not a wild one. If he got the rights of these former officers at £100 each, and carried through the patenting of their land as his own, it would cost him less than three pence an acre.

Larger profits might call for heavier investment. Washington had heard nothing that justified him, as yet, in buying any of Croghan patents, or in pursuing the idea of bargaining for Croghan's professed interest in the new Colony in Ohio; [97] but he had heard from Thomas Cresap that shares in the company might be had cheaply from some of the original members in England and he now inquired of George Mercer, who still was across the Atlantic: "Are you of this opinion? Who are they that would sell? And at what price do you think a share could be bought?" [98]

This correspondence was part of the labor of Washington after his return on the 11th of November from Williamsburg. [99] When he reached home, he found ten guests in the house but he contented himself with listing the names in his diary and with noting thereafter the various departures. [100] He was not inhospitable and, within limits, was glad to have company at Mount Vernon. Later that same year he was to welcome with much pleasure Governor Eden and a group of other Maryland notables, [101] but he probably was beginning to wonder whether he was a planter or an inn-keeper. His kinsfolk and associates, members of Martha's family, and the friends of "Jack" and of "Patsy" descended in flocks and sometimes did not allow him sufficient time for the untroubled transaction of increasing business. [102] "Jack" himself now gave promise of being an excellent host and of entertaining elegantly, if his tastes in dress were any indication of what he would do when he had an establishment of his own. In his studies, the heir of the Custises now had an added excuse for being very considerate of himself: Mr. Boucher had been so engrossed in his own affairs that he had not spent much time instructing his pupils. The dominie's amendment, fervently prom-

---

[96] See 3 *G. W.*, 69.   [97] Cf. 3 *G. W.*, 78.
[98] Letter of Nov. 22, 1771; 3 *G. W.*, 72.
[99] He left the capital November 7. See 2 *Diaries*, 40–41.
[100] 2 *Diaries*, 40–41.   [101] 2 *Diaries*, 44.
[102] This is said with reservation as to date. Abundant evidence exists that Washington's state of mind concerning visitors was pronounced, though it never led him to the least discourtesy. The conclusion that this feeling began in the early seventeen-seventies is based on the increasing number of references to guests and to the duration of their visits, but this must not be tied to any specific year.

ised, could not compensate for the hours the boy had lost.[103] Washington did not lose faith in the teacher on this account, but he must have concluded that if "Jack" was to have the schooling needed by a man of business and of culture, the youth must seek it farther from home than at Annapolis.[104]

In the late autumn, Washington received news of the death of Joseph Valentine, who had been in charge of all the Parke and Custis plantations on the York and its tributaries when Washington married Martha. In that position Valentine remained to the end of his days. Washington visited him occasionally but wrote him seldom and always accepted his statements without audit or cavil. Valentine, in short, was not an overseer of overseers but was the steward of properties left almost completely in his care,[105] and he had no assistant on the Custis estates able to manage them as he had, Washington could not hope to find another such man, already qualified, but he did not lack applicants, some of whom were endorsed by close friends.[106] His choice was to fall eventually on James Hill who, regardless of his proficiency or lack of it in other respects, was to prove himself a most accomplished Jeremiah. Before many months, Washington could be reasonably sure that every letter from Hill would catalogue so many agricultural calamities that it seemed miraculous the farms themselves had not disappeared.[107]

Washington himself was of different temper. Now that he was closing the books of 1771 and was approaching his fortieth birthday, he was inured to such vexations as debtors who could not pay, tenants behind on their rent, unreasonable applicants for counsel or assistance, "Jack's" procrastination, and the idolatry of the mother for the boy. "Patsy's" pathetic illness was hard to bear and the more so because none of the physicians seemed able to do anything to relieve her. In the larger

---

103 4 *Hamilton*, 83. Boucher wrote in his memoirs, *op. cit.*, 42, that he drank heavily "tho' never, I thank God to intemperance," during at least a part of his residence in America, but as he subsequently tore eight pages from the manuscript at that point in his narrative, it is impossible to say whether overindulgence was the reason for his inattention to "Jack" in the autumn of 1771. The MS is in the Library of the United States Naval Academy.

104 Washington's letters of the winter of 1771–72 and the spring of 1772 to Boucher (3 *G. W.*, 79, 83), are distinctly in the mood of friendship. It is possible, of course, that his reply to Boucher's confession of negligence was verbal.

105 This is plain from Washington's endorsements on Valentine's papers and from his ledger entries of payments by Valentine. The date of the death of the steward has not been found. First reference to it in Washington's correspondence appears to be James Hill's application, Dec. 9, 1771, for the position Valentine had held (4 *Hamilton*, 87). Valentine's will is dated Nov. 30, 1771 and was probated Dec. 16, 1771 (22 *York Co. Wills and Inventories*, 48).

106 *Ibid.*, 91, 93, 95, 96, 99.

107 See as typical his letter of July 24, 1772, in 4 *Hamilton*, 134. Hill was named prior to May 14, 1772.

affairs of fortune, there was at the end of the year the old uncertainty concerning the outcome of the Dunbar suit which had been postponed once more, and equal uncertainty regarding the security of the veterans' lands in event the Walpole Grant was approved and a new Colony was established on the Ohio.

The other sheet of the general ledger of hope and dread, gain and loss, progress and rebuff in 1771, was full of cheerful entries. On the 1st of December, Washington again was elected to the House of Burgesses and was host at the usual ball.[108] During the month he had eight fine days of fox hunting.[109] The mill was working profitably; all the farm industries, the fisheries in particular, were thriving; tobacco was certain to bring a good price.[110] The previous June, he had sold approximately 180 acres of his Bullskin farm for £400—the first land of any importance with which he had parted[111]—but he held at Michaelmas on quitrents to Lord Fairfax 12,463 acres[112] and he might look forward, not unreasonably, to doubling his entire land holdings. In spite of the shortage of specie, cash at Mount Vernon amounted to £371, almost enough to pay the family expenses for a year at the standard that prevailed on most plantations of the first order.[113]

There still was no young heir at Mount Vernon, nor, after twelve years of married life, could much hope of issue remain; but in nearly all other respects, Washington could say once again, at the beginning of 1772, that life never had been so rich or the promise of the future so bright in all that made for the opulent comfort of a restored plantation. Minor perplexities of course attended the New Year as always they had. Settlement of one of the main controversies over the estate of Thomas Colville[114] was followed almost immediately by an unpleasant dispute with John and William Barry over a boundary-line. They professed that Washington was cutting timber on their land; his belief was that this allegation was advanced to conceal the fact that they were encroaching on his property and were felling trees there. The matter had to go before the County Court, which named a committee to examine

[108] 2 *Diaries*, 43, with a note on the cost. Apparently Washington and John West had no opposition.
[109] 2 *Diaries*, 43–46.
[110] With the death of Joseph Valentine, accurate figures for the tobacco crop ended. No totals of actual production have been found for 1771 or for any other years prior to 1775.
[111] 2 *Diaries*, 23.   [112] *Ledger B*, folio 53.
[113] Landon Carter had written Mch. 12, 1771, in his Diary: "I find it has not been for some years less than £400 the year that has maintained my family in everything, tools, etc." (13 *W*(1), p. 158).
[114] 2 *Diaries*, 52–53.

the facts and to establish the line.[115] Like contention persisted in the
effort of Doctor Savage to withhold and of Washington and Fairfax to
collect the annuity of £100 a year due Mrs. Savage under the deed of
trust given by her first husband, Rev. Charles Green. By this time Mrs.
Savage was living in Ireland and was close to want. Washington sent
her £53 of his own money in the hope that he could collect it and all
the arrearages of the mistreated woman's money from Savage—a hope
that increased somewhat as the Doctor was driven from one legal
defence to another.[116]

The spirit of this gift to Mrs. Savage was more and more manifest in
Washington's actions. His beneficences increased with his means. He
now was paying regularly the £25 per annum that he had promised
for the schooling of William Ramsay; [117] entries of small charities were
more and more numerous in his ledger. During 1771, for example,
Washington received £20, 18s which apparently he had regarded as
lost. He decided that he would make a present of it to Dr. James Craik,
"for services done me whilst I was in the Virginia Regiment," though
the fact probably was that the duties performed by Craik were those
that a commissioned surgeon would have discharged as a matter of
course.[118] The whole community was the gainer by Washington's larger
wealth and ready cash, because he was increasingly the banker of his
neighbors and even of distant friends. He now subscribed £50 toward
the erection of a new warehouse at Alexandria,[119] and he lent £150 to
Bryan Fairfax under a somewhat complicated scheme of repayment.[120]
Most of his personal loans to acquaintances were fairly well secured,
though numerous small advances to tenants were chronically overdue.
Washington still considered Bernard Moore's debt to the Custis estate
safe because of the surety of John Baylor; but the new personal loan of
£100 to Moore was now of doubtful return, in spite of Washington's
effort to secure it adequately.[121]

The Colonel did not have to bend his shoulders so unremittingly
over these accounts that he had no time for hunting. On most of his

[115] *Fairfax Orders*, 1772–74, p. 114; survey of Jan. 18, 1772, Survey Notes, 1770–99, *Papers of G. W.*; LC; *Pocket Day Book*, 1772–74, entry of Aug. 30, 1772, of fee paid Harrison and Ellzey for services in the suit, 391 *Papers of G. W.*; LC; 2 *Diaries*, 79; 4 *Hamilton*, 102.

[116] 3 *G. W.*, 79, 101; *Ledger B*, folio 51; 4 *Hamilton*, 108, 141. It is manifest from an advertisement in the *Penn. Gazette* of July 7, 1773 that Doctor Savage was residing at or near Dumfries then.

[117] *Ledger B*, folio 47.   [118] *Ledger A*, folio 354.

[119] *Ledger A*, folio 349.   [120] 2 *Diaries*, 53.

[121] *Ledger A*, folio 151; *Ledger B*, folio 46; 4 *Hamilton*, 124; Edmund Pendleton to John Baylor, Sept. 14, 1771; *Baylor Papers*.

rides with his friends and neighbors to the matchless music of the hounds, he had the excitement of the "kill," but fate mocked him on the 4th of January. That morning the dogs got on the trail of a bear and pursued furiously. When he eluded them, they sprang a fox and harked him, too, in vain.[122] Field sports ended unhappily and with suddenness. On the 26th of January, snow began to fall in tons, as if the gods of wind and rain had repented the mercy they had shown the Potomac Valley during the floods of the previous May. By the 29th, when the storm ended, the snow was "up to the breast of a tall horse everywhere" on the plantation, according to the ready-made measure that Washington employed.[123] So deep was the fall that roads disappeared, unless their course could be followed by trees that lined them. Life on the farm became a struggle to feed the stock and to keep the fires alive. Washington had to enter in his diary that thirteen times within three weeks he was "at home all day alone" or words of like import. He became so bored, indeed, that for three days all he could add to his record was, "Ditto—Ditto." [124] The snow was, Washington wrote, "the deepest . . . I suppose the oldest man living ever remembers to have seen in this country," [125] or, in Jonathan Boucher's words, "a kind of Greenland winter." [126] Not until February 21 could an open boat cross the Potomac.[127] Even on the 25th, when Washington started to Williamsburg to attend a session of the General Assembly that had begun on February 10,[128] Accotink Creek was so high from rains which had washed away the deep snow, that he had to turn back and wait a day for the water to fall.[129]

When Washington arrived at the capital on the 2nd of March [130] and received his usual committee assignments the next day,[131] little had been done by the House of Burgesses, and little of importance, in his opinion, was done thereafter. The theatre was open; entertainment was extensive, though somewhat below the activity of most sessions;[132] the principal amusement of gentlemen who exhausted conversation was cards, at which the senior Burgess from Fairfax found himself more

122 2 *Diaries*, 49–51. 123 2 *Diaries*, 29.
124 2 *Diaries*, 53–55. 125 3 *G. W.*, 79.
126 4 *Hamilton*, 109.
127 3 *G. W.*, 79.
128 *Journ. H.B.*, 1770–72, p. 153. From February 6 onward, there had been successive one-day prorogations on account of the adverse weather. See *E. J.*, P.R.O., C.O. 5: 1350, p. 68; VSL Photostat.
129 2 *Diaries*, 55. Route and charges on the road appear in *Ledger B*, folio 3.
130 2 *Diaries*, 56. 131 *Journ. H.B.*, 1770–73, p. 204.
132 2 *Diaries*, 57–59.

often worsted than winning. He conscientiously kept the record of his play and ended the session the loser by £24; but he could write it down that on the evening of the highest battle, he had taken his adversaries into camp for £9, 10s.[133] In other respects, Martha and "Patsy" not being with him, his stay in Williamsburg was inexpensive.[134] The debate over the proposal for an American bishop interested him mildly; [135] he doubtless watched closely, also, the terms of a bill to amend the law for the inspection of tobacco,[136] and he perhaps had an active part in the passage of a measure to open and extend the navigation of the Potomac from Fort Cumberland to Tidewater.[137] His private stake was in a bill to authorize him to put a gate across the road that led to Captain Posey's ferry, a privilege not infrequently granted by the Assembly to save a planter from the necessity of having to fence both sides of a road that led through his property to a river-crossing.[138] Still more personal and distinctly painful was the work of Surgeon-Dentist Baker who extracted £4 and perhaps several teeth in an effort to save what was left of Washington's feeblest physical equipment.[139] By April 9, the dentist had done his best and the Assembly had nearly reached the end of its calendar. Washington prepared to start home,[140] but before he left Williamsburg he called on the Governor and received the promise of help in completing the grant of the soldiers' lands under the proclamation of 1754.[141]

Then it was the familiar, tedious road through the sand and the forest, with the stops at the least-bad ordinaries—a routine so frequent that Washington doubtless had forgotten long previously how many times he had endured it. Now, as often, it ended in the happiness of home and in the reassumption of duties that had been well performed in his absence, as far as they could be performed at all, by the faithful Lund Washington. Some disease had killed nearly 100 sheep that spring, but the fisheries were active [142] and the mill was busy.[143] There was, too, much talk in the neighborhood about the new law for opening the navigation of the Potomac from Fort Cumberland eastward through

[133] Ledger B, folio 48.　　　　　　　　　[134] Ibid., folio 3, 4.
[135] 3 G. W., 80.　　　　　　　　　　　　[136] 8 H 511.
[137] 8 H 564. A similar measure was passed for opening the falls of the James (8 H 564).
[138] Journ. H.B., 1770–72, p. 235. Cf. ibid., 198.
[139] Ledger B, folio 4.
[140] He drew pay for thirty-nine days (Ledger A, folio 303). The Assembly was prorogued on the 11th (Journ. H.B., 1770–72, p. 317), to meet June 25, 1772.
[141] 3 G. W., 85.　　　　　　　　　　　　[142] 3 G. W., 82, 83.
[143] Ledger B, folio 9, 25, 29, 33.

the falls to the deep water and the welcome tide above Mount Vernon. The law provided for private subscription, management and construction and for public tolls, with permission to organize a lottery of 20,000 tickets at £5 each.

Execution had to wait on similar legislation by Maryland [144] and on the willingness of merchants, shipowners and planters to subscribe the necessary funds which some honest and qualified engineer would expend wisely. The man foremost in zeal was John Ballendine with whom Washington had encountered trouble soon after he had taken over the management of Mount Vernon. Ballendine had given Washington short weight of iron then and had compelled the Colonel to carry the case to court. Now Ballendine appealed to Washington for letters of introduction to Maryland notables he believed he could interest. With reluctance Washington wrote a few lines to Governor Eden and to others, and then he felt that in justice to them, to Ballendine and to the undertaking, he should be explicit. A letter accordingly went to Thomas Johnson, the Annapolis attorney who already was displaying the high qualities that soon made him a leader in Maryland. Washington balanced the equities in this complicated sentence: "At the same time that I acknowledge that, Mr. Ballendine has a natural genius to things of this sort, which if properly encouraged may lend much to public utility, I cannot help adding, that, his principles have been loose; whether from a natural depravity, or distressed circumstances, I shall not undertake to determine; how far therefore a man of this cast is entitled to encouragement everyone must judge for themselves, for my part I think, if he applies the money subscribed, to the end proposed, the public will derive great advantages from it; on this account it is, alone, I wish to see him encouraged, and on this principle it is, I have taken the liberty of mentioning of him to Governor Eden, Colonel Sharpe, Major Jenifer and yourself; because, I think the opening of the Potomack will at once fix the trade of the western country at least till it may be conducted through the Mississippi, (by New Orleans) through that channel, and end, in amazing advantages to these two Colonies." [145] In short, as Washington judged him, Ballendine was an able rascal who might be useful if carefully watched by subscribers to an enterprise which Washington now endorsed. He had not previously

[144] 3 *G. W.*, 81.
[145] Letter of May 5, 1772; 3 *G. W.*, 83. The punctuation has been preserved; capitalization has been modernized.

done so. From the time he had reported to Thomas Lee in 1754 on his trip down the river [146] he had believed in the possibilities of developing the Potomac, but as late as 1770 he had not thought the money for the enterprise would be forthcoming.[147] He never had discouraged the project; he simply had deferred it.

The weeks that followed this endorsement of the new effort to develop the upper Potomac were full of activities which showed more than ever that the life of a speculating planter of station could not be spent in ease and idleness. Always something demanded attention at home or a journey from the plantation. Most particularly, Charles Willson Peale who lived then at Annapolis,[148] had succeeded so well in portrait-painting that to sit for him had become quite the fashion of the Potomac Valley. Washington of course was one of those whose countenance must be put on canvas for the delight of his household and the adornment of his walls, but it proved a new and not entirely pleasant experience.[149] The decision was to have Washington appear in the uniform of the First Virginia Regiment [150] with his sword and gorget and with a rifle over his shoulder. Either the uniform or his own embarrassment in posing gave him a measure of self-consciousness. Occasionally, too, as he sat immobile while Peale worked, Washington would nod. "[I am]," he wrote, "in so grave, so sullen a mood, and now and then under the influence of Morpheus, when some critical strokes are making, that I fancy the skill of this gentleman's pencil will be put to it in describing to the world what manner of man I am." [151] On the 22nd of May, the sittings ended; [152] soon the portrait was finished. It was a success in every way except, perhaps, that the "grave mood" made the line of the mouth a little too taut. Perhaps, also, Peale's desire to give Washington the appearance he had in the French and Indian War

[146] 1 G. W., 100. Needless to say the addressee was not "President" Lee. He had died in 1750.

[147] 3 G. W., 17.

[148] He spent a considerable part of his time in Philadelphia.

[149] In spite of the display of what are supposed to be authentic earlier portraits of Washington, it should be stated that no item has been found in Washington's accounts to indicate that he paid anything for portraiture of himself prior to 1772, or that he had any close contact with any artist prior to the time Peale came to Mount Vernon in the winter of 1771–72. Washington sat for a second portrait by Peale in June, 1774 (Ledger B, folio 115). This may be C. W. Peale No. 2 mentioned in John Hill Morgan and Mantle Fielding, The Life Portraits of Washington, 24–25, but it is to be noted that Washington paid for this portrait, which he scarcely would have done if the picture had been intended, as was surmised, for Peale's museum in Philadelphia.

[150] The emphasis on "First" is necessary because, it will be remembered, Byrd's Second Virginia originally was outfitted in French uniforms from a vessel captured at sea.

[151] Letter of May 21, 1772 to Jonathan Boucher; 3 G. W., 83–84.

[152] 2 Diaries, 64–65.

made him look youthful at 40 years of age.[153] Miniatures of Martha, of "Jack" and of "Patsy" were finished by Peale on the same visit [154] that was not without amusing incidents. Peale wrote later: "One afternoon, several young gentlemen, visitors at Mount Vernon, and myself were engaged in pitching the bar, one of the athletic sports common in those times, when suddenly the Colonel appeared among us. He requested to be shown the pegs that marked the bounds of our effort; then, smiling, and without putting off his coat, held out his hand for the missile. No sooner did the heavy iron bar feel the grasp of his mighty hand than it lost the power of gravitation, and whizzed through the air, striking the ground far, very far, beyond our utmost limits. We were indeed amazed, as we stood around all stripped to the buff, with shirt sleeves rolled up, and having thought ourselves very clever fellows, while the Colonel, on retiring, pleasantly observed, 'When you beat my pitch, young gentlemen, I'll try again' . . ." Before the artist said farewell, Washington was off with Bryan Fairfax to inspect and to survey some lands that friend owned in Loudoun and in Fauquier. While in that fine pastoral country, Washington purchased two horses [155] and decided to buy a tract of 600 acres in Fauquier County that Bryan had inherited from his brother "Billy." [156]

On his return to Mount Vernon, June 5,[157] Washington found Captain Posey ensconced as a guest. The Captain had arrived about the time Washington left and had decided to wait until he could see Washington and transact this business of his usual sort: He was in desperate need of money and was anxious to sell the last six acres of his land at Rover's Delight, his ferry and house there, his horse, his saddle and his

---

[153] This portrait, which is reproduced as the frontispiece of the present volume, was bequeathed to George Washington Parke Custis and by him was left to his grandson G. W. Custis Lee, who gave it to Washington and Lee University. It hangs in the chapel of that institution.

[154] On May 30 he was paid £18, 4s for the portrait and £13 for each of the miniatures, a total of £57, 4s (Ledger B, folio 50). The odd figures are due to the fact that Peale followed the usual practice of artists and made his charge in guineas. His receipt for the miniature of Mrs. Washington, ten guineas, at the cost of "Jack," is among the Washington MSS of the Huntington Library. See also 2 Diaries, 64–65. "Jack" was beginning to spend somewhat freely. In the Custis Papers, VHS, is an entry of £67 cash paid Boucher on "Jack's" account, together with note of a bill of exchange to "pay some old debts" the boy had accumulated. Young Custis appears in C. C. Sellers, Charles Willson Peale, where, p. 108–09, is narrated the incident quoted in the text.

[155] Ledger B, folio 50. He left home May 24. His day-by-day movements, which have no special interest, are recorded in 2 Diaries, 65–66.

[156] Fitzpatrick's note in 2 Diaries, 65. Bryan was younger than "Billy" and not older, as Fitzpatrick stated. The transfer of this tract, which was valued at £150, was not completed until March, 1773 (Ledger B, folio 13).

[157] Washington attended a vestry meeting at the "new church" on his way home that day. See 2 Diaries, 66.

bridle. A bargain was struck. For £50, cash in hand, Captain Posey yielded all that he had specified and, in due time, rode off to new unhappiness—to imprisonment for debt and to the virtual pauperizing of his children.[158] When next he was to appear it was to be to sell to Washington for £11 what probably was his last asset, his "rights" to 3000 acres of unlocated land under the proclamation of 1763.[159]

These were bargains. So, doubtless, Washington regarded the purchase, later in the summer, of 203 acres of land from Charles West.[160] There may have been profit, too, in a sale Washington had agreed to make of some of his land adjoining Wormeley, Alexander and others;[161] but he was not confining himself to the purchase and sale of land only. He received £150 for pork[162] and sold about 900,000 herring;[163] he was working his mill steadily; from all these he had money and he laid it out for pleasure and for future gain—in a whale boat purchased from Governor Eden,[164] in an indentured servant of Doctor Savage's,[165] in three Negroes from Adam & Co.[166]—and in much besides. The invoices of July, 1772, were for the most expensive clothing, food and furnishings Washington ever had ordered. This, for instance, was the specification for "a gentleman's hunting cap": it was to be "covered with black velvet, to fit a pretty large head, cushioned round or stuffed to make it sit easy thereon. A silk band and handsome silver buckle to it."[167] A watchmaker was admonished: "I again wish to have two [watch keys] very different from this common sort . . . to be of the best kind and much handsomer and neater than either [of those sent]."[168] All the clothing was to be "fashionable" and of quality. Most particularly Washington ordered: "A riding frock of a handsome, drab colored broad cloth with plain, double gilt buttons [and] a riding waistcoat of superfine scarlet cloth and gold lace, with buttons like those of the coat."[169]

Not so long after this invoice was filled in London and sent across

158 2 *Diaries*, 66; 4 *Hamilton*, 169; *Ledger B*, folio 50. A price of £50 for Posey's property seems very low, but its condition is not known.

159 This was in October, 1772 (*Ledger B*, folio 61, 112).

160 *Ledger B*, folio 59, 62, 66. Cf. *ibid.*, folio 41.

161 2 *Diaries*, 53. Nothing further is known of this transaction, which was being negotiated in January, 1772.   162 *Ledger A*, folio 356.   163 *Ledger B*, folio 42.

164 *Ledger B*, folio 50, 60. His first excursion in this boat appears to have been June 28, when he took a party "to the spring at Johnson's place" (2 *Diaries*, 69).

165 This was Andrew, for whose services Washington paid £35. (*Ledger B*, folio 63).

166 *Ledger B*, folio 5. It is not altogether certain that this purchase was in 1772, though the evidence is to that effect. The Negroes may have been transferred to reduce the debt of Adam & Co. to Washington.

167 3 *G. W.*, 92.   168 *Ibid.*, 95.   169 *Ibid.*, 96.

the Atlantic, the Colonel could hope to wear his new clothes to a new church. Truro Parish had two of these, old Pohick, which was three miles from Gunston Hall, and the recently constructed Payne's Church, located on the site Washington as a vestryman had voted to approve.[170] Now it was agreed that a new Pohick should be erected, but where? Should a new church rise near the old foundation, above the graves of early believers, or should the edifice be reared "whither the tribes go up," on a main road and closer to the homes of a majority of the worshippers? George Mason advocated a new building close to the old; Washington favored a central location and probably submitted a drawing to show where the building could serve the largest number of the faithful. Convenience triumphed over sentiment; Washington won.[171] It was a friendly victory that left no scars in a happy year.

All the while, Washington continued to prod or to exhort the men who could help in bringing to a conclusion the grant of the Ohio lands he wanted. He discharged, too, some further troublesome duties as executor of Thomas Colville, brother and one of the heirs of John Colville,[172] and he attended to his part of a new transaction, the shipment of 273 barrels of his flour to Jamaica or another of the West Indies. Washington was specific in his instructions to Daniel Jenifer Adams, who, as part owner, went with the vessel, the brig *Fairfax,* Samuel Brodie, master.[173] The flour was consigned to Adams, so that no question might be raised concerning his right to dispose of it. Adams was told where to proceed, what price to demand, and where to leave the consignment, should there be an outlook for a rising market and a reasonable prospect that the flour would "keep." Washington was under no illusion regarding the quality of this particular flour: "I recommend its being lumped of rather than sold in small parcels for trial, as it was ground out of indifferent wheat and will, I fear, look better

[170] See *supra,* p. 178. Washington was having a modest part at this time in what might be termed the ecclesiastical politics of Virginia. Among his letters at William and Mary College is one, dated July 30, 1772, in which he recommended a successor to Rev. James Horrocks as Commissary of the Bishop of London.

[171] This tradition of the present (1950) Pohick Church is old, see 2 *Meade,* 227, and includes the impossible detail that Washington had measured all the distances and had "marked down all the houses of the parishioners," for which, in reality, he possessed no "base map." There is no reason to question the general accuracy of the tradition. It is "in character" for both Washington and Mason. Most amusingly, at the foot of the page that describes this incident in Kate Mason Rowland's *George Mason,* some reader carefully pencilled on the copy in the Virginia State Library, "That d—d surveyor had no sentiment."

[172] *Ledger A,* folio 246; *Ledger B,* folio 21; *Pocket Day Book,* 1772–74, entries of Aug. 18, 20, 1772; 391 *Papers of G. W.,* LC.

[173] 3 *G. W.,* 106. For freight charges, see 4 *Hamilton,* 131.

to the eye than it will prove agreeable to the taste, being a little musty." The proceeds were to be laid out in Negroes, provided the cost of "choice ones" was less than £40 sterling. If the price was above that, then rum, molasses, sugar and other products were to be taken.[174] At the price he was willing to pay, Washington was somewhat exacting in his requirements for the slaves: ". . . let there be two-thirds of them males, the other third females. The former not exceeding (at any rate) 20 years of age, the latter 16. All of them to be straight-limbed and in every respect strong and likely, with good teeth and good countenances, to be sufficiently provided with clothes."[175] He already had more than his quota of old, dependent Africans.

Washington had no reason for explaining to Adams why he was trying to turn somewhat musty Virginia flour into youthful West Indian Negro flesh, but he was planning to increase his slaves because he wanted a considerable number of workers for the early, extensive cultivation of the new lands he hoped to acquire on the Youghiogheny and on the Ohio. In any small development of western lands, he might be able to supply some servants from Mount Vernon. The change from tobacco to wheat had reduced the demand for field hands on Washington's Potomac properties, except at the seasons of plowing and harvesting. He planned, for example, to sow almost 900 bushels of wheat[176] in September and apparently he did not think this would over-tax the manpower available on the farms, though the acreage was the largest Washington ever had given to that grain. Milling must go on. Even if the flour sometimes was disappointing, as the consignment to the West Indies proved to be,[177] Washington believed in the future of his industry and soon was to register his brand as "G. Washington."[178]

After his shipment to the West Indies, he had one more special duty to perform before turning to the work that was uppermost in his mind, the patenting of the soldiers' western lands. He had, in September, to

[174] In describing one of the smaller items he desired, Washington outdid his own spelling. He wanted "1 lb. of Kian Pepper."

[175] 3 *G. W.*, 98.　　　　　　　　[176] 2 *Diaries*, 81.

[177] Robert McMickan wrote from Kingston, Jamaica, Nov. 13, 1772 that the flour he had seen in Washington's consignment "was not of the best quality and, I believe, sold not for more than common flour" (4 *Hamilton*, 160). A London letter in the *Va. Gazette* of Oct. 15, 1772, noted of American flour in general that it was not ground properly but the wheat was average in quality.

[178] December 2, 1772; *Fairfax Orders*, 1772–74, p. 158. The choice of this as his brand name no doubt is responsible for the tradition that Washington was so conscientious in the manufacture of good flour that the inspectors would pass it if he merely had his name stamped on the barrel.

visit his mother and to make further arrangements for her comfort. The journey on the 14th covered the entire distance from Mount Vernon to Fredericksburg between 7 A.M. and dusk, with time for dinner and for feeding the horses at Aquia.[179] He lodged with his mother who by this time almost certainly was residing in a house on the lots he had bought the previous year. The dwelling was small but it was well built and its woodwork was excellent. Located at the corner of what later became Charles and Lewis Streets, the residence was close enough to Betty Washington Lewis's for the daughter to be quickly at her mother's side in case of need, while normally she would be sufficiently far off for Mrs. Washington to retain cherished independence.[180] Washington observed all this, conferred with his brother Charles and with Fielding Lewis, inspected the farms across the river and, on the 17th of September, returned home. Apparently he was satisfied that his mother now was well sheltered and that she no longer would be burdened by the care of fields and animals.[181]

These affairs of duty and of business had interrupted one of the most delightful seasons of pleasure the family at Mount Vernon had enjoyed in thirteen years of residence on the river. There had been hunting, fishing, visiting in Maryland and in Virginia, entertainment of numerous guests,[182] and now, on the 4th of October, a journey to Annapolis for the races, the plays and much feasting.[183] After that came ten days at home and then, on the 21st, Washington left with Martha and the young Custises [184] for Eltham, where once more they were to enjoy the hospitality of the Bassetts. In addition, through the kindness of the host, Washington was to work there with Capt. William Crawford, who was to bring with him the field notes of the new surveys of soldiers' lands. From these notes Washington was to make the plats of the tracts on the Ohio and on the Great Kanawha; and, when these were completed, he would take them to Williamsburg, would lay them before the

179 2 *Diaries,* 79. Reference to "horses" in the Diary suggests that Washington made this journey in his "chair" and not astride one of his numerous mounts.

180 Old maps of Fredericksburg show that, after 1761, the site of Mary Washington's house did not directly join Fielding Lewis's residential property, as often is stated. On the contrary, there were two streets and four rows of lots between Mary Washington's and the noble dwelling of Lewis's, subsequently known as Kenmore.

181 For his movements, see 2 *Diaries,* 79. The uncertain questions concerning the time and circumstances of Mrs. Mary Ball Washington's removal from Ferry Farm are discussed in Appendix III—3.

182 2 *Diaries,* 74–81.

183 *Ibid.,* 82–83. Apparently, "Jack" was with Washington part of this time. See *Ledger B,* folio 60. The two returned to Mount Vernon together (2 *Diaries,* 83).

184 2 *Diaries,* 84.

Governor and Council, and would try to procure final orders for the patents.

The first stages of this were exactly as Washington wished them to be. He and his charges reached Eltham on the 24th of October. Crawford already was there or else arrived immediately; and from the 25th through the 30th, he labored with Washington over the surveys. The notes were adequate, and all the lines could be drawn, but with the best effort, Crawford had been able to cover 127,899 acres only.[185] Including those surveyed the previous year, there now were thirteen tracts, one of which covered 51,302 acres, another 28,627, and another 13,532. From what Washington had seen of the country, he apprehended trouble in dividing these tracts because good land and bad would be mingled. If certain of the allotments manifestly were of a better average than the others, jealousies would be aroused and charges of partiality would be made. Besides, the surveys covered less than two-thirds of the required total. Some of the veterans would have to wait. Washington did not think the private soldiers should be denied any of their land but, on the contrary, should be awarded forthwith everything they were to have. The same treatment was deserved by those officers who had met all the calls for money with which to provide the surveys and to cover the various costs. With several who had held commissions, the case was different. Much to Washington's resentment, they had contributed nothing, but they wanted now to share to the fullest. Washington reasoned, as did other contributors, that if these delinquents had to wait, it was no more than they deserved. In this bounty, as in defence of the Colony, the first afield should be rewarded first.

Possible inequities in the quality of the land assigned different beneficiaries involved the justice that Washington had put among the essential "principles" of his life. How was justice to be assured all the officers and men? In what manner, he reasoned, could it be done so surely as by returning to the plan he originally had urged—that of designating large regions in which every man would be free to patent the best unoccupied land he could find? Washington, wrestling with the question, decided he would make another plea for free choice in the form of a large increase in the number of permissible surveys. At the same time, he would try to put the Council to the test by asking the members how he should proceed.

[185] *Rind's Gazette*, Jan. 14, 1773.

Every opportunity seemed open to him. After he reached Williamsburg, the Governor invited him to breakfast, to dinner and to supper on the 3rd of November.[186] The next day when Council met, the friendliest possible reception seemed to await Washington's formal petition, which had been drawn to make plain the points he had decided to advance. The paper reviewed the restrictions imposed by limiting the surveys to twenty and then it solicited a greater number of surveys in the name of the other officers and the soldiers of the First Virginia. Further, the petition asked that the Council direct how patents should issue for the lands already surveyed.

Councillors listened as the petition was read and, sensing the possibility of trouble over the form of the patents, voted to defer an answer for two days. On the other question, the Council held its ground without compromise: It had declined previously to increase the permissible number of surveys; twenty had been the figure; twenty it would remain. Without postponement or friendly gesture or regretful phrase, that part of the petition forthwith was rejected.[187]

Washington probably had anticipated this but he had asked for a reversal because he thought it just and also because it would be proof of his complete good faith in seeking the maximum for the men of his old Regiment. He now had to make the best of the thirteen existing surveys of less than 128,000 acres. On the 5th he dined with the Council and no doubt explained then some of the perplexities that beset him.[188] The next morning he was introduced formally into the Council Chamber and was permitted to present a plan for the apportionment among officers and men of the various tracts that had been surveyed by Crawford. It had been difficult to do. On tracts that ranged in size from 927 to 51,302 acres, the task was to allot each man all his land, if possible, within the same boundary lines—15,000 acres for each field officer, 9000 for each Captain, and so on down to the privates, each of whom was to have 400 acres.

In his own case, Washington had been careful. Some of the best land of all that had been surveyed by Crawford was in the great tract of 51,502 acres. If Washington had been free to make his choice under conditions identical in all cases, he would have preferred to take out the whole of his patent in that wide stretch of bottom land, rolling country

186 Washington arrived on the 2nd. See 2 *Diaries*, 85.
187 *E. J.*, Nov. 4, 1771; P.R.O., C.O. 5: 1440, p. 6, VSL Photostat.
188 2 *Diaries*, 86.

and forest; but this land had now to be resurveyed for subdivision. Should any or all of the patents be contested, those properties that had been "seated" and were under cultivation, with the strictest regard for the letter of Virginia law, would be least liable to attack. Seating and farming in turn, could most quickly be undertaken on tracts already surveyed. "I thought," Washington said in absolute candor a few months later, ". . . if any additional trouble was to be encountered . . . it might as well fall upon others as me, as my shoulders had supported the whole weight heretofore, and inasmuch as I might add without much arrogance that if it had not been for my unremitted attention to every favorable circumstance, not a single acre of land would ever have been obtained." [189]

He found, as he addressed the Council, that members were entirely of one mind with him on his basic propositions—that the private soldiers should receive their full allotment forthwith and that the officers should have their acreage in proportion to the financial support they had given the effort to establish their claims. Those who had met the assessments were to receive all the land due them; those who had contributed nothing must await the second distribution of land. Where a man had paid half, he would get 50 per cent of his allotment.

Then the Council took up the suggestions Washington had prepared for apportioning the different tracts among the individuals according to their respective shares. Washington recommended that the tract of 51,302 acres be divided among George Muse, Adam Stephen, Andrew Lewis, Peter Hog and a few others. The survey of 13,552 acres fitted almost precisely the acreage that George Mercer was entitled to have on his account and through rights he had purchased. Provision next was made for the heirs of Col. Joshua Fry and for Doctor Craik. Then came Washington's turn. He sought his own allowance of 15,000 acres as a field officer and he had bought the claim to 5000 of the 15,000 acres due George Muse, together with the claim of "Sergeant Brickner" for 600 acres [190]—a total of 20,600 acres. For the satisfaction of these claims, Washington asked one surveyed tract of 10,990 acres, another of 4395, a third of 2448, and a fourth of 2314. The total of these, 20,147, was 453 below Washington's claim. Like the other officers he would wait to have this remainder filled out from the subsequent allotment; but if he

---

[189] 3 G. W., 124.
[190] This evidently was Sergt. Rudolph Brickner of van Braam's Company.

got these four tracts, he would have no more surveying to do and could proceed as quickly as he might to occupy, to "seat," to clear and to develop.[191]

After these allotments to Washington were passed, those to the non-commissioned officers and the privates were made easily. Then came the question, Was the distribution equitable as respected the quality of the land? With the surveys limited in number, was it not probable that when the land actually was divided, some veterans would fare much better than others? The quantity of land had been fixed in October, 1771; that could not be reviewed; but the quality—was that assured in equity as far as practicable? [192] Washington might have answered that equity on the basis of initiative would have been assured if the Council had done as he had requested and had permitted every man to make his own survey, but that now had been decided. Nothing was gained by arguing it. Some other proposal must be made. Washington struck out boldly: A conference of the officers of the First Virginia, he said, was to be held November 23 at Fredericksburg: If complaint then were made that the distribution of land was inequitable in quality, he would bring the allegations before the Council, and if the Council found the complaint justified "he would give up all his interest under his patent and submit to such regulations as the Board [193] may see fit to prescribe." [194] This was enough for the Council. If the officers and men themselves were satisfied with the distribution, nobody else had any right to protest.

Washington was closer now than ever he had been to the acquisition of the lands he had been seeking for more than three years. Until the veterans' meeting, there was pleasure in Williamsburg and ample work in going over the details of crops and management and livestock and sales with the new steward of the Custis plantations, James Hill.[195] The merchants, too, were due to gather in Williamsburg at this season for the settlement of accounts in several of which Washington had an

---

191 *Rind's Gazette*, Jan. 14, 1773. It is interesting to note that the tract of 10,990 acres, which was near the mouth of the Great Kanawha, and the tract of 2314, which was on the Little Kanawha, remained in Washington's possession, unchanged, to the time of his death. The other properties were enlarged later.

192 Washington made the issue plain in his letter of Mch. 12, 1773 to Charles Mynn Thruston: ". . . the matter under contemplation . . . was the quality of the soil, it being supposed that the difference therein might cause an unequal division, though each man should obtain his quantum of land" (3 *G. W.*, 122).

193 That was the name which the Council used in referring to itself in its Journal.

194 *E. J.*, Nov. 6, 1772; P.R.O., C.O. 5: 1440, p. 47., VSL Photostat; *Rind's Gazette*, Jan. 14, 1773.

195 2 *Diaries*, 86–87.

interest; but for some reason, the traders were exasperatingly slow in arriving, so slow, in fact, that Washington had not been able to transact any of his business with them when the time came for him to go to the meeting in Fredericksburg. It was most inconvenient to leave,[196] but imperative that he be present at the gathering of his old command. On the 20th he carefully paid the fees for the patenting of the 200,000 acres, so there could be no future question about the entry.[197] That afternoon, he left the town, stopped for the night at Eltham and, on the afternoon of the 22nd, stepped out of his chariot at Fielding Lewis's in Fredericksburg.[198] The next day and the next, Washington explained the surveys to the officers, answered their questions, and reviewed the proceedings before the Council. When he had made everything plain, the officers approved the distribution he had recommended to Council. More than that, the veterans who had known him since 1754 passed a resolution in which they asked Council to relieve him of the offer to turn back his own lands if complaint were made and the Council found it justified.[199] He could have asked for no finer addendum to the letter in which his officers jointly had bidden him farewell at the end of 1758.[200] Then, their expression of confidence had involved no more than kindly feeling and a signature on a sheet of paper; now their endorsement recorded their conviction that he would not give them the worse of lands he had seen and they had not.

Another day was spent in Fredericksburg; still another was devoted to riding over the plantations and then up to Deep Run to examine the quarter he seldom had visited there.[201] After the start for home at length was made, he and his party spent two nights and a day at Col. Henry Lee's.[202] It was the afternoon of the 29th when the driver pulled up the horses at the entrance to Mount Vernon.[203] The hunting season

---

[196] 3 G. W., 121.

[197] Ledger B, folio 62. The fee was £20, 16s. For the patents, see Land Office Records, v. 41, p. 66 ff, 68, 69, 73.

[198] 2 Diaries, 87. From Washington's reference to "we" in his entry of November 27, it would appear that Martha and "Patsy" returned with him, but this is nowhere stated explicitly.

[199] E. J., Dec. 9, 1772, P.R.O., C.O. 5: 1440, p. 12, VSL Photostat.

[200] See Vol. II, p. 399.

[201] Incidentally his reference to "my plantations" and to the "upper place" makes it plain (2 Diaries, 88) that when he wrote in 1771 and in 1772 of "my plantations" or "my two plantations" he meant Ferry Farm and his mother's "lower plantation" or "quarter," and not Ferry Farm and the Deep Run or "upper" quarter.

[202] For its relation to the other plantations of the vicinity, see Vol. I, p. 207. On this visit, Washington probably did not see at Leesylvania young Harry Lee, who was in his seventeenth year. This young man, so soon to be renowned as "Light Horse Harry," almost certainly was at Princeton then.

[203] 2 Diaries, 88.

was at the crispest, when every fox left his scent on the damp earth. Washington was anxious to be afield, but he had to report to the Council the result of the meeting in Fredericksburg and he doubtless had to make ready other papers concerning transactions he had not been able to complete before he left Williamsburg.[204] Two days he spent in writing and, probably, not until he had signed the fair copies of his various letters and had started them to Williamsburg by his own messenger did he mount and sound his horn and set off with four companions to seek another fox. He might have reasoned that after so much diligence, he deserved a brush at least, but that day he found no fox, no trail even.[205]

Word from Williamsburg came about the 13th of that same December,[206] probably in the form of this entry from the Council Journal of December 9 to this effect:

Col. Washington's Letter of the 4th Inst to the Clerk and the resolves of the Conference of the Officers of the First Va Reg't at Fredericksburg of the 23rd of last month were laid before the Board; which resolves principally respect the engagement of Col. Washington at the conference held the 6th ult. to submit to a redivision of the lands granted him in case the partition then established should appear to be unequal & setting forth the reason of the meeting for desiring an absolution therefrom, all which being duly considered the Board approved of the partition before ordered and were of opinion that there would be no complaint against it; yet as possibly there might it was determined that at any time between this and the end of the Oyer and Terminal week in June next, the Board would hear any complaint on that subject but if none should be preferred within that they would then consider Col. Washington as absolved from the said engagement and the Clerk was directed to inform that gentleman that it would be agreeable to the Board if he would in the *Va. Gazette* or in some other publication or public manner advertise the several persons concerned of the orders read in their favour.[207]

In other words, unless the Council by June, 1773, received and affirmed the justice of a complaint that the land had been allotted with disregard of quality, then all that Washington had included in those four grants would be his! Later in the month he received the formal patents, issued

---

[204] It is manifest from the payment of the fees that Washington prepared the patents before he left Williamsburg.

[205] 2 *Diaries*, 88.

[206] Unfortunately for the purposes in hand, Washington gave Giles, the messenger, cash in advance of the journey (*Ledger B,* folio 62) and did not settle with him after the Negro's return, which would have fixed the approximate time the man brought back the good news.

[207] *E. J.*, Dec. 9, 1772; P.R.O., C.O. 5: 1440, p. 12, VSL Photostat.

"for divers good causes, but more especially for the consideration mentioned in the proclamation of Robert Dinwiddie, Esq., late Lieutenant Governor of Virginia bearing date Feb. 19, 1754 for encouraging men to enlist in the service of our late Royal grandfather for the defence and security of the said Colony." The first, for 2448 acres in the County of Botetourt, began on the east side of the Ohio about sixteen miles below the Little Kanawha.[208] Next covered by patent were 4395 acres in the same County on the east side of the Ohio, below the Little Kanawha and just above the great bend in the Ohio.[209] Then, in the third patent, were 10,990 acres on the south side of the Great Kanawha, about two miles above the confluence of that river with the Ohio.[210] The final parchment was for 2314 acres on the Ohio "about three or four miles below the mouth of the Little Kanawha, on the lower side of a small run and opposite a small island, by the side of a large one." [211] All four were duly signed and sealed. Together they would increase Washington's patiently accumulated 12,738 acres [212] by 20,147 to a total of 32,885.

It was a nice Christmas present.

[208] Va. *Land Office Records,* v. 41, 1772–73, p. 66.
[209] *Ibid.,* 68.   [210] *Ibid.,* 69.   [211] *Ibid.,* 73.
[212] As of Michaelmas, 1772; *Ledger B,* folio 59.

CHAPTER XIV

Death and Bounty Lands May Clear Debt
(1773)

IN ACCORDANCE with the request of Council, Washington devoted part of the Christmas season of 1772 to preparing for publication a suitable notice of the allotments of land made on the 9th of December. He felt that he would be criticised, if he had not already been assailed privately, for asking the Council to allot him separate surveys that almost exactly corresponded to the lands due him, though others had to slice their acres from large tracts that had yet to be surveyed in detail. To justify himself, Washington reported at length on the different tracts. Then he explained the request of Council that he advertise what had been done, and next he told how he had promised to return his quota if inequity were alleged by veterans and were proved to the satisfaction of Council. He dipped deeply into his ink horn and went on: "It remains, however, to be observed, that, as his Excellency and their Honours thought proper to adopt this method of having the lands surveyed, rather than permit each claimant, after the proportion were settled, to locate and survey his own particular quantity separately, it was found, after repeated trials, difficult, if not impossible, to associate different claims in the same patent, so as to make the total amount of them correspond with the quantity of the survey on the one hand or the several surveys nearer to the amount of the claim on the other, than they now do; and there being a necessity to have recourse to both in order to [make?] the distribution, I could not help wishing (as I was desirous of proceeding to the immediate cultivation of my portion) to be classed among the latter; which if considered as an indulgence, it is an indulgence I conceive myself in some degree entitled to, as I have already experienced much trouble, and felt many expenses peculiar to myself. The necessity of a division in order to cultivation and improvement, is a measure too obviously necessary to remind the officers of; but it may not be amiss to hint it to the soldiers and at the same time to add (to prevent any unnecessary application and journeys which cannot fail being attended with loss of time and expense to themselves) that I have now nothing more to do with their land." He proceeded to recommend that some of the soldiers call a meeting at which one of their number might be named to act for the others.[1]

This last part of the report was intelligible, but any veteran who read the first sentence and continued to wrestle with it until he understood it had an achievement to his credit. He might, indeed, have been excused if he asked that his allotment be doubled because of the extra duty he had performed in ascertaining what the Colonel meant. For his own part, Washington believed that he had earned all that he had pursued. Even before he wrote the article for the Williamsburg paper, he had undertaken to drive from his new Kanawha land men who had no right to be there [2] and he sought to collect what he could from those beneficiaries who, in his own figure of speech, had objections to the purchase of lottery tickets but would be "fond enough of partaking in the prizes." [3]

Recovery of his costs from officers who had contributed nothing to the surveys was only one of a number of difficulties that confronted Washington during a winter that was soft and beneficent in comparison with the preceding icy season.[4] First of all, Washington had much trouble with his tenants on his newly acquired property in Loudoun and Fauquier. These small farmers complained that his rents were high and his leases short,[5] and some of them resisted payment so stubbornly that he had to sue them and even then sustained loss.[6] A second unpleasantness was the prospect that his nearest and dearest friends, the Fairfaxes of Belvoir, were going to leave Virginia for a prolonged visit and perhaps for permanent residence in England. George William Fairfax had inherited property there that required attention; his health was frail; [7] Sally was sick and in need of greater medical knowledge than was available in Virginia. Their absence would be deprivation. Much had happened since those days in 1758 when Washington was

[1] *Rind's Gazette*, Jan. 14, 1773.
[2] 3 *G. W.*, 104–05. The familiar term "squatter" does not appear to have come into general use until after the American Revolution.
[3] 3 *G. W.*, 123.
[4] 3 *G. W.*, 115.
[5] 4 *Hamilton*, 171.
[6] *Ledger B*, folio 132.
[7] See William Nelson to S. Athawes, Aug. 12, 1767; *Nelson Letter Book*, 39. Fairfax had taken the oaths as Collector of Customs for the South Potomac, June 5, 1763, and had become a member of Council May 31, 1768. Sally's father, Col. Wilson Cary of Ceely's, died Nov. 28, 1772 (*Rind's Gazette*, Dec. 10, 1772).

about to set out for Fort DuQuesne and wished to know above everything else what Sally's feelings toward him were. Regard for her and
delight in her company had not vanished and probably had not diminished.[8] Close social contacts, visits and occasional journeys, together
with Martha and with George William Fairfax, had satisfied his desire
to see her and to hear her talk. Still . . . the happiest hours of his life
had been spent in her company;[9] it would be sad to have her and her
husband leave Belvoir. Washington, of course, would collect Fairfax's
accounts and would do what he could to look after the absent proprietor's interests: there could be no new neighbors at Belvoir like those
who were about to depart.[10]

Distress of a different sort was involved for Washington in the
case of Daniel Jenifer Adams.[11] Early in January, 1773, Washington received inconsistent and contradicting reports of what had been done by
Adams. He wrote Washington that he had sold 220 barrels of the flour
at 20s each and would dispose of the remainder immediately at the
same price.[12] Other accounts were to the effect that Adams and Captain Brodie had quarreled, that the brig had been put up for sale and
had been purchased by Adams, and that he then had sailed with freight
for Honduras.[13] Nothing was said of what had been done with the
remainder of Washington's cargo or with the money due him for the
flour Adams had marketed. It seemed not unreasonable to apprehend
that the sum due Washington had gone for the purchase of Brodie's
interest in the vessel, but Washington wished to be quite sure no injustice was done Adams. A power of attorney consequently was prepared and was dispatched to a merchant in Jamaica. ". . . if you find,"
Washington wrote, "as I have much reason to fear, that the proceeds of
my flour have been misapplied, [I beg] that you will use your best

---

[8] It was remarkable that on the two adjoining plantations, Mount Vernon and Belvoir, neither
of the owners had offspring.

[9] 36 *G. W.*, 263.

[10] 3 *G. W.*, 108; *Birch Cat. 663*, item 60; 4 *Hamilton*, 186. A number of circumstances,
most of them unknown, detained the Fairfaxes for months. Cf. *Va. Gazette*, June 3, 1773.
Washington's last word from George William in America was a note from York River, Aug. 5,
1773, in which Fairfax explained that sickness of the "chief mate" and of the crew had kept the
ship from sailing but that it would leave with the next favorable wind (*Washington MSS*,
Huntington Library). For the arrival of the Fairfaxes in England, see *John Norton & Sons*,
359. Details of Fairfax's property offered for sale and later facts concerning the management of
his estate will be found in 37 *G. W.*, 501–02; *Va. Gazette*, Feb. 25, 1773; *Birch Cat. 663*,
items 6 and 90; James Crane to Washington, Apr. 2, 1774 (*Washington MSS*, Huntington
Library). See also Johnson's preface to *Fairfax Correspondence*, v. 1, p. cxxxiv; *Burnaby*, 153.

[11] 3 *G. W.*, 105–07 and *supra*, p. 295.   [12] *Ibid.*, 112.

[13] *Ibid.*, 106.

endeavors to obtain redress for me . . ." [14] Accompanying this was a
letter to Adams, notifying him that Washington was withdrawing the
property from the young adventurer's hands; [15] and with these two was
dispatched a third, private letter to the Jamaican merchant. Washington
explained: ". . . it is not my wish to proceed to any harsh or rigorous
measures by which a man just setting out in trade may be injured if
there is a possibility of avoiding it . . . If, contrary to expectation you
should find things in a better way than is apprehended, please to withhold the letter directed to him, and suffer him to proceed without interruption, taking no notice of your having received any power on this
head . . ." [16] This was considerate but futile. Time showed the situation to be as bad as Washington had thought it might be. [17] Soon Washington had to undertake to catch Adams in some port where the vessel
could be attached. [18]

There was much more that was disagreeable or troublesome or wasteful, or all three, in the winter of 1772–73. Washington found himself
charged with responsibility for tickets in Lord Stirling's lottery, [19] involved in an effort to protect one of his dead brother "Austin's" tracts of
land, [20] and engaged in a controversy over the right the vestry of Christ
Church, Alexandria, asserted to reclaim its pews by repaying him and
others the amount of their original subscription. [21] Washington denied
vigorously, almost hotly, that the vestry could do this when he still
wanted his pew. Again, for trouble, in the course of crowding business,
Washington lent James Mercer some money in March on the security of
slaves and neglected to have the mortgage recorded. The result was that
he had later to ask for renewal of the bond or for different security. [22]

The superlative vexation was the attempt to establish a mill on the
land William Crawford had patented for Washington on the Youghiogheny in Pennsylvania. To improve this land and to direct the building
of the mill, Washington entered into a partnership with Gilbert Simpson, member of a family who had been among Washington tenants as
early as 1762. [23] Gilbert had acquired some property and a wife and had
learned to write and to spell well enough for his meaning to be clear.
Although his spouse was opposed, he agreed to go to the Youghiogheny

14 3 G. W., 106.   15 Ibid., 107.   16 3 G. W., 105–06.
17 Ibid., 115.   18 Cf. 3 G. W., 137.
19 Ledger B, folio 83. For delay in the drawing of the lottery, see Penn Gazette, June 23,
1773.
20 3 G. W., 111.   21 3 G. W., 112–13.
22 3 G. W., 146–47.   23 Ledger A, folio 137.

with some of Washington's slaves, tools and implements, and with his own horses and utensils, and to start a joint adventure. This seemed so promising an arrangement that Washington sent with him everything that seemed needful and told him to look to Capt. William Crawford for all additional help that might be required.[24] From the time Simpson wrote his first report to his new partner he was despairing. There was no better land in that part of the world, Simpson said, but he never was in good health from the time of his arrival. "I intend to do the best I can to improve your land until the Fall," the unhappy, homesick man wrote, "and then to quit the concern . . ."[25] That was about as unpromising a beginning as a partner could make on a frontier enterprise!

All disappointments were sharpened and all business transactions were snarled that winter and spring by one of the strangest disasters that had been visited on Virginia. In January, 1773, the Treasurer observed peculiarities in some paper £5 notes of the issues of 1769 and 1771 that had been returned for retirement. On examination he found that this currency was well-executed counterfeit in which even the watermark of the notepaper had been duplicated by impression. The Treasurer promptly published in the *Virginia Gazette* a warning of the circulation of the false notes and a description of them. A few days later he discovered that forged £1 currency also was in circulation and was identifiable by the water marks and wiring.[26]

Announcement of the existence of counterfeit almost halted business in the Colony. At first it was thought that such clever forgeries must have come from Holland;[27] but soon there was suspicion, if not actual proof, that counterfeit dollars, half doubloons and doubloons also were on the market. Washington's new steward on the Custis plantations probably acted as many others did after the news spread. He refused to accept any financial settlements because, as he said, "there was so much bad money of the new koin that I could not receive it with safety."[28] Public apprehension convinced the new Governor he must act. Council, hurriedly assembled, was of opinion that he should call the General Assembly in session to enact needed laws, and that he should offer rewards—£500 for the apprehension of the principal offenders and £100 for the arrest of any person who knowingly undertook to pass

[24] 3 *G. W.*, 117. [25] 4 *Hamilton*, 194–95.
[26] *Va. Gazette*, Jan. 28, Feb. 8, 1773.
[27] Thomas Adams to Perkins, Buchanan & Brown, Feb. 1, 1773; 23 *V* 62.
[28] James Hill to Washington, Feb. 5, 1773; 4 *Hamilton*, 181.

the counterfeit.[29] Soon there appeared in Williamsburg a man named John Short, who was described as a former under-sheriff[30] and as a one-time participant in the counterfeiting. Short asserted that the workshop of the guilty men was in the new County of Pittsylvania at a place known to him. The criminals, he said, included a ringleader who resided in North Carolina, and fifteen or sixteen men of influence in Virginia. Unless arrests were made quickly, Short warned, it soon would be exceedingly dangerous to deal with the culprits.[31]

This was exactly the sort of information for which Dunmore had been waiting. He called in Peyton Randolph, Attorney General John Randolph and Treasurer Nicholas, and sought their advice concerning his authority in dealing with the alleged criminals. The conclusion of these lawyers apparently was that the Governor as titular Chief Justice of the General Court could issue his warrant which an individual designated by him for that purpose could serve through the regular local officers of the law. Persons arrested under the Governor's warrant could be brought to Williamsburg for examination.[32] Dunmore thereupon placed the necessary warrants in the hands of Capt. John Lightfoot, a man of known resolution, and gave him full authority to call for help from the County Lieutenant and other trustworthy men of Pittsylvania.

Back to Williamsburg on the 23rd of February came Lightfoot. In his custody, under a strong guard, were Benjamin Cooke, Joseph Cooke, James Cooke, Benjamin Woodward and Peter Medley, who had been caught at work in what proved to be a complete counterfeiting shop. They had engraving-tools, dies for doubloons, half-doubloons and dollars, frames for papermaking, a rolling press, a plate for forty-shilling currency, and a large number of the familiar £5 counterfeit notes. Several suspects—Gideon Rucker and Shem Cooke of Pittsylvania and John and William Hightower of Lunenburg—were said to have fled. Still others were reported to have been locked up in county jails.[33] The

29 Williamsburg dispatch of February 4 in *Penn. Gazette*, Feb. 17, 1773; *E. J.*, Feb. 6, 1773; P.R.O., C.O. 5: 1440, p. 13, VSL Photostat. The general narrative of these developments is Dunmore to Dartmouth, Mch. 31, 1773; *Journ. H.B.*, 1773–76, p. ix–x.

30 There was no such office as under-sheriff in Virginia. The man may have been a Deputy Sheriff or a Constable.

31 *Va. Gazette*, Feb. 25, 1773; Dunmore to Dartmouth, *loc. cit*. For the North Carolina connection, see Peyton Randolph, *et al*. to the Speaker of the House of Representatives [sic] of North Carolina, Apr. 6, 1773; *Journ. H.B.*, 1773–76, p. 43.

32 Dunmore to Dartmouth, *loc. cit*. The statement by Dunmore is so brief on this point that part of the advice given him has to be reconstructed from the events that followed.

33 *Va. Gazette*, Feb. 25, 1773, *Penn. Gazette*, Feb. 17, 1773.

men caught by Lightfoot were examined by Speaker Randolph in the presence of the Governor and other notables, all of whom agreed that the accused, with one exception, should be held. Soon afterward the prisoners were given a hearing before the Court of York County and were remanded to the Williamsburg jail where they were joined by another suspect, Moses Terry, who showed a disposition to confess and to become the King's witness.[34] At this stage of the proceedings the General Assembly met, Mch. 4, 1773, in answer to the Governor's summons.[35]

Washington's departure for this session was somewhat hampered by plans he was making for Mr. "Jack." That young gentleman manifestly was wasting time with Rev. Jonathan Boucher, who was ready to admit new neglect of his pupil because of his own "political pursuits."[36] Washington's decision to send the boy to college now had become fixed. "As his guardian," Washington soon was to explain, "I conceive it to be my indispensable duty (to endeavor) to carry him through a regular course of education, many branches of which, sorry I am to add, he is totally deficient of . . ."[37] From what he had seen and heard of the College of William and Mary, Washington wrote, "I cannot think [it] a desirable place to send Jack Custis to; the inattention of the masters, added to the number of holidays, is the subject of general complaint, and affords no pleasing prospect to a youth who has a good deal to attain and but a short time to do it in."[38] Philadelphia College[39] seemed to Washington to stand "equally fair with any other" and to make particular appeal to "Jack's" mother because it was considered nearer.[40] Boucher agreed both that "Jack" should be sent to college speedily and that he should not be entered at William and Mary. "I had, as you know," the minister wrote Washington, "been endeavoring to believe the many stories we are perpetually hearing of the mismanagement at William and Mary as partial and exaggerated, but the

[34] *Va. Gazette*, Feb. 25, Mch. 4, 1773.   [35] *Journ. H.B.*, 1773–76, p. 6.

[36] They concerned chiefly the much debated question of the American episcopate. (4 *Hamilton*, 192; Campbell, *History of Virginia*, 561–62).

[37] Letter of Apr. 3, 1773, to Benedict Calvert; 3 *G. W.*, 130.

[38] Letter of Jan. 7, 1773, to Jonathan Boucher; 37 *G. W.*, 497.

[39] Needless to say, this became the University of Pennsylvania. At the time, its official name still was the one granted in 1755 to the "Trustees of the College, Academy, and Charitable School in the Province of Pennsylvania."

[40] *Ibid.* Actually, Mount Vernon was almost equidistant between Williamsburg and Philadelphia, a fact subsequently not without a certain symbolic significance. By some roads, Williamsburg was closer to Washington's home than was Philadelphia. The advantage of the northern route was in the superiority of its highways and ferries.

carefulness of your enquiries on the spot precludes all farther doubt about the matter." [41] As between Philadelphia College and King's College, Boucher was all for the New York school, because it was located in what he understood to be "the most fashionable and polite place on the continent," [42] and he was able to bring Washington to acquiesce in this choice. The Colonel made plans for going to New York and entering "Jack" in the college before he had to make the journey to Williamsburg for the spring settlement of accounts; [43] but, of course, the summons to an early session of the Assembly upset this schedule.

With Martha and "Patsy" in the chariot, Washington followed the route through Maryland to Hooe's Ferry and reached Williamsburg about 5:30 P.M., March 4,[44] the day the Assembly met. This time, Martha had elected to come directly to town and not to remain at Eltham. Wherever she went, the talk was of the counterfeiting and of the concern it had aroused, concern no less for the methods Dunmore had used in dealing with it than for the effect of the bad money on the trade of the Colony. Every Burgess admitted, of course, that so extreme a case had called for strong measures. It had to be allowed, also, in any argument on the question, that Dunmore had selected determined agents who had done their work thoroughly. At the same time, Burgesses were disturbed by the Governor's employment on a small scale of the very procedure against which the General Assembly had protested when the British ministry had invoked the forgotten statute of Henry VIII for the trial in England of persons accused of treason overseas: Dunmore had disregarded altogether the Court of Pittsylvania County and had taken men from their own vicinage for trial before the Court of a County where they had no friends.

Should this be permitted to pass without protest? Must Dunmore be tyrannical in dealing with the lawless? The answer of the Burgesses was creditable to them. When they prepared and approved the usual address to the Governor, in reply to his speech on opening the session, they thanked him for endeavoring to bring the counterfeiters to justice; "*but*," they affirmed in sharpest antithesis, "the proceedings in this case, my Lord, though rendered necessary by the particular nature of it, are

---

41 4 *Hamilton*, 175.   42 *Ibid.*, 176.
43 37 *G. W.*, 498. This had been Washington's decision while he still favored sending "Jack" to Philadelphia.
44 "About half an hour by sun" was Washington's phrase (2 *Diaries*, 103–04). This journey, begun on the 2nd, was one of the most rapid Washington made with the chariot.

nevertheless different from the usual mode, it being regular that an examining court on criminals should be held, either in the County where the fact was committed, or the arrest made." The address proceeded: "The duty we owe our constituents obliges us, my Lord, to be as attentive to the safety of the innocent as we are desirous of punishing the guilty; and we apprehend, that a doubtful construction and various execution of criminal law does greatly endanger the safety of innocent men. We do therefore most humbly pray your Excellency, that the proceedings in this case may not in future be drawn into consequence or example." [45]

Dunmore did not like this. In replying to the address, he expressed surprise that when he was seeking to punish the guilty, his conduct "could by any means be thought to endanger the safety of the innocent." He served this notice: "Permit me to say that all laws, doubtful in their construction, must be interpreted by the courts of justice. If I have done amiss the same method will not be repeated; but if it should be determined to be regular, I shall continue to exercise the powers I am invested with, whensoever the exigencies of government and the good of the country requires such exertion; and under such circumstances, I am persuaded that no one (not even the most timid) will be under the least apprehension that this proceeding may in future be drawn into consequence or example." [46] Later he wrote the home government, ". . . there was but one person who has the least knowledge of the laws of this Colony, and hardly a man of sense in the House of Burgesses who did not approve of this mode of proceeding, although a majority were for the address . . ." [47] He held his ground and had the support of more than half the members of the General Court that the proceedings were legal. [48] During the investigation and trial, one member of the House of Burgesses was accused of complicity [49] and some of the alleged culprits were discharged because John Short, their principal accuser, was proven to be a worthless witness, "a most atrocious villain," whose "word" was not to be taken. [50]

The other acts of the House prior to the 12th of March accorded with the spirit the majority displayed in the address. Adequate provision of

---

[45] *Journ. H.B.*, 1773–76, p. 22.
[46] *Journ. H.B.*, 1773–76, p. 33.
[47] *Ibid.*, xi.
[48] *Rind's Gazette*, Apr. 15, 1773.
[49] Paschal Greenhill, member from Prince Edward, who denied under oath that he had circulated the counterfeit (*E. J.*, Mch. 6, 1773, P.R.O., C.O. 5: 1440, p. 14, VSL Photostat; *Rind's Gazette*, Apr. 8, 1773; *Journ. H.B.*, 1773–76, p. 12).
[50] *Va. Gazette*, Apr. 22, 1773.

£200 was made for John Lightfoot;[51] his expenses and those of other participants in the affair were paid;[52] a bill was passed to punish the counterfeiting of the currency of other Colonies in the hope of reciprocal action;[53] all the notes of 1769 and 1771 were called in, and a new issue of the outstanding volume, £36,834, was authorized.[54]

Other legislation, most of it local, was in final stages of passage, and Washington was preparing to leave Williamsburg when, in the midst of routine proceedings on the 12th of March, a motion was made that the House resolve itself into Committee of the Whole on the state of the Colony.[55] Washington may have known, in general, what this presaged. He may have heard that some of the members who followed the leadership of Patrick Henry had been conferring on the course of action Virginia should take to establish the truth or falsity of what was being reported concerning stern measures the home government was to employ against Colonies that resisted the Ministry. Rhode Island and Massachusetts, especially, were in controversy with Britain, but how they proposed to defend their rights, the Virginians did not know. Discussion in the taverns consequently had dealt with proposals for the establishment among the Colonies of committees similar to the one Virginia long had maintained in order to correspond with her agent in England.

The motion was passed, the chair was vacated, the House was in Committee of the Whole. Recognition was given Dabney Carr, junior Burgess from Louisa who, in 1772, had succeeded Thomas Johnson. At 30 years of age, Carr was not known widely in Virginia, but he was respected and admired by Thomas Jefferson whose sister Martha he had married. Jefferson, though of the same age as Carr, was now a veteran member and a leader of the younger element in the House of Burgesses. Usually he stood with Patrick Henry and with Richard Henry Lee among those who were impatient of prerogative and not restrained by

---

[51] *Journ. H.B.*, 1773–76, p. 20. The Governor apparently advanced Lightfoot £100 from the "two shilling tax" on tobacco. *E. J.*, Mch. 11, 1773; P.R.O., C.O. 5: 1440, p. 16; VSL Photostat.

[52] *Journ. H.B.*, 1773–76, p. 24.

[53] *Ibid.*, 21, 29–30, 31, 32. Cf. Peyton Randolph *et al.* to the Speakers of various colonial Assemblies, *ibid.*, 43. For the statute, see 8 *H* 651. A reading of the preamble of this act, without details of the relevant circumstances, may create the impression that the greater part of the excitement over the circulation of counterfeit was due to the passing of the forged treasury notes of other Colonies, but the only specific instance of this observed in the present study was warning in the *Va. Gazette*, Apr. 1, 1773, that forged North Carolina inspectors' notes, "signed by Archer and Epes," were in circulation.

[54] This total was to be reduced by such amount, if any, as the Treasurer might be able to borrow at 5 per cent for the redemption of the issues of 1769 and 1771. The act is in 8 *H* 647. See also *Penn. Gazette*, Mch. 24, 1773.

[55] *Journ. H.B.*, 1773–76, p. 28.

precedent or by awe from criticising King as well as Ministry and Parliament. Jefferson had not forgotten how, when he was a young Burgess, Edmund Pendleton had afforded him means of a conspicuous hearing, and he had arranged to give Carr a similar opportunity now.

That was why Carr had the floor. He read a brief preamble to this effect: "Whereas the minds of his Majesty's faithful subjects in this Colony have been much disturbed, by various rumors and reports tending to deprive them of their ancient, legal and constitutional rights [;] and whereas, the affairs of this Colony are frequently connected with those of Great Britain, as well as of the neighboring Colonies, which renders a communication of sentiments necessary; in order therefore to remove the uneasiness and to quiet the minds of the people, as well as for the other good purposes above mentioned"—he proposed that eleven Burgesses [56] be named as a Committee of Correspondence. These eleven were "to obtain the most early and authentic intelligence of all such acts and resolutions of the British Parliament, or proceedings of administration, as may relate to or affect the British Colonies in America, and to keep up and maintain a correspondence and communication with our sister Colonies, respecting these important considerations; and the result of such their proceedings, from time to time, to lay before this House." The Committee was to be instructed especially to ascertain the principles and authority for a recent Rhode Island Court of Inquiry which was said to have had power "to transmit [sic] persons accused of offences committed in America, to places beyond the seas, to be tried." [57] This last reference was to the proceedings that had followed the burning in Narragansett Bay, June 10, 1772, of a small British armed schooner, *Gaspee,* which had run aground after her commander had irritated the population of the shoreline by zealous pursuit of smugglers. The Court of Inquiry that attempted to punish the boarding party had failed to procure the identification of any of the participants, but the Court was understood to have had power to send to England for trial any person even suspected of complicity.[58]

---

[56] Their names appear in the resolution reported to the House but they may not have been in Carr's original draft. Jefferson's reference to the committee (14 *Jefferson*, 399), suggests though it does not prove positively, that the members were "appointed" by the chair or on nomination from the floor.

[57] *Journ. H.B.*, 1773–76, p. 28.

[58] See J R. Bartlett, *History of the Destruction of the Gaspee; 7 Pubs. RIHS*, new ser. v. 4, no. 7, p. 238 ff; *Va. Gazette*, Jan. 21, Feb. 18, 1773. An unsigned article in *Washington Republican*, Sept. 14, 1822, described the hot wrath of Washington when a British guest at Mount Vernon, discussing the case of the *Gaspee*, affirmed with much arrogance that he could march through America with 5000 men. Given notice, said Washington angrily, he would engage to check them "with the Virginia riflemen alone."

As far as the facts in the case of the *Gaspee* were known in Virginia, Dabney Carr explained them to the Burgesses. It was imperative, he argued, that all the Colonies know what was threatened against any one of them. He spoke, Jefferson proudly wrote afterwards, "with great ability, reconciling all to [his motion], not only by the reasonings, but by the temper and moderation with which it was developed." [59] There was no opposition from those who in 1765 had taken such pains to expunge the firmest of Patrick Henry's resolutions against the Stamp Act. Accepted in Committee of the Whole, Carr's proposals were adopted unanimously by the House.[60] Washington approved, of course, and probably in so convinced a spirit that he thought eloquence wasted and argument unnecessary. A man who had wished the association of 1769 ten times as strict as it was fashioned in Williamsburg might have been excused in 1773 if he regarded correspondence among the Colonies as something to be undertaken without delay or ado. He was not named to the Committee of eleven [61] but, busy as he was and far distant in residence from the natural meeting place, he could not have regretted the omission of his name from the list.

Estimates of the resolutions varied greatly. When Jefferson and Dabney Carr started home after the Assembly was prorogued on the 13th,[62] they talked of the measure and agreed that the effect would be a call for a meeting of representatives of all the Colonies for maintenance of common rights. In New England, Samuel Adams said the "truly patriotic resolves" of Virginia would gladden "the hearts of all who are friends of liberty." Massachusetts would reprint and circulate the paper. Governor Dunmore was not inclined to take seriously the action of the Virginia lawmakers. "Your Lordship will observe," he wrote the Earl of Dartmouth, "there are some resolves which show a little ill humor in the House of Burgesses, but I thought them so insignificant that I took no matter of notice of them." [63] Washington, as usual,

---

[59] Jefferson to Dabney Carr, son of the orator, Jan. 19, 1816; 14 *Jefferson*, 399. The familiar account of the meeting of Patrick Henry, Richard Henry Lee, Francis Lightfoot Lee, Dabney Carr and Thomas Jefferson "in a private room of the Raleigh," before the presentation of the resolutions, appeared in Jefferson's Autobiography (1 *Jefferson*, 7).

[60] *Journ. H.B.*, 1773–76, p. 28.

[61] It consisted of Peyton Randolph, Robert Carter Nicholas, Richard Bland, Richard Henry Lee, Benjamin Harrison, Edmund Pendleton, Patrick Henry, Dudley Digges, Dabney Carr, Archibald Cary and Thomas Jefferson, any six of whom could act (*Journ. H.B.*, 1773–76, p. 28).

[62] Various writers have copied Jefferson's mistake in his Autobiography (1 *Jefferson*, 8), that the Assembly was dissolved; but the prorogation was clearly set forth in the Journal. See *Journ. H.B.*, 1773–76, p. 36.

[63] Letter of Mch. 31, 1773; *Journ. H.B.*, 1773–76, p. x. For the remarks of Adams, see H. A. Cushing, ed. *The Writings of Samuel Adams* (cited hereafter as *Samuel* Adams) v. 4, p. 27.

awaited developments [64] and occupied himself, during his leisure hours at Williamsburg with more personal plans for the future. He heard some echoes of complaint from officers who had not shared in the first allotment of lands under proclamation of 1754, but there was nothing, as yet, to indicate a protest serious enough by the date of the June Court of Oyer and Terminer in 1773 to call for action on his offer to submit his own land for apportionment by Council.[65] Efforts to collect from some of the beneficiaries of the grants continued to disappoint and to irritate.[66]

At intervals during the session, Washington had numerous opportunities of talking with Governor Dunmore, a hard-headed Scot of Washington's own age, who had a kindred appetite for land. Like Dinwiddie and Botetourt among his predecessors, Dunmore had particular interest in the West where he probably designed in fancy a vast domain worthy of the Murray name he bore and not altogether beneath the dignity of the royal Stuarts from whose female line he was descended. The Governor wanted to see for himself what the country looked like, how rich its lands were, and how its streams ran. Washington of course answered the Governor's questions with descriptions that were accurate but not imaginative except perhaps where he talked of trees. As a result, in part, of their conversation, Dunmore engaged to go with Washington to the Ohio country that summer. The understanding was that they would communicate with each other after the Colonel reached home and found when he could undertake the journey. Dunmore then was to come to Mount Vernon, whence the start was to be made.[67]

While Dunmore was turning his eyes to the Ohio, Washington was looking to West Florida [68] where, it was reported, fine tracts could be acquired on most generous terms. As Washington understood the facts, bounties of land in this region were available to veterans of the French and Indian War, in accordance with the proclamation of October, 1763.[69] Washington had never exercised his rights under that

[64] As far as has been observed, he never mentioned in his extant correspondence the organization of this Committee.

[65] This is in inference from Washington to Charles Mynn Thruston, Mch. 12, 1773; 3 *G. W.*, 120–24.

[66] Cf. Washington to John Fry, and Washington to John Nicholas, Mch. 10, 1773; 3 *G. W.*, 118–20. In the second of these letters Washington remarked that he had inquired of "Mr. Jefferson" if that gentleman was not a neighbor of the heirs of Col. Joshua Fry, from whom he sought to get £31, their part of the cost of prosecuting the claims. That was the first time the name of Thomas Jefferson appeared in any of the surviving letters of Washington.

[67] Cf. 3 *G. W.*, 132.

[68] As then defined, West Florida ran from the Appalachicola River to the Mississippi and from the Gulf of Mexico northward to latitude 32° 30′.

[69] See *supra*, p. 245.

proclamation and he looked now to James Wood [70] who was about to go to West Florida to explore the country, and he commissioned that young man to take up there for him all the land to which a field officer was entitled, 5000 acres. In addition, Washington had bought up Captain Posey's claim, which was for 3000 acres, and the claim of Charles M. Thruston for 3000. With his usual care in such matters, Washington had all three of these papers certified by Governor Dunmore, and he wrote minute instructions to Wood concerning the nature of the land he desired.[71] His hope was to talk further with his new agent before leaving Williamsburg but on his last evening in town he missed the young man, who was dining out.[72] When he could do so, Washington wrote Wood again and repeated the interpretation the colonials had of the proclamation of 1763 as exempting the tracts from quit rents and from cultivation and improvement for a period of ten years. If Wood found the land good and the tenure easy, then Washington would take up 15,000 or 20,000 or even 25,000 acres.[73] The bottoms on the Great Kanawha and the Ohio were welcome but they had not satisfied Washington's appetite for western land; on the contrary they merely had made him anxious to have more and still more acreage of high quality.

Back at Mount Vernon on the 16th of March,[74] Washington had two days in which to catch up with his accumulated business. Then he enjoyed a few spirited fox hunts.[75] After that he had a surprise of first magnitude: without telling his mother or his stepfather or even giving a hint to the dominie in whose house he was living, "Jack" Custis, though only 18,[76] had become engaged to marry. The girl was Eleanor, more familiarly "Nelly" Calvert, second daughter and one of the ten children of Mr. and Mrs. Benedict Calvert of Mount Airy, across the Potomac in Maryland. Benedict Calvert, in youth called Benedict Swingate, was the illegitimate son of Charles Calvert, fifth Lord Baltimore, who acknowledged paternity and gave the young man a start but never let the name of the mother be known. In 1745 Benedict became Collector of Customs at Patuxent, the next year he received appoint-

[70] This was the same James Wood later distinguished as a Revolutionary officer and as Governor of Virginia. He was a son of Washington's friend and political sponsor, Col. James Wood of Frederick, and he was at this time 22 or 23 years of age. See Katherine Glass Green, *Winchester*, 108, 160, 362. Washington's letters indicate that young James Wood was a good judge of farmland, was trustworthy, and was acquainted with Gist and other frontiersmen of Virginia.

[71] 3 *G. W.*, 124–25.　　　[72] *Ibid.*, 127.　　　　　　　[73] 3 *G. W.*, 129.

[74] 2 *Diaries*, 105. He had left Williamsburg on the 12th.

[75] *Ibid.*　　　　　　　　　　[76] As of November, 1772.

ment to the Council, and in 1748 he married a distant cousin, Elizabeth Calvert, daughter of Gov. Charles Calvert. As Benedict Calvert's connections were of this eminence, his accident of birth was not regarded as a social stigma. One of his well-reared daughters consequently would be a suitable wife for "Jack," except for the fact that her father's moderate estate would be subject to long division when he passed on.[77]

Washington and "Jack's" mother both were hurt, of course, that the boy had not confided in them on a matter that might shape his entire life, but the Colonel's special distress was that the young man wished to get married at the very time plans were being made to send him to college to undertake seriously the study he so long and so skillfully had evaded. It was no help in this to have "Jack" explain that he had been unable to devote himself to his books for twelve months because he had been so much in love.[78] Washington wrote somewhat anxiously: "I could have wished ['Jack'] had postponed entering into that engagement till his studies were finished. Not that I have any objection to the match, as she is a girl of exceeding good character; but because I fear, as he has discovered much fickleness already, that he may either change, and therefore injure the young lady; or that it may precipitate him into a marriage before, I am certain, he has ever bestowed a serious thought of the consequences; by which means his education is interrupted and he perhaps wishing to be at liberty again before he is fairly embarked on those important duties." [79]

The decision was to accept the engagement—what else could be done?—and by joint consent to have the marriage postponed until Custis had gone to college. Whether the young man assented to this with a convinced mind or acquiesced in the belief that he later could have his own way, the immediate procedure was for Washington to write Calvert, to approve the match, and to state his hope that "Jack" would progress further in his studies before the marriage should be solemnized. It was a task which, Washington confessed, was embarrassing to him, but one he discharged forthrightly. After telling Calvert in a letter that an alliance with the Maryland family would be welcome, Washington proceeded: "This acknowledgment being made, you must

[77] Charles Lowe to Benedict Leonard Calvert, Aug. 31, 1728; 3 *Md. His. Mag.*, 323. See also 16 *ibid.*, 313; Hammond, *Colonial Mansions of Maryland*, 185, 187; Boucher to Washington, Apr. 8, 1773, 4 *Hamilton*, 191; Benedict Calvert to Washington, Apr. 8, 1773; *ibid.*, 188; 3 *G. W.*, 129 ff.

[78] 4 *Hamilton*, 193.

[79] Letter of Apr. 25, 1773 to Burwell Bassett; 3 *G. W.*, 134.

permit me to add, sir, that at this, or in any short time, his youth, in-experience and unripened education is and will be insuperable obstacles in my eye, to the completion of the marriage." Then he argued, without dwelling on "Jack's" fickleness, that the boy should learn more and should acquire some experience before matrimony. With a verbal running start, Washington took this long leap: "Delivering my senti-ments thus will not, I hope, lead you into a belief that I am desirous of breaking off the match; to postpone it, is all I have in view; for I shall recommend it to the young gentleman with the warmth that becomes a man of honor (notwithstanding he did not vouchsafe to consult either his mother or me on the occasion) to consider himself as much engaged to your daughter as if the indissoluble knot was tied; and, as the surest means of effecting this, to stick close to his studies, (in which I flatter myself you will join me) by which he will, in a great measure, avoid those little flirtations with other girls which may, by dividing the attention, contribute not a little to divide the affection." Thereupon Washington disclosed what "Jack" possessed, and ex-pressed his hope that Calvert "would also be willing to do something genteel by your daughter." The gentleman on the right bank of the Potomac closed with an invitation for the Calverts to cross the river for a visit to Mount Vernon, and he sent, along with his own, the "respect-ful compliments" of Mrs. Washington and of Miss Custis.[80]

This was a new adventure in letterwriting but it was well done and well received. Benedict Calvert replied with modest thanks for the praise of "Nelly" and expressed his entire agreement that "it is, as yet, too early in life for Mr. Custis to enter upon the matrimonial state." Calvert hoped that "Jack's" attendance on college would make for the future happiness of the young people and that "this separation will only delay, not break off, the intended match." Then the girl's father man-fully admitted that it was a match much superior to any he had hoped "Nelly" could make. He could do little for her, financially, because of the size of his family, but "Nelly's" portion of his personal estate should at least be equal to that of any of his other children.[81]

If, then, "Jack" was fated to become engaged to a girl when he should have been engaged only in his studies, Washington well may have hoped that the boy had escaped, without dishonor, from premature marriage. The task immediately ahead was that of getting young Custis off

[80] 3 G. W., 129-31.   [81] Letter of Apr. 8, 1773; 4 Hamilton, 188-90.

promptly to New York with the least reluctance and the fewest tears. In proceeding to do this, Washington and Martha did not attempt to keep "Jack" from Mount Airy on the theory that the more he saw of "Nelly" during the interval between his known engagement and departure, the more would he be disposed to renounce all intention of going to college. The mother and the stepfather of "Jack" acted as if the engagement and the postponement of the marriage were matters of course. They visited the Calverts, entertained them at Mount Vernon and made some of "Nelly's" friends a part of their own circle. When the date for departure approached, it was agreed that "Jack" should start two days ahead of Washington and should spend the time at the home of his fiancée, where Washington called for him on the 10th of May, 1773.[82]

The journey to Philadelphia was without incident except that Washington tried a different route from Annapolis. Instead of proceeding up the western shore of Chesapeake Bay, he crossed on a packet to Rock Hall on the Eastern Shore and thence he proceeded by Georgetown on the Sassafras, Newcastle, Wilmington and Chester to Philadelphia.[83] Arrival on the 16th at the Quaker capital was followed immediately by invitations from all the notables. The Governor had Washington to dinner that afternoon and again on the 19th. Washington himself gave a dinner on the 18th, went to the Assembly that evening and, on the 20th, had his midday meal as the guest of John Cadwalader. Not content with all this, the Virginian that night attended a ball. Other activities were of the same sort. It must have impressed "Jack" no little that his stepfather was a welcome friend of the most distinguished residents of the greatest city he ever had seen. Truth was, the former Colonel of the First Virginia Regiment always had been received cordially in Philadelphia but never with so much overflowing hospitality as now.[84]

When he left on the 23rd, he was accompanied by an interesting man who called himself Lord Stirling and had friends who always so styled him. He was American born, the son of James Alexander who fled to the Colonies after sharing in the cause of the "Old Pretender" in 1715. James had distinguished himself for many things and most of all for his defence of the printer Peter Zenger who was jailed for criticizing

82 2 Diaries, 107–10.
83 Ibid., 111. The Diary gives the dates of his halts and the places where he lodged.
84 2 Diaries, 111–12.

the Governor of New York in 1735. William, who was six years older than Washington, had deep interest in mathematics and in astronomy. During the French and Indian War, Alexander had served as aid and secretary to General Shirley and had attended him to England.[85] There, with the encouragement of men of high station, the young colonial had entered claim to the presumably extinct title of the Earl of Stirling. He convinced a jury by the testimony of two old men that he was descended from an uncle of the first Earl and that he was "heir male of Henry, fifth Earl." Satisfied with this, Alexander returned to America and thereafter used the title; but when the Committee of Privileges of the House of Lords passed on the case, they ruled that he had not established his descent.[86] Thus was he Lord Stirling in America, and William Alexander in Great Britain. In either country he would have been distinguished for a fine, martial appearance and for his social arts if not for his intellect. Washington, who had handled some of his lottery tickets,[87] took pleasure in his company and rode with him for two days to Lord Stirling's fine seat, Basking Ridge, where he spent the nights of May 24 and 25.[88] Having proceeded by way of Trenton and Princeton, Washington went on to Elizabeth on the 26th and that night lodged in New York.

Washington found the town, or at least the conservative element of it, preparing for a farewell to an old acquaintance of his, Thomas Gage, now a Lieutenant General and still Commander-in-Chief of the British military forces in America. Gage had been on the continent almost continuously after 1755, but now he was going home and was to leave with all the ceremonies New York could stage for him. While Washington never had been as intimate with Gage as he had been with some of Braddock's staff officers, relations between the two had been friendly, if not close, and had justified the Virginian in asking Gage in the spring of 1758 to commend him to Forbes.[89] Thereafter, apparently, correspondence lapsed but with no cooling of relations. It was pleasant to share on May 27 in the "elegant entertainment" the merchants and

---

[85] A. D. Mellick, Jr., *The Story of an Old Farm*, 307 ff; 15 *NJHSP* (4), 265. There is a possibility that Washington had met Alexander in Boston on his visit there in February-March, 1756, but from what is known of Stirling's movements that winter, it seems more probable he was not in the city at the time.

[86] See *DAB* with citation of Charles Rogers, *Memorials of the Earl of Stirling*, v. 1, p. 282.

[87] *Supra*, p. 308, cf. 396. Stirling had visited Mount Vernon in January, 1773 (2 *Diaries*, 97).

[88] Basking Ridge, Somerset County, New Jersey, was burned in 1920.

[89] 2 *G. W.*, 176-77. This was the letter in which Washington naïvely told Gage he wished to be distinguished in Forbes's eyes "from the general run of provincial officers."

other citizens gave the General. "The cheerfulness and harmony which presided at every table," one newspaper reported, "spoke the highest sense of His Excellency's affable and benevolent deportment during his ten years' residence in this province."[90]

Three days later Washington dined with Gage and, meantime, enjoyed numerous social affairs that were pleasant if not quite on the scale of those in Philadelphia, where Washington was better known.[91] At King's College no difficulty was encountered in registering "Jack." The President, Rev. Myles Cooper, M.A., proved to be a man of 36, full of zeal for King and church, a warm advocate of an American episcopate and a vehement enemy of dissenters. Whitefield's followers, he had denounced as "knaves or madmen."[92] Quarters for "Jack" and his body servant were provided—a large parlor and two bedrooms, one for "Jack" and the other for his servant, who was to cook his breakfast, clean the rooms and give some attention to Custis's two horses, a gray and a bay.[93] Washington probably arranged, also, for "Jack" to dine with the faculty, "a liberty," the boy soon was to boast "that is not allowed any but myself."[94] For the cost of all this, Washington deposited £100 sterling[95] and, on May 31, started for home.[96] This time he did not allow himself the luxury of Philadelphia. He arrived on the evening of June 2 and was off the next morning by 11. For the rest of the journey, he started early, rode ten or fifteen miles before breakfast and, keeping steadily to this schedule, reached home in the early afternoon of June 8.[97] He promptly set down the cost of the trip for himself, "Jack" and the Negro, £40, 11s 5d.[98]

Much pleased that the boy was at a good school and away from the temptation to marry under a sudden impulse, Washington resumed his normal enjoyments and encountered the usual vexations, together with some he had not known previously. Troublesome boundary-disputes had developed on the Custis Eastern Shore property and on one

[90] *Penn. Gazette*, June 9, 1773. For Gage's own "grand entertainment" of June 4, and for the ceremonies of embarkation, see *Rind's Gazette* of July 1, 1773, and *Va. Gazette*, July 8, 1773. See also *N. Y. Journal*, June 10, 1773; *Rivington's Gazette*, June 10, 1773; *Penn. Gazette*, June 9, 1773. As long previously as February, Gage had offered his "country seat" for sale (*N. Y. Journal*, Feb. 15, 1773).

[91] 2 *Diaries*, 113.

[92] One is tempted to sketch this argumentative educator who did much for the advancement of the institution that became Columbia University, but as his life did not influence that of Washington, detailed treatment does not seem to be justified.

[93] 4 *Hamilton*, 232–33, 233.
[94] *Ibid.*, 233.
[95] 3 *G. W.*, 134.
[96] 2 *Diaries*, 113.
[97] 2 *Diaries*, 113–14.
[98] *Ledger B*, folio 90.

of the plantations near the White House.[99] Edward Violett, at the time overseer of Muddy Hole, had died not long before Washington left home for New York; a successor had to be found.[100] It developed, also, that tobacco was selling very poorly and that Col. John Baylor's security for Bernard Moore's debts, which included many besides that to the Custis estate, would not suffice by £3000.[101]

These were developments Washington could not prevent and therefore did not long bemoan. What angered him was that Gilbert Simpson had abandoned the new joint settlement and mill-site on the Youghiogheny, had left Washington's slaves and property there, and had returned to his own farm in Loudoun County. Simpson had elaborate excuses for his failure to remain on the rich Pennsylvania lands that Capt. William Crawford had patented for Washington. ". . . my wife never let me fairly know her intentions," Simpson wrote, "until your Negroes and other things came to me, and then I thought it was best to go out and settle in hopes she would come into another way of thinking, but the more I strove to persuade the farther she seemed to be off, and to give a person so nearly connected as a wife is uneasiness perhaps all their days." On arriving, Simpson said, he had been forced by bad weather to remain for fifteen days in a bark cabin nine feet square. One of Washington's man servants had proved worthless; the Negro girl knew nothing of work. Exposure had given Simpson a bad cold that had been followed by fever. When spring at length had come, the flies had almost killed Simpson's horses. To save them, he had to leave. In doing so, he had put one of his own Negroes in charge and had arranged for a neighbor to take a look at what was being done. Washington, he insisted, had been well served. Six acres had been cleared, planted in corn, and fenced. Two other acres had been rid of trees. An eighteen-foot cabin had been erected.[102] Washington was angered by Simpson's behavior [103] but at the moment he was unable to do anything. The venture had to be abandoned or left in uncertainty until Simpson or someone else could be persuaded to proceed to the Youghiogheny and to assume the direction of what could be a rich plantation— Simpson himself gave assurance of that. ". . . I am certain," said he,

[99] 4 *Hamilton,* 200.
[100] Violett's articles of agreement are in *Papers of G. W.;* LC. His will, offered for probate May 17, 1773, appears in *Fairfax Orders,* 1772–74, p. 194. *Ledger A,* folio 186, 205, shows some of his accounts.
[101] 4 *Hamilton,* 203.   [102] 4 *Hamilton,* 217–19.
[103] Cf. Simpson: "I find you are much disturbed . . ." (4 *Hamilton,* 217).

"that is not such another place to be found as yours is, both for the goodness of the land and the convenience of the place . . ." [104] Fine as was
the country, its development was not to be easy.

Simpson left the Youghiogheny during the first week of June; [105] his
letter announcing his abandonment of "the concern" probably reached
Washington about the 18th of that month. Mount Vernon was crowded
with guests at that time. "Nelly" Calvert and one of her girl friends
were there; on the 18th, "Jack" Washington, his wife and two children
arrived for a visit. The next day, June 19, Washington remained at
home all the forenoon and, at the usual hour, sat down with his family
and guests at a bountiful dinner. The meal was pleasant and prolonged;
it was 4 o'clock when the chairs were pushed back. "Patsy," in particular, seemed to have enjoyed herself greatly and was, to the observant
eyes of her mother and stepfather, in better health and spirits than
normal. The guests scattered to their afternoon pursuits; Washington
went about his work. Shortly before 5 o'clock there was a stir of a sort
that came often and unhappily at Mount Vernon—"Patsy" had been
seized with one of her fits. This time it was different. The girl did not
utter a word. Not a groan and scarcely a sigh escaped her lips. In less
than two minutes she was dead.[106]

Martha, of course, was overwhelmed. Washington himself was
shaken, and, as "Jack" was away, he was most anxious that Mrs. Dandridge, Martha's mother, should be with her.[107] Immediately, there
was nothing he could do except to comfort Martha as best he could,
to notify "Jack" and the kinsfolk around Williamsburg, and to have
the body of the seventeen-year-old girl made ready for burial.[108] A
coffin could be had in Alexandria of James Connelly; [109] first mourning had to be procured in Williamsburg and sent by the post; [110] as
soon as the shock was over, second mourning could be put on the invoices for shipment from London; [111] a pall that belonged to Wash-

104 *Ibid.*, 219. To correct Simpson's spelling is perhaps to give too favorable an opinion of
the man, but, on the other hand, to reprint his incredible phonetics would be to make too
heavy a demand on the time of a reader who wished to interpret Gilbert.

105 *Ibid.*, 218.   106 2 *Diaries*, 115; 3 *G. W.*, 138.   107 3 *G. W.*, 138.

108 She may have been 18 by June, 1773; her birthday is not known. "Patsy," needless to
say, was a victim of epilepsy, which, as noted *supra,* does not appear to have shown itself in
strong convulsions, if at all, until 1768; but the symptoms then must have been sufficiently
pronounced to put marriage out of question. None of the many guests at Mount Vernon, mentioned in Washington's Diary, can be identified as possible suitors for "Patsy's" hand, though
she was among the wealthiest girls in Virginia. Compare the tragic case of Elizabeth Turberville,
Vol. I, p. 118.   109 *Ledger B,* folio 90.   110 *Ibid.*, folio 117.

111 3 *G. W.*, 139. This second mourning, listed in detail, was ordered July 10, 1773, about
three weeks after "Patsy's" death.

ington but had been lent in Alexandria could be recalled; [112] Rev. Lee Massey of Pohick would be available to read the service.[113]

Everything was done decorously and quietly. Condolence was as candid as kindly. Governor Dunmore understood instinctively that the proposed western journey with Washington had to be delayed. He wrote: ". . . as the poor young lady was so often afflicted with these fits, I dare say she thinks it a happy exchange." [114] Fielding Lewis said: "Poor 'Patsy's' death must have distressed Mrs. Washington very much, but when she considers the unhappy situation she was in and the little probability of ever getting well, she must conclude that it's better as it is, as there was little appearance of her ever being able to enjoy life with any satisfaction." [115] Washington himself had written his wife's brother-in-law, Burwell Bassett, that spring concerning the loss of Burwell's own daughter: ". . . The ways of Providence being in-scrutable, and the justice of it not to be scanned by the shallow eye of humanity, nor to be counteracted by the utmost efforts of human power or wisdom, resignation, and as far as the strength of our reason and religion can carry us, a cheerful acquiescence to the Divine Will, is what we are to aim . . ." [116]

"Patsy's" death might end the greater part of Washington's fi-nancial distress. Thanks to small expenditure during her childhood and to her stepfather's prudent administration from 1759 onward, her estate had increased to £16,000 and more. Half this went to "Jack" and half, through Martha, to Washington. He wrote his merchants briskly: ". . . as I would choose to discharge my debt to you I would apply her money in the [stock of the] Bank [of England] to that purpose, pro-vided I can sell out without loss; be so good therefore as to let me know as soon as you can what steps are necessary to be pursued, in order to do this, and upon what terms it is to be done. In the meanwhile please to place the balance due to this deceased young lady to my credit and carry the interest arising from the dividends of stock to my account current regularly, till I either transfer or dispose of it in some other manner." [117]

112 4 Hamilton, 261.
113 For which he was paid £2, 6s 3d (Ledger B, folio 90).
114 4 Hamilton, 229.   115 4 Hamilton, 237.
116 Letter of Apr. 25, 1773; 3 G. W., 133.
117 Letter of Nov. 10, 1773 to Robert Cary & Co.; 3 G. W., 165. On Oct. 27, 1773, Wash-ington paid Edmund Pendleton a small fee "for the settlement of my guardianship" which evidently was of "Patsy" (Ledger B, folio 93).

There might be no more interest charges against George Washington on the books of Robert Cary & Co., but there was abundance of other trouble, petty and time-consuming. Disappointments were numerous. Washington's superfine flour, for example, found a ready local market that yielded a good profit; his "seconds" had few buyers. Puzzled and disappointed by this, he decided to try two devices. One was to mix with the "seconds" enough of his best flour to make an acceptable product for bread; the other was to send part of the unwanted flour to Jamaica and the remainder to the Madeira Islands, along with some of his superfine, and to barter the whole for wine.[118] The profit or loss of these diversified transactions was not calculated. In return for the shipment to the "wine islands," Washington had to be content with four pipes of Madeira and two boxes of citron.[119] In circumstances somewhat analagous, the Negro, Tom, sold in St. Kitts,[120] had brought sixty-six gallons of spirits and various small delicacies.[121]

Washington the miller now became Washington the land broker. Whether or not his holdings on the Ohio and the Kanawha were to be in the proposed new Colony, he was resolved that he would comply promptly with all the statutory conditions of "seating" new lands in Virginia. Furthermore, even if the patents under the proclamation of 1754 were construed to exempt veterans from the requirements of regular grants, he was determined to comply with the letter of the Old Dominion act, in the belief that he then could hold his rich bottoms, no matter what new and stern conditions subsequently were imposed by a separate government. Washington reasoned, too, that settlers who went to his new western lands in order to advance their own fortunes would do better by him than would overseers or managers on such a contract as the one for the Youghiogheny tract. He did not want another Gilbert Simpson but tenants who would have every incentive to develop his land for their own profit.

To this end, he drew up a general advertisement that was designed to elicit inquiry. When interested persons asked terms, he would state the other requirements, which covered leases for twenty-one years or three lives. Tracts of desired size could be held rent free for four years and after that at £4 current money per hundred acres, provided: (1) three acres of every fifty were cleared, fenced and under cultivation by Oct.

---

[118] 3 *G. W.*, 109, 143, 167; 4 *Hamilton*, 207, 216, 236, 238, 247. For the sale in the West Indies of Washington's surplus corn, see 3 *G. W.*, 147.
[119] *Ledger B*, folio 92.   [120] See *supra*, p. 168.   [121] *Ledger A*, folio 245.

1, 1775, as demanded under Virginia law; (2) five acres of every hundred were enclosed, laid down and kept in good grass for meadow; (3) fifty good fruit trees were planted on every 100 acres or in proportion for larger or smaller farms; (4) a dwelling house and barn "fit for a common farmer" were built within seven years.[122]

Settlers who were inclined to accept these terms were assured that transportation to the eastern settlements could and would be improved. Already, Washingon asserted in his advertisement, there was easy communication between the mouth of the Great Kanawha and Fort Pitt. Thence "vessels of convenient burden" passed up the Monongahela to Redstone. In time, Washington wrote, "[from Redstone] by means of Cheat River and other navigable branches of the Monongahela, it is thought the portage to Potomac may, and will, be reduced within the compass of a few miles . . ." [123]

On these terms and with this prospect Washington undertook to draw settlers to his lands which, he said in his advertisement, were "among the first which have been surveyed in the part of the country they lie in." [124] He had, at the outset, a prospect that some Scottish families might go to the Kanawha [125] and, soon afterward, a hint that bargains might be struck with certain Irishmen who "could not live under the exactions" their landlord made in negotiating new leases.[126] Apparently it did not occur to Washington that his terms might be subject to the same condemnation. Instead, he felt that the conditions he imposed were warranted by the excellence of the bottoms on the Ohio and the Kanawha. To protect his title and to develop the tracts, he would wait for those who would pay what he asked. None came.

Difficulties attending the development of this Kanawha land were not considered a barrier to the acquisition of more land, and more and more. Washington was committed fully in his mind to his view that the road to wealth ran on the frontier, and he set no limit to what he would patent if he could find low-lying, easily-developed tracts of the

---

[122] 3 *G. W.*, 144–46; 37 *ibid.*, 502–03.

[123] 3 *G. W.*, 145. The distance is thirty-five miles up the Monongahela from the mouth of Redstone Creek to the point where Cheat River empties its waters into the Monongahela. Overland portage between the mouth of Redstone and that of the Cheat River is twenty miles. On the line of the present West Virginia Counties of Preston and Tucker, the distance from the upper waters of the Cheat to those of the north branch of the Potomac is about fifteen miles. It is not likely that Washington knew these distances or had any detailed information concerning the navigability of the more remote streams. He probably reasoned only that where streams were so close together on the Appalachian Divide, they could and would be opened when the volume of transportable goods from the interior justified the outlay.

[124] 3 *G. W.*, 145.   [125] 2 *Diaries*, 122.   [126] 4 *Hamilton*, 256.

first quality. On the Scioto River, beyond the western limit of the proposed Colony under the Walpole Grant, Thomas Bullitt, an irrepressible Captain of Washington's old Regiment and the hero of Grant's defeat,[127] had been arousing great curiosity by making surveys for which there was no understood reason.[128] Soon the report spread that Governor Dunmore had said he would recognize in Virginia's back country the land claims of Pennsylvania veterans who qualified under the proclamation of 1763.

As Washington had asked Col. John Armstrong for information concerning grants in the Penns' domain,[129] that old comrade of 1758 wrote Washington to ascertain the truth of the stories that Virginia was opening her undeveloped western realm to former soldiers from other Colonies.[130] Washington undertook, of course, to procure promptly the information Armstrong wanted.[131] As Governor Dunmore had gone to the Ohio country and thereby had given color to the reports of large and mysterious enterprises, a new opportunity seemed to be opening to Washington. He wrote to Captain Crawford and to Captain Bullitt to survey 10,000 unclaimed acres for him, 5000 in his own right and 5000 on account of purchased rights of other officers.

This land must be of the first quality, in one tract if possible, as near as might be to the mouth of the Scioto, which he understood the Crown had set as the western boundary of the proposed new Ohio Colony.[132] A little later, Washington was to appeal to Governor Dunmore to permit the patenting of veterans' lands on the Scioto, under the proclamation of 1763.[133] Simultaneously, he was warning an influential trespasser—no less a person than Michael Cresap—to get off part of his Kanawha lands;[134] and, with equal vigilance he was doing what he could to facilitate the surveys of the lands still due veterans of the First Virginia who had not received the whole or even any part of their allotment in the distribution of December, 1772.[135] Nor did Washington forget altogether the possibility of procuring vast new plantations on the Mississippi in West Florida, though the prospect of this was

---

127 See Vol. II, p. 340.   128 4 Hamilton, 249.
129 2 G. W., 471; 3 Hamilton, 302.
130 Letter of Aug. 17, 1773; 4 Hamilton, 248.
131 Cf. 3 G. W., 155.
132 3 G. W., 149. In terms of modern place names, Washington thus was advancing his speculative land interests from the approximate site of Point Pleasant, West Virginia, to the vicinity of Portsmouth, Ohio.
133 3 G. W., 157. This was Nov. 2, 1773. See infra, p. 332.
134 3 G. W., 152, 153–54.   135 3 G. W., 151.

dimming.[136] The design of it all was clear in his mind: he wanted land, land, more land, but the most fertile of it only, and in large tracts of river bottoms—always there and never on the infertile uplands off the enriching streams.

To find time for steadfast, undeviating pursuit of wealth in the West, Washington had learned daily new lessons in how to organize and to perform the work he had to do as plantation-owner, as counsellor of his neighborhood, as executor and administrator, as stepfather of the somewhat unstable Mr. "Jack" Custis, as the husband of a grief-stricken wife, as a private gentleman who enjoyed his rightful share of sports— and so endlessly. He never could have finished all his duties—to say nothing of keeping his books and conducting his correspondence—had he not risen early and ordered his hours. That summer and autumn he had, in addition, to study the financial affairs of his brother Samuel and had to lend that gentleman £400 with which to buy land.[137] Trouble was had, also, with James Hill, steward of the Custis estate, who excused his occasional confusion of mind by giving the somewhat unusual explanation that he had been caught in a squall and had never recovered entirely.[138]

These and matters like them [139] were not to be escaped and therefore were best endured and soonest dispatched if they were handled cheerfully; but Washington now disclosed once more his familiar weakness in being unwilling to say "No" to a request that meant a material increase in the load of business he already carried. John Mercer, the able and contentious attorney who possessed vast appetite for land,[140] had died on the 14th of October, 1768, at the age of 64.[141] He left much property of many sorts—700 ounces of plate, a coach-and-six, a chariot, 400 books, scores of scattered tracts large and small [142]—and many debts.[143] His son James was so interested in the law that he neglected his own affairs; [144] George, the other son, Washington's former aide,[145] remained in England, where he had a romantic but, for the time being,

---

[136] *Ibid.*

[137] *Ledger B*, folio 36. Samuel acted on occasion for his brother George in business matters. See a letter the master of Mount Vernon wrote him, July 28, 1772, concerning claims against tenants (*L. W. Smith Coll.*).

[138] 3 *G. W.*, 143–44; 4 *Hamilton*, 239.

[139] Among them an effort to collect a bond from "Montgomerie and others to us" in a land transaction that was not handled as Washington had expected. See his letter of July 4, 1773 to John West Cameron (*Mount Vernon MSS*).

[140] See Vol. I, p. 63.   [141] *Va. Gazette*, Oct. 27, 1768.

[142] *Ibid.*, May 16, June 13, 1771.   [143] 4 *Hamilton*, 286.

[144] See his card in *Va. Gazette*, May 20, 1773. Various other attorneys signed this notice.
[145] A sketch of him will be found in 17 *W* (1) p. 88.

an impoverished marriage.[146] Soon it was thought that George Mercer's bride would receive a fortune, in anticipation of which he had high-priced slaves purchased in considerable number for his Virginia plantations. At the next turn of the wheel, George and James Mercer were at cross purposes and with their interests so confused that Washington and one or two other of their friends had to try to untangle many transactions. Washington, as usual, had most of the work to do and spent much time on it, with ultimate results less disastrous than he had anticipated.[147]

Most of the other events of the fruiting season of 1773 were pleasantly pitched. At the end of July, there was another of the delightsome family visits to Maryland,[148] visits that were becoming more frequent now that Belvoir was closed. Then in September was the usual journey to Annapolis for the races [149]—likewise a diverting but at the same time a humiliating experience because the master of Mount Vernon did not pick the horses with the judgment he displayed, for example, in his selection of lands. He was the poorer by almost £15 as a result of his wrong choices, his encounters with the card-playing Marylanders, and his normal expenses of entertainment.[150]

A document of doubtful meaning awaited him on his return, though perhaps it was not altogether unexpected. Before leaving for Annapolis, Washington had written Dunmore to ascertain if it were true, contrary to expectations, that the Governor was granting patents beyond the western boundary of the projected new Colony on the Ohio, to soldiers who had rights under the proclamation of 1763. If this were being done, said Washington, he hoped his efforts to get lands in West Florida in accordance with that proclamation would not be a barrier to filing a claim on the lower Ohio. He had little prospect of getting the Florida

[146] His letters of 1771 to Thomas Adams are in the *Adams Papers*, VHS, and are precisely such as might have been written by Samuel Richardson for the youthful hero of a romance of 1750.

[147] As this episode added little to Washington's experience and contained scarcely any detail not repeated in a dozen familiar stories of financial distress in colonial Virginia, it is not reviewed here. See Washington to George Mason, Aug. 20, 1773, MS, L. W. Smith *Coll.*, Ledger B, folio 84, 129, 221; Lund Washington to G. W., Dec. 30, 1775, MS, Thom *Coll.*, Mount Vernon; 37 *G. W.*, 507–08. This last item covered the sale of Colonel Mercer's property. In writing of bills of exchange for Mercer, who still was in England, Washington urged that care be taken to get bills that "were esteemed good, but," he added emphatically, "I will never by any indorsation of mine, make my estate liable to be rent and torn to pieces, if they should prove otherwise." For the handling of Mercer's affairs in 1774, see 3 *G. W.*, 249–53; 37 *ibid.*, 507 ff; 2 *Diaries*, 144–45, 171, 172.

[148] 2 *Diaries*, 119–20.

[149] *Ibid.*, 125–26. The start from home was September 26; return was October 2.

[150] Ledger B, folio 93. A list of the prizes offered in these races appeared in *Va. Gazette*, Oct. 14, 1773.

lands; but if he had to wait for report of failure there, before applying in the district Dunmore was said to be opening, then he would be "hung in suspense between two chances" and would "more probably fall through in both." He would appreciate a "line or two by post." [151] Governor Dunmore's reply—at hand on the return from Annapolis— was to the effect that he did not mean to grant any patents on the "Western waters" under the proclamation of 1763. The tone of the letter and the inclusion of the words "I do not think I am at present empowered to do so" raised some hopes for the future.[152] Washington put the phrase "at present" away in his mind for future use, but he had to conclude that nothing could be done immediately.

He turned to a gratifying task—the enlargement and further adornment of Mount Vernon. A gardener had been employed in January for £25 a year, washing, lodging and diet; [153] much painting was in contemplation; [154] 60,000 brick had been burned for new foundations and buildings; [155] close to 15,000 shingles had been purchased.[156] Although "Patsy" was missed hourly, the place was more beautiful than ever it had been when, on October 19, Washington set out for Williamsburg to settle his business with the merchants who would assemble there at the end of the month.

Martha traveled with him, as did "Jack," who had come home from New York for vacation. The boy had been much shocked by the unexpected news of "Patsy's" death. He had put himself and his servant in deep mourning [157] and, in the ponderous words of President Cooper, was in a state of mind that did not "admit of any intentness of application"; [158] but he rallied somewhat and, when he left in September, brought with him good reports from Cooper and from a tutor, John Vardill.[159] Washington had been pleased [160] to hear this and, now as always, he had satisfaction in the company of Martha and her son as they rode on to Eltham, which they reached on the 23rd of October.

---

[151] Letter of Sept. 12, 1773, *Dunmore Papers*, William and Mary Lib.; 20 *W* (2) p. 164–65. In this letter, Washington referred to an Order in Council, Apr. 7, 1773, that forbade western grants except to officers and soldiers under the proclamation of 1763. He evidently had read of this in *Va. Gazette*, July 15, 1773.

[152] Quoted in 3 *G. W.*, 155–56.

[153] He was David Cowan of Fredericksburg, whose contract, Jan. 11, 1773, is in 13 *Papers of G. W.*, 81, LC.

[154] 3 *G. W.*, 155.   [155] *Ledger B*, folio 77.

[156] *Ledger B*, folio 82.   [157] 4 *Hamilton*, 235.

[158] 4 *Hamilton*, 227.

[159] This is the same Vardill who later was a clergyman, controversialist and spy on Americans in England. For the reports on "Jack," see 4 *Hamilton*, 262–63.

[160] 3 *G. W.*, 148.

After two days there, Washington went on to Williamsburg,[161] and renewed vigorously the veterans' agitation for land. In so far as the proclamation of 1763 was a basis of claims, he could do no more than submit the petition he had prepared in the name of the prospective beneficiaries.[162] Those of the volunteers of 1754 who had received the tract of 51,302 acres had called a meeting at the mouth of the Great Kanawha, October 20, to make a final partition.[163] Delinquent contributors, passed over in the first distribution, were now to receive their acreage. At the same time, Washington and a few others who had benefited in the first allotment had a new chance of increasing their holdings, thanks to Washington's forethought two years previously. The surveys approved in 1772 had been for 127,899 of the 200,000 promised in 1754 by Governor Dinwiddie. That left 72,101 acres to be divided. For those officers and men who had as yet received nothing, Crawford made five new surveys of tracts from 7276 to 28,400 in size. The total of these five tracts was 72,299 acres, or substantially the total needed to make up the entire 200,000. Against this there were outstanding soldiers' claims of 53,432 acres. There consequently remained 18,887 —the difference between claims and the total set in the proclamation. Originally, the Council had ordered that 30,000 be reserved for late claimants, but when Washington presented the figures, no claimants remained and no formal protests over inequitable distribution had been received. All claims appeared to be satisfied. The 18,887 acres were "left over." In tabular form:

	Acres
The original promise of 1754 was for	200,000
In December, 1772, the Governor and Council had allotted	127,899
This left for the second distribution	72,101
Crawford had made five surveys that approximated this or, in precise figures	72,299
Outstanding claims for this second distribution were	53,432
Which left unallotted and unneeded	18,867

161 Washington's ledger entries contain nothing to indicate that Martha went to town except perhaps for a day or two at a time. "Jack" must have remained in Williamsburg during most of Washington's stay, because he contrived to spend £19, 12s 9d while there. (*Ledger B,* folio 96.)

162 See 3 *G. W.,* 157.

163 *Rind's Gazette,* Sept. 30, 1773. The notice of the meeting was signed by Adam Stephen, Peter Hog, John West and Charles M. Thruston.

When Washington presented these figures to the Governor and Council on the 5th of November, he proposed that the balance of 18,867 be divided among those who "had been at all the trouble and whole risk" of advancing their full part of the cost of exploration, surveys and patents. He urged that each of these men share in percentages that corresponded to the proportions of the original allotment. Field officers had received 15,000 acres and Captains 9000; those of like rank who qualified now were to receive 3500 and 2100 each of the residue—the Captains 60 per cent of what the field officers had. None could assail this as a new plea. In October, 1771, carefully at Washington's instance, had not the Governor and Council provided that part of the reservation of 30,000 should be for those who sustained extra expense in seeking to procure suitable lands for the soldiers? [164] The colonial officials now were as good as their reservation. They made the regular "second apportionment" as Washington recommended and added what Washington termed "the dividend" to those who had footed the bills for exploration and surveys. Washington, for example, had an unfilled claim of 453 acres because he had not "come out even" on his original 15,000 acres. He now received that balance and 3500 acres of the "remainder" of 18,867. As in the apportioning of lands the previous year, he saw to it that his new acreage was in one of the smallest tracts, which he shared with George Muse.[165]

So far as Washington was involved directly, one thing only remained for him to do. That was to collect what he could from those officers and men who had received their full bounty and had contributed meagrely or not at all. He soon was to take up this task, which proved exasperating and scarcely yielded enough to repay him for his vexing

[164] See *supra*, p. 283. In his report of Nov. 5, 1773 to the Governor and Council, Washington introduced the proposal for the distribution of the "left over" land in this manner: "—this . . . leaves of the 30,000 acres (set apart in October, 1771, for satisfying any claims which might thereafter come in, and for the further purpose of reimbursing the few who had been at all the trouble and whole risk) 18,867 acres, which if appropriated to those who were full in advance at that time, and distributed according to the former proportions, will go thus . . ." (3 *G. W.*, 160). Council minutes for the 31st of October, 1771, have not been found; but it will be recalled that in his letter to George Mercer, Nov. 7, 1771, Washington noted that the reservation of 30,000 acres included compensation for "those who have been and must necessarily continue to be saddled with this expense . . ." (3 *G. W.*, 69). The language of Washington's advertisement, *Rind's Gazette*, Jan. 14, 1773, and of his announcement in *ibid.*, Nov. 25, 1773, was substantially the same. This is made plain because casual examination of the circumstance might leave the impression that Washington and some of the other former officers simply gobbled up 18,867 acres because they could.

[165] *E. J.*, Nov. 4, 1773, P.R.O., C.O. 5: 1440, p. 40, VSL Photostat; 3 *G. W.*, 160; *Rind's Gazette*, Nov. 25, 1773.

trouble.[166] Even so, Washington had not been rewarded poorly for presenting and pursuing the promise of bounty made in 1754, a promise which most certainly would never have been redeemed without his money, his determination and his persistence. This was the result: On his own account, he had received 18,500 acres and at small expense he had bought up claims for an additional 5600, a total of 24,100 acres of as good land as his discriminating eyes and the honest effort of the experienced William Crawford had been able to find on the Kanawhas and the left bank of the Ohio.

A good deal of the business of the Custis estate as well as of Washington's own had to be transacted in Williamsburg before a start for home was made. The guardianship account of "Patsy" had to be settled, with Edmund Pendleton as the attorney;[167] some new moves in the Dunbar case had to be countered by the same skillful lawyer,[168] in circumstances the reverse of those that irked John Custis in his lifetime. The "old Colonel" had fretted often over the law's delays; now it was to Washington's interest, as administrator of the estate, to wear down the claimants. He may have rejoiced over a condition of which a merchant then was complaining to an English correspondent—that eight to ten years were required in Virginia to get a final decree in chancery.[169]

In addition to these two matters, Washington had to make a major decision on the investment of the credit balance that was accumulating on "Jack's" account with London merchants. Most of the money "Jack" inherited from his sister was outstanding in loans at the time of her death, but the sum left in the hands of the men who handled the Custis tobacco on the English market was larger than Washington wished it to be. It was better laid out, he thought, in Virginia lands that could be worked by the increasing Custis slaves.

Opportunity seemed to be offered for the holdings of William Black, who had acquired in King and Queen the principal estate of Treasurer Robinson, and also one of Bernard Moore's plantations, Woromonkoke, in King William County. Washington examined the plantations, liked

---

166 Cf. his circular of Dec. 30, 1773 in 3 G. W., 171. All the early funds handled by Washington on account of "The Officers and Soldiers Concerned in the grant of 200,000 acres of land" appear in Ledger A, folio 322, 324; Ledger B, folio 40. No final statement has been found, as yet, of the excess of Washington's expenditures over the amounts paid him by the other beneficiaries.

167 Ledger B, folio 93. See supra, 326, n. 117.

168 Ledger B, folio 93. The details are not known.

169 23 V 64.

them, and at length bought them for "Jack" at £3679 sterling.[170] The price was accounted fair, but Mrs. Black was so much opposed to the sale, presumably for fear of losing her dower rights, that months had to be spent in persuading her to sign.[171] Washington hung on patiently through the whole because, as he said, the purchase was too advantageous for "Jack" to forego it.[172] Patience was rewarded, also, while Washington was in Williamsburg, by receipt of news from Jamaica that Daniel Jenifer Adams's brig, now styled *Anne and Elizabeth*, had been served with bottomry papers on return to that island and was ready to sail for Norfolk, subject to Washington's claim. He ordered her to proceed.[173]

Back at length Washington went to Mount Vernon, by way of Fredericksburg, where he paid his mother £30 and took pains to note that he did so in the presence of his sister, Betty.[174] He arranged, also, to have Mrs. Washington's lot paled.[175] At home, December 9, he found himself at once subjected to a new plea—that "Jack" be not required to go back to college but be permitted to follow the desires of his heart and marry "Nelly" Calvert as soon as arrangements could be made. Determined as Washington was by nature, it was futile for him to attempt to resist the forces arrayed against him. ". . . I have yielded, contrary to my judgment, and much against my wishes," he wrote President Cooper, "to [Jack's] quitting college, in order that he may enter soon into a new scene of life, which I think he would be much fitter for some years hence than now; but having his own inclination, the desires of his mother and the acquiescence of almost all of his relatives to encounter, I did not care, as he is the last of the family, to push my opposition too far, and therefore have submitted to a kind of necessity."[176] There remained nothing to do except to settle "Jack's" outstanding New York bills, which were found to reach a total of about £80.[177] One of them, in the eyes of that avowed foe of dissenters, President Cooper,[178] deserved scrutiny. He wrote Custis: "Graham's bill is

[170] *Pocket Day Book*, unpaged, Dec. 4, 1773, 394 *Papers of G. W.*, LC; *Ledger B*, folio 96. The properties were described in some detail by Black in his advertisement, *Rind's Gazette*, Oct. 21, 1773. A typographical error in 2 *Diaries*, 129 n, makes it appear that the cost of the land was £6375 instead of £3675 sterling. This became the Romancoke estate.

[171] 3 *G. W.*, 164, 174, 176, 181; 4 *Hamilton*, 282, 297, 328, 330, 365, 375.

[172] 37 *G. W.*, 503.

[173] Letter of Nov. 29, 1773 to Capt. Thomas Pollock; 3 *G. W.*, 166, 169.

[174] *Ledger B*, folio 45.   [175] *Ledger B*, folio 56.

[176] Letter of Dec. 15, 1773, 3 *G. W.*, 167, somewhat drastically repunctuated.

[177] 4 *Hamilton*, 313.   [178] See *supra*, p. 323.

a heavy one; but you best know what articles you had of him. I always heard him reckoned a *dear* fellow—as I once told you;—whether he is *honest* or not, is another question: but it is certain he is a violent Presbyterian."[179] Washington's comment was that had he known how brief "Jack's" stay at college was to be, "I should not (as his guardian) have thought myself justified in incurring so great an expense . . ."[180]

Thus did the prospects of "Jack's" marriage and increasing expenses make Washington more careful than ever about the frugal administration of the Custis trust. On his own account, though he was unrelaxing in his study of how he could acquire more land and could drive off those who encroached on his new possessions,[181] he continued to enlarge his benefactions. In his service to his neighbors he was so generous of his time he now was close to the limit of his resources,[182] great as was his skill in ordering his days. Something deep in him—perhaps his old combativeness and his sense of justice—made him persist in his unrelenting efforts to get Mrs. Savage's annuity from her husband.[183] Washington paid quietly for the schooling of Doctor Craik's son[184] and, in spite of all his unhappy experience with John Posey, gave the Captain money with which to keep off the sheriff and to drive off the wolf.[185] On the plea of the weaver, Thomas Davis, he advanced £19 in order to bring to America the man's mother and sister—money that never was repaid.[186]

Washington could afford these larger charities in the year that was dying in the Christmas logs on the hearth, but when he came to balance the books of 1773—or rather to attempt to balance them—he could not account for £144 that had disappeared somewhere, somehow.[187] Other accounts were favorable. Even if the year had not been a good one on the tobacco market,[188] the master of Mount Vernon stood to lose nothing on that account because he received 8000 pounds only from tenants.[189] The flour industry was profitable, though the "seconds" from the mill were slow to move from the wholesalers' warehouses. Washington was pondering that unpleasant reality and also was asking himself whether he might not find a market for ships' biscuit. Plantation fisheries were undergoing a change. Some of the salt herring were being sent to

[179] Letter of Feb. 5, 1774; 4 *Hamilton*, 323.
[180] Letter of Apr. 15, 1774; 3 *G. W.*, 207.
[181] Cf. 4 *Hamilton*, 293–94.
[182] Cf. Robert Brent in 4 *Hamilton*, 333–35.
[183] 3 *G. W.*, 169; 4 *Hamilton*, 267.
[184] *Ledger B*, folio 44.
[185] *Ledger B*, folio 93; cf. 4 *Hamilton*, 246.
[186] *Ledger B*, folio 86.
[187] *Ledger B*, folio 98.
[188] 4 *Hamilton*, 203.
[189] *Ledger B*, folio 52.

Norfolk for sale; [190] there was a prospect of building and of leasing a fish house on the river front of the Potomac to an enterprising Philadelphia merchant, William Milnor, who probably was hoping to handle Washington's catch as well as his own.[191]

"Patsy's" death was both grief and relief in 1773; "Jack's" unwillingness to remain at King's College was a distress; vexations had been numerous. The great event was the prospect of cancelling all of the debt to Robert Cary & Co. and the completion of the patenting of the lands under the proclamation of 1754. A year of proud and profitable achievement ended before word came to Virginia of strange occurrences in Boston harbor on the night of December 16.[192]

[190] *Ledger B*, folio 85; 3 *G. W.*, 109.
[191] 4 *Hamilton*, 271; 3 *G. W.*, 168–69; Milnor's account, *Ledger B*, folio 123.
[192] The first report published in the Old Dominion appears to have been that in the *Virginia Gazette* of Jan. 13, 1774. In the issue of January 6 had been printed an account of the arrival in Boston of a tea ship, which went to a wharf where another similar vessel already was moored, "so the same persons who watch the one can the more easily take care of the other."

CHAPTER XV

"An Innate Spirit of Freedom"
(January–August, 1774)

THE BACKGROUND of those occurrences in Boston was familiar in part to Washington at the beginning of 1774.[1] He knew that after the repeal in April, 1770, of all the Townshend duties except that on tea, the edge of the issue of taxation had been dulled. Some of the tea-drinking colonials gradually had disregarded their covenant not to use that beverage. At Virginia ports, for example, between Dec. 1, 1770 and Jan. 5, 1773, duty had been paid on almost 80,000 pounds of tea.[2] New York and Philadelphia became notorious centres of tea-smuggling, though the people kept up the form of non-importation agreements.[3] By 1773, official silence might have produced public forgetfulness, had not Lord North's ministry approved a new policy in order to enforce the tax on tea and to relieve the financial distresses of the East India Company, which as a result of various governmental and corporate blunders, had a surplus of 17,000,000 pounds of the leaves.[4] Under an act of May, 1773,[5] the East India Company was authorized to ship tea directly to its own agents or to individual merchants in the English Colonies of America. On entry, the produce was subject to the detested tax of 3d a pound, which had been in force since 1767.[6] One London merchant expressed the general opinion of the new policy when he wrote Virginia correspondents: "Some of my friends in the India Direction tell me they have thoughts of sending a quantity of tea to Boston, New York, Philadelphia, Virginia and South Carolina, which

---

[1] This is the year in which the mass of material on Washington's activities becomes so great that it is not practicable to include all the incidents of his life without obscuring the main events. From 1774 onward, much minor detail of a repetitious nature is omitted.

[2] Schlesinger, *Colonial Merchants,* 246.　　　[3] *Ibid.*

[4] This merely paraphrases *Schlesinger,* 262, a work from which, it may be remarked, many authorities have drawn with surprisingly little credit to the author. The most succinct statement of the various changes in the British taxes, drawbacks, etc., is in G. E. Howard, *Preliminaries of Revolution,* 266. For a more detailed study, see M. Farrand, "The Taxation of Tea, 1767–73," in 3 *A.H.R., 267.* See also Hutchinson, *History of Massachusetts Bay,* v. 3, p. 179.

[5] 13 George III, c. xliv; *Statutes at Large,* v. 30, p. 77

[6] Howard, *op. cit.,* 268.

government seems to approve, but they suspect their motives are to make a catspaw of the Company and force them to establish the 3d per pound American duty." [7] It did not seem a hopeless undertaking. Tea sent to America and taxed in this manner would be cheaper than it ever had been in the Colonies and far less expensive than in England. In fact, not even the widely used Dutch tea of the smugglers could be sold profitably in competition with it.

The new plan for the sale of tea did something besides reawaken American colonials to the tax which they had denounced as a tyrannical levy imposed without their assent. Previously, the East India Company, which alone could bring tea into Great Britain, had been required to offer it at public auction to merchants who then sold it either to other dealers with factors in America,[8] or directly to distributors in the Colonies. None of these men could take a middleman's profit under the new law of 1773. All existing commercial organization in the trade might topple to its ruin when the Company itself supplied the American dealer who dispensed the tea over the counter. To the citizen's familiar cry of taxation without representation, the merchant class now added that of monopoly without recourse. Tea was denounced as the drug of the tyrant, the scourge of the master, the bane of health. A correspondent of the *Virginia Gazette* wrote from Boston: "Since our last, arrived here Captain Coffin not only with PLAGUE (tea) on board but also with smallpox. As tea is of a drawing quality, it is suspected it has sucked in the distemper and therefore, if permitted to be landed, it is presumed there would be no purchaser." [9] On three counts, therefore, the demand was that the tea must not be brought ashore: [10] To frustrate the changes in the trade, merchants used New England "Sons of Liberty," who demanded that the British government should not tax the Colonies; the champions of popular rights were glad to make common cause with the powerful mercantile class. As a result of their

---

[7] John Norton to Peyton Randolph et al., July 6, 1773; *John Norton & Sons*, 337.

[8] As the terms then were employed, a "factor" was agent in America of a merchant in Great Britain; an American merchant was an independent dealer.

[9] *Rind's Gazette*, Jan. 13, 1774. Cf. *ibid.*, Dec. 30, 1773: "That bane to America, that poison to health, the East India Company's tea." Schlesinger, *op. cit.*, 264 ff traced the history of merchants' incitation of resistance to the new plan for distributing tea. The same author (p. 276–77), quoted some remarkable allegations of the responsibility of tea for human ailments.

[10] Numerous detailed and informative accounts of British shipments and of the preliminaries of Dec. 16, 1773 will be found in that reliable colonial newspaper, the *Penn. Gazette*. See particularly issues of August 11, November 17, December 1, 8, and "Postscript" of December 9. See also *Rind's Gazette*, Nov. 11, 1773, with reports of October 25–28 from Philadelphia and New York.

joint agitation, directed with skill and vehemence by Samuel Adams, a large number of men carelessly disguised themselves as Indians, clambered aboard three ships at the dock on the night of Dec. 16, 1773, and dumped into the waters of the harbor 342 chests of tea belonging to the East India Company.[11] No resistance was offered by the crews or by British soldiers or warships.[12]

Information of this affair reached Mount Vernon about New Year's Day.[13] It did not excite Washington greatly, nor did it produce any general upstir in Virginia, where the merchants were not as numerous or as influential as in Massachusetts. Resentment over the tea tax was revived somewhat in the Old Dominion, perhaps, by events in Massachusetts, but the "Boston tea party" was not approved by Washington and apparently was not regarded by him as immediately serious. Six months elapsed before he mentioned the incident in any of his letters.[14] He could not be unmindful of what might be the response of a proud King to so defiant an act—especially after so stern an inquiry had been ordered in the affair of the Gaspee—but Washington was busy that January, 1774, and for many weeks afterwards, with an accumulation of troubles over tenants and leases, land claims and controversies.

Both to Washington's regret and to his indignation, Robert Cary & Co. professed to have found obstacles that delayed the sale of "Patsy's" stock in the Bank of England and the conversion of the proceeds to the settlement of Washington's long standing unfavorable balance. The

11 Of the various contemporary accounts, two especially to be commended for accurate detail are Samuel Cooper to Benjamin Franklin, Dec. 17, 1773, and John Scollay to Arthur Lee, Dec. 23, 1773, MHS. Cols., (4) v. 4, p. 373, 379. The excellent report in the Penn. Gazette is in the special issue of Dec. 24, 1773.

12 Cf. Admiral Montagu to Philip Stephens, Sec. of the Admiralty, Dec. 17, 1773: ". . . during the whole of the transaction, neither the Governor, magistrates, owners or revenue officers of the place ever called for my assistance; if they had I could have prevented the execution of this plan but must have endangered the lives of many innocent people, by firing upon the town." Lt. Col. Leslie similarly reported that he had his Sixty-sixth Regiment ready but that he received no appeal for help. He added: "I am informed the Council would not agree to the troops going to town, however it must end in that" (R. Hist. MSS. Comm., 11th Report, Appendix, p. 344).

13 The news was printed in the Penn. Gazette, special edition of Dec. 24, 1773, a paper that should have reached Annapolis by the 28th. Unfortunately there is a gap in the files of the Maryland Gazette for that period. This is true, also, of Rind's Gazette. Its issue of Dec. 30, 1773, included a report from Boston dated November 29, and its edition of Jan. 13, 1774 contained a letter of Dec. 13, 1773 from Boston. The edition of Jan. 20, 1774, had only a report of what was done in Philadelphia when the news was received there. In general, a month elapsed between the date of an event in Boston and the publication of it in Williamsburg, unless the news was conveyed by express or by a vessel that enjoyed favorable winds.

14 The first observed reference is in a letter of June 10, 1774, to George William Fairfax, mentioned infra, but there is of course a possibility that Washington referred to the incident in some lost letter.

merchants wished the debt extinguished, of course, but they seemed to encounter endless legal barriers at the Bank, and they permitted months to pass without pressing for a decision on the basis of the papers transmitted them. What seemed to Washington a simple procedure was dragged on indefinitely. The result was that Washington considered himself actually out of debt but still on the wrong side of Cary's books.

Another unpleasant affair of 1774 was with George Muse, who in spite of his admitted cowardice at Fort Necessity, had entered his claim and had received allotment of the 10,000 acres due a field officer under the accepted interpretation of Dinwiddie's proclamation of 1754. Muse in some manner concluded that he had not received his full acreage and he wrote in protest a vehement letter to Washington, as if the Colonel had cheated him. The man who brought this paper, or some other person, told the gentleman of Mount Vernon that Muse was intoxicated when he penned the letter, but the recipient of the insult became infuriated as he read, and he made no allowance for the fact that Muse, sober, might repent of what Muse, drunk, had alleged. Washington "slept on" the letter for a night but still felt so much resentment that he scarcely could control himself when he addressed Muse in this fashion: "Sir, Your impertinent letter of the 24th ulto., was delivered to me yesterday by Mr. Smith. As I am not accustomed to receive such from any man, nor would have taken the same language from you personally, without letting you feel some marks of my resentment; I would advise you to be cautious in writing me a second of the same tenour; for though I understand you were drunk when you did it, yet give me leave to tell you that drunkenness is not excuse for rudeness; and that, but for your stupidity and sottishness you might have known"—and with that he explained the apportionment. He added: "all my concern is that I ever engaged in behalf of so ungrateful and dirty a fellow as you are." [15] Addressed to some men, this would have provoked an immediate challenge to a duel. Sent to Muse in full knowledge of the individual, it doubtless brought an apology. Relations were resumed at least to the extent of credits for surveys and patents until Muse wrote to say that because of his "infirmness and old age" he was transferring his remaining interest in a certain western tract to his son. [16]

[15] Letter of Jan. 29, 1774; 3 G. W., 179–80. For the account of Washington with Cary & Co., see *infra*, p. 453.

[16] The Washington-Muse grant of 7276 acres, Dec. 1, 1773, is in *Land Office Records*, 42, p. 50. Muse's account was recorded in *Ledger B*, folio 114. His letter concerning the transfer bore date of Jan. 6, 1775, and appears in 5 *Hamilton*, 81–82.

Washington continued ready to buy any good claims in the region assigned the veterans of 1754 but he worked principally that winter to "seat" his own grants in the manner required by Virginia law.[17] He wished he might journey to the Kanawha again and supervise this in person [18] but as this seemed impossible, he began to search for someone to transact his business there, and he soon found Capt. William Crawford's brother Valentine, former wagon master of war days, with whom he started negotiations. Gilbert Simpson received another chance and new equipment for building the mill on the Youghiogheny—proof either of Washington's increasing tolerance of the weakness of men, or else of his inability to get a genuinely responsible agent.[19]

Washington had not been successful either with the Scottish or with the Irish, who had been regarded as possible settlers. A better prospect seemed to be offered by getting Germans from the Palatinate.[20] Good reports had reached him of these "Palatines," as he termed them, but he was rigid in his requirements, though admittedly ignorant of the conditions under which they might be brought to America. He did not wish men and their wives with more than one child for each family because, he said, "families encumbered with many children . . . would only add to my expenses without contributing to my design." If such persons were available on the usual indenture, he wrote, he would consider them as his "property" during their agreed term of service, or he would bargain with them as tenants under a general covenant.[21] Here, as in seeking native tenants, he found that his terms were not sufficiently attractive in an enterprise that proved more and more difficult for him the further he explored it.[22] He was again to advertise for settlers [23] but he found the customary methods the surest, so he bought labor for the frontier—four male convicts, four indentured servants and a man and wife. The gross price, £110, was considered high for persons on in-

---

[17] For his difficulty in getting a tenant on the upper Potomac, see his correspondence with Angus McDonald (4 *Hamilton*, 305; 37 *G. W.*, 305; see also Washington to unnamed correspondent, Jan. 28, 1774; *Prussing Papers*, LC). The possible acquisition by purchase of soldiers' claims under the proclamation of 1763 is outlined partially in 4 *Hamilton*, 325, 329 and in 3 *G. W.*, 191. Renewed controversy with Michael Cresap over the "Round Bottom" on the Kanawha is to be found in 3 *G. W.*, 209 and 4 *Hamilton*, 387.

[18] 3 *G. W.*, 180.

[19] *Pocket Day Book*, Mch. 24, 1774; *Washington MSS*, Huntington Library. For Valentine Crawford's connection with the wagons during the French and Indian War, see Washington to Dunmore, Feb. 11, 1774; William and Mary Lib.; 20 *W* (2) p. 165–66.

[20] That part of Bavaria west of the Rhine, known more generally as the Pfalz.

[21] 3 *G. W.*, 193. Cf. *ibid.*, 185, 187.

[22] *Ibid.*, 195. See also 4 *Hamilton*, 355, 356, 368–69.

[23] 3 *G. W.*, 211.

denture.[24] As soon as practicable, he organized these and some of his
domestics into a party, more than twenty in number, to proceed to the
Kanawhas.

Some of Washington's other duties of management had to be discharged immediately, but some of them fortunately could be deferred
until the celebration of the event that most interested the entire Mount
Vernon household—the marriage of "Mr. Custis," as he now was styled
respectfully. The date was set for the 3rd of February; the place was
Mount Airy, the Calvert home in Maryland. Washington had an early
dinner that wintry day and then, with Lund Washington, set out across
the Potomac.[25] That evening he witnessed the ceremonies and shared
in the celebration. Generously, as became the stepfather of the groom,
he remained for the festivities of the "second day." [26] Then, leaving the
bride, her husband and the friendly hosts, the Colonel and Lund returned to Mount Vernon, whence, in a few days, he sent to the young
couple what "Jack" gratefully described as "many kind offers." [27] It was
Martha's hope and doubtless Washington's expectation that "Jack" and
"Nelly" would spend the greater part, and preferably all of their time
at Mount Vernon, until a decision concerning a permanent home was
reached.

Washington seldom went from home now, even for a few days,
that he did not find on his return an accumulation of business, most
of it troublesome, to which he had to devote long hours in patient
equanimity. Almost every post yielded a perplexity. It never had been
quite so true as it now was in 1774; but after "Jack's" wedding and

---

[24] 4 *Hamilton*, 354.

[25] 2 *Diaries*, 140. No mention is made of Martha's presence. She may have considered it
"unbecoming" to attend a wedding so soon after the death of her daughter, even though her
son was the groom.

[26] No evidence has been found to justify the surmise of Fitzpatrick (2 *Diaries*, 140 n), that
after "Jack" decided to go on with his marital plans when his stepfather counselled delay,
Washington "seemed to have lost interest in the matter." Such remarks as occur in Washington's
correspondence and all the inferences reasonably drawn from his diary indicate that he accepted
in good spirit what he could not prevail on the young man to defer.

[27] 4 *Hamilton*, 336. A sentimental, undated letter alleged to be from Martha Washington to
"Nelly" Custis appears in Lossing, *Mary and Martha . . . Washington*, 126. It reads: "My dear
Nelly,—God took from me a daughter when June roses were blooming. He has now given
me another daughter about her age when winter winds are blowing, to warm my heart again. I
am as happy as one so afflicted and blest can be. Pray receive my benediction and a wish that
you may long live the loving wife of my happy son and a loving daughter of your affectionate
mother, M. Washington." Like the letter Washington is alleged to have written Martha, July 20,
1758 (see Vol. II, p. 319 n and 405–06), this missive is said to have been copied by Benjamin
Lossing "from the original at Arlington." It is almost certainly forged and probably by the
same hand as the pretended letter to Martha from Washington. None of Martha's surviving
letters suggests the style or diction of this document.

before Washington began to struggle again with deeds and debts and the troubles of tenants, he and his household had one high satisfaction: To the great joy of the parishioners, the long-desired Pohick church was completed and, on February 24, was received formally by the officials, who proceeded almost immediately to advertise for bids on a vestry house.[28] Washington regarded the newly finished edifice as the one with which he would be associated, though he had, also, in the church at Alexandria an interest which his effort to prevent a reassignment of pews had strongly bespoken.[29] In his pew of the Pohick church, he had drawers put for the safe-keeping of prayer-books and papers, and soon he was to have his cipher placed on the door.[30]

A whirl of new and continuing business at Mount Vernon was rendered the more difficult because of a daily coming and going of visitors whose entertainment consumed hours. Washington did not permit himself to engage in foolish hurry and he did not pass hasty judgment on weighty affairs, but he found himself fully occupied and often annoyed. Foremost among his troubles was that of *Anne and Elizabeth,* Daniel Jenifer Adams's brig. Washington's bottomry bond had required that the vessel be delivered into his hands at Alexandria, though he would have preferred that she be put under the hammer at Norfolk. By a succession of accidents, she was damaged and delayed so that, as he later wrote, he was "thirty odd pounds deeper in the mire" when she finally was advertised for sale at Alexandria.[31] Young Adams had asserted that if the brig were offered at that port, his friends would assist him in redeeming her by paying the amount of the judgment Washington had procured for the money Adams had pocketed after he sold the cargo of flour in the West Indies. None of these "friends" appeared, with the result that Washington, much against his wishes, had to "bid in" the vessel for £175. His hope was to sell her for at least what she cost him, and, if that was impossible, to use her in his fish-and-flour trade. Actually, the brig was not a bad bargain. She was not more than four years old and, when refitted, was a good vessel, for which Washington ere long refused an offer of £300. *Anne and Elizabeth* was renamed *Farmer* and soon was a part of the equipment of the Mount Vernon enterprises.[32]

[28] *Truro Parish Vestry Book,* Feb. 24, 1774, p. 61; *Md. Gazette,* Mch. 24, 1774.
[29] See *supra,* p. 308.   [30] *Ledger B,* folio 6, 120.
[31] 3 *G. W.,* 212, 213. The advertisement was published in *Va. Gazette* of Mch. 10, 1774 and was reprinted in 10 *V* 325.
[32] *Ibid.;* 3 *G.W.,* 204; 4 *Hamilton,* 374; 2 *Diaries,* 146.

If Washington had to add a brig to his belongings, he had the good fortune to sell a farm. It was one he did not want, though it included the "home place" on the Rappahannock, the first realty that ever had been his. Now that his mother had removed to Fredericksburg, the land of Washington's youthful residence had been consolidated with Mary Washington's "lower quarter" in a tract which had never been surveyed but was believed to contain about 600 acres. Poor as most of the land was, it had become valuable because it included a fine site, close to the growing town of Fredericksburg. Washington had advertised the property shortly after his mother moved to Fredericksburg[33] and he believed, if he could sell it, he could use the purchase-price advantageously in the acquisition of better ground that would increase similarly in value. Sentiment did not enter into the transaction; he felt no attachment to the farm, though he had lived there from the time he was seven years of age until he began his service in the French and Indian War. Dr. Hugh Mercer of Fredericksburg became as anxious to buy as Washington was ready to sell. In April, 1774, a ready bargain was struck at the excellent price of £2000 Virginia currency, to be paid in five equal parts in successive years.[34]

There was much more of the same sort of experience in the spring of 1774, gain to offset loss, irritation to match satisfaction. Even to Washington himself, the detail must have been tedious—an accident that put the treasured chariot into the river whence it had to be fished,[35] a judgment of £600 in Mrs. Savage's behalf that might be difficult to collect,[36] the seizure of Captain Crawford by law officers while he was visiting Mount Vernon,[37] the forced abandonment of the dream of patenting Florida lands[38] and so through time-consuming trifles to one matter of

[33] See *Rind's Gazette*, Nov. 5, 19, 1772 and Appendix III–3, *infra*.

[34] 3 *G. W.*, 198–99, 205; 4 *Hamilton*, 356, 366. In the absence of all transfer deeds of part of this property to Washington from his mother, or from Washington to Mercer, some doubt might be raised whether Ferry Farm itself was included in this transaction. This doubt is set at rest by mention in Washington's advertisement of the fact that the property included "one of the most agreeable situations for a house that is to be found on the whole river, having a clear and distinct view of almost every house in the said town and every vessel that passes to and from it" (*loc. cit.*). Ferry Farm corresponds precisely to this description. No tract farther down the river would. As noted in Appendix III–3, this advertisement is basis for the assertion that as an operating farm, the property on which Mrs. Washington resided for twenty-eight years after the death of Augustine included, in 1772, about 200 acres only of cleared land.

[35] *Pocket Day Book*, 1772–74, *Washington MSS*, Huntington Library, entry of May 4, 1774. The expense was 18s.

[36] 3 *G. W.*, 208; 4 *Hamilton*, 395, 398; *Ledger B*, folio 51.

[37] 4 *Hamilton*, 364. The Captain had decided that he would open an ordinary at his farm near the Youghiogheny, because he was ruining himself by the ceaseless entertainment of travelers. "Some days now," he wrote, "if I had rum I could make £3 a day" (4 *Hamilton*, 318).

[38] 37 *G. W.*, 506.

large moment—a calamitous frost on the 4th of May. This appeared at the moment to have destroyed about half of the wheat on the 1000 acres Washington had planted in that grain.[39] As compensation, there was hope that good prices might be offered for the short tobacco crop of 1773,[40] but the staple was doomed to yield so little on the London market[41] that Washington, in disgust, debated whether he should not abandon the culture of the leaf on the Custis plantations precisely as he had at Mount Vernon.[42] Herring, likewise, were not selling to advantage.[43] It was fortunate for Washington in this discouraging situation that he had a large store of wheat on hand and that he did well with it when he marketed it as flour.[44]

So far, then, as his own foresight and management could extend, Washington had protected his interests and had secured for himself an opulent if busy life on the Potomac; but along with the killing frost of May there came evil news. From the scene of Washington's earliest military adventure, the report was that John Connolly on the authorization of Governor Dunmore had seized Fort Pitt in the name of the Colony of Virginia, which asserted title to the forks of the Ohio. That meant strained relations between Virginia and Penn's Colony and it might jeopardize negotiations Washington was reopening for some of Croghan's land on Chartier's Creek.[45] Worse still than any previous development of the year, was a threat of renewed Indian warfare. Connolly was expected to proceed against the Shawnees and to punish them for outrages committeed against Virginians, but the result, as in all such border conflict, was uncertain. Defeat for the whites would mean massacre on the frontier. More immediately, so far as Washing-

---

[39] 3 *G. W.*, 214, 220; 4 *Hamilton*, 394. Fithian, *op. cit.*, 151, recorded a current rumor that in Loudoun County, wheat and rye had been destroyed so completely that they had been cut for fodder. "In these lower Counties" said he, "many of the leaves are falling as in November." As usual, damage was distinctly less than anticipated (3 *G. W.*, 225).

[40] 4 *Hamilton*, 333. The crop of 1773 had been damaged greatly by mould from wet, hot weather soon after the leaf had been cut. See 1 *Ballagh, Lee Letters*, 105.

[41] Cf. 5 *Hamilton*, 7.

[42] 3 *G. W.*, 217.

[43] 4 *Hamilton*, 374.

[44] *Ibid.* and *Ledger B*, folio 119, 133. Sales to Hooe and Company, Alexandria, amounted to £1054 and those to Robert Adam reached £407 (*ibid.*). For evidence of the shift in Northern Virginia from tobacco to wheat, see Vol. I, p. 142, n. 549. An interesting note was supplied in August, 1774, by William Herbert who estimated that in the preceding twelve months 27,325 barrels of flour and 150,000 bushels of wheat had come to the Alexandria market (15 *Papers of G. W.*, 43, LC).

[45] Scarcely any details of the acquisition of 2813 acres there have been brought to light; but in 14 *Papers of G. W.*, 128, LC, is a survey, Apr. 18, 1774, of 2000 acres in Fincastle County that Washington had patented under the assignment made him by Lieut. Charles Mynn Thruston.

ton was involved, the upstir caught at Redstone the expedition he was sending out to "seat" his Kanawha lands.[46]

Before the extent of this financial reverse was known, Washington made ready to go to Williamsburg for a meeting of the General Assembly, most inconveniently called for the 5th of May. He had hoped he might excuse himself from this session because of the state of his own affairs, but he found that county interests required his attendance.[47] Remaining at home as long as he could after the frost of May 4, in order to appraise the damage, he set off on the 12th for the capital, in the usual manner and at the normal pace. When he arrived on the 16th[48] and received his regular committee appointments,[49] he found little done but much dreaded.

King, ministry and Parliament had made their first response to the action of the Boston mob in throwing tea overboard from three ships on the night of the 16th of December, 1773. No protest, no threat, no action of violence by the Colonials had so outraged their critics in England or had alienated so many of their friends. A majority even of those who had been firmest in defence of the rights of the Americans admitted that the people of Boston should be punished. Benjamin Franklin had written in dejection: "I suppose we never had since we were a people so few friends in Britain. The violent destruction of the tea seems to have united all parties here against our province . . ."[50] A bill had been introduced promptly to close the port of Boston after June 1 to all vessels large and small, until the town paid for the destroyed tea, gave "reasonable satisfaction" to injured revenue officers, and convinced the King "that peace and obedience to the laws shall be so far restored in the said town of Boston, that the trade of Great Britain may be safely carried on there, and his Majesty's customs duly collected

---

[46] 3 G. W., 498. See infra, p. 398. This occurred at the beginning of the operations known as Dunmore's War. It has not been thought necessary to go into detail here because Washington had no part in the "war" otherwise than to the extent that he lost servants and property and shared the dismay of all Virginians over a revival of border fighting at a time when controversy with Britain became acute. Cf. 3 G. W., 224. Most of the documents of Connolly's activities at Fort Pitt, and a mass of material on the military campaign appear in Peter Force, American Archives (cited hereafter as Force) ser. 4, v. 1, p. 260 ff, 455 ff, 677, and in R. G. Thwaites and L. P. Kellogg, ed., Documentary History of Dunmore's War, 1774, based on the Draper MSS, Wis. H. S. See also 17 V 388. Numerous important papers on the Virginia claims to lands in Western Pennsylvania appear in the third series of Penn. Arc.

[47] 3 G. W., 180. The particular matter probably was a bill for the extension of the corporate limits of Alexandria (Cf. 4 Hamilton, 393).

[48] 2 Diaries, 151.   [49] Journ. H.B., 1773–76, p. 107.

[50] Letter of Mch. 22, 1774 to Thomas Cushing; 6 Smyth's Franklin, 223. An important London letter of Feb. 18, 1774, concerning Franklin's part in the transmission of the Hutchinson letters appeared in Penn. Gazette, Apr. 20, 1774.

. . ." [51] Whether Boston survived or starved, she was to be chastised till she both paid and repented. The other Colonies were to be warned by that example. Lord North said: "Let us continue to proceed with firmness, justice and resolution: which, if pursued, will certainly produce that due obedience and respect to the laws of this country, and the security of the trade of its people, which I so ardently wish for." [52] Gov. George Johnstone [53] replied: "I now venture to predict to this House, that the effect of the present bill must be productive of a general confederacy, to resist the power of this country." He concluded that the bill "instead of quieting the disturbances of Boston . . . will promote them still further, and induce the inhabitants to cut off all communication with your ships of war, which may be productive of mutual hostilities and most probably will end in a general revolt." [54] This warning and even the thunderous logic of Burke were in vain. The bill passed the Commons March 25 without a division [55] and on the 30th received the unanimous approval of the Lords. [56]

The text of the law reached Boston May 10 [57] and both angered and appalled. A town meeting showed a determination to resist to the utmost. All the Colonies were to be asked to break off trade with Britain and Ireland till the act was repealed. "I hear from many," General Gage wrote Lord Dartmouth, "that the act has staggered the most presumptuous, but minds so inflamed cannot cool at once . . ." [58] Virginians did not learn of the precise terms of the act until shortly before May 19. [59] Then the universal comment, in varying phrase, was that if one port could be closed in this manner, all could be—to the complete destruc-

---

[51] Text conveniently printed in 1 *Force* (4), 61–65. The substance of the debate appears in *ibid.*, 35–61. See also *Md. Gazette*, Apr., 7, 1774, and *Penn. Gazette*, May 11, 1774, for colonials' information of the receipt in Britain of the news of the "tea party," together with first accounts of the response of government.

[52] 1 *Force* (4), 43.

[53] This was the somewhat notorious George Johnstone who will reappear as a man with whom Congress refused to accept a negotiation of peace because he attempted to bribe an American commissioner. See *Journals of the Continental Congress*, ed. 1904–1937 (cited hereafter as *JCC.*), v. 11, p. 770.

[54] 1 *Force* (4) p. 56.   [55] *Ibid.*, 57.   [56] *Ibid.*, 60.

[57] *Penn. Gazette*, May 18, 20, 1774; T. Newell's Diary, May 10, 1774, *MHSP.*, 1876–77; MS. Comm. Corres. to Peyton Randolph et al., May 21, 1774; 1 *Sparks Transcripts*, VSL.

[58] Letter of May 19, 1774; 1 *Gage*, 355.

[59] The exact date is not known. Richard Henry Lee wrote his brother Arthur, June 26, 1774 (1 *Ballagh, Lee Letters*, 114): "We had been sitting in Assembly near three weeks when a quick arrival from London brought us the tyrannic Boston Port Bill," but Lee was speaking in general terms. The Assembly met on the 5th of May, and the resolution for the fast was passed on the 24th, within two days less than three weeks. *Rind's Gazette* of May 19, 1776, contains references which show that the main provisions of the Boston Port Act and the date of its passage by Parliament were known in Williamsburg.

tion of American rights. "The Parliament of England," wrote Landon Carter, "have declared war against the town of Boston and rather worse." He recorded the force being mustered and affirmed, "This is but a prelude to destroy the liberties of America . . ." [60] Washington's disapproval of the violent destruction of private property in Boston did not obscure for an instant his view of the larger issue,[61] but he did not belong to the small, inner group of new leaders in the House of Burgesses who were accustomed to determining in private the action they later called on their colleagues to take.[62] Perhaps he knew that the plan was to delay the full protest of the General Assembly until the closing days of the session so that necessary legislation would have been passed and nothing of importance would be lost if, as anticipated, the Governor dissolved the Assembly for speaking out. More than this, Washington probably was not told.

The session continued without important action until May 24. Then, when petitions had been presented and referred in the usual order, the grave and religious Treasurer, Robert Carter Nicholas, took the floor and presented a paper that began: "This House, being deeply impressed with apprehension of the great dangers to be derived to British America from the hostile invasion of the city of Boston in our Sister Colony of Massachusetts Bay, whose commerce and harbor are, on the first day of June next, to be stopped by an armed force, deem it highly necessary that the said first day of June be set apart, by the members of this House, as a day of fasting, humiliation and prayer, devoutly to implore the divine interposition, for averting the heavy calamity which threatens destruction to our civil rights and the evils of civil war; to give us one heart and one mind firmly to oppose, by all just and proper means, every injury to American rights; and that the minds of his Majesty and his Parliament, may be inspired from above with wisdom, moderation and justice, to remove from the loyal people of America all cause of danger from a continued pursuit of measures pregnant with their ruin." The remainder was an order for the House to assemble on the 1st of June

[60] Diary, June 3, 1774; 14 W (1) p. 184. This part of Carter's Diary fortunately is printed and is, all in all, among the most informative commentaries on events in Virginia at this period. Valuable, also, though more restricted in argument, are the letters of Thomas Nelson, addressed principally to mercantile correspondents in England and preserved in the Nelson Letter Book.

[61] His first detailed review of the situation, to repeat, was on July 4, and is quoted infra, but there can be no doubt he held the same opinions in May.

[62] Cf. Geo. Mason to Martin Cockburn, May 26, 1774: "Matters of that sort here are conducted and prepared with a great deal of privacy, and by very few members, of whom Patrick Henry is the principal." (1 Rowland, Mason, 168.)

and to proceed, with the Speaker and the mace, to the church where prayers were to be said and a sermon delivered by a designated clergy-man.[63] Publication of the resolutions was directed, also, in order that the public might share in the services and in the fast.

The House approved with little argument and no division. Nor, apparently, did any member think it worth while to point out how different the language was from that of ten years previously. Members had described themselves in 1764 as "your Majesty's dutiful and loyal subjects" who gave assurance of their "firm and inviolable attachment to your sacred person and government." Now they spoke for the "loyal people of America" who were resolved "to oppose, by all just and proper means, every injury to American rights."

Something no less significant would have been observed had members of the House been told of the precedents consulted in the drafting of Nicholas's resolution. The previous evening, the leaders of Patrick Henry's contingent in the House had gathered in the Council Chamber —Henry, Richard Henry Lee, Francis Lightfoot Lee and two or three other Burgesses, along with George Mason, the inspirer of so much of their action, who happened to be in Williamsburg on private business.[64] The meeting place was chosen so that the men could consult the books there. Jefferson wrote afterward: "No example of such a solemnity [as a call for a fast] had existed since the days of our distresses in the war of '55, since which a new generation had grown up. With the help, therefore, of Rushworth, whom we rummaged over for the revolution-ary precedents and forms of the Puritans of that day, preserved by him, we cooked up a resolution . . ."[65] Even Jefferson did not elaborate in after years on the singular fact that the depository of the precedents should have been the *Historical Collections* of John Rushworth, who had been secretary to General Fairfax and to Oliver Cromwell . . . and had recorded the execution of a King of England.

George Washington did not have Rushworth's eight folio volumes among his own few books or among those that had been brought to Mount Vernon from the collection of Daniel Parke Custis at White House. In fact, Washington may never have heard of the worthy col-lector, but he voted for Nicholas's resolution to observe a fast and he

63 *Journ. H.B.*, 1773-76, p. 124; *Rind's Gazette*, May 26, 1774.

64 1 *Rowland, Mason*, 169.

65 1 *Jefferson*, 9. Robert Carter Nicholas, who was not present at the meeting, was asked the next day to introduce the "order" because of his known standing as a man of firm, religious faith (*ibid.*, 10).

determined to respect it literally and in spirit. The understanding was that members who could afford to do so would dispatch to their Counties the resolution for the fast, in the hope that sympathetic clergymen would read the text from the pulpits and would exhort the congregation to observe the designated day or some other fixed by them. Washington sent such an express to his minister, Rev. Lee Massey. Almost simultaneously, the philosopher George Mason forwarded this message in a letter to a friend: ". . . should a day of prayer and fasting be appointed in our County, please to tell my dear little family that I charge them to pay a strict attention to it, and that I desire my three eldest sons and my two eldest daughters may attend church in mourning, if they have it, as I believe they have." [66] Washington did not order mourning at Mount Vernon where it already was being worn for "Patsy," but the injustice of the Boston Port Act was burning in his heart. The need of action was plain to him. If he knew of certain vigorous resolutions that Richard Henry Lee had written and intended to introduce in the last days of the session, he was ready to endorse them, also. Washington did not lead in drafting such measures—he had not overcome his awkwardness in phrasing—but he did not have to be persuaded to give his voice to those that asserted the ancestral rights of Americans.

He had not long to wait for a new test. The resolutions of Nicholas had been adopted on Tuesday the 24th; Wednesday week would be June 1. Burgesses expected they would be dissolved, but not until they had completed their major legislation, which might not be finished before the latter part of June.[67] The House consequently went on with its work at its usual pace and on the 25th contrived to hear a number of petitions and to advance a few bills. Much the same order of business was in progress between 3 and 4 P.M. on the 26th [68] when the Clerk of the General Assembly brought the familiar message, "The Governor commands the House to attend his Excellency immediately, in the Council Chamber." In a few minutes the life of the legislature was ended in a single sentence from Dunmore: "Mr. Speaker and Gentlemen of the House of Burgesses, I have in my hand a paper published by order of your House, conceived in such terms as reflect highly upon his Majesty and the Parliament of Great Britain; which makes it

[66] George Mason to Martin Cockburn, May 26, 1773; 1 *Rowland, Mason*, 169.
[67] George Mason to Martin Cockburn, May 26, 1774; 1 *Rowland, Mason*, 168.
[68] 1 *Force* (4), p. 350.

necessary for me to dissolve you; and you are dissolved accordingly." [69]

It had happened that way in May, 1769. Burgesses who had been present then remembered how they had gone from the Capitol to Raleigh Tavern and there had begun the discussion that led to the drafting of the first association. Without argument they flocked now to the same building on the 27th and, in the same Apollo room, took counsel for the future. They were angry but they were convinced their Governor had blundered. "It certainly deserves notice," Landon Carter wrote a few days later, "that it is the very first time the praying that His Majesty and his Parliament may be inspired from above with wisdom and justice and moderation was ever thought derogatory to the honor of either of them especially in an established church whose liturgy proposes collects for that very purpose and in words almost tantamount." [70] That was the logic: what of the course Virginia now must pursue? A basis of action was suggested in the resolutions Richard Henry Lee already had drafted. One of these called for the non-use in Virginia of the tea of the East India Company so long as the tax remained. Another of Lee's proposals denounced the Boston Port Act as "a most violent and dangerous attempt to destroy the constitutional liberty and rights of all British America." Then came a paragraph for the appointment of Deputies to meet with like representatives from other Colonies in order to consider means of stopping exports and of securing the constitutional rights of America.[71]

A paper containing substantially the same ideas was drawn up at the tavern by the Burgesses and was adopted without haggle or hesitation. The central conclusion was this: "We are further clearly of opinion, that an attack, made on one of our sister Colonies, to compel submission to arbitrary taxes, is an attack made on all British America, and threatens ruin to the rights of all, unless the united wisdom of the whole be applied. And for this purpose it is recommended to the Committee of Correspondence, that they communicate, with their several corresponding committees, on the expediency of appointing deputies from the several Colonies of British America, to meet in general congress, at

[69] *Journ. H.B.*, 1773–76, p. 132. Dunmore acted when he did, with the unwilling, silent assent of the Council (Landon Carter's Diary, 14 *W* (1) p. 184) because he had wind of Lee's resolutions, though he did not know their author or their full import. See his letter of May 29 to Lord Dartmouth, May 29, 1774; 1 *Force* (4) p. 352. See also Dunmore to Dartmouth, May 29, 1776; Dartmouth to Dunmore, July 6, 1774; Aspinwall Papers, *MHS Cols.*, (4), v. 10, p. 718, 719.
[70] Diary of June 3, 1774; 14 *W* (1), p. 186.
[71] Text, somewhat mutilated, in 1 *Ballagh, Lee Letters*, 115.

such place annually as shall be thought most convenient; there to deliberate on those general measures which the united interests of America
may from time to time require." A warning was added that persistence
in unconstitutional taxation might "compel us against our will, to
avoid all commercial intercourse with Britain";[72] but the proclamation
of a common cause and the suggestion of an annual Congress were the
revolutionary developments. Virginia had not been represented at the
Albany Conference twenty years previously or at the Stamp Act Congress of 1765; now she was discussing the desirability not merely of a
meeting of protest and planning but of an annual Congress of all the
Colonies.

Action was firm but, so far as Dunmore was concerned, it was singu-
larly impersonal. Washington had dined and had spent the evening at
the Governor's on the 25th, the day the resolutions for a fast had been
adopted. The next morning, before the dissolution, he had ridden with
Dunmore to the Governor's farm and had breakfasted there. On the
27th, along with many of those who had joined him in saying "Aye" to
the new resolutions, he went to a ball the House of Burgesses previously
had arranged for Lady Dunmore. It was an extraordinary, a para-
doxical, an amusing and, withal, an enjoyable affair: the hosts were to
be put to the bother and expense of a canvass and a new election for
no other reason than that they had decided to have a fast day; all the
same, as gentlemen, and at £1 per capita,[73] they bowed low to the wife
of the man who had dissolved their House.

On the 28th, the day after the ball, most of the Burgesses went home,
but Washington stayed in Williamsburg to complete arrangements for
the deeds to the Black property.[74] Several other members of the dissolved House remained to attend a meeting of the Committee of Correspondence. With eight of the committeemen present, this body took
up the duty assigned it of communicating with the other Colonies on
the "expediency" of an annual Congress of Delegates from all the
Colonies. Every member saw, of course, the immense potentialities of
a regular meeting; nobody was disposed to press in committee for any
binding action: the idea should be allowed to ferment. Perhaps, in a
different metaphor, the committeemen felt that the club should not
be wielded at the moment but should be held over the head of colonial

[72] Text in *Journ. H.B.*, 1773–76, p. xiii–xiv. The punctuation of this historic document is
preserved.
[73] *Ledger B*, folio 112.   [74] *Ledger B*, folio 112.

Governors. So, that 28th of May, the Virginians approved a circular letter in which, first of all, the dissolution of the House was explained. Then the committee wrote: "The propriety of appointing deputies from the several Colonies of British America to meet annually in general Congress, appears to be a measure extremely important and extensively useful, as it tends so effectually to obtain the united wisdom of the whole, in every case of general concern. We are desired to obtain your sentiments on this subject which you will be pleased to furnish us with." A later and fuller letter was promised; this one was sent by the day's post.[75]

That was on Saturday. The next day, May 29, Washington in grave mood went to church for both the morning sermon and the afternoon prayers.[76] It perhaps was during churchyard conversation following the second service that Washington heard of the arrival of important dispatches from Maryland, with enclosures of serious moment from Philadelphia and Boston.[77] Soon word spread that Peyton Randolph asked that all the Burgesses in Williamsburg assemble the next morning. Calls were dispatched, also, for those in nearby Counties. Washington of course responded and, on the morning of the 30th, found that twenty-four of his former colleagues had done likewise. The paper from Maryland was read to them. With it were a letter and a notice of a meeting held in Philadelphia. These, in turn, had been prompted by a communication Samuel Adams had addressed on May 13 to the Philadelphia Committee of Correspondence to cover resolutions adopted in Boston. The chain ran all the way down the coast: Boston had acted and had advised Philadelphia; the Quaker town had deliberated and had passed on its conclusions to Annapolis; Marylanders had taken their stand and now were advising the Virginians, who were expected to transmit the whole file to the Committee in North Carolina.

Some of the resolutions of the Colonies above the Potomac were enough to make even the calm eyes of Washington flash. Samuel Adams enclosed the text of the Port Act, which already had been received in Virginia, and he reported the expectation of enemies and the fear of friends that Boston alone could not "support the cause under

[75] Minutes of the Committee of Correspondence, May 28, 1774; *Journ. H.B.*, *1773–76*, p. 138.
[76] 2 *Diaries*, 152. There is no record that Washington ever previously had attended two services the same day.
[77] Virginia Comm. Corr. to North Carolina Committee, May 31, 1774; *Journ. H.B.*, *1773–76*, p. 139.

so severe a trial." He went on: "As the very being of each Colony, considered as a free people, depends upon the event, a thought so dishonorable to our brethren cannot be entertained, as that this town will now be left to struggle alone." Attendants on the Boston meeting had called for the suspension of all trade with Britain and the West Indies until the Port Act was repealed.[78] In Philadelphia, May 20, a conservative, almost meaningless exhortation to "firmness, prudence and moderation" had been coupled with assurance of the city's "firm adherence to the cause of American liberty." [79] Maryland's Committee, writing May 25, was in favor of ascertaining what the people thought of a drastic plan of resistance—commercial non-intercourse, an association "on oath" to assure compliance, refusal of lawyers to enter suits for debts due in Britain, and abandonment of all dealings with any Colony that declined to join with a majority of the others.[80]

These were the papers Peyton Randolph presented: regarding them, what was the pleasure of the gentlemen who had assembled? The argument quickly centred on a severance of all trade relations with Britain. Washington could not endorse this. He favored cutting all imports to absolute necessities, but he did not believe Virginians should refuse to pay their debts to Britain, and he reasoned, of course, that if planters and merchants were to pay, they had to export their goods.[81] In this stand he was by no means alone. "Most gentlemen present," the participants were to report, "seemed to think it absolutely necessary for us to enlarge our late association, and that we ought to adopt the scheme of nonimportation to a very large extent; but we were divided in our opinions as to stopping exports." [82] It was argued, also, that where so small a part of the subscribers to the existing association were present, they should not undertake to modify the agreement. Any action of any sort should represent as many freeholders as possible. The unanimous decision accordingly was to invite all the members of the former House to meet in Williamsburg and to consider what should be done. A date two months later, August 1, was set, in order that ample time might be given to arrange private business in advance of the gathering. Mean-

[78] *Journ. H.B.*, 1773–76, p. 148.

[79] Minutes of meeting of May 20, 1774; *ibid.*, p. 148.

[80] Letter of Maryland Comm. Corr., May 25, 1774; *ibid.*, p. 146.

[81] These were Washington's sentiments in July. See 3 *G. W.*, 229, 234. There is every reason to believe he was of this mind at the end of May.

[82] Letter of the twenty-five to the other members of the former House of Burgesses, May 31, 1774; 3 *Hamilton*, 354–56; printed Williamsburg folder of May 31, 1774 in 15 *Papers of G. W.*, 19; LC.

time, members would "have opportunity of collecting the sense of their respective Counties."[83] The meeting adjourned with the understanding that the names of those present were to be signed to a letter that would be dispatched to the entire membership of the House.[84] Washington's name, by chance or otherwise, was the first of those in the right-hand column of the two on the printed folder.[85]

That afternoon, May 30, all the males of the town were invited to meet and to hear a report of the deliberations of the forenoon. The townspeople assembled, listened and approved—"cheerfully" the members maintained.[86] The Governor growled: ". . . these circumstances give too much cause to apprehend that the prudent views, and the regard to justice and equity, as well as loyalty and affection, which is publicly declared by many of the families of distinction here, will avail little against the turbulence and prejudice which prevails throughout the country; it is, however, at present quiet."[87] Very different in spirit was this concluding sentence in the letter of the twenty-five Burgesses to their former colleagues: "Things seem to be hurrying to an alarming crisis, and demand the speedy, united council of all those who have a regard for the common cause."[88]

The day after his name was signed to this, Washington fulfilled to the letter the resolves that had precipitated the dissolution. All he entered in his diary was, "Went to church and fasted all day."[89] It was much the same in all parts of Virginia reached by the men who carried the Burgesses' call for public participation. Harrower, the indentured schoolmaster, looked on the services with the eyes of a newcomer and wrote in his diary: "This day there were prayers in all the churches in Virginia on account of the disagreement at present between Great Britain and her Colonies in North America on account of their not paying a duty on tea laid on them by the British Parliament and the Bostonians destroying a quantity of tea belonging to the British East India Company in 1773."[90] In contrast, the deeply steeped colonial, Landon Carter, reported: ". . . our rector, it seems, appointed a meeting in his lower church . . . and, it is said, did very pathetically exhort the people in his sermon to support their liberties, concluding with the

83 3 Hamilton, 354-56.
84 Ibid., 355-56.
85 Williamsburg folder, as supra, n 82.
86 Ibid., 355.
87 Dunmore to Dartmouth, June 6, 1774; 1 Force (4), 387; Aspinwall Papers, MHS Cols., (4), v. 10, p. 719.
88 Letter of May 31, 1774; 3 Hamilton, 355.
89 June 1, 1774; 2 Diaries, 153.
90 6 A. H. R., 80, with his abbreviated words spelled out.

resolve for the fast, and in the room of 'God save the King!' he cried out 'God preserve all the just rights and liberties of America.' " [91]

That, doubtless, was the unvoiced prayer of Washington as he turned, after the fast day, to the considerable volume of private business that had to be performed, and to the errands that had to be discharged at Williamsburg.[92] He went about this as methodically as ever and he did not interrupt good relations with Governor Dunmore, at whose house he dined on the 16th of June.[93] If there was any evidence of excitement on Washington's part, it was that his card playing was for higher stakes.[94] Governor Dunmore had assumed that "it was intended by the solemnity of a public fasting and praying to prepare the minds of the people to receive other resolutions . . ."; [95] but he did not sense that these would be resolutions of popular meetings, rather than of the Burgesses. In most of the older Counties, plans were being made for freeholders' meetings to pass judgment on the Boston Port Act and the threat to the liberties of Americans. Washington shared heartily in this, and did so easily, because when he got home on June 22,[96] he found good reports of affairs on the plantation, but soon afterwards, he had more of bad news from England. Passage of the Boston Port Act had been followed by the introduction of other drastic measures in Parliament. One of them,[97] styled a "bill for the better regulating the government of the Province of Massachusetts Bay, in New England," removed the Council of the Colony, authorized the Governor to name virtually all officials, limited sternly the meetings of the local governing bodies, the selectmen, and placed in the trusted hands of Sheriffs practically the whole control of the impanelment of juries.[98] The second supple-

[91] Diary of June 3, 1774; 14 *W* (1) p. 184, heavily repunctuated. Cf. Christopher Marshall, *Diary* (cited hereafter as *Marshall, Diary*), p. 6.

[92] He visited the land purchased from Black (2 *Diaries*, 153); he performed a variety of services for George William Fairfax (3 *G. W.*, 218, 221); he attended the meeting and paid his subscription to the somewhat unprosperous Society for the Advancement of Useful Knowledge; (*Ledger B*, folio 115; 2 *Diaries*, 154; *Rind's Gazette*, May 19, 1774); he contributed to a fund to get one of his former Lieutenants out of jail (3 *G. W.*, 226); and he spent several days of ease (June 2–5) at Colonel Bassett's (2 *Diaries*, 153).

[93] 2 *Diaries*, 154.

[94] *Ledger B*, folios 112, 115. About this same period, Landon Carter observed that a guest arrived at Sabine Hall Thursday noon and remained at play till Saturday night, with young men of the family and neighborhood, though the winnings and losses were small. "A gamester," observed Carter, "must keep his expectation of winning constantly engaged" (14 *W* (1), p. 250). Washington never permitted gambling to get any such grip as that on him.

[95] 1 *Force* (4), 352.

[96] He left Williamsburg on the 18th and, en route, spent one day at Eltham (2 *Diaries*, 154).

[97] This usually is regarded as the second bill with the Boston Port Act considered the first.

[98] Presented Apr. 15, 1774; received the royal assent May 19, 1774 (text in 1 *Force* (4) p. 104–12).

mentary measure, for the "impartial administration of justice" in Massachusetts, gave the Governor power to transfer to England or to other Provinces the trial of any official or citizen who might not get a fair hearing in Massachusetts if charged with the murder of any person engaged in mob violence, smuggling, or resistance to law enforcement. Witnesses, also, could be transported.[99] The ostensible object of this, needless to say, was to give protection to officials and to individuals they might call to their assistance in dealing with men who defied the King's government in the Colony;[100] but to the colonials it appeared to be the reverse of the act of Henry VIII that had been cited as warrant for transporting patriots to a strange land to face trial for treason. That law denied an accused person the protection of trial by men of his vicinage; the new bill would deny freeholders the right of passing judgment on what might seem to them to be official murder. It was for this reason that the measure became known as "the Murder" or "the Murderers' Bill." As for the legislation to "regulate" the government of Massachusetts, it seemed to many Americans a warning that the charters of their Colonies no longer could be regarded as a permanent guarantee by the King of popular rights. If an act of Parliament could take away the essential liberties imbedded in the charter of Massachusetts, which the King had granted, then no colonial charter and consequently no civil right was secure.

Washington sat himself down on July 4, 1774, to review this ominous change. He did not undertake this because of any doubt in his own mind but because of a letter from Bryan Fairfax. That son of Washington's early friend, Col. William Fairfax, had been asked by some of his close associates to be a candidate for the Fairfax County seat in the House of Burgesses that John West had decided to vacate. Bryan Fairfax was ambitious to succeed West but was checked by the conviction that he favored a more moderate policy of dealing with Great Britain than a majority of the voters would approve. Fairfax believed

[99] Presented Apr. 15, 1774; received the royal assent May 20, 1774 (text in 1 Force (4), p. 129–31).

[100] Still another bill was "for the better providing suitable quarters for officers and soldiers in His Majesty's service in North America." This was introduced May 2, 1774 and was made law June 2, 1774 (text in 1 Force (4), p. 170). The final measure was a bill "for making more effectual provision for the government of the Province of Quebec, in North America." This came before the House of Lords for the first time May 2, 1774, and received the royal assent, June 22, 1774 (text in 1 Force (4), p. 216 ff). Apparently, little was known in detail of the "Quartering Act" or of the "Quebec Act" at the time of Washington's observations of July 4, 1774, infra. His first known written reference to the "Canada Bill" was on Aug. 24, 1774 (See 3 G. W., 242).

the King should be implored to prevail on Parliament to wipe out the offensive new laws—if they yet had become laws—and he thought the appeal should "be unaccompanied with any threats or claims . . ." In Fairfax's opinion, a new, inclusive non-importation agreement should be postponed "till the effect of a petition be tried." [101]

Washington's answer was almost impatient: ". . . have we not tried this already? Have we not addressed the Lords and remonstrated to the Commons? And to what end? Did they deign to look at our petitions? Does it not appear, as clear as the sun in its meridian brightness, that there is a regular, systematic plan formed to fix the right and practice of taxation upon us?" Did not the Boston Port Act and the measure for transferring trials to England convince anyone that the government was "determined to stick at nothing to carry its point"? Washington's conclusion from his question was instant: "Ought we not, then, to put our virtue and fortitude to the severest test?" More could be done, he said, through a non-importation agreement than men generally believed, but withholding remittances from Britain was another matter. On this, Washington wrote: ". . . whilst we are accusing others of injustice, we should be just ourselves, and how this can be, whilst we owe a considerable debt, and refuse payment of it to Great Britain, is to me inconceivable. Nothing but the last extremity, I think, can justify it. Whether this is now come, is the question." [102] There he stood—with no misgiving other than that he might be unjust to his adversary.

The Colony was running far ahead of him. Meetings planned in accordance with the suggestion made by the twenty-five Burgesses were now being held in most of the Eastern and Midland Counties. Some of the gatherings were convened before the participants had learned the details of any repressive measure besides the Boston Port Act, but the tone of early resolutions was to differ scarcely at all from that of papers drafted after word reached the Counties of the bills to regulate the government of Massachusetts and to provide for a change of the place of trial of officials accused of crimes of violence. [103] The Boston Port Bill in itself was enough to stir resistance and to fire reprisal. A few Counties took precisely the view Washington did—that non-importa-

---

[101] Letter of July 3, 1774 to Washington; 5 Hamilton, 19–22.

[102] 3 G. W., 228–29.

[103] The term "change of venue" scarcely seems applicable inasmuch as that phrase implied in Washington's time no greater change than that from one English County to another.

tion of British goods was necessary but that a ban on exportation was not yet desirable and might be unjust because it would make impossible the payment of debts to England.[104] Most of the Counties demanded more than this and either approved non-importation and other retaliatory measures short of non-exportation,[105] or else went all the way and called for complete severance of trade relations with Britain.[106] One County contented itself with advocating any action that might be necessary.[107] Two Counties, only, Middlesex and Dinwiddie, were in opposition to any stern action.[108] Several of the Counties urged that a general Congress of all the Colonies be assembled[109] and in one instance, that of Prince George County, the call was for a general association to limit importation and for a Congress of all the Colonies "to consult and agree upon a firm and indissoluble union and association for preserving by the best and most proper means their common rights and liberties."[110] In the resolutions the same assurance was repeated again and again—that the cause of Boston was the cause of all the Colonies.

All these papers were designed to be laid before the proposed Convention and before the new General Assembly. Washington intended to seek re-election to the House of Burgesses and to do his full part in the name of his constituents and on his own account, but he had hoped that a deft writer, such as George Mason or Bryan Fairfax, would be a candidate for the seat vacated by John West. When Bryan declined because he was out of step with his neighbors, Washington renewed his appeal to George Mason, though with the warning that he could be of small help in getting his neighbor elected. "I early laid it down as a maxim," he explained, "not to propose myself and solicit for a second."[111] Mason's declination left Charles Broadwater the only new

104 E.g., Chesterfield (1 Force (4), p. 537-38) and York (ibid., 597). York added a special exhortation "that industry and frugality" be adopted and "that horse racing, and every species of expensive amusement, be laid aside . . ."

105 Prince George (1 Force (4), p. 493-95), Surry (ibid., 593), Hanover (ibid., 615-16), Elizabeth City (ibid., 634), Caroline (ibid., 539-40), Henrico (ibid., 550-51), Princess Anne (ibid., 640-41).

106 Prince William (ibid., 387), Frederick (ibid., 392-93), Westmoreland (ibid., 437), Spotsylvania (ibid., 448-49), James City (ibid., 499), Albemarle (ibid., 637).

107 Accomac (ibid., 639). The general line of argument advanced at these meetings probably was that outlined in Landon Carter's Diary, June 8, 1774 (14 W (1) p. 247). See also Thomas Nelson to Samuel Athawes and to T. & R. Hunter, Aug. 7, 1774 (Nelson Letter Book, 315, 317).
108 1 Force (4), p. 551-52.

109 New Kent (ibid., 535-36), Caroline (ibid., 539-40), Henrico (ibid., 550-51).

110 This set of resolutions (ibid., 494-95), was signed by Theodorick Bland as Clerk of the meeting. He may have been the author of the paper.

111 3 G. W., 227-28.

candidate—a worthy man but, in Washington's candid language, one who "might do as well in the discharge of his domestic concerns as in the capacity of a legislator." [112]

The Fairfax election was held July 14, in accordance with writs issued by Governor Dunmore on the 17th of June,[113] and was completed in about two hours, as a young stranger wrote, "with great order and regularity." [114] There was a hogshead of punch for all comers,[115] but if Washington furnished this, he was not so informed. He paid for the cakes served freely [116] and he left the details of the ball that evening to Capt. John Dalton, who computed Washington's share of the cost at approximately £8.[117] The greater part of this doubtless was for music and for the coffee and chocolate. No tea was served. "This herb," a visitor explained, "is in disgrace amongst them." [118]

During the preliminaries of the election, and on election day itself, no resolutions on the Boston Port Act were passed. The reason probably was a desire the leading men of the County had expressed on the 5th of July that George Mason prepare deliberately for a selected committee a paper that would set forth the principles at stake.[119] When he had completed a draft of resolutions and a designated committe had approved them, the final text was to be presented at a county meeting over which Washington was to preside. On the 17th, Mason brought to Mount Vernon his resolutions, which he doubtless discussed that evening. The next day, Monday, July 18, the two friends rode to Alexandria and there reviewed with the other committeemen, paragraph by paragraph, the long statement Mason had fashioned. With no acrimony and with little debate, various amendments were made at the instance of the committeemen. Then the party went to the assembly [120] at the

[112] *Ibid.*, 228.

[113] 1 *Force* (4), p. 419; Dunmore to Dartmouth, June 20, 1774, on the appeal of Council that he issue writs of election, Aspinwall Papers, *MHS Cols.*, (4) v. 10, p. 720. On the 8th of July, before the election had been completed, the Governor had prorogued the Assembly from August 11, the date set in the writs, to November 3 (*ibid.*, 523).

[114] *Journal of Nicholas Cresswell*, 1774–77 (cited hereafter as *Cresswell*), p. 28.

[115] Cresswell (*op. cit.*, 28) described it as "a Hogshead of Toddy (what we call Punch in England)"; but the word "toddy" was used somewhat loosely in Virginia. Strictly speaking, "toddy" was water, spirits and sugar, flavored with nutmeg or similar spice, but more broadly, the term was used to include almost any distilled liquor that was drunk with water or even without it. For example, to say of a man that he "loved his toddy" was equivalent merely to stating that he drank heavily. The beverage served at election doubtless was rum punch, a "standard drink" in eighteenth-century Virginia.

[116] The bill was high—£3, odd money (*Ledger B*, folio 117).

[117] *Ledger B*, folio 126.　　　　　　　　　[118] *Cresswell*, 28.

[119] Such, at least, was the interpretation Fitzpatrick gave in 2 *Diaries*, 156 n. It seems reasonable, but no authority was cited.

[120] One of the unanswered questions of this era in Virginia and in most of the "Tobacco" or

Court House, where Washington and the other members of the committee mounted the bench. The proceedings had been opened when someone handed Washington a bulky letter. He broke the seal and found the contents to be a lengthy argument by Bryan Fairfax for petition and reconciliation, rather than for protest and reprisal.[121] After looking over the paper, Washington passed it down the bench. One only of those who examined Fairfax's appeal was favorable to it. All the others were for ignoring it as unlikely to have the slightest support. Several asked why they should submit a view contrary to the very one they had met to record.[122]

Mason's resolutions then were presented, explained and adopted[123] in the form of a statement of principles applied to the controversy between Colonies and Parliament. The observations on the rights of Americans contained little that had not been expounded previously by Mason, but they now were phrased with deliberate simplicity. The colonials, Mason protested, in no sense were a conquered people but were the descendants of conquerors who had brought with them to the new world all their "rights, advantages and immunities" as British subjects. Americans were as much entitled to enjoy all their rights under the British constitution as if they had remained in "the realm of England." Then Mason repeated that the doctrine of legislation by freely-chosen representatives was the basic provision of the British constitution. As Americans could not have representation in the British Parliament, the only exercise of their rights had to be through their own assemblies.

The duty of the Colonies to contribute to the support and defence of the British Empire was admitted; but, Mason said sharply in fresh

"Plantation Colonies" is the extent of participation of small farmers, artisans and "common men" generally in public meetings. It would appear that all inhabitants were invited but that freeholders only were expected to share in the deliberations. At Williamsburg, it will be recalled, all white males of twenty-one years and over had been asked to attend the gathering called by the twenty-five Burgesses (see *supra*, p. 357). The usual introduction to published resolutions was, "At a meeting of the freeholders and other inhabitants of" etc., (Cf. 1 *Force* (4) p. 417) but the general impression left by most of these Virginia resolutions is that they represented chiefly the "gentlemen, merchants and members of the bar." If "common men" attended in any considerable number, they were overawed by their "betters." While no proceedings of meetings in Virginia include any evidence that men of the humbler economic classes dissented from the policy advocated by "the gentry," it is by no means certain that the small independent farmer or tenant knew anything more about the issues than that they somehow concerned his taxes and his liberty.

[121] Text in 5 *Hamilton*, 22 ff.
[122] Washington to Bryan Fairfax, July 20, 1774; 3 *G. W.*, 230–31.
[123] They appear in 1 *Rowland, Mason*, 427 ff, in 18 *V* 159 ff, and in 1 *Force* (4) p. 597 ff.

language, "no argument can be fairly applied to the British Parliament's taxing us upon a presumption that we should refuse a just and reasonable contribution but will equally operate in justification of the Executive power's taxing the people of England upon a supposition of their representatives refusing to grant the necessary supplies." [124] Action by Parliament in defiance of these principles "must, if continued, establish the most grievous and intolerable species of tyranny and oppression that was ever inflicted on mankind." This vigorous language was followed by the firm declaration "that it is our greatest wish and inclination, as well as interest, forever to continue our connection with and dependence upon the British government; but, though we are its subjects, we will use every means which Heaven hath given us to prevent our becoming its slaves." [125]

There followed a denunciation of the course of the ministry and of the Parliament, and then almost a score of specific recommendations on non-importation, aid to Boston, colonial association, and eventual refusal to grow and to export tobacco if the punitive acts regarding Massachusetts remained in force. Most of these proposals were subject to the same criticism that had weakened the association of 1769: they were too rigid, too detailed. This could not be said of the twelfth resolution—"that nothing will so much contribute to defeat the pernicious designs of the common enemies of Great Britain and her Colonies as a firm union of the latter, who ought to regard every act of violence or oppression inflicted upon any of them as aimed at all: and to effect this desirable purpose that a Congress should be appointed to consist of deputies from all the Colonies to concert a general and uniform plan for the defence and preservation of our common rights and continuing the connection and dependence of the said Colonies upon Great Britain, under a just, permanent and constitutional form of government." One duty of this Congress would be to draw up an "humble and dutiful remonstrance to the King, who was to be conjured and besought to reflect—ominous words next!—"that from our Sovereign there can be but one appeal . . ." [126]

Washington felt that this petition to the King would be futile and he would not have voted for that particular resolution if he had not been

---

[124] Fourth resolution, *loc. cit.* The original is sprinkled with meaningless and confusing commas that have been eliminated here.

[125] Eighth resolution, *loc. cit.*, again with the punctuation modernized.

[126] Twenty-third resolution, *loc. cit.*

satisfied that the appeal to the throne would in no wise interfere with action he considered genuinely defensive and perhaps effective. His objection to an agreement that would stop all exports was staked on the same ground, that "if we owe money to Great Britain, nothing but the last necessity can justify the non-payment of it . . ." [127] On virtually all the other Fairfax resolutions, his mind was so firmly convinced that when he returned home and explained to Bryan Fairfax why he had not read that friend's letter to the meeting in Alexandria, he powdered no phrases: ". . . what further proofs are wanted," he said, "to satisfy one of the designs of the ministry than their own acts, which are uniform and plainly tending to the same point, nay, if I mistake not, avowedly to fix the right of taxation? What hope then from petitioning, when they tell us that now or never is the time to fix the matter? Shall we, after this, whine and cry for relief when we have already tried it in vain? Or shall we supinely sit and see one province after another fall a prey to despotism?" [128]

A strong non-importation agreement Washington still regarded as the first imperative. ". . . I think, at least I hope," he wrote Bryan Fairfax, "that there is public virtue enough left among us to deny ourselves everything but the bare necessities of life to accomplish this end." Washington continued: "This we have a right to do, and no power upon earth can compel us to do otherwise, till they have first reduced us to the most abject state of slavery that ever was designed for mankind." [129] He wrote this with all earnestness and then he courteously expressed regret that his views were so much at variance with those of his friend. A few added clauses were as self-revelatory as any of the letters he had written in the seventeen-fifties when his military ambition was soaring: ". . . [I] should much distrust my own judgment upon the occasion, if my nature did not recoil at the thought of submitting to measures which I think subversive of everything that I ought to hold dear and valuable, and did I not find, at the same time, that the voice of mankind is with me" [130]—the old regard for the good opinion of others! It was as strong as ever. He would support the simpler form of resistance, which was non-importation. If that did not suffice, he would join in a pact to withhold all exports to Britain; and if the ministry still

[127] 3 *G. W.*, 233–34.
[128] Letter of July 20, 1774; 3 *G. W.*, 232–33.
[129] *Ibid.*, 234. Mason had used substantially this language in December, 1770. See 1 *Rowland, Mason*, 150 and *supra*, p. 275, n. 50.
[130] 3 *G. W.*, 234.

persisted in denying the Colonies the right of making their own laws
and of imposing their own taxes, then there remained the "one appeal"
from the Sovereign mentioned in the Fairfax resolutions. That was to
the same "last resource" of which Washington had written George
Mason five years previously.[131] Washington had set the very steel in
his soul on full, if patient resistance. Neither fear nor argument could
shake him. In all the earlier discussion he had assumed that somehow,
sometime, differences with Britain would be adjusted. When the Ministry had been particularly inept, he had shared the resentment of the
Colony, but always without thinking of America as separated permanently from Britain. Independence had not been a part of his
political creed. Now his view was changing. Valuable as were the ties
of trade, of defence and of inheritance, a deliberate attempt on the part
of King George's counsellors to deny Colonials their fundamental rights
and to demand their submission, would justify complete separation.
The Boston Port Bill and the related measures of repression did more
than all the previous controversy had, from the days of the Stamp Act
onward, to turn Washington from faith in reconciliation to a belief
that a struggle for independence might be the only recourse of a people
determined to preserve the liberties they always had enjoyed as the
inheritance of free-born Englishmen.[132]

He had a direct duty to perform now. Among the final resolutions
adopted at the meeting in Alexandria on the 18th of July was one that
named him first on a committee empowered to call another general
meeting or "to concert and adopt such measures as may be thought
most expedient and necessary." This involved no immediate action,
but another resolution of the same gathering had named him and
Charles Broadwater to attend the convention the twenty-five Burgesses
had recommended for the 1st of August. Little time remained for the
transaction of private business between the date of appointment and that
of departure, but, fortunately, the season was one in which most of the
calls on Washington were social. By July 28, he had everything in
order and he set out with "Jack" Custis, whom even the charms of a
young wife could not keep at home when there was prospect of gaiety

---

[131] Letter of Apr. 5, 1769; 2 G. W., 500–01. See supra, p. 211.
[132] Cf. Tench Tilghman to his father, Apr. 24, 1778: "I have heard [Washington] declare
a thousand times, and he does it every day in the most public company, that independence was
farthest of anything from his thoughts, and that he never entertained the idea until he plainly
saw that absolute conquest was the aim and unconditional submission the terms which Britain
meant to grant" ([Samuel Alexander Harrison, compiler]: Memoir of Lt. Col. Tench Tilghman, 166).

or excitement or both at Williamsburg in the company of his distinguished "Pappa." [133]

When Washington rode into Williamsburg on the 1st of August, 1774,[134] he found a large number of delegates already there. Others arrived hourly until the convention had more members present than Washington ever had seen at any session of the House of Burgesses.[135] Nearly all the old leaders were in attendance; so were the younger spokesmen of a vigorous policy, with the regretted exception of Thomas Jefferson. He had fallen sick on the way to Williamsburg and had sent on to friends in the convention the text of an uncorrected paper, "A Summary View of the Rights of British America, Set Forth in some Resolutions Intended for the Inspection of the Present Delegates of the People of Virginia, now in Convention." [136] This was laid on the table and was so often read and discussed that it was published immediately. Washington was one of the first purchasers.[137]

He doubtless discovered that a majority of the Delegates were unwilling to go to the full conclusion of Jefferson's argument, but that most of them were in accord with the bulk of the Fairfax County resolutions. Debate must have been primarily over the justice and the expediency of recommending that colonial products be withheld from the British market at the same time that importations from Britain were barred by a binding popular agreement. On the one hand, the argument was that the suspension of all shipments would bring about the speedy repeal of the offending laws against Massachusetts. By some, the contrary policy was advocated, first, because the crop of 1774, half-grown already, had been relied upon by planters as a source of income, and, second, because if tobacco were not sold, honest debts to British merchants could not be paid.[138]

---

[133] 2 *Diaries*, 158, with the itinerary via Eltham.

[134] 2 *Diaries*, 158.

[135] At least this seems to be what he meant to say on August 5 in a letter to Thomas Johnson of Maryland: "We never before had so full a meeting of delegates at any one time, as upon the present occasion" (3 *G. W.*, 236). It is possible he intended to make the comparison between the convention and the previous meetings of "Associators" or Burgesses whose House had been dissolved, but it seems more probable that he used "Delegate" as synonymous with "Burgess" and that the comparison was the one suggested in the text.

[136] It has been reprinted many times. One easily accessible text is in 1 *Force* (4) p. 690 ff; another is in 1 *Jefferson* 184–211. The circumstances of composition, etc. are given in *ibid.*, 183, in Jefferson to John W. Campbell, Sept. 3, 1809; 12 *ibid.*, 307, and in several other letters or notes of Jefferson's later life. See Dumas Malone, *Jefferson and His Time* (cited hereafter as *Malone*) v. 1, p. 181–90, for an admirable summary of the place this paper had in the developing philosophy of the Revolution.

[137] *Ledger B,* folio 120, entry of Aug. 6, 1774 "For Mr. Jefferson's Bill of Rights 3s 9d."

[138] There is no Journal of the Convention of August, 1774, and no unofficial report that is more than fragmentary. Such inferences as seem justified at all must be based on the evidence the finished resolutions and instructions afford of compromises on divisive issues.

Daily deliberations were searching and detailed; the evenings were free, so far as Washington was concerned, of festivities that did not fit the times. He dined out twice only and devoted his spare time to study of the situation [139] and to the transaction of his own business, which included an unpleasant experience with the firm of Hanbury. Younger members of that house of London merchants had protested, though they subsequently paid, a bill of exchange that Washington had drawn on account of "Jack" Custis, whose credit was superlatively good even at those rare intervals when his balance of funds temporarily was not large. The humiliating protest was more than could be endured by a man as jealous of his financial integrity as Washington was. In a coldly polite letter, behind which was manifest wrath, he terminated trade relations that had existed with the Hanburys long before he took over the management of the Custis estate in 1759. [140] It was the second time only, in twenty years of dealing with British merchants, that Washington formally had abandoned correspondence of this nature. The other instance was that of Richard Washington from whom he never had been able to collect a balance of £36 sterling. [141]

While Washington wrote, the Convention reached its decisions. By August 5 there was agreement among the Delegates to accept Philadelphia as the place and September 5 as the time for the meeting of the General Congress. [142] On the 6th, the participants unanimously approved their declaratory resolutions and their instructions to the seven men who were to be sent to Philadelphia to represent Virginia. The opening statement was an uninspired paper that contained few new ideas and did not express the accepted views with the ring of high determination. Import of British goods was to be halted, along with the purchase of newly-entered slaves, as of November 1. Unless "American grievances" were redressed before Aug. 10, 1775, the export of tobacco and of all American products to Britain likewise would be stopped. Most of the other resolutions dealt with the encouragement of industry and the enforcement of the association. One additional pledge was to the effect that if Boston were forced to pay for the tea destroyed in the "party" of Dec. 16, 1773, Virginia would not import or use any tea of the

[139] Cf. his letter of Aug. 7, 1774, to Richard Henry Lee concerning figures on Virginia exports and imports; 3 G. W., 236.

[140] 3 G. W., 234–35.

[141] Letter of Sept. 20, 1765; 385 Papers of G. W., LC; Ledger B, folio 45, charge-off entry of Jan. 1, 1772.

[142] 3 G. W., 235.

East India Company until Boston was recompensed.[143] Still another resolution not anticipated by any previous action of Virginia was to this effect: "Being fully persuaded that the united wisdom of the General Congress may improve these our endeavors to preserve the rights and liberties of British America, we decline enlarging at present; but do hereby resolve that we will conform to and strictly observe all such alterations or additions assented to by the Delegates for this Colony, as they may judge it necessary to adopt, after the same shall be published and made known to us."[144]

Instructions to the Delegates were written in the same spirit and with a stubborn repetition of familiar arguments, to which was added sharp denunciation of arbitrary orders issued not long previously by General Gates in Boston. Pains were taken to make clear the reasons why Virginia did not favor the immediate prohibition of exports. The Delegates were told: "The earnest desire we have to make as quick and full payment as possible of our debts to Great Britain, and to avoid the heavy injury that would arise to this country from the earlier adoption of the non-exportation plan, after the people have already applied so much of their labor to the perfecting of the present crop, by which means they have been prevented from pursuing other methods of clothing and supporting their families, have rendered it necessary to restrain you in this article of non-exportation; but it is our desire that you cordially cooperate with our sister Colonies in General Congress, in such other just and proper methods as they or the majority shall deem necessary for the accomplishment of these valuable ends."[145]

Washington, himself an unimaginative man, may have been altogether content with these resolutions, which reflected his opinions almost to the letter and omitted any reference to another useless petition to the Throne; but there must have been some Delegates who wished that the proposal for united resistance through a General Congress had been proclaimed by Patrick Henry in the full sweep of his eloquence or phrased with the sonority of the resolutions adopted in Hanover County.[146]

---

[143] *Rind's Gazette* of May 26, 1774, had reported the value of the destroyed tea to be £8000. The resolution concerning non-payment was a reversal of the argument advanced soon after the party—that Boston should not be punished until she had been given opportunity of paying for the tea.

[144] Tenth resolution; 1 *Force* (4) p. 688.   [145] *Ibid.*, 689–90.

[146] These resolutions (*ibid.*, p. 615–17) do not appear to have been attributed to any writer and as they were addressed to Henry, they may not be his work, but they have the rhythm of his utterance when his "blood was up."

Even if the declaration did not echo the spirit of Virginia, it was historic in its provision for seven Delegates to the proposed Congress. Who should they be? The Speaker of the House, Moderator of the Convention, was deferentially the first choice. Next on the printed list and probably next by selection, was Richard Henry Lee, whose effort had in large part been responsible for the convention. Washington came next. Then, in order, were Patrick Henry, Richard Bland, Benjamin Harrison and Edmund Pendleton.[147] In the absence of Jefferson, the length of whose disability was uncertain, and the preoccupation of Robert Carter Nicholas with his duties as Treasurer, these seven were the most distinguished members of the House. George Wythe, it will be remembered, was Clerk and not a member. John Randolph, the Attorney General, had royalist sympathies and doubtless would have declined appointment, had he been chosen.[148] When Washington was put on this list, he probably did not regret his election, even though it meant long absence from home; but he could not have realized, by any human power of reason, what that relatively unimportant incident of being chosen one of seven Delegates to a new, experimental Congress was to mean in his life. Had he not been named on the delegation in 1774, he might not have been known to Northern members of Congress the next year and . . .

Now he had to ride back to Mount Vernon, with the £90 voted each delegate for expenses,[149] and had to arrange his affairs in the knowledge that, if all went well, Patrick Henry would join him at his house on the 30th and would go with him to Philadelphia.[150] Strangely enough, both the principal incidents of the days that preceded the start for the Quaker City concerned the sons of that good friend William Fairfax who gave him the news that led him to tender his services in 1753 for what proved to be his first great adventure—the journey to Fort Le Boeuf.[151] George William Fairfax was gone, gone permanently; the contents of

---

[147] *Ibid.*, p. 689. The familiar story that each of these men was selected because of his special qualities (see 1 *W. W. Henry*, 196, with citation of 1 Tucker's *Jefferson*, 63) probably is mythical.

[148] In 1 *Meade*, 220, quoted in 1 *W. W. Henry*, 197, there appears, incorrectly printed, part of a letter of Oct. 1, 1774, wherein Roger Atkinson described to James Pleasants the characteristics of the seven Delegates. According to the text in 15 *V* 356 Atkinson said of Washington: "[He] was bred a soldier—a warrior, and distinguished himself in early life before and at the death of the unfortunate but intrepid Braddock. He is a modest man, but sensible and speaks little—in action cool, like a Bishop at his prayers."

[149] *Ledger B*, folio 30.

[150] This was arranged before Washington left Williamsburg. See 3 *G. W.*, 236.

[151] See Vol. I, p. 273.

Belvoir were for sale; Washington had to assume some of the direction of this sad vendue.[152] He was improving his own house at the time and he bought furniture, fittings, carpets and utensils on August 15 at a total cost of £169. Included were a mahogany chest of drawers, a mahogany sideboard, the dining room chairs and window curtains, a large looking glass in a gilt frame, and the coverlets, pillows and bolsters that probably included Sally's own.[153] It was grim business to have men and women of every station peering and poking through the handsome chambers of that beloved house, but it was consoling to know that some of the furnishings most delightfully associated with Belvoir would adorn Mount Vernon. By no means the whole of the effects was sold on the 15th; another auction would be held in the late autumn.

The other experience with the Fairfaxes that August was an attempted renewal by Bryan of the argument which the committeemen on the bench had declined to read to the meeting on the 18th of July at Alexandria. Bryan had felt some dissatisfaction that his views had not been made known, especially when his one avowed supporter in the audience told him afterward that a "great many" were of his opinion but felt that it would be useless to speak in opposition to the committee.[154] In a few days, Fairfax overcame his feeling on the subject and disavowed any desire to create a party, but he held to his views and wrote Washington a disquisition of some 2500 words on the rights of Parliament and of colonials.[155] Washington read it but realized that where opinions were as far apart as his and Fairfax's it was useless to argue. His answer was modest and at the same time convinced: ". . . I am sure I have no new lights to throw upon the subject, or any other argument to offer in support of my own doctrine, than what you have seen; and could only in general add that an innate spirit of freedom first told me that the measures which administration hath for some time been, and now are most violently pursuing, are repugnant to every principle of natural justice; whilst much abler heads than my own hath fully convinced me that it is not only repugnant to natural right, but subversive of the law and constitution of Great Britain itself . . ."[156] There he stood: his "innate spirit of freedom" was his rock.

---

[152] The advertisement of the property for lease appeared in the *Va. Gazette* of Sept. 25, 1774 and in the *Penn. Gazette* of Oct. 19, 1774, and is conveniently at hand in *Conway's Barons*, 216. In *ibid.*, 218, is the inventory of the goods sold Aug. 15, 1774.
[153] *Havemeyer MSS*, L. W. Smith *Coll.*   [154] 5 *Hamilton*, 34–35.
[155] *Ibid.*, 34–44.   [156] 3 *G. W.*, 240–41.

One more duty remained. It was infinitesimal in comparison with the future of a continent but it was personal and, in its small way, reflected some of the determination Washington had displayed in this new conflict with Britain. The affairs of Mrs. Savage still were his to carry, because her husband had sought an injunction in chancery when the hand of the law was about to be laid on the money he was withholding from his wife.[157] As the law fixing officers' fees had expired and had not been renewed before the Assembly was dissolved, the courts temporarily were stalled. Washington painstakingly explained all this to Mrs. Savage's benefactress in Dublin, and he carefully reminded her that Mrs. Savage's bond was devisable. The cheated woman should make a will, he said, because it would be "wrong to suffer the small pittance she reserved to herself [at] the time of her unhappy marriage to fall into the hands of a v——n who has not only endeavored to wrong [her] of it but would, I suppose, deprive her of the very means of existence if he could do it." [158] Washington would see to it that Savage did not succeed. The interest of a defrauded wife would not be disregarded even when he was about to begin a struggle with a King.

The time for that struggle was at hand. Punctually on the 30th of August, Patrick Henry arrived at Mount Vernon. With him was Edmund Pendleton, likewise bound for Philadelphia as a Delegate.[159] George Mason came also, spent the night, and the next day discoursed no doubt on the rights of free peoples and the blindness of rulers. Henry listened and shared—"the first man upon this continent," in the opinion of Mason. The counsel of Pendleton was as always conservative but penetrating. Washington probably said little and that little not argumentative. His mind was made up. All through the morning they reasoned and planned. Then, after dinner, the three delegates bade Mason goodbye and started for the ferry.

Mason, Henry, Pendleton, Washington—history was cheated when no record was made of what they said that August day. History? They went their way to make it!

---

[157] See *supra*, p. 288, 337, 346.   [158] 3 *G. W.*, 244, slightly repunctuated.
[159] As noted *supra*, Washington's information on the 7th of August (3 *G. W.*, 236), was that Henry would travel via Mount Vernon. Nothing was said then of Pendleton's intention to be a welcome third traveller. He may have notified Washington subsequent to the 7th.

CHAPTER XVI

A Delegate Glimpses a Continent
(September–October, 1774)

When Washington, Henry and Pendleton reached Philadelphia on the 4th of September, 1774,[1] they found Delegates assembling from all the Colonies except Georgia. The day was the Sabbath but by no means all the bustle was of church going.[2] Introductions were being made; invitations to dinner were tendered and accepted, luggage was moved to visitors' lodgings.[3] Washington himself spent the night at the home of his friend, Dr. William Shippen, already a distinguished physician and anatomist.[4] After breakfasting there the next morning, Washington went to the City Tavern[5] where the Delegates were to meet. His five earlier visits to the city—one of them in the previous year—made him feel at home. On its face, moreover, the work ahead was in a measure similar to that which he had performed for fifteen years as a member of Virginia House of Burgesses, but the drama was tenser and on a continental stage. At Williamsburg, Washington knew all the powerful Burgesses, played cards with some of them, and served on committee with two score. Here he was on friendly terms with several of the Maryland and Pennsylvania Delegates, as well as with his colleagues from Virginia, but most of the other Delegates were strangers to him.[6]

At the tavern it was explained that the Pennsylvania Assembly had voted the Congress the use of the State House and that the carpenters of the city had offered their handsome hall for the meeting. Although Washington may have been unaware of it, politics were involved: The

[1] Their itinerary, via Annapolis and the Eastern Shore of Maryland, is given in 2 Diaries, 162.
[2] For two of the religious services of the day, see 2 John Adams, 364. This citation is from John Adams's Diary, which is one of the basic documents of the Congress of 1774.
[3] 2 Diaries, 162; John Adams, loc. cit.; E. C. Burnett, ed., Letters of Members of the Continental Congress (cited hereafter as Burnett), v. 1, p. 5.
[4] 2 Diaries, 162–63. An acceptable sketch, with a good bibliography, will be found in DAB.
[5] Called by others the New Tavern or Smith's Tavern (1 Burnett, 8 n).
[6] Strictly speaking, it cannot be established that he knew any of the Delegates other than those of the three Colonies named, but on such a question there manifestly cannot be certainty.

THE POLL THAT STARTED WASHINGTON ON HIS WAY

To a gentleman's sporting interest in politics is due the unique document reproduced on the adjoining page. When the Delegates to the Virginia Convention of Aug. 1, 1774, assembled, they elected a secretary who kept minutes that apparently were not printed or preserved. All that survive of official records are a summary made public after adjournment and the credentials of the men chosen on the 5th to represent Virginia in the proposed Continental Congress. Fortunately, Edmund Berkeley of Middlesex County wished to see how the "candidates" were esteemed. After the balloting, he wrote on a blank page of his copy of the *Virginia Almanac* for 1774 the result of the poll. Washington stood third on the list with ninety-eight votes compared to 104 for "Mr. Speaker" Peyton Randolph, and 100 for Richard Henry Lee. Fourth on the list was Patrick Henry, with eighty-nine. Then followed Richard Bland, Benjamin Harrison and Edmund Pendleton.

The significance of the penciled figures to the right is not certain. A natural guess would be that a second ballot was taken, with a considerable shift in the standing of the men chosen. One objection to this theory is that all seven of those at the top of the list had a majority vote. Besides, on the credentials filed with the Continental Congress, the order of the Delegates' names is that of the first poll. Had the penciled list been followed in making out the credentials, Pendleton would have been the fifth instead of the seventh. It may have been, of course, that the Secretary was at fault, or that the first vote was taken with no clear understanding of the number to be sent. On a second vote the next day for seven, most of those who had voted for Thomas Nelson and for Thomas Jefferson may have "switched." As this concerns Washington, it means that if there was a second ballot, he polled 106 and stood next to Peyton Randolph, who had 107. In its wider bearings, Edmund Berkeley's list is the first extant document to record the decisive step in the rise of George Washington as a continental leader. Suppose he had stood eighth on the list and had not gone to the First Continental Congress—could he have had the opportunity that came to him the next year?

(Through the Generosity of Francis L. Berkeley, Jr., University of Virginia, Owner of the Original)

Delegates

Peyt: Randolph — — — 104
R: H: Lee — — — — — 100
Geo. Washington — — 98
P. Henry — — — — 89
Rich: Bland — — — 79
Benj: Harrison — — 66
Edm: Pendleton — — 62
Thos: Nelson — — — 51
Thos: Jefferson — — 51
T. Mason — — — 16
Jas: Mercer — — — 7
F. L: Lee — — — — 4
Archd: Cary — — — 4
R: C: Nicholas — — 4

A MOUNT VERNON GUEST WHO LATER
PLAGUED HIS HOST

No portraits of demonstrable authenticity exist of Charles Lee or of Benedict Arnold—a regrettable gap in the picture gallery of the American Revolution. Had a discerning artist painted either of these men, it might be possible to read in their faces some characteristics that would help to explain their acts. Ironically, the lineaments of Charles Lee survive only in two cartoons, one a crude affair by Thaddeus Kosciusko, the other a skillful, mocking sketch by Barham Rushbrooke, made in 1776, after Lee had returned from Poland. Kosciusko's effort is reproduced in the *Pennsylvania Magazine of History and Biography*, v. 15, p. 26; Rushbrooke's, reprinted on the facing page, was said to be recognizable. The uniform is that of an aide to King Stanislaus; Lee's companion is of the species he esteemed above humankind.

Charles Lee had in America the reputation he assured all his admirers he enjoyed in Europe. He wished the revolutionary officers to believe that he was one of the "great captains of the age" and he spoke of his acquirements with a respect that proved contagious. In New England, his dirty habits and obscenity gave offense in 1775, but he was endured for what he was supposed to know. It was the same at all his subsequent stations—New York, Virginia, South Carolina, and again in New York. When his counsel was lost to America temporarily, by reason of the events described in Chapter X of Volume IV, Congress was most solicitous for his safety and comfort.

When he returned, it was as a conqueror. The rest was anticlimax, set forth in Volume V, but the whole story of his adventures in America was not known until 1858. No personality of the Revolution arouses quite the same curiosity that Charles Lee does: what manner of individual was he in his heart? Those warm friendships that he professed, were they real? Had he any deep loyalties? Washington attempted no more of an answer than that Lee was "fickle" and in that belief he always was cautious in his dealings with his senior lieutenant. An enigma Lee was—and still is.

carpenters were adherents of the cause of the Colonies; the State House was the stronghold of a conservative element, under the leadership of Joseph Galloway, a cold, austere man of approximately Washington's age.[7] Delegates decided to view both places, but when they examined the Carpenters' Hall, they liked it so much that a member asked whether they need look any further. In questioning this, a Delegate from Massachusetts spoke up, a man of middle height or slightly below it, somewhat stout, with a large round head, a wide brow and kindly, half-humorous eyes. If Washington had not heard his name and had not identified him earlier he did so now—John Adams, lawyer, aged thirty-nine. Adams's argument was not heeded; the hall was accepted; the Congress proceeded to organize; Peyton Randolph was unanimously named Speaker; Charles Thomson of Philadelphia was made Clerk.

Argument began almost immediately over a motion to name a committee to draw up "regulations" for the Congress. This motion was construed to involve determination of the fundamental if disturbing question, whether each Colony should have one vote or a number proportionate to the population. In due time, Washington saw Patrick Henry rise, dressed in parson's gray,[8] and heard his colleague maintain that the heavily peopled Colonies should have the larger vote. The orator soon warmed to his theme and, as in Virginia, had his audience breathless with suspense and emotion. His peak was reached in the cry that distinctions among the Colonies had been effaced. "I am not a Virginian," Henry protested, "but an American."[9] His argument, no less than his eloquence, deepened the favorable impression the resolutions of the Virginia Convention had made in advance of the Congress.[10] The individual members from His Majesty's Old Dominion appealed to Silas Deane as "sociable, sensible and spirited."[11] To John Adams they seemed to be "the most spirited and consistent of any delegation."[12]

Bland, Pendleton and probably Lee spoke during the initial sitting of the Congress or the next, when the decision was to allow each Colony

---

[7] Cf. Silas Deane to Mrs. Deane, Sept. 5–6, 1774; 1 *Burnett*, 11.

[8] Thomson, quoted second hand, in 1 *Burnett*, 10 n.

[9] 2 *John Adams*, 367. In Wirt (*op. cit.*, 106) is a fanciful description of this speech, the only reports of which are those of John Adams (*op. cit.*, v. 2, p. 365, 366) and James Duane (1 *Burnett*, 12). Neither of these men spoke of Henry's deliverance as if it had been sensational, but the tradition of the effect on the audience probably is founded on fact.

[10] Cf. 2 *John Adams*, 352, entry of August 23: ". . . the spirit of the people is prodigious; their resolutions are really grand."

[11] See his letter of Sept. 1–3, 1774 to Mrs. Deane in 1 *Burnett*, 4. Cf. Caesar Rodney in *ibid.*, 27.

[12] 2 *John Adams*, 362.

a single and equal vote.[13] The second and third days of the Congress were exciting. After the Delegates had met on the morning of the 6th, an express from the North brought confused rumors that Boston had been bombarded by cannon of the British garrison that occupied the town. Details were lacking. Before the most apprehensive member could conclude that artillery fire had been opened, he had to piece together and accept all the strange tales the express had heard.[14] Massachusetts men scarcely could believe such a crime had occurred, but they displayed an intense concern that all the Delegates shared. "Every gentleman," John Adams wrote his wife, "seems to consider the bombardment of Boston as the bombardment of the capital of his own province."[15]

In their uncertainty and dismay, members were conscious of the need of Divine Guidance, and were sympathetic with a proposal that the proceedings be opened with prayer. The embarrassment was that of selecting a clergyman without seeming to favor a particular creed. At length, as Washington listened and observed, a man of medium height, muscular and well knit, arose and addressed the chair. Although his hand was palsied and his hair prematurely frosted, he was in his early forties. His eyes were of a steel gray, his nose prominent, his expression mobile. This was Samuel Adams, the most conspicuous and boldest of the New England leaders, who now proposed to drop all religious differences and to request a minister of the Established Church to conduct prayers. By vote, an invitation was extended Rev. Jacob Duché.[16] The next morning, September 7, the minister duly appeared in his vestments, and, after the opening sentences, read the Psalter for the day, the Thirty-fifth Psalm. Every man thought of the reported bombardment of Boston as the clergyman began:

"Plead thou my cause, O Lord, with them that strive with me: and fight thou against them that fight against me.

[13] Here arises a problem similar to that of dating certain of the entries in Washington's Journal of 1748: It is difficult, in some instances, to tell from members' letters whether the events described by them occurred on the day the Delegates wrote or on the preceding day. This doubt does not invalidate or even affect the narrative of any day of important proceedings but it sometimes confuses. James Duane's account of Henry's speech, for example, would leave the impression that it was delivered on the second, rather than on the first day of the Congress (see 1 *Burnett*, 12). The probability is that the debate over the vote of the different Colonies covered two days, but of this there is no proof. [14] 2 *John Adams*, 368.

[15] Letter of Sept. 8, 1774, in C. F. Adams, ed., *Familiar Letters of John Adams and His Wife Abigail Adams, During the Revolution* (cited hereafter as *Adams, Fam. Let.*) p. 31.

[16] 1 *JCC.*, 26–27, with references to the contemporary accounts of this incident.

"Lay hand upon the shield and buckler: and stand up to help me.

"Bring forth the spear, and stop the way against them that persecute me: say unto my soul, I am thy salvation."[17]

As John Adams wrote, "It seemed as if Heaven had ordained that Psalm to be read on that morning." After the collect and some of the prayers of the day, Duché delivered a prayer of his own composition that "filled every bosom."[18]

Almost in direct answer to prayer, as it seemed, expresses who arrived on the 8th reported that the rumors of the bombardment of Boston had no better basis than the seizure of the Colony's powder at Charlestown.[19] The emotions of the day were not buried with its fears. Memory both of the terror and of the Psalm was kept alive while Congress briskly decided that the debates should be secret and behind closed doors, and that two committees be named. One of these, consisting of two members from each of the Provinces, was "to state the rights of the Colonies in general, the several instances in which these rights are violated or infringed, and the means most proper to be pursued for obtaining a restoration of them."[20] The second committee, including one representative of each delegation, was "to examine and report the several statutes which affect the trade and manufactures of the Colonies."[21]

As Washington was not appointed to either of these committees,[22] he had no official duties to discharge during the period from September 8 to September 17 when the Congress merely adjourned from day to day or, at most, received a new Delegate and approved his credentials.[23] These days were not wasted. They constituted the first period of the work of the Congress, the period during which the prime duty of every member was to become acquainted with the other Delegates. In this, Washington's own experience was typical. With colleagues, he dined almost daily at the home of some conspicuous and hospitable Pennsylvanian, where talk ranged far.[24] It was the largest, longest opportunity Washington ever had enjoyed of conversing with men of station

---

[17] *Adams, Fam. Let.,* 37.
[18] 2 *John Adams,* 368–69. Cf. 1 *JCC,* 27.
[19] 1 *Burnett,* 20.
[20] 1 *JCC.,* 26.
[21] *Ibid.* John Adams's later description in his Autobiography of the function of these two committees was manifestly in error (2 *John Adams,* 373).
[22] Richard Henry Lee and Edmund Pendleton were named from Virginia to the first committee, and Henry to the second (1 *JCC.,* 28–29).
[23] *Ibid.,* 29–31.
[24] The list of his dinner engagements, but not the names of fellow guests, appears in 2 *Diaries,* 163–64.

from all the Colonies. He was advantaged in making the most of their educational discourse, both because he was a good listener and because he was treated with deference and courtesy. His reputation as a soldier was known; his wealth was exaggerated. Silas Deane wrote his wife: "Colonel Washington is nearly as tall a man as Colonel Fitch,[25] and almost as hard a countenance; yet with a very young look, and an easy, soldier like air and gesture. He does not appear above forty-five,[26] yet was in the first actions in 1753 and 1754, on the Ohio, and in 1755 was with Braddock, and was the means of saving the remains of that unfortunate army. It is said that in the House of Burgesses in Virginia, on hearing of the Boston Port Bill, he offered to raise and arm and lead one thousand men himself at his own expense, for the defence of the country, were there need of it.[27] His fortune is said to be equal to such an undertaking."[28] Where Washington already was the subject of talk of this sort, guests at sumptuous Philadelphia dinners were apt to address many of their remarks to him.

They were likely, also, to take particular pains to answer his questions; but Washington did not rely altogether on this method of extending his knowledge of the issues before the Congress and the country. Philadelphia at this time, as previously, had a press that was quick to print pamphlets [29] and it now had both supply and demand. In some of these political papers, Washington invested more than seventeen shillings [30] and he doubtless read from his purchases during the rare evenings [31] he spent alone at his lodgings. Occasionally there were card-games, in which Washington fared somewhat better than usual,[32] but more frequently able men engaged in speculative, informative discussion of the work of the Congress and of a thousand things besides.

As he moved among the Delegates, Washington must have seen, as others did, that during this first period of the Congress, the difficulty of

[25] This evidently was Col. Thomas Fitch of Norwalk, Conn., (1725–95), son of Gov. Thomas Fitch. Traditionally, Colonel Fitch was the original Yankee Doodle Dandy. See Roscoe C. Fitch, *History of the Fitch Family*, v. 1, p. 136–48 and F. B. Dexter, *Yale Graduates*, 2nd Ser., p. 79—two references generously supplied by Clarence S. Brigham.

[26] Deane evidently did not know that Washington was only six years older than he was.

[27] This unfounded story had preceded Washington to Philadelphia. John Adams heard it, August 31, from Thomas Lynch, one of the Delegates from South Carolina (2 *Adams*, 360).

[28] Letter of Sept. 10, 1774 to Mrs. Deane; 1 *Burnett*, 28.

[29] Cf. Washington's own experience with his Journal of 1754; vol. II, p. 236–37.

[30] *Ledger B*, folio 125.   [31] 2 *Diaries*, 163–65.

[32] Cf. *Ledger B*, folio 125, entry of Oct. 30, 1774: "To cash won at cards during stay in Philadelphia, £7. 0. 0." Entries in his *Pocket Day Book* of 1772–74 (Washington MSS, Huntington Library) show that on three evenings between October 9 and 20 he was net winner by more than £6.

becoming acquainted was more serious than would have been thought. Private dinners helped to overcome this, and so did a great entertainment given by Philadelphians at the City Tavern on September 16;[33] but lack of previous contact made some of the Delegates a little awkward, not to say suspicious, in dealing with strangers, even though all were met for the same purpose. As the Connecticut members subsequently wrote their Governor, "An Assembly like this, though it consists of less than sixty members, yet, coming from remote Colonies, each of which has some modes of transacting public business peculiar to itself, some particular provincial rights and interest to guard and secure, must take some time to become so acquainted with each one's situation and connections, as to be able to give an united assent to the ways and means proposed for effecting what all are ardently desirous of."[34]

Most of the Delegates were impressed, also, by the magnitude and intricacy of the task assigned them. The humble-minded were disturbed by their lack of familiarity with the problems of neighbors whose cause was now theirs.[35] Some members, too, who were esteemed eminent in their own Colony felt they must vindicate their reputation by eloquence and profundity. "Every man in [the Congress]," John Adams was to write wearily, "is a great man, an orator, a critic, a statesman; and therefore every man on every question must show his oratory, his criticism, and his political abilities."[36] The prominence of the conservative Joseph Galloway in the Pennsylvania delegation and in the social life of Philadelphia led some of the members to shake their heads. Galloway's pipes might lead them far afield. Instead of leaving them to determine how the manifest wrongs of the Colonies could be righted, he and his followers might compel the members to discuss, ad infinitum, the natural rights of man[37] and the precise limits of the constitutional authority of Parliament. Further, some of the Massachusetts Delegates were fearful their Colony would be considered quarrelsome and revolutionary, and they were convinced they must proceed with great circum-

---

[33] Approximately 500 were present; more than two score toasts were proposed (*Phila. Journal*, Sept. 21, 1774).

[34] Letter of Oct. 10, 1774; 1 *Burnett*, 70.

[35] *Ibid.*, 45, 60, 62, and frequently, almost repetitiously, in John Adams's Diary and letters.

[36] 1 *Burnett*, 66–67. Cf. Adams's Diary, Oct. 10, 1774, cited in *ibid.*, 67.

[37] Galloway in 1 *Burnett*, 22; 2 *John Adams*, 373 ff. Some caution is suggested in the use of John Adams's Autobiography, which the second of these references quotes. Needless to say, Adams's intellectual honesty was above dispute, but he wrote his unfinished account of his life soon after his retirement from office in 1801 (see 1 *John Adams*, 604 and 2 *ibid.*, 375 n), without consulting the records. Inevitably, his recollection of some of the events of 1774 was confused, though he retained the "feel" of the times.

spection and restraint if they were to win the support of all British America.[38] The leaders of the Bay Colony would have been surprised during the early days of the session had they known that a Delaware member, Caesar Rodney, was writing his younger brother, "the Bostonians who (we know) have been condemned by many for their violence are moderate men when compared to Virginia, South Carolina and Rhode Island." [39]

The cautious fencing and the deliberate finesse, the suspicious aloofness and the formal delivery of ciceronian speeches, took a realistic turn with the first major event of the session, the submission to Congress on September 17 of resolutions adopted on the 6th by citizens of Suffolk County, Massachusetts.[40] The paper was an ordered, vigorous and somewhat rhetorical statement of the position the people of Boston and its vicinity had taken in their controversy with the Crown, with Governor Hutchinson, who now was in England, and with General Gage. If those "Suffolk Resolves" in most respects were merely a restatement of the colonial defence of liberties, they had an undertone of defiance and this bold endorsement of reprisal: In event any of the leaders of the popular cause were arrested, the people should "seize and keep in safe custody every servant of the present tyrannical and unconstitutional government throughout the County and Province, until the persons so apprehended be liberated from the hands of our adversaries and restored safe and uninjured to their respective friends and families." [41] The author of these resolutions, Dr. Joseph Warren, had been instructed by the meeting which adopted them to wait on Gage with a committee and to express the County's alarm over the military preparations the British troops were making. Warren and his fellow-committeemen accordingly had prepared an address to the General in the same spirit of the resolves. One stiff sentence of this address had been sharpened on both its antithetical edges: it informed Gage that the men of Massachusetts had resolved "never to submit" to the repressive acts of Parliament, "but have no inclination to commence a war with his Majesty's troops . . ." [42] At first the British Commander

---

[38] This note runs through John Adams's correspondence during the early days of the Congress.

[39] Letter to Thomas Rodney, Sept. 9, 1774; 1 *Burnett*, 27.

[40] These resolutions were brought to Philadelphia by Paul Revere and were delivered on the 16th to the Massachusetts Delegates (1 *JCC.*, 39 n).

[41] Resolve No. 13; 1 *JCC.*, 35.

[42] *Ibid.*, 38.

and now the Congress might wonder how keen the cutting edge of that sharp verb "commence" would prove to be.

Boston, in a word, was expressing the full argument of the colonial cause and was serving notice sternly that reprisal would be the answer to arrest, that scuffs would be returned as blows, and, if need be, that war would be met with war. The principle in all this was one that Washington long previously had decided for himself. To his way of thinking, Massachusetts' determined stand did not justify hesitation or warrant discussion. The position was right, and, being right, must be defended. Congress' answer was equally decisive and in the same spirit, and was given that very day, September 17, after what must have been brief, undissenting debate: "Resolved unanimously that this assembly deeply feels the suffering of their countrymen in the Massachusetts Bay, under the operation of the late unjust, cruel, and oppressive acts of the British Parliament, that they most thoroughly approve the wisdom and fortitude, with which opposition to these wicked ministerial measures has hitherto been conducted, and they earnestly recommend to their brethren a perseverance in the same firm and temperate conduct . . . trusting that the effects of the united efforts of North America in their behalf will carry such conviction to the British nation of the unwise, unjust and ruinous policy of the present administration as quickly to introduce better men and wiser measures." A second resolution called for a continuance of gifts to the needy of Boston.[43]

This measure delighted and relieved the members from Massachusetts[44] at the same time that it afforded an opportunity of testing the sentiment of Congress as a whole. Thereafter, in what proved to be the second period of the life of the Congress, more confidence was shown in preparing the committee reports and in urging resolutions on the floor of the Congress, though there still was caution and a lack of planning and leadership. "Our business . . . proceeds slow," Silas Deane wrote with a measure of good cheer, "but it is not in consequence of any divisions or altercation in the Congress, but from the vast, extensive and lasting importance of the questions before us."[45] Convinced and impatient Delegates were willing to go more slowly if all the Colonies would move together. Unity was worth the time spent in assuring it. By the 22nd, Delegates were agreed that the entire continent

[43] 1 JCC., 39–40. [44] Cf. 1 Burnett, 34, 35, 37.
[45] Letter to Mrs. Deane, Sept. 23, 1774; 1 Burnett, 45.

should enter into a non-importation pact, a traitor-proof "association." Consequently, by resolution, merchants were advised to send no new orders to England and to call for the suspension of outstanding orders there until Congress decided on the scope of the covenant it would recommend.[46]

That same day, September 22, a report was presented by the committee named to set forth the rights of America and their infringement by Parliament and the Ministry. Consideration of this document was deferred until the 24th when to the relief of those who feared abstract discussion would be endless, the decision was to limit the review of violated colonial rights to events after 1763, the year of the first agitation in Parliament to make America bear part of the direct costs of garrisoning the western frontier.[47]

It probably was while members were debating a report on these violated rights that Washington received from the hand of a homeward-bound Virginian a letter written him by his friend and former Captain, Robert Mackenzie, who now was a Lieutenant in the 43rd Foot and was stationed in Boston.[48] The strife in that city was the theme of Mackenzie's letter. He spoke of the citizens' "fixed aim at total independence, of the weakness and temper of the main springs that set the whole in motion" and of the necessity that "abler heads and better hearts should draw a line for their guidance . . ." Mackenzie then went on to explain that the recent British fortification of Boston had been necessitated by the "rebellious and numerous meetings of men in arms, their scandalous and ungenerous attacks upon the best characters in the Province, obliging them to save their lives by flight, and their repeated but feeble threats to dispossess the troops . . ."[49]

Washington read and disagreed and put the letter by for answer when a decision had been reached on two questions that now had developed in the Congress. The first of these was the date when a proposed non-importation agreement should become effective. After debating the choice between November 1 and December 1,[50] the Congress was unanimous for the later date.[51] The second question was consideration

---

[46] 1 *JCC.*, 41.

[47] 1 *JCC.*, 41, 42. See the explanation given by the South Carolina Delegates (1 *Burnett*, 85).

[48] Washington, it will be remembered, had expressed in November, 1760, his interest in Mackenzie's transfer to the regular establishment. See 3 *Hamilton*, 193 and 2 *G. W.*, 355.

[49] 5 *Hamilton*, 49–50.

[50] See Adams's notes of the debates in 1 *Burnett*, 48–49.

[51] 1 *JCC.*, 43.

or deliberate disregard of a plan of settlement put forward on September 28 by Joseph Galloway. He had a vast design for the Colonies, a Grand Council, with an elected membership that was to meet annually and was to possess "all the like rights, liberties and privileges, as are held and exercised by and in the House of Commons of Great Britain." A President General was to direct affairs in which Great Britain and one or more of the Colonies were concerned. He and the Grand Council were to "be an inferior and distinct branch of the British legislature, united and incorporated with it . . ." Either Parliament or the Grand Council should have authority to originate and enact "general regulations" for the Colonies, but the assent of both legislative bodies would be required to make effective these meekly named and feebly disguised statutes at large.[52]

Objection to the Pennsylvanian's plan was immediate and varied—that action on it would be beyond the authority given the Delegates, that it reduced the ancestral rights of the Colonies, that it made changes in legislative practice concerning which the Delegates first should consult the Assemblies, and that it set up a general legislature which might be bribed precisely as Parliament was.[53] Washington's colleagues, Richard Henry Lee and Patrick Henry, were among the critics of Galloway's proposal[54] and were influential in having it laid aside, six votes to five, for future consideration. In the debate of this outline, Washington had no hand, but the contents of the paper may have been among the subjects Washington and Richard Henry Lee discussed that afternoon with John Adams and the other members of the Massachusetts delegation.[55]

[52] Except for bills which the Grand Council might pass in wartime for granting aid to the Crown (1 *JCC.*, 49–50).

[53] 1 *Burnett*, 53. [54] *Ibid.*, 59.

[55] 2 *Diaries*, 165; 2 *John Adams*, 386. In *MHSP.*, 1858–60, p. 69, Charles F. Adams interpreted Mackenzie's letter, quoted *supra*, as designed to "prejudice [Washington's] mind against the action of the people of Massachusetts, and to induce him to exert his influence to counteract the policy their Delegates were advocating in Philadelphia." A visit Washington paid Adams and others on September 28 was said by C. F. Adams to have convinced the Virginian that the men of the Bay Colony were not "noisy, brawling demagogues, meaning mischief only," but were "plain, downright practical men, seeking safety from oppression and contemplating violence only as a result of an absolute necessity forced on them by the government at home." This conference, said C. F. Adams, removed all Washington's doubts, "if he had any," concerning the sound patriotism of the Massachusetts representatives. It is not believed that Charles Francis Adams could have made such a statement if the records now available had been at his command when he wrote in 1857 or 1858. Washington had condemned the violence of the Boston "Indians" and the destruction of the tea, but there is not a shred of evidence to indicate that he was in the least doubt concerning the character of the Massachusetts Delegates or the justice of the course they were pursuing. It is inconceivable that Washington, after three weeks with the spokesmen of the Bay Colony, should have failed to appreciate them. There was no

By the date of its vote to defer consideration of the Galloway proposals, the Congress had been in session more than three weeks, and,
in positive enactment, had done nothing more than to express support
of Boston and to agree that a non-importation plan was to come into
operation December 1. John Adams had to complain, "Tedious indeed
is our business—slow as snails"; and he reverted to issues that should by
this time have been resolved or, at worst, simplified: "Fifty gentlemen
meeting together, all strangers, are not acquainted with each other's
language, ideas, views, designs." He added, "They are therefore jealous
of each other—fearful, timid, skittish." [56] In contrast, his cousin Samuel
Adams, the real leader of the opposition in Boston to Hutchinson and
to Gage, was displaying unwonted patience: "[The Delegates]," Samuel
wrote Doctor Warren, "have not yet come to final resolutions." Adams
explained: "It becomes them to be deliberate. I have been assured, in
private conversation with individuals, that, if you should be driven to
the necessity of acting in the defence of your lives or liberty, you would
be justified by their constituents, and openly supported by all the means
in their power"; but beyond that, Samuel Adams was not sure. "It is of
the greatest importance," he exhorted, "that the American opposition
should be united, and that it should be conducted so as to concur with
the opposition of our friends in England." [57]

Absence of planning continued to give the Congress a winding path;
impatience and caution made an uncertain team. In the fourth week of
the Congress they pulled now forward, now backward, until progress
seemed to be measured in single resolutions, after each of which there
would be a pause for panting. On the 30th of September, the Congress
resolved to recommend that no American products be exported after
Sept. 10, 1775, unless the grievances of the Colonies were redressed
before that date. A committee, of which Washington was not a member, received instructions to bring in a plan for "carrying into effect the
non-importation, non-consumption and non-exportation resolved on." [58]
The day after this was ordered, the Congress decided to have a loyal

---

reason, moreover, why conference between the Virginians and the Massachusetts Delegates had
to do with this question, or with this one only. Aside from Galloway's plan, the policy to be
pursued on exportation was a single item of several questions Washington and Lee may have
wished to discuss with the spokesmen of the Bay Colony. They doubtless had been together on
numerous social occasions, as, for example, at Chief Justice Chew's dinner on the 22nd of
September. See 2 *John Adams*, 381.

[56] Letter of Sept. 25, 1774, to Mrs. Adams; 1 *Burnett*, 47.
[57] Letter of Sept. 25, 1774; *ibid*.   [58] 1 *JCC.*, 51, 53.

address to the King prepared, though many regarded this as a futile and humiliating plea for indulgence when the issue was one of rights. Two consequential resolves, spaced forty-eight hours apart as if by design, were that the address to the King should set forth the willingness of the Colonies to pay their just taxes, and, next, that the address should assure his Majesty the repeal of the obnoxious laws would remove the grievances of the Colonies.[59] Every detail of this was debated at sittings which began at 9 A.M. and continued until 3 in the afternoon. At 4, most of the Delegates would dine, and frequently at the table of wealthy Philadelphians who served ample meat and abundant wine. After hungry, tired men had filled themselves, most of them could do little more for the remainder of the day than to sit and talk or to play cards.[60] It was expensive, it continued to be wasteful of time as well as of money, but it remained useful, in a cumulative sense, because it was breaking down one provincial barrier after another and was bringing the Delegates to see more clearly, even amid gathering clouds, that theirs was a common cause that called for a joint defence.

In the fifth week of the Congress came a letter on October 6 from the Boston Committee of Correspondence, which described the stern military rule there and asked the advice of the Congress [61] on the course the people should follow. Congress' first decision, duly matured, was to name a committee to draft a letter of protest to General Gage.[62] Not content with that, the Congress spent a day of sharpening discussion and came to the sternest resolution Delegates thus far had adopted—"that this Congress approve of the opposition by the inhabitants of the Massachusetts-bay to the execution of the late acts of Parliament; and if the same shall be attempted to be carried into execution by force, in such case, all America ought to support them in their opposition." [63] In another day's deliberations, October 10, the people of Boston were advised not to leave their town unless compelled to do so; but they were told that if the provincial Council should consider removal of the population necessary, the Congress would recommend that all America contribute toward making good the loss citizens would sustain. Further, the people were counselled to dispense, where practicable, with the administration of justice, if it could not be procured "in a legal and peaceable manner" under the charter and the laws of the Colony.

[59] *Ibid.*, 53, 54, 54–55.
[61] 1 *JCC.*, 55, 56.
[63] *Ibid.*, 58.
[60] *Adams, Fam. Let.*, 42, 43.
[62] *Ibid.*, 57–58.

Finally, Congress was mindful of the enemy within the gates. It resolved that all persons who accepted office or served in any way under the parliamentary act changing the government of Massachusetts "ought to be held in detestation and abhorrence by all good men, and considered as the wicked tools of that despotism which is preparing to destroy those rights which God, nature and compact have given to America."[64] Some doubt regarding the wisdom of rigid and precise recommendation was voiced during the course of this debate. One proposal, voted down, was that the Colony should be left to make its own decisions as need developed or circumstance demanded.[65]

It was at this stage of the proceedings, on Sunday October 9, when Washington attended a Presbyterian service in the morning and a Roman Catholic in the afternoon,[66] that he found time to answer Robert Mackenzie's letter about the turbulent and lawless spirit alleged to exist in Boston. Deliberately or unconsciously, Mackenzie's former Colonel employed the direct, friendly style he had used almost twenty years previously in his relations with his company officers. Writing in some haste, Washington repetitiously echoed, also, some of the phrases he had been hearing every day in Carpenters' Hall. At the same time he unmistakably showed his former Captain where he stood on the controversy in Boston: ". . . You reason from effects, not causes; otherwise you would not wonder at a people who are every day receiving fresh proofs of a systematic assertion of an arbitrary power, deeply planned to overturn the laws and constitution of their country, and to violate the most essential and valuable rights of mankind, being irritated, and with difficulty restrained from acts of the greatest violence and intemperance . . . give me leave, my good friend, to tell you that you are abused, grossly abused [in what is told you], and this I advance with a degree of confidence and boldness, which may claim your belief, having better opportunities of knowing the real sentiments of the people you are among, from the leaders of them in opposition to the present measures of the administration than you have from those whose business it is, not to disclose truths but to misrepresent facts in order to justify as much as possible to the world their own conduct . . ."

Washington became more emphatic: ". . . it is not the wish or interest of that government [of Massachusetts] or any other upon this

64 1 JCC., 59–60.
65 Ibid., 60 n, with quotation from John Adams to Edward Biddle, Dec. 12, 1774.
66 2 Diaries, 167.

continent, separately or collectively, to set up for independency; but this you may at the same time rely on, that none of them will ever submit to the loss of those valuable rights and privileges which are essential to the happiness of every free State, and without which life, liberty and property are rendered totally insecure." He asked how it could be "wondered at" that men who wished to ward off an impending blow were preparing for defence if they could not divert that blow. ". . . give me leave to add as my opinion," he went on, "that more blood will be spilt on this occasion, if the ministry are determined to push matters to extremity than history has ever yet furnished instances of in the annals of North America . . ." [67]

It was the first time he ever had used that word "independency" in any of his letters—even to deny that the Colonies sought it.[68] Never previously had he essayed to speak so vigorously in behalf of all the Colonies. He was himself exemplifying the great value of the Congress in that he was learning more about the other Provinces every day and was increasingly conscious of the unity of their cause. On the great fundamental of colonial rights, deliberation and conference could not carry him further because he had gone the whole way. Justice and fairplay, two of his most cherished "principles," were threatened. He would remonstrate, he would cooperate, he would sacrifice to defend them, and then, if he must, he would fight.

This was the sentiment of most of the Delegates, but some seemed to have whetted their appetite for argument. Without any inclusive "re-solve" to express the feeling of the Congress, some of the constitutional lawyers concluded, moreover, that when they voted for non-intercourse with Britain, they should give their reason for doing so and should seek the support of like-minded men in America and in Great Britain. With this in view, preparation of a memorial to the people of North America and of an address to the people of Great Britain was entrusted to Richard Henry Lee, William Livingston and John Jay.

There followed a three-day debate, October 12–14, on the rights of the Colonies. This was based on reports the committee had made on the 22nd and 24th of September,[69] but as the debate progressed the report was made an omnium gatherum of affirmations, of reiterations of action already taken, and of resolutions on contingencies.[70] When the whole

[67] 3 *G. W.,* 245–46. See *supra,* p. 366 for the development of his views on independence.
[68] Reservation has to be made, of course, concerning the possibility that Washington spoke of "independency" in some earlier, lost letter, but this does not seem probable.
[69] 1 *JCC.,* 42.   [70] *Ibid.,* 63–73.

was adopted, October 14, even its authors would have had difficulty in saying what the document made final and what it left the Congress to elaborate. In the absence of any plan or leadership, men who had been successful lawmakers in their own Colonies found it difficult to put together an orderly plan of action, even after their differences had been reconciled. Members were aware of this and were becoming restive. The Virginians served notice on the 16th that some of them would have to leave not later than that day week,[71] in order to attend the meeting of the House of Burgesses, which was due to open on the 3rd of November.[72] For his own part Washington decided that the larger issue would be determined in Philadelphia: he would remain there to see the end of deliberations concerning which Abigail Adams wrote her husband: "The people in the country begin to be very anxious for the Congress to rise; they have no idea of the weighty business you have to transact, and their blood boils with indignation at the hostile preparations they are constant witnesses of." [73]

Consciousness of this feeling, the exhaustion of argument, a desire to get home, the completion of reports over which committees had spent uncounted hours—some or all of these circumstances were responsible for a less leisured tempo of discussion after October 17, in the final period of the Congress. On the 18th, the terms of association were adopted in form for transcription and signature. The completed paper reviewed the "ruinous system of colonial administration" and the specific acts of which America had complained. "To obtain redress of these grievances, which threaten destruction of the lives, liberty and property of his Majesty's subjects in North America"—so ran the last paragraph of the preamble—"we are of opinion that a non-importation, non-consumption and non-exportation agreement, faithfully adhered to, will prove the most speedy, effectual and peaceable measure . . ." The Delegates accordingly committed themselves and the people of their respective Colonies to a broad agreement against the importation of British and Irish goods, and of all slaves after Dec. 1, 1774. Non-consumption of tea and of other taxed goods was pledged; non-exportation was set at the time first agreed upon—Sept. 10, 1775. Local committees were recommended to see that the association was enforced.

All these matters were put together in a long document, so long, in

---

[71] George Read to Mrs. Read, Oct. 16, 1774; 1 *Burnett*, 77.
[72] *Journ. H.B.*, 1773–76, p. 165.
[73] Letter of Oct. 16, 1774; *Adams, Fam. Let.*, 48.

fact, that after it was signed by the members present on the 20th of October and was delivered to the printer, it had to be issued as a pamphlet.[74] Whether it represented a practical plan of non-intercourse, calculated to assure repeal of the offensive laws, Washington and the Virginians well might question. The experience of their Colony with similar detailed, over-precise regulations was monitory, not to say discouraging; but, of course, they and others who had witnessed the failure of stern, separate provincial associations were agreed that if this policy could prevail at all, it had to be on the continental basis now proposed.

The decision on non-intercourse came on a day otherwise unhappy to the Virginia delegation and personally humiliating to their most active member, Richard Henry Lee. He had prepared the draft of the address to the people of Great Britain and, on the 18th, he presented it to a Congress that had a fondness for verbal pyrotechnics and shining syllogism. This time the paper fell flat. Nobody praised it; nobody knew what to say that would not embarrass Lee. At length a motion was made to lay the address on the table. The next day it was recommitted after William Livingston had read a much superior address written by John Jay. This, slightly amended, was adopted on the 21st.[75] That very day, as it happened, Patrick Henry presented his text of an address to the King, authorized October 1.[76] In spite of the reputation Henry had gained as an orator, the Congress did not like and would not approve his text. It was sent back to the committee where acceptable changes were made by an added member, John Dickinson of Pennsylvania.[77]

While the Congress was in a mood of decision that day, October 21, it took into account the repeated rumors that some of the members were to be arrested and transported to England for trial there. This created no fear but it dictated a warning that the colonials would pursue the lex talionis. Congress resolved "that the seizing, or attempting to seize, any person in America, in order to transport such person beyond the sea, for trial of offences committed within the body of a County in America, being against law, will justify and ought to meet with resistance and

[74] 1 JCC., 75–80, 81. The front page of the first printed edition is reproduced in ibid., opp. p. 74.

[75] 1 JCC., 81 ff. The story of Richard Henry Lee's failure was told by Thomas Jefferson to William Wirt in a letter of Aug. 4, 1805, quoted in 1 Burnett, 79 n. Although this account is second-hand, from Edmund Pendleton and Benjamin Harrison to Jefferson, all the stated incidents conform to facts, as far as these are determinable. John Adams's account of Nov. 12, 1813, to Jefferson (13 Jefferson, 434), contains some confusion of detail.

[76] 1 JCC., 53, 102.   [77] Jefferson, loc. cit.; 1 JCC., 102, 103.

reprisal." [78] Further, the next day, October 22, the Congress dismissed Galloway's plan for a Grand Council of all the Colonies,[79] and recommended, instead, that the Colonies choose Delegates to a new Congress that would assemble in Philadelphia on the 10th of May, 1775.[80]

Was there anything more a Congress could do? Most of the Virginians did not think the remaining deliberations of particular importance and, on the 23rd or 24th of October, all of them except Washington and Richard Henry Lee acted in accordance with their previous warning and started homeward. Bland, Harrison, Randolph and probably Pendleton left in Washington's hands a power of attorney to sign their names "to any of the proceedings of the Congress." Patrick Henry entrusted a similar paper to Lee.[81] The two Virginians who remained, along with the Delegates from most of the other Colonies, still had to consider the final form of their address to the King and the text of an appeal to the people of Quebec. This second paper had been authorized on the 21st [82] and now, on the 24th, was ready, but it was not acceptable either to the literary or to the legalistic purists of the Congress. They must have spent the better part of the day "nibbling and quibbling," in John Adams's words, and then they recommitted it. The Massachusetts Delegate wrote in disgust: "There is no greater mortification than to sit with half a dozen wits, deliberating upon a petition, address or memorial. These great wits, these subtle critics, these refined geniuses, these learned lawyers, these wise statesmen, are so fond of showing their parts and powers as to make their consultations very tedious." [83] It doubtless was precisely so on the 25th, when the address to the King was approved [84] and it was that way, too, on the 26th in considering the new version of the letter to the inhabitants of Quebec.[85] Before the day was out, Washington probably observed once more what he had seen on many tedious days in the House of Burgesses—that beyond a certain limit lawmakers would not listen and would vote for a clumsy measure

[78] 1 *JCC.*, 102. Cf. Joseph Hewes to James Iredell, Oct. 31, 1774: "Our friends are under apprehension that administration will endeavor to lay hold of as many Delegates as possible, and have them carried to England and tried as rebels . . . I have no fears on that head, but should it be my lot, no man on earth could be better spared. Were I to suffer in the cause of American liberty, should I not be translated immediately to Heaven, as Enoch was of old?" (1 *Burnett*, 83).

[79] Diary of Samuel Ward; 1 *Burnett*, 80.   [80] 1 *JCC.*, 102.

[81] See 1 *JCC.*, opp. p. 54; 1 *Burnett*, lxiv, 81   [82] 1 *JCC.*, 101.

[83] Diary, October 24, 1774; 2 *John Adams*, 401.

[84] Reported in amended draft on the 24th, this address was "laid over" for consideration on the 25th (1 *JCC.*, 103, 104).

[85] 1 *JCC.*, 105.

sooner than wait for promised perfection they did not believe the drafters could attain. That limit had now been reached. All the remaining papers on the calendar were completed and approved; fair copies of the address were signed.[86] Richard Henry Lee subscribed for himself and for Patrick Henry, whereupon Washington attached his signature and those of Pendleton, Bland and Harrison.[87] Then, at long, long last, the Congress was dissolved, Wednesday, Oct. 26, 1774.[88]

So lacking in plan had been the deliberations and so meandering the stream of slow-flowing debate that when members undertook to say what the Congress had done, they might have had difficulty in stating in one-two order the resolves and recommendations. There had been so much of hesitation and of confusion that many must have been disappointed. In detail, the rights of the Colonists had been asserted, and the nature of their grievances had been set forth. Delegates had endorsed a continental association to stop all British and Irish imports. Non-exportation was pledged as of September, 1775, should non-importation fail to produce a repeal of the punitive laws before that time. Addresses to the King, to the people of North America and to the inhabitants of Quebec had been drafted. These documents were soundly logical and instructive, even though comparatively few of the people could understand the arguments in the papers designed to strengthen them in their resolution to resist parliamentary taxation. The patriots of Massachusetts were given the fullest assurance that they had the sympathy and should receive the support of all America in their resistance to execution of the laws enacted for their chastisement. No threat of war had been made by the Congress; but neither had there been any hint of willingness to compromise by the sacrifice of any right. Warning had been given that any attempt to arrest an American and to transport him overseas for the trial of an offence committed in the Colonies would "justify and ought to meet with resistance and reprisal." Opinion was divided concerning the probability of repeal of the laws directed against Massachusetts; but there was an overwhelming majority in Congress and out, for inflexible resistance to those acts. If force were used to execute them, then it would be met with force, the force not of

---

[86] 1 *JCC.*, 113.

[87] See the facsimiles in 1 *JCC.*, opp. p. 120. Washington did not use his power of attorney for Peyton Randolph, perhaps because he thought Randolph's name, as President, would appear at the head of the list, along with that of his successor, Henry Middleton, for whose election see 1 *JCC.*, 102. Cf. 1 *Burnett*, lxiv.

[88] 1 *JCC.*, 114.

a single town or province—Boston or Massachusetts—but of all the Colonies. John Dickinson spoke the mind of many when he wrote: "The first act of violence on the part of administration in America, or the attempt to reinforce General Gage this winter or next year will put the whole continent in arms, from Nova Scotia to Georgia." [89]

More important than all that the Colonies had pledged in their Congress was the fact that all had pledged it. "A determined and unanimous resolution animates this continent," said Dickinson, "firmly and faithfully to support the common cause to the utmost extremity in this great struggle for the blessing of liberty—a blessing that can alone render life worth holding . . ." [90]

In contributing to this, Washington had displayed no deftness of pen or skill of exhortation. His had been a silent rôle in a body where most of those who were not trying their hand at the drafting of a state paper were preparing an address or were delivering a speech which, they flattered themselves, would enchant the sympathetic and bewilder the critical.[91] From that company, Washington had not been selected to serve on a single committee, nor had he often been mentioned in the letters of members, otherwise than as a visitor at lodgings or as a guest at dinner.[92] In a list of convention celebrities, compiled by the observant John Adams, he was not mentioned.[93] Among the Virginia Delegates, Richard Henry Lee and Patrick Henry had displayed more of parliamentary leadership and had outshone him completely, even though these two had not escaped humiliation.

Unpraised, he had not been unobserved. Members had esteemed him for his military reputation and had found that the soundness of his judgment compensated for the awkwardness of his public utterance. They respected him more, rather than less, for his lack of desire to parade his opinions on the floor. While he had made no overwhelming conquest by force of character, he had impressed his colleagues as a

[89] Letter of Oct. 27, 1774 to Arthur Lee; 1 Burnett, 83.

[90] Ibid. Dickinson, it will be remembered, was accounted one of the "timid" members of the Congress (Cf. John Adams, 1 Burnett, 81). See also Charles Lee to Edmund Burke, Dec. 16, 1774: "I have conversed with every order of men, from the first estated gentleman to the poorest planters, and cannot express my astonishment at the unanimous, ardent spirit reigning through the whole." See The Lee Papers, NYHS. Cols., 1871 (cited hereafter as Lee Papers) v. 1, p. 145, quoted also in F. A. Mumby, George III and the American Revolution, 359.

[91] Some apocryphal stories of the impression he made at Philadelphia will be found in 2 Ford, 444 n.

[92] It will be understood, of course, that this remark applies to extant letters only, though these are sufficiently numerous to be representative.

[93] Cf. 1 Burnett, 67.

resolute man of integrity. He had bowed attendance at most of the social affairs, had spent pleasant evenings at taverns or at the quarters of the various delegations, and had made many acquaintances. Four times only had he gone to eat a second time at any of the thirty-one private homes where he had been a guest at dinner,[94] but he had strengthened ties with several of the Virginia Delegates, Benjamin Harrison in particular, and he had found much to admire in Joseph Reed, Thomas Mifflin and several other Philadelphians.[95] Washington, moreover, had widened his horizon to the North and to the South. Never narrow after boyhood, his view now was increasingly continental. At Williamsburg, he had watched silently the processes of law-making under the direction of a group of long-schooled, suave lawyers and planters who managed everything, and then he had seen the sceptre of the Burgesses pass to Patrick Henry, to Richard Henry Lee and to other men less instinctively loyal to the throne than the old leaders had been. In Philadelphia, Washington observed the suspicions, personal and provincial, that had to be overcome, the hesitation that contact had to disarm, and the clash of interest that candor must recognize and good faith reconcile before agreement among all the Colonies could be assured. The patience he had acquired in defending the frontier was aroused anew in enduring the Congress, and it had not failed him. Apparently he never fumed as John Adams had over the interminable argument he seldom shared. He accepted it stoically and, having sat for fifteen years in the Virginia House of Burgesses, he knew there was no way of avoiding debate. Prolonged discussion had to be accepted as the preliminary of enactment, exactly as drill had to precede combat.

A propos of combat, the Congress had not made any formal recommendation that the Colonies prepare for their defence. The possibility of war could not be blinked; the probability of it was believed to hang on offensive action by the British, in Boston particularly. Argument was unnecessary where agreement was almost unanimous that if hard blows were struck, harder would be returned. In private conversation

[94] Even this assumes that "Mr. Allen," with whom he dined September 29 was either Andrew or James Allen, who previously had entertained him. Further, it is assumed that "Mr. Willing," host on October 19, was Thomas Willing, who had Washington to dinner on the 24th of September. See 2 *Diaries*, 163–168.

[95] In part, this statement of the impression made and the friendships formed by Washington in Philadelphia during the Congress of 1774 is inferential, but it is certain he would not have received early and general recognition in 1775 if he had not earned good opinion the previous year.

there must, of course, have been surmises concerning the armed strength the Colonies might muster. An oddly dressed, eccentric British half-pay officer, Charles Lee, who had been in the service of the pro-Russian faction in Poland, had talked much in Philadelphia about the organization of a battalion which it was manifest he wished to command.[96] Washington of course met him but made no record of it. In the eyes of some members—Silas Deane for example—Washington himself was essentially a soldier,[97] but of his employment by the Congress, there had been no suggestion. At home, toward which he now hastened,[98] it was different. In his absence, his younger neighbors of Fairfax County had organized an Independent Company and had written to ask if he would inquire in Philadelphia whether the new volunteers could procure there a pair of colors, two drums, two fifes and two halberts. "We leave it to you, Sir," the committee had written, "to determine whether it may be proper or necessary to vary from the usual colors that are carried by the regulars or militia." [99]

"Proper or necessary to vary from the usual colors," British colors— did pride or preparation shape that question?

[96] 1 *Burnett*, 81.

[97] See *supra*, p. 377, and 1 *Burnett*, 28.

[98] The journey consumed three and a half days only, October 27–30 (2 *Diaries*, 169).

[99] William Ramsay *et al.* to Washington, Oct. 19, 1774; 5 *Hamilton*, 57. This probably was the young William Ramsay whose bills at Princeton had been paid in part by Washington. See 2 *G. W.*, 499 and *Ledger B*, folio 47.

CHAPTER XVII

Preparation for a Brief Absence If . . .
(October, 1774–April, 1775)

A GREAT change was observable when Washington reached home on the 20th of October. The people of Virginia were much more in a mood of preparation for defence. Older men and matrons busied themselves with enforcing the association or adapting plantation life to it; the young men were intent on organizing Independent Companies, on finding arms, and on drilling.[1]

By chance, too, these volunteers were confident even beyond the norm of youth on a first introduction to arms because men of their blood had just won a victory in Governor Dunmore's War. At Point Pleasant, where the Kanawha enters the Ohio—the very district in which Washington had taken up land under the proclamation of 1754—Col. Andrew Lewis and a force of Virginia militia had encountered a mass of savages on the 10th of October. For some hours the Indians had stood and had fought as stubbornly as the redskins who had combatted Henry Bouquet's men on Bushy Run in August, 1763; but in the new battle, as in the old, the savages at length had broken and had quit the field.

News of this success reached the Potomac about the time of Washington's return. It was followed soon by reports that the Indians were asking peace and had given hostages for the delivery of the white prisoners in their villages.[2] It was the swiftest and, in the judgment of many, the most decisive campaign the Virginians had waged against the redmen, and for that reason was tonic to the young men in Fairfax and nearby Counties who looked to Colonel Washington for instruction and for help in procuring arms. He knew of no manufactory except those in Philadelphia from which muskets could be purchased

---

[1] Cf. Dunmore, to Dartmouth, Dec. 24, 1774; *R. Hist. MSS. Comm., Dartmouth MSS, American Papers*, v. 2, p. 242; abstract in 17 *V* 435–36.

[2] See the references *supra*, p. 348 and 1 *Force* (4) p. 1015 ff, 1169, 1222; 9 *V* 395 ff, 10 *ibid.*, 255; 5 *Hamilton*, 54, 61.

and he had to forward to his commercial correspondent there the order of a Dumfries Independent Company for forty muskets.[3] Fortunately no crash occurred to make the use of arms immediately necessary. Not one mob assembled. The only reported violence was in the throwing overboard of two half-chests of tea at Yorktown from the hold of the ship *Virginia*; but in stiff and stern resolutions the planters of Gloucester County and the inhabitants of York proscribed the vessel, denounced the London merchant, John Norton, who dispatched the tea, and verbally pilloried the firm of Prentis &˙Co., Williamsburg, who had ordered it.[4] In all this threatening and preparation was warning that did not dismay Washington, whose resolution was fixed more firmly than ever, if that were possible, and there also now was growing probability that he would be called to command the Virginia volunteers. Andrew Lewis had a good record as a fighter but he was distant and taciturn in manner and lacked art in dealing with persons of station. There was a chance, too, that Col. William Byrd might seek command; it was no more than a chance; Byrd was royalist in sympathy and was too deeply in debt to be able to turn from his own tragic affairs. Another who might be qualified for high command was the half-pay officer Washington had met in Philadelphia, Gen. Charles Lee, who had come to Virginia and was acquiring land "over the mountains" in Berkeley County. Lee visited Mount Vernon early in the winter, doubtless talked of war and of liberty, and, departing, borrowed £15.[5] Virginians might like him or might have suspicions of him; there was no chance they would prefer him to the man who had won fame on the bloody field of Braddock's defeat.

Washington found that committees could be set up readily enough in accordance with the resolutions of the Philadelphia Congress.[6] In Fairfax no difficulty was encountered, after organization of the committee, in dealing with a shipment of forbidden linens, to the value of £1101, reported by the consignees, Fitzgerald & Peers. The goods were sold by package to the highest bidder; the net proceeds were set aside for the relief of the poor of Boston.[7] When it came to regular committee

---

[3] Among a people who loved display, there was as insistent a demand for officers' sashes as for weapons. See 5 *Hamilton*, 65, 68, 78, 80, 112, 132; 3 *G. W.*, 266; 2 *Diaries*, 170.

[4] 1 *Force* (4) p. 964–65. Norton and Prentis were not without their defenders. See *John Norton & Sons*, 368; *Va. Gazette*, Nov. 7, 24, Dec. 8, 15, 1774.

[5] He was there Dec. 30, 1774–Jan. 4, 1775 (2 *Diaries*, 175, 181).

[6] Cf. 1 *Force* (4) p. 986 ff. These are indexed adequately under the heading "Virginia,"

[7] 1 *Force* (4) p. 1051.

meetings, Washington on at least one occasion made the journey to
Alexandria only to find that circumstances, indifference or preoccupation had kept his associates from attending.[8] An adversary of the cause
of the Colonies might have said that experience with human selfishness
was being repeated and that the continental association, like those
formed earlier by the individual Colonies, would fail of general
observance. Even so, nothing similar to the feeling aroused by the
Boston Port Act, the suppression of the Massachusetts Council and
Assembly, and the occupation of Boston by British troops ever had been
witnessed in Virginia. Commercial fear had been aroused along with
patriotic wrath. A daily-tightening shortage of money made every man
a miser. Debts of trade were difficult to collect, and gentlemen's obligations to one another completely so.[9] Sterling exchange rose to 35 per
cent; [10] even Washington had to admit himself embarrassed for lack of
specie; [11] but fortunately he found a continuing good market for his
flour and a temporary demand for his sea biscuit which previously had
found few buyers.[12] In addition, though it was more a consolation than
a marketable asset, he heard that he had won two prizes in Lord
Stirling's lottery.[13]

Calls on him seemed endless. Early in 1775, his old friend and fellow-
Burgess, John West, wrote that he was near death and was desirous of
naming Washington as guardian of the son of the house. Washington
replied in genuine distress of spirit that he could not possibly discharge
the duty as he felt it should be performed. He could not bring himself
to a "flat refusal," he said, but he hoped West would perceive from a
statement of his obligations that the boy might be placed "in better
hands." Washington explained: "For what with my own business, my
present wards', my mother's (which is wholly in my hands), Colonel
Colville's, Mrs. Savage's, Colonel Fairfax's, Colonel Mercer's (for
Colonel Tayloe, though he accepted of the trust jointly with myself,
seems no ways inclined to take any part of the execution of it), and the
little assistance I have undertaken to give in the management of my
brother Augustine's affairs (for I have absolutely refused to qualify as

[8] 2 *Diaries*, 173.

[9] For typical instances of Washington's troubles on this score, see *infra*, p. 415 and his
account of the unsecured loan of £300 to John Page (37 *G. W.*, 510).

[10] 3 *G. W.*, 249 n.

[11] *Ibid.*, 273, 275, 290. For the general situation, see 5 *Hamilton*, 72. Arthur Lee's suggestion of measures to strengthen the economy of America at this time, is in 1 *Force* (4) p. 1040.

[12] 5 *Hamilton*, 73, 157; contract in 15 *Papers of G. W.*, 81, I.C.

[13] 3 *G. W.*, 264.

an executor) keeps me, together with the share I take in public affairs, constantly engaged in writing letters, settling accounts, and negotiating one piece of business or another in behalf of one or other of these concerns; by which means I really have been deprived of every kind of enjoyment, and had almost fully resolved to engage in no fresh matter till I had entirely wound up the old." [14] In this, there was not a touch of exaggeration. Washington was busy from early morning until 3-o'clock dinner. He still was able, once in a while, to go fox-hunting,[15] but that was the limit of all recreation not incidental to some ride on business.

Details must have been tedious, even to a man of disciplined mind and ordered habits. An abortive effort to organize a project for the improvement of the Potomac,[16] an extended journey into Fauquier to dispose of some of the Mercer lands,[17] a further attempt to satisfy a sobered George Muse concerning lands under the proclamation of 1754,[18] supervision of a second sale at Belvoir and continuing effort to correct poor management there,[19] a contest to protect some of the lands of "Austin's" children from being gobbled up by the Cresaps,[20] another round with Doctor Savage,[21] maneuver to collect from Daniel Jenifer Adams and to get out of the shipping business[22]—these things were a part only of Washington's load in the winter of 1774–75.[23] One of the most troublesome affairs of all was the breakup of the party of indentured servants[24] and slaves[25] sent in March to the Kanawha lands and

[14] Letter of Jan. 13, 1775; 3 G. W., 261–62. G. Chinard in his George Washington as the French Knew Him, 45, quoted the translator of Chastellux's Travels to this effect: "Before the war there was not a gentleman within the circle of [Washington's] neighborhood who, having important concerns, or a family to leave behind him, did not close his eyes in peace could he be so fortunate as to get Mr. Washington for an executor." When the same translator went to see Washington about a matter of business, late in the war, the General said he had little knowledge of his own affairs, but he proceeded to take up the matter in the most precise detail.

[15] Two days in January, 1775, and four days in February (2 Diaries, 182–87).

[16] 2 Diaries, 170, 183; 5 Hamilton, 84 ff, 133. Cf. supra, p. 290–91.

[17] Nov. 20–Dec. 1, 1774; 2 Diaries, 171; 3 G. W., 249, 283 ff, 286 ff; 37 ibid., 507; 5 Hamilton, 114.

[18] 5 Hamilton, 66, 82; 3 G. W., 263.

[19] 2 Diaries, 173; 5 Hamilton, 121; Birch Cat. 663, item 143.

[20] 3 G. W., 267.   [21] 5 Hamilton, 120, 159.

[22] 3 G. W., 256, 273–75; 5 Hamilton, 92, 116, 118. Washington sold the brig Farmer Apr. 11, 1775 (5 Hamilton, 156), after the vessel had completed a voyage to Jamaica, (Ledger B, folio 122).

[23] Cf. 37 G. W., 509. Some of these tasks were carried over into the early spring of 1775.

[24] Washington, it will be remembered, had given up all hope of procuring Palatines and was adding to the English and Irish he "purchased" on indenture. He noted, Jan. 26, 1775, that he "stayed in Alexandria all night and bought a parcel of servants" (2 Diaries, 183). Trouble was encountered with runaways. See 3 G. W., 289; Rind's Gazette, May 4, 1775; Va. Gazette, May 5, 1775; 5 Hamilton, 176.

[25] In Armstrong Papers at Mount Vernon is a list in Washington's hand of the slaves on that

halted at Redstone by the outbreak of Dunmore's War. Lacking firm control, one after another of the workers disappeared, and with them the implements and supplies Washington had entrusted to the men in charge. Washington computed his loss at £300.[26]

The larger interests held first place in his mind. On Sunday, Jan. 15, 1775, George Mason, Martin Cockburn and others returned with Washington to Mount Vernon, after service at Pohick Church, and that afternoon and evening they doubtless talked of plans for having their County do its full part in armed defence of colonial rights.[27] This was not easy. The County possessed no ammunition beyond that which individuals had for hunting and the small quantity that merchants kept in stock to meet the normal requirements of planters. Fowling pieces were the only weapons. Besides this lack of essentials, there was an odd obstacle of law: by whose authority were the Independent Companies being organized? In the event officers were challenged for taking up arms, what would be their justification?

Discussion of these subjects was resumed on the 16th of January at Alexandria, whither Washington rode, probably in the company of his overnight guests.[28] The decision on all three perplexities was clear-cut. Ammunition could not be purchased with money raised by formal county levy for that purpose unless the prior consent of the General Assembly was had,[29] but powder and shot could be bought at the common cost of the inhabitants of the County. The Committee therefore voted: "It is . . . recommended that the sum of three shillings per poll . . . be paid by and for every tithable person in this County, to the Sheriff or such other collector as may be appointed, who is to render the same to this Committee, with a list of the names of such persons as shall refuse to pay the same, if any such there be."[30] Washington and Mason agreed to advance the money required immediately for the pur-

---

estate, classified by farm, by sex and by adults and youths. Included are the Negroes he acquired personally and those of the Custis estate. Total numbers were as follows: River Plantation, 32; Muddy Hole, 10; Ferry Plantation, 11; Dogue Run, 13; Mill [sic] plantation, 6; home, 34.

[26] 3 *G. W.*, 498. Cf. *ibid.*, 273.   [27] 2 *Diaries*, 182.

[28] He did not mention them as traveling companions on the 16th, but if it be true, as reasonably assumed (1 *Rowland, Mason*, 182) that the resolutions to be mentioned in the text were the work of George Mason, it is altogether likely that he attended Washington to the committee meeting.

[29] This was implicit in the general tax laws; no specific prohibition has been found.

[30] 1 *Force* (4) p. 1145. It probably was to this unofficial levy that Governor Dunmore referred in his dispatch of Mch. 14, 1775, to Lord Dartmouth (P.R.O., C.O. 5: 1353, p. 145, LC Transcript). Dunmore said: "One County has already laid a capital tax of 3s."

chase of the explosive.[31] As for the weapons, the Committee concluded these could be provided quickly in no other way than by conforming to the principle of the militia law and requiring every man to have his own firelock and to keep it in good order.[32]

A solution of the other perplexity—that of arming without risk of arrest—already had been offered in Maryland and now was adopted, tongue in cheek. Citizens across the Potomac had decided that the colonials would be safe if they acted on the ostensible theory that they simply were making the authorized militia more effective. So, some good draftsman with a sense of humor—almost certainly George Mason—prepared this "resolve," which might have made even the stern-visaged Washington smile: ". . . that this committee do concur in opinion with the Provincial Committee of the Province of Maryland that a well regulated militia, composed of gentlemen freeholders and other freemen, is the natural strength and only stable security of a free government, and that such militia will relieve our mother country from any expense in our protection and defence, will obviate the pretence of a necessity for taxing us on that account, and render it unnecessary to keep standing armies among us—ever dangerous to liberty; and therefore it is recommended to such of the inhabitants of this County as are from 16 to 50 years of age to form themselves into Companies . . . that they provide themselves with good firelocks, and use their utmost endeavors to make themselves masters of the *Military Exercise,* published by order of his Majesty in 1764, and recommended by the Provincial Congress of the Massachusetts Bay on the 29th of October last." [33]

George Mason was of opinion that the entire body of free citizens of military age must be organized; [34] Washington realized better than did any other Virginian how frail a rod the militia would be, even though they had shown improvement in Dunmore's War, and he consequently provided in the military "association" for the organization of special Companies of riflemen who were to be uniformed in hunting shirts.[35] Poor as the initial equipment of volunteers might be, the general plan of organizing Fairfax County, as thus worked out, probably was as good as could be formulated at the time. In a knowledge, finally, that a few men, well trained, could defeat a far larger raw force, Washington

---

[31] They found repayment slow and difficult, though one man only, the Alexandria merchant William Hartshorn, flatly refused to contribute to the fund (5 *Hamilton,* 107, 110–11, 135; 1 *Rowland, Mason,* 185–87).

[32] Text of Fairfax County Association; 1 *Force* (4) p. 1146.

[33] 1 *Force* (4) p. 1145–46.   [34] 5 *Hamilton,* 94.   [35] 1 *Force* (4) p. 1146.

undertook to go to Alexandria at intervals and to drill its Independent
Company.[36] It was another beginning from nothing, as in the darkest
days of the Virginia Regiment, but it had the same fundamental maxim,
"Discipline is the soul of an Army." [37]

During the first stages of this training, hope of an early, peaceful
settlement with Britain rose again. On the 25th of February, 1775,
Washington wrote John Connolly: "With us here, things wear a disagreeable aspect and the minds of men are exceedingly disturbed at
the measures of the British government. The King's speech and address
of both Houses, prognosticate nothing favorable to us; but by some
subsequent proceedings thereto, *as well as by private letters from
London,* there is reason to believe the ministry would willingly change
their ground, from a conviction that forcible measures will be inadequate to the end designed. A little time must now unfold the mystery,
as matters are drawing to a point." [38] The purpose of that underlining
of a phrase was, of course, to indicate to Connolly that the Virginians
had specific information from London at variance with reports of an
inflexible resolution on the part of the ministry to bring the Colonies to
submission. A new Parliament had met on Nov. 29, 1774, and the next
day had listened to a belligerent speech from the throne. After reviewing briefly the "most daring spirit of resistance and disobedience to
law" still prevailing in Massachusetts, the King had said that he had
given proper orders for executing the laws designed to protect commerce and to restore order. "And you may depend on my firm and
steadfast resolution to withstand every attempt to weaken or impair the
supreme authority of this Legislature over all the Dominions of my
Crown, the maintenance of which I consider as essential to the dignity,
the safety and the welfare of the British empire . . ." [39] The address
from the Philadelphia Congress to the King had not been mentioned at
that time or, officially, until a month and a half later. Then, on the 19th
of January, 1775—the day that Washington had gone from the committee meeting in Alexandria [40]—Lord North had laid before the
Commons a packet of 149 numbered papers. Five of these [41] concerned
the proceedings of the Congress; any one of three might, from the
docket, have covered the address; [42] none was labeled specifically.

[36] Cf. 2 *Diaries*, 185.
[37] See Vol. II, p. 263.
[38] 3 *G. W.*, 268.
[39] 1 *Force* (4) p. 1465.
[40] 2 *Diaries*, 182.
[41] Nos. 43, 57, 58, 122, 158.
[42] 1 *Force* (4) p. 1489–93.

When Edmund Burke had inquired why no papers from Maryland had been included, Lord North had replied that he had brought the papers but had not examined them.[43] In the House of Lords, the Earl of Chatham on the 20th of January had moved an address to the King for the recall of the troops sent to Boston, but after a furious debate, he had been defeated eighteen to sixty-eight.[44] Undaunted, Chatham on the 1st of February had presented a compromise entitled, "A provisional act for settling the troubles in America and for asserting the supreme legislative authority and superintending power of Great Britain over the Colonies." This measure had called for the repeal of all the acts that had inflamed America and it had provided that no tax for revenue could be imposed by Parliament on the Colonies without the consent of their provincial assemblies. In return for this recognition of their rights as "British freemen in America," all the colonials were to recognize the supremacy of Parliament and, at a joint Congress, were to grant the King an unspecified perpetual revenue. After another fiery debate, this measure was rejected by the Lords on its first reading, sixty-one to thirty-two.[45]

None of these developments of midwinter was known to Washington when he wrote Connolly, but he doubtless had cheerful assurances from merchants in London—always traffickers in hope till colonials' balances were struck—that the King would relent and the Ministry fall. Virginia was encouraged but was wary. A new convention was called in line with the recommendation of the Philadelphia Congress of 1774 that each Colony select Delegates to a similar Congress in May, 1775.[46] Peyton Randolph probably consulted the Committee of Correspondence on this, and, exercising liberally the authority given him by the Virginia Convention of 1774,[47] "requested" the election in each County of Delegates who were asked to meet in the town of Richmond, March 20, at a safe distance from Dunmore.[48]

Washington was named Fairfax's representative on February 20 along with his new fellow-Burgess, Charles Broadwater,[49] and he was prompt to make all necessary arrangements for absence from Mount

---

43 *Ibid.*, 1513.
44 *Ibid.*, 1504.
45 1 *Force* (4) p. 1503-14.
46 1 *JCC.*, 102.
47 1 *Force* (4) p. 188. Strictly speaking, he merely had authority to bring together the same Delegates and to recommend that vacancies caused by death or absence be filled.
48 See his notice in *Va. Gazette*, Feb. 3, 1775. As this issue is the earliest of 1775 in known collections, the probability has to be taken into account that the notice may have appeared also in editions of prior date.
49 2 *Diaries*, 186. George Mason gave his blessing (5 *Hamilton*, 94).

Vernon. En route[50] to the little town at the fall line of James River,
he stopped to review the Dumfries Independent Company, but he
reached his destination the day the large body of Delegates organized
and named Peyton Randolph their presiding officer. All the Counties
were represented, and all except six of them by two members.[51] James-
town, Norfolk and Williamsburg, each of which had one Burgess, now
sent one Delegate each. The College of William and Mary was without
a spokesman, but as every man knew, that was because her Burgess,
Attorney General John Randolph, was antagonistic to the popular
movement. Nearly all the other leaders of the House of Burgesses,
including the Virginia Delegates to the Congress of 1774, were present
in the little church on top of the hill in Richmond. Three of Washington's comrades of the French and Indian War, Andrew Lewis, Adam
Stephen and Thomas Walker, had seats.

The Convention met with many auguries of peace with Britain.
Some of the Delegates doubtless had seen copies of the *Virginia Gazette*
of March 17, which contained tares of foreboding but a sheaf of cheerful news and of reassuring prediction—how Lord North wished to have
more information concerning the sentiment of America, how the greater
part of the military were to be removed from Boston and the fleet alone
left to enforce the blockade, how merchants in British centres of trade
were preparing to appeal to the House of Commons in behalf of the
Colonies, and how the reasonableness of the Philadelphia Congress of
1774 had turned the tide of public opinion in England and Scotland to
the side of the colonials. All this, of course, was meat and drink to the
Virginia Delegates who still had faith in their King, and it was un-
palatable argument to those who believed the monarch a tyrant. Initial
division among members did not interfere with a sympathetic review
of the recommendations of the Philadelphia Congress. At the end of
two days' discussion, the entire proceedings of the Congress were
approved by unanimous vote, and the Delegates were thanked.[52] On
the 23rd of March, the fourth day of the Convention,[53] the Delegates
considered in detail a memorial and petition the General Assembly

[50] His route was via Fredericksburg, Bowling Green and Hanover Court House, approximately the present U. S. Route 1 to Fredericksburg and thence Route 2 to Richmond.

[51] Augusta had three; West Augusta sent two who were admitted on the 21st (2 *Force*
(4) p. 167).

[52] 2 *Force* (4) p. 167.

[53] It has been traditional that the dramatic events to be described in the text occurred on the
"third day of the Convention," which would have been the 22nd, but this could have been the
case only if Henry addressed the chair the day before the passage of the resolutions.

of Jamaica had sent the King in an effort to mediate the differences with the colonies of the mainland. As it seemed no more than courtesy to acknowledge this, a formal resolution of thanks was drafted. To it was attached assurance "that it is the most ardent wish of this Colony (and we are persuaded of the whole continent of North America) to see a speedy return of those halcyon days when we lived a free and happy people."

Patrick Henry then won recognition and offered a series of resolutions,[54] which the clerk read. They repeated substantially the now-familiar Maryland and Fairfax argument regarding a "well regulated militia, composed of gentlemen and yeomen" as the "natural strength and only security of a free government." After that came words with a rumble: ". . . the establishment of such a militia is at this time peculiarly necessary, by the state of our laws for the protection and defence of the country, some of which have already expired, and others shortly will do so; and that the known remissness of government, in calling us together in a legislative capacity, renders it too insecure, in this time of danger and distress, to rely that opportunity will be given of renewing them in General Assembly, or making any provision to secure our inestimable rights and liberties from those farther violations with which they are threatened. Resolved, therefore"—the Convention must have become tense as the Clerk read on—"that this Colony be immediately put in a posture of defence; and that [blank] be a committee to prepare a plan for the embodying, arming and disciplining such a number of men as may be sufficient for that purpose." [55]

Henry now took the floor. With little of his studied, half-awkward hesitation in an exordium, he launched into a bold argument that the increase of British force in America was intended for the enslavement of the Colonies. Memorials and petitions were futile: In one way only could Americans retain their liberty. "We must fight!" he cried, as if the command were from Heaven. At the words, most of the older sympathizers with the royal house stirred and mumbled: why should Henry pronounce conflict unavoidable? War would not, could not

---

[54] William Wirt Henry, *op. cit.*, v. 1, p. 257, thought these resolutions were offered as an amendment to those on Jamaica, but there is no reason for assuming this other than that they follow immediately in the Journal, with nothing to indicate separate action on them. This may have been the mistake of John Tazewell, who had served as Clerk of the Committee of Correspondence (*Journ. H. B.,* 1773–76), but never as Clerk of the House of Burgesses. He may not have been familiar with journal keeping in the House, where all resolutions were separated to prevent just such confusion of unrelated measures.

[55] 2 *Force* (4) p. 167–68.

come, unless fools and brawlers provoked it. Members less convinced of the certainty of peace sat as if they had been paralyzed by the orator's prediction. Henry swept furiously onward in the charge of his eloquence until, to younger ears, his majestic words were the call of bugles and the roar of guns. His voice filled the little church and the crowded yard and seemed to descend over the brim of the hill and on to the river that would carry his challenge across the seas. He was transfigured—orator, actor, the personification of his country—as he shouted at the end: "Is life so dear, or peace so sweet, as to be purchased at the price of chains and slavery? Forbid it, Almighty God! I know not what course others may take; but as for me, give me liberty or give me death!" [56]

Men sat as if they had been stunned or condemned or called to a task so much beyond their strength but so lofty and so commanding that it awed them. Then they stirred, looked about, and wondered what they could say and what they should do. A few were vain or reckless enough

[56] Wirt, *op. cit.*, 123. No contemporary report of Henry's speech of Mch. 23, 1775, exists. His early biographer, William Wirt, writing at intervals from 1805 to 1817, relied chiefly on accounts given him by John Tyler and by St. George Tucker, both of whom were present when Henry spoke. As Judge Tyler died in 1813, it is fair to assume that he was at least 60 years of age when he described in, say, 1807, the events of forty-two years previously. This would eliminate him as a witness on anything that involved absolute precision of statement; but as he was a young man of 28 when he heard Henry's appeal, he is to be credited with a general memory of so tremendous an utterance. He doubtless had like memory, perhaps somewhat distorted by hindsight, of the impression the speech produced. St. George Tucker, like Tyler, was a jurist and an intelligent man. Born in 1752, he was 23 when Henry spoke and he was approximately 55 to 60 when he gave his recollections to Wirt. All that applies to Tyler's testimony may be said of Tucker's also. As one or the other of these men was responsible for "we must fight" and "I know not what course," etc., those two quotations may be accepted as substantially correct. It is a thankless duty to have to add that the other testimony concerning the content of this famous oration is not entitled to credence. To list this so-called evidence is to discard it. Included are: (1) an account H. S. Randall received after 1826 from a clergyman who had it from an old minister said to have been present; (2) a "verification" in 1834 by another auditor, John Roane, of that part of the speech Judge Tyler had written out for Wirt from memory; (3) sundry "unsigned notes" on Wirt's life of Henry prepared by some unidentified person who found fault with the summary of the arguments credited by Wirt to the adversaries of Henry's resolution, though the critic entered no complaint against Wirt's version of Henry's speech; (4) the account given by Edmund Randolph in his MS *History of Virginia*, which may contain some echoes of reminiscence by Edmund's uncle, Peyton Randolph, who died in October, 1775. Washington nowhere wrote of the speech, which he certainly heard. His sole comment on the events of the day was: "Dined at Mr. Patrick Coote's and lodged where I had done the night before" (2 *Diaries*, 189). Washington, in fact, did not mention the convention itself but once during his stay in Richmond and then merely to say that he returned to a particular session (*ibid.*). It is strange that Jefferson did not describe in his writings this renowned utterance, though he recorded in detail Henry's denunciation of the Stamp Act in 1765. The account left by Thomas Marshall, father of John Marshall, is useful only for the generalization Henry's was "one of the most bold, vehement and animated pieces of eloquence that had ever been delivered." (*W. W. Henry*, v. 1, p. 270–71). From the whole of this evidence, it seems safe to conclude that a few sentences burnt themselves into the memory of auditors. The remainder of the speech probably is far more Tucker, Tyler and Wirt, chiefly Wirt, than Henry. See *infra*, n. 58 for discussion of the hits and misses of some of the arguments Wirt put in the mouths of Henry and of the men who opposed the resolutions.

to attempt to match their eloquence against Henry's; others felt they must dispute his logic though they could not rival his delivery. The voice of caution was not that of cowardice. Bland and Nicholas urged further delay before Virginia defiantly took up arms. They and other members [57] could not believe the King would permit the controversy to reach the dreadful pass where British subjects would be at one another's throat. Convention Delegates of short temper or of realistic training would not have it so. Britain, they said, was preparing to subjugate the Colonies; every act of government demonstrated that.[58] Richard Henry Lee and Jefferson led in support of Henry; the vote, in the end, was for putting the Colony "into a posture of defence." Henry was named first on a committee of twelve to bring in a plan for "embodying, arming and disciplining such a number of men as may be sufficient for that purpose." [59]

Washington was assigned to the committee along with his old comrades in arms, Adam Stephen and Andrew Lewis, and with most of the leading members of Henry's following. This committee probably worked from a draft prepared in advance but it could do so little for the immediate strengthening of the Colony's defence that it had its report ready by the time the convention met the next day, March 24.[60] This

[57] Judge Tyler was of opinion that Benjamin Harrison and Edmund Pendleton were among those who sided with Nicholas and Bland, but he was not sure. See *W. W. Henry*, v. 1, p. 258.

[58] If the greater part of Henry's speech, as printed, is in reality Wirt's, several passages of it represented a discerning interpretation of the arguments that were being advanced at that time in Virginia by those who had become convinced that the royal government was determined, at any cost, to establish the authority of Parliament over the Colonies. In more than one furious challenge put on Henry's lips by Wirt is the echo of phrases then current in the Dominion. Wirt's most serious blunder was in having Henry hint of foreign intervention to aid America if war should come. The evidence examined in this study contains nothing to show that this argument was advanced in Virginia during the spring of 1775. Wirt, moreover, was not successful in his presentation of the views held at that time by those who opposed Henry's resolutions (Wirt, *op. cit.*, 117 ff). Bland, Nicholas and most of the others were closer to the popular cause in 1775 than Wirt thought they were. Nicholas's conservatism, which is analyzed most discerningly by T. P. Abernethy in *DAB*, was positive but never was carried to the point where Nicholas refused to go on with the majority. Bland, though perhaps of more stubborn mind, held substantially the same ground as Nicholas. Wirt, in short, seems to have attributed to the opposition in 1775 the opinions held several years previously. In particular, Wirt apparently postdated to 1775 some observations on the speed of political revolution in Virginia that Thomas Jefferson manifestly intended to apply to an earlier crisis. W. W. Henry followed William Wirt in this.

[59] *2 Force* (4) p. 168.

[60] *2 Force* (4) p. 168. Washington spent the night in Richmond and did not go out, as previously he had, to Archibald Cary's residence, Ampthill, across James River in Chesterfield County. It consequently is safe to assume that the committee spent the afternoon and evening working on its report (see *2 Diaries*, 189). Nothing is known of the authorship of any scheme of organization prepared in advance. If there was such a paper, it may have been an elaboration of a plan "for embodying the people" of Fairfax County that George Mason had sent Washington Feb. 6, 1775, which document, said Mason, "I have made . . . as general as I well could" (*1 Rowland, Mason*, 184).

paper was discussed by the convention on the 25th, the sixth day of the
session. As then debated, amended and adopted, the report was essentially an appeal for the organization of volunteers. Each of the Counties
on and East of the fall line was asked to raise one or more Troops of
Cavalry, thirty men to the Troop; the other Counties were called on to
furnish at least one foot Company of sixty-eight rank and file. All these
men were to be equipped substantially as required by the militia act.
Nothing was said concerning the method by which the officers of the
volunteers were to be selected. Under the law 1738, which was declared to be the only statute still in effect for governing the militia,[61]
the Colonel of the militia in a given County appointed the Captains.[62]
Field officers were commissioned by the Governor. The act of 1738 was
much inferior to the military measures Washington had prevailed upon
the House of Burgesses to adopt and to strengthen temporarily during
the French and Indian War, but the convention plan presented a sharp
innovation and an anticipated improvement not only in the emphasis
on volunteers but also in the provision for so large a force of Horse. As
the weakness of Virginia's defence was certain to be the lack of arms, of
ammunition and of equipment of every sort, the committee recommended that each County levy the equivalent of a head tax, as in Fairfax, for the purchase of ammunition. A central committee of three was
created to buy military supplies for Counties that did not know how
to procure them. All this was approved by the Convention, which likewise selected on the 25th a committee of thirteen to "prepare a plan for
the encouragement of arts and manufactures in this Colony," a bland
euphemism for employing the pitifully undeveloped resources of war.

Washington, as a military man, was on this committee, too, though
the majority of the members were political leaders or individuals who
were supposed to have special familiarity with trade.[63] A third and far
more important assignment was his. When the seven members of the
Virginia delegation to the new General Congress were elected on the
25th, Washington was the second chosen. Peyton Randolph's name
alone preceded his; Henry's followed. All the other members of the
delegation to Philadelphia in 1774 were re-elected.[64]

By the time this was done, Delegates were becoming anxious to leave

[61] 2 *Force* (4) p. 169; the act is 5 H 16.
[62] And presumably the other company officers, though the act did not so state.
[63] 2 *Force* (4) p. 170.
[64] 2 *Force* (4) p. 170. On the last day of the Convention, Jefferson was selected as an
alternate to Peyton Randolph "in case of the non-attendance" of the Speaker (*ibid.*, 172).

the little town that offered few conveniences for tavern guests. So, over the Sabbath, the committee on the encouragement of arts and manufactures threw together a plan that covered a diversity of objects, from the strict enforcement of the vagrancy laws to the encouragement of steelmaking. Almost the only proposals that could be made for immediate and specific defensive preparation were, first, that sheep be conserved for wool and, second, that financial assistance be given a specified individual who was anxious to establish salt works. The Convention approved the report and, after transacting a variety of other business, adjourned that same day, March 27.[65]

Counselling in some of these decisions and concurring in all, Washington maintained the resolute calm that had been his from the time he heard the distant rumble of the coming storm. At the end of a letter to his brother "Jack," written during the Richmond convention, he said: "I had like to have forgot to express my entire approbation of the laudable pursuit you are engaged in of training an Independent Company. I have promised to review the Independent Company of Richmond [County] sometime this summer, they having made me a tender of the command of it[.] At the same time I could review yours and shall very cheerfully accept the honor of commanding it if occasion requires it to be drawn out, as it is my full intention to devote my life and fortune in the cause we are engaged in, if need be." [66] That was all. The quiet dedication seemed little more than an incidental explanation of his reason for being willing to take command of still another Independent Company.

In this spirit and with promises to meet his fellow-Delegates in Philadelphia or en route, Washington left Richmond on the 28th of March, and spent a day and a half in Fredericksburg,[67] where he may have accepted the general supervision of a volunteer Company.[68] Then, riding northward by the usual route, he reached home March 31 after an absence of half the month.[69] He scarcely had rested when he heard an alarming rumor—nothing less than that Governor Dunmore was going to cancel all the land patents issued under the proclamation of

---

[65] 2 *Force* (4) p. 170–72.

[66] Letter of Mch. 25, 1775; 3 *G. W.*, 276–77. It is a singular fact that this first of the few letters Washington ever wrote from the town of Richmond should have related to arms, the grim subject destined to be associated above all others with the history of that city.

[67] While there, he noted that he paid his mother "part of her income, £30" (2 *Diaries*, 190). See Appendix III–4.

[68] It reported to him for orders the next month. See *infra*, p. 410.

[69] 2 *Diaries*, 190.

1754, because William Crawford who surveyed the tracts for the veterans of the Virginia Regiment was alleged to have failed to qualify in the manner prescribed by statute. Washington was aghast. Twenty-three thousand acres of his land were involved! They could not and must not be lost. His informant, Captain Floyd, assuredly was mistaken or else had been imposed upon by surveyors who were trying to collect fees for doing Crawford's work over again.

Washington was concerned but skeptical when John David Wilper [70] came to Mount Vernon and made the same report. Wilper was an old Sergeant of the First Virginia who later had become a Lieutenant, and he had traveled intermittently for a long time on the frontier as a seeker after lands. He had talked with many settlers and he explained now that those who had grants under Dinwiddie's proclamation of '54 were alarmed and at a loss to know what to do.[71] Even after hearing this statement of Wilper's, made by a mature and experienced though uneducated man, Washington was loath to believe the surveys would be nullified, but he concluded he should inquire directly of the Governor whether the story had anything more behind it than the excited gossip of ignorant frontier-folk. In a letter to Dunmore he reviewed the history of the grant and advanced an argument he never had employed before—that under the proclamation of Dinwiddie the veterans of 1754 had been entitled to have their lands surveyed by the Colony without cost to them. When the applicants decided to make their own surveys, Washington explained, they received instructions to apply for the appointment of a Surveyor. This had been done; all the requirements of the law had been met. He would not trouble the Governor, Washington concluded, except for the importunity of some of the landholders and, in addition, because he wished to know the facts so that, if anything further had to be done to secure the titles, he could ascertain what it was.[72]

Promptly enough there came a terse and formal answer from his Lordship, who wrote as if he never had entertained Colonel Washington and did not distinguish the Fairfax Burgess, the former commander of the Virginia troops, from any adventurer who might be attempting to defraud the Colony. The Governor wrote: "Sir, I have received your letter . . . The information you have received that the patents granted for the lands under the proclamation of 1754 would be

[70] The name frequently is given as Woelper and often was so spelled by Washington.
[71] 3 G. W., 280.   [72] Ibid., 283.

declared null and void, is founded on a report that the Surveyor who surveyed those lands did not qualify agreeable to the act of Assembly directing the duty and qualification of surveyors. If this is the case, the patents will of consequence be declared null and void." [73]

The letter was one to ponder. If in some manner unknown to the man most heavily concerned, Captain Crawford had failed to qualify, all the cost and all the labor of Washington's journey to the Ohio in 1770 would have gone for nought. The expenses of attempted "seating," including the £300 lost in 1774, might never be recovered. Those lush bottoms on the Kanawha might be taken from the volunteers who had fought for the King in 1754, and might be given to persons who would support him now against his old defenders. Could the whole disconcerting affair be an attempt to bribe Washington and the others into acceptance of the royal policy? Was it a threat that if they persisted in their "disobedience" they would be deprived of lands that later would be worth a fortune; or was it simply by chance that Crawford's surveys had been brought into question at a time when Washington was reviewing volunteers and was preparing for the dread eventuality of war?

If Washington suspected blackmail or reprisal, it did not deter him from a single act of military preparation or from the utterance of a word he would have spoken in aid of the colonial cause. On the very day that he explained to Lord Dunmore the surveys of Crawford, he reported approvingly to George Mercer: ". . . the people [are] resolved, although they wish for nothing more ardently than a happy and a lasting reconciliation with the parent State, not to purchase it at the expense of their liberty and the sacred compacts of government." [74] That last, incidentally, was a phrase he had not used before—"compacts of government." He was learning from the constitutional lawyers. Relations between Britain and the Colonies, as he now conceived them, were not based on a grant by a monarch in whom all power adhered, a King from whom all rights emanated. The rights were those of freeborn Englishmen; the division and the exercise of power by Parliament and by the representative bodies of the Colonies were matters of mutual acceptance, not of royal grace only. In the letter that set forth this faith, as in all that Washington wrote at this time, there was not a provocative stroke, but neither was there an erasure of any opinion he had expressed from the beginning of the controversy. As formerly, he

[73] Letter of Apr. 18, 1775; 5 *Hamilton*, 158   [74] 3 *G. W.*, 288.

held that if Britain persisted, she would be resisted, and that, if she
struck a blow, it would be returned; but still he would affirm, un-
grudgingly and without reservation, that if the King and the Ministry
ceased to threaten punishment and restored to Boston and to Massachusetts the rights that had been taken away, the old amity could be
restored. That was Washington's simple, untheatrical view.

Now came a visit to Alexandria for the muster of the Independent
Company, and five days of discourse by Gen. Charles Lee who returned
to Mount Vernon on a visit [75] and had as companion a charming young
fellow of nineteen, Harry Lee, son of Henry Lee of Leesylvania.[76] After
that, when lengthening April days brought spring to the Potomac, the
greater part of Washington's time was given to the direction of plantation affairs. The wheat was green and fully two months from the
cradlers, but the spring plowing was completed, the long rows were all
laid off, and corn planting was under way. The scene on the river was
busy, too, because it was the season for the herring to run, the time for
more of those fabulous "catches" that filled the seine with shining,
writhing fish. There was no sweeter season on the Potomac than that
of the last week in April when every plot in the flower garden sought
to outdo its neighbor, and the bees were drunk with pollen.

It was late on the 26th, after Washington returned from a day in
Alexandria,[77] or it was on the 27th, at the very peak of the glory of
spring, that a hurrying express brought a startling letter from Fredericksburg, signed by Hugh Mercer and three other men interested in
organizing troops for the defence of the Colony. They had heard from
Williamsburg that on the night of the 20th–21st, the Captain of a
British armed schooner had landed with fifteen marines, had gone to
the magazine in Williamsburg and had taken from it the powder
stored there. Mercer and the committee in Fredericksburg reported:
"The gentlemen of the Independent Company of this town think this
first public insult is not to be tamely submitted to and determine with
your approbation to join any other bodies of armed men who are willing
to appear in support of the honor of Virginia as well as to secure the
military stores yet remaining in the magazine. It is proposed to march
on Saturday next [the 29th] for Williamsburg properly accoutred as
light horsemen. Expresses are sent off to inform the commanding
officers of Companies in the adjacent Counties of this our resolution,

[75] 2 *Diaries*, 191–92.   [76] See Vol. I, p. 207.   [77] 2 *Diaries*, 193.

and we shall wait prepared for your instructions and their assistance." [78]
Although Mercer's letter omitted mention of it, Mann Page, Jr. had
been sent from Fredericksburg to the colonial capital in order to ascertain the situation there and to ask the counsel of Peyton Randolph.[79]

Besides this exciting news from Fredericksburg, Washington had an
express from Dumfries. Volunteer officers reported that they had received and had voted to answer a summons from Mercer to join him at
the Rappahannock, but they awaited Washington's further instructions.[80] These defenders of their Colony were not acting in the dark or
on the basis of false information. Events in Williamsburg had been substantially as they were reported in Fredericksburg and at Dumfries.
Between 3 and 4 A.M. on the 21st, Captain Collins of the royal armed
schooner *Magdalen* had come to the magazine with fifteen marines and
Governor Dunmore's wagon. All the powder in the magazine, approximately twenty barrels, had been removed and transported to the bank
of James River, whence it had been conveyed to the H. M. S. *Fowey*.[81]
When the townspeople discovered what had happened, wrath rose. The
call was "To the Palace." They would demand the immediate return
of the powder; it was theirs of right, theirs with which to defend themselves. Before the crowd could start up the street from the vicinity of
the Capitol, Peyton Randolph, Treasurer Nicholas and some others
urged that the Common Hall of the city was the proper body to act:
Let the citizens wait and see what could be accomplished by a decent
and respectful protest; threats and clamor might make the Governor
resist as a matter of self respect. This seemed reasonable to men who
had not yet lost their heads completely. The Common Hall met, debated, drafted a paper and proceeded in a body to the Governor's residence, where Peyton Randolph presented the address. It was a simple
argument that the magazine and its contents were for the security of
the Colony, which might require ammunition quickly in event of an
uprising by the slaves. Would the Governor explain why he had
removed the powder, and would he return it?

The reference to a rebellion by the Negroes gave Lord Dunmore a
peg on which to hang a cloaking excuse: Reports of a servile insurrec-
tion in a neighboring County, he said, had led him to remove the

[78] Letter of Apr. 26, 1775; 5 *Hamilton*, 162–63.
[79] 2 *Force* (4) p. 426.
[80] Letter of Apr. 26, 1775; 5 *Hamilton*, 163–64.
[81] 2 *Force* (4) p. 465; Dunmore to Dartmouth, May 1, 1775 (P.R.O., C.O. 5: 1353; LC
Transcript). Most accounts state that the powder was put on the *Magdalen*.

powder to a place of security, whence—upon his word and honor—it could be returned in half an hour were it needed to combat the uprising. He had been led to send it off at night to avoid excitement and he was surprised to hear that the people had taken up arms. In that situation he did not think it prudent to put powder in their hands.[82] The members of the Common Hall left the Palace, unsatisfied; Dunmore armed his household and the naval officers who happened to be in town. Outside the Palace, the townspeople showed a temper that seemed to threaten attack, but, after a time, they listened to Nicholas and Randolph and began to disperse. Dunmore was a liar, they told one another. He had no information about a revolt of the slaves; no such thing had occurred: all that Dunmore was doing was for one purpose only—to make the people defenceless! They must have their powder.

That had been the state of affairs when messengers had left Williamsburg with the information that was received in Fredericksburg and was passed on to Colonel Washington. As the muster of the Independent Companies at Fredericksburg had been set already for the 29th, nothing could and nothing need be done meantime except to see that the Alexandria volunteers were ready if they were needed. Dunmore might restore the powder; a clash might be avoided. Washington hoped for a settlement or, at the least, for delay. Unless it was imperative that he remain in Virginia, he would leave home for Philadelphia early in May to attend the Congress, which was to begin its sessions on the 10th.[83]

At the very time when peace or conflict in Virginia appeared to hang on the temper of Dunmore and the restraint of the colonials, the news that had been half dreaded and half awaited for weeks arrived from the North: a clash had occurred in Massachusetts; much blood had been shed.[84] In the early morning of April 19, a British infantry force

---

[82] 2 *Force* (4) p. 371–72.

[83] No letters of Washington for this historic week are extant. All that is known of his movements is that he was in Alexandria on the 26th and 30th of April and the 1st of May. Two of these three journeys were to "meet the Independent Company" (2 *Diaries,* 193).

[84] The first report of the clash at Lexington, with no details except incorrect figures of American casualties, was written at Watertown, "near 10 o'clock, April 15, 1775," was received in New York on the 23rd, and was in Philadelphia on the 24th of April. At Annapolis it was printed on the 27th in the *Md. Gazette.* Information of so much importance would, of course, have been carried quickly from Annapolis to the Potomac. If it came by express, it may have reached Washington on the evening of the 27th. The *Gazette* with the dispatch from Watertown almost certainly was in his hands before night-fall on the 28th. In Williamsburg, the information appeared in the *Va. Gazette* of April 29 (*W. W. Henry,* v. 1, p. 279). More detailed information, sent by a second express, reached New York at 2 P.M. on the 25th, Philadelphia at noon on the 26th, Annapolis at 9 A.M. on the 28th, and Alexandria at 6 P.M. that day (2 *Force* (4) p. 363–66). More than once, the dates of the second express have been published as if they were those of the first intelligence of hostilities at Lexington.

had appeared ten miles Northwest of Boston in the village of Lexington, where part of a volunteer Company, forewarned, was awaiting them. The British commander called on these provincials to disperse and, when they did not move swiftly enough to suit him, he ordered his front ranks to fire. At the volley, the Company scattered, but the Americans left eight dead on the ground. Ten more were wounded. The British then marched on to Concord, twenty miles from Boston and ten miles Southwest of Lexington. At Concord, Massachusetts volunteers were gathering but they fell back on the approach of the regulars. Then, while 100 Britishers held the bridge over the Concord River, the others searched the town for military stores they had been told the colonials had hidden there. Little was found but fires were lighted that angered the volunteers, who, after a time, returned to the bridge, where an exchange of musketry occurred. This and the menacing advance of the provincials caused the British guard of 100 to break and leave the little stream. Presently the whole body of regulars reassembled, hesitated for a time and at length started back on the march to Boston. Word of their presence or the sound of the fire had been heard throughout the countryside near the villages. Most of the men hurried out with their rifles to reenforce the volunteers, and soon the Americans opened fire on the flank and rear of the retiring British. A running fight began and kept up for miles, until a relief column from Boston joined the retreating regulars and held off the provincials with artillery while the exhausted redcoats caught breath and rested their weary legs. Even when the strengthened column got underway again, the colonials harassed it to Charlestown, within range of the British men-of-war. Casualties had been considerable; north of Roxbury the colonials remained on "Boston Neck"; Boston virtually was besieged.

By no means all this information was conveyed in the first or even in the second report, but sufficient was transmitted to make plain the fact that the British had struck the blow the colonials had served notice they would resist.[85] War might follow this bloody encounter:

[85] The British column had consisted at the start of 700 men and had left Boston on the evening of the 18th of April. During the fighting of the 19th, a total of seventy-three British and forty-nine Americans had been killed. The wounded numbered 366. All the essential American documents, including the depositions of many American witnesses, will be found in 2 Force (4) p. 391, 435 ff, 490 ff, 626 ff, 673 ff. Gage's brief report is in 1 Gage 396–97. His explanation of his casualties was that the troops, returning to Boston, "were so fatigued from their march that it was with difficulty they could keep out their flanking parties to remove the enemy to a distance." Gage did not dwell on the fact that he manifestly had underestimated the likelihood of resistance. He recklessly had dispatched 700 men to an objective twenty miles distant, without artillery and with no alternative to completing a march of forty miles if they met with so much opposition that they could not bivouac at Concord or on the road. The most detailed modern authority on the action is Allen French, *The Day of Concord and Lexington*.

Washington was not the man to blink the reality or to change plans based on the probability. If he must, he would stay in Virginia to combat any violent acts of Dunmore; but if the semblance of peace were preserved in his own Colony, he would continue with his plans to go to Philadelphia, there to share common council for the continental cause. Washington waited anxiously for more news from the North or from the South, news of further conflict in Massachusetts or of some outcome, pacific or sanguinary, of the controversy with Governor Dunmore over the powder. The 30th brought information that fourteen Troops of Light Horse to a total of about 600 men had rendezvoused the previous day at Fredericksburg for a march on Williamsburg, but that they had delayed their start because of a letter of advice dated April 27 and received by express on the night of the 28th from Peyton Randolph. To consider his answer to their request for advice, the men chose a council of 102 that included nearby members of the Virginia Convention and officers and representatives of the different Companies. On his own account and for the corporation of Williamsburg, the wise Speaker of the House of Burgesses reported that Dunmore had given private assurance he would return the powder, though the Governor had not said when he would. "So far as we can judge from a comparison of all the circumstances," Randolph wrote, "the Governor considers his honor at stake; he thinks that he acted for the best, and will not be compelled to what, we have abundant reason to believe he would cheerfully do, if left to himself." Randolph continued: "If we, then, may be permitted to advise, it is our opinion and most earnest request that matters may be quieted for the present at least; we are firmly persuaded that perfect tranquility will be speedily restored. By pursuing this course we foresee no hazard, or even inconvenience that can ensue, whereas we are apprehensive, and this we think upon good grounds, that violence may produce effects which God only knows the effects of." [86]

This was counsel not to be disdained by men of sanity. The committee of volunteers and other citizens approved a strong written summary of the colonial case and recommended: "Whilst the least hope of reconciliation remains . . . that the several Companies now rendezvoused here do return to their respective homes; but considering the just rights and liberty of America to be greatly endangered by the violent and hostile proceedings of an arbitrary ministry, and being firmly

[86] Letter of Apr. 27, 1775, to Mann Page, Jr. *et al.*, Campbell's *History of Virginia*, 609, wrongly cited as from *So. Lit. Mes.*, 1858, p. 26. The correct citation is *ibid.*, July, 1858, p. 26.

resolved to resist such attempts at the utmost hazard of our lives and fortunes, we do now pledge ourselves to each other to be in readiness, at a moment's warning, to reassemble, and by force of arms, to defend the law, the liberty and rights of this or any sister Colony, from unjust and wicked invasion." There followed brief reference to like action by other Companies and then a deliberate, dramatic contrast: In place of the "God save the King" that ended the Governor's proclamation, the officers who read the volunteers' paper to their men shouted boldly and defiantly: "God save the liberties of America." [87] In an echo of that cry, there on the flats under the hills of the Rappahannock, the Companies unanimously approved this decision, broke ranks and went home, but not without a lesson to themselves and an implied warning to their Governor: Never had so many armed volunteers been mustered so quickly in Virginia.[88]

Washington doubtless concluded from this report that he was justified in looking now to Philadelphia instead of to Williamsburg. He had half a score of trusteeships and other semi-public duties that would have to await his return which, to judge from the duration of the previous Congress, would be about the 1st of July. Work on the residence at Mount Vernon was progressing acceptably and would go forward in his absence and without excessive delay, under the guidance of Lund Washington. Even so, Washington's affairs were in a condition that would make prolonged absence disadvantageous and perhaps expensive. Armistead's executors owed Washington £104; the executors of Col. John Baylor were in his debt for £528 on account of Bernard Moore's bond; Balfour & Barraud had not paid for flour, biscuit and perhaps other plantation products, to a total of £880; John Page's bond of £300 was unsettled.[89] These accounts must be entrusted to the generous

---

87 2 *Force* (4) p. 443. The identity of the author of this fine paper is not known.

88 In 3 *Burk*, 406, are further details that cannot be accepted. Randolph and Pendleton, en route to Philadelphia, are alleged to have sent written advice to the assembled volunteers to defer action until the Congress had adopted a plan. Washington is said to have given similar counsel, but the decision of the committee to recommend temporary suspension of a march on Williamsburg is stated to have been reached by a majority of one vote only. This last "fact" is enough to arouse suspicion regarding the story, because might-have-beens of Virginia history often are hung on the peg of a single vote. In this instance, the minute of the committee meeting is a refutation of the greater part of Burk's account, which manifestly is a confused repetition of the incident described in the text and not, as Campbell thought, another incident of the same day.

89 Total accounts due in Virginia to the Custis estate were £954 and, to Washington himself (Statement of May, 1775, *Washington MSS*, Huntington Library), £1078. Certain other debts by persons outside the Colony were listed in a memorandum of Apr. 30, 1775, prepared for Lewis (37 *G. W.*, 509–10). The delay in settling the account of Balfour & Barraud may have been due to the death of James Balfour. See *Va. Gazette*, Apr. 14, 1775.

stewardship of Fielding Lewis, who was not the man to complain at being called to render so onerous a service.[90] Neither Lewis nor Lund could do anything about the losses entailed in the attempt to "seat" the Kanawha property in 1774. Unescapable hazard, running to large figures, was involved in the possibility that Dunmore might nullify the land grants under the proclamation of 1754 on the ground that William Crawford had not qualified as a Surveyor. All that Washington could undertake, in order to protect his interests and those of his former comrades was himself to conform and to urge them to conform, most scrupulously to the letter of the Virginia statute on the "seating" of patented lands. A Governor at odds with nearly all the colonials manifestly was not in a mood to interpret the law generously for a resolute member of the colonial convention and of the Continental Congress. Dunmore must stop growling, at the very least, before he should be approached. Perhaps that would be possible, if all went well, after Washington came back from Philadelphia.

The hours of the last days before departure were eaten up by visitors. Among others, came Washington's long-time friend, Horatio Gates, who had added many adventures to an interesting life after the days when he had commanded an Independent Company in Braddock's expedition. Gates now was a half-pay Major, residing in Berkeley County, a cherished neighbor of Washington's brother, Samuel,[91] and he was wondering, no doubt, what place, if war came, he could find in the armed forces of the Colonies whose cause he had resolved to espouse. Washington could not answer, of course, but he considered the Major an excellent officer who could aid materially the cause of the Colonies that had dismally few good soldiers. On the 3rd of May, while Gates still was at Mount Vernon, Richard Henry Lee arrived, with his brother Thomas Ludwell Lee, and with Charles Carter.[92] The season was unusually hot, with wind from the South;[93] the lawn by day and the parlors in the evening were a rostrum for much discourse on the part of the two Lees, of Carter and of Gates. As host, Washington listened and, when he had observations, made them briefly. Perhaps, when the guests had gone to their rooms, and Washington was alone with Martha, there was some of the sadness of farewell, but optimism had the upper hand of grief: it was only another journey he was making, another

---

[90] 3 *G. W.*, 290; 37 *ibid.*, 509–10.
[91] Samuel Washington to Gates, Jan. 16, 1776; *Gates Papers*, NYHS.
[92] 2 *Diaries*, 194.   [93] Cf. *infra*, p. 483.

visit, unpleasantly prolonged, perhaps, though in a pleasant city. When the Congress adjourned, he would come back, of course, to the comfortable house, to the beauties of the garden, and to a view of the lovely Potomac with the gentle ebb and flow of the tide—unless that affair at Concord and Lexington, that bloody clash of colonies and ministerial troops, meant war. Even in that event, one campaign would decide whether Britain would recognize the rights of the colonials or would suppress the uprising and punish the leaders. Should the darker fate be America's, then there would be a refuge on those frontier lands Washington was trying to save.[94]

94 Washington to Burwell Bassett, Feb. 28, 1776; 4 *G. W.*, 539.

CHAPTER XVIII

"Not Think Myself Equal to the Command"
(May 4–June 22, 1775)

It was on the morning of the 4th of May that Washington climbed into his chariot and rode off with his colleagues.[1] Twenty years previously, on the corresponding date, he had been at Winchester, in the first uncertain discharge of vague duties as volunteer aide to Braddock, and he had been stormily impatient over the delay that lack of wagons necessitated.[2] Military ambition had soared then; he had coveted and zealously had sought to win "honor" and reputation. Now, at 42, he faced the uncertainties of duty on a road that might prove far rougher, in a different sense, than the one that stretched in rock and mud and marsh from Winchester to Fort Cumberland and on past Laurel Hill and Fort Necessity and Chestnut Ridge. This time, instead of the testy kindness of Braddock, the violence of Sir John St. Clair and all the bickerings of staff and line in the regular establishment of Britain, there might be participation as a Delegate in the task of creating an army from nothing except the vigor of untrained men and the ingenuity of artisans who had few tools.

That possibility was a grim and silent companion on the first leg of the journey which this time led by way of Alexandria, and not directly across the Potomac opposite Posey's old landing.[3] From the thriving county seat Washington drove at a moderate pace to Marlborough, and the next day he reached Baltimore, where he was invited to review on the 6th the ardent volunteer Companies[4] organized in that patriotic

[1] 2 *Diaries*, 194. The use of Washington's chariot for this journey is shown by the reference in his revolutionary accounts to his purchase of five horses "having sent my chariot and horses back to Virginia." See *Monuments of Washington's Patriotism: Containing a Fac Simile of His Publick Accounts Kept During the Revolutionary War* . . . Washington, P. Force, Printer, 1838 (cited hereafter as *G. W. Rev. Accts*), p. 1.

[2] See Vol. II, p. 32.

[3] The reason for this is not known, but it probably was to meet in Alexandria fellow-Delegates who were to make the journey with him. There is no direct reference to joint travel, but, as will appear in a later sentence of the text, most of the Virginians arrived simultaneously, if not together, in the vicinity of Philadelphia.

[4] 2 *Diaries*, 194.

town. There was significance, of course, in the invitation. For ten
years and more—in fact from the time of his marriage to a rich widow—
Washington had been welcomed as a wealthy planter who had been a
conspicuous colonial soldier. Now the scale of values was tipped the
other way: he was one of the few experienced military officers in the
Colonies and, by chance, a man of high financial standing. As a soldier
he was received; through the eyes of an officer of the seventeen-fifties
he looked at the young Marylanders who stood with straight shoulders
while he walked past. After the review, the townsmen gave a dinner
which he attended. It was a day to stir old memories and to carry him
back to November, 1754, when he had declined the invitation to serve
with Governor Sharpe but had confessed, "my inclinations are strongly
bent to arms."[5] There were other "inclinations" now, among them the
delights of such a home as he never had in boyhood and just such an
opulent plantation life as had been among the most determined ambitions of his youth. Still, his state of mind was fundamentally the same
as that in which he had written his brother from Richmond: "it is my
full intention to devote my life and fortune in the cause we are engaged
in, if need be."[6]

On the 9th of May when Colonel Washington and a number of other
Virginians were within six miles of Philadelphia,[7] they met a party of
horsemen later reckoned at 500. These were the officers of all the military Companies, together with leading private citizens of the town, who
had come out to welcome the Delegates. After an exchange of amenities
and a display of firm restraint in speech-making, guests and hosts rode
four miles toward the city, and there they found a band and an escort of
foot and riflemen. From that point onward, the column was a parade,
much applauded and doubtless admired.[8] In the comfortable Pennsylvania capital, the Virginians greeted numerous Southern representatives and the members from New Hampshire. About noon the next day,
the Eastern Delegates arrived in a cavalcade,[9] which was received with
cheers and ceremony. The spirit of almost everything that day seemed
encouragingly different from that which had prevailed at the opening
of the Congress of 1774. Most of the suspicious rivalry of the previ-

[5] See Vol. I, p. 445.
[6] Letter of Mch. 25, 1775; 3 *G. W.*, 277; *supra*, p. 407.
[7] His itinerary is in 2 *Diaries*, 194–95.
[8] *Marshall's Diary*, 25; Richard Henry Lee to William Lee, May 10, 1775; 1 *Ballagh, Lee
Letters*, 134.
[9] 1 *Burnett*, 89 and 90 n.

ous year had been dissipated by the volleys on the Concord Road; the necessity of united action was manifest now to all except the unyielding Loyalists and the most provincially minded members. Richard Henry Lee was able to write at the outset: "There never appeared more perfect unanimity among any set of men than among the Delegates, and indeed all the old Provinces, not one excepted, are directed by the same firmness of union and determination to resist by all ways and to every extremity." [10] A Massachusetts supporter of the royal authority, who had come to Philadelphia in the hope of finding there more of the spirit of reconciliation with England, was depressed by what he heard at Joseph Reed's, where Washington, Benjamin Harrison and Richard Henry Lee spent the evening of the 9th. The guest from New England thought Washington "a fine figure and of a most easy and agreeable address," but, the Loyalist wrote in dejection, "I could not perceive the least disposition to accomodate matters." [11]

Where that temper prevailed, no time was lost in organization. On the 10th, the Delegates met in the Pennsylvania State House, re-elected Peyton Randolph President and, on the 11th, ordered the doors closed for deliberations that were to remain secret until a majority voted otherwise. [12] Procedure was smooth; papers were submitted to the Congress as if it were an established Parliament of recognized authority. In the mass of communications, the one that meant most was from Dr. Joseph Warren, acting President of a body that had a new name, soon familiar—the "Provincial Congress" of Massachusetts. "We have . . . passed," he wrote, "an unanimous resolve for thirteen thousand, six hundred men, to be forthwith raised by this Colony; and proposals are made by us to the Congress of New Hampshire, and governments of Rhode Island and Connecticut Colonies for furnishing men in the same proportion." Never before, in any war, had a Colony spoken in terms of so many soldiers. Thirteen thousand from Massachusetts alone! Warren justified the number with sound military logic: ". . . We beg leave to suggest," he wrote the Philadelphia Congress, "that a powerful army, on the side of America, hath been considered by [Massachusetts] as the only mean left to stem the rapid progress of a tyrannical ministry." Clearly he saw: "Without a force, superior to our enemies, we must reasonably expect to become the victims of their relentless fury:

[10] Letter of May 10, 1775 to William Lee; 1 *Burnett*, 90.
[11] Samuel Curwen, *Journal*, May 10, 1775, p. 27, quoted in 1 *Burnett*, 90 n.
[12] 2 *JCC.*, 11, 22.

With such a force we may still have hopes of seeing an immediate end put to the inhuman ravages of mercenary troops in America . . ." That much said, he trailed off into rhetoric;[13] but in the very hour of the conception of an American army, he had laid down the germinating ideal—superiority of force.

The first application of military policy by Congress came during the opening week of the session, in answer to an inquiry by New York: British troops were en route to the busy city at the mouth of the Hudson:[14] what should American sympathizers do? The decision of Congress, promptly given, was that so long as the redcoats remained in their barracks, quietly and peaceably, they should be left alone, but that if the British constructed fortifications, attempted to cut off the town from the surrounding country, committed hostilities, or invaded private property, they must be resisted.[15] This raised a question in answering one: If that was the policy for New York City, what of the Colony? Where and in what number should American troops be posted outside the principal settlement? To aid in deciding this, Washington received his initial assignment. He had sat in his place throughout the Congress of 1774 and until this fifth day of the second Congress, and had not once received the President's nod or his colleagues' majority vote for a place on a special committee. Now that hostilities seemed nearer and the experience of soldiers had to be invoked, he was named to head a group that included Samuel Adams of Massachusetts, Thomas Lynch of South Carolina, and all the New York Delegates.[16]

While this Committee was studying the map of New York in the dim light of the little information they possessed of the military situation in that Colony, Washington had his thoughts turned for a few hours to his own Virginia. Patrick Henry arrived on the 17th or early on the 18th[17] and gave the authentic details of occurrences regarding which the Virginia Delegates already had a variety of rumors. It developed that word of the fighting at Lexington and Concord had reached Henry and his neighbors ahead of information concerning Randolph's letter of April

---

[13] 2 *JCC.*, 24–25.

[14] Although it would be most convenient on occasion to refer to New York City at this time as Manhattan Island, and thus to distinguish it from the Province and from the other parts of twentieth-century New York, Washington apparently never used the term Manhattan Island. The name does not even appear in the index to *G. W.*

[15] 2 *JCC.*, 52.   [16] 2 *JCC.*, 53.

[17] That is to say, he first attended Congress on the 18th (2 *JCC.*, 55) and doubtless had just arrived, though Marshall listed him among the Virginians who reached the city on the 9th. It presently will appear that Henry did not leave home till May 11.

27 to the troops at Fredericksburg. The wrath of Henry already had been aroused by the seizure of the powder at Williamsburg; this intelligence of a British march to purloin the supplies of the Massachusetts people convinced him that the Ministry was proceeding swiftly and systematically to destroy the colonials' means of defence. Outraged by this, the orator sent for the Hanover County Committee and had the commanding officer order the volunteer Company to assemble at Newcastle on the 2nd of May.[18] That day, Henry addressed them in the conviction he expressed privately to two of his friends: "You may in vain talk to [the people] about the duties on tea, et cetera. These things will not affect them. They depend on principles, too abstracted for their apprehension and feeling. But tell them of the robbery of the magazine, and that the next step will be to disarm them, you bring the subject home to their bosoms, and they will be ready to fly to arms to defend themselves." [19] He did not mistake his constituents. When he proposed at Newcastle that they make reprisal on the royal government in an amount large enough to purchase as much powder as Dunmore had seized, the crowd shouted its approval. Capt. Samuel Meredith, the company commander, enthusiastically resigned his commission so that Henry might succeed him and exercise full authority.[20] Henry thereupon had the County Committee pass a resolution for the detachment of a party of seventeen to proceed to Laneville, the home of Receiver-General Richard Corbin, and to demand the money. If it was not forthcoming, the detachment was to seize Corbin and bring him to Henry who would be moving meantime toward Williamsburg with the remainder of the Company.

Corbin chanced to be in Williamsburg, but when news reached the town that Henry had demanded payment for the powder, and was marching on the colonial capital, the Governor arranged that a bill of exchange for £330, the estimated value of the powder, be sent in Corbin's name to Henry. The leader of the expedition triumphantly receipted for the money, which he said he would turn over to the Virginia Delegates in Philadelphia, to be laid out in powder.[21] Then, after

18 Nothing in the minutes shows that the Company was ordered formally to muster but it scarcely would have come together, virtually in full strength and with its officers, unless orders had been issued. Newcastle, the place of meeting, was then a hopeful settlement and ferry-landing on the Pamunkey River. Subsequently, the village almost disappeared.

19 Third-hand in Wirt, op. cit., 137, but in the spirit of Henry and with the ring of authenticity. On the other hand, "the heads of his harangue," as given in ibid., 139, appear, once again, to be at least nine-tenths Wirt and not more than one-tenth Henry.

20 Wirt, op. cit., 140.

21 Minutes of Hanover Committee, May 9, 1775; 2 Force (4) p. 540.

conference and assurances that all was quiet in Williamsburg, the men of Hanover marched home again. Going and returning, they were attended by most of the adult males in that part of Virginia. The elders were eager to observe any fight that might occur, and the younger men were ready, if need be, to take a hand in it.

Next in Virginia came a variety of appeals and addresses, a vigorous dispute in the Council of State, and, on the 6th, a proclamation directed against Henry "and a number of deluded followers." All persons were strictly charged by the Governor "upon their allegiance, not to aid, abet, or give countenance to the said Patrick Henry, or any other persons concerned in such unwarrantable combinations; but, on the contrary, to oppose them and their designs by every means; which designs must otherwise inevitably involve the whole country in the most direful calamity, as they call for the vengeance of offended majesty, and the insulted laws to be exerted here to vindicate the constitutional authority of governments." [22] This proclamation led to a report that Governor Dunmore intended to order the arrest of Henry. For that reason, when the orator started for Philadelphia on the 11th of May an armed guard of mounted men attended him all the way to Hooe's Ferry and across the Potomac.[23] His followers soon laughed at their own concern. The threat to Henry increased his popularity, which already was great. One County after another approved his action and pledged him support or, without naming him, endorsed resistance to Britain.[24]

Washington and the other Virginia Delegates, hearing Henry's story in Philadelphia, might feel relief that the storm had blown over in the Old Dominion. They might distrust the Governor and they might wonder precisely where the majority of the Council would stand if a choice had to be made between the King's authority and the Colony's rights, but they could have no doubt of the support of the popular cause by the great body of those Virginians still classified separately as "gentlemen and yeomen." Washington, then, temporarily could dismiss his concern for his own Colony and could devote his undivided mind to his committee assignment, which now had new importance because of surprising news from upper New York.

[22] Printed in Wirt, op. cit., 145–46. See also 2 Force (4) p. 464–66, 504, 547; 8 V 412. The more detailed accounts are in W. W. Henry, v. 1, p. 279 ff, and in Campbell, History of Virginia 611 ff. In writing Dartmouth, May 15, 1775, Dunmore spoke of Henry as "a man of desperate circumstances and active in encouraging disobedience and exciting revolt" (P.R.O., C.O. 5: 1355, p. 195).

[23] 2 Force (4) p. 541 n.

[24] 2 Force (4) p. 451, 475, 476, 524–27, 539, 612, 622, 641 ff, 681, 702–03, 710–11, 718.

On the 10th of May, a loose organization of colonials had overrun Fort Ticonderoga at the northern end of Lake George,[25] and, without bloodshed, had captured its garrison of two officers and forty-three men. The fort itself was in ruins and almost certainly beyond repair, but it contained about sixty cannon and mortars, which were believed to be serviceable. If that site or Crown Point or even the southern end of Lake George could be held, then the British route between Canada and the waters around New York City would be blocked. That possibility was of first importance to Washington and his committee in their study of the defence of the Colony of New York; but, the daring of the plan for the seizure of Ticonderoga and the boldness of the execution somewhat startled Congress. One of the most cherished arguments of many Delegates had been that the "ministerial forces," as they preferred to term the royal soldiery, had been responsible for the affair at Lexington and Concord; now colonials had assumed the offensive. The result was a recoil on the part of Congress—the first of the session —and the adoption forthwith of a resolution in which the occupation of Ticonderoga was justified on the ground that the hostile ministry of Britain was preparing the invasion of the American Colonies from Quebec. Recommendation was made by Congress that the provincial committees of New York should move the captured cannon from Ticonderoga to the southern end of Lake George,[26] where the ordnance could be stored. Congress hastened to counsel: ". . . that an exact inventory be taken of all such cannon and stores in order that they may be safely returned when the restoration of the former harmony between Great Britain and these Colonies so ardently wished for by the latter shall render it prudent and consistent with the overruling law of self-preservation." [27] At the moment, it was well, perhaps, that Delegates who were stunned by the success on the New York Lakes did not know of the jealousies and animosities that had developed between the two men who had contended for the command in the attack on Fort Ticonderoga, Ethan Allen, who was acting under Connecticut commission, and Benedict Arnold, whom Massachusetts had sent out.[28]

[25] A most useful map of the region, drawn under the supervision of Robert W. Bingham, will be found in *Atlas of American History*, Plate 45.
[26] This was the site of the earlier Fort William Henry.
[27] 2 *JCC.*, 56.
[28] These rivalries are disclosed aggressively in the first reports of Benedict Arnold and Edward Mott, for which see 2 *Force* (4) p. 556–58. See also *ibid.*, 450, 507, 540, 605, 618, 623, 624, 638, 1085–88.

With such information as could be supplied by the messenger who brought the dispatch from Ticonderoga, Washington and his committee finished their report in time to submit it to Congress on the 19th of May.[29] It was referred forthwith to the Committee of the Whole and soon was involved in a long, serious debate over general defence, bounties, the employment of troops on garrison duty, and the possibility of reconciliation with Great Britain. Peyton Randolph did not remain to preside over all this discussion. On the 24th of May, he left to attend the session of the General Assembly that Dunmore at length had called. In Randolph's place, John Hancock, of Massachusetts, was named unanimously.[30] It was under his rulings, that the committee's report concerning the defence of New York was approved, May 25, in six common-sense resolves—that ground near King's Bridge on Harlem River be fortified so that the city could not be cut off from the country North of it,[31] that batteries be erected on either side of the Hudson to prevent the passage of hostile vessels, that a force be organized immediately to hold New York City, that the total of these troops should not exceed 3000, that there be no bounties or pay in excess of that allowed in New England, and that enlistment be to December 31, 1775, unless Congress directed that the men be discharged sooner.[32] Before argument was concluded, a proposal was made that New York be admonished to diligence in preparing her defence "as it is very uncertain whether the earnest endeavors of the Congress to accommodate the unhappy differences between Great Britain and the Colonies by conciliatory measures will be successful." This was disapproved by believers in a policy of conciliation, and was carried over until the 26th. It then was endorsed,[33] but debate on the warning to New York proved to be merely the first skirmish in a furious battle over new, optimistic resolutions for still another petition to the throne. These, too, were passed and were attached to the resolves on New York.[34]

No sooner had Washington discharged the instructive duty of preparing this defensive plan than he received another and still more formidable assignment—the chairmanship of a committee of six, named "to consider ways and means to supply these Colonies with ammunition and military stores and to report immediately." [35] With him were to

[29] 2 JCC., 57. [30] 2 JCC., 58–59.
[31] The necessity of this appears clearly in *Atlas of American History*, Plate 70.
[32] 2 JCC., 59–60. [33] *Ibid.*, 61, 64.
[34] *Ibid.*, 64–66. Details of this contest will be found in John Adams's Diary, 2 *John Adams*, 408 ff. [35] 2 JCC., 67.

work Philip Schuyler, Thomas Mifflin, Silas Deane, Lewis Morris and Samuel Adams—as solid counsellors on this baffling business as the Congress could have provided from its membership.[36] The committee proceeded to confer, but its deliberations could not be prolonged for the unhappy reason that little could be done immediately except to recommend that the Colonies collect the supplies already in America and that they undertake to manufacture gunpowder where practicable. Discussion of these fundamentals called for no night meetings. Washington dined out frequently[37] and, when not privately entertained, had his afternoon meal at the City Tavern with Lee and Benjamin Harrison, his own colleagues, Alsop of New York, Chase of Maryland and Caesar Rodney and George Read of Delaware.[38] About one evening in three he spent in his own lodgings with his correspondence, his newspapers and his pamphlets.[39]

Washington continued to vote with the majority of the Delegates for all measures that looked to a reconciliation, but he had no faith in the success of any of them. As he fashioned plans and read reports from the North, his soldierly impulses rose. He had brought with him from Mount Vernon a red-and-blue uniform he had worn in the French and Indian War—the one in which Charles Willson Peale had painted him[40] —and now he was wearing it daily, as if to signify to his fellow-Delegates that he believed the time had come to take the field. "Colonel Washington," wrote John Adams on the 29th of May, "appears at Congress in his uniform, and, by his great experience and abilities in military matters, is of much service to us."[41] Not the least of that service was in arousing

---

[36] Schuyler, approaching his forty-second birthday, had extensive and varied business interests and a special familiarity with transportation; Mifflin was a successful large merchant of great energy, aged 31; Silas Deane, 38, was a prosperous trader as well as an able lawyer; Lewis Morris, who was 49, was among the largest landowners of New York; Samuel Adams, needless to say, at 53 years of age, knew much of Massachusetts industry, though himself possessed of no wealth.

[37] 2 *Diaries*, 196–97.

[38] George Read to Mrs. Read, May 18, 1775; 1 *Burnett*, 92.

[39] 2 *Diaries*, 196–99. Only one letter survives of those written by him from Philadelphia prior to June 16. He evidently had no one to assist him with his correspondence during this period and he kept no copies of any of it.

[40] At least this seems by elimination to have been the uniform because, to the date on which he is known to have worn military dress, there is no entry in his accounts for any new uniform. In an article quoted in 2 *Ford*, 477, Charles Francis Adams stated that Washington wore buff and blue, and he cited John Adams as authority, but the older Adams (1 *Burnett*, 102) named no color. Buff and blue apparently was introduced in Philadelphia, as uniform colors, by the Light Infantry Company of the First Battalion of the city forces (2 *Force* (4) p. 1034).

[41] 1 *Burnett*, 102. This is the first reference to Washington's appearance in uniform at the Congress but, needless to say, he may have worn it and probably had for some days previously, perhaps from the beginning of the session.

confidence that hard effort would create an army that could stand up against the British. He scrutinized all the authentic accounts he could get of the fighting at Concord and Lexington and he found encouragement in them. "I believe . . ." he said, "that if the retreat [of the British] had not been as precipitate as it was (and God knows it could not well have been more so) the Ministerial Troops must have surrendered or been totally cut off: For they had not arrived in Charlestown (under cover of their ships) half an hour, before a powerful body of men from Marblehead and Salem were at their heels, and must, if they had happened to have been up one hour sooner, inevitably [have] intercepted their retreat to Charlestown." [42] Gratifying as it was to Washington to know that Americans could and would fight, the tragedy of fraternal conflict oppressed him. He wrote on: "Unhappy it is, though, to reflect that a brother's sword has been sheathed in a brother's breast and that the once-happy and peaceful plains of America are either to be drenched with blood or inhabited by slaves. Sad alternative! But can a virtuous man hesitate in his choice?" [43]

More and more of Washington's colleagues were giving the same implied answer to the identical question; but even those who subscribed to revolutionary methods—defiance, attack and reprisal—were willing, as formerly, to proceed slowly for the sake of the unity they believed to be essential to successful resistance. No proposal, Silas Deane wrote his wife, could be advanced without being subjected to much canvassing "before it will pass with the unanimous approbation of thirteen Colonies, whose situation and circumstances are various." He reiterated: "And unanimity is the basis on which we mean to rise; and, I thank God, it hitherto prevails to a most surprising degree." [44] All the while, one issue after another was presented that appeared to have no solution either through delay or through honorable reconciliation. Daily, it seemed, there was a higher barrier to renewal of the old ties between England and the Colonies.

Letters from London were discouraging now. On the 20th of February, North had fulfilled expectations by introducing a motion [45] to the effect that if any Colony made provision for its part of the cost of the common defence and promised to meet the expenses of its own government, Parliament might vote "to forbear, in respect of such Province or

---

[42] Letter of May 31, 1775, to George William Fairfax; 3 *G. W.*, 291–92.
[43] 3 *G. W.*, 292, with the punctuation drastically revised.
[44] 2 *JCC.*, 80 n.   [45] 1 *Force* (4) p. 1598.

Colony, to levy any duty, tax or assessment" otherwise than for the regulation of commerce. The aim of this patently was to divide the Colonies, but it was so clumsy a maneuver and so certainly foredoomed to rejection in America that the House of Commons showed no enthusiasm for it. The debate on the side of the Ministry was halfhearted and shamefaced. By strange chance the final speech for the bill was by a soldier under orders to go to Boston with reenforcements for General Gage. The martial M.P. was by avocation a dramatist and he carefully worked up to a climax on the theme of the absolute necessity of maintaining the supremacy of Parliament: "I shall enforce [these principles] to the best of my power," said he, "if called upon to act in the line of my profession, conscientiously convinced that upon the due support of them both here and on the other side of the Atlantic, the existence of this country and constitution directly, emphatically and conclusively depends." [46] If colonials read any report of this speech, they probably knew nothing of the man who delivered it. His name was John Burgoyne. One other address followed his, on the 27th of February. Then Lord North's resolution was passed without a division over its terms— and without faith in their effect.[47]

The government was not through. In the eyes of the Ministry, vindication of Parliament justified reprisal as well as repression. Lord North previously had introduced (Feb. 10, 1775) a bill that denied the New England Colonies the right to fish off Newfoundland and confined their trade to Great Britain, Ireland and the British West Indies. His argument was that "as the Americans had refused to trade with this Kingdom, it was but just that we should not suffer them to trade with any other nation." [48] The House of Commons passed this on the 8th of March and transmitted it to the Lords [49] who amended it and, on the 21st, sent it back to the Commons.[50] It was the return of this measure to the House that gave Edmund Burke an advantageous occasion for an argument in behalf of conciliation with the Colonies, a speech that must have made many an American wish the great Irish orator headed the government and shaped its policy. By dramatic chance, this renowned appeal to reason had been followed the very next day in Richmond, Virginia, by Henry's fiery deliverance on his resolutions to arm the Colony. Now, in Philadelphia, almost two months later, May 30,

[46] 1 *Force* (4) p. 1622.
[48] *Ibid.*
[50] *Ibid.*, 1691.
[47] *Ibid.*
[49] *Ibid.*, 1660, 1661,

the report was that English friends of America thought the Colonies should be, or must be, satisfied with Lord North's plan. Sympathizers in London had been told, "no further relaxation can be admitted." [51]

With the echo of this came the din of many voices. Benedict Arnold sent a most urgent call for reenforcements with which to meet anticipated attack.[52] Following that, on June 2, Congress had before it this puzzling question from Massachusetts: What should the Colony do about the establishment of civil authority, which had in effect been suspended? To their own inquiry on this subject, leaders of the Bay Colony added counsel to Congress: "As the Army now collecting from different Colonies is for the general defence of the right of America, we would beg leave to suggest to your consideration the propriety of taking the regulation and general direction of it, that the operations may more effectually answer the purposes designated." [53] Still again, money was demanded in large amount for everything the Congress undertook, but in what sums it might be required for a campaign, or for a year's military operations, nobody knew. On the 3rd of June, therefore, Congress voted to appoint a committee of five to make an estimate of the funds that had to be raised. Although Congress had not yet acted on the report Washington and his colleagues had filed June 1 on procuring ammunition and military stores,[54] this did not excuse him from additional service. Along with Schuyler and Deane, he was named to this new committee of financial estimate,[55] while to still another committee, consisting of the Pennsylvania Delegates, was assigned the task of raising £6000 immediately for the purchase of gunpowder. Assurance was given that Congress would "make full and ample provision" for repayment,[56] though actually that body had no revenue and possessed no power of taxation.

There was zeal; there were endless proposals for advancing the American cause; so much was urged on the floor or asked in letters from the Colonies that members doubtless became confused. When they took up proposals for active defensive preparation, they could do little so long as they were uncertain whether differences were to be reconciled

[51] 2 *JCC.*, 72.   [52] *Ibid.*, 73–74.
[53] *Ibid.*, 76–78.   [54] *Ibid.*, 74.
[55] *Ibid.*, 80. The other members were Thomas Cushing of Massachusetts, one of the most astute of the merchants who had given themselves to the public service, and Joseph Hewes, a most delightful person, who had large mercantile and shipping interests at Edenton, North Carolina.
[56] *Ibid.*, 79.

or a struggle for independence had to be faced. Specifically, in the matter of government for Massachusetts, the committee could suggest and Congress could approve no more than that the people follow the procedure set out in their charter and choose representatives to the assembly who, in turn, would name the council "which assembly and council," the resolution read, "should exercise the powers of government, until a Governor, of his Majesty's appointment, will consent to govern the Colony according to its charter." [57] Few Delegates had the heart to say that Congress was clinging to mere straws of compromise when it spoke now of an acceptable "Governor of his Majesty's appointment." Similarly, for provisioning the troops around Boston, the Provincial Convention of New York was requested to "convey" 5000 barrels of flour to Rhode Island or to a port of Massachusetts Bay, where the authorities of one or the other of those Colonies were "desired to receive and forward it to the camp before Boston." [58] In courageous disdain of its complete lack of money, the Congress resolved that it would "make provision for defraying any expense incurred for this service." [59]

It was cruel how tasks were multiplied and difficulties were piled up hourly. The best minds, after hardest effort, could suggest little that was genuinely useful. When, for instance, agreement was reached on Washington's report concerning a supply of ammunition, this was the whole of it: The interior towns of Massachusetts and all areas of the adjoining New England Colonies were implored to forward secretly to the "American army" in front of Boston all the powder they could "possibly spare"; New England, New York and the "eastern division" of New Jersey were asked to collect the saltpetre and brimstone in their confines and to send the whole to the New York convention, which was besought to put the powder mills of that Colony in operation; from similar collections in the Middle Colonies, a stock was to be transported to Philadelphia to be turned into explosive; each of the Southern Colonies was called upon to collect the materials and to establish factories to utilize them; a new committee was named "to devise ways and means to introduce the manufacture of saltpetre in these Colonies." [60] When this sifted down to instant procurement of powder for the volunteers who were trying to confine the British to Boston, it meant that no more could be expected immediately than neighboring communities would give of their meagre hoard.

[57] *Ibid.*, 84.
[59] *Ibid.*

[58] *Ibid.*
[60] *Ibid.*, 85–86.

The confidence of the early days of the session was changing now to something not far short of discouragement. When Delegates spoke of any question, certain of them of course would seek to display their eloquence and to arouse their colleagues, but even Henry and Lee fashioned no phrases that flamed.[61] Orators had lost their power to rally Congress; the minds of nearly all the members still were resolute to defend the rights of the Colonies; moral courage remained, but with it was new and startled consciousness of the poverty of America, in all material things, save food and timber, required for successful resistance to the strongest of Kings and the richest of states. It might be honorific to sit in council and to continue to pass resolutions, sage or bellicose; but wearisome wrestling with detail, exacting and unrewarding effort, daily frustration, the clumsy response of inexperienced men, and the immediate certainty of adverse odds were the lot of those members who sought to turn legislative "resolves" into armies, weapons and successful combat. How could colonials face the almost intolerable ordeal of spirit unless they made themselves realize daily, hourly, that the alternative was loss of liberty? This was no time for the enjoyment of the flattering society a rich provincial might have coveted ten years previously! If it was ease he sought, it must be among his slaves on a plantation; and if he lived within reach of despotism then he might prepare a refuge, like the one Washington had planned to establish on the Kanawha, so remote that no enemy would think the loot worth the labor of the journey. Was it "honor" an ambitious leader of martial impulse coveted—"honor" of the sort young Washington had pursued over the mountains and on the "Beautiful River" of the French? It was better for any man to renounce that sort of "honor" when he considered the weakness of the Colonies. If a pampered pleasure-lover must take sides in a coming conflict, it might be fortunate for him if the older allegiance proved the stronger. All the might and all the power were on the side of his Majesty.

Some of this spirit appeared in the resolution Congress adopted on the 12th of June for the observance of a fast day, July 20. Inhabitants of the English Colonies were urged to pray God "to forgive our iniquities, to remove our present calamities, to avert those desolating judgments with which we are threatened, and to bless our rightful Sov-

---

61 Wirt wrote: "I cannot learn that Mr. Henry distinguished himself peculiarly at this session of Congress" (*op. cit.*, 148). Letters of Delegates contain scarcely any references to brilliant addresses.

ereign, King George the Third, and [to] inspire him with wisdom to discern and pursue the true interest of all his subjects, that a speedy end may be put to the civil discord between Great Britain and the American Colonies without further effusion of blood . . ." There was more in the same idiom, but by no means everything was compliant or conciliatory. Even in its fast-day resolves the Congress incorporated a firm assertion of the "just rights and privileges of the Colonies"; [62] and two days later, it authorized the raising in Pennsylvania, Maryland and Virginia of a total of ten Companies of "expert riflemen" to march to Boston. Provision was made for officers' pay and the form of enlistment; another resolution named Washington and four of his former committeemen to prepare regulations for the army.[63]

The next decision had been shaping itself for days, perhaps for two weeks, because imagination, as always, outran action. In the paper for raising the ten Companies, it was specified that when these troops reached Boston they should be employed as Light Infantry "under the command of the chief officer in that army." [64] Correspondence of the Massachusetts Delegates had contained warnings of a possible crumbling of the lines around Boston unless the troops there had assurance that the United Colonies would support them. Although the letters from New England did not so state in clear-cut words, it was becoming manifest that the retention of a sufficient force to confine the British to Boston depended in large part on assurance that all the Colonies would stand behind the men in Roxbury and around Cambridge. Action to this end had been postponed from week to week in the hope of winning to a strong, positive course of unanimous action the few Delegates who still clung to the hope that the final appeal to the King would be answered favorably if the Colonies did not resort to common violence and defiant rebellion before they laid their petition at the foot of the throne. The majority were weary now of deferring to what they regarded as the illusion of this element of their membership. Necessity could not wait any longer on diplomacy. Americans must demonstrate by their acts what they so often had asserted—that the cause of Massachusetts was the cause of all. Compulsion was absolute. A leader of ability and character must be commissioned in the name of the United Colonies and must be sent to Boston to take command of troops paid

[62] 2 JCC., 87–88.
[63] Ibid., 90.
[64] Ibid., 89.

and fed by "the continent" and reenforced promptly with volunteers from every province.

Such a leader must personify the unity of Americans, their character, their resolution, their devotion to the principles of liberty: Who should that leader be? Perhaps a majority of the New Englanders favored the selection of Artemas Ward, Commander-in-Chief of the Massachusetts troops in front of Boston. If, as some feared, Ward's health would not permit his continued service in the field, one or another of several general officers familiar with their own region was preferred by most of the Delegates from the Northeastern Colonies. John Adams, who increasingly was the spokesman of the best judgment of Massachusetts, thought it politic to name a man from a different part of America and thereby to dissipate the suspicion some were supposed to nurture that New Englanders wished to impose their will on the other Colonies.[65] Elbridge Gerry and Joseph Warren favored Charles Lee. If he was unacceptable because he had not been born in America, they looked with favor on "the beloved Colonel Washington." [66]

Washington of course had heard all of this and had known for days that he was being advocated by some Delegates. They regarded him as the most experienced of the younger soldiers, the member of Congress who had displayed in committee the greatest familiarity with military matters and, as far as they could ascertain, the best judgment. One after another had told him, in effect, "You are the man." Every such expression alarmed and depressed him. He enjoyed so much happiness in the life he had been leading at Mount Vernon that he could not think of exchanging it for army command otherwise than with dismay. He felt, also, that he did not have the training, and he did not believe he had the ability to discharge so overwhelming a task. His reluctance was manifest to his colleagues.[67] He did not once "insinuate"—the verb was of his choosing—that he wished the command,[68] and he did his utmost to restrain his friends from advocating his election. Soon he had to face the possibility that in spite of wish and inclination, he might be subjected to so strong an appeal by Congress that he might be compelled

[65] Cf. Eliphalet Dyer to Joseph Trumbull, June 17, 1775, with reference to the fear "lest an enterprising Eastern New England General, proving successful, might with his victorious army give law to the Southern or Western gentry" (1 *Burnett*, 128).

[66] J. T. Austin, *Life of Elbridge Gerry*, v. 1, p. 79, cited hereafter as *Austin's Gerry*.

[67] Cf. 1 *Burnett*, 124.

[68] Cf. to Burwell Bassett, June 19, 1775: ". . . it will be remembered, I hope, that no desire or insinuation of mine placed me in this situation" (3 *G. W.*, 297).

to yield. On the 16th of May, he had written the Fairfax Committee to name some one to serve in his stead, should a Virginia Convention be called in his absence,[69] but he had inserted "pro tem" with reference to his substitute as if he felt sure he would return soon to Virginia. Now, because of the stronger prospect of a call to military duty for the Congress, he had Edmund Pendleton draft a will for him; [70] and in his letters to Martha, he avoided any mention of the probable time of his home-coming.[71] As the pressure on him continued, he urged his friends to help him resist it and he probably prevailed upon Edmund Pendleton openly to oppose his election,[72] but as the middle of June approached, he began to feel that destiny and nothing less than destiny, was shaping his course.[73]

On the 14th, Washington went to the Congress and listened to discussion of the number and type of troops that should be raised, a subject of liveliest interest to him. At length John Adams rose.[74] In the eyes of those who believed reconciliation still possible, Adams was a convinced advocate of separation from Great Britain; but his reputation as a revolutionary did not weaken his position as perhaps the wisest and most influential representative of New England. He proceeded now to show the need of action to save the New England army in front of Boston. If it dissolved, said he, through despair or lack of supplies and ammunition, the organization of another force of like numbers would

[69] 37 *G. W.*, 511.   [70] See *infra*, p. 453.
[71] 3 *G. W.*, 294. Detailed references to Washington's state of mind are not given here, because his letters, presently to be quoted, are a mirror of his feelings.
[72] Pendleton's opposition is of record (2 *John Adams*, 416) but the grounds of it nowhere have been stated. David J. Mays, of Richmond, Virginia, who (1949) has been working for some years on a biography of Pendleton, is of opinion that Pendleton took his stand for a New Englander rather than against Washington, because Pendleton believed it proper to have the operations directed by a man from the threatened region. This may have been the fact. On the other hand, Pendleton had been Washington's private counsel in important matters, such as the Dunbar case and, as noted in the text, he was the man Washington selected at this very time for drawing a will. No matter how independent the mind of either man, personalities were weighty in the Congress and in the politics of the time. Pendleton scarcely would have opposed the advancement of his friend and client had he not done so at Washington's instance.
[73] 3 *G. W.*, 294. A precise date for this conclusion on the part of Washington is not determinable. The suggestion by the Massachusetts Provincial Congress that the Philadelphia Congress take over the army at Boston had been received on June 2 by the Delegates of that Colony. Adams recorded (2 *John Adams*, 418) that, at the end of the first debate on the subject, it was "postponed to a future date," which may suggest a later time than the morrow; but an unidentified Virginia delegate quoted as of June 14, 1775 (2 *Force* (4) p. 979), said that "Washington had been pressed to take the supreme command . . . and I believe will accept the appointment, though with reluctance." This is the first specific reference and it may refer to the efforts made that day, and during the immediately preceding days, to prevail on Washington to consent.
[74] From this point, to the close of the day's debate, the narrative does not depend on the accuracy of the assumption that the date was June 14.

be extremely difficult. Before a new army could be collected, the British, no longer under siege, might march out of the city and spread desolation.[75] The colonial forces already in service, Adams argued, must have heartening evidence that the whole of British North America was behind them; this could best be done by placing the army under the direction of a man who represented the Congress and the continent.

Washington of course approved without interrupting to say so. Then he heard Adams admit that this might not be the proper time to nominate a General, and that the choice of a particular individual probably was going to be the question that presented the largest difficulty. For his part, Adams went on, he did not hesitate to say that he had one person in mind, one only. At the words, John Hancock, who was in the chair, showed manifest pleasure, as if he were certain Adams was about to call his name. Washington, fearing otherwise, felt embarrassment creep over him. Adams did not prolong the suspense: The commander he had in mind, he said, was a gentleman from Virginia. On the instant John Hancock's expression changed: his disappointment was beyond concealment; the tightening of his lips and the flash of his eye showed that he felt Adams had betrayed his expectations. Adams observed this but went straight on: he referred, he said, to one whose skill and experience as an officer, whose independent fortune . . . With that, Washington bolted for the adjoining library: Adams could be talking of no other than of him.[76]

He went out; he stayed out; but after adjournment, he of course was told of what happened: John Adams paid high tribute to Washington and predicted that the choice of the Virginian would be approved by "all America" and would be a means of uniting the efforts of the Colonies more cordially than would be possible under any other leader.[77] Somewhat to John Adams's surprise and to the deepened mortification of John Hancock in the chair, Samuel Adams seconded his cousin's recommendation. Mild dissent was immediate, though not general. Several members reasserted the familiar argument that as the whole of the army came from New England and had succeeded in confining the British in Boston, the men were entitled to a General of their own. In this view, Edmund Pendleton concurred. All the Delegates who expressed this opinion were careful to state that their objection was not to

[75] Adams overlooked the fact that the British had no transportation for a long advance. See *infra*, Vol. IV, Chap. III, n. 41.

[76] 2 *John Adams*, 417.   [77] *Ibid.*

"GEO. WASHINGTON ESQ: WAS UNANIMOUSLY ELECTED"

Six lines near the bottom of the manuscript reproduced on the next page shaped the destiny of George Washington and, through him, the destiny of the United States in so far as one man could mould the life of a growing nation. Those half-dozen lines from the pen of Charles Thomson, Secretary of the Congress, differ scarcely at all in form from thousands of other stretches of black ink he spread across the pages of the Journal of the Continental Congress. Thomson, as usual, was in a hurry when he elaborated his notes and set them down as the permanent record of the deliberations in Philadelphia, June 15, 1776. He did not pause and tell himself he was recording a great event in history. If he made that ugly blot immediately after he described the proceedings of the Committee of the whole on "the ways and means of raising money and the state of America," he could not have been in good humor. So he wrote straight on: "The report of the committee being read and debated, Resolved that a General be appointed to command all the continental forces raised or to be raised for the defence of American liberty That five hundred dollars per month be allowed for his pay and expenses The Congress then proceeded to elect a general and by a unanimous vote"—Thomson found his sentence was becoming involved at this point and he cancelled the reference to a unanimous vote—"when George Washington Esq: was unanimously elected." Then, or afterward, he changed "elect" to the more elegant "the choice of"—and there he left the record for posterity.

As the text on p. 436–37 explains, Washington did not attend Congress the day he was named Commander-in-Chief, but he knew what might occur behind the closed doors of the Hall and he dreaded the result. He was willing to lead the troops his own Colony might supply; continental command seemed to him beyond his experience and abilities. "Remember, Mr. Henry," he told his fellow-Delegate, "what I now tell you: from the day I enter upon the command of the American armies, I date my fall, and the ruin of my reputation." Seldom in American history, if ever, has achievement been in such amazing contrast to a man's expectations.

(After the Original Journal in the Library of Congress)

American continental army for one year unless sooner discharged and to bind
myself to conform in all instances to such rules & regulations as are or shall be
established for the government of the sd. army.—

Upon motion Resolved that Mr. Washington Mr. Schuyler Mr. Deane Mr. Cushing & Mr. Hewes
be a committee to bring in a draft of Rules & regulations for the government of
the Army.

A letter from the Convention of New york dated 10 June 1775 respecting
a vessel which is stopt there on suspicion of having provisions on board
for the army & navy at Boston was read & referred to the delegates of New york
Massachusetts bay Connecticut & new york.

Resolved that this Congress will to morrow resolve itself into a committee of the whole
to take into consideration the ways & means of raising money & the state
This to be a standing order until the business is compleated.

Adjourned till to morrow at 9 oClock.—

Thursday June 15. 1775

The Congress met according to adjournment
The committee to whom the letter from the convention of New york was
referred brought in their report which being read
Resolved That the thanks of this congress be given to the convention of New york
for their vigilance in the case of Capt Coffin's vessel & that it be recommended
to them that the vessel be unloaded & the cargo safely stored until all just
claims be the destination of it shall be removed.

that the same be transmitted by the Prest. in a letter to the chairman
of New york.

On the order of the day the Congress resolved itself into a committee
to take into consideration the ways & means of raising money & the state
of America after some time spent therein the president resumed the
chair & Mr Ward reported that the committee had come to certain resolutions
but they desired him to report but not having come to a conclusion
ordered him to move for leave to sit again.

The report of the committee being read & debated —
Resolved, That a General be appointed to command all the continental
forces raised or to be raised for the defence of american liberty
That five hundred dollars ⅌ month be allowed for his pay
and expences

The Congress then proceeded to the choice of a General by
& when George Washington Esq: was unanimously elected.
Resolved that the congress will to morrow again resolve itself into
a committee of the whole to take into consideration the state of America

Adjourned till to morrow

Friday June 16. 1775.

The Congress met according to adjournment. The President the orders of Congress being ---

The President from the Chair informed Geo: Washington Esq[r] that the Congress had by a unanimous vote made choice of him to be general to take the supreme command of the forces raised & to be raised in defence of American Liberty, and desired his acceptance of it.

Upon motion resolved that a committee of three be appointed to draught a commission for the general — and instructions

The committee to consist of the following persons, W[m] Lee M[r] E Rutledge & J. Adams ——

Upon motion resolved i[em]: That a committee of 5 be appointed to take into consideration the papers transmitted from the convention of New York relative to indian affairs & report what in their opinion necessary to be taken for preserving the friendship of the Indian nations

That the committee consist of the following persons viz M[r] Schuyler M[r] Henry M[r] Duane M[r] Wilson & M[r] Livingston ——

Agreeable to the order of the day the Congress resolved itself into committee of the whole to take into consideration the state of America, and after some time spent therein the President resumed the chair & M[r] Ward reported that the committee had come to certain resolutions which they had ordered him to report but not having come to a conclusion they desired him to move for leave to sit again ——

The resolves of the committee being read the Congress came to the following Resolutions.

Resolved, That two major general be appointed for the american army

That the pay of each of the major general be one hundred & sixty six dollars

That when any of these act in separate departments he be allowed for his pay & expences three hundred thirty two dollars p[er] month. —— That the pay of each

That the Brigadiers general be one hundred twenty five dollars p[er] month

That there be one adjutant General and his pay one hundred and twenty five dollars p[er] month

That there be one Commissary general of stores & provisions and that his pay be eighty dollars p[er] month. ——

That there be one quarter master general for the grand army and a deputy under him for the separate army & that the pay of the quarter master general be eighty dollars p[er] month, that of the deputy forty dollars p[er] month.

That there be a paymaster general and a deputy paymaster general

BIRTH CERTIFICATE OF THE UNITED STATES ARMY

The scrawled, unlovely folio reproduced on the opposite page is, in reality, part of the "birth certificate" of the American Army. In the proceedings that included the election of Washington as Commander-in-Chief on the 15th of June was an entry, scarcely legible, to the effect that "Mr. Washington, Mr. Schuyler" and three others "be a committee to bring in a draft of Rules and regulations for the government of the Army." That was the beginning of the Army Regulations, familiar now to generations of American soldiers.

The Journal of June 16 covered the formal notification of Washington and the appointment of a committee to draw up his commission and instructions. Then, after an important discussion of Indian affairs, Congress voted on the organization of the line command and of the staff departments. The highest rank, after Washington's own, was to be that of Major General. No Lieutenant Generals were provided. Even the number of Major Generals was contested. Three, four and two were successively agreed upon. Five Brigadiers appeared to be a sufficient number, but on review, eight seemed the minimum that would satisfy provincial pride. The subsequent growth of the Army required more general officers within a year, though Washington never had as many of this rank as the service required.

There follow in the text of the Journal the first entries on the establishment of the Adjutant General's Department, the creation of the office of "Commissary general of flour and provisions," and the choice of a "quartermaster general for the grand army" and a deputy under him for the separate army. The last entry on the folio is for the inclusion in the staff departments of a Paymaster General. On the next page of the Journal, not reproduced here, is provision for "one chief engineer of the grand army," with two assistants. The same arrangement was authorized "for the army in a separate department." Standards of compensation were low, even before colonial currency began a progressive depreciation, but at the time of the original appointments, few complaints of poor pay were heard. During this stage of the Revolution—a brief stage—every patriot was willing to make a sacrifice for the preservation of his political rights.

(After the Original Journal in the Library of Congress)

Washington personally but to the employment of any other commander than one who was known to the men and had shared their hardships.[78]

The debate ended that day without any decision, but now that Washington's name had been proposed on the floor, those who advocated him did not hesitate in seeking to convert their friends. Southerners who cherished regional pride but had deferred to New England needed to hear no other argument than that the choice of Washington would be acceptable to Massachusetts and Connecticut; men from the threatened Colonies had no answer to those of their neighbors who told them the election of Washington was politically expedient, because it would assure full Southern support of the struggle against the British. No advocate of Washington's preferment showed any disposition at the outset, to attribute superlative military qualities to him. The Virginian veteran was admired; he was accounted able and experienced; he was of unchallenged character and rectitude; reliance could be placed on his sound judgment and on his wide acquaintance with business affairs. Eliphalet Dyer probably spoke the mind of numerous Delegates when he said of Washington: "He is a gentleman highly esteemed by those acquainted with him, though I don't believe, as to his military and real service, he knows more than some of ours . . ."[79] Expediency prevailed even where the impression of Washington's martial ability did not convince some of the members that he was preeminently the man to head the army. Within a few hours after Adams spoke, the opposition to Washington evaporated.

On Thursday, June 15, 1775, when the discussion was resumed in Congress, everything pointed to the selection of Washington. He stayed away and knew nothing of the deliberations until, about dinner time, the Delegates left the hall and, as they met him, shook his hand, congratulated him, greeted him as "General," and told him how, when the Committee of the Whole finished its debate and went through the formality of reporting, Congress resolved "that a General be appointed to command all the continental forces, raised, or to be raised, for the defence of American liberty."[80] Then Thomas Johnson of Maryland [81]

---

[78] *Ibid.* [79] Letter to Joseph Trumbull, June 17, 1775; 1 *Burnett*, 128.
[80] 2 *JCC.*, 91.
[81] At least, that was John Adams's recollection (2 *John Adams*, 418). It sometimes is assumed mistakenly that his tribute to Washington constituted the actual nomination, when choice of a General first was under discussion. Johnson would have been an appropriate person to present Washington: as a resident of Maryland, he knew the Colonel well and, at the same time, he did not come under accusation of advocating the election of a member of his own delegation.

rose to his feet and proposed Washington. No other name was put forward; election was unanimous;[82] adjournment followed almost immediately.

Washington was overwhelmed, but he had so many duties to discharge that he did not have time that afternoon to think at length of the immense task he had taken upon himself. Following dinner at Burns's "in the fields,"[83] he had to attend a meeting of the committee to draft rules and regulations for the government of the army. Some hours had to be found during the evening, also, for the preparation of a reply to the formal notification he was to expect the next day. In this labor he probably had the aid of Edmund Pendleton, who wrote more readily than Washington did,[84] but he doubtless specified that Pendleton make it plain he did not seek the command and did not feel qualified for it. With all his old anxiety to avoid censure, Washington wanted it understood, also, that he did not accept the position for the pay of $500 a month that Congress had attached.[85] Were he to take the salary, critics would complain of the amount and would say he wanted to make money rather than to serve his country. If he waived all pay and failed later, he could not be accused of having acted from mercenary motives, and, if he won, he would have the warmer praise and gratitude because he had no monetary compensation.

The answer to Congress was shaped accordingly and, no doubt, was in Washington's pocket when, the next day, he walked to the State House for the ceremonies. John Hancock by this time had recovered somewhat from his disappointment over his failure to receive the command and he made the best of the vote that left him in the chair when he had thought of himself, perhaps, as being addressed from the chair. Solemnly Hancock began: The President had the order of Congress to inform George Washington, Esq., of the unanimous vote in choosing him to be General and Commander-in-Chief of the forces raised and to be raised in defence of American liberty. The Congress hoped the gentleman would accept.[86]

[82] 2 JCC., 91.
[83] In the *Diary of Jacob Hiltzheimer*, 205, entry of Apr. 23, 1794, the site of Burns's Tavern is given as Tenth Street. J. T. Scharf, in his *History of Philadelphia*, v. 1, p. 476, fixed the location on Ninth, above Arch. Eberlein and Hubbard in their *Diary of Independence Hall*, 260, stated that the tavern was on the Commons, about at Tenth and Vine Streets.
[84] The only known copy of this paper, apparently the manuscript used by Washington, is in 152 *Papers of the Continental Congress*, pt. I, p. 1, LC. With the exception of a single interpolation it is in the autograph of Pendleton. See 3 *G. W.*, 293 n.
[85] 2 JCC., 91.   [86] 2 JCC., 92.

Washington bowed, took out the paper and read:

Mr. President: Tho' I am truly sensible of the high Honour done me in this Appointment, yet I feel great distress from a consciousness that my abilities and Military experience may not be equal to the extensive and important Trust: However, as the Congress desires I will enter upon the momentous duty, and exert every power I Possess In their Service for the Support of the glorious Cause: I beg they will accept my most cordial thanks for this distinguished testimony of their Approbation.

But lest some unlucky event should happen unfavourable to my reputation, I beg it may be remembered by every Gentn. in the room, that I this day declare with the utmost sincerity, I do not think my self equal to the Command I am honoured with.

As to pay, Sir, I beg leave to Assure the Congress that as no pecuniary consideration could have tempted me to have accepted this Arduous employment [at the expence of my domestt. ease and happiness] [87] I do not wish to make any proffit from it: I will keep an exact Account of my expences; those I doubt not they will discharge and that is all I desire.[88]

There was applause, no doubt, and widely voiced gratification that he was willing to serve his country without pay, but, of course, so plain and personal an answer made no deep-cutting impression on men accustomed to eloquence in every utterance on the floor.[89] With no more ado, Congress agreed to name a committee of three to draft a commission and formal instructions for the General; [90] and then, after some discussion of Indian relations in New York, the Congress decided that it later would choose two Major Generals, five Brigadiers and various staff officers whose pay was fixed forthwith.[91] Next—as if deliberately exhibiting the range of the perplexities with which it wrestled—Congress debated the means whereby the troops in New York could be reenforced.[92] At the end of a long session, Washington went to dine with Dr. Thomas Cadwalader.[93]

The next day, Washington's commission was reported by the committee—Richard Henry Lee, Edward Rutledge and John Adams—who

[87] The bracketed phrase is in Washington's handwriting.
[88] 3 *G. W.*, 292–93, verbatim.
[89] None of the letters of members, printed in *Burnett*, refers to the response of Washington.
[90] 2 *JCC.*, 92.
[91] *Ibid.*, 93–94. The original MS of the Journal shows the changes made when additional Major Generals were authorized.
[92] *Ibid.*, 94.
[93] 2 *Diaries*, 199. The index-entry of *ibid.*, is incorrectly under the name of the doctor's son, John Cadwalader.

had framed it. The paper ran in the name of "The Delegates of the United Colonies," each of which was specified. It proceeded to assign him the command of all the forces for the defence of American liberty and for repelling invasion; "and you are hereby vested with full power and authority to act as you shall think for the good and welfare of the service." Obedience and diligence were enjoined on Washington's subordinates; he was himself exhorted to "cause discipline and order to be observed in the army," to see that the soldiers were exercised, and to provide them "with all convenient necessities." In every particular, he was to regulate his conduct "by the rules and discipline of war . . . and punctually to observe such orders and directions, from time to time, as you shall receive from this, or a future Congress of these United Colonies, or committee of Congress." [94] When they had approved this document, the members unanimously declared in a vigorous resolution that "they [would] maintain and assist him, and adhere to him, the said George Washington, Esq., with their lives and fortunes in the same cause." [95] All this was as well done as members knew how to do it and it could not be otherwise than acceptable to Washington. If his experience as a soldier made him realize that it would be difficult for a committee of Congress to direct a military campaign, his common sense told him there was at the time no source of authority other than Congress, which had to act through committees. Besides, his own troubles during the French and Indian War had not been with members of the General Assembly but with the Governor, Robert Dinwiddie. In the best of circumstances, with the most sympathetic consideration by the wisest of committees, the morrow of organization, discipline, supply, training, combat and all the contingency of war would be dark, dark, dark! Washington knew that and he agonized over it. As he talked with Patrick Henry of his lack of training for the task assigned him, the new General had tears in his eyes. "Remember, Mr. Henry," he said, "what I now tell you: from the day I enter upon the command of the

---

[94] 2 *JCC.*, 96. Washington's commission was to continue in force "until revoked by this, or a future Congress." The original paper is in LC and is reproduced in 3 *G. W.*, opposite p. 292. In the library of the Morristown National Historical Park is a document presumed for a long time to have been an early draft of the commission, signed by Hancock, that Washington carried with him. It is, in reality, a clumsy copy on paper with a watermark of 1809. Strangely, too, the person who transcribed the document referred in the preamble to "The Delegates of the United States of America," instead of to "the Delegates of the United Colonies . . ." See V. H. Paltsits, "The Bogus Washington Commission," *Autograph Collectors' Journal,* v. 1, p. 4.

[95] 2 *JCC.*, 97.

American armies, I date my fall, and the ruin of my reputation." [96] His friends did not take so pessimistic a view but they sympathized. At a dinner given Washington by some of the leaders at a tavern on the Schuylkill, below the city, the first toast was to "The Commander-in-Chief of the American Armies." Benjamin Rush recorded later: "General Washington rose from his seat, and with some confusion thanked the company for the honor they did him. The whole company instantly rose and drank the toast standing. This scene, so unexpected, was a solemn one. A silence followed it, as if every heart was penetrated with the awful but great events which were to follow the use of the sword of liberty which had been put into General Washington's hands by the unanimous voice of his country." [97]

The next action of Congress was an unescapable part of the vast, inevitable gamble—the choice of the two Major Generals, who were to be Washington's senior subordinates, and of an Adjutant General, who would keep the headquarters records and perform minor executive duties for the Commander-in-Chief. In 1755, Washington had wanted to pick the officers of his Regiment,[98] and many times afterward he had reason to lament Governor Dinwiddie's unwillingness to let him do so. Now he resolved that he would use his influence to procure the election of some, at least, of those on whose military qualities he had to depend. In the initial selection, he could not intervene. If New England stood aside for a Southerner in chief command, the Eastern Colonies naturally expected the General who held Boston Neck to receive immediate recognition. The ballot of Congress for "first Major General" [99] consequently was in favor of Artemas Ward,[100] General and Commander-in-Chief of the troops of Massachusetts. He was 47 years of age, had been in public life since young manhood, had seen arduous service in Abercromby's campaign, and possessed the good will and support of most New Englanders. Washington had never met him and knew nothing of him except what was said in his praise by the Massachusetts Delegates, whose judgment Washington respected. It is not

---

96 George W. Corner, ed., *The Autobiography of Benjamin Rush,* 113. This is second-hand—Doctor Rush's recollection of what Henry told him, but it has the ring of sound money on the historical counter.

97 *Ibid.,* 112–13.   98 See Vol. II, p. 108 ff.

99 The Journal of Congress originally read, "first Major General and second in command," but the last four words were stricken out (2 *JCC.,* 97).

100 In the Journal, the spelling was Artemus (*ibid.,* 98). In *Moore's Lee,* 27, is a statement, with no authority cited, that Charles Lee described Ward as a "fat old gentleman, who had been a popular church warden but had no acquaintance whatever with military affairs".

likely that Washington was told—if indeed the New England members of Congress themselves knew then—that Ward had a belief, almost fanatical, in the rightness of his own Massachusetts people, through the protection and favor of the Almighty.

Next chosen by Congress, again on ballot, was the Adjutant General, who forthwith was voted the rank of Brigadier. The man selected for this post was Major Horatio Gates,[101] about 46 years of age, whose name almost certainly had been put forward by Washington.[102] The new Commander-in-Chief had formed a good opinion of Gates during the years they had served together and he had confirmed that judgment by what he had seen of Gates after the Major had moved to Virginia.

The second Major General elected by Congress was another man Washington recommended[103]—Charles Lee, who at the time was in Philadelphia[104] and had made already a favorable impression on some Congressmen by his manifest knowledge of European affairs and by his confident familiarity with military organization. Lee did not fail to put a high valuation on his services. Before he accepted, he insisted on a pledge from Congress that he would be indemnified for any financial loss he might sustain by devoting his sword to the colonial cause,[105] a somewhat ominous display of self-regard on the part of a man who had been loud in affirming his devotion to political liberty.

These long proceedings were on Saturday, June 17, 1775, the last day of what had been probably the most fateful week in Washington's forty-three years of life. That evening, almost for the first time after the morning of the 14th, Washington could draw breath and, alone[106] in his lodgings, could survey the outlines, vague as yet in detail, of a task

101 The sketch in *DAB* by Randolph G. Adams is penetrating and is an admirable approach to an understanding of the man. It is necessary to remember that while Gates assisted Washington in many ways and performed certain assigned executive duties at various times, he was in no sense the equivalent of a modern-day Chief of Staff. As will appear in connection with the later service of Timothy Pickering as Adjutant General, the prime duties of the position were clerical and custodial—the keeping of army records, the distribution of orders and the preparation of such returns as were not exclusively in the care of the Commissary of Musters.

102 1 *Burnett*, 136. Cf. Samuel Washington to Horatio Gates, June 22, 1775: "As my brother has been prevailed upon to take the command of the Continental Army, I am happy in your being with him in the capacity you and he mentions, as your greater experience will assist him in the arduous business . . ." (*Gates Papers*, NYHS).

103 1 *Burnett*, 136.

104 He probably had been there for the greater part, if not for all, of the session. Cf. *supra*, p. 433.

105 2 *JCC.*, 97–99. Cf. Alexander Hamilton, quoted in *Moore's Lee*, 29: "[Charles Lee] had a certain preconceived and preposterous notion of his being a very great man [which always] operated in his favor."

106 That is to say, in his Diary he did not list any caller (2 *Diaries*, 199), nor did any of the Delegates whose letters appear in *Burnett* mention any visit to him that evening.

that would appal any man. He had no figures on the population of the
English Colonies in America, but if the total was roughly two and a
quarter million, black and white,[107] the number of able-bodied freemen and white indentured servants could not exceed 175,000.[108] These
were scattered over a land area of slightly more than 200,000 square
miles.[109] The largest city was the one in which Washington then was
sojourning, with about 34,000 residents. New York sheltered about
22,000, Boston some 15,000 and Charleston, South Carolina, 12,000.[110]
These four made a combined total of 83,000, comparatively few of
whom were skilled artisans.

Washington did not know precisely what part of the arms-bearing
population of 175,000 already was afield on Boston Neck, Northeast of
Roxbury, or on the Northern New York Lakes,[111] and he had no reliable information concerning the number of volunteer Companies
being organized and drilled. If what he had observed in Virginia was
typical of conditions in the other Colonies, it was far easier to get men
than to arm them. Expanded manufacture of firelocks and explosive
would be difficult to begin and of doubtful issue. As for cannon, Washington probably had information concerning those taken at Ticonderoga, and he doubtless had heard some of the New England Delegates
mention artillery in position around Boston, but here again he had no
formal "returns" from any quarter, nor any list of cannon stored in
America after they had been removed from armed merchantmen at
the close of the French and Indian War.[112]

There was much the same ignorance as respected the volume of shipping. The colonials owned many vessels, which they readily could commission as privateers, but they had not kept up the armament these and
earlier ships had carried in 1755–63. Even if refitted and granted letters

[107] In *A Century of Population Growth,* p. 9, the estimate for 1770 is 2,205,000 and for 1780,
it is 2,781,000. Indians are not included.

[108] On the basis of J. F. Jameson, *The American Revolution considered as a Social Movement,* Ralph B. Flanders estimated the slave population as 506,000 at the beginning of the
Revolution. This left a white total of about 1,750,000. The usual figure of one fighting man
in ten persons of the general population yields the number given in the text.

[109] The land area of those parts of the United States enumerated in the census of 1790
was 417,000 square miles, of which 239,000 had at least two residents per square mile. The
estimate in the text is the very modest one that the "settled" area, in the census definition of
the word, increased 20 per cent only between 1775 and 1790.

[110] *Century of Population Growth,* 11, where the basis of each estimate is explained.

[111] As used in the text, this term covers Lake George, Lake Champlain and the connecting
waterways. All other New York lakes are mentioned specifically.

[112] Details concerning the supply of ordnance are given in the chapters on the Siege
of Boston.

of marque, these merchantmen could not hope to stand up against British men-of-war, certainly not against ships of the line. The royal navy was much weaker than it had been a decade previously, but it still could blockade the coast, could send armed vessels up any of the larger tidal rivers, and could cover the movement of transports anywhere that troops were to be landed from deep water. In all of this the odds were so crushing that a naval war seemed hopeless except against British traders that were operating without convoy. Again, if distance from England was itself a protection, in that it gave the Colonies time to prepare their defence and to train their troops, there was no existing American military establishment that could be expanded, no group of men who had done the same thing before and had some official tradition of how to go about it. A few more half-pay officers of the type of Horatio Gates and Charles Lee might be sympathetic with the cause of the Colonies and might be willing to accept military commission, but these former soldiers did not constitute a staff. No organization of the commissary, the ordnance, the medical department or the quartermasters' service existed. Staff, command, army, equipment, supplies— all these had to be created from nothing! Washington was not feigning modesty when he told Congress his "abilities and military experience [might] not be equal to the extensive and important trust" the members put in his hands.

"Extensive" was about the most conservative word he could use to describe a task for the performance of which he had certain qualifications of experience and still greater equipment of character.[113] A number of conditions had made his five-year command of a small Virginia Regiment a more informative and educational experience than slothful officers of his rank often had acquired; but those five years had taught him little that any intelligent and ambitious Colonel would not have mastered in like circumstances. Washington's military training had ended, if not in actual frustration, at least in the grim conviction that he would find no rewarding future in a career of arms. When he became a planter, he deliberately put behind him all military ambition, but he had not shunned casual talk of arms, even though he had neglected study of them. Youthful experience had been ripened by the reflec-

113 Before reading this analysis of Washington's character in 1775, at the beginning of the American Revolution, a person who wishes to follow in detail the remarkable development of the man may find it worthwhile to review the sketch of Washington at the end of the French and Indian War, as given in Vol. II, p. 369 ff.

tion of a maturing mind. He believed as firmly as ever that "discipline is the soul of an army" [114] and that the first reliance of a commander had to be on a body of well-trained troops who would do what competent officers directed.

As Washington undertook to begin anew on a larger scale where he had left off as temporary Brigadier, he did not have to adjust himself to changed tactics. Twelve of his sixteen years at Mount Vernon had been a period of peace for the countries of Western Europe. Russia had been at war; Poland had been partitioned; but in France and in England, grass had grown under the wheels of parked cannon, and the authors of books on tactics had not been called upon to revise their texts. Armies fought as they had when Washington took off his uniform at the end of 1758. This persistence of a tactical system gave less of reassurance to the new Commander-in-Chief than might be assumed, because his scanty combat experience had been with Indians or with French in woodland warfare. From the day he surprised Jumonville in 1754, his only exchange of anything approaching line-fire had been in the twilight of the unhappy 12th of November, 1758, when his command and George Mercer's had exchanged volleys.[115] If, now, Washington could lure the British into the forest, the advantage would be his; but if he had to give battle in the open, he would have no past lessons on which to draw, and no knowledge other than that which he had gleaned from books before 1759. To refresh himself on field evolutions and deployment, he would have to apply the counsel he had given his officers in the winter of 1755–56: "As we now have no opportunities to improve from example, let us read for this desirable end." [116] Even that poor preparation might be by the grace of a hesitant or lazy opponent.

Washington's other apparent military deficiencies in 1775 included almost complete lack of training in the formulation and subsequent practical test of strategical plans of any magnitude. In person, he never had directed artillery or cavalry, or, indeed, any considerable body of men. His acquaintance with the care of wounded and with the administration of hospitals was slight. In raising an army, the best that could have been said of him was that his failures had been no worse and no

---

[114] See Vol. II, p. 263. Cf. Charles Willson Peale to Edmond Jennings, Aug. 29, 1775: "I am well acquainted with General Washington who is a man of very few words but when he speaks it is to the purpose. What I have often admired in him is he always avoided saying anything of the actions in which he was engaged in the last war" (C. C. Sellers, *Charles Willson Peale*, 122).

[115] See Vol. II, p. 357–58.   [116] 1 *G. W.*, 271; see Vol. II, p. 150.

more numerous than those of other officers. Such skill as he had displayed individually in prevailing upon young men to enlist in the
service of Virginia during 1754–55 had evaporated, somehow, when he
had undertaken to supervise recruiting by his subordinates.

Fundamentally, his chief experiential weakness was in scale. He who
had operated a Regiment on a frontier was now, after sixteen years, to
direct an Army on a continent. It was as if a beginner at the law had
been called to preside as chancellor. From the post of mate on a merchantman, he was summoned overnight, as it were, to direct a convoy.
Had he been a tenant on a hundred-acre tract, suddenly promoted to
manage the Fairfax proprietary, his orders now to recruit, to arm,
to train and to lead a large Army could not have been more of a
gamble.

Some of his colleagues in Congress believed he would win the gamble
because, primarily, they credited the myths that had grown up concerning his early exploits, the magnitude of his acquisitions and the valor
of his Virginia troops of the seventeen-fifties. The more the colonials
came to hate the British, the more did they depreciate the redcoats and
exaggerate the part natives had played in such campaigns as that of
Braddock.[117] In the same way, the reported offer of Washington in
1774 to enlist a thousand men at his own expense and to march to the
relief of Boston had persisted in spite of its absurdity, and it had added
to his fame. All this, of course, had the transience and the fragility
of "the bubble reputation" but at the moment it was an advantage to
Washington in assuring the support of a Congress on whom he would
be dependent. It was an advantage increased by the fact that he looked
the part of a soldier. Good health was his more surely than at any time
since boyhood, except for the badness of his teeth. Men caught their
breath in admiration when they saw him on a spirited horse. Everything
about him suggested the commander—height, bearing, flawless proportions, dignity of person, composure, and ability to create confidence by
calmness and by unfailing, courteous dignity. The only personal quality
of command that he lacked in 1775 was the dramatic sense. He was a
bit too cool to fire the imagination of youth.

Discerning members of Congress had additional ground for believing

117 In explanation of this deprecatory attitude of most of the colonials, it should be said
that the genuinely distinguished achievements of British arms in America during the French
and Indian war had been at Louisburg and at Quebec and were relatively unfamiliar to most
of the people of the English Colonies to the southward.

that Washington would win the gamble with fate and with the circumstance of war, because they had observed how wisely he described in committee and in private the military pitfalls America must avoid and the hard road she must travel. No man had proclaimed him a genius. Most members of Congress could outdo him in a public speech; few of them wrote more awkwardly. All the lawyers had larger knowledge of affairs of state, probably; some of the Delegates were as good in business and as easy in manner. It was the essential, practical wisdom of his advice, the balance of his parts that made men regard him as Silas Deane did: "I have been with him," said this Connecticut Delegate, "for a great part of the last forty-eight hours in Congress and Committee and the more I am acquainted with, the more I esteem him . . ." [118] Washington counselled as a Commander-in-Chief should. All the Delegates would have affirmed that.

In dealing with Congressmen and in winning their support, Washington's experience as a member of the Virginia House of Burgesses was of value beyond calculation. Nothing he possessed, save integrity, helped him so much, from his very first day of command, as his sure and intimate knowledge of the workings of the legislative mind. In the discharge of every duty to Congress and in the presentation of every request, his approach could be accurate, informed, and deferential. He might blunder in New England, but not in Philadelphia so long, at least, as men of the type with whom he had served in Congress kept their seats and their sanity. In 1758, he had known intimately Virginians, Marylanders and Pennsylvanians. Now that he had met and had conversed with some of the best men of every Colony, he was able to understand their problems and those of America. His horizon never had been provincial but it had been regional. Service in two Congresses had made it continental.

In the matter of equipment for his task, Washington had acquired, also, at least something of most forms of honest and useful experience that America had to offer in farming, manufacturing, shipping, frontier development, lay service on the bench, foreign purchasing, finance and exchange. While his only large-scale manufacturing had been as a miller, he had touched the edge of other industries as a plantation manager, and he had a family tradition of iron-making. Although he still was inclined to do too much paper work, he was increasingly systematic,

[118] Letter of June 16, 1775 to Mrs. Deane; 1 *Burnett*, 126.

also, from the very necessity of handling everything in an orderly manner if he was to perform his many duties. In making decisions he was no faster, but in adhering to them, he was, if anything, more tenacious. Caution and daring were close to a balance in his mind. As one venture after another had succeeded, he had become increasingly disposed to take chances in reliance on his judgment which had matured steadily and without the cancerous growth of prejudice. Gradually he had built up the feeling, "I overcame that obstacle, I can triumph over this one." His was not the type of recklessness that may have led some of the planters the more readily to defy King and Parliament because they were financially ruined anyway. He was solvent but he was bold, deliberately, coldly bold, and, at the same time, he was patient in waiting for an advantageous opening and was wary until he found it.

Along with daring, he had developed skill in adapting and in improvising. He had shown ingenuity during the French and Indian War in employing feeble materials, human and man-made, to create and to equip a Regiment. After the war he had learned additional homely lessons in utilizing what he could get, instead of what he desired, and in making shift where he lacked a machine. Few Americans not directly in mercantile business had a clearer understanding of the Colonies' pathetic, costly dependence on England for manufactures, and of the resulting necessity of building up colonial industry at once. Moreover, while it would not be regarded as a compliment to the men who might have to fight for American freedom, Washington's large experience in the subsistence of slaves would be of use in the commissariat. He would find for his troops the best food he could; but if gaunt hunger threatened, he knew on what simple rations, and of what kind men might keep their health. Even his frustrated efforts to establish frontier plantations supplemented everything he had learned during 1754–58 about the victualing of forts and outposts.

Admirable as was this equipment, unique as it perhaps was among Americans who lived in a simple, essentially agrarian society, it did not give Washington conceit, arrogance or overconfidence. Always he kept his head. Careful in what he said before strangers, he was candid among friends and, at the same time, always as modest in manner as he was just in judgment. He never quoted and seldom read St. Paul, but he adhered unswervingly to the exhortation "not to think of himself more highly than he ought to think." Somehow, too, he made his companions conscious of his modesty, though he never defaced the virtue by professing himself humble.

In his undeviating adherence to what he called "principles," Washington had not changed from 1755 to 1775. The same thing was true of his conception of duty that could not be declined otherwise than with discredit. When Washington wrote of his reluctant acceptance of continental command, he soon was to say: "It was utterly out of my power to refuse this appointment, without exposing my character to such censures as would have reflected dishonor upon myself, and given pain to my friends." [119] Doubtless he had forgotten it, but almost twenty years previously, when he had an intimation that he was to be offered the command of the Virginia Regiment, he had written his mother: ". . . if the command is pressed upon me by the general voice of the country, and offered upon such terms as can't be objected against, it would reflect eternal dishonor upon me to refuse it; and that, I am sure must, or ought, to give you greater cause of uneasiness than my going in an honorable command; for upon no other terms I will accept of it if I do at all . . ." [120] Two or three similar parallels existed. Although he now was acquiring a nascent taste for humor, he still was too sparing with the tonic of laughter. Fear of censure continued. In most qualities of mind and spirit the Washington who put on his shoulders the heavy burden of continental defence in 1775 was different from the disappointed and half-embittered young officer who had ridden eastward from Fort Pitt in December, 1758. If it justly could be said that ambition had been the dominant of his life until that time, then the epitome of 1759–74 was development. Many other men matured after 25; Washington was almost transformed. The goodness of youth had not perished in manhood; modest characteristics had grown into positive virtues. The surest evidence of this, certainly the most striking, was in his attitude toward money. He had not lost his acquisitiveness and he was as stiff as ever in his dealings with overseers, tenants and tradesmen. His form of contract was fixed and printed. Those who wanted to work his land must sign the paper as it was. In other ways, he was less exacting financially. Lack of need restrained him unless the stake was large or he felt he was imposed upon. If any man had flattered himself that he could cheat Colonel Washington, let him beware! In all other transactions, Washington was increasingly disposed to think

---

[119] Letter of June 18, 1775; 3 *G. W.*, 294.   [120] Letter of Aug. 14, 1755; 1 *G. W.*, 159.

of the other party, even if that party of the second part did not belong to the ruling class, the members of which might borrow and return when and as they would. Assured position, broadened sympathy and the financial ease that had come through his marriage to Martha—the most influential single event of the sixteen years after 1758—had multiplied his benefactions. If it had to be said that his finest example of generosity was in the case of William Ramsay, the son of a friend,[121] it would have been possible to list a score of gifts where neither friendship nor gratitude for anything except for his own good fortune was responsible.

Washington was far simpler in character, and clearer in his sense of values. In 1755, even for service with Braddock, there had been the most careful weighing of advantage against disadvantage, cost against "honor" and, at the last, reservation concerning the date he was to begin his service and the time at which he might leave it. Now, the defence of justice and the maintenance of the liberties of Americans were so manifestly compelling that there were no provisos, no qualifications. He took his stand, moreover, with little or none of the self-consciousness that earlier had made him awkward and in some things unlikeable. Whether this particular change was because he was more confident of himself and more certain of his position, perhaps he would have had difficulty in saying. Whatever the reason, the reality was beyond dispute. He did not seem now to be thinking always of his own advancement or of the public approval he might win.

Still deeper, Washington was distinctly more religious than in the days of the French and Indian War, and he was more frequently mindful of Providence, though he still was puzzled to distinguish Providence from destiny. He indulged in no theological disquisition and he wrote no homilies, but as he served the church, he developed new reverence for its Head, and as he lengthened his own journey of life, he had to conclude that a Guide directed his path. It is not certain that he attributed to religion the self-mastery in which he had achieved his most notable and most beautiful development. His sensitiveness doubtless was as sharply painful as ever, but he was capable now of combatting every expression of it—not because he was callous but because he soon learned that he had to endure hurt lest he hurt his cause. This self-mastery, this conquest of his proneness to take offence, was the

121 See *supra,* p. 211.

more to Washington's credit by reason of the change in his circumstances after 1758. For fifteen years, as an affluent planter, he had been responsible only to his conscience, to his constituents in a polite, perfunctory fashion, and to the court as far as the Custis estate was concerned. Outside those narrow bounds, he had been the lord of his manor, the owner of slaves who could not dispute his will, the master of indentured servants, bought by the "parcel." [122] Now, though styled Commander-in-Chief, he was himself to be the servant of all.

The influence of religion on Washington was not confined, directly or indirectly, to this development of self-mastery. Performance of some of the most unpleasant service of the years between the wars had spiritual aspects that perhaps were unrealized. Captain Posey had been a burden; Dr. Savage's rapacity had opened before Washington's eyes a gulf of degradation; every mention of Gilbert Simpson made Washington angry even now; [123] Daniel Jenifer Adams had disgraced the society to which he belonged. Yet Washington had continued to help Posey, had hired Gilbert Simpson a second time, and had refrained from action against Adams as long as there was any possibility of an honest explanation of the young man's conduct or any prospect of atonement for it. As for the long controversy over Rev. Charles Green's trust, Washington had persisted though he found it almost as difficult to endure Mrs. Savage's changes of mind as it had been to outwit and outwear Doctor Savage's villainy. These and like affairs—defalcations, broken promises, indolence and lying—had been ugly and depressing at the time but they had taught Washington not to expect too much of the frail or of the feeble. Had he sat down to analyze himself, which he seldom did, Washington might have counted it a strange paradox, but it was true: high among his qualifications for command were spiritual attributes that some might have accounted weaknesses—patience, pity, understanding of the shortcomings of men.

What Washington did not realize and consequently could not gauge at the time was the extent to which his inherently sound judgment had matured. To be sure, he modestly could have said that he would have a fair prospect of reaching a correct answer to some questions that had come within the range of his experience. The same Magister Optimus had taught him that certain things were not to be done, because they inevitably would end in disaster. Moreover, as he often had taken

---

[122] See *supra*, p. 397 n.   [123] 3 *G. W.*, 432.

chances and had won, he could reason that in still other cases the odds, whether long or narrow, were measurably determinable. Beyond these ventures, he now had to expect that he must deal with equations difficult in themselves and infinitely complicated by every sort of pride and greed, appetite and ambition, on the part of governors and lawmakers, rivals and subordinates. Washington had nothing in his experience and nothing in the previous range of exercised judgment to reassure him that he would be able to resolve these long equations in terms of wisdom, justice and action. Perhaps the utmost that could be affirmed on this score was negative: he had not come to any blank wall of reasoning or of judgment beyond which he knew, in his heart of hearts, that he could not penetrate.

His dignity was innate; his calm was in part deliberate and in some degree the unconscious expression of his sense of rectitude. Goodwill begat the amiability that shone in his countenance without effusiveness or any lack of self-respect. The habit of command, as soldier and as master, had become so fixed in his bearing that it kept men from presuming on him, but it did not mar with austerity the benevolence of his visage. Although there was as yet no marked restraint in his mien, his continuing lack of facility of speech disposed him to be cautious in expressing himself outside the circle of trusted friends who would not abuse confidence. This wariness might become more pronounced when Washington was surrounded by officers who were curious to know what he thought of his companions-in-arms and what he planned to do against the enemy. Reticence might become reserve that would give a certain frigidity to his address. Apart from this possibility that his native kindliness might be covered with ice, his gracious, unfailing good manners were consonant with his appearance as Commander-in-Chief, and were to prove both lubricant and emollient in the management of men.

If, then, the balance of circumstance was against Washington, because the visible resources of colonial America were not comparable to those of Britain, the balance of personal character and qualification was decisively and indisputably favorable to him. The final casting of the fateful account could not be that simple. To what extent did he possess two of the supreme qualities demanded of the man who was to head so small and feeble an army as his country would put into the field? If he and his colleagues were justified in expecting that a single campaign would end in reconciliation or accommodation, the question might not be one on which the fate of a continent hung, but if a long war lay ahead, those two special virtues must be displayed by a General dutiful to the Philadelphia Congress and in command of soldiers of such temper as could be brought into colonial ranks. He would need many elements of strength but, most of all, patience and determination, inexhaustible and inextinguishable. Washington had shown during the French and Indian War that though he might become impatient and even lose his temper over small vexations, he could command patience almost in direct proportion to the drafts then made on it. Did he have as much patience as he now might be called upon to display? Would pride outride patience, or would he be able to endure cowardice, quarrelsome rivalries and the hideous greed of a continental struggle? As for the other essential, men who had known him well from 1754 onward would have credited him with steadfastness of a sort to be admired if the end of man was honest self-advancement; but even those who appreciated his achievements might have believed that his unrelenting efforts to make more money, to win new "honor," to acquire other thousands of acres did not go beyond the ambition of other energetic and calculating men of intelligence. There perhaps had been no special virtue in it, no evidence of any dedication of spirit, except as Washington had adhered unflinchingly to the cause of American liberty regardless of the effect on his private estate. He was a patriot who did not equivocate; he was a man of affairs who had shown persistence. That would be conceded. Did he have, in addition, the higher order of determination that could be combined with his patience in self-effacing leadership of a desperate cause in its most desperate hour?

Before he faced any part of that test he had to acquaint Martha with his decision and he had to ease, if he could, the emotion he knew his letter would stir. He waited until next day, Sunday, June 18, and then he penned this:

My Dearest: I am now set down to write you on a subject which fills me with inexpressible concern, and this concern is greatly aggravated and increased, when I reflect upon the uneasiness I know it will cause you. It has been determined in Congress that the whole army raised for the defence of the American cause shall be put under my care, and that it is necessary for me to proceed immediately to Boston to take upon me the command of it.

You may believe me, my dear Patsy, when I assure you in the most solemn manner that, so far from seeking this appointment, I have used every endeavor in my power to avoid it, not only from my unwillingness to part with you and the family, but from a consciousness of its being a trust too great for my capacity, and that I should enjoy more real happiness in one month with you at home than I have the most distant prospect of finding abroad, if my stay were to be seven times seven years. But as it has been a kind of destiny that has thrown me upon this service, I shall hope that my undertaking it is designed to answer some good purpose. You might, and I suppose did perceive, from the tenor of my letters, that I was apprehensive I could not avoid this appointment, as I did not pretend to intimate when I should return. That was the case. It was utterly out of my power to refuse this appointment, without exposing my character to such censure as would have reflected dishonor upon myself, and have given pain to my friends. This, I am sure, could not, and ought not to be pleasing to you, and must have lessened me considerably in my own esteem. I shall rely, therefore, confidently on that Providence which has heretofore preserved and been bountiful to me, not doubting but that I shall return safe to you in the fall. I shall feel no pain from the toil or the danger of the campaign; my unhappiness will flow from the uneasiness I know you will feel from being left alone. I therefore beg that you will summon your whole fortitude and pass your time as agreeably as possible. Nothing will give me so much sincere satisfaction as to hear this, and to hear it from your own pen.

If it should be your desire to remove into Alexandria (as you once mentioned upon an occasion of this sort) I am quite pleased that you should put it into practice, and Lund Washington may be directed by you to build a kitchen and other houses there proper for your reception. If on the other hand you should rather incline to spend a good part of your time among your friends below, I wish you to do so. In short my earnest and ardent desire is that you will pursue any plan that is most likely to produce content, and a tolerable degree of tranquility; as it must add greatly to my uneasy feelings to hear that you are dissatisfied or complaining at what I really could not avoid.

As life is always uncertain, and common prudence dictates to every man the necessity of settling his temporal concerns while it is in his power, and while the mind is calm and undisturbed, I have, since I came to this place (for I had not time to do it before I left home) got Colonel Pendleton to draft a will for me, by the directions I gave him, which will I now enclose. The provision made for you in case of my death will, I hope, be agreeable: I have included the money for which I sold my land (to Doctor Mercer) in the sum given you as also all my other debts. What I owe myself is very trifling, Cary's debt excepted, and this would not have been much if the bank stock had been applied without such difficulties as he made in the transference.

I shall add nothing more at present as I have several letters to write, but to desire that you will remember me to Milly and all friends, and to assure you that I am, with the most unfeigned regard

My dear

Patcy Yr affecte
Go Washington

PS

Since writing the above I have received your letter of the 15th and have got two suits of what I was told was the prettiest muslin. I wish it may please you. It cost 50/ a suit, that is 20/ a yard.[124]

In the same spirit he wrote "Jack" Custis and confessed to "very anxious feelings" on account of the boy's mother. Short of issuing a direct parental command, Washington said everything he could to induce the young Custises to reside at Mount Vernon in his absence.[125] Characteristically and with all of his sensitive regard for the good opinion of men, he wrote Burwell Bassett: "May God grant . . . that my acceptance of [the appointment as Commander-in-Chief] may be attended with some good to the common cause, and without injury (from want of knowledge) to my own reputation. I can answer but for three things, a firm belief of the justice of our cause, close attention to the prosecution of it, and the strictest integrity. If these cannot supply the place of ability and experience, the cause will suffer, and more than probably my character along with it, as reputation derives its principal support from success; but it will be remembered, I hope, that no desire or insinuation of mine placed me in this situation. I shall not be deprived therefore of a comfort in the worst event if I retain a consciousness of having acted to the best of my judgment." [126]

There was little time for these or for any other letters, because duties with Congress and preparations for departure for Boston occupied every hour of the long summer days. When the Delegates came together Monday, June 19, they proceeded to put into effect some political agreements that had been reached over the week-end. Besides the two Major

[124] 3 *G. W.*, 293–95. What appears to be the original of this letter is owned by E. L. R. Smith of Luthersville, Md., who most generously permitted collation with the typically "edited" text 3 *Sparks*, 2–4. The additions from the Smith version are personal but highly interesting. Punctuation is revised somewhat here.   [125] 3 *G. W.*, 296.

[126] 3 *G. W.*, 297. A letter of much the same purport to "Jack" Washington, June 20, 1775, appears in *ibid.*, 299–300.

Generals already chosen, two others now were authorized and forthwith were elected.[127] This was a dangerous decision, because it involved the assignment of large powers and wide discretion to men whose mistakes might hamper the Commander-in-Chief if actually they did not wreck the colonial cause. It would have been more nearly safe to have given these officers provisional rank or to have commissioned them Brigadiers; but pride and jealousy and assumed necessity combined to make a bargain: If Virginia and Massachusetts had respectively the General and a Major General, Connecticut and the Middle Colonies must not fail of recognition equal that of the Bay Colony. A commission as Major General was voted Philip Schuyler, a rich New York landed proprietor and man of business who had seen some service in the war of 1754–63 and had been active in the colonial cause. Schuyler was then in Philadelphia as one of the New York Delegates [128]—popular, influential and in many respects the Northern counterpart of Washington, who was Schuyler's senior by almost two years. This appointment, needless to say, was quid pro quo for the Middle Colonies.[129] The other command as Major General was awarded to Israel Putnam of Connecticut,[130] 57 years of age, a picturesque, little-schooled representative of the New England small farmers who were rallying to the colonial cause. Although Putnam was personally unknown to his new commander and to most of the Delegates in Philadelphia, he was a legendary figure to humble folk of his own Colony. Impossible feats were attributed to him; he enjoyed as a soldier in New England much the same sort of following that Patrick Henry had in Virginia.[131] Equally with those of Washington, Ward and Gates, this fifth nomination was approved readily by a Congress that praised Putnam: not one vote was cast against him.[132] The negotiation had been troublesome and, to some of the members, humiliating. "Nothing has given me more torment," John Adams wrote James Warren, when the last choice had been made, "than the scuffle we have had in appointing the general officers." Adams explained: "We could not obtain a vote upon our seat for L[ee] . . . Dismal bugbears were

---

127 2 *JCC.*, 99.
128 He had taken his seat May 15. See 2 *JCC.*, 48. Cf. Richard Montgomery to Robert Livingston, June 3, 1776: "[Philip Schuyler's] consequence in the Province makes him a fit subject for an important trust, but has he *strong nerves?* I could wish to have that point well assured with regard to any man so employed." *Livingston Papers*, 31, NYPL.
129 Cf. Dyer in 1 *Burnett*, 137.
130 He was born in Salem Village, later Danvers, Massachusetts.
131 For the election of these Major Generals, see 2 *JCC.*, 99.
132 *Ibid.*

raised. There were prejudices enough among the weak and fears enough among the timid, as well as other obstacles from the cunning: but the great necessity for officers of skill and experience prevailed." [133]

When Washington had been assigned these principal lieutenants, he received his instructions, which were intelligently drawn to cover his journey to Massachusetts, his assumption of command, his discretionary powers, and the steps he should take to organize, recruit and supply the Army. He was authorized to make brevet but only brevet appointments of Colonels and of officers below that rank until vacancies were filled by the Convention or Assembly of the Colony from which the troops and their commanders came. [134] The guiding rule, not set forth explicitly in the paper given him, was to be this: Congress would name the general officers of the soldiers in continental pay; all the officers of the different Colonies were to be appointed and, if need be, replaced by the colonial law-making bodies, according to such differing rules and practices as each might formulate. The supply of equipment and blankets and the issuance of new commissions were not explained in the instructions but were discussed with a friendly committee named on the 21st and then were determined, if only on paper, by Congress. [135]

The day that brought decision on these matters witnessed the choice of eight Brigadier Generals. Doubtless by previous agreement, [136] three of these were from Massachusetts, Seth Pomeroy, William Heath and John Thomas, and two from Connecticut, David Wooster and Joseph Spencer. New Hampshire was honored by the commissioning of John Sullivan; Rhode Island was credited with Nathanael Greene. An Irish resident of New York, Richard Montgomery, completed the list. Washington's respect for Congress' right of free choice and his inborn sense of justice made him wait hopefully to see what qualities these men possessed; but he knew none of them personally and he could not have been pleased to hear then, or to learn later, that the first-named of the Brigadiers, Pomeroy, was 69 years of age, and that Wooster was 64. Washington was entirely uninformed, also, concerning the seniority of the general officers of the different Colonies. He had no idea, probably—if indeed any of the Congressmen knew—whether the order of the selection of these commanders in Philadelphia conformed to that of their names on the rolls of their provinces.

[133] Letter of June 20, 1775; 1 *Burnett,* 137.
[134] 2 *JCC.,* 100–01.   [135] *Ibid.,* 103.
[136] See John Adams to Joseph Warren, June 21, 1775; 1 *Burnett,* 141.

By his restrained attitude toward this delicate and dangerous business of appointments, and by all his other dealings with Congress, Washington almost overnight increased as a General the good opinion he had won as a Delegate. Once the members had made him their choice, they instinctively became his champion in order to justify themselves. Some who probably had regarded him as no better a soldier than Ward or Pomeroy began now to extol him. The enthusiastic John Adams wrote of him as "the modest and virtuous, the amiable, generous and brave George Washington," [137] the "sage . . . and amiable General Washington." [138] As Silas Deane continued the close relations of which he had written previously, he found Washington's acceptance "modest and polite" and he reported admiringly that Washington "is said to be as fixed and resolute in having his orders on all occasions executed, as he is cool and deliberate in giving them." [139] John Hancock, manfully overcoming the hurt to his pride at not being offered the command, introduced Washington to his Massachusetts friends as "a fine man," and "a gentleman you will all like," and he urged an appropriate reception and a suitable residence. [140] How long this good opinion would prevail, Washington himself could not foresee in the least. Charles Lee, Ward, Putnam, any of these or some unknown man might become quickly the hero of the Revolutionary cause. The only certainty in this was that none of the distinguished seniors of earlier wars would come back to dispute first place in command. All these figures had passed from the stage or had grown old. Sir William Shirley's was now a name fast being forgotten after his death at Roxbury, Mass., in March, 1771; Sir William Johnson had come to the end of his days in July, 1774; Col. John Bradstreet had succumbed that same year; Sir William Pepperell had not survived to read of the Peace of Paris in 1763; if there would have been any prospect that Col. Henry Bouquet's affection for the colonials would have led him to change his uniform, fever had taken him off in 1765 at Pensacola. [141]

Thus did Washington have the initial advantage, if no more than that, on the fields in front of Boston, to which he had now to proceed. On the 19th he wrote a last casual entry in his brief Diary—"Dined at Col. Ried's. Spent the evening at Mr. Lynch's"—and then he tucked

137 Letter of June 17, 1775 to Mrs. Adams; *ibid.*, 130.
138 Letter of June 20, 1775, to James Warren; *ibid.*, 136.
139 Letter of June 18, 1775 to Joseph Trumbull; *ibid.*, 133.
140 Letters of June 18, 1775 to Joseph Warren and Elbridge Gerry; *ibid.*, 134–35.
141 The inventory of Colonel Bouquet's effects is in Br. Mus. Add. MS 21660, 1–5.

the little volume away.[142] Even the two or three minutes spent daily
on that thin record must be saved. He purchased five new horses and a
light phaeton on public account and he started his own chariot and
team homeward.[143] Two able young Philadelphians, Thomas Mifflin
and Joseph Reed [144] agreed to go with him temporarily as members of
his staff. Soon Washington completed his meetings with Congress or
its committees on the compelling questions that had to be settled before
his departure. Neither he nor the New England leaders felt he could
wait in Philadelphia to deal directly with small issues when his presence
with the troops in Massachusetts was required. Charles Lee and Philip
Schuyler were making ready to depart with their Commander-in-Chief.

Dramatically, on the 22nd, as Washington was engaged in his final
preparations, there arrived vague, scarcely credible news of another and
bloodier clash near Boston. As elaborated within a few hours,[145] the
story ran in this wise: colonials who held crude lines around the city
had heard on the 16th of June a report that a British force was about to
sally and to seize hills in Charlestown and on Dorchester Neck. In an
effort to anticipate this hostile movement, about 1200 Americans had
set out during the night of the 16th–17th, for Bunker Hill in Charlestown, a position that dominated the port of Boston. Unfortunately the
men went by mistake to Breed's Hill, a lower eminence than Bunker
Hill, but they dug diligently during the night and laid out a small
redoubt. Soon after daylight, officers on one of the British ships discovered the work and opened fire. As the morning wore on, the British
increased their cannonade and about 2 P.M. landed troops to storm the
hill. After two repulses by colonials, who had now been reenforced, the
British succeeded in their frontal assault and drove off the Americans.
The New England commanders admitted considerable losses, though
charging the enemy with more, and while they had to confess failure in
their attempt to seize and to hold the high ground, they reported that
their men had behaved well and would have done even better if ammunition had not been exhausted.[146]

142 2 *Diaries*, 199. "Mr. Ried" was Joseph Reed. Either Thomas Lynch or Thomas
Lynch, Jr. was the other person mentioned.
143 *G. W. Rev. Accts.*, p. 1; *Washington's Journey of 1775*, p. 22.
144 Reed was a native of New Jersey but he had made himself so much a part of the life
of the Quaker City after he established himself there as a lawyer in 1770 that he was regarded
as a Philadelphian.
145 See *supra*, p. 461, n. 6.
146 According to the return in 2 *Force* (4) p. 1328, American casualties were: killed and
missing, 145; wounded, 304; total 449. British losses summarized by Gage were: killed, 226;

Washington could not manufacture powder but he could, and now he must, be at the front. On the morning of the 23rd, Charles Lee and Philip Schuyler and the others who were to go with them were ready. Washington had one last duty to perform, one only. He sat down and wrote:

My Dearest: As I am within a few minutes of leaving this city, I could not think of departing from it without dropping you a line, especially as I do not know whether it may be in my power to write you again till I get to the camp at Boston. I go fully trusting in that Providence, which has been more bountiful to me than I deserve and in full confidence of a happy meeting with you sometime in the Fall. I have no time to add more as I am surrounded with company to take leave of me. I retain an unalterable affection for you which neither time or distance can change. My best love to Jack and Nelly and regards for the rest of the family; Conclude me with the utmost truth and sincerity, Your entire [147]

Now—to mount and be off! Gentlemen are very kind to extend their good wishes and to ride in their carriages a short distance on the way. Here are all of the Massachusetts Delegates—our compliments to you— and here other members. Numerous officers of militia have taken pains to dress the occasion; members of the Light Horse of Philadelphia, fully uniformed, have turned out to do the honors and to escort the General at least as far as New York. A band is playing; [148] the open road leads northward, not far from a little place named Germantown, with one to the Northwest styled Valley Forge, and on to the Delaware, to Trenton, to Princeton, to Long Island and on, on . . .

Gentlemen of the Congress, gentlemen of the militia, again, thanks and farewell!

---

wounded, 804; total 1032 (*ibid.*, 1099). These figures were raised slightly by later deaths to an announced 1054. The first report of the Massachusetts Provincial Congress, June 20, probably contains much more than reached Philadelphia on the 22nd, but still is a somewhat meagre document. See 2 *Force* (4) p. 1039, 40. Gage's report is in *ibid.*, 1097–99 and, perhaps more conveniently, in 1 *Gage*, 405–06. Privately on the same date, June 25, 1775, Gage wrote Lord Dartmouth: "The trials we have had show that the rebels are not the despicable rabble too many have supposed them to be, and I find it owing to a military spirit encouraged amongst them for a few years past, joined with an uncommon degree of zeal and enthusiasm, that they are otherwise." A picturesque account of the battle as seen by General Burgoyne, who did not participate actively, will be found in 2 *Force* (4) p. 1094–95.

[147] 3 *G. W.*, 300–01, corrected by the text belonging to E. L. R. Smith, Luthersville, Md.
[148] 1 *Burnett*, 142; *Penn. Gazette*, June 28, 1775.

CHAPTER XIX

First Train an Army and Bottle a Foe
(June 23–July 3, 1775)

It was an interesting cavalcade. Washington himself started on horseback [1] but later rode in a light vehicle drawn by two white horses; [2] his companions and his escort were mounted. His immediate attendants, Thomas Mifflin and Joseph Reed, were handsome, attractive young men of charming manners. Reed, 34, was of distinguished courtesy, considerate in all things, and was accustomed to dealing with men in high station. For many months he had conducted a correspondence with the Secretary of State for the Colonies, Lord Dartmouth, and had presented the American point of view with some acumen. Because Reed had seen something of the world, and was a skillful writer as well as a man of high intelligence, Washington was gratified to have him even temporarily as military secretary and as a conspicuous member of the headquarters "family." [3] This was true, also, of Thomas Mifflin, who was ranked as aide-de-camp. Thirty-one years of age, rivaling Reed in good looks, and finely athletic in form, Mifflin had wealth, established position, a charming young Quaker wife and much felicity in speech-making. As long as he had Reed to prepare his letters and Mifflin his addresses, Washington was equipped to overcome his two greatest deficiencies in the transaction of public business.

His other companions, Charles Lee and Philip Schuyler, had a training to complement his own as a soldier and as a purveyor to the needs of fighting men in the field. Lee had every mark of the "careless, hardy

---

[1] 1 *Burnett,* 142.

[2] It scarcely matters, but there is a doubt whether it was a four-wheeled phaeton, for which he had procured harness in Philadelphia (16 *Papers of G. W.,* 52, LC), or a two-wheeled sulky, in which he was said by Mrs. Richard Montgomery to have entered New York (*Biographical Notes concerning General Richard Montgomery . . .* cited hereafter as *Mrs. Richard Montgomery's Notes,* p. 6–7).

[3] As this term has not been used in these pages since the narrative dealt with the French and Indian War, it may be proper to note again that a General's "family" at this period was a synonym for the staff officers and civilian headquarters personnel who ate at his table. In more restricted usage, the word covered the staff only.

veteran," as Abigail Adams soon was to style him,[4] and he talked, as always on military matters, with authority and complete self-confidence.[5] Schuyler owned mills and dams, vast farms and virgin forests, diversified machinery and a light squadron of his own on the Hudson— the very man, it seemed, to equip and to lead expeditions to control the Northern New York Lakes. He had done some of this military work in 1759–60, when he had forwarded from Albany provisions for Amherst's army. Schuyler's bearing fitted his station. Piercing eyes lighted a strong face; his dress was flawless; he moved among his fellows with a high austerity that the unfriendly and the affronted denounced as arrogance. For him and for Washington, the escort of some of the foremost young men of the Quaker City, the detachment of the Philadelphia Light Horse under Captain Markoe, seemed altogether appropriate.

The journey of the 23rd was without sensation, except for vague bad news from Boston [6] and a discouraging, day-long rain.[7] On the 24th, when Washington reached Brunswick, General Schuyler became apprehensive that the British warships in New York harbor might prevent a crossing or, more probably, might send out boats to halt a barge and, at

---

[4] *Adams, Fam. Let.*, 78.

[5] A detailed character sketch of Lee will be found *infra*, p. 472.

[6] Washington Irving, v. 1, p. 488, gave a paragraph to this tradition: "They had scarcely proceeded twenty miles from Philadelphia, when they were met by a courier, spurring with all speed, bearing dispatches from the army to Congress, communicating tidings of the battle of Bunker's Hill. Washington eagerly inquired particulars; above all, how acted the militia? When told that they had stood their ground bravely; sustained the enemy's fire—reserved their own until at close quarters, and then delivered it with deadly effect; it seemed as if a weight of doubt and solicitude were lifted from his heart. 'The liberties of the country are safe!' exclaimed he." No authority was cited by Irving or by any of those who copied or paraphrased his account, but evidently Irving used the brief reference in John Adams' *Autobiography*, to this effect: "They [i.e., Washington and his entourage] had not proceeded twenty miles from Philadelphia before they met a courier with the news of the battle of Bunker's Hill, the death of General Warren, the slaughter among the British officers and men, and the burning of Charlestown." (2 *John Adams*, 418). Even this germ of the tradition, if put under the microscope, will show some of the treacherous effects of lapse of memory. Adams confused the dates of the various reports that reached Philadelphia. Two accounts, received on the 22nd, covered no more than snatches of information (See 1 *Burnett*, 141, 145, 147; NYHS Cols., 1886, *The* [Silas] *Deane Papers* (cited hereafter as *Deane Papers*) v. 1, p. 63). The second of these so-called reports undoubtedly was that contained in the final sentences of Jonathan Trumbull's letter of June 20, 1775, to the Continental Congress (2 *Force* (4) p. 1035). On the 24th, two expresses from the North reached Philadelphia. An afternoon messenger brought a somewhat full account of the battle as observed from Winter Hill by Capt. Elijah Hide of Lebanon. In the care of the evening express was a Watertown newspaper that had a few general sentences and a statement that the "confusion of the times renders it impractical to give a particular account of what has already occurred but hope to give a good account in our next." (See Dunlap's *Penn. Packet*, June 26; *Penn. Gazette*, June 28, 1775). Washington probably met one or both of these riders (for their route see 3 *N. J. Col. Docs.* (3) p. 140) but he could not have made any such out-of-character remark concerning militia as Irving attributed to him. The instance is an informative one in the growth of tradition.

[7] 3 *G. W.*, 301. Presumably, the halt for the night of June 23–24 was at Trenton, but no positive record has been found.

one step, to capture three Generals and some of their staff officers. Washington had been talking en route with Schuyler about the defence of New York, and he wished, of course, to push on, but he could not disregard a native's exhortation to be careful. By friendly compromise, it was agreed that the party would go on the next morning to Newark, fair weather or foul, and that Schuyler would send an express to the New York Provincial Congress. That body would be asked to appoint a committee, who would meet Washington in the Jersey town and advise whether the party could pursue its course or should take another.[8]

Off dashed the express; at a less furious pace Washington later rode to Newark, where the General had told his companions he expected to arrive at 9 A.M. on the 25th,[9] a schedule that accorded with the habit he had formed some years previously of making an early start without waiting for breakfast, so that he would get a good part of a journey done before the heat wore down his horse. If this exacting travel clashed with the comfort of his comrades they were too polite to say so, or else, after they reached Newark, they received information that made them forget how long their dawn-challenging chief had made them ride to get their morning meal: A committee of the New York Provincial Congress arrived during the late forenoon and announced among other things, that Governor William Tryon, an uncompromising Loyalist, was returning to New York and had sent word that he would disembark the next day, Sunday, June 25.[10] The King's Governor and the Congress' General to land in the divided town the same day—the oddness of it had humor and presented manifest danger. A clash between the supporters of the two causes, on a summer Sunday afternoon when the streets were full of strollers, might transfer the battle of Charlestown to New York. It was not a pleasing prospect but certainly not one over

[8] Schuyler to P. V. B. Livington; *19th Report American Scenic and Historic Preservation Society,* 257. In *ibid.,* 255, is a description of the three routes then in use between New Brunswick to New York. One was via Perth Amboy and Staten Island, whence there was a ferry to New York. The second was by way of Elizabeth Point. A third road, gaining in popularity, ran from Newark to Powles Hook. See also on New Jersey routes, NJHSP., new ser., v. 7, p. 97, with a good note, p. 109, on the Staten Island Ferry.

[9] Schuyler, *loc. cit.*

[10] 2 *Force* (4) p. 1318. The committee named by the New York Provincial Congress shortly after 9 o'clock on the morning of the 25th consisted of Thomas Smith, J. S. Hobart, Gouverneur Morris and Richard Montgomery (*ibid.*), but it is not known whether these were able to hurry off immediately, to catch the ferry and to ride to Newark at the breakneck speed required to meet Washington in time to participate in the remainder of the known events of the day. Lest the uncorrected dates of Washington's correspondence deceive a reader, it should be noted that he was one day behind the calendar in all his extant papers from June 25 until he reached Cambridge, July 2. He stated, for example, that he reached New York on the 24th of June; the correct date was June 25. Arrival at Cambridge was on July 2.

which Washington would hesitate. To avoid, if he could, the chance of being seized on the ferry by a boat's crew from one of the royal ships, he accepted the advice of the committee and of some Jersey men [11] that he go up the west shore of North River beyond the usual crossing at Powles Hook, and that he then cross from Hobocken.[12] Notice to this effect was sent ahead; Washington and his cavalcade made their way to the ferry.[13] For his first appearance in New York as American Commander-in-Chief, Washington put on a new purple sash with his blue uniform, and laid aside his travel hat for one that bore a fine plume.[14] Thus appareled, he and as many of his companions as could find space got aboard the ferry and started for the New York shore, which spread before him all its early summer beauties. He never previously had enjoyed that view of New York, with the handsome residence and fine lawn of Col. Leonard Lispenard immediately ahead. On the right, distant about one mile from Colonel Lispenard's, was the outer, northern rim of the town. Beyond that, southward for another mile, the houses extended to the fort which Washington had seen on his three previous sojourns. North of Colonel Lispenard's were a few fine dwellings, and open land above them up North River as far as the eye could reach.

Much more exciting to the approaching soldiers was the immense crowd around the mansion toward which the ferry was headed. Men in uniform were there in considerable number, evidently the greater part of the nine volunteer Companies of the city. With them were many persons of all ages and both sexes, who had walked all the way from town to see and to greet their new General. Washington never had faced a like ceremonial on comparable scale. Philadelphia's generous reception and grateful farewell were small affairs when set against the welcome that awaited him and Lee and Schuyler. Twenty years previously, this would have been one form of the "honor" he coveted;[15] now it was gratifying only as it gave the lie to the reports that the people of New York were indifferent to the American cause. Time must not be lost on display and formal etiquette. He had to press on to Boston and, meantime, had to draft instructions for Schuyler.

[11] 3 *G. W.*, 301.

[12] Some of the narratives and maps give Hobock and Hocken as other early renderings of the name of the present Hoboken.

[13] Two routes, neither of them direct, ran from Newark to Hoboken. W. Hawkes's map of 1776 would indicate that the shorter of these roads was the one via Bergen. Beyond that town, when a traveler proceeding eastward was close to Powles Neck, he would take the left turn and would ride slightly East of North to Hoboken.

[14] *Mrs. Richard Montgomery's Notes*, 5–6.   [15] See Vol. II, p. 390.

It was about 4 o'clock Sunday afternoon, June 25, 1775, that Washington stepped ashore at Colonel Lispenard's, shook hands with the officials and acknowledged the huzzas by taking off his plumed hat.[16] He proceeded from the landing to the house and, after more introductions, accepted Lispenard's invitation to dinner.[17] Something besides savory viands awaited him. Eager and excited members of the Provincial Congress told him that an express had arrived from the vicinity of Boston with a number of papers, among which was a letter to the President of the Continental Congress from the corresponding body in Massachusetts. It doubtless contained additional news of the battle of Bunker Hill: would not the General open it and give the New York authorities the information it contained of that fight? Washington hesitated to break the seal of a communication addressed to the presiding officer of the body to which he was responsible, but the New Yorkers hinted politely that the paper might contain facts that would be of value on the journey he had ahead of him.[18] Reluctantly Washington took the letter from the express, who had been brought to Lispenard's to await the General's decision. The paper bore date of Watertown, June 20, carried the signatures of James Warren, President, and Samuel Freeman, Secretary of the Provincial Congress of Massachusetts,[19] and was in every way as sensational as the guests at Colonel

[16] Penn. Gazette, June 28, 1775; George Livingston to Peter Tappan, June 29, 1775, in *19th Report Am. Scenic Preservation Soc.,* 259; cf. Thomas Jones, *History of New York During the . . . Revolution,* v. 1, p. 55. The hour of arrival is given variously as 12 M and 2 and as 4 P.M. All the circumstances indicate that the later hour is more nearly correct.

[17] According to the map of New York, published in 1789, Colonel Lispenard's residence was directly East of the road to Greenwich, which followed the eastern shore of the Hudson. As the map places the house about 700 yards North of Reed (Reade) Street, the site of the dwelling probably was close to the Canal Street approach to the Holland Tunnel. A swampy area on either side of the present Canal Street was known as "Lispenard's Meadow." The name Lispenard survives in a short street between Broadway and Sixth Avenue, just South of Canal. More in detail, the authors of *Washington's Journey of 1775* state (p. 30–31) that as Lispenard's place occupied seven or eight acres, it was approximately in the area bounded by Canal, Varick, Laight and Hudson Streets. The house is believed by these writers to have been on a line with Desbrosses Street. Washington is assumed, by the same authorities, to have proceeded from the Greenwich Road, where Greenwich Street now is intersected by Laight, southeasterly along the southern side of Lispenard's grounds about to the present Varick Street, thence to the Northeast along the eastern side of the property, thence westward into the grounds and to a circular drive in front of and to the East of the house. This may be correct, but it is difficult to see why hungry men, in something of a hurry, might not have walked across the lawn from the landing while batmen conducted the horses and vehicles along the road and the lane.

[18] 3 *G. W.,* 304. The time of Washington's explanatory note to the President of Congress, "5 o'clock P.M." makes it almost certain that the incident occurred at Colonel Lispenard's.

[19] 2 *Force* (4) p. 1039–40. Although Washington (*loc. cit.*) did not give the date of the letter he opened, the paper summarized here precisely accords with all the circumstances and with Washington's reference to part of its contents. The same express brought a somewhat inclusive, unofficial account of the battle of Bunker Hill. This document was put in type immediately by John Holt and was sold as a broadside. It is reproduced in C. K. Bolton, *The Private Soldier Under Washington* (cited hereafter as *Bolton*) p. 16.

Lispenard's had hoped it would be. The battle of the 17th was described in some detail, with this grim announcement near the end: "Though this scene [of the destruction of Charlestown] was almost horrible, and altogether new to most of our men, yet many stood, and received wounds by swords and bayonets before they quitted their lines. At 5 o'clock the enemy were in full possession of all the posts within the isthmus." The number of "Americans killed and missing was unknown but supposed by some to be about sixty or seventy, and by some considerably above that number." The former President of the Provincial Congress, Dr. Joseph Warren, was among the victims. Other officers had been slain, and three Colonels "and perhaps one hundred men . . . wounded." One report put casualties among the ministerial troops at 1000, "but," said the Massachusetts legislators honestly, "this account exceeds every other estimation." Washington, reading this with the eyes of a veteran, knew that casualty lists usually are to be corrected the morning after a battle by adding to one's own losses and subtracting from those of the enemy; but even if the final figures were half as favorable as the first estimates were, Americans could stand up against British regulars. That first conclusion from James Warren's letter burned its way into the mind of Washington.[20]

The General doubtless gave the substance of this good news to the guests at Colonel Lispenard's but he spoke to a few only concerning this ominous paragraph which immediately followed the report of the battle: "As soon as an estimate can be made of public and private stocks of gunpowder in this Colony, it shall be transmitted without delay, which we are well assured will be small, and by no means adequate to the exigence of our case. We apprehend that the scantiness of our stock of that article cannot fail to induce your Honors still to give your utmost attention to ways and means of procuring a full supply of it. We feel ourselves infinitely obliged to you for your past care in this respect."

Powder shortage! It had been known, deplored and discussed in Philadelphia,[21] but it had not been relieved, and now it was a threat to the defence of an army which had earned by its valor the right to protect itself and the colonial cause. There was some relief, forthwith, in the assurance of New York leaders that 1000 pounds of powder had been sent to Boston from the city on the 22nd, though the heart sank at the additional remark that New York had been stripped of explosive to

[20] His subsequent repeated emphasis on the disparity of losses makes this plain.
[21] Cf. R. T. Paine to Elbridge Gerry, June 10, 1775; 1 Austin's *Gerry*, 80–81.

provide this small assistance. Not more than four barrels of powder remained in town. At least that was the estimate the gentlemen at Colonel Lispenard's made. Washington talked with them and then excused himself briefly to recite the facts in a short letter he had one of his aides prepare for the President of Congress in explanation of his breaking the seal of the dispatch from Massachusetts.

All this occurred while the volunteer Companies waited on the grounds of Colonel Lispenard and the crowd idled or shifted or came and went. Outside was confidence and good cheer; indoors was dark reflection on the desperate possibility that the American troops around Boston might not be able to hold off the enemy because they would not have powder for their muskets. Such were the contrasts of the Sabbath afternoon. It was past 5 o'clock [22] when the letter to Congress was copied and delivered to the express. Then, at last, the parade was formed—nine New York Companies in front,[23] next the members of the Provincial Congress, after them the Generals, and, following the gentleman with the plume, the Philadelphia Light Horse. The cheering populace closed the rear [24] in such numbers as never had assembled at one time in the town.[25] Loyalists looked on in disgust or dismay. The "shouts and huzzas" to the ears of Judge Thomas Jones, were those of a "seditious and rebellious multitude"; parade to New York was "conducted in the same tumultuous and ridiculous manner" as the reception of the Generals.[26] Knowledge of this state of mind on the part of the King's supporters served only to heighten the enthusiasm of the "Sons of Liberty" and to hearten the cheers when the parade disbanded at Hull's Tavern.[27]

[22] 3 G. W., 304.

[23] The number of Companies is given in Washington's Journey of 1775, p. 32, from the Va. Gazette of July 7, which reprinted an article from some unidentified New York correspondent.

[24] 19th Report Am. Scenic Preservation Soc., 259. The same work concludes that the marchers "followed Greenwich Road, probably turning as they passed King's College grounds." In Washington's Journey of 1775, p. 33, the theory is advanced that the parade followed Greenwich Road at least as far as the present Chambers Street, and perhaps to what now is Murray Street, into which it turned. It passed the old site of the college and entered Broadway opposite "The Fields," the present City Hall Park.

[25] Shewkirk's and William Smith's Diaries, quoted in 5 Stokes, Iconography of Manhattan Island, 894–95; George Livingston to Peter Tappan, loc. cit.; Dawson, New York City, 82.

[26] Thomas Jones, New York During the Revolution, v. 1. p. 56. This amusingly venomous work is the closest approach in existence to a history of the Revolution from the viewpoint of an American Loyalist.

[27] In 19th Report Am. Scenic Preservation Soc., 259, it is stated that Washington's resting place on the night of June 25 is unknown; but as the parade ended at Hull's Tavern, (William Smith's diary in 5 Stokes, Iconography, 894) it is not improbable that Washington lodged there. Hull's Tavern was near Trinity Church. In its early days the tavern was known

Washington lost no time at his temporary quarters. In the closing paragraph of the letter from the Massachusetts Congress, James Warren had written: "We beg leave to suggest that if a Commander-in-Chief of the Army of the United Colonies should be appointed, it must be plain to your Honours that no part of this continent can so much require his immediate presence and exertions as this Colony." [28] Washington's sense of duty underscored "immediate" and prompted him to spur on toward Boston, but at the moment he had to consider the instructions he was to give Philip Schuyler. For that officer, as commander in New York, the welcome being accorded at that very hour to Governor Tryon might present the most delicate of the many difficult decisions he would be compelled to make.

The Governor, who had been absent in Great Britain for fourteen months, had sent word from the *Juliana* that he would land in the evening at the Exchange, on North River, close to the tip of the island.[29] This announcement was accepted as a call for a rally of all the members of his Majesty's Council, the judges of the Supreme Court, the Mayor, the clergy, the governors of King's College and those, in general, whom one of their number described as "his Majesty's well affected and loyal subjects." [30] It was an assembly to make proud the men who believed their self-respect, their offices or their fortunes depended upon continued allegiance to Great Britain, but this ominous circumstance was observed by every participating Loyalist: the volunteer Companies enlisted in the continental cause were not represented even by a guard of honor, though they were to be seen patrolling the Battery, while admirers watched and walked with them.

At 8 o'clock, the Governor came up the ferry stairs. He looked grave, in spite of the cheers of the throng, and he had little to say as he went with the committee to the house of Hugh Wallace, where he was to lodge.[31] The larger crowds of the day and the greater enthusiasm mani-

as the Province Arms (Vol. II, p. 162); subsequently it was Burns's, and still later the Bunch of Grapes (Abbott, *New York in the Revolution*, 64). Mrs. Montgomery stated in her *Notes* (6–7) that Governor Tryon "nearly fainted" when he saw Washington pass in parade, but it is not probable that the events now to be described in the text occurred before the crowd from Lispenard's reached Hull's Tavern and dispersed.

[28] 2 *Force* (4) p. 1040.

[29] Whitehall Slip was nearest the lower point of the island; then came Exchange, and then Coenties Slip, around the point and up East River. The Exchange itself was a small structure in Broad Street, about seventy yards from the water's edge. Exchange Place, South of Wall Street, and nearby Whitehall preserve these old names in modern Manhattan.

[30] Jones, *New York During the Revolution*, v. 1, p. 56.

[31] William Smith's Diary in 5 Stokes, *Iconography*, 895; *Mrs. Richard Montgomery's Notes*, 6–7, with some manifest errors; Jones, *op. cit.*, v. 1, p. 55.

festly were on the side of the continentals. If there was any satisfaction
for the Loyalists it was a sort of ironic amusement over the equivoca-
tion of some of the New Yorkers. Judge Jones remembered bitterly
afterward: The very men who had been pouring out flattery and
adulation to the rebel Generals now joined the Governor's train, welcomed him to the Colony and hoped he would remain long in his
government.[32]

Suppose Tryon did remain and, in seeking to suppress "rebellion,"
locked up some of the opposing leaders or attempted to dissolve the
Provincial Congress—what should Schuyler do as American commander? This was a question with which Washington wrestled that
evening in preparing instructions for the man he was about to leave in
the city of strife. Manifestly, if Tryon attempted any action inimical
to the common cause, he had to be frustrated; but if that necessitated
the arrest of the Governor, should Washington authorize it? The new
Commander-in-Chief told himself that he should not hesitate over
forcible measures if the responsibility rested exclusively on him and the
Continental Congress were not in session. As it was, the Congress being
in Philadelphia, he directed Schuyler to consult that body in such an
emergency. On the practical military issues that had to be decided,
Washington requested Schuyler to report to Congress and to him as
frequently as developments required. Beyond that, orders could not be
explicit or restrictive: "Your own good sense must govern in all matters
not particularly pointed out," Washington said, "as I do not wish to
circumscribe you within narrow limits."[33] In his very first orders
Washington thus abdicated the right of a Commander-in-Chief to have
every decision of importance made at his headquarters. Distance itself
vested discretion. The channel of command was not to run from New
York to Boston and back through Philadelphia on doubtful subjects that
required prompt decision. Schuyler could operate independently of
the Commander-in-Chief when, in his judgment, such a course was
expedient.[34] Washington would advise and perhaps could supervise;
he could not direct or administer, and he neither would try nor would
pretend to do so.

[32] Jones, loc. cit.

[33] 3 G. W., 303–04. While these instructions are headed "June 25," they were written the
next morning. See supra n. 10 on the misdating of Washington's papers for a week and more.

[34] It is impossible to say whether this most important decision concerning the channels of
command was reached deliberately, was based on knowledge that a crisis might develop suddenly in New York, or was due to Washington's confidence in Schuyler.

The next morning, Monday, June 26, while Colonel Mifflin was shopping for Lee and for him,[35] Washington was told that William Morris and Isaac Low wished to see him on behalf of the Provincial Congress. Shown in, they explained that the Congress desired to present Washington an address and would like to know when it suited his convenience to receive the paper. Anxious though the General was to start for Boston, he of course could not decline this civility, and as he still had matters to discuss with Schuyler before he left New York, he set 2:30 P.M. as the hour. Meantime, he directed his companions to have everything ready for departure as soon as the ceremonies were concluded. At the designated hour, the members of the Congress waited on him with an address diplomatically fashioned to attest their devotion to the continental cause without giving unendurable offence to those who feared military rule in America and still hoped for reconciliation with England. The brief paper read: "At a time when the most loyal of his Majesty's subjects from a regard to the laws and constitution by which he sits on the throne, feel themselves reduced to the unhappy necessity of taking up arms to defend their dearest rights and privileges; while we deplore the calamities of this divided Empire we rejoice in the appointment of a gentleman from whose abilities and virtues we are taught to expect both security and peace. Confiding in you, Sir, and in the worthy Generals immediately under your command, we have the most flattering hopes of success in the glorious struggle for American liberty and the fullest assurance that whenever this important contest shall be decided, by that fondest wish of each American soul, an accommodation with our Mother Country, you will cheerfully resign the important deposit committed into your hands and reassume the character of our worthiest citizen." [36]

Washington had his answer ready: "Gentlemen, at the same time that with you I deplore the unhappy necessity of such an appointment as that with which I am now honored, I cannot but feel sentiments of the highest gratitude for this affecting instance of distinction and regard. May your every wish be realized in the success of America at this important and interesting period; and be assured that every exertion of my worthy colleagues and myself will be equally extended to the reestablish-

35 He bought wine to the total of £7, 10s 6d, some stationery and a trunk, and he paid an "upholder" i.e., a dealer in small wares, £16, 13s (16 Papers of G. W., 65, LC).

36 Badly misprinted in N. Y. Gazette and Weekly Mercury, July 3, 1775. What appears to be a correct text is in 2 Force (4) p. 1321. The punctuation is revised slightly in quotation here.

ment of peace and harmony between the Mother Country and these Colonies, as to the fatal but necessary operations of war. When we assumed the soldier, we did not lay aside the citizen; and we shall most sincerely rejoice with you in that happy hour when the establishment of American liberty, upon the most firm and solid foundations, shall enable us to return to our private stations in the bosom of a free, peaceful and happy country." [37] The suggestion regarding the return of the military leader to civilian life originated with the New York committee, not with Washington or with his staff; but his reply had a clear simplicity that reassured. "When we assumed the soldier we did not lay aside the citizen"—the words, widely circulated, came to represent Washington in the eyes of many Americans.[38]

There followed polite addresses to Lee and Schuyler, and replies no less courteous on the part of the two Major Generals,[39] with the result that 3 o'clock had many minutes added to it before the ceremonies ended. Even then there was delay because numerous citizens and several Companies of the New York volunteers wished to join the faithful contingent of the Philadelphia Light Horse. The column followed King's Road to King's Bridge over Spuyten Duyvil.[40] There the New Yorkers again wished the General the best of fortune, bade him a cheerful farewell, and turned back. Washington probably was so intent on his duties that he scarcely observed the absence from the cortege of the two residents with whom he had been associated most closely on his previous visits to the city: Beverley Robinson at the moment was indisposed to have any part in the quarrel between mother and daughter; [41] Dr. Myles Cooper, President of King's College, months previously had shaken the dust of an unbelieving city from his resentful feet and had returned to England.

[37] Garbled in N. Y. Gazette and Weekly Mercury, July 3, 1775. A correct text is in 3 G. W., 305. The form of this answer, which probably was the work of Mifflin or of Reed, would indicate that the committee informally had given Washington a copy of the address far enough in advance of the ceremonies for an appropriate answer to be prepared. This was more or less standard practice in addresses to royal Governors, though it seldom was avowed, if ever.

[38] Cf. Landon Carter's Diary, May 3, 1776: "I never knew but one man who resolved not to forget the citizen in the soldier or ruler and that was G. W., and I am afraid I shall not know another" (17 W (1) p. 8).

[39] N. Y. Gazette and Weekly Mercury, July 3, 1775.

[40] Needless to say, there always is a question where Spuyten Duyvil ends and Harlem Creek, now Harlem River, begins. According to the 20th Report of Am. Scenic Preservation Soc., 106. the route North was substantially that of the present Broadway to McGown's Pass Tavern, near the upper end of what now is Central Park. Beyond that, the left fork continued up Broadway to King's Bridge.

[41] For his gradual conversion to the Loyalist cause, see Sabine, American Loyalists, v. 2, p. 221.

Washington ended the short day's journey near the bridge,[42] where Schuyler, as well as the other officers, remained with him. The next day they proceeded to New Rochelle and there they found Brig. Gen. David Wooster and Col. David Waterbury, Jr., with 1800 Connecticut troops, bound for New York.[43] Washington had no previous acquaintance with the senior of these officers, who was older even than his sixty-four years. In 1741, Wooster had been named Lieutenant of a sloop his native Connecticut had commissioned to guard its coast, and from that time onward, he shared in most of the Northern campaigns of the two wars with France until, in length of military experience, he was one of the elder soldiers of America. Although he was a graduate of Yale and had married in 1746 a daughter of President Clap of that institution, Wooster had no suavity or polish. He seemed to think that a blunt heartiness of manner was enough to animate his troops without subjecting them to a harassing, if instructive discipline. His own way was the better way. Of that he was sure. In addition, he now had a grievance: he had been a Major General of Connecticut troops but he had been made a continental Brigadier General, had been demoted in short, for giving himself to the common cause.[44] He could not understand it; he did not pretend to like it.

Washington probably did not spend much time in Wooster's company at New Rochelle, because the dissatisfied Connecticut officer was to pass at once under the command of Schuyler at a time when Washington's whole impulse was to put on to Boston. At 10 A.M.,[45] with quiet courtesy and earnest good wishes, he said adieu to Schuyler and Wooster, and to the Philadelphia Light Horse, also, and for the first time after he left Philadelphia, he went forward without a dust-raising, clattering escort. In the smaller company, his relations were closer with

---

[42] N. Y. *Gazette and Weekly Mercury*, July 3, 1775. By some New York local historians, it is thought that Washington almost certainly spent the night at Cox's Tavern, a part of which is believed to have been incorporated later in the Macomb mansion at the northwest corner of Broadway and 230th Street. So far as is known, there then was no other dwelling in that vicinity except the Van Cortlandt mansion, built in 1748 and distant, in what is now Van Cortlandt Park, about one mile from the bridge. In *Washington's Journey of 1775*, p. 39, the statement is made that Washington may have established himself that evening at Hyatt's Tavern, also known as Kingsbridge Inn. This was located at what is now the intersection of Broadway and 223rd Street.

[43] N. Y. *Gazette and Daily Mercury*, July 3, 1775; *Rivington's Gazette*, June 29, 1775. Cf. W. S. Baker, *Itinerary of General Washington, 1775–1787* (cited hereafter as *W. S. Baker*).

[44] It has been said that he was the only general officer of a Colony to receive lower rank in continental service, but this was not the case. To cite two other instances, Artemas Ward, Massachusetts General, became continental Major General, and John Thomas, who had been commissioned by the Bay Colony as a Lieutenant General, was created a Brigadier by Congress.

[45] Schuyler to Congress, June 28, 1775; 2 *Force* (4) p. 1123.

his fellow-travelers and, in particular, with his strange second in command. Charles Lee at 44 was odd in appearance and in manner. About five feet eight inches in height and unhealthily thin, he seemed deliberately careless in dress and disdainful of appearances. By his own admission, he much preferred the company of dogs to that of men. So devoted was he to these animals that he never went anywhere without a number of trotting, barking canines, two of which he usually took to table with him at mealtime.[46] Lee protested: "When my honest quadruped friends are equalled by the bipeds in fidelity, gratitude, or even good sense, I will promise to become as warm a philanthropist as Mr. Addison himself affected to be—to say the truth I think the strongest proof of a good heart is to love dogs and dislike mankind." [47] Adhering to both his conclusions, he did not fail to show by his manners his contempt for his fellow mortals. He was blunt, contemptuous of all the amenities, and sometimes he seemed deliberately rude. When his temper, which naturally was acid, was stirred by contention, he scarcely was master of his words or even of his acts. Yet he was the best-traveled and at least experientially, the best-schooled of the officers with whom Washington was now to associate. Lee wrote readily, if sometimes volubly, and when he wished to impress an individual who might be useful to him, he displayed a convincing familiar style of speech and argument that won for him numerous correspondents and friends in high places. On any theme, he would express his opinions quaintly and confidently, even dogmatically, no matter how alien to the matters entrusted to him. Men listened and decided, usually, that if he spoke with so much authority, he must know whereof he spoke. His acquisitiveness was as remarkable as his cleverness: he would ask for anything and, if denied it, would seek something else. Withal, he seemed wholly devoted to the cause of American liberty. Just before leaving Philadelphia, after having solicited and received the pledge of Congress to secure him in his Virginia properties,[48] he renounced his British half-pay in a brief letter he circulated among his friends. Nor did he complain when the letter

---

[46] Although it does not matter greatly, Lee's contemporaries differed in their record of the number of dogs he carried with him. James Thacher in his *Military Journal of the American Revolution* (cited hereafter as *Thacher*) p. 463, said merely that "a number always followed him." Samuel Richards in his *Diary* (p. 18) remarked: "I occasionally saw General Lee—accompanied by his two hounds." Other writers suggest that he kept a small pack at his headquarters.

[47] Letter of Sept. 19, 1775 to Benjamin Rush; 1 *Lee Papers*, 207.

[48] See *supra*, p. 441.

appeared in print.[49] He manifestly regarded himself as a destined leader of the revolutionary cause in America and in that rôle he had written his friend Gen. John Burgoyne of the British army a long argumentative letter he had shown to the Massachusetts Delegates and to others.[50] All the while, his conduct in his dealings with Washington was militarily correct and not, so far as one could observe, flattering, supercilious or ostentatiously subordinate. Lee was in almost every respect so much quicker than his commander and was of a nature and a way of living so wholly different that Washington might well have wondered how this lieutenant would behave under the stresses of campaigning; but as Lee was professionally well equipped, by comparison with everyone of Washington's other juniors, except Gates, all peculiarities were to be endured. The carpenter needed keen-edged tools; he had to use one that was sharp, even though it was rough-handled.[51]

With Lee and the staff officers, Washington on the 28th reached New Haven, where he lodged at the house formerly occupied by Isaac Beers.[52] The coming of the new head of the Army either had been known in advance, or else news of it was spread quickly through the town. Yale students who had established a volunteer Company sent to ask if he would review them; two other Companies made arrangements to muster the next morning and to escort him part of the way on the road to Boston. Washington found satisfaction, of course, in the fact that one small town had three Companies already organized, and he cheerfully agreed to see how the young academicians were learning to handle their arms; but he chafed a little as he reflected how much time he was losing on the road.[53] The day might not be far down the calendar when the United Colonies would need every man who was drilling on every town green in America; at the moment, Boston was "the front," Boston the place where, if anywhere, success might produce an honorable settlement, without the acute agony and ruinous cost of a long struggle.[54]

[49] It was published in the N. Y. Gazette and Weekly Mercury, July 3, 1775. The letter, Lee to Lord Barrington, June 22, 1775, will be found conveniently in 1 Lee Papers, 185–86.

[50] 1 Lee Papers, 193. This letter was not delivered until after Lee reached Cambridge, Mass. See infra, p. 488.

[51] Other of Lee's characteristics and aptitudes, with which Washington could not have become acquainted at this date, are sketched infra.

[52] The Beers House is said to have been at the corner of Chapel and College Streets, on the site of the old New Haven House and of what is now the Hotel Taft. Cf. Washington's Journey of 1775, p. 41–42.

[53] Cf. 3 G. W., 320–329.

[54] For the day at New Haven, see the newspaper reference in W. S. Baker, 7.

"OLD PUT"—HOW GOOD WOULD HE BE IN NEW CAMPAIGNS?

One of the first official acts Washington performed after arriving at Cambridge, Massachusetts, on the 2nd of July, 1775, was to present to Israel Putnam the commission as Major General that Congress had voted unanimously on the 19th of June to a man who was, above everything else, distinctly himself. Putnam had not made any effort to rub off the marks of the farmer and tavern keeper, though his second marriage in 1767 to a widow of some estate had carried him into a new circle. As he had been, so he was, with pride of performance and no apologies of any sort. He did not represent the Massachusetts of John Hancock and John Adams and James Warren, but the Massachusetts that had gone to Connecticut and had kept alive the spirit of the early settlers. What mattered it if Israel scarcely could write? He most certainly could fight. Had he not survived capture in 1758 by Indians who were about to burn him alive? He had been shipwrecked off Cuba and had been one of the few to survive; after that he had shared Bradstreet's campaign in Pontiac's war; and still later he had ascended the Mississippi to ascertain what land speculators in the valley of that river might hope to gain. What more practical school of the soldier could there have been than these adventures had offered? In every phase of the trouble with Britain after his return home, Putnam had a part— from the time he drove a herd of sheep to Boston for the relief of the city's needy, to the great day on Bunker Hill when he had been a rock and a rallying-post. Some of those who knew his picturesque and gallant record might have asked themselves, when he was commissioned, whether the lesser soldier might not be attempting to honor the more renowned by giving him the sheet of paper Peyton Randolph had signed. Putnam at 57 seemed in almost every respect a more experienced warrior than Washington at 43.

What would be the outcome? If the two were able to work together, would "Old Put" continue to have, on the wider field of conflict, the amazing good luck that long had been his? War had offered many contrasts as marked as that between Washington and Putnam. Let the drama test the players!

(Probably the most faithful and perhaps the sole surviving sketch of Putnam made from life is that of John Trumbull, now in the Wadsworth Atheneum, Hartford, Conn., the property of the Putnam Phalanx of Hartford, Hartford, Conn., by whose generous permission it is reproduced here. The portrait, based on Trumbull's sketch, is the work of H. I. Thompson and now is in the Connecticut State Library, Hartford, Connecticut.)

IS GATES'S FACE THAT OF AN AMBITIOUS RIVAL?

This is Charles Willson Peale's conception of the Horatio Gates of the Revolution—about 49 years of age, with a well-shaped head and a face not then narrowed by time. His mouth is positive but not unfriendly; his eyes, if Peale portrayed them accurately, have a penetration and a straight gaze that scarcely seem to reflect the indirection sometime charged against him.

A more familiar portrait of Horatio Gates is the one from the brush of Gilbert Stuart, in the Metropolitan Museum of Art, New York. It was painted about 1794, when the General was 67 and had both honor and wealth. In the Stuart portrait Gates appears in his continental uniform and in his most dignified mood. Conspicuous on his left breast are his "Saratoga medal," presented by Congress, and his "eagle" of the Society of the Cincinnati. It is a famous portrait but to some eyes, at least, it is less attractive than the simple painting that hangs on the wall of Independence Hall, Philadelphia.

During the early months of the Revolutionary War, Gates's service as Adjutant General was of the greatest value to Washington, but after Gates went to the Northern Department, the two seldom worked together. Gates became increasingly anxious to have separate command; Washington did not insist on Gates's return to headquarters, though he would have been glad to utilize again the abilities of his first Adjutant General. The acclaim Gates received for the victory over Burgoyne in October, 1777, perhaps made him susceptible to the flattery of Thomas Conway, the Irish-born French officer who had come to America in the hope of winning honors that would bring promotion in the service of King Louis. Whether Gates actually hoped to supersede Washington is doubtful, but naturally he was willing to make the most of what appeared to be a rising tide of favor. He had been angrily incautious on one occasion in appearing before Congress, and in like unwisdom he was guilty of a blunder in sending to President Laurens in December, 1777, a copy of a letter he should have kept within the "military family" by dispatching it to Washington only. From the hour of that rash mistake of judgment, Gates's star began to wane. It was a strange story.

(After the Original, Independence Hall, Philadelphia)

Even if that contest was unavoidable, the camps around Boston must be the training school of victory. The sooner the start, the earlier the ending.

On June 29, the officers set out for Wethersfield, with the Yale students and the two other Companies, and, when the young men turned back,[55] the seniors pressed on. Washington the new commander could not shake Washington the farmer out of the saddle. He saw that the summer had been dry in the lower Connecticut Valley and along the northern shore of Long Island Sound, but he observed with admiration "a great deal of delightful country," as he described it, "covered with grass . . . in a very different manner to what our lands in Virginia are."[56] At New London, which he had visited in 1756, he saw some familiar edifices, and at Wethersfield, where the day's journey ended, he found the family and friends of Silas Deane, the Connecticut member of Congress who was among his most confident admirers.[57] Fortunately, the town was not large enough to stage a ceremonial overnight, zealous though most of Deane's fellow-townsmen were in the colonial cause. The place itself was most pleasing. Its streets were wide; its houses were set well apart, each with a garden; a handsome brick church gave to everything the appearance of righteousness and stability.[58]

The ride from Wethersfield[59] to Springfield occupied the 30th of June and put Washington in touch for the first time with men who were sharing as Massachusetts legislators in the contest with the British in Boston. Dr. Benjamin Church and Moses Gill presented themselves as a committee named on the 26th of June by the Provincial Congress of Massachusetts to proceed to Springfield and to receive the Generals "with every mark of respect due to their exalted characters and stations."[60] These hosts explained that the Massachusetts Congress had directed that gentlemen of each of the larger towns on the road to Cambridge be requested to serve as escort to the new Commander-in-Chief

---

55 *Ibid.* Tradition is that the students went with him as far as "Neck Bridge" where State Street crosses Mill River. See *Washington's Journey of 1775,* p. 41–42.

56 3 *G. W.,* 371.

57 W. S. Baker noted, *op. cit.,* 8, that if Washington lodged at Deane's home, as seemed probable, the dwelling was the one next South of the Webb House, which had later associations with Washington. For Deane's letter to Mrs. Deane, introducing Washington, see 1 *Deane Papers,* 63.

58 *Journal of Ennion Williams,* in *Penn. Arc.* (2) v. 15, p. 10–11.

59 Jeremiah Wadsworth lent his horse to be used for the carriage of the commanding General. *Washington's Journey of 1775,* p. 45.

60 See the proceedings in 2 *Force* (4) p. 1447.

and his second. That prospect was equivalent to prolonging the highway to the besieged city, but, once again, there was no avoiding what manifestly was meant to be honor and courtesy. As Church and Gill were to attend him all the way to Cambridge, Washington could hope to learn something of conditions in front of Boston, and something, likewise—if less important—of his informants. Benjamin Church, the more conspicuous of the pair, was two years younger than Washington, who probably had met him in May when Church had gone to Philadelphia to present to Congress the defensive needs of Massachusetts. After graduating at Harvard and studying medicine under Joseph Pynchon, he traveled to London to see the "great world" and there he married a Hertfordshire girl. When he returned to Massachusetts he established himself at Raynham and practiced his profession with some success while developing other tastes. About 1768 he built a house so expensive that his neighbors marvelled, and he soon made his literary bow as a poetic defender of the Whig cause. There was some suspicion later that he was not wholly on the side of the Colonies, but the vigor of his writing and his subsequent activity in the Provincial Congress led many to rank him high among the "friends of America." He knew much of what was happening at Boston and in the camps and he informed Washington usefully on many subjects that soon would be put on the General's office table.

With Church and Gill and a number of the leading men of Springfield, Washington rode on the 1st of July to Brookfield, where his escort was changed, and thence to Worcester, where the same thing happened. From Worcester the next stage was to Marlborough, the halting-place for the night.[61] Sunday, July 2, with the Company of horse from Marlborough, he covered early the distance to Watertown. The Provincial Congress was holding its sessions there, and the week previously had named a committee of six to prepare for the reception of the General.[62] At the head of the committee was the President of the body, James Warren; among the other members were Benjamin Lincoln, who held a colonial commission as Lieutenant Colonel, and Elbridge Gerry, chairman of the Committee of Supply. To two of these gentlemen

[61] This assumes what there is no reason to doubt—that he adhered to the schedule and route previously arranged. In *Washington's Journey of 1775*, p. 46, is reference to the traditions of Washington's stopping places on the road. No direct evidence has been found to sustain these traditions, though some of them have probability.

[62] *Journ. Prov. Cong. Mass.*, 1774–75, p. 391.

Washington had special letters of introduction,[63] which he scarcely needed, because the entire Congress gave him a grateful welcome and presented him an address that was cordial in spirit and honest in warning the General he would not find "such regularity and discipline" in the army as he might expect. He was told, also: the "greatest part of [the troops] have not before seen service, and, although naturally brave and of good understanding, yet, for want of experience in military life, have but little knowledge of divers things most essential to the preservation of health, and even life. The youth of the army are not possessed of the absolute necessity of cleanliness in their dress and lodging, continual exercise and strict temperance to preserve them from diseases frequently prevailing in camps, especially among those who, from their childhood, have been used to a laborious life." As this paper could not be shown to the new commander in advance of its actual delivery, he could not do more than to express his thanks and to promise a later reply.[64] Washington then listened as another address was read to Charles Lee, who replied in six modest sentences. "You may depend, gentlemen," he said "on my zeal and integrity," and he added at once: "I can promise you nothing from my abilities." [65]

Then Washington was able to start on the last, short stretch of his journey, the three miles to Cambridge.[66] In that college town, some of the troops had been paraded the previous morning because it was reported that Washington and Lee were to arrive,[67] and again on the 2nd soldiers had marched out to do honor to the Generals; but rain had fallen, and no positive word of the hour of Washington's arrival had come. The men had been dismissed [68] with the result that when at length the officers entered the town on the wet road, they found Sun-

---

[63] Mercy Warren, *History of the . . . Revolution,* v. 1, p. 233; Samuel Adams to Elbridge Gerry, June 22, 1775; 1 *Austin's Gerry,* 90–91; Mercy Warren to unnamed correspondent, July 4, 1775; *Mercy Warren Papers,* MHS. The three-volume work on the American Revolution, written by this remarkable woman, is cited hereafter as *Mercy Warren.*

[64] The address is conveniently in 2 *Force* (4) p. 1472–73. Washington's answer is in *ibid.,* and in 3 *G. W.,* 307–08. It is dated July 4, 1775, but is entered in the Journal as if delivered the day of the address.

[65] Address and answer in 1 *Lee Papers,* 186–87. The brevity of the reply suggests that it may have been extemporaneous.

[66] The halt at Watertown must have been brief. A dispatch from Watertown, July 3, to the *Penn. Gazette,* issue of July 12, 1775, stated that Washington "passed through this town yesterday . . ." Nothing was said of any ceremonies. He had been expected there on the 1st (7 *N. H. Records,* 555).

[67] *Journal of James Stevens* in 48 *Essex Inst. His. Cols.,* 49. Loammi Baldwin, on the other hand, had been told to expect the General on the 4th or 5th. See his letter of June 29, 1775, to his wife; *Baldwin Papers,* Harvard Coll. Lib.

[68] James Stevens, *loc. cit.*

day-afternoon idlers around the college but no committee with an address, and no column to line Harvard Yard.[69] Even a noisy bombardment of Roxbury that might have served as a salute of honor, had died away.[70] Probably without ceremony, trumpet-flourish or roll of drums [71] Washington was conducted to the residence of President Samuel Langdon where, he was advised, the Massachusetts Provincial Congress had given orders that he and General Lee were to have all the rooms, except the one that was allotted Langdon.[72] This arrangement probably did not please Washington, who would be embarrassed to confine the owner of a house to a solitary chamber while he, Charles Lee, and their staff occupied the remainder of the residence, but the hour of arrival was not a time to find fault with the choice of quarters the committee, his hosts, had made for him. Washington went in and met the officers who already had assembled or called as soon as they heard of his arrival. Conspicuous among them was Artemas Ward, in general command—medium in height, with strong, stern features, heavy in body and slow of speech.[73] Another to welcome the new commander was Israel Putnam, a powerfully built man of low stature, with a jaw so square that he looked as if he might have fallen on his chin and mashed it to a flatline with his cheeks.[74] As Putnam had been the unanimous choice of Congress for one of the

[69] The hour of arrival is variously given. Noah Chapin, Jr., (MS *Diary*, LC) was told that Washington reached the town "about 11 o'clock." General Heath in his *Memoirs of the American War* (cited hereafter as *Heath*, with page reference to the edition of Rufus R. Wilson, 1904), p. 31, gave the time as 2 P.M. Charles Lee (1 *Lee Papers*, 188) said it was "before dinner," which would accord substantially with the hour Heath gave.

[70] *Diary of Samuel Bixby*, in MHSP., 1875-76, p. 289. The fire was by the British from 4 to 7 A.M.

[71] This statement has to be introduced with "probably" because the instance is one of many in which tradition is strong, though the evidence is frail, indeed negligible. It is customary to say, in paraphrase of Irving, *op. cit.*, v. 1, p. 496, that as Washington "entered the confines of the camp, the shouts of the multitude and the thundering of artillery, gave note to the enemy beleaguered in Boston of his arrival"; but not one diary consulted in this research mentions any such occurrence, or any other ceremonial on the 2nd of July. Ward's orderly book contains nothing to indicate that a review was held. See the orders in MHSP., 1876-77, p. 133.

[72] For the action of the Provincial Congress, see its *Journal*, 1774-75, p. 398, 441. The structure assigned Washington, it scarcely need be said, was the Wadsworth House, erected in 1726, for the Harvard President whose name it still bears. The various references to it were assembled by Justin Winsor in *The Memorial History of Boston*, v. 3, p. 107. See Amory, *Old Cambridge*, 11 ff., for a description of nearby buildings.

[73] See Charles Martyn, *Artemas Ward* (cited hereafter as *Martyn's Ward*), p. 91. Although Mr. Martyn quoted the tradition that Ward entertained Washington on the evening of the third, he found no evidence of a specific character to that effect. As Ward was then residing at the Hastings or Holmes House in Cambridge, and was mindful of the amenities, it is to be assumed that he received Washington on arrival or, if absent, called as soon as he returned to the town.

[74] A British prisoner at Hartford described Putnam later in 1775 as about five feet, six inches tall. See 1 *CHS Cols.*, 197.

commissions as Major General, Washington thought it appropriate to hand him immediately the formal paper that attested his rank.[75] Putnam received it with heartiness and accepted it without hesitation, but the delivery of the paper or some incident of the meeting brought Washington a first, unpleasant surprise: It was manifest that the seniority prescribed by Congress for the New England Generals did not accord with the opinion the leaders had formed of the relative merits of those commanders. Experience with this delicate matter of officers' sensibilities and perhaps his memory of his own troubles with Captain Dagworthy[76] prompted Washington to keep in his military chest the other commissions of the Generals. Soon he learned, also, that Seth Pomeroy, for whom he had a Brigadier's commission, had left the army because of disappointment, though Pomeroy was said to charge this against the Provincial Congress and not against the Delegates in Philadelphia.[77] Still another new Brigadier, Joseph Spencer of Connecticut, was said to be angry because Israel Putnam, whom he had outranked in the service of that Colony, had been given a higher continental commission.[78] This was not the last or the most embarrassing case. Dr. John Thomas was regarded as one of the best officers of Massachusetts, and had been Lieutenant General of its forces,[79] but in ignorance of existing seniority, Congress had made him a Brigadier and had listed him as junior to William Heath and Seth Pomeroy, both of whom he had outranked in Massachusetts service. It was assumed among those who told Washington these facts that Thomas, like Pomeroy and Spencer, would refuse to accept.

Nine generals[80] named for the troops over whom Washington was to exercise direct command and three of the nine probably to decline— that was a glum greeting for a new Commander-in-Chief! It was a blow and it might prove a calamity in an army for which, as none knew better than did Washington, few qualified senior officers could be found. An enemy could not have outdone a well intentioned but manifestly misinformed Congress in so ranking the New England Generals

[75] 3 G. W., 326. Ward's commission had been sent him direct (Martyn's Ward, 151).

[76] See Vol. II, p. 132 ff.

[77] Washington was not quite certain about the reasons for Pomeroy's departure. Cf. 3 G. W., 326.

[78] Ibid., 2 CHS Cols., 285, 288, 290.

[79] Notification of Thomas, May 25, 1775, that he had been named Lieutenant General, and his acceptance, Thomas Papers, 18, MHS. Cf. Charles Coffin, Life and Services of Major General John Thomas, 5 ff.

[80] Exclusive of the Adjutant General of the Army, Horatio Gates, who of course was not counted as a line officer.

OUTLINE SKETCH OF THE BOSTON AREA, 1775–76

Forster's Hill and Signal Tree Hill often were styled the "Twin Hills." Little remains of
Signal Tree Hill, but the other fine eminence, frequently called "Telegraph Hill," is now a
memorial park.

479

as to create the widest dissatisfaction. Washington was immediately and intently on the alert. Whether the end of the summer campaign was victory and the restoration of rights or compromise and reconciliation with England, quarrels must not be permitted to cripple the training and to divide the leadership of the Army on which the vindication of the colonial cause depended.

After the disclosure of the disturbed feeling of the camp and the uneasiness of the Provincial Congress because of the blundering choice of Generals, it must have been with a heavy though still resolute heart that Washington rode out in the company of Putnam, Lee and some of the other officers on the afternoon of July 2 for a preliminary view of the fortifications. In a short time the horsemen covered the three-quarters of a mile from the Wadsworth House to the edge of a long ridge that ran roughly from Northwest to Southeast about 1200 yards South and Southwest of the Mystick River.[81] At the eastern end of this ridge was an elevation known as Prospect Hill. This was not as high as Spring Hill at the other end of the ridge, but it deserved its name because it afforded a view of a long sweep of country to the eastward. When Washington had climbed the hill,[82] he had almost immediately in front of him at a distance of a little more than a quarter of a mile an excellent gun position his guides called Cobble Hill.[83] Thence on all sides, thin woodland and cleared fields fell away to the salt marshes and the open water.[84] East and Southeast of Prospect Hill, across a wide millpond, and at a distance of slightly more than a mile was Bunker Hill where Washington, with a glass,[85] could see British sentinels, the first footmen wearing the King's coat on whom he ever had looked as enemies. Below their post and under Breed's Hill were the ruins of

[81] Needless to say, Winter Hill lies between the river and a part of this ridge. The name "Mount Pisgah" was applied somewhat loosely to the eastern end of the area by natives but was not a name used generally by continental officers.

[82] His presence there on the afternoon of the 2nd is attested by Noah Chapin. See his *Diary*, July 2, 1775, LC.

[83] To be precise, from the crest of Prospect Hill, the bearing of Cobble Hill is East, 25 degrees South. To Bostonians it is not necessary to explain that Prospect Hill is in Somerville, directly North of Union Square, and that what is left of Cobble Hill lies in the nearby yards of the Boston & Maine Railroad.

[84] Cf. the preface to *Deacon Tudor's Diary*, p. iv. In comparing the description that follows in the text with any portrayal of the Boston area as of 1950, the large-scale reclamation of flat, tidal lands will be kept in mind by the reader. This change in the geography is most pronounced in East Boston, formerly Noodle or Noodle's Island, and in South Boston, styled Dorchester Neck on the maps of the Revolution. Concerning these maps and the elevations of the Boston area in 1775–76, see Appendix III–5.

[85] This was the term most frequently employed during the seventeen-seventies by Americans, though "spy-glass" was good usage. "Field-glass" does not seem to have been a familiar word until the time of the later Napoleonic wars.

the town of Charlestown, which had been set afire and almost had been consumed in the fighting of the 17th of June. Taken as a whole, the Charlestown Peninsula was about a mile and a half in length, from Northwest to Southeast, and was slightly more than three-quarters of a mile across at its widest point. To the North of it was the Mystick River, in which were two English floating batteries. The entire peninsula thus was British ground, isolated and easily defended, except perhaps against night raids by men in boats.

When Washington turned his view southeastward across the hillside that led down to shallow water, he could see a considerable part of Boston, distant about two miles. He never had looked at the town from that angle previously but he knew the odd conformation of the peninsula—how it extended northward from Boston Neck like the three-toed footprint of some monster. The Neck at its narrowest point was then not quite a quarter of a mile across, East to West. From this isthmus, the town extended irregularly northward two miles to the water's edge. The width of Boston from the western end of Cambridge Street to South Battery, which overlooked Dorchester Flats, was approximately a mile and a half. Distinctly visible to the Southeast, from the top of Prospect Hill, were the village of Roxbury and stretches of Dorchester Neck.[86] Beyond Boston, toward the sunrise and in the fine harbor, were the ships of the British fleet with high masts that an observer likened in homely phrase to the trees of a "dry, cedar swamp." [87] The waters in which the vessels were riding easily on the lazy summer tide could be swept by the naval guns. In addition, two miles and a half from the eastern rim of Boston, familiar Castle Island had its armament and its garrison. Thus land and harbor were commanded by the King's long arm, his cannon. Had Providence designed the picturesque sweep of hill, of peninsula and of waterways in order to give security both to mother and to daughter, while they were contemplating and reconciling their differences, the lines of the shore could not have been drawn more mercifully. Washington saw at a glance that the redoubts prepared by the Americans were feeble and in several instances badly placed,[88] but he could observe, also, that some of the

---

[86] Long doubt concerning the extent of the view from Prospect Hill would seem to be set at rest by the detailed description given by a returned traveler and printed in the *Penn. Gazette* of Aug. 25, 1775.

[87] *Jabez Fitch's Diary*, in *MHSP.*, 1894–95, p. 43.

[88] 3 *G. W.*, 330–31.

positions were strong naturally. With vigor and good engineering, he could hope to confine the British to Boston and to the hills above Charlestown. By choosing advantageous ground for batteries, he might discourage landings from the fleet. Together, these possibilities shaped his first mission: He must bottle up the British while he trained his Army.

CHAPTER XX

PREPARATION DISCLOSES A SHORTAGE

(July 3–Aug. 1, 1775)

THE THIRD of July, Washington's first full day in Cambridge, began with sparkling weather. During the morning, the temperature rose steadily until men accustomed to a Northern climate pronounced it very warm,[1] but to the General, the heat doubtless was reminiscent of the far-off Potomac, peaceful under the summer sun. The little college town, even when crowded with troops, was charming. Cambridge was, he soon wrote his brother Samuel, "in the midst of a very delightful country, and is a very beautiful place itself . . ."[2] He could enjoy the scenery even if it made him reflect on the pity that a scene of so much loveliness should be the theatre of war,[3] war that demanded what he had told Burwell Bassett he was resolved to give to the contest, "a firm belief of the justice of our cause, close attention in the prosecution of it, and the strictest integrity."[4] Transfer of command by Ward was more or less formal, but did not impress itself on witnesses as ceremonious,[5] probably because Washington had too much to do to wait on marching columns or strutting drummers. Morning General Orders of the 3rd, the first issued by Washington,[6] included a call for a "return" of the troops around Boston, in conformity to his instructions from Congress to ascertain immediately the number of men under his direct command and the strength of the different Regiments.[7] Along with their returns, the Colonels were to file a statement of the ammunition in the hands of

---

[1] *Ezekiel Price's Diary*, in MHSP., 1863–64, p. 194.
[2] Letter of July 20, 1775; 37 *G. W.*, 513.   [3] *Ibid.*
[4] See *supra*, p. 454.
[5] See the testimony, most of it negative, cited in *Martyn's Ward*, 152 and n. There is no detailed contemporary account, nor even passing mention of the "Washington elm" or of the Cambridge Common where tradition has it that the General took over the Army. The tree was there at the time—that was manifest from its rings when it fell in 1924—but there is no proof that the transfer from Ward to Washington occurred there or nearby. See S. F. Batchelder, *Bits of Cambridge History*, 239 ff.
[6] They read as if they came from Ward rather than from the new commander who as yet did not have his Adjutant General with him, but Washington's name is attached to them in Ward's (Henshaw's) Orderly Book, *MHSP.*, 1876–77, p. 114.
[7] 2 *JCC.*, 100; 3 *G. W.*, 306.

their men. Washington was most careful about this, both because he
had been told in Philadelphia that powder was in exceedingly short
supply everywhere in America and also because he had been alarmed in
New York by the letter of the Massachusetts Provincial Congress [8]
regarding the special needs of the Army. To his surprise and annoyance
he found that the returns could not be supplied that day, but he had a
prompt and satisfying report on powder: The store was 308 barrels, or
roughly sixteen tons.[9] This was enough for current operations, if they
were economically conducted, but of course the store must be replenished and increased.

For the moment, then, as the shortage of powder would not be serious,
Washington could devote his energies primarily to strengthening the
fortifications. That very afternoon, as it chanced, there was an alarm
of a threatened attack. It did not materialize but it deepened Washington's concern lest the enemy, if alert, would assault speedily the
feeble American earthworks.[10] Not a day must be lost in making the
defences as nearly impregnable as they could be in the hands of such
inexperienced troops as manned them.

After a more detailed examination of the ground on his left, Washington went with Lee to the other flank in front of Boston Neck and
again discouraged any parade or escort.[11] On the 5th, riding to Roxbury,
they met young Henry Knox, a former Boston book-dealer, 25 years of
age, who had interested himself in artillery and engineering and, at the
moment, was serving with General Ward as a volunteer. Knox was a
powerful and bulky man, whose martial bearing was not diminished in
the least by a maimed left hand. He now was riding to Cambridge but,
at the instance of the Generals, he turned about and went back to
Roxbury to show them the works there.[12] Washington found that
Boston Neck was shaped like a hand bell, with open, shallow water to
the East and a marsh to the West. The narrow "handle" of the "bell"
was about half a mile long, from North to South, and of an average

---

[8] See *supra*, p. 465.
[9] 3 *G. W.*, 394. The contents of a barrel are here estimated at 110 lbs., on the basis of
Jonathan Trumbull's statement in 2 *Force* (4) p. 1035, but many barrels weighed 100 lbs. net.
[10] 3 *G. W.*, 306. The threat was against the lines held by Nathaniel Folsom's New Hampshire troops.
[11] *Noah Chapin's Diary*, July 4, 5, 1775, LC; *E. Clarke's Diary*, July 4, 1775, p. 13.
[12] Henry Knox to his wife, July 6, 1775; F. S. Drake, *Life and Correspondence of Henry
Knox*, 18. There is some question whether Washington did not go to the right on the 4th as
well as on the 5th, but it is possible that the confusion arose over a delayed entry in *Clarke's
Diary*. Samuel Bixby (*MHSP.*, 1875–76, p. 289) was among those who saw Washington at
Roxbury on the 5th.

width, between marsh and water, of approximately 350 yards. South of the "handle," the "bell" spread southward to the end of a little inlet to the East. Still farther southward, at a distance of some 500 yards beyond the inlet, was the village of Roxbury. There, as everywhere on the front, the purpose of the American dispositions was, of course, to confine the British. Fortification by the King's engineers was designed to repel the continentals, if an attack was delivered, and to cover a sally in event one was undertaken. The American works had little strength. Abattis had been placed on the Boston Road; a crude entrenchment had been erected on either side of the highway at a point close to the George Tavern. Another had been dug across the main street of Roxbury. Still another breastwork had been thrown up on the Dorchester Road near the burying ground. The one formidable work was a fort on the hill near the meeting house, though this was overlooked by a rocky eminence to the South and East. With work and skill, Roxbury and its environs could be made strong enough to resist successfully any assault the British were apt to deliver, but to render this certain, at least as much fortification had to be undertaken as already had been completed.[13]

East of Roxbury, at a distance of about a mile was the western extremity of a long irregular peninsula styled Dorchester.[14] This was an area of irregular dimensions, about three miles in extent from East to West and of width, North and South, that varied from half a mile to a mile and more. "Dorchester Neck," strictly speaking—the stretch of land leading into the peninsula—was about a mile and a quarter, high tide to high tide, from Northwest to Southeast. The importance of the Dorchester district was in its hills which dominated the approaches to Boston from the sea. One of these hills, styled Dorchester Hill or

[13] 3 G. W., 321, 331; Samuel Gray's description in Frothingham's Siege, 212; "private letter" of July 10, 1775, quoted in ibid., 217. Although there is reason to question the accuracy of some of the small details of the accounts cited by Frothingham, reliance has to be placed on these and on Washington's summary reports because it is impossible to date some of the maps and equally impossible to ascertain when and whether later entrenchments were entered on one or two of the dated maps. It is manifest, for example, that Trumbull's early map of the area incorporated some fortification ordered by Washington after this visit. Similarly, the revision of this map reproduced on a small scale in The Memorial History of Boston, v. 3, p. 80, though marked "Sept. 1775, J. T.", does not include some works erected during July and August. The subject is one that lends itself to the tedious presentation of details of small importance, but general warning is in order: The student should not rely on any of the known maps for information concerning the extent of particular American works at any stage of the siege unless he finds documentary proof of the completion of the works at a given date.

[14] Contemporary authorities used indiscriminately the terms "Dorchester Neck" and "Dorchester Point" to describe the entire peninsula. Occasionally a British writer would style it "Dorchester Peninsula," but colonials seldom did.

Nook's Hill, fairly looked down on Boston. From this high ground on "The Neck," the principal redoubt in the eastern part of the town, Fort Hill, was distant only five-eighths of a mile. British gunners in a redoubt on Boston Neck might be able to enfilade from a lower elevation an American force that climbed Nook's Hill, but this and nearby ground that Gage had planned to take prior to the Battle of Bunker Hill was unoccupied still by either side and was not even disputed, though heavy cannon placed there could sweep the inner harbor.

Washington rode over the ground, examined the works, and had his first glance at the colonial troops around Roxbury, two Connecticut and nine Massachusetts Regiments.[15] The discipline of none of these was good, by professional standards, but was least bad, as always, where the officers were intelligent and alert. Arms were poor and of every age and type; many of the men were almost naked because they had lost their clothing at Bunker Hill and had not received that which the Provincial Congress had voted them cheerfully.[16] It was manifest, too, that many officers did not know what their duties were or how they were to do what was required of them. Washington already had sensed this and, before riding to Roxbury, he had written the Massachusetts Congress, in answer to the members' address, that it was too much to expect troops collected as had been those on the Boston lines to "possess the order, regularity and discipline of veterans." He had added that deficiencies would, he hoped, "soon be made up by the activity and zeal of the officers, and the docility and obedience of the men."[17] As for the feebleness of the defences and the mistakes made in locating them, he attributed these shortcomings primarily to the small number of trained engineers and to the scarcity of tools and implements.[18] He was tolerant and was resolved to be patient because he knew the human material out of which an army and its command had to be created. On the hills of Massachusetts, he remembered the Valley of Virginia.

Charles Lee was not so long-suffering or so indulgent of inexperience. After he had been two days at Cambridge he wrote a friend: "We found everything exactly the reverse of what had been represented. We were assured at Philadelphia that the army was stocked with engineers. We found not one. We were assured that we should find an expert train of artillery. They have not a single gunner and so on. So far from being

15 3 G. W., 322.   16 Cf. ibid., 313.
17 3 G. W., 307.   18 Ibid., 322.

prejudiced in favor of their own officers, they are extremely diffident in 'em [19] and seem much pleased that we are arrived." He went on: "The men are really very fine fellows, and had they fairplay would be made an invincible army." [20]

In this contrast of view—both states of mind very different from the pleasure and surprise that Henry Knox thought they felt after they had examined the situation at Roxbury [21]—the two Generals went back to Cambridge and to divergent tasks. Washington took up his administrative duties vigorously and with his usual regard for detail; Lee pursued his diplomatic correspondence. Dr. Benjamin Church, to whom had been entrusted the letter to Gen. John Burgoyne, stated that he had not been able to have it delivered. Burgoyne was now conspicuous in Boston and was no less disposed than Lee to have the scratch of his pen accompany the rattle of his sword. The Englishman was not only a letter writer but a dramatist also and had quite a name, at the moment, because David Garrick was staging in London a play of his. Lee's argument in his letter had been that Burgoyne and Howe were men of too much character to be the tools of a wicked ministry in the attempted subjugation of a people resolved and able to defend their liberties. "America," Lee had written, "is the last asylum of persecuted liberty." He had continued: "Here should the machinations and fury of her enemies prevail, that bright Goddess must fly from the face of the earth and leave not a trace behind. These, sir, are my principles, this my persuasion, and consequently I am determined to act." [22] The day before Washington had arrived at Cambridge with Lee—so ran the tale—trumpeters had come from the British lines with what was said to have been a letter from Burgoyne to Lee. A newspaper reported that the messenger had been blindfolded and conducted to headquarters where he had delivered the communication. Then with his eyes again covered, he had been escorted back. The incident had created much talk and, on the day after Lee returned with Washington from Roxbury, it found its way into a Gazette, though it was dismissed as a "mere exchange of courtesies." [23] If any officer or member of the Provincial Con-

[19] This was entirely good eighteenth-century use of "diffident" in the sense of "lacking confidence in."

[20] To Robert Morris, July 4, 1775; 1 *Lee Papers,* 188.

[21] Letter of July 6, 1775, to his wife; *loc. cit*   [22] 1 *Lee Papers,* 180–85.

[23] *New England Chronicle and Essex Gazette,* July 6, 1775. No reference is made to this occurrence in the communications that passed between Burgoyne and Lee. If the flag of truce actually was sent in the manner indicated, it may have been dispatched to inquire whether Lee had arrived.

gress had not heard already of the trumpeter and the mysterious letter from General Burgoyne, the article informed even the deaf and doubtless served to raise the stature of Lee in the eyes of New Englanders. Here, surely, said admirers, was a man acquainted with the "great world," a diplomatist as well as a soldier, though there was, of course, some criticism and ridicule of Lee. British in Boston asserted that he merely was making himself conspicuous by "sending impertinent letters to his old friends here." [24] Now that Lee was close to Burgoyne, he formally sounded a truce on the front and on the 5th of July sent through the lines his letter of June 7 [25] with a verbal request for immediate delivery and prompt reply.[26]

This doubtless was done with the consent of the Commander-in-Chief. For his own part, Washington was pondering a letter from James Warren and Joseph Hawley. Those leading members of the Massachusetts Provincial Congress believed they had found a way of righting the wrong they thought Congress had done General Thomas when the Philadelphia lawmakers had put Seth Pomeroy and William Heath ahead of Thomas in continental service, though that officer had outranked both of them on the Massachusetts roster. The inactive Pomeroy, said Washington's correspondents, was 100 miles away. If the Commander-in-Chief found it consistent with his instructions to withhold Pomeroy's commission until he could hear from Congress, they would try to prevail on Heath to acquiesce in the restoration of Thomas's seniority. In this way, they said, "we humbly conceive that the way would be open to do justice to Thomas." [27] Washington had no objection to this and realized immediately that it would be desirable to give

[24] Letter from Boston, Dec. 21, 1775, in *London Morning Post and Daily Advertiser*, Feb. 22, 1776, quoted in Margaret Wheeler Willard, *Letters on the American Revolution, 1774–76* (cited hereafter as *Willard*) p. 241. A forthright citizen of Piscataway, George Kendrick Fisher, declared that General Lee was a "damned impudent fellow for writing such a letter as he did to General Burgoyne." The remark and sundry other observations by Fisher brought on him formal condemnation as an enemy of his country. Somehow, too, the minutes of the hearing in Fisher's case found their way into Washington's papers (17 *Papers of G. W.*, LC, 8).

[25] Kemble stated in his Diary, *NYHS Cols.*, 1883, (cited hereafter as *Kemble*), p. 46, that Lee began the correspondence on July 4, which may have been the date of a note, now lost, to cover the delayed letter of June 7. The correct date appears in Henry Knox to Mrs. Knox, July 6, 1775 (See 1 *Knox Papers*, 160, MHS). This letter makes plain that Church previously had Lee's paper which, as will appear presently, undoubtedly was the one dated June 7. Knox told his wife: "You may remember General Lee's letter which Dr. Church was to have sent into Boston to General Burgoyne. Yesterday Mr. Webb took it to the lines at Bunker Hill where Major Bruce of the 38th came out to him . . ."

[26] Knox, as *supra*. A reference in Samuel Webb to Silas Deane, July 11, 1775, identifies "Mr. Webb" as Samuel's brother Joseph. See W. C. Ford, ed. *Correspondence and Journals of Samuel Blachley Webb* (cited herafter as *Webb*) v. 1, p. 76,

[27] Letter of July 4, 1775; 2 *Force* (4) p. 1573.

seniority to John Thomas if that officer was as good as Massachusetts leaders said he was. No injustice would be done Heath in this, were that officer voluntarily to comply with the request that Thomas be given again the seniority that had prevailed before the continental commissions had been issued. In a positive way, all that Washington had to do in the matter was to retain the Generals' commissions till the pleasure of Congress was known. He decided to do this and to write Congress. The Massachusetts conciliators meantime might try their hand with Heath—a corpulent, bald-headed man of 38, fond of parade and able to maintain discipline of a fair standard, but not credited by his fellows of the Bay Colony with initiative.[28]

This affair out of his way, Washington could devote himself to fundamental needs of the army that were plainer every day, secure fortification, accurate intelligence, the discipline of understanding minds and the strength of good organization.[29] Cover and training both might soon be imperative, because Gage's men were working hard to raise their works and gave every indication of a purpose to attack somewhere on the long half circle of American defences.[30] Because the British had command of the waterways, they were able, as Washington wrote Richard Henry Lee, to proceed "to any point of attack, without our having an hour's previous notice of it, if the General will keep his own counsel; whereas we are obliged to be guarded at all points, and know not where, with precision, to look for them."[31] Reconnaissance[32] confirmed Washington's belief that the American positions were insecure against attack of this sort and perhaps against bombardment by the close and powerful British artillery on Bunker Hill.[33] He had, above all and first of all, to build up his army defensively but he saw at the same time an opportunity of using his extended works as a cordon to intercept the supply of the British in Boston from the surrounding country. The sea still was the King's; the land must be America's and

28 Cf. *Thacher*, 413. In describing this incident, there would be a gain in compactness if the word overslaugh were used, but that term in its present-day American military sense was not employed in the British or Continental army of the period.

29 Cf. Washington to the President of Congress, July 20, 1775: "Next to the more immediate and pressing duties of putting our lines in as secure a state as possible, attending to the movements of the enemy and gaining intelligence, my great concern is to establish order, regularity and discipline, without which our numbers would embarrass us and in case of an action, great confusion must infallibly ensue" (3 *G. W.*, 349).

30 1 *Webb*, 75: "We hourly expect [the British] to sally out and attempt to carry our lines."

31 Letter of July 10, 1775; 3 *G. W.*, 330. Cf. similar statements in a letter of July 27, 1775, to John Augustine Washington, 3 *G. W.*, 372, and in one of July 20, 1775, to Samuel Washington; 37 *G. W.*, 512.

32 3 *G. W.*, 321.   33 3 *G. W.*, 321, 330, 371.

must not yield the redcoats a saddle of mutton, a bushel of wheat or a cord of wood. If, as Washington hoped and believed, the summer's campaign would effect a settlement of some sort and would end the war, then he had no greater duty, in a strategical sense, than that of confining the British, hungry and helpless, in Boston.[34]

For this reason, Washington directed that breastworks be built from Prospect Hill to the Mystick River [35] and that new defences be constructed or old fortifications be stiffened wherever it appeared feasible for the British to effect a landing.[36] When these redoubts and batteries were finished, there would be protected positions from which the colonial troops could direct a fire of cannon, of small arms, or of both against British who pushed ashore anywhere between the Charles and the Mystick Rivers.[37] On the right, around Roxbury, new defences were begun on Col. Joseph Williams's rocky high ground to the West of those already erected above the Work House on Meeting House Hill.[38]

Discipline, order and sound organization could not wait on the raising of parapets to the required height. Washington felt that his men might become good soldiers [39] and as he did not believe it safe to rely on the militia,[40] he set out to train the troops he had, as far as he knew how to do it, in such a manner as to make their numbers count to the fullest. As commander, he would do his best to provide clothing, ample fresh provisions and palatable bread; [41] they must measure up to the requirements of duty and to the terms of the newly formulated army regulations.[42] Officers must set an example and must exemplify the discipline they imposed. Some of them justified the warning Massachusetts lawmakers had given Washington. Numbers of men in charge of troops seemed to think they were above the law and could deal with their own men as they saw fit. Two, for example, had taken military prisoners from lawful custody; [43] a Quartermaster was charged with drawing provisions for more men than his Regiment included.[44] These and a number of cases involving men in the ranks [45] had been pending, in

[34] 3 G. W., 371–72. Washington's belief in the probability of a settlement and his plan of containing the enemy will be elaborated in later chapters.

[35] 1 Reed, 75.   [36] 3 G. W., 321.   [37] Cf. 1 Reed, 75.

[38] Heath, 33. Heath did not identify Williams, but he could have meant none other than Joseph, one of the best-known men of Roxbury, whose residence long was a landmark. It should be noted, also, that Heath gave the location of the new works as Southwest of those above the Almshouse, but they were more nearly West than Southwest. See F. S. Drake, The Town of Roxbury, edition of 1905, p. 382, 384.

[39] 3 G. W., 328.   [40] Ibid., 327.   [41] 3 G. W., 313.

[42] 2 JCC., 111.   [43] 3 G. W., 318, 343.   [44] Ibid., 311.

[45] Ibid., 312, 313.

some stage, when Washington assumed command: he saw to it that they were brought before a court martial. In addition, officers were reminded sharply of their military sins of omission, their negligence in circulating and heeding orders,[46] and their slowness in making returns.[47] All this could be dealt with summarily, but a matter brought up by Joseph Hawley called for more delicate handling. Hawley took as his text Washington's statement that the British might attack soon, and he went on to "suggest" that while there were in his Colony's troops "divers brave and intrepid officers, yet there are too many, and even some Colonels, whose characters, to say the least, are very equivocal with respect to courage." The communication continued: "There is much more cause to fear that the officers will fail in a day of trial, than the privates. I may venture to say that if the officers will do their duty, there is no fear of the soldiery."[48] It would be well, Hawley concluded, if Washington issued an exhortation to courage and gave warning that those who failed their country would be denounced and punished.[49] Washington painfully had witnessed one torrential summer night long before at Fort Necessity an incredible example of an officer's feebleness of fibre[50] and now, upon inquiry, he learned that Capt. John Callender had been found guilty of cowardice at Bunker Hill and had been sentenced to be cashiered.[51] There were, also, what Washington subsequently described as "several strong circumstances and a very general opinion against" certain other officers for their behavior in that battle.[52] Among those under strange suspicion was Col. James Scammon[53] who was alleged to have kept out of the fight by moving deliberately to a secure position, which he knew his commander could not have intended him to occupy.[54] Washington decided after he received Hawley's letter to bring Scammon before a court[55] and to confirm the sentence in the case of Callender. In cashiering the Captain, Washington could deliver the admonition that Hawley recommended.[56]

Prior to Washington's arrival, sentences against enlisted men had been

---

[46] 3 *G. W.*, 311–12. [47] *Ibid.*, 319.
[48] Letter of July 5, 1775; 2 *Force* (4) p. 1589.
[49] *Ibid.* [50] See Vol. I, p. 413.
[51] 3 *G. W.*, 314. [52] *Ibid.*, 348.
[53] Washington habitually wrote the name as "Scammons."
[54] See 3 *G. W.*, 336 n. [55] *Ibid.*, 335.
[56] *Ibid.*, 313–14. It is pleasing to note that Scammon was acquitted (*ibid.*, 345–46), and that Callender, after being cashiered, volunteered as a cadet in the New York artillery and fought so gallantly that the sentence against him was revoked by Washington (*ibid.*, 314; F. B. Heitman, *Historical Register of Officers of the Continental Army during the War of the Revolution* . . . edition of 1914, cited hereafter as *Heitman*, p. 140).

imposed usually in the same form and with almost the fullness of the severity that had prevailed in the French and Indian War. A man who had "taken" two horses in Connecticut, and subsequently had made restitution, was given nothing worse than a reprimand, after which he was turned out of the camp; [57] but in other cases, punishment with lashes "on the bare back" and even with a ride of specified duration on "the wooden horse" [58] had been meted out. To penalties and to appeals, the men in the ranks responded, as always, according to their own temperament and their individual sense of justice. If a culprit was to receive thirty-nine lashes, the savage and the seekers after sensation would walk miles to see them well laid on. In his diary, one soldier had set it down regretfully: ". . . went to Roxbury to Major Meigs encampment where a soldier was to be whipped at 8 o'clock 39 lashes but before we got there he was executed then I see them set off with the drums to drum him out of camp." [59] The general effect of these disciplinary measures was gradual and probably wholesome except where furious resentments were fired. Slowly the men began to see that the aim of discipline was to protect the individual and to shorten a victorious war.

During the first days that fortification and discipline were being improved in this rudimentary fashion, Washington was calling for "returns" of the strength of the Army. He kept prodding his Generals not only because of his orders to make prompt report,[60] but also because his own mathematical mind demanded a basis of precision for the dispositions he was to make. He was told by the senior officers at Cambridge that from 18,000 to 20,000 men were on the lines,[61] but nobody could speak with certainty. General Ward had found it difficult to get his self-willed subordinates to make returns; [62] Washington fretted over the clumsy delay in compiling figures he thought every regimental commander would have had at hand as a matter of course.[63] "Could I have conceived," he wrote later, "that what ought, and, in a regular army, would have been done in an hour, would employ eight days, I should have sent an express on the second morning after I arrived, with a gen-

---

[57] 3 G. W., 306.   [58] 3 G. W., 333.   [59] E. Clarke's Diary, 13.
[60] His instructions from Congress read, in part: "You are to make return to us as soon as possible . . ." 2 JCC., 100.
[61] 3 G. W., 330.
[62] 3 G. W., 322. The return of the "Massachusetts Regiments in Roxbury," July 5, 1775 (Thomas Papers, 92, MHS.) is an example of the confusion that existed.
[63] 3 G. W., 317–18, 330.

eral account of things; but expecting in the morning to receive the returns in the evening, and in the evening surely to find them in the morning, and at last getting them full of imperfections, I have been drilled on [64] from day to day, till I am ashamed to look back at the time which has elapsed since my arrival here." [65] As delivered on July 9, one week after Washington reached Cambridge, the returns were alarming. Instead of the 18,000 to 20,000 that he had been told he had, Washington found only about 16,600 enlisted men and n.c.o's, of whom the rank and file, present for duty, fit,[66] numbered 13,743 foot.[67] The artillery were listed as 585.[68] Of Massachusetts troops, supposed to be by far the strongest element in the army, there were less than 9000.[69]

The health of the men was encouraging [70]—the sick being less than 10 per cent of the army [71]—but in every other respect, effective strength was so much below estimates that it raised immediately a question larger than any that Washington ever had been called upon to answer: Should these half-trained and poorly disciplined colonials attempt to continue the siege and to invite attack, or for safety's sake should they retire beyond the range of the British heavy guns, land and naval? This seemed to Washington to involve so weighty a decision that he determined immediately to refer it to a council of war and, regardless of his Generals' advice on the question of siege or withdrawal, to proceed at once, by every legitimate means, to get more men into the Army. It might be possible to meet the immediate shortage of enlisted strength by calling out the militia, but aside from his old distrust of those temporary soldiers,[72] Washington the farmer could not overlook the fact that July and August were months when every man who lived on the land should be in the fields.[73]

The council—the first Washington held as continental Commander-

---

[64] "Drilled on" in the sense of "put off" was good usage as early as the fourteenth century but apparently was becoming old-fashioned even in Washington's time.

[65] Letter of July 10, 1775, to Richard Henry Lee, 3 *G. W.*, 329–30.

[66] It may be out of order to note again that the British army organization, which at this time was being followed by the Americans, counted "rank and file" as those enlisted men present in the line with arms in their hands. This classification included Corporals and privates, but excluded Sergeants and drummers.

[67] Washington had ample reason to complain of these returns. They were made up in such a manner that even now non-commissioned officers and the rank and file are confused easily. It is impossible to say whether the list of the sick included or excluded n.c.o's, drummers and fifers. Commissioned officers present were set down at 965, of whom 493 were Lieutenants. Staff officers—Chaplains, Adjutants, Quartermasters, Surgeons and Surgeons' Mates—numbered 144. Sergeants were reckoned at 1192, drummers and fifers at 576.

[68] 2 *Force* (4) p. 1630.   [69] 3 *G. W.*, 319.

[70] *Ibid.*   [71] 2 *Force* (4) p. 1630.

[72] 3 *G. W.*, 327.   [73] *Ibid.*

in-Chief—was unanimously of one mind: Members estimated the enemy's total strength at 11,500, and they computed that the American force should be approximately twice that, or 22,000. Dangerous as continuance of the siege might be, withdrawal would give Cambridge, Roxbury and Watertown to the enemy, would encourage the British, would dispirit the entire continent, and would create widespread dissatisfaction in Massachusetts. Besides, if the American army abandoned the siege of Boston and evacuated the defences constructed with so much labor, at what point would the Regiments be able to make a stand? Conditions of combat admittedly were bad: where would they be better? The British could be drawn from the cover of their ships, yes; but would the continentals be in positions as strong as those they now held? The answer of the council was that the army must continue the siege, if possible, and must offer the sternest resistance it could in event the British made a sally. If retreat was unavoidable, it should be to the high ground known as "the Welsh Mountains" near Cambridge and in rear of Roxbury.[74] Washington concurred in the decision wholeheartedly but he could not shut his eyes to the risks he had to take. "Between you and me," he told Richard Henry Lee, "I think we are in an exceedingly dangerous situation, as our numbers are not much larger than we suppose those of the enemy to be, from the best accounts we are able to get." He laid particular stress on the condition he had observed from the first—that command of the waters around Boston made it possible for the enemy to concentrate secretly in superior force and to deliver a surprise attack on any part of the American lines.[75]

Once again, then, if the army was to stand in front of Boston, it must stand on the A-B-Cs of war: it must be thoroughly disciplined, well organized, ceaselessly vigilant and numerically stronger. To this basic policy, after the council of war, Washington returned even more positively than ever. He stressed it in his initial detailed dispatch to the President of Congress and he dealt tactfully with the need of new troops of the right fibre. In particular he said: "From the number of boys, deserters and Negroes which have enlisted in this Province, I entertain some doubts whether the number required can be raised here . . . This unhappy and devoted Province has been so long in a state of

---

[74] Washington's epitome of the controlling reasons for the main decision will be found in his letters of July 10 to the President of Congress (3 *G. W.*, 322), and to Richard Henry Lee (*ibid.*, 330–31). The minutes of the council of war, July 9, 1775, are in 2 *Force* (4) p. 1628. A rough draft, much amended and simplified, is in 16 *Papers of G. W.*, 82, LC.

[75] 3 *G. W.*, 330.

anarchy, and the yoke of ministerial oppression so heavily laid, that great allowances are to be made for their troops collected under such circumstances. The deficiencies in their numbers, their discipline and stores can only lead to this conclusion, that their spirit has exceeded their strength." It was desirable, he said with much deference, to enlist troops from other Colonies. While this was being done, difficulty would be encountered in disciplining the army with the enemy in sight and an attack expected daily, but the task would be undertaken.

The one cheerful passage in a realistic report was that "there are materials for a good army, a great number of men able bodied, active, zealous in the cause and of unquestionable courage." [76] At headquarters there were other encouraging conditions. Horatio Gates arrived and on the 9th assumed his duties as Adjutant General, greatly to the relief of Washington.[77] When the Massachusetts Provincial Congress learned that the President's house at Harvard was not altogether adequate as headquarters in the circumstances that developed,[78] it directed the Committee of Safety to procure and to place at Washington's disposal and at Lee's any other dwelling that suited them.[79] As a result, the two Generals transferred headquarters to the house of John Vassall, who had left it, well furnished, and had gone to Boston when the colonials occupied Cambridge.[80]

Another encouragement was a new turn in the case of Gen. Joseph Spencer. After that Connecticut commander had taken offence at the appointment of Putnam over him, he had left his quarters on July 6 [81] without farewell and without leave from the new Commander-in-

[76] 3 G. W., 327–28.
[77] 3 G. W., 318. Gates's plans for joining his new chief were given in Gates to Washington, June 22, 1775; 16 Papers of G. W., 60, LC.
[78] Vagueness cannot be avoided here. The tradition is that a cannonball penetrated the structure and gave warning that it was too much exposed (See Amory, Old Cambridge, 22, and Francis Le Baron, 73 Century Mag., 487) but it seems improbable in the extreme that this could have occurred without some mention of the incident in any of the numerous contemporary diaries, which often recorded incidents far less important and dramatic. In the absence of all evidence, a safe guess is the one already advanced—that it was embarrassing to Washington to have to occupy a house the master of which, a distinguished man of 52, was present and was allowed one room only. Whether Mrs. Langdon or any of their five surviving adult children were with him, the record does not show. See F. B. Sanborn in MHSP., 1903–04, p. 192 ff.
[79] Journ. Prov. Cong. Mass., 1774–75, July 8, 1775, p. 460. Cf. ibid., 455, 592.
[80] Amory, Old Cambridge, 22. See the proceedings of the Massachusetts Congress, July 8, 1775, op. cit., p. 593 for the appointment of a committee to procure a steward and serving woman for the residence which, needless to say, is the famous Craigie or Longfellow House. Charles Lee's residence there was of less than three weeks. Prior to July 26, he moved about four miles to General Royall's place at Medford, which he soon styled Hobgoblin Hall. See 1 Reed, 116; Samuel Cooper's Diary in 6 A. H. R., 326 n; Dr. Belknap's Journal in MHSP., 1858–60, p. 82–83.
[81] E. Clarke's Diary, 13.

ARTEMAS WARD, WHO MIGHT HAVE HAD WASHINGTON'S TASK

When younger, the gentleman whose portrait appears to the right might have been the Commander-in-Chief of the continental armies and might have established a reasonably good claim to that position. Around Boston, in June, 1775, the opposing armies were conducting what they hoped would be the only campaign of the war. Should not the Americans be under an officer thoroughly familiar with the people and the militia of that region? Ward met that requirement. Massachusetts was supplying the largest number of troops: should not the Bay Colony name one of its sons as leader? Ward, who was 48 years of age in 1775, counted it first among his distinctions that he was of Pilgrim stock. He had been, moreover, a Colonel of militia in the French and Indian War and he knew the resources of the New England States. Should he be supplanted by a man from a remote Colony that had not been called on, as yet, for sacrifices comparable to those of Massachusetts?

It would have been expecting too much of human nature to suppose that these and similar questions were not asked when announcement was made that Congress had elected Washington, not Ward, as Commander-in-Chief of the American armies. Ward did not relish that action and did not pretend to do so. He received Washington with full regard for all the proprieties but without personal cordiality. His prime rule of conduct seemed to be to obey orders and to keep his distance. Although no clash occurred, neither man cared for the other. After the siege of Boston ended, and Washington transferred the greater part of the Army to New York, Ward resumed general command in Eastern Massachusetts. He had little to do and, as his health appeared to be failing, he repeatedly sought to resign until Congress at length consented.

Perhaps he deserved more credit than he received. He kept the Army together in front of Boston until Washington came, and after that, however much he felt aggrieved, he did not add to his successor's difficulties by organizing the discontented. Charles Lee laughed at Ward's generalship and sneeringly termed him a church warden. Perhaps it was a compliment. Had Ward possessed the spirit of the man who assailed him, he might have ruined Washington.

(After the portrait in Independence Hall, Philadelphia, painted late in his life. No earlier picture of him has been found.)

JOHN SULLIVAN, WHOSE ZEAL COULD NOT
WIN GOOD LUCK

When John Sullivan reported for military duty a few days after Washington's arrival at Cambridge, the Commander-in-Chief greeted him as a colleague, who, like himself, had left the Continental Congress to take the field. Sullivan had served both in 1774 and in 1775 as a Delegate from New Hampshire and he had highly interesting antecedents. His father and his mother had come to America as redemptionists—the New England synonym for indentured servants—and by hard work they had established themselves in decent independence that had made it possible for John to study law. Although prone to sue when he might compromise, he had attained some success at 35, when he was elected a continental Brigadier. He had zeal, ambition and all of an eighteenth-century Irishman's hate of England. While he labored industriously and not unskillfully as a soldier, he never forgot the lawmakers and the voters at home. They were his constituents as well as his companions in revolution, and he gave them a regular accounting of his leadership. One eye always was on the hills of New Hampshire.

Of all Washington's Generals, Sullivan was the most human in the sense that his responses to a situation could be predicted with virtual certainty. Was a fight in prospect? Sullivan was ready for it. Did the Commander-in-Chief give him an opportunity? He grasped it avidly, with over-optimistic assurances of success. If the clouds of adversity gathered, Sullivan gave instant warning of a deluge and declared himself entirely willing to die in it. He thirsted for recognition and always was hungry for good will. Perhaps this was because he was unchangeably the politician; perhaps he had a half-conscious craving for what he suspected men of station might deny a redemptionist's son, but the feeling was there—an excessive desire to be popular. It tempted him often into unwise correspondence, without destroying his fundamental loyalty to Washington. One other disadvantage was to develop later, the strange run of the cards, the inexplicable contradiction of chance that Napoleon had in mind when he said it was not enough that a General be a good soldier: he must be lucky, too.

(After the Original in Independence Hall, Philadelphia)

Chief,[82] and he either inspired or else said nothing to prevent a written protest on July 5 by forty-nine of his officers.[83] This paper was addressed to the Connecticut Assembly and was primarily a complaint that General Spencer "who came here first in command of the Connecticut forces" had been "degraded" from his previous rank. The petitioners affirmed that they had "no objection to the appointment of Generals Washington and Lee," but they maintained, "the late arrangement so far removes General Spencer from his former command that he cannot and will not continue in the service under this arrangement." Warning was given: "We apprehend the morals and good order and discipline of our troops will be greatly endangered under the present arrangement." The General Assembly of Connecticut was invoked to urge that the previous action of the Continental Congress might "be altered so as to continue General Spencer in command as before." [84] Obligingly, and somewhat in the spirit of being all things to all men, the Connecticut Assembly requested Governor Trumbull to write the Colony's Delegates "and acquaint them with the estimation in which General Wooster and General Spencer" were held. At the same time, the Governor was to testify to the Assembly's appreciation "of the singular merit of General Putnam" and was to ask the Delegates in Philadelphia "to devise some method of obviating the difficulties apprehended." With this was joined an appeal to Spencer not to resign, because this, among other things, would "give great anxiety and dissatisfaction to his country . . ." [85] The effect of this agitation was to bring Spencer into general disfavor. Even the officers who had signed the petition in his behalf were said to have become ashamed of themselves. In the end, Spencer had the good sense to swallow his pride and to return on the 18th of July [86] to his troops, at the rank of Brigadier, assigned him by the Continental Congress.[87] This relieved Washington of a delicate situation which he had not created and could not himself correct. Wooster's discontent persisted; Pomeroy might perhaps be disregarded; if Thomas could be reconciled to the rank given him or could be made the senior Brigadier, then jealousies of this nature might cease for the time to threaten the precarious cause of the aspiring Colonies.

To this there was a proviso, one that Washington overlooked, pur-

---

[82] 3 G. W., 326.
[83] Included were Col. Samuel H. Parsons and his officers of the Sixth Connecticut.
[84] 2 Force (4) p. 1585.   [85] Ibid., 1585–86.   [86] 3 G. W., 349.
[87] 7 CHS Cols., 205, 208, 209; 1 Burnett, 164, 166–67; 1 Webb, 79–80.

posely disregarded, or refused to credit as a possibility, lest admission of it be unjust to a patriot: Continuance of restored amity among the general officers around Boston depended, above all, on the conduct of Charles Lee. If his growing reputation and popularity led him to become independent—not to say insubordinate—he could make endless trouble. At the moment, there was just enough of the unexpected in his conduct to create an uneasiness that many felt and none voiced. When Lee's most recent utterance or odd act was described, persons of sensitive spirit might hesitate a moment and then would say that General Lee was of course a great soldier and a true friend of liberty.[88] Immediate developments were not of a sort to alarm. By a flag of truce, Burgoyne replied under date of July 8 [89] to the letter Lee had passed through the lines on the 5th.[90] After presenting his argument in behalf of the King, Burgoyne proposed a meeting at a specified place on Boston Neck "to renew the 'rights of fellowship' " and, in the British officer's words, perhaps to "induce such explanation[s] as might tend in their consequences to peace." Burgoyne went on: "I feel, in common with all around me, for the unhappy bulk of this country; they foresee not the distress that is impending over them. I know Great Britain is ready to open her arms upon the first overture of accommodation; I know she is equally resolute to maintain her original rights; and if the war proceeds, your 150,000 men will not be a match for her power." To assure an easy conference on these things, safe conduct was pledged and asked. "If this plan is agreeable to you," the Englishman said, "name your day and hour." [91]

It manifestly was an attractive opportunity. Washington no doubt

[88] It is almost impossible to say when this misgiving began. Abigail Adams appears at first to have had doubts that she subsequently overcame (*Adams, Fam. Lett.*, 78). Another doubter was James Warren who wrote of Lee, July 9, 1775: "I admire the soldier, but think civility or even politeness not incompatible with his character. But this *inter nos.* I shall take care to speak highly of him on all occasions" (*Warren-Adams Letters*, 72 MHS Cols., cited hereafter as *Warren-Adams Letters*, v. 1, p. 69). It was not until October that Dr. Belknap wrote of Lee as "full of fire and passion and but little manners, a great sloven, wretchedly profane . . ." (*Belknap's Journal* in *MHSP*, 1858–60, p. 82–83). These criticisms were of the man, not of the soldier or of the patriot.

[89] The letter was not presented by a trumpeter, sounding a truce, until July 10. Henry Knox to Mrs. Knox, July 11, 1775; 1 *Knox Papers*, 163, MHS.

[90] As printed in 2 *Force* (4) p. 1611–12, Burgoyne's answer contained numerous references that almost positively identify it as a reply to Lee's letter of June 7, 1775, and not some later, lost communication. One sentence of Burgoyne clinches the matter. Lee had written under date of June 7: ". . . I request you to lay your hand upon your heart, and then answer with your usual integrity and frankness, whether" etc. (1 *Lee Papers*, 181). In his reply, Burgoyne said: "Now, sir, lay your hand on your heart, as you have enjoined me to do on mine, and tell me to which" etc. (2 *Force* (4) p. 1611).

[91] 2 *Force* (4) p. 1611–12.

heard the details from Lee, but in what followed, the initiative was that of the senior lieutenant, not that of his superior. On the 10th of July, Lee sent the Massachusetts Congress the original of Burgoyne's letter and begged leave "to receive their commands with respect to the proposed interview." He would accept or decline the interview as the Congress advised. If the decision was for a meeting, he would like for the Congress to name one of its members to attend and to hear the entire conversation, and he welcomed an immediate answer, he said, because he had promised to notify Burgoyne by 4 o'clock that afternoon whether the interview was to take place.

The answer of the Massachusetts members was cautious. They voiced their faith in Lee but asked, ". . . as the confidence of the people in their General is so essentially necessary to the well-conducting the enterprise in which we are engaged; and as a people contending for their liberties are naturally disposed to jealousy, and not inclined to make the most favorable construction of the motives of conduct which they are not fully acquainted with, whether such an interview might not have a tendency to lessen the influence which the Congress would wish to extend to the utmost of their power to facilitate and succeed the operations of war." To prevent as far as they could any "disagreeable consequences which may arise from the jealousy of the people on such an occasion," the Congress reported that they had appointed Elbridge Gerry to attend the interview if Lee thought proper to proceed. The members added that they did not "think themselves authorized to counteract the General's inclination," but they hinted strongly that he would be wise to take the advice of the council of war in a matter of such apparent delicacy.[92]

Lee might well have asked himself whether this statement bespoke confidence or suspicion, trust or jealousy; but while he could not quarrel with the form of the answer, he could not fail to see that the Massachusetts Congress disapproved negotiations by him, without the approval of higher authority. He concluded that he had better drop the plan and he forthwith wrote Burgoyne that he must "defer the happiness of embracing a man whom he most sincerely loves, until the subversion of the present tyrannical ministry and system, which he is persuaded must be in a few months, as he knows Great Britain cannot stand the contest." [93] This ended the correspondence but not the independent activi-

92 2 *Force* (4) p. 1504.   93 Letter of July 11, 1775; *ibid.*, 1638–39.

ties of Lee outside his military duties. He denounced with venom the treatment the British were alleged to be according American prisoners in Boston and he let it be known that he intended protesting to the royal authorities with a threat of reprisal.[94] Washington did not reprimand Lee for this or write to Congress concerning it. He said nothing and did nothing to indicate that he regarded Lee's actions otherwise than as the zealous service of a peculiar but devoted man, perhaps the best trained General the continent had.

If Lee thought that he, and not Washington, should be at the head of the army, he gave no intimation of it. One sentence only from his pen, in a letter to General Thomas, might have raised a question, and even this was part of an episode creditable to Lee. When Washington sent Congress on the 10th of July his first detailed report of the conditions he had found in the Army,[95] he included a reference to the dissatisfaction over the appointments of general officers. After telling of Spencer's disgust and Pomeroy's withdrawal, Washington remarked cautiously: "General Thomas is much esteemed and most earnestly desired to continue in the service, and as far as my opportunities have enabled me to judge, I must join in the general opinion that he is an able good officer and his resignation would be a public loss. The postponing [96] him to Pomeroy and Heath, whom he has commanded, would make his continuance very difficult and probably operate on his mind, as the like circumstance did on that of Spencer." [97] That was all Washington said. With ingrained respect for civil authority, he left action, if any was taken, to Congress and, more particularly, to those Massachusetts Delegates in Philadelphia who now were aware of the esteem in which the soldierly virtues of Thomas were held. Bay Colony members scarcely needed prodding, because James Warren already had written of a contrast that left nothing to be added. He had said in a letter to John Adams: "[Thomas's] merits in the military way have surprised us all. I can't describe to you the odds between the two camps. While one has been spiritless, sluggish, confused and dirty, I mean where General Putnam's and our friend [Joseph] Warren's influence have not had their effects, the other has been spirited, active, regular and clean. He

---

[94] 1 *Webb*, 77.   [95] 3 *G. W.*, 320–29.

[96] This is an earlier use of the word in this particular sense than the *New English Dictionary* records. Its example of postpone as "to place after in serial order or arrangement; to put at, or nearer to, the end" dates from 1620; but it assigns 1893 to its example of postpone, with the definition "to place after in order of precedence, rank, importance or value."

[97] 3 *G. W.*, 326.

[Thomas] has appeared with the dignity and abilities of a General." [98]
On receipt of this, John Adams solicited votes to give Thomas the
seniority assigned Pomeroy, and he soon found the members willing to
do this if Washington approved.[99] Thomas meantime conducted himself with the moderation and reserve that became his erect six feet, his
finely proportioned body, his distinguished face and his commanding
presence.[100] Warren reported: "He seldom talks imprudently, and
I believe he has never done it on this occasion." Thomas's one disquieting remark was at the same time patriotic: If he quit the army, he told
his friends, he soon would return as a volunteer.[101] This assurance was
enough to make all his admirers bestir themselves. Both Washington
and Charles Lee were asked to write Thomas and to urge him not to
resign. In compliance, Washington had Joseph Reed prepare a letter
which he revised slightly and sent to the offended General.[102] It was an
eloquent paper, built around two questions: "What matter of triumph
will it afford our enemies, that in less than one month, a spirit of discord should shew itself in the highest ranks of the army, not to be extinguished by anything less than a total desertion of duty? How little
reason shall we have to boast of American union and patriotism, if at
such a time and in such a cause, smaller and partial considerations cannot give way to the great and general interest?" [103]

Lee's letter—the one that might have been said to disclose the author
while reenforcing his plea—was written Thomas the same day Washington's was, and it was penned in courteous camaraderie. In terse
acknowledgment that he did not feel Thomas had received just treatment at the hands of Congress, Lee asked: ". . . is this a time, sir, when
the liberties of your country, the fate of posterity, the rights of mankind are at stake, to indulge our resentments for any ill treatment we
may have received as individuals." Here Lee took the centre of the
stage: "I have myself, sir, full as great, perhaps greater reason to complain than yourself. I have passed through the highest ranks, in some
of the most respectable services in Europe. According then to modern
etiquette notions of a soldier's honor and delicacy, I ought to consider
at least the preferment given to General Ward over me as the greatest
indignity, but I thought it my duty as a citizen and asserter of liberty

[98] Letter of June 27, 1775; 1 *Warren-Adams Letters*, 68.
[99] *Ibid.*, 79; 1 *Burnett*, 161.   [100] Arthur Lord in *MHSP.*, 1903–04, p. 421.
[101] 1 *Warren-Adams Letters*, 95.   [102] 1 *Reed*, 109.
[103] Letter of July 23, 1775; 3 *G. W.*, 359.

to waive every consideration. On this principle, although a Major General of five years' standing, and not a native of America, I consented to serve under General Ward, because I was taught to think the concession would be grateful to his countrymen, and flatter myself that the concession has done me credit in the eye of the world . . ." With this he brought the argument back to Thomas,[104] who doubtless was too much concerned with his own case to analyze Lee's letter as a clue to the character of its writer. If Washington saw the communication, he may not have attached importance to two words in the clause, "I ought to consider at least the preferment given to General Ward over me as the greatest indignity." What was the full implication of "at least"? Manifestly, Lee thought he "at least" should outrank Ward, and at maximum —where should his place be? Ahead of Washington?

This question did not arise, nor did that of seniority of Thomas continue to disturb and to divide the camp. Field officers of Thomas's command joined in urging him to stay, though they professed entire willingness to abide his decision.[105] He deferred action of any sort temporarily,[106] but Congress promptly voted to make him senior Brigadier, vice Pomeroy, who, in the language of the resolution, "never acted under the commission sent him." To remove all ground of future difference, the Delegates stipulated that Thomas's commission bear the same date as Pomeroy's.[107] If this displeased Heath, he made no formal protest and by his silence let the controversy end to the relief of all those who admired Thomas's accomplishments and feared that if the Brigadier resigned, many subordinates would, also.[108] Washington could mark off his list of difficulties the "great dissatisfaction," as he had termed it,[109] with the original appointments of general officers. Not till this was past did he admit the full seriousness of the danger he thought the controversy carried in it. Then he confided to Philip Schuyler that because of the incompetence and clashes among the officers, "confusion and disorder reigned in every department, which in

---

104 1 *Lee Papers*, 197–98.

105 *MHSP.*, 1902–03, p. 428–29. The original, dated July 25, 1775, is in the *Thomas Papers*, p. 53, MHS.

106 Probably at the instance, among others, of James Warren who assured him of an early "handsome appointment in the Army, and such an one as we presume would be satisfactory to you" (Letter of July 22, 1775, *Thomas Papers*, p. 50, MHS).

107 2 *JCC.*, 191.

108 Cf. Abigail Adams, July 25, 1775: "If Thomas resigns, all his officers resign" (*Adams, Fam. Lett.*, 89). For felicitations on the settlement of the affair, see 3 *G. W.*, 358, 374; 1 *Warren-Adams Letters*, 85, 95, and 1 *Burnett*, 173.

109 3 *G. W.*, 325.

a little time must have ended either in the separation of the army or [in] fatal contests with one another." He added, "the better genius of America has prevailed . . ."

Relief in this was attended by a reminder to Washington that in wartime it often is as difficult to bar politely the ambitious and the unqualified as it is to find the diligent and the able. From Philadelphia, on the 10th of July, John Hancock wrote to say that nothing of concern to the Army had been decided since his previous letter. Hancock then became personal: "I must beg for the favor that you will reserve some berth for me in such Department as you may judge most proper, for I am determined to act under you if it be to take the firelock and join the ranks as a volunteer." [110] Hancock, as Washington was aware, had wished the refusal of the army command, if indeed, he had not hoped to lead the troops in the field, though his experience in war was nil. Whether or not Washington knew the depths of Hancock's resentment over what the rich Massachusetts merchant regarded as a slight at the hands of his fellow-Delegates, the General made the most direct answer. On the 21st he wrote: "I am particularly to acknowledge that part of your favor of the 10th instant, wherein you do me the honor of determining to join the Army under my command. I need certainly make no professions of the pleasure I shall have in seeing you: At the same time I have to regret that so little is in my power to offer, equal to Colonel Hancock's merits and worthy his acceptance. I shall be happy in every opportunity to show the regard and esteem with which I am, etc."—Just that, no more. [111]

There was no telling, of course, when or whether Hancock would descend on headquarters, but there was in reality no place for him as an officer of the line. Hancock compromised, temporarily, by getting married; Washington proceeded to battle with mounting duties and in particular, to execute a plan for dividing the Army into three "Grand Divisions" of two Brigades each. Artemas Ward was named to command the right, with the Brigades of John Thomas and of Joseph Spencer. The central Grand Division, lacking as yet an organized second Brigade, was to be Israel Putnam's. Its existing Brigade, in which Putnam had been ranking officer, was entrusted to its senior Colonel. On the left were the Brigades of John Sullivan and Nathanael Greene, with Charles

[110] 16 *Papers of G. W.*, 83, LC.
[111] 3 *G. W.*, 353.

Lee in general command.[112] Provision was made by Washington for the insignia of these senior officers;[113] a Judge Advocate General was named to organize the work of the military courts;[114] similarly, a Commissary General was appointed in the person of Joseph Trumbull;[115] cleanliness of quarters and a score of other improvements were enjoined.[116]

Many of the articles required for the camps and for the decent dress and equipment of the men would be crude, and some, of course, were unprocurable in a region deprived of imports; but Washington found gratefully that he could count on everything the nearby New England Colonies could supply. New Hampshire was remote and had little; Connecticut, Rhode Island and Massachusetts were better stocked than might have been assumed and were diligent in answering Washington's calls. The Massachusetts Provincial Council was within arm's reach, so to say, at Watertown. Under the leadership of James Warren and of men like-spirited, the Congress gave sound, intelligent counsel along with all the Bay Colony could provide in food and powder and arms.[117]

Washington had like support in July and August from the Governor of Connecticut, Jonathan Trumbull. The Governor was 65 and in spite of business adversity that had wrecked a fortune made in skillful trade, he had faith and fervor, energy and positive eagerness to aid the Army in every way. His first letter to Washington, written to congratulate the new General, echoed characteristically in some of its phrases the language of the Old Testament: "[The Congress] have, with one united

[112] The GO of July 22, 1775, covering this organization, was poorly drawn. Ward's command was termed "the right wing or division," though the term "Grand Division" was used in an earlier paragraph. Lee was announced as commander of "the left wing or second division" of the army. Although one Brigade only was listed as Putnam's, the order read: "These two Brigades to be under the command of Major General Putnam, also a Corps-de-Reserve, for the defence of the several posts, North of Roxbury, not already named" (3 G. W., 355–56).

[113] The Commander-in-Chief was to wear "a light blue ribband . . . across his breast, between his coat and waistcoat. For the Brigadiers and the Major Generals a pink ribband was prescribed. The badge of staff officers was green (3 G. W., 339). As of July 24, the pink ribband was restricted to the Brigadiers. The Major Generals were assigned a purple (ibid., 362). Field and company officers were to be distinguished by cockades of different colors, n.c.o's by a strip of colored cloth on the right shoulder (3 G. W., 357).

[114] Deacon Tudor's Diary, July 13, 1775; 3 G. W., 378. This official was William Tudor, son of the deacon and diarist.

[115] July 31, 1775; 3 G. W., 378–79. Trumbull was a son of the Governor of Connecticut presently to be mentioned.

[116] For the camps, see 3 G. W., 338. Daily GO's of the early summer frequently contained instructions of some sort that indicated regular visitation of the camps by Washington and close observation of deficiencies and of neglected discipline.

[117] However the equities may be determined by historical investigators of the ugly political rivalry between Warren and John Hancock, any student of events during the period of Washington's presence in front of Boston in 1775–76 is apt to be impressed by the patriotism and wisdom James Warren displayed as President of the Massachusetts Congress.

voice, appointed you to the high station you possess. The Supreme
Director of all events hath caused a wonderful union of hearts and
counsels to subsist among us. Now, therefore, be strong and very
courageous. May the God of the armies of Israel shower down the
blessings of his Divine Providence on you, give you wisdom and fortitude, cover your head in the day of battle and danger, add success,
convince our enemies of their mistaken measures, and that all their
attempts to deprive these Colonies of their inestimable constitutional
rights and liberties are injurious and vain." [118] This descent from the
words of the Almighty to the parlance of the constitutional dispute—
this blending of exhortation to Joshua, son of Nun, with hope for recovered ministerial sanity—was typical of Governor Trumbull and in the
pattern of his aid. He would invoke the God of Israel but he would lose
no time in raising two new Regiments and in forwarding precisely 1391
barrels of flour.[119] Lieut. Gov. Nicholas Cooke of Rhode Island was 58,
somewhat younger than Trumbull, and was less known but no less
diligent or devoted. He, too, sent congratulations and a pledge of
support to which he adhered.[120]

Abatement of jealousies over rank, first steps in organization and
discipline, the progress of fortification, the support of the New England
Colonies—all these were facilitated by hearty acceptation of Washington as a man of character and as a leader of judgment and resolution.
In the Bay Colony as in Pennsylvania, he was credited with so great a
fortune [121] that his willingness to risk it in the colonial cause bred
confidence in him. Young soldiers and observant, clear-eyed women
confirmed after Washington's arrival all that had been written by
Massachusetts members of Congress before he set out. Henry Knox
told his wife: "General Washington fills his place with vast ease and
dignity, and dispenses happiness around him." [122] Abigail Adams
assured her husband, the man who had done more than any other to
have the Virginian sent to New England: "You had prepared me to
entertain a favorable opinion of General Washington, but I thought the
half was not told me. Dignity with ease and complacency, the gentle-

[118] Letter of July 13, 1775; Jared Sparks, ed. *Correspondence of the American Revolution;
being Letters of Eminent Men to George Washington* . . . (cited hereafter as *LTW*) v. 1,
p. 2–3. For a somewhat earlier use of much the same language by Trumbull, see 7 *N. H. Prov.
Rec.*, 532–33.
[119] 1 *LTW.*, 4–5.
[120] See his letter of July 12, 1775, in 1 *LTW.*, 1.
[121] *Bristol*, (Eng.) *Gazette*, Aug. 24, 1775; quoted in *Willard*, 160.
[122] Letter of July 9, 1775; Drake's *Knox*, 18.

man and soldier, look agreeably blended in him. Modesty marks every line and feature of his face." [123] Said Samuel Webb hopefully: "Our General and the other gentlemen from the southward will be the means of disciplining the army, which was much needed." [124] In the opinion of Surgeon James Thacher, the appearance of the new General was: "truly noble and majestic; being tall and well proportioned. His dress is a blue coat with buff-colored facings, a rich epaulette on each shoulder, buff underdress and an elegant small sword; a black cockade in the hat." [125] Mercy Warren, James Warren's wife, writing later but in the memory of Washington's first weeks at Cambridge, recalled how "in his character was blended a certain dignity with the appearance of good humor." [126]

Washington was fortunate, more than fortunate, in his adversary. Bunker Hill had shaken both the strength and the confidence of the British.[127] Although some of the officers around Charlestown expressed special confidence in the commander of that "wing," Gen. William Howe, they had respect for American marksmanship and resentment of the colonials' vigilance. One participant wrote: "Never had the British army so ungenerous an enemy to oppose; they send their riflemen five or six at a time who conceal themselves behind trees, &c till an opportunity presents itself of taking a shot at our advance sentries, which done they immediately retreat. What an unfair method of carrying on a war!" [128]

Day by day, the British delayed the attack Washington expected. On the 8th of July, some of General Thomas's men surprised the guard at Brown's House, an advanced post on the Roxbury line, and destroyed the dwelling and barn there.[129] After that nothing happened until the 25th of July, when three men-of-war and six transports sailed out of Boston and disappeared on a course ESE. Where were they going?

---

[123] Letter of July 16, 1775; *Adams, Fam. Let.,* 78.
[124] 1 *Webb,* 73 ff; letter of July 11, 1775, to Silas Deane.
[125] *Thacher,* 30; entry of July 20, 1775.   [126] *Mercy Warren,* v. 1, p. 233.
[127] Lord Percy wrote, July 28, 1775: "For . . . our army is so small that we cannot afford even a victory, if it is attended with any loss of men" (*Lord Percy's Letters,* 58). General Gage's comment was, July 24: "Our situation is not advantageous but I will endeavor to make the best of it" (1 *Gage,* 409).
[128] William Carter, *A Genuine Detail . . . in Letters to a Friend* (cited hereafter as *Carter, Letters to a Friend*) 5, 7.
[129] The fullest account and certainly the most accurate, is Thomas to his wife, July 8, 1775, *Thomas Papers,* 24, MHS. See also 3 *G. W.,* 321; *N. Y. Gazette and Weekly Mercury,* July 24, 1775; Samuel Haws's Diary in Abraham Tomlinson, compiler, *The Military Journals of Two Private Soldiers, 1758-1775,* (cited hereafter as *Samuel Haws's Diary*), 60–61; *Diary of N. Morgan* in 7 *CHS Cols.,* 102; *Diary of Samuel Bixby* in *MHSP.,* 1875–76, p. 289.

Washington asked himself the question and concluded the commander in Boston was conducting a raid, with naval assistance, to procure supplies. It so proved. The raid was on the smaller islands of Long Island Sound, which had to be defended, if at all, by forces from Connecticut, rather than from Boston.[130] In the belief that its turn might be next, Massachusetts immediately appealed to Washington to "know of him if he can, consistent with his instructions and the general service, order a detachment [to the eastern parts of this Colony] to prevent the enemy from ravaging the country and plundering the inhabitants of their sheep, cattle, wood &c., to supply themselves." [131]

This was action of the House of Representatives which on the 19th of July had come into being as the lower branch of the Legislature that had succeeded the self-dissolved Provincial Congress. The new lawmaking body included many of those who had served in the Congress but it was sufficiently different for Washington to make particular effort to establish with it the close and trustful relations he had enjoyed with the Provincial Congress. At the same time, its resolution dealt with a dispersion of force against which all his soldierly impulses protested. The House of Representatives, in fact, might have asked him for any honorable thing he could do, and it would have had better prospect of getting his approval than it had of prevailing on him to divide a force he considered too small to meet the anticipated British attack. He replied as politely as he could but firmly and clearly with what was, in effect, his first verbal application in his new command of the doctrine of the concentration of force. He wrote: "It has been debated in Congress and settled that the militia or other internal strength of each Province is to be applied for defence against those small and particular depredations which were to be expected, and to which they were supposed to be competent. This will appear the more proper when it is considered that every town, and indeed every part of our seacoast, which is exposed to these depredations would have an equal claim upon this Army. It is the misfortune of our situation which exposes us to these ravages, against which, in my judgment, no such temporary relief would possibly secure us. The great advantage the enemy has of transporting troops by being master of the sea, will enable them to harass us

---

130 For the details of this raid on Fisher's, Gardiner's, Plumb and Block Islands, see 1 *LTW*, 11, 19, 21; 3 *Force* (4) p. 73, 87, 134; a copy of Wooster to Trumbull, the last of the preceding items, is in 17 *Papers of G. W.*, 55, LC. General Gage reported, Aug. 20, 1775, that the raid had yielded 1800 sheep and more than 100 oxen (1 *Gage*, 413).

131 3 *Force* (4) p. 291; resolve of July 29, 1775.

by depredations of this kind; [132] and should we be tempted to pursue them upon every alarm, the army must either be so weakened as to expose it to destruction, or a great part of the coast be still left unprotected. Nor, indeed, does it appear to me that such a pursuit would be attended with the least effect. The first notice of such an incursion would be its actual execution; and long before any troops could reach the scene of action, the enemy would have an opportunity to accomplish their purpose and retire." [133]

This might not please the Massachusetts legislators but it represented a position Washington was resolved to maintain unless he had explicit contrary orders from Congress. He could not afford to send off part of his troops in futile pursuit of landing parties at any time and most certainly not when indications multiplied that the enemy might be preparing by regular approaches to break the siege.[134] On the night of the 29th of July, two patrols were sent out to capture a prisoner and to ascertain what was happening at Charlestown, where the British appeared to be extending their lines. The patrols crept forward on their hands and knees from opposite flanks and were about to join forces when they ran into the British relief guard and had an exchange of fire. Two British prisoners were taken without loss.[135] This brush led to scattered fire more or less steadily along the line and to two small actions. On the 30th, the British demonstrated both on Boston Neck and West of Bunker Hill. Late in the night of the 30th–31st, a British party advanced toward Roxbury from the North but failed to gain a complete surprise because a deserter from the British ranks had slipped ahead and had given warning. In spite of this, the defence was badly handled, with the result that the attacking party burned the George Tavern, which was at the northern end of Roxbury, about 1800 yards from the advanced British position on the Neck.[136] By prearrangement, rather than in reprisal, an American force of 300 landed from whaleboats about 2 o'clock that same night of July 30th–31st on the island where the British were repairing the Light House. The object of the attack was to

---

132 The original reads "kinds."

133 3 G. W., 379–80. It will be noted that Washington uniformly referred to the enemy as "they." In the next century, the enemy usually was mentioned as "he."

134 3 G. W., 393.

135 3 G. W., 393; some details in Frothingham's Siege, p. 229.

136 3 G. W., 394; Carter, Letters to a Friend, 9; Samuel Cooper's Diary in 6 A. H. R., 315; Ezekiel Price's Diary in MHSP., 1863–65, p. 201; Stephen Kemble's account is in 1 Kemble, 51. For the commanding location of the tavern property, with a view both of Boston Harbor and of Cambridge Bay and the mainland, see Drake's Roxbury, ed. 1905, p. 278.

stop the work and to capture the carpenters and a guard of thirty-two marines under a subaltern. Thanks primarily to the good leadership of Maj. Benjamin Tupper, the American success was complete.[137] Although the party lost its tide and had to wait till the next, it suffered only two casualties and killed or captured all the British and all the carpenters—a total of fifty-three slain or made prisoners.[138] Tupper brought off the enemy's wounded, who otherwise might have perished,[139] and he and his men received next day Washington's commendation in orders: "The General doubts not but the Continental Army will be as famous for their mercy as for their valor." [140]

These activities, though relatively small, might forecast the anticipated major attack. Washington's intelligence reports contained nothing to contradict what general restlessness on the lines seemed to presage. The American commander knew that a fleet of transports had brought reenforcements to Boston, and he had learned that these consisted of four identified Regiments, with an estimated strength of 1110 men, "a miserable relief," as one British officer put it.[141] Washington's estimate of the total strength of the British was 10,000 to 12,000,[142] admirably equipped in every particular, with good artillery. The effectiveness of this force was increased vastly by its ability to concentrate at almost any point in superior numbers.

Washington never let himself forget that British advantage, which he feared he could not offset with such troops as he had. Soon after his arrival, he had written: "The abuses in [the continental] army, I fear, are considerable, and the new modeling of it, in the face of an enemy,

---

137 Gates to Thomas, July 25, 1776, *Thomas Papers*, 52, MHS, contains instructions concerning whaleboats that doubtless were being assembled for this expedition. As of July 18 Washington had ordered an alert (Gates to Thomas, *Emmet Coll.*, 9249, NYPL).

138 Tupper's report, 3 *Force* (4), p. 19.

139 3 *G. W.*, 394; *Cheever's Diary* in *MHSP*, 1926–27, p. 93; *London Chronicle*, Oct. 10–12, 1775, quoted in *Willard*, 185; a description of the firing that night appeared in *Morning Chronicle and London Advertiser*, Oct. 4, 1775 (*ibid.*, 186).

140 3 *G. W.*, 381. The British apparently were somewhat ashamed of this affair. Mentioning it in a general report of Aug. 20, 1775, General Gage said the Americans "made prisoners of a few marines posted there by the Admiral, and ten or twelve carpenters who were repairing the house" (1 *Gage*, 413).

141 Letter of June 27 in *London Evening Post* of Aug. 8–10, 1775, quoted in *Willard*, 153–54. The troops were the 22nd, 27th, 40th, and 44th Regiments (*Carter, Letters to a Friend*, 8).

142 3 *G. W.*, 372; 37 *ibid.*, 512. For estimates of the actual British strength. see Allen French, *The First Year of the American Revolution* (cited hereafter as *French's First Year*), p. 321–23, 672–73, and 2 *Gage*, 690. The last of these references is to a return of July 19, 1775, showing 7475 rank and file, but it does not give the strength of the two Battalions of marines. A total of 8500 enlisted men, sick and fit, probably is a maximum figure. To this figure should be added the officers, n.c.o's and the personnel of the fleet. In March, 1776, (*French's First Year*, 672), total army strength, officers included, was 8906.

from whom we every hour expect an attack, is exceedingly difficult and dangerous. If things therefore should not turn out as the Congress would wish, I hope they will make proper allowances." [143] Now, at the beginning of August, he increasingly suspected that the British would make the most of their superiority in cannon and would begin heavy bombardment of the American lines in the hope of driving the troops from them.[144] He scarcely could hope to answer this fire, gun for gun, round for round, because he did not have the powder for such an exchange, even though nothing had occurred during July to reduce materially the stock of 308 barrels he had been told was in store. In any event, if the enemy was stirring, cartridges must be issued the men. Charles Lee alone called for 200,000. As the continental stock amounted to 35,000 only, appeal was made forthwith to the Massachusetts authorities to furnish the remainder from their store. Elbridge Gerry replied at once that the supply of the Bay Colony amounted to no more than thirty-six barrels of powder.[145]

Thirty-six barrels? Impossible. What did the troops of the other Colonies have?

Their total was about fifty-four barrels.

Thirty-six and fifty-four—ninety barrels or 9900 pounds.

Was that all? Absolutely! When the return had been made up after Washington's arrival, the men who gave the General the figure of 308 barrels had included all the powder that had been collected—what had been fired at Bunker Hill and elsewhere as well as what remained.

If the British attacked, the army had barely powder enough to issue each man nine cartridges.[146]

[143] Letter of July 10, 1775, to Richard Henry Lee; 3 G. W., 331.
[144] Ibid., 388.
[145] Gerry to Washington, Aug. 1, 1775; 3 Force (4), p. 4.
[146] 3 G. W., 394–95. Washington's figures for the powder stores of Rhode Island and Connecticut have been reduced to barrels, at 110 lbs a barrel (2 Force (4), p. 1035), to make them comparable to the return of the Massachusetts store. See supra, p. 484, n. 9.

CHAPTER XXI

BALANCE OF OFFENSIVE AND DEFENSIVE

(August–September, 1775)

THE FACTS were there, on the papers before Washington, to prove statements that otherwise would have seemed incredible. In addition to the startling letter from Gerry,[1] the Commander-in-Chief received through Brig. Gen. John Sullivan information that of the powder supplied by New Hampshire, only nineteen barrels of 100 lbs. weight each remained.[2] Lead and flints likewise were so limited that a single fight would exhaust them, but powder was the supreme concern. If the total amounted to no more than 9940 pounds, then something must be done immediately to lessen the danger that the exchange of nine volleys would leave the continentals only gun butts and stones, bayonets and a few frail pikes.[3] One brisk action might render the Army defenceless: it must not be!

The very next day brought reports that 80,000 flints and eight tons of lead were in transit to the Army and that "fifteen hogsheads of powder" had been received in New York and would be reported to the Commander-in-Chief; but "reports" were one thing and deliveries quite another. Washington had to be miserly with every grain of explosive the Army possessed, and he had to call for every pound left in New England, without being at liberty to tell the people how overwhelming was the need. Unless there was the tightest secrecy, the British would hear of the colonials' plight. Then out of Boston would stream the redcoats, covered by unstinted artillery fire the Americans could not answer. Faced with that prospect the Army, first of all, must stop

---

[1] Letter of Aug. 1, 1775; 3 *Force* (4) p. 5. For the reported stock of powder in Worcester and Hampshire Counties, Mass., and for deliveries prior to June 30, see 2 *Force* (4) p. 1467. Deliveries from June 14 through Aug. 17, 1775 from "the Colony Magazine for the use of the Army before Boston," to a total of 17,825 pounds, are listed in 6 *Force* (4) p. 419.

[2] 3 *Force* (4) p. 15. If written reports of the stock of powder supplied by Connecticut and Rhode Island were filed, they have not been found. Their combined store was about thirty-five or thirty-six barrels. Cf. 3 *G. W.*, 394–95.

[3] They were styled "pikes" in GO, July 14, 1775 (3 *G. W.*, 338), but were termed "spears" on July 23 (*ibid.*, 357). Officers' half pikes were called "espontoons."

wasting cartridges. This was enjoined by an order of August 4 that touched in the lightest way possible on the depletion of the magazines. All the stress was on disobedience of orders that prohibited unauthorized "firing of guns." The language was shaped to make the offender look foolish: "It is with indignation and shame," the order read, "the General observes that . . . contrary to all orders, straggling soldiers do still pass the guards and fire at a distance, where there is not the least probability of hurting the enemy, and where no other end is answered but to waste ammunition, expose themselves to the ridicule of the enemy, and keep their camps harassed by frequent and continual alarms, to the hurt of every good soldier, who is thereby disturbed of his natural rest, and will at length never be able to distinguish between a real and a false alarm. For these reasons" . . . then the order put an absolute ban on going beyond the outguards, otherwise than on written pass. The sentinels were to treat violators as a common enemy and were to fire on them. Every man's ammunition was to be examined at evening roll call. Those soldiers who were short of their allotment were to be confined.[4]

Next, the Governors—what could they do to relieve so desperate an hour? Governor Cooke of Rhode Island must be acquainted with the essentials if he was to be stirred to a dangerous enterprise some members of the council of war had advocated. With few preliminaries Washington wrote: "I am now, sir, in strict confidence to acquaint you that our necessities in the articles of powder and lead are so great as to require an immediate supply. I must earnestly intreat you will fall upon some measure to forward every pound of each in the Colony which can possibly be spared. It is not within the propriety or safety of such a correspondence to say what I might on this subject. It is sufficient that the case calls loudly for the most strenuous exertions of every friend of his country and does not admit of the least delay. No quantity, however small, is beneath notice, and should any arrive, I beg it may be forwarded as soon as possible."[5]

An appeal of substantially the same urgency was forwarded the Governor of Connecticut and the New Hampshire Committee of Safety.[6] Further in a belief that the secret of the beggared condition of the magazine was too critical to be entrusted to any large body of men, however patriotic, Washington went to Watertown and personally put the facts

---

[4] 3 *G. W.*, 384–85.   [5] Letter of Aug. 4, 1775; *ibid.*, 385–86.
[6] *Ibid.*, 388–90.

before James Warren, whom he besought to collect with few words and great diligence as much as possible of the meagre supply of the explosive in the towns of Massachusetts.[7] The next and obvious step was to report the stark danger to the President of the Continental Congress. This was done as briefly as might be, with the stern conclusion: "I need not enlarge on our melancholy situation. It is sufficient to say that the existence of the Army and salvation of the country depends upon something being done for our relief both speedy and effectual and that our situation be kept a profound secret."[8]

Washington knew little of what had been undertaken by Congress to procure powder after he had left Philadelphia six weeks previously. He could not be optimistic concerning the collection that might be made in New England, which already had depleted its store. More must be done—anything, indeed, that would bring even one barrel of powder to the troops. Washington confided to Governor Cooke: "I have resolved in my mind every other possible chance and listened to every proposition . . . that could give the smallest hope . . ."[9] By chance, a resident of Bermuda had come a short time previously to the American camp in front of Boston and had told of the existence of a large magazine of powder in a remote part of that island. This newcomer, Harris by name, affirmed that the people of Bermuda were sympathetic with the colonial cause in America and, instead of resisting an effort to seize and remove the powder, would be willing to assist. Out of this information came quickly a scheme for the dispatch of an expedition to Bermuda, under American command but with Harris in attendance, to procure the precious kegs of black grain. "I am very sensible," Washington wrote Governor Cooke, "that at first view the project may appear hazardous and its success must depend on the concurrence of many circumstances; but we are in a situation which requires us to run all risks." Then he added in unconscious echo of the reasoning on which he had based many a speculative venture as a planter and landseeker: "No danger is to be considered when put in competition with the magnitude of our cause and the absolute necessity we are under of increasing our stock." He broadened the base of his argument: "Enterprises which appear chimerical often prove successful from that very circumstance. Common sense and prudence will suggest vigilance and care when the danger is plain and obvious, but where little danger is apprehended, the

[7] *Ibid.,* 395. [8] *Ibid.* [9] *Ibid.,* 386.

more the enemy is unprepared and consequently there is the fain'd prospect of success." [10]

This was an argument to which the devoted Governor of Rhode Island was certain to respond. In fact, Cooke had been urging the closest economy in powder and had elicited already from the commander of his Colony's contingent with Washington a pledge of fullest care in avoiding waste. "As my fate, your fate and all the continent depends on that article to make a proper defence," Nathanael Greene had assured Cooke, "I should think myself criminal to the last degree to neglect so capital a matter." [11] Now, unhappily, Cooke could send no powder and little lead [12] but he entered immediately into plans to arm and equip a vessel to go to Bermuda for powder or, failing there, to seek it elsewhere. [13]

In all this, time ran against America. Weeks must pass before Washington would know whether there actually was a magazine in Bermuda and whether the contents could be procured and brought to the continent. Meantime, what? How could such desperate danger be abated? Within approximately a week after the discovery of the critical nature of the shortage, Washington received an answer of an unexpected nature: From Philadelphia, under date of August 1, Richard Henry Lee wrote [14] to inform Washington that Congress had adjourned for ap-

[10] *Ibid.*, 386–87. "Fained" in the sense of "favorable" or "sought after and welcome" was passing from English speech in Washington's day but was familiar if somewhat rhetorical two centuries previously. The corresponding verb appears twice in the King James version and at least once in the Psalter, xxxiv, 12. The King James version used in this last instance changed "would fain see good days" to "loveth many days." Shakespeare used "fain" at least sixty-three times.

[11] Letter of June 22, 1775; *American Antiquarian Society Proceedings* (cited hereafter as *AASP*), 1926, p. 240.

[12] 1 *LTW*, 17, 20.

[13] *Ibid.*, 18, 20, 26, 30, 34, 35; 3 *Force* (4) p. 631; 3 *G. W.*, 420–21, 475–76. The last of these references is to a letter in which Washington asked the help of the people of Bermuda in seizing the powder. This letter was not to be used unless it was needed to win the Bermudians to the cause of the American Colonies. See 3 *G. W.*, 477.

[14] The lapse of time between the dispatch and the receipt of letters varied so much with season and circumstance that a student is most grateful for such care as that displayed always by Philip Schuyler and often by Nicholas Cooke and John Hancock in stating when papers written on a given date by Washington came into their hands. In general, after expresses were organized adequately in 1776, their service was much more rapid than it had been the previous year. The mud of winter of course slowed down an express. At the period under consideration in this chapter, August–September, 1775, an express from Cambridge to Providence, R. I., took three to five days (1 *LTW*, 11, 17, 30, 34); to Lebanon, Conn., the home of Governor Trumbull, one and a half to two days (1 *ibid.*, 21, 31; 3 *G. W.*, 411); to Albany a week (1 *LTW*, 22); to Ticonderoga, eight to nine days (*ibid.*, 13, 59); to New York, five to six days (*ibid.*, 173, 191); to Philadelphia, nine days (*ibid.*, 65, 164). Later, relays of expresses, riding continuously day and night, under orders to make the best time possible, covered the long road from Boston to the Quaker City in five days (*ibid.*, 175) and, it would appear, on one occasion, in four days (*ibid.*, 188).

proximately a month.[15] "The capital object of powder," Lee said, "we have attended to as far as we could by sending you the other day six tons, and tomorrow we shall propose sending you six or eight tons more, which, with the supplies you may get from Connecticut, and such further ones from here, as future expected importations may furnish, will I hope enable you to do all that this powerful article can in good hands accomplish."[16]

At least some of the powder in those hogsheads at New York might reach Boston. If that supply in New York did not include the six tons started from Philadelphia prior to August 1, then, manifestly, the arrival of this supply before an attack by the British would give the continentals a fighting chance. The odds against the Army no longer would be hopeless. Eagerly Washington traced the progress of the wagons with the powder, and learned that if all went well, they would draw up in his camp on the 16th—"a most seasonable relief in our present necessity."[17] So he wrote Philip Schuyler in words that sounded like the first deep, free breath of a man just passing from the reach of the arm of instant Death. To be sure, the promised minimum supply would not give the Army more than 184 barrels, according to Washington's calculation, or a bare thirty cartridges per man;[18] but that would be a condition at least three times better than the one that had existed. It would raise the spirits of the men, too. "We are just in the situation," Joseph Reed said, "of a man with a little money in his pocket." Reed explained: "He will do twenty mean things to prevent his breaking in upon his little stock. We are obliged to bear with the rascals on Bunker's Hill when a few shots now and then in return would keep our men attentive to their duty, and give the enemy alarms."[19] Besides, the arrival of the powder, with the prospect of more to follow,[20] would be heartening proof that Congress had been mindful of the Army and both energetic and successful in seeking supplies.[21]

Congress was not the only contributor to the magazines. The powder it collected or purchased from forehanded importers in Philadelphia

---

15 Adjourned Aug. 1 to reassemble Sept. 5, 1775; 2 *JCC.*, 239.

16 1 *LTW.*, 12. The same letter appears in 1 *Burnett*, 185, and in 1 *Ballagh, Lee Letters*, 145–47.

17 3 *G. W.*, 424.   18 3 *G. W.*, 442.

19 Letter of Aug. 24, 1775, to Thomas Bradford, 1 *Reed*, 119.

20 3 *G. W.*, 436–37, 438.

21For the action of Congress, see 2 *JCC.*, 85–86, 184, 191, 204, 210, 212, 223, 238; 1 *Burnett*, 178–83, 1 *Warren-Adams Letters*, 66, 74. Scores of detailed references to the powder shortage throughout the Colonies will be found in the index to 3 *Force* (4).

was supplemented by lead that Schuyler, on order, forwarded from Ticonderoga.[22] Governor Cooke likewise purchased for the army, at what he considered an excessive price, 7000 pounds of powder, seventy hundredweight of lead and 500 stand [23] of arms [24] from dealers who subsequently were said to have procured the cargo in Africa by bartering rum.[25] Soon, also, two additional tons of powder were sent from Philadelphia.[26] Gradually, then, the situation was being changed for Washington to the extent that instead of dreading an attack, he ere long was to lament the fact that his supply still did not suffice for him to take full advantage of his positions.[27] Charles Lee's observation was, "Although we want powder most cruelly, we rather approach than retire from the enemy." [28] What powder the Army had, it would keep against the coming of the day of action. Washington was resolved upon that, and, to assure it, was prompt in appointing a commissary of artillery stores.[29]

Through these anxious weeks of the late summer, Washington still hoped against hope that the war would be concluded in 1775 and that peace would be restored. He even wrote Lund to urge that work on the chimneypiece in the new dining room at Mount Vernon be hastened because, he said, "I could wish that end of the house completely finished before I return." [30] The possibility that Dunmore might seize Martha by way of revenge on him was one that Washington could not efface from his mind, but he reflected that she probably would go down into New Kent County and would be safe for two or three months, "in which time," he reasoned, "matters may and probably will take such a turn as to render her removal either absolutely necessary or quite useless." [31] What Washington could not understand, as his mind came

[22] 3 *G. W.*, 424; 1 *LTW*, 28.
[23] American usage of this plural form of the noun was not universal but was more frequent than "stands."   [24] 3 *G. W.*, 477, 482; 1 *LTW*, 30; 3 *Force* (4) p. 631.
[25] William Gordon, *History of the Rise, Progress and Establishment of the Independence of the United States of America* (cited hereafter as *Gordon*), v. 2, p. 128. A critique of this discredited work that once was regarded as almost a primary source will be found in the Bibliography, Vol. VIII.
[26] Robert Morris to Washington, 17 *Papers of G. W.*, 130, LC.
[27] 3 *G. W.*, 487; 3 *Force* (4) p. 683.   [28] 1 *Lee Papers*, 205.
[29] Ezekiel Cheever (3 *G. W.*, 427–28).
[30] 3 *G. W.*, 435. Cf. *ibid.*, 432, for the injunction to press the work of spinning on the estate, "as we shall have nothing else to depend upon if these disputes continue another year." See also *ibid.*, 484, 487–88.
[31] By "quite useless," he probably meant "unnecessary," because hostilities would have ended (*ibid.*, 433). Washington had no knowledge at the time, of course, that King George on the 23rd of August had proclaimed the existence of rebellion in North America and had called on "all our officers, as well civil as military," and all "obedient and loyal subjects, to use their utmost endeavors to withstand and suppress such rebellion" (3 *Force* (4) p. 241).

sharply back from Virginia to Boston, was why the British withheld the blow that might decide the campaign in a victors' stern peace or in an admission that the home government could not tax the Colonies. Again and again he asked himself, was Gage preparing by regular approaches to force the Americans from their lines; or were the British counting winter as an ally before whose blasts the Army would scatter? Could there be truth to the rumor that the King's men would take ship, use their seapower, and transfer the war to New York, where the waters of the Hudson and of the Northern Lakes might give them contact with their comrades in Canada?[32]

For such light as could be shed on these questions, Washington undertook to develop a rough-and-ready intelligence system that had been established before his arrival. Chelsea, North of the approaches to Boston harbor, was an ideal place from which to observe movements of all British shipping. After Washington's coming,[33] Col. Loammi Baldwin was made responsible there and at Malden, July 24–26, for daily intelligence reports.[34] It was not an easy assignment. Baldwin had no glass worth focusing on the enemy. When one or the other of the express horses at Chelsea was lame for lack of shoes, or was used to carry a man to get medicine from Cambridge, the dispatch of intelligence reports was rendered uncertain or was suspended altogether for the day.[35] Besides the results of Baldwin's direct observation, much of fact and more of rumor was supplied at Chelsea, in Cambridge and at Roxbury by Boston residents who were passed through the lines in spite of orders to the contrary.[36] Almost a full history of what had happened in the city could be pieced together, in time, from questioning those whom General Gage authorized to leave the town in order to reduce the consumption of food there[37] or, as the Americans thought later in the year, to spread smallpox.[38] Of the deserters, another traditional and unreliable source of intelligence reports, a few knew much;[39]

---

[32] 3 *G. W.,* 389–90, 407, 415.

[33] *Baldwin Papers,* Harvard Coll. Lib., notably Gates to Baldwin, July 26, 1775.

[34] Some of these survive in the Library of Harvard College and in 16 and 17 *Papers of G. W.,* LC. Of more interest than the average are the reports of July 28, 29, Aug. 8, 11 and 13, in 16 *Papers of G. W.,* 116, 117, and in 17 *ibid.,* 31, 32, 45.

[35] 17 *ibid.,* 45, 64.   [36] 3 *G. W.,* 366.

[37] *Ibid.,* 397, 401–02.

[38] Mercy Warren to John Adams, Aug. 2, 1775; *Mercy Warren Letter Book,* 153; MHS. 4 *G. W.,* 78, 154; Harrison to Baldwin, Dec. 13, 1775, *Baldwin Papers, Harvard Coll. Lib.*

[39] Cf. Kemble's reference of July 27, 1775, to the desertion of a "sensible, intelligent fellow [with] some knowledge of fortification" (1 *Kemble,* 50)—perhaps the man who helped John Trumbull prepare his map of the Boston defences. See John Trumbull's *Reminiscences,* 22.

others knew or would tell nothing.[40] In addition to these sources, some of the British in Boston credited the Americans with a system of explosions by night and signals from church-steeples in daytime. A gullible correspondent in the besieged city wrote a friend in England: "About three weeks ago a man was taken from a steeple who confessed he had been employed for seven days at this. Another was caught last week swimming over to the rebels with their General's passes in his pocket. He will be hanged in a day or two." [41] These and like tall tales were more apt to spread suspicion than they were to stop the smuggling of reports, trivial or otherwise, to American headquarters.

If Washington could not procure from these sources of intelligence much information of real value concerning British plans, he could not fail to be pleased at the success of efforts to keep secret the shortage of powder. The public, in fact, overconfidently exaggerated the size of the supply instead of presenting the scarcity as worse than it was. False reports circulated of large importation and of great stores. Ezekiel Price had heard in July that 1800 barrels of powder had reached Philadelphia; [42] the next month, from its printing house across the salt marshes, the *Boston Gazette* had boasted that "the needful" was "not wanting"; [43] Ezra Stiles was told he might rely on it that the Colonies had fifty tons.[44] This, in a sense, was a triumph of the American intelligence service. So was the deception of the British. Royal officers were being misled and, in some instances, were deceiving their own people at home. Those who would listen to such things heard tall tales of the magnitude of desertion from American ranks,[45] and of the unexplained "arrest" of Charles Lee by his own commander's order.[46] London newspaper readers soon were to be regaled with reports that on August 7, the British, 5000 strong, had attacked "the rebels" and after slaughtering a host had captured Putnam and Lee, 2500 other prisoners, a vast number of carefully specified cannon, 6000 stand of small arms, and £100,000 in specie.[47] If these absurdities later were found in newspapers that were smuggled across the Atlantic, they would amuse the Americans who meantime did all they could not only to confuse the enemy but also to create discontent in British ranks. One device was to tie to a

---

[40] Cf. 3 *G. W.*, 420.
[41] Letter of July 25, 1775 in *Morning Chronicle and London Advertiser*, Sept. 11, 1775, quoted in *Willard*, 175.
[42] *MHSP.*, 1863–64, p. 194. [43] Issue of Aug. 10, 1775.
[44] 1 Ezra Stiles's *Literary Diary*, 600. [45] *Carter, Letters to a Friend*, 10.
[46] 1 *Kemble*, 1883, p. 58. [47] Reprinted in 3 *Force* (4) p. 82–83 n.

rock and then to throw to the redcoats a strip of paper that had been printed to this effect:

	Prospect Hill		Bunker Hill
I.	Seven Dollars a Month	I.	Three pence a day
II.	Fresh provisions, and in plenty	II.	Rotten salt pork
III.	Health	III.	The Scurvy
IV.	Freedom, ease, affluence and a good farm.	IV.	Slavery, beggary and want.[48]

This was clever; it might make mouths water in the British camps, and it might bring to the American lines some deserters who might know a few facts worth passing on to the General; but Gage—was he merely waiting for further reenforcements? [49] Because the answer was fogged in doubt, Washington continued steadfast in his refusal to detach any large part of his Army to serve as garrison or to combat raids, even though he told himself, with some of his former sensitiveness, that he would "be accused of inattention to the public service and perhaps with want of spirit to prosecute it." [50] With equal determination he continued his work of securing his positions and of improving his organization and discipline. It was not enough to be safe against attack; he must place his guns where he could answer the enemy's bombardment as soon as he had the powder with which to do so. On the right, this involved a considerable addition to the fortifications at Roxbury. "This village," a soldier wrote in his diary, "has been a pleasant place, but the regulars have spoiled it much with their cannon balls and it is now in a manner desolate, the people having left their houses and given them to the soldiers for to make barracks of them for to protect their rights and liberties." [51] On the other, or northwestern flank of the American lines,

[48] Facsimile in *Bolton*, 90. For the throwing of these papers into the British lines, see H. Bedinger's *Journal* in Danske Dandridge, *Historic Shepherdstown*, 107.

[49] Cf. 3 *G. W.*, 488.

[50] *Ibid.*, 443. For his other arguments at this time against dispersion of force, see *ibid.*, 466, 470.

[51] Aug. 13, 1775; Daniel McCurtin, "Journal of the Times at the Siege of Boston . . ." in Thomas Balch, ed., *Papers Relating to the Maryland Line During the Revolution* (cited hereafter as *McCurtin's Journal*, with reference to Balch's pagination) p. 13. McCurtin gives more detail than any other diarist concerning the works undertaken around Roxbury, but in this instance, as with the maps, it sometimes is difficult to say when particular fortifications were taken in hand. Among the facts that McCurtin does establish definitely is that the works on Lamb's Dam were being raised August 14 (*ibid.*), though Frothingham (*op. cit.*, 242), stated that the "strong work" there was not completed till September 10. Doctor Belknap (cited *ibid.*, 254), explained that the breastwork across the road, "just below where the George Tavern stood" until burned by the British, extended "to Lamb's Dam which makes a part thereof." See also Drake's *Roxbury*, 76, 80, 110.

about halfway between Winter Hill and the scene of the battle of
June 17, was an eminence known as Plowed Hill. This elevation did
not obstruct in the least the fire from Prospect Hill or Bunker Hill, but
there were rumors that the British intended to seize Plowed Hill [52] in
order to command the low ground between that eminence and Bunker
Hill and thereby to render their position more secure.[53] It was the
ground worth fighting for. Washington resolved to seize it, to fortify
and thereby to invite the British to contest it. With their picks and their
shovels, their gabions and their fascines, 1200 colonial troops moved out
to Plowed Hill on the night of the 26th of August and there they threw
up so much earth that when daylight came they had cover against the
enemy's fire. The British cannon slumbered until 9 A.M. but when they
did wake up, they barked all day, though with little hurt to the Americans. Four men only were killed, and two of them, in Washington's
judgment, because of their own carelessness.[54] Even after the first vain
trial of their blasts, the British kept up their bombardment until it was
estimated they had expended more than 300 shells.[55] For making the
fortifications proof against this fire, Charles Lee was given credit.[56]
Washington was pleased and at the same time was distressed because he
did not feel he could expend the powder required to answer the British
effectively from this new position.[57] He promised himself that if sufficient ammunition arrived he would not take in silence the challenge
of the British guns.

Organization must progress along with fortification while Washington waited either for the enemy to attack or for the coming of powder
with which to seize the initiative if the enemy did nothing. The commissioning of Thomas as senior Brigadier on the Boston front and the

---

[52] 3 *G. W.*, 453.

[53] According to Washington's diagram of the ranges, the distance from Prospect Hill to
Bunker Hill was calculated with some accuracy at 430 rods or 2365 yards, though this was at
least 400 yards less than the distance shown on the best of the contemporary British maps.
Several of these maps vary so much that the only safe course to be pursued by a careful student
of the siege is to re-locate the old positions, as far as possible, on a modern contour map. This
done, the actual distance from the crest of Prospect Hill to the top of Bunker Hill is about 2450
yards. From Winter Hill to Bunker Hill is 3400 yards. Plowed Hill, which is 1450 yards from
Bunker Hill, later was called Mt. Benedict. It lies in the angle of Broadway and Mystic Avenue,
East Somerville, and is about half way between Foss Park to the Northwest and Sullivan Square
to the Southeast.

[54] 3 *G. W.*, 453 and 462 n, with quotation from Wilkinson's *Memoirs;* 1 *Sullivan Papers*,
79, with the letter misdated July 29; John Chester's letter, Aug. 28, 1775; 8 *Mag. Am. His.*,
pt. 1, p. 125; *N. Y. Gazette*, Sept. 11, 1775.

[55] *Boston Gazette*, Sept. 11, 1775.

[56] Extract from [misdated] letter of Aug. 27, 1775; *London Evening Post*, Oct. 26–28, 1775,
quoted in *Willard*, 204.

[57] 3 *G. W.*, 462.

return of General Spencer put an end, apparently, to what one officer described as "uneasiness in camp," [58] though there still was a vacancy because of Seth Pomeroy's non-acceptance of his commission.[59] A little further down the scale of rank, the venality or incompetence of several field and company officers was brought to light. When appointed by the colonial authorities, these men had been granted continental commissions without any inquiry into their fitness.[60] Washington had to deal vigorously with the inevitable result of this bad system and, in particular, with the inertia of ignorance. ". . . It is among the most difficult tasks I ever undertook in my life," he confided, "to induce these people to believe there is, or can be, danger till the bayonet is pushed to their breast; not that it proceeds from any uncommon prowess, but rather from an unaccountable kind of stupidity in the lower class of these people which, believe me, prevails but too generally among the Massachusetts *part* of the Army who are *nearly* of the same kidney with the privates, and adds not a little to my difficulties; as there is no such thing as getting of officers of this stamp to exert themselves in carrying orders into execution—to curry favor with the men (by whom they were chosen, and on whose smiles possibly they may think they may again rely) seems to be one of the principal objects of their attention." [61] He made himself a list of those officers who had been cashiered and of those who were awaiting trial. Before the end of August he was able to write confidentially: "I have made a pretty good slam among such kind of officers as the Massachusetts government abound in since I came to this Camp, having broke one Colonel and two Captains for cowardly behavior in the action on Bunkers Hill—two Captains for drawing more provisions and pay than they had men in their company —and one for being absent from his post when the enemy appeared there and burnt a house just by it.[62] Besides these, I have at this time one Colonel, one Major, one Captain and two Subalterns under arrest for trial. In short I spare none yet fear it will not do as these people seem to be too inattentive to everything but their interest." [63]

[58] Jed. Huntington, Aug. 6, 1775; 20 *CHS Cols.*, 226.

[59] 3 *G. W.*, 396–97.　　　　　　　　　[60] 1 *Burnett*, 160; 3 *G. W.*, 451, 472.

[61] Letter of Aug. 29, 1775, to Richard Henry Lee; 3 *G. W.*, 450–51. See the note, Chapter XXII, p. 558, on the disposition of some writers to generalize loosely regarding troops from different Colonies.

[62] Several of these cases are covered by GO's in 3 *G. W.*, 383, 397, 410, 427, 472, 490. Cf. Boardman's approving comment of August 3 on one of the sentences, *MHSP.*, 1892–93, p. 400.

[63] 3 *G. W.*, 451–52. He saw to it, also, that relatively minor offenses were punished— intimidating a soldier (*ibid.*, 410–11), swearing and beating men (*ibid.*, 410), abusing a superior

One larger, surer remedy, he thought, was in naming officers from other Colonies, now that the Army was continental. "I submit . . . to your consideration," he asked of a friend in Congress, "whether there is or is not a propriety in that resolution of the Congress which leaves the ultimate appointment of all officers below the rank of Generals to the governments where the Regiments originated . . . To me it appears improper in two points: first, it is giving that power and weight to an individual Colony, which ought, of right, to belong only to the whole, and next it damps the spirit and ardor of volunteers from all but the four New England governments as none but their people have the least chance of getting into office." [64]

A second means of improving the quality of officers, as Washington saw it, was for Congress to keep open a number of commissions as rewards of merit, especially for those who had done well at Bunker Hill.[65] Still another means, never proclaimed but always regarded, was that of setting an example of what an officer should be. On occasion, too, as when Col. William Woodford of Virginia wrote for his advice on the duties of an officer, Washington could put on paper some of the essentials of his code of command: "Be strict in your discipline; that is, to require nothing unreasonable of your officers and men, but see that whatever is required be punctually complied with. Reward and punish every man according to his merit, without partiality or prejudice; hear his complaints; if well founded, redress them; if otherwise, discourage them in order to prevent frivolous ones. Discourage vice in every shape, and impress upon the mind of every man, from the first to the lowest, the importance of the cause, and what it is they are contending for." [66] In applying this personally to his immediate subordinates, Washington undertook to see that their rights were not disregarded, that their seniority was established and respected,[67] and that they were treated as individuals and as gentlemen. The rotating officer of the day, the officer of the guard and the Adjutant of the day, no matter who they might be, had standing invitation to dine at head-

---

officer (*ibid.*, 464–65). After the third week in August, most of the courtmartial charges were drawn in terms of violation of specific articles of war and consequently cannot be catalogued in detail with accuracy otherwise than by reference to the specifications in individual cases.

[64] *Ibid.*, 451. Cf. *ibid.*, 405, 447.   [65] *Ibid.*, 400, 410.

[66] Letter of Nov. 10, 1775; 4 *G. W.*, 80. The remainder of the letter deals with precautions against surprise, the need of precision and simplicity in orders, and the admonition, "Be easy and condescending in your deportment to your officers, but not too familiar, lest you subject yourself to a want of that respect which is necessary to support a proper command."

[67] Cf. *ibid.*, 402–03, 435–36.

quarters:[68] Washington was resolved, having done what he could in ridding the officers' corps of cowards, rascals and incompetents, to acquaint himself thoroughly with the others and to develop their good qualities.

Even when Washington himself could recommend or temporarily could appoint officers, he could not always find men equipped to fulfil the ideal he set before Colonel Woodford, but he selected them with care from the class he thought most conscious of obligation and best qualified to meet his special needs. He made Thomas Mifflin Quarter-master General with rank of Colonel;[69] he approved the best Brigade Majors he could procure,[70] and after some delay and a bit of finessing in avoiding political appointments,[71] he named Edmund Randolph and George Baylor as aides.[72] Both were Virginians and both of the upper stratum of the Colony's society. Baylor was accepted primarily on Edmund Pendleton's recommendation,[73] though Washington had known the young man's father well and had large acquaintance with the Baylor family. Edmund Randolph was the son of John Randolph, former Clerk of the House of Delegates and then Attorney General, who had taken the side of the King in the Colonies' quarrel. The revolutionary zeal of Edmund, a handsome youth of 22 years, was as pronounced as was his father's devotion to the royal cause. Moreover, Benjamin Harrison endorsed Edmund Randolph and regarded him as one of the cleverest young men of America. Harrison's recommendation was shared by Richard Henry Lee and by Thomas Jefferson.[74] As Washington's acquaintance with Randolph had given him a high opinion of the character of the young gentleman,[75] he did not hesitate to accept the new aide.

While improving in these respects the organization of his officers during the time he was awaiting Gage's attack, Washington continued his efforts to make the troops comfortable and healthy and to better their discipline. This second task was rendered more difficult by the arrival in camp of the riflemen recruited in accordance with the resolution of Congress adopted June 14, when Washington still was in attendance.[76]

[68] Ibid., 474–75.
[69] GO Aug. 14, 1775; 3 G. W., 419.
[70] Ibid., 425, 427.
[71] Ibid., 447, 459; 37 ibid., 514.
[72] Ibid., 425.
[73] Pendleton to Washington, July 12, 1775; 16 Papers of G. W., 86, LC.
[74] 1 Cal, Wash. Papers, 14; 2 Force (4) p. 1698; 1 Ballagh, Lee Letters, 144.
[75] 3 G. W., 450.
[76] 2 JCC., 89. The original resolution provided (see supra p. 432), in careful detail, for six Companies from Pennsylvania, two from Maryland and two from Virginia; but two additional

The idealized argument for Companies of this type had been compressed by Richard Henry Lee into a few clauses when he wrote of these men's "amazing hardihood, their method of living so long in the woods without carrying provisions with them, the exceeding quickness with which they can march to distant parts and above all, the dexterity to which they have arrived in the use of the rifle gun." Lee added almost with awe: "There is not one of these men who wish a distance less than 200 yards or a larger object than an orange—Every shot is fatal." [77] In at least some colonial camps, so many marksmen volunteered that an embarrassed Captain was said to have set up a board one foot square on a tree distant 150 yards from the line. On this board he outlined in chalk a human nose and announced he would accept as volunteers those men who, at a single shot, would come close to this mark. The first forty or fifty obliterated the nose. By the time the maximum strength of a Company was enrolled, the board itself had been blown in bits from the tree. At least that was the story proudly told and retold.[78] Washington doubtless heard it and knew enough about frontier riflemen to realize that their indiscipline was as remarkable as their skill with a rifle. He wanted some of them; he probably [79] did not desire too large a contingent. When they began to arrive late in July, he and everyone else marvelled at the speed with which the men had enlisted,[80] had settled their affairs at home, and had covered on foot the hundreds of miles to Boston. Stephenson's Company from the vicinity of Berkeley County, Virginia, marched thirty to thirty-six miles a day and then never caught up with the Company of Capt. Daniel Morgan with whom they had expected to proceed.[81] One of the Maryland Companies had as its Cap-

---

Companies were approved for Pennsylvania (*ibid.*, 104), and through some misunderstanding, two Companies, instead of one, were raised in Lancaster County, Pennsylvania, and were accepted (*ibid.*, 173).

[77] Letter of Feb. 24, 1775 to Arthur Lee; 1 *Ballagh, Lee Letters,* 130–31.

[78] John Harrower to James Craigie, Aug. 28, 1775; 6 *A. H. R.,* 100.

[79] The reason for stating this probability is a remark by Charles Lee in a letter to Robert Morris, July 27, 1775, in 1 *Lee Papers,* 200: "If I were General Washington however I should jump at the offer of your third Battalion Riflemen." As Washington did not have his full authorized strength of 24,550 and did not think he could attain it (3 *G. W.,* 322), it scarcely seems reasonable that he would have declined a Battalion on the ground that it would raise the establishment above the permitted total. The type of the troops, rather than the number, may have been the explanation.

[80] Cf. Gates to Washington, June 22, 1775; 16 *Papers of G. W.,* 50, LC.

[81] Stephenson's men left Shepherdstown July 17 and reached Cambridge August 11. See Dandridge, *Historic Shepherdstown,* 81, 97, 101. Morgan arrived on the 6th. See 3 *G. W.,* 424 n. Tradition has it that Washington received these troops with deep emotion and shook each of "Morgan's men" by the hand. He undoubtedly welcomed them with pride, because they impersonated the unity of the American cause, but the handshaking scarcely seems "in character" for the Commander-in-Chief.

tain no less a person than Michael Cresap, with whom Washington had been in some unpleasant dispute over land rights.[82] Many of the men under these officers were physically magnificent and some of them wore already the hunter's shirt that Washington always had advocated and now sought vainly to procure for those who did not have that garb.[83] Time was to show that the ranks included numbers who had enlisted for adventure and not because of skill with the rifle,[84] but the very first comers showed a marksmanship that taught the British to keep their heads below the nearer parapets.[85] The anticipated deficiency of most of the riflemen soon was apparent: These "shirtmen," as the infantry styled the members of the rifle Companies,[86] had no such word as "discipline" in their vocabulary. They had marched to Boston as self-contained bands of fighting men—at least one Company with its own "Surgeon"[87]—and they saw one duty and one only. That was to kill the British, precisely as their fathers and elder brothers had slain the Indians, by stalking them. As soon as they had established their camps, the riflemen began to slip through the line of guards and to make their way toward the British outposts. Some went alone; a few crept forward in pairs. Whenever they saw a "lobster," as all the Americans now styled the redcoat, they would take a shot at him if he was within the farthest range of their rifles. The result was much wastage of powder and no increase in British casualties. This endless pop-pop by the riflemen at extreme distance was one reason for Washington's bristling order of August 4 against futile firing.[88] For grumbling riflemen as for the more malleable foot soldiers, Washington continued to make the best provision he could. He sought to have their ration palatable and to keep its cost reasonable by combatting artificial shortages;[89] every attempt by officers to use soldiers on their farms was repressed, as previously, with stern words and sterner court martial;[90] prompt pay,[91] serviceable clothing,[92] and humane hospital care were set as

[82] Captain Cresap died in New York, Oct. 17, 1775, and had a sumptuous military funeral (Frank Moore, *Diary of the American Revolution, from Newspapers and Original Documents,* cited hereafter as *Moore,* v. 1, p. 152; *Anon. N. Y. Journal,* LC, entry of Oct. 19, 1775).

[83] 3 *G. W.,* 387, 389, 404, 415, 422, 445, 511; *Thacher,* 31. The shortage of tow cloth was the reason for failure. See 3 *G. W.,* 511 and 1 *LTW.,* 26. For the history of the hunting shirt, see A. B. Gardner in 1 *Mag. Am. His.,* 60, 461 ff.

[84] 3 *JCC.,* 400.   [85] 1 *Reed,* 117.

[86] Norfolk, Virginia, letter of Feb. 20, 1776; *Willard,* 262–63.

[87] See petition of Garret Tunison, 23 *Papers of G. W.,* 94, LC.

[88] *Supra,* p. 511, and 1 *Warren-Adams Letters,* 100.

[89] 3 *G. W.,* 396, 408, 455.   [90] *Ibid.,* 406, 408–09.

[91] *Ibid.,* 413, 446, 460, 477; *Boston Gazette,* Aug. 14, 1775.

[92] 3 *G. W.,* 415, 444.

ideals [93] constantly to be pursued even if never achieved. Wisdom and advantage both demanded that they be not forgotten.

In adherence to what he soon was to write Colonel Woodford about discouraging "vice in every shape," Washington undertook to reduce the use of liquor by the men.[94] He went so far as to try to keep them from imbibing of new cider, not for the advancement of temperance but for the prevention of stomach-aches and diarrhoea. ". . . Nothing," he wrote in general orders, "is more pernicious to the health of soldiers, nor more certainly productive of the bloody flux . . ." [95] In like spirit the men were admonished to respect property, particularly gardens.[96] They were to enjoy outdoor bathing while the weather was warm; but this was forbidden "at or near the bridge in Cambridge, where," said the General, "it has been observed and complained of, that many men, lost to all sense of decency and common modesty, are running about naked upon the bridge, whilst passengers, and even ladies of the first fashion in the neighborhood are passing over it, as if they meant to glory in their shame . . ." [97]

It is not of record whether the young men of the Continental Army heeded this particular admonition of a General who himself, at their age, had suffered the humiliation of having his money stolen by two women while he was splashing in the waters of the Rappahannock.[98] In general, the foot soldiers accepted discipline and, like their commander, waited to see whether their adversary intended to attack. All went well until September 10. That day, the Adjutant of Thompson's Battalion, which included all of the Pennsylvania riflemen, arrested and confined one of the Sergeants. The men of the rifle Companies thought this unjustly done and they began rioting on Prospect Hill. Commands from their officers to abstain from further outcry were defied. Before long, the "shirtmen" were in a turmoil so close to open mutiny that some of the Generals had to ride out to the hill.[99] The ringleader, John Seamon, and thirty-two others were arrested and the next day were brought before a general court martial over which Col. John Nixon presided. On a charge of disobedient and mutinous behavior, each of the men was mulcted 20s, which was to be deducted from the

---

[93] 20 *CHS Cols.*, 229; 3 *G. W.*, 440, 480–81; 16 *Papers of G. W.*, 113, LC.
[94] 3 *G. W.*, 474–75; *E. Clarke's* Diary, Aug. 19, 1775.
[95] 3 *G. W.*, 449.   [96] *Ibid.*, 414.
[97] *Ibid.*, 440.   [98] Vol. I, p. 246–47.
[99] One report was that Washington, Lee, and Greene had to quell the mutiny. See the reference in *Martyn's Ward*, 179 n, to a lost letter of Jesse Lukens.

next pay. Seamon, in addition, was imprisoned for six days.[100] These penalties were fitted to the culprits who probably would have staged a real mutiny had they been given the usual punishment of lashes "on the bare back." Fines restrained the men somewhat but did not reconcile them to discipline. They continued to irk the soul of the order-loving Washington, who did not find compensatory solace in the good behavior of most of the other troops. Even before the riflemen's riot on Prospect Hill, Washington's patience had snapped under the strain of stupidity and venality around him. Publicly, he maintained his amiable calm; privately he spoke his mind to Lund: "The people of this government [Massachusetts] have obtained a character which they by no means deserved; their officers, generally speaking, are the most indifferent kind of people I ever saw . . . In short they are by no means such troops, in any respect, as you are led to believe of them from the accounts which are published, but I need not make myself enemies among them, by this declaration, although it is consistent with truth. I dare say the men would fight very well (if properly officered) although they are an exceedingly dirty and nasty people . . ." [101]

It was a disillusioning experience, as well as an arduous and, withal, a lonely task. The Generals would come, of course, when called, would counsel wisely or ill and, if they had grievance or complaint, would spur with it to Cambridge. The burden rested finally on the gentleman from Virginia who, after those blessed sixteen years of quiet at Mount Vernon, had to make the decisions on which, perhaps, the fate of America hung. There was help, to be sure, from some of the staff, and especially when close argumentative logic had to be shaped for public reading. Early in August, reports filtering from Boston told of the indiscriminate herding of American prisoners of war in the common jail of the city. At Washington's instance and in his name, Joseph Reed wrote a protest that included a formal threat of reprisal in this language: "My duty now makes it necessary to apprize you that for the future I shall regulate my conduct toward those gentlemen who are or may be in our possession exactly by the rule you shall observe towards those of ours now in your custody. If severity and hardship mark the line of your conduct (painful as it may be to me) your prisoners will feel its effects: But if kindness and humanity are shown to ours, I shall with

---

[100] 1 *Warren-Adams Letters,* 107; Aaron Wright, 6 *His. Mag.,* 209; 3 *G. W.,* 490. The fines were to go to the hospital.

[101] Letter of Aug. 20, 1775; 3 *G. W.,* 433.

pleasure consider those in our hands only as unfortunate and they shall receive from me that treatment to which the unfortunate are ever entitled." [102] This, of course, was written with an eye to publication and was an epistolary challenge of a sort not to be declined by a General who had to do no more in the matter than to say to Gen. John Burgoyne, "Answer it." Back came promptly a reply that Burgoyne as a dramatist and parliamentary debater doubtless considered adequate, not to say devastating, except for its final paragraph, which was Gage's own. The substance of the reply was that behind the American lines, faithful British subjects were being worked "like negro slaves, to gain their daily subsistence, or [were being] reduced to the wretched alternative to perish by famine or take arms against their King and country." Tartly it was said: "Those who have made the treatment of the prisoners in my hands or of your other friends in Boston a pretence for such measures found barbarity on falsehood." Britons, it was said, "overlooked the criminal in the captive." There was flat assurance that "by the law of the land" the American prisoners "are destined to the cord," but, Gage added, they "have hitherto been treated with care and kindness, and more comfortably lodged than the King's troops in the hospitals, indiscriminately, it is true, for I acknowledge no rank that is not derived from the King." [103]

That adverb "indiscriminately" was regarded by Americans as a palpable give-away. Washington's own attitude toward prisoners who held commissions was precisely that which he had taken after his first skirmish, twenty-one years previously, when he had "disfurnished" himself, as he said, in order to clothe two French officers, La Force and Druillon, though he thought "in strict justice they ought to be hanged as spies of the worst sort." [104] Much as Washington desired to remain the gentleman at the same time that he was the soldier, he felt he could not allow easy imprisonment to British officers, if Americans were denied it. He accordingly directed Reed to write the Massachusetts Council and to request that all privileges be taken from the British officers in American hands.[105] This done, Reed replied for Washington in another somewhat florid letter which concluded: "If your officers, our prisoners, receive a treatment from me different from what I wish to shew them, they and you will remember the occasion of it." [106]

[102] *Ibid.*, 417.
[104] See Vol. I, p. 376.
[106] Letter of Aug. 20, 1775; 3 *G. W.*, 430–31.

[103] Text in 3 *Force* (4) p. 246.
[105] 3 *Force* (4) p. 328.

Washington threatened: he punished briefly in reprisal; he could not persist in severity. While he was carrying on the correspondence with Gage, he was urging tactfully that the baggage of British officers captured in July on Machias River, Maine, be restored to them,[107] and soon he recommended that the greatest leniency be shown British officers who were in districts from which they could not escape. This involved, among other things, a most tedious correspondence with a captive British Major, Christopher French of the 22nd Regiment, who waged with much persistence a long epistolary campaign for the right to wear his sword.[108] Washington usually answered French patiently and in person, but there were many matters in which the members of his staff could be of service to the General. This was increasingly true of Reed, whom James Warren described as "a man of sense, politeness and abilities for business." [109]

Horatio Gates was similarly useful and soundly versed in military affairs. By the second week in September, the Adjutant General was operating quietly and as smoothly as could be expected where he had to deal with men still inexperienced in military usages. More generally, Washington was not far from the point where he could say that the Army was improving. If it was not yet good, it was less bad by far than it was at the beginning of July. The General doubtless would have been reluctant to have his men attempt, as yet, to stand up against the British in the open field; but, assuming that powder and ball sufficed in quantity, he would not be afraid to meet a British attack—if only the British would come out and assault the American positions.

If . . . if . . . if—that continuing, gnawing uncertainty was worse than the indiscipline of riflemen, the venality of the basest of the Colonels, and all the remaining woes and perplexities of the Army put together. Suppose Gage still refused to attack as the brief New England summer passed and autumn brought warning of the long dark months when sentries might freeze at their posts and the tents of the camp be deep in snow. Farewell in that event to hope of a conclusion of the conflict in a single campaign! The war might drag on—who could say

---

[107] *Ibid.*, 426–27. For the capture, see 3 *Force* (4) p. 98.

[108] See 3 *G. W.*, 463, 522–23; 4 *ibid.*, 35, 42–43; 3 *Sparks*, 105; 4 *Force* (4) p. 996; 18 *Papers of G. W.*, 5, 62, 66, LC; 1 *CHS Cols.*, 189–225. This last reference includes some details of the career of Major French, whose Diary from Jan. 1 to Sept. 13, 1776 is printed. A Philadelphia dispatch in the *New England Chronicle and Essex Gazette* of Aug. 17, 1775, stated that he and two junior officers were taken off a ship from Cork.

[109] 1 *Warren-Adams Letters*, 168.

for how long? The summer had been mild and dry; [110] the cold months might accord or might offer a rebellious contrast. Winter quarters would be required, and they would have to be built with much labor and at burdensome cost. America would be called upon to erect within three months decent shelter for more persons than dwelt in Boston and for almost as many as resided in New York.[111] Besides, virtually all the enlistments had been to December 7 or to the end of 1775; what would happen then? Would the Army disintegrate, or reenlist, or would it be necessary to raise an entirely new force and go through all the turmoil and confusion of training officers and of disciplining the stubborn-minded youth of America?

Whatever had to be done, Washington would do. He had set his hand to the plow; he would not look back. If winter quarters had to be provided, then manifestly all buildings of Harvard College that could house soldiers must be used; temporary shelters against sun and rain must be closed in; those officers who were erecting board-covered retreats must not make them of large dimensions unless they were to be occupied by as many persons as could be accommodated; there must be no waste of boards, no amplitude of barracks; the Commissary General must formulate immediately his plans for feeding the men who would be crowded into these rooms.[112]

This was protective, defensive in the larger sense, and it was not enough to satisfy Washington's military mind or his conscience as a steward of public money. He considered it as shameful as it was militarily unsound and humiliating to have close to 19,000 men eat their heads off and do nothing but drill, mount guard and wait behind parapets. Impatiently, at last, Washington cast aside his earlier theory that his strategical task simply was to confine the British to Boston. He must do more—but what and where and how? Washington reflected on the possibilities, deliberated at intervals of three weeks with Massachusetts lawmakers and congressional Delegates on vacation, and decided to undertake three things: First, now that he had stopped all deliveries to Boston by land, he would arm some coastal vessels and would try to cut off the supplies that were reaching the British by sea.

---

[110] *Deacon Tudor's Diary*, Aug. 1, 1775.

[111] According to *A Century of Population Growth*, 11, New York had a population of 21,863 in 1771, and Boston 15,520 in 1770.

[112] 3 *G. W.*, 366, 393, 410, 425, 482; Loammi Baldwin to Washington, Sept. 1, 1775; *Baldwin Papers*, Harvard Coll. Lib. For the use of Harvard buildings, see 4 *Force* (4) p. 844–46, and S. T. Batchelder, *Bits of Harvard History*, 244, 247, 252.

Second, he would attempt to give help to Schuyler, if the New York commander was able to formulate a plan and to carry out the decision Congress had reached after Washington left Philadelphia, for the early invasion of Canada. Third, Washington would himself deliver with his Army a direct attack of some sort on Boston.

The effort at sea had to be made with armed schooners, by some of the numerous mariners in the Regiments from the coastal towns. Nicholson Broughton [113] was appointed a Captain in the Army of the United Colonies and was directed to proceed to sea with the armed schooner *Hannah* and to capture, if he could, any craft laden with men, arms, ammunition or provisions inward or outward bound from Boston. Broughton was to avoid an engagement with any warships of the enemy, because, Washington reiterated, "the design of this enterprise [is] to intercept the supplies of the enemy, which will be defeated by your running into unnecessary engagements." [114] Besides the *Hannah,* other American vessels were to be equipped with cannon and put in service.

Plans for a diversion in Canada probably originated in reports that the British had few troops in the region wrested from France, and that the native population was still hostile to the redcoats and by that very fact sympathetic with the Americans. The weakness of the enemy was one thing on which there was agreement among officers who had been on duty in Northern New York and had been at odds over everything else.[115] On the basis of what had been told him, Governor Trumbull was convinced that about 200 men were at St. John's, that Chambly was defended by 100, that not more than fifty soldiers were at Montreal, and that Quebec could count as its garrison a bare twenty or thirty. "The whole number of regulars in Canada, these included," said Trumbull, "does not exceed 700." [116]

[113] See 3 *G. W.,* 467 n for the varied spelling of Broughton's given name.
[114] Instructions, undated, in 3 *G. W.,* 467–69. Fitzpatrick recorded (*ibid.,* 469 n), that the draft of these instructions, in the autograph of Joseph Reed, subsequently was endorsed by Richard Varick: "Captn B. sailed the 5th Sept."
[115] See Justin H. Smith, *Our Struggle for the Fourteenth Colony* (cited hereafter as *Justin Smith, Struggle*), v. 1, 129–34, 150–55, 183–92. While Smith's narrative is so detailed that it often is difficult to follow, it contains in text and footnotes substantially all that is to be known about the attempted American conquest of Canada. His earlier work, *Arnold's March from Cambridge to Quebec,* is precisely what its title indicates and is of small use in the present study; but the two books together are so comprehensive that it seems best to deal only with the larger strategy of Canadian operations and, more particularly, with Washington's part in them. Readers who wish more than is given here and less than is found in Smith are referred to *French's First Year.*
[116] Letter of Aug. 24, 1775, to Gov. Nicholas Cooke; *AASP.,* 1926, p. 270.

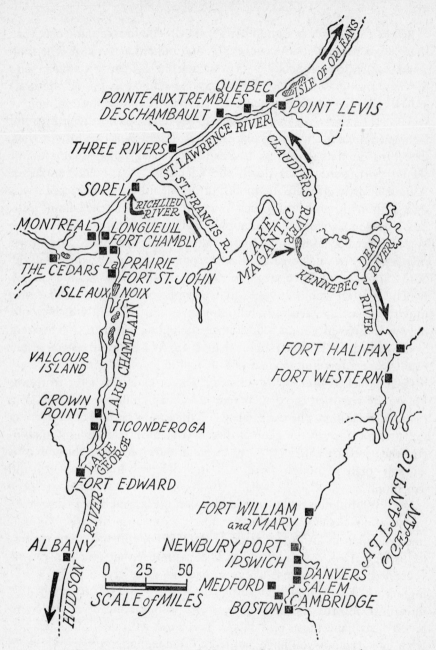

POINTE AUX TREMBLES
DESCHAMBAULT
QUEBEC
ISLE OF ORLEANS
POINT LEVIS

THREE RIVERS

ST. LAWRENCE RIVER

CLAUDIERS RIVER

SOREL
RICHLIEU RIVER
ST. FRANCIS R.

MONTREAL
LONGUEUIL
FORT CHAMBLY

LAKE MAGANTIC

DEAD RIVER

THE CEDARS
La PRAIRIE
FORT ST. JOHN

KENNEBEC RIVER

ISLE AUX NOIX

VALCOUR ISLAND

LAKE CHAMPLAIN

FORT HALIFAX
FORT WESTERN

CROWN POINT

TICONDEROGA

LAKE GEORGE

FORT EDWARD

HUDSON RIVER

FORT WILLIAM and MARY

ATLANTIC OCEAN

ALBANY

NEWBURY PORT
IPSWICH

0   25   50

DANVERS
SALEM

MEDFORD

SCALE of MILES

BOSTON
CAMBRIDGE

THE QUADRILATERAL OF THE NORTHERN CAMPAIGNS OF 1775–76

This outline shows in simple form the relationship between Arnold's advance to Quebec and
Montgomery's march on Montreal and thence down the St. Lawrence.

531

Before this extreme estimate was made, Washington learned that there was a route, known to several New England leaders, by which he could cooperate with Schuyler in attacking the British in Canada. The previous spring Col. Jonathan Brewer had offered to follow this trail and, if 500 men were assigned him, to make a demonstration against Quebec. His proposal, in effect, was to move troops northward up the Kennebec River to a carrying place opposite a stretch of Dead River, then westward on that stream to its headwaters near Lake Megantic and thence northward again down the Claudière to the St. Lawrence. Almost directly opposite the mouth of the Claudière was Quebec itself, then as in the French and Indian War, the bastion and the base of military power in Canada.[117] Substantially as Colonel Brewer had reasoned, Washington concluded that the advance up the Kennebec and down the Claudière would force the British commander in Canada, Gen. Sir Guy Carleton, "either to break up and follow this party to Quebec," by which Carleton would leave Schuyler unopposed, or else to "suffer that important place, [Quebec] to fall into our hands, an event which would have a decisive effect and influence on the public interests." [118] So long as the British in Boston remained inactive, Washington felt he easily could spare a force of 1000 or 1200 to make this diversion,[119] and even if Gage attacked him, or he perfected a plan of his own for storming Boston, he regarded the detachment of a small column to Canada as a risk worth taking. The essentials were, first, to be certain Schuyler was going to advance in the general direction of Montreal; second, to procure the necessary batteaux for the ascent of the rivers; and, third, to find an able man of tough fibre and inflexible resolution to lead the expedition.

Once Washington had made up his mind, he lost no time in ascertaining whether General Schuyler intended to move northward. He outlined the plan in an urgent letter of August 20, which he sent express to his New York comrade, and in it he admitted that much of success depended on the response of the Canadians themselves. Then Washington asked a prompt decision: "You will . . . by the return of this messenger inform me of your ultimate resolution. If you mean to proceed, acquaint me as particularly as you can with the time and force, what late accounts you have had from Canada, and your opinion as to

---

117 1 *Justin Smith, Struggle,* 498–99, with quotation from Brewer's undated proposal.
118 3 *G. W.,* 437–38.   119 *Ibid.,* 437.

the sentiments of the inhabitants, as well as those of the Indians upon a penetration into their country; what number of troops are at Quebec, and whether any men of war, with all other questions which may be material in the consideration of a step of such importance. Not a moment's time is to be lost in the preparations for this enterprise, if the advices from you favor it. With the utmost expedition the season will be considerably advanced so that you will dismiss the express as soon as possible." [120] Schuyler had written Washington of some of the difficulties he had been encountering because of slothfulness and jealousy and greed,[121] but in reality he had been having a worse time, in a wallow of exasperating detail, than he had described. Some of this trouble, if not of Schuyler's making was certainly not of his correction by sharp orders. He was too patient and conscientious and at the same time too businesslike to proceed otherwise than in orderly steps; [122] but under the spur of Washington's letter of the 20th, he was prompt to reply. By the 2nd of September,[123] Washington had a new account of his colleague's troubles with the Indians, whom the British in Canada were trying to arouse against the Americans. Schuyler then expressed his agreement with Washington's proposals and gave assurance that Gen. Richard Montgomery was making ready to leave Ticonderoga for Canada. He would join his Brigadier at Crown Point, Schuyler said, but he would not have in the two columns more than 1700 men. These would be too few to employ against Quebec after necessary detachments had been left at the places he would undertake to seize. There were, Schuyler reported, as far as he could ascertain, 350 or 400 regulars at St. John's, 150 to 200 at Chambly, about fifty at Montreal, and one Company at Quebec. Besides these, the British had a mixed force in Canada, chiefly Indians, to a total from 300 to 500. No report had been received of ships; Schuyler was inclined to think there were none in the St. Lawrence. Then he said positively: "Should the detachment of your body penetrate into Canada, and we meet with success, Quebec

---

[120] 3 G. W., 438. [121] See 1 LTW., 3, 6, 8, 13.

[122] The account in French's First Year, Chap. xxv, appears just and, as it was prepared carefully from the sources, its research has not been duplicated. French's conclusions are accepted here as correct.

[123] Washington's letter of the 20th reached Schuyler on the sixth day; Schuyler's answer of the 27th should, on that schedule, have been delivered at Cambridge on the 2nd. The headquarters correspondence of that date reads as if the orders to be described in the text were issued after Washington had heard from Schuyler, but, unfortunately, in Washington's reply of September 8, there is no mention of the date of the receipt of Schuyler's of August 27, though direct references are made to the contents of that letter. See 3 G. W., 485-86.

must inevitably fall into our hands. Should we meet with a repulse, which can only happen from foul play in the Canadians, I shall have an opportunity to inform your party of it, that they may carry into execution any orders you may give, in case such an unfortunate event should arise." [124]

The letter came at a time when Washington was engulfed in all the vexations of the effort to buy powder in Rhode Island and to seize it in Bermuda; he was planning simultaneously the cruise of *Hannah* and the commissioning of other vessels; the hope of an attack on Boston was rising; he was pressing for speed in the construction of winter quarters, and he was saying "No" once again to those who pleaded for detachments of troops to protect them against coastal raiders. All the while, of course, Washington had to see that vigilance was unrelaxed on the entire arc from Chelsea to Dorchester Neck. He could not have been called upon to formulate still another detailed plan at a time when he was more nearly absorbed in his duties, if, indeed, he could keep his temper, his patience and his sound judgment. Still, he felt a measure of confidence about the enterprise, first because he was reassured concerning the attitude of the Canadians and the Indians, second, because everyone who knew anything about the country said the route of the Kennebec-Claudière was practicable, and, third, because he believed the limitations of transport and supply could be overcome by the man he now selected to lead the expedition.

This was Benedict Arnold. For his exploit in seizing Ticonderoga with Ethan Allen, May 10, 1775, Arnold had received much applause, and he had proceeded without loss of time to the head of Lake Champlain where he had destroyed Fort St. John. Then had followed an ugly succession of quarrels over the command of a pitifully equipped little force to which four Colonies and the Continental Congress were contributing meagrely. Arnold had wished to attack Canada without delay, but his violence and the stubbornness of his rivals had paralyzed effort. At length, when he was told to recognize the seniority of his most persistent rival, Col. Benjamin Hinman, he resigned his Massachusetts command, dismissed his men and, before many weeks, appeared at Watertown for the settlement of his accounts. [125] Rightly or

---

[124] Letter of Aug. 27, 1775; 1 *LTW*, 22–24. In the *Journal of Du Roi the Elder*, 84 ff. are descriptions of Forts Sorel, Chambly and St. John as they were in June, 1777.

[125] He apparently was there by August 5 (see 3 *Force* (4), p. 311) and certainly was in the town and was on pleasant terms at nearby headquarters in Cambridge for some time prior to August 24. See Gates to Arnold, Aug. 25, 1775; *Gates Papers*, NYHS.

wrongly, he thought the Bay Colony was suspicious and miserly toward him in this settlement, and for days afterward he must have lived in a fury, but he had boldness, energy and ambition of a sort that would not permit him to be unoccupied in wartime. Soon he presented himself to Washington—a man of middle height or slightly below it, sturdily put together, 34 years of age, of dark hair and swarthy, full-blooded complexion, with strange, light eyes in challenging contrast to his dark skin.[126] Washington quickly saw that Arnold was furnished with much of the stuff that must be in a man called to head a swiftly-moving expedition that was to fight water and wind and winter. Besides, as a trader before the war, Arnold had been to Quebec and probably knew more about the town and the approaches to it than did any officer of Washington's immediate command. Arnold could get there! He must have commission as Colonel in continental service and without the loss of an hour he must organize the troops, speed the building of the batteaux, accumulate provisions on the Kennebec, and start his march before the summer slipped away.[127] Washington, for his part, undertook to see that vessels were assembled by Nathaniel Tracy for the movement of Arnold's men to the mouth of the Kennebec;[128] Gates drew up the papers for the construction of the flatboats and for the purchase of flour and meat under the direction of Reuben Colburn;[129] the drafting of an address to the people of Canada was another task for the staff—probably for Joseph Reed—and was regarded by Washington as one of the most important of the preliminaries. The more he reflected on the plan, the more did the General become convinced that success depended, above everything else, on preserving the friendship the French residents of Canada were said to have for the colonial cause.[130]

Next, the troops—how were they to be designated? Washington's discussion with Arnold and with others led him to conclude that the

---

[126] John Joseph Henry's Journal of the Campaign against Quebec in 15 *Penn. Arc.* (2) p. 65 ff. Much information about Arnold's movements, though surprisingly little about his personal appearance, is presented by contemporary diarists in Kenneth Roberts, *March to Quebec, Journals of the Members of Arnold's Expedition.*

[127] It is much to be regretted that the date of Washington's decision to dispatch Arnold is not known, because this would show with what speed, not to say haste, the expedition was staged. Gates's letter to Arnold, Aug. 25, 1775, cited in n. 125 *supra* shows that Washington was considering Arnold for some mission—almost certainly this one—that depended on Schuyler's answer; but Gates added: "I have laid your plan before the General, who will converse with you upon it when you next meet"—proof enough that a final decision had not been reached.

[128] 3 *G. W.,* 470–71.

[129] *Ibid.,* 471. The original is in Gates's autograph.

[130] Cf. 3 *G. W.,* 485–86.

force should consist of the equivalent of a Battalion, or 676 men, with the normal complement of officers and n.c.o's, and that three Companies of riflemen should be provided—roughly 1100 men altogether.[131] These soldiers would do better if they went of their own free choice. Consequently, Washington apportioned the footmen among the Regiments, pro rata, with the understanding that volunteers would be accepted at a parade on September 6. In event a sufficient number did not step forward, the remainder were to be assigned; but whether they offered their services or came under orders, they must be "active woodsmen and well acquainted with batteaus." [132] Washington decided, also, that the riflemen should include two Companies of the Pennsylvania Battalion and one of the Virginia Companies.[133] These were chosen by lot and as units—William Hendricks's Cumberland County Pennsylvanians, Matthew Smith's riflemen from Lancaster County in the same Colony, and Daniel Morgan's Virginians.[134] Two of the three Captains were recognized as men of ability. Hendricks, tall, mild-mannered, and handsome, had manifest qualities of character, a leader of the sort to be relied upon in a pinch. Morgan, aged 39, was the personification of the frontier soldier. Smith was a man of good looks and soldierly bearing, but he was illiterate and incurably talkative.[135]

For service with these riflemen, many volunteers from the Regiments were forthcoming; [136] preparations were hurried to equip the force and to begin the march by September 13 at latest; [137] a resounding address to the people of Canada was completed in Washington's name and was translated into French, which Charles Lee agreed to correct.[138] One passage read: "Come, then, my brethren, unite with us in an indissoluble union. Let us run together to the same goal. We have taken up arms in defence of our liberty, our property, our wives and our children: we

---

[131] 3 G. W., 473; Journal of Capt. Henry Dearborn, in Roberts, op. cit., 129; Henry's Journal in ibid., 300. Morison, in ibid., 500, gave the strength of the force as 1200. Justin Smith was of opinion (Arnold's March, 57) that the total was "almost exactly 1050."

[132] GO of Sept. 5, 1775; 3 G. W., 473.

[133] Ibid. Washington spoke of the Pennsylvanians as "Colonel [William] Thompson's Regiment" but the command often was styled synonymously a Battalion.

[134] For the choice by lot, see William Hendricks's Journal in 15 Penn. Arc. (2) p. 31.

[135] See the brief sketches of the three in John Joseph Henry's Journal in Kenneth Roberts, op. cit., 301–02. It should be noted that while Daniel Morgan's name is associated with Virginia and with Virginia arms, he was born on the Delaware. Both New Jersey and Pennsylvania claim him.

[136] Cf. Kenneth Roberts, op. cit., 619, 653, for the statements of Ephraim Squier and of John Pierce that they volunteered.

[137] 3 G. W., 485. Cf. ibid., 482–83.

[138] Ibid., 480 n. The address appears to be in the best hortatory style of Joseph Reed.

are determined to preserve them or die. We look forward with pleasure to that day not far remote (we hope) when the inhabitants of America will have one sentiment and the full enjoyment of the blessings of a free government. . . . The Great American Congress have sent an army into your province under the command of General Schuyler, not to plunder but to protect you. . . . To cooperate with this design and to frustrate those cruel and perfidious schemes which would deluge our frontier with the blood of women and children, I have detached Colonel Arnold into your country, with a part of the Army under my command. I have enjoined upon him, and I am certain he will consider himself, and act as in the country of his patrons and best friends. . . . The cause of America and of liberty is the cause of every virtuous American citizen[.] Whatever may be his religion or his descent, the United Colonies know no distinction but such as slavery, corruption and arbitrary domination may create.[139] Come, then, ye generous citizens, range yourselves under the standard of general liberty, against which all the force and artifice of tyranny will never be able to prevail." [140] In this same spirit, Arnold's instructions were given final form,[141] with the particular injunction that the men were not to ridicule the service of the Catholic church or affront its priests and votaries.[142] More personally, Washington told Arnold: "Upon your conduct and courage and that of the officers and soldiers detached on this expedition, not only the success of the present enterprise, and your own honor, but the safety and welfare of the whole continent may depend." [143]

At each stage of the hasty arrangement of Arnold's expedition, Washington remained hopeful, almost confident of success, though he took the precaution of calling on Governor Trumbull for the immediate dispatch to Boston of new levies from Connecticut, so that his effective strength would not be reduced by the detachment of Arnold's column.[144] Washington's chief concern was over Schuyler's lack of almost everything a force invading Canada would require. On this, the optimistic language of the Commander-in-Chief was scarcely more than an assumption: ". . . I trust you will have a feeble enemy to contend with, and a whole province on your side, two circumstances of great weight

---

139 The proper punctuation of these sentences is debatable. No period is placed in the original after "citizen," but "Whatever" is capitalized.
140 3 G. W., 479–80.
141 Ibid., 491 ff. These instructions are dated Sept. 14, 1775.
142 Ibid., 495–96.   143 Ibid., 491.   144 3 G. W., 486.

in the scale." [145] In the absence of information, Washington soon felt certain that Schuyler already had advanced as far as St. John's. To his brother "Jack," the General wrote on the 10th of September: "If [Schuyler] should succeed there, he will soon after be in Montreal without opposition; and if the detachment I am sending (though late in the season) from hence, should be able to get possession of Quebec, the ministry's plan, in respect to that government, will turn out finely." [146] Where so much was at stake, it was unpleasant to hear that some of the volunteers had refused to start their march until they received a month's pay,[147] but that could be provided. Obstacles were created in order to be defied! Even if it already was close to the middle of September, everything *must* and would work out; the resisting waters of the Kennebec could be ascended; the portages would not be intolerable; provisions would be at hand; intelligence reports could not be at fault in their assurance that the French of Canada eagerly awaited deliverance!

Arnold rolled the drums as soon as the different parts of his force could take the road to Newburyport [148]—and the senior officers who shook his hand and wished him luck must come together at Cambridge to consider the third of Washington's proposals. The Commander-in-Chief had written his Major Generals and his Brigadiers on the 8th of September and had asked them to consider in advance of a formal council of war whether he should undertake a dual attack on Boston, up the "Neck" from Roxbury and by boats from other parts of the front. Season and circumstance might be a demand for action. The approach of winter, he reasoned, would involve heavy expense for barracks, wood and clothing; blankets, though greatly needed, could not be provided in sufficient number. How, then, could a shivering, half-frozen Army be held together, even if expense were disregarded? Again—a new aspect of an old question—if the existing Army would not reenlist, another must of necessity be raised: were two different forces, then, to be kept simultaneously on the payroll, or was the country to be exposed to ruin between the time the old Regiments were disbanded and new ones were made ready? The foe might be relying

---

[145] *Ibid.*, 486. In the original the first quoted clause read "but, I trust," etc.
[146] *Ibid.*, 487–89.
[147] *Ephraim Squier's Diary*, Sept. 11, 1775, in Kenneth Roberts, *op. cit.*, 619.
[148] The route to Medford, Salem, Danvers, Ipswich, and Newburyport on the Merrimac, a march of about thirty-six miles, can be followed conveniently on the general map of the expedition in *Atlas of American History*, Plate 67.

upon that very development! Meantime, powder was being wasted with no certainty of replenishment. Costs had leaped above the highest estimate. In spite of all effort at saving—and here the businessman of the Potomac made himself heard above the soldier—"the expense of supporting this Army will so far exceed any idea that was formed in Congress of it that I do not know what will be the consequences." On the other hand, much as a "speedy finish of the dispute" was to be desired, "we are not," said Washington the soldier, "to lose sight of the difficulties the hazard and the loss that may accompany the attempt, nor what will be the probable consequences of a failure." [149]

On September 11—the very day Arnold's men were put under marching orders [150] and the day after the riflemen's mutiny on Prospect Hill [151] —Washington repeated to the eight members [152] of his council of war substantially this argument. No detailed plan of attack had been prepared by him for review and criticism: At the moment, Washington wished to know only whether his Generals believed the outline of an offensive should be taken in hand.

The approach of the council was half military. Lee wrote shortly afterwards that he believed an attack should be delivered; in the same letter he had to admit, "the fatal persuasion has taken deep root in the minds of the Americans from the highest to the lowest order that they are no match for the regulars but when covered by a wall or breastwork." [153] His fellow-commanders did not take precisely that view: their concern, as one after another voiced it, was over the strength of the British positions and not over the alleged reluctance of the soldiers to face the bayonet, the red line and the cannon's mouth. Boston Neck was too narrow, the officers maintained, and the approaches by water too much exposed to give the colonials a decent chance of success.

The other half of the argument was political and was hung on the hope—indeed, on the expectation—that the ministry of Lord North would fall and that friends of America would come into power. No

---

[149] 3 G. W., 484.

[150] See Dr. Isaac Senter's Journal in Kenneth Roberts, op. cit., 197.

[151] Supra, p. 525.

[152] Ward, Lee, Putnam, Thomas, Heath, Sullivan, Spencer and Greene.

[153] Letter of Sept. 19, 1775, to Benjamin Rush; 1 Lee Papers, 206. Cf. Joseph Reed to Thomas Bradford, Sept. 14, 1775: "It has been in very serious contemplation to strike a decisive stroke but we are so well posted, provided with all necessities, and our troops so young, that we know not how to continue them on a service which would put veterans to the test; and should they happen to fail in the trial, the consequences would be very fatal" (Papers of Joseph Reed, NYHS, with the punctuation considerably revised).

word had been received, as yet, of the King's action on the appeal of
the Continental Congress; [154] but news probably had arrived of the
"Humble Address, Remonstrance and Petition" which the Lord Mayor,
Aldermen and Livery of London had adopted on June 24 and were
seeking to present to the Monarch. This paper was all that Americans
could have asked. It began: "We have already expressed to your
Majesty our abhorrence of the tyrannical measures pursued against our
fellow-subjects in America," and it repeated, "the power contended for
over the Colonies, under the specious name of dignity, is, to all intents
and purposes, despotism." Without qualification or apology, the Lon-
doners asserted, "We have seen with equal dread and concern a civil
war commenced in America by your Majesty's Commander-in-Chief."
At the end, the petitioners called on the King to dismiss forever his
present ministers and advisers, to dissolve Parliament, and to put his
future confidence in servants whose attachment to the constitution,
when joined to the King's own wisdom and integrity, "may enable
your Majesty to settle this alarming dispute upon the sure, honorable
and lasting foundations of general liberty." [155] Colonials who read this
would conclude, not unnaturally, that even if the King ignored the
appeal of the Continental Congress, he certainly must consent to
receive and to answer the address of the most powerful single body of
his subjects.[156]

In the light of all this, an attack on Boston—if any attack were feasible
—well might be delayed until the arrival of the next ship, which might
bring announcement of the King's dismissal of Lord North and a
hostile ministry.[157] Officially, then, the council adjourned in a mood

[154] It had not been presented to Lord Dartmouth until Sept. 1, 1775.

[155] 2 Force (4) p. 1073–74.

[156] Some doubt exists concerning the date the address reached America.

[157] Congress itself was expectant, though divided. On Sept. 25, 1775, Silas Deane was to
write his wife: "We expect intelligence from Great Britain every hour. I am impatient for
it; not that I think it will alter our measures, for I am very confident as to the complexion of it,
before it arrives; but that the least and every shadow of excuse for not pursuing the most vigorous measures may be removed . . ." (1 Deane Papers, 80). In contrast, William Lee had
written, in the letter of July 13, already quoted, that the King's answer to the address of the
Corporation of London might be received from the vessel that carried his communication and
the text of the address. Largely on the basis of William Lee's letter, his brother Richard Henry
Lee was to say on the 26th of September: "We have no late accounts from England, but from
what we have had that can be relied on, it seems almost certain that our enemies there must
shortly meet with a total overthrow" (To Washington; 1 Ballagh, Lee Letters, 151). Recruiting
had failed in England, Lee reported; shipbuilders had mutinied; the Ministry had been compelled to send to the Highlands to find willing recruits. Benjamin Franklin, as usual, was
looking deeper for a decision by the British: "All depends upon that nation's coming to its
senses" (Letter of Sept. 12, 1775, to Jonathan Williams, 6 Smyth's Franklin, 429).

of cautious optimism. When the members had clattered out, Washington had to approve minutes that concluded: "After duly weighing the above proposition [for an attack on Boston] considering the state of the enemies' lines and the expectations of soon receiving some important advices from England, it was unanimously agreed that it was not expedient to make the attempt at present at least." [158]

"Unanimously" was not precisely the word for the rejection of the plan. Lee doubted; Washington at heart dissented. "I cannot say," he told Congress, "that I have wholly laid it aside"— [159]

[158] 18 *Papers of G. W.*, 30, LC; printed in 3 *Force* (4) p. 768.
[159] Letter of Sept. 21, 1775; 3 *G. W.*, 511.

A STRANGE CRYPTOGRAM THAT SMELLED
OF TREASON

When Nathanael Greene put into Washington's hands the strange paper of which one folio is reproduced on the next page, the Commander-in-Chief knew of course that it was in "secret writing," though he had not handled many such documents, if any, in his previous military service. When folded with a letter given Washington at the same time, September, 1775, the paper smelled of treason. As soon as Washington received a woman's confession that Dr. Benjamin Church, Director General of the Hospital, had written the mysterious communication, Washington had inquiry made for persons who might decipher the cryptogram. Two men were found, a clergyman and a militia Colonel. They worked separately and soon ascertained that symbols were used for letters and that as the paper originally had been in English, decipherment was merely a matter of counting the symbols and giving to each the place it had in frequency of occurrence in ordinary English speech and writing. The process, in short, was the one Edgar Allan Poe described long afterward, with so much gusto, in "The Gold Bug."

Both texts submitted to Washington by the amateur cryptographers were identical. They left no doubt that Doctor Church was communicating important information to some British agent in Boston. Washington soon became convinced of Church's guilt and in this, as in many a case that developed subsequently, he had no inclination to show mercy to a traitor. Frequently during the Revolution Washington remitted the death sentence of ignorant deserters, even of some who had been captured after they had gone over to the enemy, but when he spared these culprits, he did so from policy and not from pity. The deserters were denounced as villains who should get the noose; they were saved from the gallows solely because over-frequent executions lost their value as deterrents. It was still different with intelligent men who gave information to the enemy and thereby sinned against the liberties of their country. The life of the nation was being defended, Washington reasoned, by patriots who were risking their own necks and all their possessions. These Americans deserved protection from the traitor in the camp as vigilantly as from the foe in the field, and Washington tried to give that protection.

(After the Original in the Library of Congress)

Dear Sir

I now sett down to right a few lines hopeing thay
will find in god helth as thay leave me [at] present you
would have wrote to me be for this But now forget
to see you hear every Day I such wonder you never
sent me you promised to send if you Did never rite
it so pray lett know By the first opertunity wen you
expect to be bear & let the same time whether you
ever sent me not & wether you ever got as answer
from my sister I am alittle unesey that you never
wrote thear is a certen person hear wants to see
you very much so pray con as turn as posebell

If you right Direct your letter to me

Edward Hawton Living on Mr Haythorps farm
in Little Lamberig

The letter on the facing page was written by a woman who had no intention of betraying Dr. Benjamin Church or his treasonable correspondence with the British. On the contrary, if it be true, as alleged, that she had been a demimondaine in Boston, she may have felt she owed a debt of gratitude to the man of distinction who gave her the less precarious station of mistress. She seems to have acted willingly as Church's messenger in getting his letter to Newport for transmission to the beleaguered city, and here she shows herself fearful the information from Church was not forwarded. Her statement that "asertin person hear" wished to see the man she addressed, Godfrey Winwood, probably meant she wanted him to think that if he visited Cambridge he might resume the illicit relations he previously had with her. Once she got him there, she doubtless thought she could learn from him what had happened to the letter.

When she was apprehended and brought to headquarters, Washington and his aides had the greatest difficulty in persuading her to disclose the identity of the man she had been assisting, perhaps without realizing what

Church was doing. From the time she mentioned him, she disappears from the story. Her name, her age, her appearance, her fate—none of these is of record. The use of "j" for "I" in her surviving letter and her "jexpected" suggest the possibility that she was of French origin, but that scarcely matters one way or the other. She had played her little part in the strange drama of Doctor Church.

Women of her vocation appear with some frequency in reports of the rival armies' occupation of cities. Conditions in New York were particularly shocking and doubtless were exaggerated in some of the diaries that have been printed. On the whole, females of this type did not serve often as spies. Elias Boudinot mentioned one dame who smuggled information to him, though there is no suggestion that she was of the underworld. The "honest women" who acted as secret agents for the Army in the operations around Philadelphia in 1777–78 usually were humble persons who brought provisions to the market. Some worked for money and some for love of country, but the allegiance of most of the women was that of husband or sweetheart.

CHAPTER XXII

December Brings a Dark Crisis

(September–December, 1775)

The council's review of plans for an offensive against Boston was made when Washington had been at Cambridge about two months and a half. He kept so busy, every hour of the day, that he had no time to look over his shoulder or to turn the pages of correspondence that told what he had accomplished. Most of his subordinates accepted his direction of the Army as a matter of course. He proceeded as if he knew what he was about. Almost everyone assumed that he did. In any event, he had far better acquaintance with military affairs than did any of his lieutenants except, of course, Charles Lee and Horatio Gates. If those two doubted Washington's ability or secretly mocked his errors, they were silent, and even they must have felt respect for a man who so quickly had adapted himself to unfamiliar duties vastly more complicated than any he ever had attempted to discharge. In April, Washington had been the private gentleman of Mount Vernon, the host of many guests who were enjoying their first liberation from the imprisoning mud of late winter. He could have said then that he had not signed a military order for field forces in more than sixteen years and that he seldom had worn a military uniform except when he had posed for his portrait. Now he had to act as if he always had been a soldier and had been master of all the mysteries of army usage. It was an incredible mutation, almost as great a change as if he, by some incomprehensible process, had become an entirely different man in everything except character. No less amazing, perhaps, was the fact that he had been able to do what Congress had demanded of him. He doubtless had made mistakes, but he could tell himself in all honesty that they had not been numerous and that none, thus far, had been fatal to the cause in his keeping. His responsibilities were out of scale to his experience, but, somehow, they had been measured and met. He felt that he was out of his depth, but he still was keeping afloat.

For a fortnight and longer, after Arnold's volunteers marched away, there was a spiteful dispute of the artillery, but nothing that indicated preparation by the British for an immediate attack.[1] "The almost constant fire of the enemy," wrote one American soldier, "produced one effect, probably not contemplated by them: it hardened our soldiers rapidly to stand and bear fire." When a cannon ball had struck the earth, one man and then another and another would run out and would try to be the first to seize it when its velocity was sufficiently reduced for anyone to lay hands on it. A winner would guard the missile vigilantly until he could carry it to a sutler and trade it for spirits.[2] The British made ten such shots or more for every one from an American cannon, because Washington demanded unrelaxed care to prevent the wastage of powder. Each grain was guarded as if it were a coin in the last treasure of America. Some additional powder arrived at the camp, few knew whence, but almost as much went out of the store as ammunition for the men.[3] If possible, custody of the powder supply became even more exacting when it was known that the expedition to Bermuda had found no stock of explosive on the island.[4]

All the while, the feeling grew in Washington's mind that if powder could be had, the enemy could be driven from Boston;[5] but, meantime, angry artillerists had to endure the annoyance of British fire, and shivering sentinels had to be clothed. "So far as regards the preservation of the Army from cold," Washington had to tell Congress, "they may be deemed in a state of nakedness." Specifically, "Many of the men have been without blankets the whole campaign and those which have been in use during the summer are so much worn as to be of little service."[6]

---

[1] N. Morgan's Diary in 7 *CHS Cols.*, 106, 107; Carter, *Letters to a Friend*, 13. As of September 17, Lieut. John Barker reported that a soldier of the King's Own had his leg shot off as the relief was going to the lines. "This," said Barker, "is the first man who has suffered by the rebels' cannon" (*op. cit.*, 64). For later intervals of silence at the batteries, see *McCurtin's Journal*, 24, 26.

[2] Diary of Samuel Richards, *loc. cit.*, 19.

[3] The following references are believed to cover most of the vicissitudes of the powder supply, except for the Bermuda expedition, to the end of December, 1775: 1 *Burnett*, 195, 199, 237, 245; Bedinger's Journal, *op. cit.*, 109; 2 *John Adams*, 517; 1 *Lee Papers*, 212; 1 *LTW.*, 66; 2 *JCC.*, 248–49, 253; 3 *ibid.*, 262, 284, 286, 338, 345, 346, 365, 388, 426, 436, 460; *Diary of Ezekiel Price* in *MHSP.*, 1863–64, p. 217, 219; 1 *Ballagh, Lee Letters*, 157; *Barker's Diary*, 67; E. *Clarke's Journal*, 28. Attention again is directed to the fact that the indices to 3 *Force* (4) contain scores of minor items on powder that the student interested in the supply of ammunition will do well to examine in detail.

[4] *AASP.*, 1926, p. 271, 276; 3 *G. W.*, 500, 501; 4 *ibid.*, 53, 63–64; 1 *LTW.*, 49 ff, 58, 67–68, 83.

[5] Cf. 4 *G. W.*, 173.

[6] Letter of Sept. 21, 1775; 3 *G. W.*, 509. Cf. 4 *G. W.*, 34, 49, 87, 155; *Bedinger's Journal*, loc. cit., 116.

If the Army were to scatter at the end of its enlistment, even these thin blankets and ragged greatcoats would be lost, and the troops who took the place of the discharged men would have to be supplied. Without the waste of an hour, new Regiments and old must be given shelter against the wind that would soon roll down from the hostile North or roar inland from the angry Atlantic. This work of constructing the barracks was pressed, though not at a speed to equal the evidences that the need would be early and inclusive. As Joseph Reed put it: ". . . We continue here in statu quo. Our present employment is building barracks and making provisions for winter, which approaches fast." [7]

Weather, rather than slow-handed workmen, was responsible for most of the delay in building winter quarters. The soldiers themselves, whether carpenters or sentinels, were not laggard or sullen. They were, in fact, so much better disciplined than three months previously that relatively as many officers as privates came before courts martial.[8] Even then, the number of officers accused of serious misconduct was not alarming in proportion to the size of the army but it was humiliating to New England leaders. Said Samuel Adams: "Some of our military men have, I fear, disgraced us; it is then important that every anecdote that concerns a man of real merit, and such I know there are, be improved, as far as decency will admit of it, to their advantage, and [to] the honor of a Colony which, for its zeal in the great cause, as well as its sufferings, deserves so much of America." [9]

Adams, Washington, everyone was unprepared for what developed at the end of September when Brig. Gen. Nathanael Greene called at headquarters and asked to see the Commander-in-Chief privately. He entered with another man and shut the door behind him. Then he introduced his companion as Godfrey Wainwood, a baker of Newport, Rhode Island, and he handed Washington a letter that Wainwood had brought from Henry Ward, Secretary of that Colony. Ward's letter and Wainwood's statement had to do with a woman who had come to Wainwood's house in Newport early in August and, on the basis of previous acquaintance in Boston, had asked him to arrange for her to see Capt. James Wallace of H.M.S. *Rose,* or the Royal Collector, Charles Dudley,

---

[7] 1 *Reed,* 120. For reports on construction, the probable necessity of using private houses in Cambridge, and the early arrangements for providing firewood, see 3 *G. W.,* 511; 4 *ibid.,* 17–18. Later developments are described *infra,* p. 582, n. 158.

[8] For officers, see 3 *G. W.,* 496, 515; 4 *ibid.,* 13, 19–20, 30, 39, 90, 95, 107–08. Cases involving enlisted men and n.c.o.'s will be found in 3 *G. W.,* 497, 514; 4 *ibid.,* 89.

[9] Letter of Sept. 26, 1775 to Elbridge Gerry; 3 *Force* (4) p. 806.

or George Rome, a known Tory, who was a rich merchant and ship-owner. The manner of the woman led the baker to wonder if she might not have some secret communication to make to a Loyalist. Wainwood thereupon proceeded to question the woman and at length got from her an admission that she had received in Cambridge a letter she was to deliver to one or another of the men she had named, in order that it might be forwarded to Boston. This of course deepened Wain-wood's suspicions and led him to give one excuse after another for not taking her to any of the men she wished to see. Finally, the woman lost patience or interest or both and acceded to Wainwood's suggestion that she entrust to him the letter, which he said he would deliver at first opportunity. The woman disappeared and presumably went back to Cambridge. Wainwood was left with the paper. For some time he kept it, not knowing what disposition to make of it, but he determined to relate the circumstances to a Newport schoolmaster named Maxwell, a stout supporter of the colonial cause. Without hesitation, Maxwell broke the seal and opened the communication the woman had entrusted to Wainwood. It was to no purpose that he scrutinized the sheet, because the letter was written in strange characters and was completely unintelligible. Maxwell gave the paper back to Wainwood, who put it away again and troubled himself no more about it until, days later, the woman wrote him in much trepidation to this effect:

Dear sir

I now sett down to right afeu Lines hoping thay will find in good helth as thay Leave me Iexpeted you would have arote to me be for this But now Iexpet to sea you hear every Day I much wonder you never Sent wot you promest to send If you Did Inever reseve it so pray Lett me know By the first orpurtunuty wen you expet to be hear & at the Same time whether you ever sent me that & wether you ever got a answer from my sister I am alittel unesey that you never rote thar is aserten person hear wants to Sea you verey much so pray com as swon as posebell if you righ Direct your Lettr to mr Ewerd Harton Living on Mr Tapthonges farm in Littel Cambrig [10]

Wainwood was a man of native shrewdness and, when he read this, he was led to the conclusion that the person who had employed the mysterious cipher had been in communication with the addressee in

[10] 18 *Papers of G. W.*, 121, LC; verbatim except that the writer used a long J for I. Her handwriting is no worse than that of a majority of her contemporaries.

Boston and had learned that the letter had not been received. Wainwood accordingly went to Maxwell, told him what had occurred and agreed that the two of them would proceed to Providence and report the circumstances to Ward. The Secretary in turn urged that Maxwell go to Cambridge and lay the facts before General Washington. It was suggested, too, that Wainwood, who might be seen in town by the woman, should ride only as far as Denham and should wait there in event he were needed. As it befell, Wainwood, not Maxwell, made the journey to army headquarters and delivered a letter of introduction from Ward to Nathanael Greene.[11]

So, there they were, Greene and Wainwood, with the letter the woman had sent the baker and with the queer cryptogram she had left with him earlier. Washington took the second of the two papers and observed that the date "22 july" was on the outside, under the fold, and that the address was "For Major Cane in Boston on his magisty's sarvice."[12] The cipher, needless to say, was as incomprehensible to him as it had been to the others. Who was the woman? Wainwood gave her name and probably confided, then or later, that she was a female of easy virtue, with whom he had consorted in Boston before the war.[13] Immediately, Washington gave orders that search be made for her. It was promptly undertaken and soon rewarded. That evening she was brought to headquarters but was obdurate.[14] "For a long time," Washington said later, "she was proof against every threat and persuasion to discover the author . . ."[15] Ignorant as she showed herself to be, she was cunning and, according to her code, loyal. It was in vain that Washington reverted to his old civilian rôle of examining justice and tried to trip her into a confession. Even when it was explained to her

[11] Ward's letter, which gives most of the essential facts, is dated Providence, Sept. 26, 1775 and is in 3 *Force* (4) p. 809. Some details and the identification of several actors in this strange drama are in Ezra Stiles's *Literary Diary*, v. 1, p. 618–20, 626–28. Washington's own account, which becomes first-hand evidence at this point in the narrative, will be found in his letter of Oct. 5, 1775 to Congress; 4 *G. W.*, 10. A few details, not in Ward's letter to Greene, are mentioned by Washington.

[12] 1 Stiles's *Lit. Diary*, 628. If the address is in the same handwriting as the woman's letter, it was written much more carefully. The date "22 july" well may be in the woman's autograph (18 *Papers of G. W.*, 119, LC).

[13] Cf. 1 Stiles's *Lit. Diary*, 619, 628

[14] There apparently is no basis of fact for the family tradition (W. F. Livingston, *Israel Putnam*, 258), that the woman was taken to the headquarters of General Putnam who made her mount behind him and rode furiously to Washington's house with her. The arrest of course was made as quietly as possible, in order that the man who was using her as his messenger might not take alarm. James Warren (1 *Warren-Adams Letters*, 121), is authority for the statement that she was brought to Washington's headquarters at night.

[15] 4 *G. W.*, 10.

that she had been carrying information to the enemy and that her one hope of escaping a frightful penalty would be to tell the whole truth, she would say nothing. Finally, the next day she was worn to the point where she could resist no longer: the man who had given her the letter to carry to Newport was . . . Dr. Benjamin Church.[16]

Doctor Church? The Director General of the Hospitals, a leader in the Massachusetts Congress and a member of the Boston delegation, along with Samuel Adams and John Hancock in the new House of Representatives?[17] Could it be possible that a man so distinguished for public service, one of those sent to Springfield to escort Washington and Lee to Watertown, could be engaged in a correspondence that certainly was clandestine and suspicious and probably was traitorous? Send at once to Watertown and ask James Warren and Maj. Joseph Hawley to come to Cambridge without delay. To those two astonished leaders, on arrival, Washington repeated the woman's story and showed the communication in cipher. What would they advise him to do? Their counsel was given with no thought that Church had any sort of legislative immunity: he and his papers should be seized.[18]

In a few hours the Doctor appeared under guard and submitted readily to questioning. Yes, the letter was his and was intended for his brother, Fleming Church, who was in Boston. When deciphered, the Doctor said confidently, the document would be found to contain nothing criminal. He accompanied this with many protestations of his loyalty to the cause of the Colonies, but he did not offer to put the contents of his letter in plain English. Nor did he explain why, if the communication were innocent, he had said nothing of the correspondence to any person but the woman who, it eventuated, Church had been keeping as his mistress.[19] With a deeper reproach than calm words expressed, Washington told Church that if he merely had wished to send a letter into Boston, he could have done so any day. Dispatching anything in cipher, via Newport and through the hands of the enemy, was as needless as it was suspicious.[20]

---

[16] *Ibid.,* 10. [17] 3 *Force* (4) p. 271.

[18] 1 *Warren-Adams Letters,* 122.

[19] 4 *G. W.,* 10. On October 3, Eben. Huntington wrote: ". . . The plot was discovered by [Church's] Miss who is now with child by him and he owns himself the father (for he has dismissed his wife)" *Eben. Huntington Letters,* 22.

[20] 1 Stiles's *Lit. Diary,* 619. In July, Henry Knox had remarked to his wife that when a trumpeter had come out to deliver Burgoyne's letter to Charles Lee, a letter from Joseph Webb to a sister in Boston was passed without difficulty. See Henry Knox to his wife, July 11, 1775; 1 *Knox Papers,* 163, MHS.

Church must be put under surveillance; the letter must be deciphered. For this purpose, one copy was given Rev. Mr. West, who was credited with some knack for cryptography. Col. Elisha Porter of the Massachusetts Militia heard of the paper and, as he, too, had some familiarity with secret writing, he offered his services. Elbridge Gerry, who suggested that Porter volunteer to decipher the paper, assisted him in working on it.[21] The key was found easily. By October 3, Washington received from West and Porter identical copies of the deciphered document that ran to only 1000 words. Although unaddressed except for the cover to Major Cane,[22] the letter evidently was to a person with whom Church previously had conducted a correspondence. The Doctor recorded his own movements, told of a visit to Philadelphia, described the strength and equipment of the colonial forces, mentioned the plan for commissioning privateers, and stated that an army would be raised in the Middle Colonies to take possession of Canada. Church wrote next: "For the sake of the miserable convulsed empire, solicit peace, repeal the acts, or Britain is undone. This advice is the result of warm affection to my King and to the Realm. Remember I never deceived you; every article here sent you is sacredly true." There was more in the same vein and then: "I write you fully, it being scarcely possible to escape discovery. I am out of place here, by choice, and therefore out of pay, and determined to be so unless something is offered in my line." The letter concluded with elaborate instructions concerning the dispatch of an answer. The last sentence was, "Make use of every precaution or I perish."[23] In Washington's eyes, this language was complete refutation of Doctor Church's statement that he had been seeking to win concessions from Britain by disclosing the great strength of the colonials. Church was in traitorous communication with the enemy— that was the clear conclusion of Washington. His sense of justice did not protest for an instant, in any particular, against the verdict of his military judgment.

[21] Elbridge Gerry to unnamed correspondent of Washington's military "family," Oct. 5, 1775; 19 *Papers of G. W.*, 5, LC.

[22] Those who have written of this affair have spelled the name of the addressee in many different forms, but there scarcely can be any doubt he was Maj. Maurice Cane, then on duty in Boston.

[23] 3 *Force* (4) p. 958–59. The text from the *Remembrancer*, printed in 2 *Force* (4) p. 1713–14 is dated July 23, 1775, and is different in paragraphing and, to a minor degree, in phrasing but in essentials is the same document. Original and deciphered copy of Church's letter are in 18 *Papers of G. W.*, 119, 120, LC. Part of the cryptogram is printed between pages 541 and 542 of this volume.

Procedure was another matter and one concerning which Washington was not certain. He felt the need of advice and, on the 3rd of October, convened a council of war. Grimly and with few words he informed the general officers of the discovery of Church's activities, and, in proof, laid before them the text of the letter of July 22 as deciphered by West.

The other Generals, like Washington, were stunned by the disclosure and were unable at the moment, to reach any other decision than that they should summon Church before them, question him, and then judge for themselves whether he was lying to save his neck or, incredibly, had undertaken in this stupid manner, as he alleged, to effect a settlement. Washington acquiesced. The next day, Doctor Church was brought before the assembled Generals and was confronted again with the deciphered text of the letter to Major Cane: did he acknowledge it to be his and to be correctly set forth from the characters he had used? Church did not hesitate. He had written the letter; it was deciphered properly; he had penned it deliberately in the hope he might deter ministerial forces from attacking at a time when the Army's supply of ammunition was low.

In other respects, the Doctor's argument was a repetition of what he already had professed to Washington, and it was unconvincing. When Church at length was taken from the room, still declaiming about his loyalty to the American cause, Washington asked members of his council for their judgment. Unanimously they were of opinion that Church beyond doubt had carried on a criminal correspondence. What, then, should be done with him; what did the army regulations prescribe? The offence was one so little contemplated among the possibilities of misconduct in the military establishment that none of the officers was quite certain of the punishment prescribed. A search of the regulations adopted by Congress in June disclosed an odd provision: Under Article XXVIII, a person communicating with the enemy, directly or indirectly, was to suffer such punishment as a general courtmartial should mete out; but under Article LI, it was disputable whether a military court was authorized in such a case to impose any penalty heavier than that of cashiering, a fine of two months' pay, or thirty-nine lashes. Apparently the Delegates in Philadelphia who had adopted a revision of the old British army regulations had not considered carefully the limitations set to the authority of courts martial—a piece of negligence that might have reminded Washington of the early days of the French and

Indian War when he had been powerless to deal with the worst military offences.[24] This time, the penalty was absurdly unfitted to the crime. There was nothing the council could do about that, except to have Washington call the attention of Congress to the inadequacy of the punishment for those who communicated with the British. Pending further instructions from the Delegates in Philadelphia, Doctor Church must be confined closely and denied all visitors except those who had the General's permission.[25]

An early and careful examination by Joseph Reed of the accused man's papers uncovered no direct evidence against Church[26] though "it appeared upon inquiry," as Washington reported to Congress, "that a confidant had been among [the papers] before my messenger arrived."[27] With this, so far as headquarters had responsibility for the case, it was closed; but the known facts of arrest and exposure were enough to puzzle and to excite New England.[28] A few of the leaders, looking back over the Doctor's career, felt that he had been party to several incidents, among them a visit to Boston during the siege, that had been disregarded at the time but were highly suspicious now.[29] Other informed persons scarcely could credit the evidence against a man, who, wrote a New Yorker, "was looked on by us all as one of the firmest friends of America."[30] Said John Adams: "The letter of Dr. [Church] is the oddest thing imaginable. There are so many lies in it, calculated to give the enemy an high idea of our power and importance, as well as so many truths tending to do us good that one knows not how to think him treacherous: Yet there are several strokes which cannot be accounted for at least by men, without the supposition of iniquity. In short I endeavor to suspend my judgment. Don't let us abandon him for a traitor without certain evidence. But there is not so much delibera-

[24] Vol. I, p. 429; Vol. II, p. 118. The text of the army regulations, as adopted, will be found in 2 *JCC.*, 111–122. Washington had served on the committee that drafted these rules, but it will be remembered that he had left Philadelphia before they were debated and adopted.

[25] The exact language is that "no person visit him but by special direction." See 3 *Force* (4) p. 958.

[26] Cf. 1 *Reed*, 120; 1 *Burnett*, 226.

[27] 4 *G. W.*, 10–11. Washington's report to Congress is one of the principal documents on the affair of Doctor Church.

[28] By Oct. 10, 1775, the broad circumstances of Church's arrest were familiar to the men in the camps. See McCurtin's Journal, *loc. cit.*, 21. Under GO of Oct. 3, 1775, without explanation, Dr. Isaac Foster was instructed "to take the direction and superintendency of the General Hospital until further orders . . ." (4 *G. W.*, 2).

[29] Cf. James Warren to John Adams, Oct. 1, 1775: Many circumstances, new and old, said Warren, were "much against" Church (1 *Warren-Adams Letters*, 122).

[30] "Unidentified gentleman of distinction" quoted in *London Morning Post and Daily Advertiser*, Jan. 1, 1776, reprinted in *Willard*, 220.

tion in many others, or so much compassion."[31] Samuel Ward, Rhode Island Delegate, fairly exploded: ". . . what a complication of madness and wickedness must a soul be filled with to be capable of such perfidy! what punishment can equal such horrid crimes; I communicated the affair to the Massachusetts Delegates. They could hardly conceive it possible."[32] Charles Lee reasoned of Church: ". . . admitting his intentions not to be criminal, so gross a piece of stupidity in so sensible a man is quite a portent; and supposing him guilty, it is terrifying to the last degree. . . . It will spread an universal diffidence and suspicion, than which nothing can be more pernicious to men embarked in a cause like ours . . ."[33]

Washington, for his part, remained firm in his conviction of Church's guilt and he determined to have the man punished, but if he was tempted to ask whether there were other potential traitors among those who huzzaed for the Colonies or rattled a sabre in the name of liberty, he was careful to say nothing that bespoke doubt or distrust. He saw to it that Church was kept in confinement to await the judgment of Congress and also of the Massachusetts Assembly, which could act independently on the treason of one of its own members.[34] When Church

[31] 1 *Warren-Adams Letters*, 142. Adams previously had said that the country could not be too careful about the persons it trusted in such times as these. "Yet," he added, "we ought not to let our caution degenerate into groundless jealousy" (*ibid.*, 137–38).

[32] 1 *Burnett*, 225–26.

[33] Letter of Oct. 5, 1775 to John Adams; 1 *Lee Papers*, 209. General Sullivan, reporting the case of Dr. Church to Josiah Bartlett and John Langdon, Oct. 4, 1775, connected the physician's treason with neglect of the sick in hospitals (1 *Sullivan Papers*, 97; cf. *ibid.*, 80–83, 84–86) though Church had defended himself previously against a somewhat similar charge, which he attributed to men who supported uneconomical methods in providing care for the sick (See Church to Samuel Adams, Aug. 23, 1775, Allen French, *General Gage's Informers*, 173 ff). William Palfrey, writing Samuel Adams, Oct. 3, 1775, thought the affair doubly embarrassing. "At a time," he said, "when prejudices against the people of this Colony are circulated—when we are represented to all strangers from the southward as a parcel of canting, hypocritical, peculating knaves, whose sole aim is to prey on the public—how extraordinarily unfortunate it is to meet with such a shocking instance of treason against the country in a person of Dr. Church's high trust and ability" (*Samuel Adams Papers*, NYPL). Church's protestation that he could not get Lee's letter to Burgoyne into Boston was itself in retrospect suspicious. The subsequent effort of the British to exchange him for an American in 1777, as explained in n. 34, was, of course, an admission of his "loyalty." Allen French sifted from the *Gage Papers* in the Clements Library at Ann Arbor all the documents that might have been written by Church. Along with some evidence that raised suspicion but did not quite convict Church of previous communication with the British commander in Boston, French brought to light an unsigned letter, received at British headquarters May 24th, that contained various items of confidential military news. At the end, a reference to a vexatious appointment to "carry the dispatches to Philadelphia," unmistakably identifies the writer as Doctor Church (*op. cit.*, 156–57).

[34] After personal examination before the Massachusetts House, which he addressed formally in his defence (3 *Force* (4) p. 1479), Church was expelled on Nov. 3, 1775 (*ibid.*, 1497–98). Massachusetts lawmakers were fearful he might not be punished properly because of the defect in the articles of war (*ibid.*, 1517–18); but Congress gave orders, which Governor Trumbull faithfully executed, that Church be kept in a safe Connecticut prison with stern restrictions

was sent to Connecticut for safe custody, Washington's only recorded comment was: "Dr. Church is gone to Governor Trumbull, to be disposed of in a Connecticut gaol, without the use of pen, ink or paper, to be conversed with in the presence of a magistrate only, and in the English language. So much for indiscretion, the Doctor will say." [35]

Had Washington been writing of his adversary in Boston, he might have added in his letter "And so much for discretion, General Gage will say." Word had reached the Americans, in the midst of the excitement over Doctor Church, that the British commander had been ordered home and that Maj. Gen. William Howe, the senior officer of the reenforcements that had come to Boston in May, 1775, had been named to act in Gage's absence as head of the armed forces in that part of America.[36] The change was one to justify the conclusion *a priori* that Gage had been recalled because he had been too cautious, too discreet in using his forces or, perhaps the vainglorious might say, too much afraid of the colonials to take the offensive against them.

Beyond this, there was no ground for rejoicing over the transfer of command. On the contrary, Washington might well have reasoned that he was exchanging an adversary he knew for one with whom he was unacquainted, except as Howe had shown fighting spirit at Bunker Hill. If some resolute and cunning spy had been able to filch from Gage's files copies of the British General's letters to the home government, Washington would have had confirmation of much that he had sus-

---

on the visitors he might see (3 *JCC.*, 334; 4 *G. W.*, 91). Later Church petitioned for a moderation of his imprisonment (1 *Burnett*, 316; 4 *G. W.*, 61), which was allowed (*ibid.*, 65). In May, 1776, on the basis of further petition and various certificates of ill health (*ibid.*, 350), Congress requested the Council of Massachusetts to bond him for appearance at trial and meantime to parole him under specified conditions (*ibid.*, 352). This was done but it was dangerous liberty. At Waltham, where Church lodged on the 3rd of June, 1776, a mob assailed him. Although the Selectmen intervened for his protection, he escaped only by leaping from a window and running off (1 *Warren-Adams Letters*, 254–55). In September, 1777, a proposal to exchange Church was made by the British but was rejected by Congress, Oct. 1, 1777 (8 *JCC.*, 758). Later, according to Sparks (*op. cit.*, v. 3, p. 505), Church received permission from the Massachusetts authorities to leave the country and to go to the West Indies. He disappeared aboard a vessel of which nothing was heard afterwards. The presumption was that the ship was lost at sea.

[35] Letter of Nov. 20, 1775 to Joseph Reed; 4 *G. W.*, 105.

[36] 4 *G. W.*, 5; *McCurtin's Journal*, 19, 21; *New England Chronicle and Essex Gaz.*, Oct. 5, 1775. Howe's regular rank was that of Major General but he was given local rank of General while serving in America. His explanation of his rank and of his subordination to Guy Carleton in event they operated together, are available in his letter of Sept. 28, 1775 to Gov. Francis Legge in 4 *G. W.*, 5 n. Gage remained titular royal Governor of Massachusetts. For his recall, see Dartmouth's letter to him, Aug. 2, 1775 in 2 *Gage*, 203, a paper that apparently reached Boston September 26. See also Howe to Dartmouth, October 5 (3 *Force* (4) p. 955). Gage's reply to Dartmouth's letter of August 2 is dated September 30 and is in 1 *Gage*, 417. His preliminaries of departure are sketched in 2 *Gage*, 203 n.

pected and an intimation of one or two advantages he had enjoyed, unknown to himself, because of General Gage's planning. His Majesty's senior officer in New England had felt after the fight on the high ground above Charlestown that his situation, as he described it, was "not advantageous," first, because he had no line of land advance from the city except by narrow Boston Neck, and, second, because, even if he could break out, he did not have a force large enough to hold the town and simultaneously to subdue the country. "There are no rivers for the transportation of supplies," he had explained, "and land carriages are not to be procured." [37] That was his main contention and one that had not been given proper weight at American headquarters: Gage had no conception of the use of seapower in the waters around Boston. He felt he could hold his position, though the Americans were stronger than the Ministry or the British people realized; he might attack and conceivably he might win, but he could not follow up a victory because his army was small and his land transport almost nil. [38] He had been considering a different plan, which his successor might approve and develop, but Washington must discover that and, meantime, must cope with troubles that multiplied on his side of the salt marshes as the leaves fell.

At the beginning of the third week in October, with the camps buzzing over Church's arrest and the recall of "Blundering Tom," as the men styled Gage, [39] it manifestly was too early to expect any important news from Arnold; but barracks had to be built and ceaseless vigilance displayed, and above everything else—if there could be a superlative among so many perplexities—the possible break-up of the army had to be faced. That was the "terror by night," a threat to the cause of freedom so affrighting that a timid man scarcely could bring himself to think of it. The enlistments of the Connecticut and Rhode Island troops would terminate December 1; none of the men from other New England Colonies had covenanted to remain in service beyond the end of 1775; [40] the riflemen, in the main, would be subject to martial law until July 1. If the majority of the foot soldiers reenlisted, the ranks might be filled by vigorous recruiting; but if most of the men marched

[37] Letter of July 24, 1775, to Lord Dartmouth; 1 Gage, 409.
[38] His views are clearly set forth in his dispatches of Aug. 19 and Oct. 1, 1775, to Dartmouth (1 Gage, 413, 418) and in a brief communication of Aug. 19, 1775 to Lord Barrington (2 ibid., 696).
[39] Cf. New England Chronicle and Essex Gaz., Oct. 5, 1775.
[40] 3 G. W., 506.

off with the assertion that they had done their part, how were they to be replaced? To abandon the contest was, to Washington's mind, utterly unthinkable; to continue it was to face a hundred snares.

Some of the complications he already had presented in his dispatches to Congress [41] only to have these and several others returned to him for his recommendations. As it chanced—for he never seemed to be allotted even a single day for the exclusive consideration of one issue— several inquiries of the highest importance had reached Washington from Congress while he was dealing with the alleged treason of Doctor Church.[42] The General had given the substance of the new questions to the officers then and, two days later, he had repeated them in a circular: Congress wished to know what number of men would suffice for a winter campaign? Could soldiers' pay be reduced? Of what should the ration consist? Were further regulations necessary for the Army? To these questions Washington added several of his own and, in particular, one concerning the length of the term of future enlistments.[43] Before the council could assemble and give its advice, the General was notified from Philadelphia that a committee of three members of Congress would come immediately to headquarters to confer with him. The reason was the belief of the lawmakers that it was unwise to attempt to pass finally, through correspondence, on issues of such importance as those under review.[44] To the prospective meetings, Washington was directed to invite representatives from the legislatures of the New England Colonies and, second, the Governors of those Colonies that had such officials. This arrangement was acceptable to Washington [45] in both its parts and not the less so, certainly, because of the members chosen for the committee of Congress: Benjamin Franklin, Thomas Lynch of South Carolina, and Washington's friend Benjamin Harrison of Virginia, the Delegate who was supposed to speak in Congress for the Commander-in-Chief.[46] Washington would have been pleased still more had he realized that Congress was seeking resolutely to do its duty by him and the country, even if the attempt to apply the methods of direct democratic action had burdened and, indeed, well nigh had exhausted that body. Its work had increased but its procedure had not

---

[41] Most particularly that of Sept. 21, 1775; 3 *G. W.*, 505 ff.
[42] See his letter of Oct. 5, 1775, to the President of Congress; 4 *G. W.*, 9.
[43] *Ibid.*, 7–8.
[44] See Hancock to Washington, Sept. 30, 1775; 1 *LTW.*, 55, and the answer, Oct. 12, 1775, in 4 *G. W.*, 22.
[45] 4 *G. W.*, 22.   [46] Cf. 1 *Burnett*, 368 n.

improved during the three months after Washington's departure. In the matter of sending a committee to confer with him, for example, the decision to do so was reached through a long argument and by formal vote; then the members who should make the journey were chosen by ballot, after a yes-and-no on increasing the number of committeemen to four because of a tie in the election of the third man to go. At torturing last, still another committee had been selected by ballot, to draft instructions for the designated counsellors.[47]

When the committeemen reached Cambridge, October 15, Washington had ready for them the advice of his council of war on the questions of organization, pay, rations and the like, which had been discussed on the 8th;[48] but in the absence of President of the Congress of New Hampshire, who was delayed by illness in his family, the committee waited until the 18th before it began discussion[49] of subjects that seemed to grow in intricacy and in number with every hour of waiting. The time was not lost. Among the instructions given by Congress to the committee was one, naturally mentioned only in the narrowest circle of senior officers, to this effect: "that [at] the conference with the General, the committee declare to him the sense of the Congress respecting an attack on the ministerial troops at Boston and on Bunkers Hill, viz., that if before the last day of December his Excellency upon consideration of all circumstances shall think it practicable and likely to defeat the enemy and gain possession of the town it will be advisable to make the attack upon the first favorable occasion and before the arrival of reenforcements which the Congress apprehend may be soon expected, the Congress having the most perfect confidence in the courage and good conduct of the General and his officers and the spirit and bravery of the men under his command." It was added that if the troops did not suffice, Washington should be authorized to call in as many minutemen as he thought proper, on such terms as he saw fit; but if he could not attack even with this temporary accession of numbers, the size of the army and the rate of pay should be reduced for the winter. A final sentence in this paragraph of the committee's instructions reiterated the desire of Congress that the attack be made, with the help of the temporary troops, "as soon as a favorable opportunity shall open."[50]

[47] *Richard Smith's Diary*, cited in 1 *Burnett*, 210. Cf. 3 *JCC.*, 265, 266.
[48] 4 *G. W.*, 7–8 n; the original is in 19 *Papers of G. W.*, 14, LC.
[49] 3 *Force* (4) p. 1155.   [50] Instructions of Oct. 4, 1775; 18 *Papers of G. W.*, 114, LC.

Washington read this from the text the committee brought. Although the council had decided as recently as September 11 that the Army should not attempt to storm Boston, he felt that he now should resubmit the question to his senior officers. He consequently called them together on the 18th of October and without going into all the terms of the instructions to the visiting committee, he told his Generals that he had "an intimation from the Congress that an attack upon Boston, if practicable, was much desired." Not one of the eight believed it feasible. Greene thought that an offensive might be successful if 10,000 American soldiers could be landed in Boston, but not otherwise. John Sullivan was of opinion the winter might bring a more favorable opportunity. Charles Lee said he was not sufficiently acquainted with the troops to judge what they could do. As this was in doubt, he thought a general assault involved too great a risk. All the other members of the council of war were content to go on record as saying that the suggested course was impracticable or that the attack would be improper.[51] Washington expressed no opinion.

The committee met with Washington that same day and before it took up matters of administration, it requested the officers of the Connecticut Regiments to ascertain how many of their men were willing to remain in service until the other troops finished their enlistment at the end of December—a necessary first step, of course, in determining what strength would be at Washington's disposal during the last month of the year. At the outset, too, the conference accepted the council's figure of 20,372 as the minimum strength of the new army, and members proceeded to deliberate on what should be done if reenlistments did not reach that total. The decision was to encourage in every way general continuance in service, to look to individual officers to fill their own ranks, and, if all else failed, to summon the militia.[52] Plans to reduce pay and to decrease or change the generous ration were dropped in haste, because they were adjudged certain to defeat the whole plan of reenlistment. At the least, in the dignified, if vague language of the committee's subsequent report, these savings "would be attended with dangerous consequences."

While the conference was deliberating, at length and in a detail to rival the proceedings of the Philadelphia lawmakers, Washington

---

[51] Minutes of the council of war of Oct. 18, 1775; 3 *Force* (4) p. 1153.

[52] *Ibid.*, 1155–58. The organization was to include 18,928 foot soldiers and 1444 riflemen and artillerists.

undertook to carry out the instruction to ascertain how many of the officers and men of the six Connecticut Regiments with a strength of about 3700, rank and file, would remain with the Army after the 1st of December.[53] In his initial order on this subject he specified particularly that regimental commanders report at once which of their officers would leave the army at the end of their current enlistment. With this, was notice that "these brave men and true patriots who are resolved to continue to serve and defend their brethren, privileges and property" were to consider themselves engaged to the end of 1776, unless sooner discharged by Congress.[54]

Optimistic early reports indicated that most of the officers would be willing to remain with the Army through 1776 and many beyond that date; but detailed reports soon led Washington to doubt whether more than one-half, or at maximum, two-thirds of the company officers would promise to stand by the colors to Dec. 31, 1776.[55] Whether the Connecticut private soldiers would agree to remain until the expiration of the enlistment of the Massachusetts and New Hampshire troops on the last day of December, 1775, was a subject of sharp division of opinion. Many officers thought the greater number of the troops would stay with the Army to the year's end if, meantime, the men could go home on furlough, see their families, and get their winter clothing.[56] Unhappy knowledge that even the warmest coats would not protect the men from cold was a special consideration with the committee in urging the utmost speed in ascertaining the sentiment of the soldiers. If the men were doubtful about committing themselves while autumn weather lingered, they almost certainly would insist on leaving, if they could, when December had frozen the fields and sent its paralyzing chill into unfinished barracks.[57]

So much for theorizing; actual polling of the rank and file of the Connecticut Regiments was disheartening. "After breakfast," one Lieutenant of the Eighth wrote in his diary, "we called out the Com-

[53] These figures are of Nov. 18, 1775, *ibid.,* 1611. For the legal basis of the right of the Connecticut troops to leave the service December 1, see *infra,* p. 572, n. 143.

[54] GO Oct. 22, 1775; 4 *G. W.,* 37.　　　[55] *Ibid.,* 55.

[56] Samuel A. Parsons to Washington; Experience Storrs to Washington, both Oct. 23, 1775; 152 *Papers Cont. Congress,* 263, 265, LC; 3 Force (4) p. 1332–33.

[57] See the committee's letter of Oct. 24, 1775 to the President of Congress, 3 *Force* (4) p. 1155. As early as September 24–25, Daniel McCurtin had complained of a "most unaccountable cold, frosty night" and he frequently made entries thereafter of the severity of the cold, but he seems to have been exceptionally sensitive to low temperature. The first ice mentioned in diaries was that of October 14. See *McCurtin's Journal,* loc. cit., 23; *Ezekiel Price's Diary* in *MHSP.,* 1863–64, p. 214.

pany and made a trial to see who would stay in the service till the 1st of January, but not a man would engage." If this was typical of what Washington had to expect,[58] the Army would be dangerously weak in December, after the Connecticut men went home. During that month, moreover, a new force must be created. Continuance of the siege and the very life of the American cause would depend upon reenlistment in December. The least difficult situation that Washington could anticipate, in short, was that of having thirty-one days in which to muster out one army and to replace it with another while in the presence of the enemy.

Would it be possible to reduce that danger by attacking the British if they would not sortie? Twice a council of war had decided against an offensive by the Americans. Was there a possibility as yet uncanvassed? The approach of winter and the talk of ice-covered waters around Boston suggested something that had not previously been mentioned in Washington's reports to Congress, though it almost certainly had been considered: Suppose the harbor of Boston were frozen so tightly that the British warships could not maneuver; suppose sufficient powder and long-range cannon were collected at suitable positions; could the city be bombarded so heavily that the British would be forced to surrender? If this was possible, would it be humane? Should the people of Boston have death that America might have liberty? Many of the first-born of their mothers were in the city: should the plague of fire take them in order that those who came after might be free-born?

These were questions for common counsel. On the last day of the conference, October 24, when Washington had made his final interrogation of the committee on the minor problems of administering the army and of dealing with the Colonies, he reviewed what had been said about attacking Boston. Then, in the formal language of the minutes, "the

---

58 There was too much disposition to base broad judgment on the geographical origin of troops. It scarcely is believable, for example, that truth inhered in the charge, heard on the streets of Philadelphia, that all the Massachusetts Regiments counted in the ranks "great numbers of boys, old men and negroes such as are unsuitable for the service" (John Adams in 1 *Burnett*, 217), though some of the Regiments doubtless were weakened in this wise. Nor was it likely, either, that all the Connecticut troops were as excellent as the levies sent to replace the men who had marched off with Arnold, even though Washington said the newcomers were "a body of as good troops as any we have" (letter of Oct. 12, 1775 to the President of Congress; 4 *G. W.*, 25). Then and thereafter, generalization about the Army was unsafe and inaccurate. Even so charming and discriminating a sketch of the Army as that of Trevelyan, *op. cit.*, v. 2, p. 182 ff, is subject to the criticism that it does not take fully into account the differences between the Regiments of alert and of indolent officers.

General wishes to know how far it may be deemed proper and advisable to avail himself of the season to destroy the troops who propose to winter at Boston by a bombardment when the harbor is blocked up; or, in other words, whether the loss of the town and the property therein are to be so considered as that an attack upon the troops there should be avoided, when it evidently appears that the town must of consequence be destroyed." The committee did not take long to answer: The matter, they said, was of "too much importance to be determined by them," wherefore they would refer it to Congress on their return to Philadelphia.[59]

What the bombardment of a town of wooden houses might involve in loss and suffering, commander and Congressmen learned in sickening detail while they were discussing future operations. On the 5th of October Washington received from an intelligent Boston refugee a report that a considerable squadron, including two transports that could provide quarters for a total of 600 men, was to have sailed from that port on the 4th—a warning that was passed on, as soon as possible, to most of the coastal towns.[60] The squadron was delayed, apparently, but on the 13th it was standing out to sea, NNE. "We presume," said Washington, "it is destined against some town of this province, or New Hampshire, or possibly gone to Quebec."[61]

After the last sail faded into the darkness, nothing more was heard of the squadron until the 24th of October, when the three members of Congress were catching up the last loose ends of their instructions.[62] That day, a man came to Washington's headquarters, introduced himself as Pearson Jones, and told a dark story. On the 16th, four British vessels had appeared off Falmouth[63] under the command of Capt. Henry Mowat, of the *Canceau*. After much bluster, warning, futile negotiation and demand for cannon and hostages, Mowat's ships opened fire on the 18th. As the residents had taken heed and had left their homes, none of them was killed by the bombardment, but the town was set afire and the greater part of the prosperous place destroyed —139 dwellings and 278 other structures. Captain Mowat was alleged to have said that he had orders to burn all the seacoast towns between Boston and Halifax. He would return to his base to replenish ammunition; then he would give Portsmouth, New Hampshire, the treatment he

[59] Minutes in 3 *Force* (4) p. 1163.   [60] 4 *G. W.*, 16.
[61] *Ibid.*, 28–29.
[62] Washington mentioned their presence in Cambridge that day (*ibid.*, 41). They left late on the 25th or, more probably, on the 26th (See *Samuel Cooper's Diary*, in 6 *A. H. R.*, 323).
[63] Falmouth is directly North of the present Portland, Maine, on the west shore of Casco Bay.

had administered to Falmouth. Pearson Jones reported most of this, while the people of Portsmouth added some hearsay details and asked Washington to send them powder. Of their own they had seventeen barrels only.[64] To supplement this, Washington could do little, but he sent Gen. John Sullivan to the New Hampshire port and he broke his rule against detachment of force to the extent of ordering a small number of riflemen to attend the General.[65] The enemy did not visit Portsmouth, as Captain Mowat had threatened; but the lesson of Falmouth could be applied in Boston. With proper artillery, mounted near the town, Boston could be destroyed if that was the only way of driving the enemy out—a different plan, most certainly, from Washington's expectation in July that his prime duty would be to confine the enemy to Boston.

The week of the committee's conferences and of the receipt of the unhappy news from Falmouth was part of a brief period of uncertainty, excitement and expectancy. In the camps, the hammer was heard more frequently than the cannon; Washington's concern was not over what the enemy might do but over what the Connecticut troops and later the whole army might *not* do in reenlistment. Then, daily, hopeful impatience mounted for news of Arnold. About the 4th of October,[66] Washington had received a letter written on the 25th of September by Arnold, who announced that he reached the Kennebec River promptly, September 20, but that he had found some of the batteaux so poorly constructed he had felt it necessary to build others. While this had delayed his general advance, he had sent forward two reconnaissance parties on the 24th and was following with two other "divisions." Col. Roger Enos was to bring up the rear.[67]

After that report, Washington received none from Arnold for days and days. The General grew anxious but he comforted himself with the recollection of one most explicit order he had given Arnold: If anything went amiss, Arnold was to notify him by express.[68] For a time, Washington was equally apprehensive of delay in Schuyler's expedition against Montreal, because the New York commander continued

[64] 1 *Gordon* (ed. of 1801), p. 411; H. Wentworth, Chairman, to Washington, Oct. 19, 1775; 3 *Force* (4) p. 1152–53. Cf. *ibid.*, 1172, 1552. Captain Mowat's letter to the people of Falmouth, Oct. 16, 1775 is in *ibid.*, 1154.

[65] Sullivan to Washington, Oct. 29, 1775; 1 *LTW.*, 70–71. Cf. Washington to the Committee of Falmouth, Oct. 24, 1775; 4 *G. W.*, 41–42.

[66] See 4 *G. W.*, 2–3, for a letter of Oct. 4, 1775, to Daniel Morgan, manifestly written after Washington received the communication about to be mentioned in the text.

[67] 1 *LTW.*, 47.   [68] 3 *G. W.*, 495.

to report obstacles that were vexatious and, in some instances, manifestly dangerous. Gen. Richard Montgomery was pushing toward St. John's [69] and Fort Chambly, above the northern end of Lake Champlain, but, said Schuyler, he himself was beset by many difficulties. "If Job had been a General in my situation," Schuyler protested, "his memory had not been so famous for patience." [70]

During the first week of November, the outlook changed. Schuyler reported that Montgomery had captured Chambly on the 20th of October, with its garrison of eighty men, 124 barrels of gunpowder and 125 stand of British arms.[71] Within three or four days,[72] Washington received a dispatch that Arnold had written on the 13th of October at the second portage from the Kennebec to Dead River.[73] With the dispatch was a terse journal that cheerfully told a tale of toil.[74] Arnold expressed the hope that the worst of his difficulties were behind and that he would reach the Claudière River within eight or ten days. He had on hand, said Arnold, provisions to last his 950 effectives for approximately twenty-five days. Washington was immensely relieved. On the 8th of November he wrote of Arnold: "I think he is in Quebec. If I hear nothing more of him in five days, I shall be sure of it." [75] Five days of silence followed, but on the sixth day good tidings from Schuyler arrived: St. John's on the Richelieu River had fallen to the Americans. On the 2nd of November, Montgomery had forced its formal capitulation after a soldierly advance and investment.[76] So fine an achievement presaged, of course, the isolation and almost certain fall of Montreal, and it led Washington further than ever he had gone in using his general orders for religious exhortation. "The Commander-in-Chief is con-

[69] On some early maps and in official correspondence the name was Fort St. John, but the Americans nearly always spoke of it as St. John's.

[70] Letter of Sept. 26, 1775, to Washington; 1 *LTW.*, 54.

[71] See Schuyler to Washington, Oct. 26, 1775; 1 *LTW.*, 68–69. All the details will be found in *Justin Smith, Struggle*, v. 1, p. 424 ff. For the receipt of this news, November 4, see Boardman's Diary, *MHSP.*, 1892, p. 412. Cf. 4 *G. W.*, 65

[72] Certainly by November 8 and probably before that time. See 4 *G. W.*, 74.

[73] See *Atlas of American History*, Plate 67.

[74] The dispatch is in 3 *Force* (4) p. 1057–58 and in 1 *LTW.*, 60; for the Journal, see 3 *Force* (4) p. 1058–62.

[75] 4 *G. W.*, 77; cf. *ibid.*, 74.

[76] See 3 *Force* (4) p. 1392 ff. Charles Carroll was told later that St. John's could not have been captured without the powder taken at Chambly (Kate Mason Rowland, *Life and Correspondence of Charles Carroll of Carrollton*, cited hereafter as *Rowland, Carroll*, v. 1, p. 394). In this connection, the eager interest of Congress in the outcome of the operations of 1775 against Canada is worth pursuing through *Burnett, Ballagh, Lee Letters*, and similar collections. While it is part of the history of the Revolution, rather than of a biography of Washington, this determination to win Canada evidenced impressively the clear understanding the congressional leaders already had of the geographical unity of America.

fident," he said on the day of the news of the capture, "the Army . . . will show their gratitude to providence, for thus favoring the cause of freedom and America; and by their thankfulness to God, their zeal and perseverance in this righteous cause, continue to deserve his future blessings." [77] In worldly terms, Montgomery had done his part well and had vindicated both the good opinion of his friends and the fine patriotism he had shown in his letters.[78] If Arnold matched him, Quebec as well as Montreal would be wrested from Britain.[79] When those towns fell, the remainder of Canada must. The ministerial forces would have no northern base from which to descend the Hudson in an effort to separate the Middle Colonies from New England.

Five days more and then, on the 19th, more news, incredible news: There arrived from Arnold another dispatch, dated at Claudière Pool, not at Quebec, and forwarded by Lt. Col. Roger Enos, commander of the rear "division" of Arnold's little force. The heading and opening words of Colonel Enos's own explanatory letter were enough to make the eyes bulge and the blood run to the face:

"Brunswick, near Kennebeck, November 9, 1775
"Sir: I am on my return from Colonel Arnold's detachment . . ."

"On a return from Arnold's detachment," a *"return"*! Washington read on:

"I brought up the rear of the whole; Captains McCobb's, Williams's and Scott's Companies were assigned to my division. We proceeded as far as fifty miles up the Dead River, and then were compelled to return, for want of provisions . . ."

Enos went on to relate how, as he had advanced, Arnold had sent back for provisions with which to feed the men in front. In response, Enos had forwarded what he could and then had decided that he should turn back with his three Companies because, if he went on, the provi-

77 GO of Nov. 14, 1775; 4 *G. W.,* 87. The date of this order fixes that of the receipt of the news that St. John's had been occupied.

78 See Montgomery to Robert Livingston, June 7, Oct. 5, Oct. n.d., 1775, *Livingston Papers,* 35, 51, 57; NYPL. Although Montgomery's surviving letters are comparatively few in number, they always are interesting and sometimes are admirable.

79 Montgomery thought the operation against Montreal should be conducted by Charles Lee, with the assistance of Arnold who, said Montgomery, "is very active, intelligent and enterprising." Letter of Dec. 17 to Robert Livingston; *Livingston Papers,* 97; NYPL.

sions of all would give out before supplies could be had from the French settlements on the Claudière.[80] Retreat seemed desertion of Arnold, an act so dastardly that Washington could not get himself in a state of mind to consider fairly whether Enos's action could have been justified. Arnold's letter, forwarded by Enos, appeared to make the withdrawal all the more infamous. From Claudière Pool, Arnold wrote to say he had been so much impeded by heavy rains that he had just arrived with seventy men. Provisions were short; Colonel Enos and Colonel Greene [81] had been directed to bring forward no more men than they could supply with fifteen days' rations. The undertone of Arnold's report was cheerful and as resolute as ever. Although the route was far worse than he had been told to expect, he would press on and would get provisions. Indications pointed to a welcome by the French in Canada; reports were that few troops, if any, were stationed at Quebec.[82]

Surely a man who wrote in the spirit displayed by Arnold should have the support of the last musket on the rivers and on the portages, even if the rearguard had to march and to fight on an empty stomach. So Washington reasoned from Arnold's letter and from that of Enos. Officially he told Congress: "I can form no judgment on [Colonel Enos's] conduct till I see him . . ."; [83] privately he wrote Joseph Reed in sarcastic wrath that Arnold's "rear division under the command of the *noble* Colonel Enos, had, without his privity or consent, left him with three Companies . . ." [84] Washington assumed that when Arnold's advance became known, General Carleton could be expected, of course, to bring together at Quebec the remnants of the British forces that survived the fall of Chambly and of St. John's and the expected occupation of Montreal by Montgomery. The task of Arnold now would be much more difficult than it would have been if, with Enos's men in support, he had reached the vicinity of Quebec a fortnight earlier. In spite of this ill fortune, Washington did not despair of the success of the resolute man who had ascended the Kennebec.[85]

Anxiety over Arnold's plight was deepened, of course, by hourly concern over reenlistments and barrack-construction. Another and serious problem was that of the reassignment of officers who would

---

[80] 3 *Force* (4) p. 1610.
[81] This was Lt. Col. Christopher Greene who had been given command of Thayer's and Topham's Rhode Island Companies and of Hubbard's Massachusetts Company. (1 *Justin Smith, Struggle*, 531).
[82] 3 *Force* (4) p. 1609-10. [83] Letter of Nov. 19, 1775; 4 *G. W.*, 100.
[84] Letter of Nov. 20, 1775; *ibid.*, 106. [85] *Ibid.*, 100-01, 106.

be left without commands when the Connecticut Regiments disbanded. Procurement of powder and artillery for offensive operations against Boston had to be taken in hand at once. There was a prospect of getting some cannon from New York and still more from Ticonderoga.[86] A further opportunity of capturing British ordnance supplies was suggested in great haste and secrecy through a dispatch from Philadelphia and was embraced instantly.[87] Still again, in the hope that cannon and explosive would be found for blasting the British out of their redoubts in Boston, Washington decided to extend his earthworks beyond the point reached on the night of Saturday, Aug. 26, 1775, when American troops on the left had occupied Plowed Hill, more than halfway to Bunker Hill from the high, dominating ground of Winter Hill.[88] As far as the Commander-in-Chief could foresee, he would not have to pay too high a price for Cobble Hill, an excellent position three-quarters of a mile South of Plowed Hill and slightly less than that Southwest of Bunker Hill.[89] The three positions were a triangle with the apex to the East, a circumstance that some day might make it possible to direct a converging fire on Bunker Hill. If Cobble Hill was to be taken, it had to be at once, because the ground was freezing fast and deep and, as Washington said, was "getting as hard as a rock."[90] Whether the British would be content to let the Americans hold this ground must be ascertained by the new move. Howe might conclude that a stop had to be put, by decisive counter-action, to the gradual shortening of the range. It seemed much like trying to tighten a noose around the neck of the enemy, but the experience at Plowed Hill was duplicated incredibly. Under Washington's own eye, high parapets were thrown up on the night of November 22–23 and, to the amazement of the Americans, were undisturbed by the British for days. Washington wrote on the 28th: "We have worked on ever since, without receiving a single shot from Bunkers Hill, the ship or floating batteries. What all this means we know not unless some capital strike is meditating."[91]

Thus many, many things seemed to be shaping to a climax, when, as an unpleasant incident and not as a part of the larger design, Col. Roger

---

86 See *infra*, p. 584.   87 *Infra*, p. 566.   88 See *supra*, Chap. XXI.
89 As noted, *supra*, p. 480, all that is left now of Cobble Hill is in the yards of the Boston & Maine Railroad between East Somerville and East Cambridge.
90 Letter of Nov. 27, 1775, to Richard Henry Lee; 4 *G. W.*, 116.
91 4 *G. W.*, 118; cf. *ibid.*, 116, 121, and, for the completion of the fort on or about Dec. 11, 1775, see *J. Baldwin's Journal*. A brush with *Scarborough* occurred Dec. 18, 1775; *Barker's Diary*, 69.

Enos returned to Cambridge with his three Companies.[92] Washington put him under arrest at once [93] and ordered a court of inquiry under the presidency of Charles Lee, to sit on the 28th.[94] This procedure rather than that of formal courtmartial was adopted because it seemed wise not to exhaust the possibility of penalties until Arnold's account of the withdrawal of Enos was received.[95] During the evening of the day on which the order for the court of inquiry was issued, November 27, an express from General Montgomery brought the joyous tidings of the unopposed occupation of Montreal on the morning of the 13th.[96] General Carleton got away with his troops and his powder, but when Montgomery wrote, at Montreal, he was hopeful he could capture the explosive.[97] Almost as important was a paragraph that began: "By intercepted letters, I find Colonel Arnold is certainly arrived in the neighborhood of Quebec; that the King's friends are exceedingly alarmed, and expect to be besieged, which, with the blessing of God, they shall be, if the severe season holds off, and I can prevail on the troops to accompany me." [98] That was as much as Washington could ask and it somewhat relieved his mind, because it held out the promise of joint operations by Montgomery and Arnold against Quebec, but it did not remove anxiety for Arnold, who might not be as close to the fortress of the St. Lawrence as the captured papers indicated. At that opportune hour, he might be crippled by the absence of Enos. "Poor Arnold," Washington wrote in a letter to Joseph Reed, "I wonder where he is." [99]

If, on the whole, the developments in Canada were favorable on the day Enos was cited to appear before a court of inquiry, there was fine news from the sea, also. The letter that Washington had received from Philadelphia in some haste during the second week of October [100] informed him that friends in London had written of the departure from England, August 11, of "two north country built brigs of no force," laden with arms, powder and other stores for Quebec. These vessels were said to be proceeding without convoy. Washington must under-

---

[92] He arrived about November 23 and certainly before November 25. See 4 *G. W.*, 113 and 3 *Force* (4) p. 1701.

[93] 4 *G. W.*, 120–21.   [94] *Ibid.*, 119.   [95] *Ibid.*, 126.

[96] 4 *G. W.*, 119. In a letter of the 28th to Joseph Reed, the General wrote: "I have this instant by express received the agreeable news of the capitulation of Montreal" (*ibid.*, 126), but if there was an express directly from Montgomery or a report by that officer to Washington, it has not been found. Indications are that the dispatch was Schuyler to Washington, Nov. 18, 1775, with the enclosure, Montgomery to Schuyler, Nov. 13, 1775 (3 *Force* (4) p. 1602).

[97] *Ibid.*   [98] *Ibid.*, 1602–03.   [99] 4 *G. W.*, 126.

[100] It may have been October 11 and certainly was by October 12. See 3 *Force* (4) p. 1037–38.

take to have Massachusetts, Connecticut and Rhode Island send out armed craft and capture, if possible, the immensely valuable prizes.[101] These instructions had reached Washington at a time when he was working through the Mustermaster General of the Army, Stephen Moylan,[102] to send light ships to sea to prey on British shipping.[103] Rhode Island could do nothing to help in the special enterprise Congress enjoined on Washington;[104] there scarcely was time to communicate with Connecticut. Washington accordingly had concentrated on dispatching ships from Massachusetts ports.[105] Many delays and much of irritating human slothfulness had been encountered,[106] but two vessels had left port October 21,[107] and the armed schooner *Lee,* Capt. John Manley, had sailed from Plymouth, November 4,[108] at a time when conflicting reports were in circulation concerning the cargoes of the supply ships en route to America.[109] Manley had the initiative and the good fortune to recapture a schooner, laden with wood, that a British prize crew was carrying into Boston.[110] Now, November 27, Washington received intelligence that the diligent Captain had brought to Cape Anne an infinitely richer prize, the large brig *Nancy* which was believed to be one of the two vessels of which word had been sent privately from England. It developed that Manley had sighted both the brigs but had not been able to overtake the leading one, which was believed to have aboard her all the ordnance of the troops intended for service in Canada.[111] The harbor of Cape Anne was open;[112] as *Nancy* had been boarded within sight of her consort, the British in Boston would learn of her fate, might ascertain quickly where she was, and might send their men of war to Cape Anne and recover her. That must be prevented.

---

101 1 *LTW.,* 56; 3 *JCC.,* 278. Information regarding these British brigs may have come from Arthur Lee. The report of the committee of Congress, recommending the effort to capture the ordnance ships, is a major document in the history of the beginnings of the American Navy. See 1 *Burnett,* 216–17 n with informative quotations from John Adams and others.

102 Appointed Aug. 11, 1775; 3 *G. W.,* 414.

103 See 3 *Force* (4) p. 946, 948, 994 and *supra,* p. 529–30.

104 1 *LTW.,* 58.   105 4 *G. W.,* 29, 32–33.

106 *Ibid.,* and 3 *Force* (4) p. 1068, 1075, 1084, 1109, 1126.

107 3 *Force* (4) p. 1134.   108 *Ibid.,* 1209, 1378.

109 *Ibid.,* 1182; *AASP,* Oct. 1926, p. 277; E. *Clarke's Diary,* 28. As of Nov. 14, 1775; Lt. John Barker recorded a rumor in Boston that Captain Parker of the *Phoenix* had sailed away and had left a convoy of thirteen vessels in clear weather, near the coast. The master of one of these vessels, laden with "mortars, guns, shot, shells and 400 barrels of powder," was alleged to have taken her into Marblehead, where he surrendered to the Americans (*Barker's Diary,* 67; *Letters of Capt. W. G. Evelyn,* 72–73).

110 3 *Force* (4) p. 1532.

111 Washington was not explicit in his antecedent of "their whole ordnance" (4 *G. W.,* 130), but his reference is assumed to be to the Canadian expedition.

112 *Ibid.,* 132.

Almost before the handshaking over the good news was ended, Washington ordered four Companies to Cape Anne, gave authority for the impressment of teams to haul away the stores, and directed the minutemen of the adjoining country to assemble and to assist in removing the cargo to a place of safety.[113] As the men went about this hurried task, every lift from the hold of *Nancy* seemed to bring a military treasure into daylight. When he saw her papers, Horatio Gates exclaimed that he could not have made out a better invoice if he had tried.[114] Although she carried no powder, she yielded 2000 stand of small arms, many flints, tons of musket shot, and a trophy of special esteem and utility, a fine brass mortar, with a maw of thirteen inches and a weight in excess of 2700 pounds.[115]

When, ere long, this giant was brought to Cambridge, General Putnam was to christen it with a bottle of rum, and Colonel Mifflin was to name it "Congress;"[116] but before that festive celebration, many things happened. First among them was the assembly of the court of inquiry in Enos's case. Contrary to Washington's expectation, by no means all the testimony was adverse. There was doubt, in fact, whether Enos had not helped Arnold by sending forward all the supplies he could spare, instead of marching ahead to add more mouths to those that already were exhausting Arnold's provisions. The court doubtless wished, as Washington did, to have Arnold's report in hand before taking final action, but Colonel Enos's commission was about to expire, and the right of a court to try him after he left the Army was in some doubt. If anything further was to be undertaken, it had to be done at once, even if the opinion of Arnold on the conduct of Enos could not be made a part of the record.[117] The court of inquiry was somewhat reluctant to recommend action in the light of the evidence, but it concluded that a formal trial was necessary "for the satisfaction of the world," as it said, and for Colonel Enos's "own honor."[118] Washington accordingly ordered a courtmartial with John Sullivan as President.[119]

Whatever the verdict in this case, Washington's regimental subordinates now presented him with a perplexity of a new sort. Because some of the Regiments were small, they had more officers than they required.

---

[113] 4 *G. W.*, 130.

[114] Letter of Capt. John Chester, Dec. 3, 1775; 8 *Mag. Am. His.*, pt. 1, p. 126.

[115] 4 *G. W.*, 149; *McCurtin's Journal*, 29.

[116] Stephen Moylan, in *Military Journal of Two Private Soldiers*, 83, quoted in *Bolton*, 164, in *Frothingham's Siege*, 270, and in numerous other works.

[117] 4 *G. W.*, 157.   [118] 3 *Force* (4) p. 1709.   [119] 4 *G. W.*, 131.

On the reorganization of the Army after the reenlistment, there would be twenty-seven Regiments only and an increase in supernumerary officers.[120] How were the best officers to be retained and the feeblest dismissed? Washington had raised that question at the council of war on the 8th of October, only to be told by his Generals that it was a "very difficult and delicate" matter, for the consideration of which they wished more time. Horatio Gates favored the direct choice of the best surplus officers and the dismissal of the others: Nathanael Greene urged that the selection be based on the recommendation of officers familiar with their subordinates; John Sullivan thought the question would answer itself, because the good officers, in the main, would be willing to stay.[121] Five meetings were held afterward to combat colonial prejudice with the weapon of common interest, but, Washington found, as he put it: "Connecticut wants no Massachusetts man in their corps; Massachusetts thinks there is no necessity [122] to be introduced amongst them; and New Hampshire says it's very hard that her valuable and experienced officers (who are willing to serve) should be discarded because her own Regiments, under the new establishment, cannot provide for them." [123] In the same spirit Washington wrote the President of Congress: "I . . . find so many doubts and difficulties to reconcile I cannot say when they are to end, or what may be the consequences . . ." [124] A little later his disgusted, if restrained exclamation was, "The trouble in the arrangement of the Army is really inconceivable." [125]

Some of his subordinates did their best to help him. One of them prepared carefully for the Adjutant General a score sheet on which the ideal rating of a Brigadier General was put at 4000, that of a Colonel at 1000, and so at lesser figures down the list of field officers. Equal value

120 The estimate of twenty-seven Regiments of Foot and of one artillery Regiment will be found in 4 G. W., 183. Prior to that time, the inclusion of militia in returns of the Army gave a number of Regiments that fluctuated from month to month. When the Army was brigaded, July 22, 1775, it consisted of thirty-one Regiments of Foot, with the Independent Companies counted as a Brigade (3 G. W., 354–56); but on July 31, 1775, there were under Washington twenty-six Massachusetts Regiments and four Independent Companies, three Connecticut Regiments, three from New Hampshire and three from Rhode Island, a total of thirty-five (3 Force (4) p. 30). At the year's end, the roster included, with the militia, a total of thirty-nine Regiments (ibid., p. 491). For part of December, the number of Regiments was thirty-four (4 G. W., 183). These later figures do not include the Regiment of Artillery. Speaking generally, if the precise number of Regiments is of importance in any study of Washington's Army at this period, it is well to consult the full returns of the nearest appropriate date.

121 3 Force (4) p. 1040–44.

122 At this point Fitzpatrick interpolated "[for a Rhode Islander]" and observed that both Sparks and Ford had introduced the same words without bracket. The original letter in 1 Reed, 126, contains neither the bracket nor the quoted words.

123 Letter of Nov. 8, 1775; 4 G. W., 77.   124 Ibid., 73.

125 Letter of Nov. 11, 1775, to the President of Congress; ibid., 82.

was assigned courage, "government," military discipline and "common honesty." John Thomas was given 3000 of 4000 points, but Heath no more than 1000 at a like "standard." Colonels, with an attainable maximum of 1000, in no instance were put above 750, though a few men of lower rank were rated at maximum.[126] Washington doubtless made the most of all information he received and he sought to identify and retain competent leaders, but at a council meeting on the 2nd of November he told his Generals that they were much better acquainted with the character and merits of the field and company officers than he was, and that he wished their help in selecting those who were to be nominated to head the twenty-seven Regiments of the new Army.[127] After that, laboriously and slowly, the nominees were chosen and were assigned, thanks in part to permission to Washington from Congress to issue temporary "warrants" in lieu of commissions, for officers he desired to retain.[128] There was no assurance, even then, that these officers would be acceptable to the men in the ranks.

If private soldiers reenlisted at all, they did so reluctantly. As of November 19, the number who had agreed in eleven Regiments to stay with the colors was 966.[129] Adverse weather retarded the construction of barracks. Because quarters were unfinished and firewood was scarce,[130] most of the soldiers were cold and miserable and consequently more convinced than ever that other men should take their place and that they should be permitted to go home and look after their families. Gloomy skies turned black. From the 16th of November onward for a week, the elements seemed to be enleagued against the Americans— high northwest winds, hard frost, snow on the 21st, and not even a wintry smile of the heavens until the 26th. There scarcely could have been more adverse conditions under which to plead with the men in the ranks to reenlist.[131]

Washington thus far had endured without flinching all the venality, all the incompetence and all the ignorance of war with which he had been confronted, but he had to face the prospect that if the long-desired British attack was delivered, it might be at the most unwelcome time

126 19 *Papers of G. W.*, 130, LC.
127 20 *Papers of G. W.*, 41, LC. Cf. Gates to unnamed correspondent, Dec. 3, 1775; *Ford MSS*, NYPL.
128 20 *Papers of G. W.*, 65, LC.   129 4 *G. W.*, 101.
130 *Ibid.*
131 See *Carter, Letters to a Friend*, 16; *McCurtin's Journal*, 28; *Barker's Diary*, 68; *E. Clarke's Journal*, 27.

conceivable, the freezing days when the Connecticut troops would be marching home. In writing Joseph Reed of this and of some skirmishing around Lechmere Point [132] he had explained that "a scoundrel from Marblehead, a man of property," had gone to Howe, had told of the reluctance of continentals to reenlist and had assured the British commander that the ministerial forces easily might make themselves master of the American lines. As best Washington could, he undertook to counter. In the hope of alarming the British as well as of improving his position he began a bomb battery at Lechmere Point on the night of the 29th–30th. [133] He could not tell whether this activity would serve its immediate purpose in deterring the British at a time when the expected departure of the Connecticut troops would weaken him dangerously, but he confided to Joseph Reed that every officer in the army expected an attack by the enemy. [134] What more perfect time for it could there be? As Washington saw the cunning of the place hunters and sensed the acuteness of a danger the slothful disregarded, he had to struggle with himself to keep his patience and his faith. In another letter to Reed he broke out: "Such a dearth of public spirit, and want of virtue, such stock-jobbing and fertility in all the low arts to obtain advantages of one kind or another in this great change of the military arrangement, I never saw before, and pray God I may never be witness to again. What will be the ultimate end of these maneuvers is beyond my scan. I tremble at the prospect. We have been till this time enlisting about three thousand, five hundred men. To engage these I have been obliged to allow furloughs as far as fifty men a Regiment, and

[132] On the 9th of November, nine Companies of light Infantry and 100 grenadiers landed at Lechmere Point, now East Cambridge, which, at high tide, was an island (*Barker's Diary*, 66). The aim of this party probably was to do no more than to seize some cows that were kept there (4 *G. W.*, 84; 1 *Moore*, 166), but as the American commanders were ignorant of the limited scope of the operations, orders were issued immediately for Col. William Thompson to use his Regiment of Riflemen and for Col. Benjamin Woodbridge to take part of his and part of Col. John Patterson's, and to drive the enemy off (4 *G. W.*, 84). Most of these men made so steady an advance (cf. *ibid.*, 79) even though they had to wade through two feet of icy water, that the British, having taken ten cows, withdrew promptly. Their naval support, consisting of a light ship and a floating battery, covered the operation, as did a battery at Charlestown Neck. The answering fire of the American artillery (4 *G. W.*, 84) seemed to their adversaries to be exceedingly slow in service (*Barker's Diary*, 66–67; *Heath*, 38). Washington congratulated the participants (GO of Nov. 10, 1775; 4 *G. W.*, 79), but he felt later that the "coloring" of the affair had been "rather too high," because the high tide necessitated a circuitous route and held the musketry at such a distance that few of the men were actually in danger (*ibid.*, 130–31). Two Americans only were wounded and those by grapeshot from the man of war (*ibid.*, 84; *Letters of Capt. W. G. Evelyn*, 74–75).

[133] 4 *G. W.*, 131. According to his *Journal*, Jeduthan Baldwin did not stake out the fort there until December 16. For its completion in February, 1776, see Vol. IV.

[134] 4 *G. W.*, 131. Cf. Eben. Huntington to Jabez Huntington, Nov. 22, 1775; *Eben. Huntington Letters*, 25.

the officers, I am persuaded, indulge as many more. The Connecticut troops will not be prevailed upon to stay longer than their term (saving those who have enlisted for the next campaign and mostly on furlough), and such a dirty, mercenary spirit pervades the whole that I should not be at all surprised at any disaster that may happen. In short, after the last of this month our lines will be so weakened that the minutemen and militia must be called in for their defence . . ."

Without the pause of a paragraph, or anything more than a semi-colon, he rushed angrily on: ". . . these [men], being under no kind of government themselves, will destroy the little subordination I have been laboring to establish, and run me into one evil whilst I am endeavoring to avoid another; but the lesser evil must be chosen. Could I have foreseen what I have, and am likely to experience, no consideration upon earth should have induced me to accept this command. A Regiment or any subordinate department would be accompanied with ten times the satisfaction, and perhaps the honor." [135]

That was the spirit and that almost the phrasing of 1756, even to the word "honor." He now was as resolute, if as resentful, as he had been almost two decades previously, but once again when he saw others of that same state of mind, he rallied himself and them. In a few days he was to be telling the discouraged Philip Schuyler: "I have met with difficulties of the same sort, and such as I never expected; but they must be borne with. The cause we are engaged in is so just and righteous that we must try to rise superior to every obstacle in its support." [136]

On the 29th of November, Washington's information was that at least 1500 men were absent on furlough as a reward for reenlistment and that the force with which he had been defending his lines thus was reduced by almost 12 per cent.[137] The report was, also, that the Connecticut troops absolutely could not be induced to continue in service beyond the 1st of the month. Something had to be done; the situation was critical; delay was dangerous. He summoned a council of war for the next morning and he hurried off a messenger to Watertown with a request that the General Court send one or two of its members to join with his senior officers in advising what he should do in the emergency.[138]

[135] Letter of Nov. 28, 1775; 4 G. W., 124–25.
[136] Letter of Dec. 5, 1775; ibid., 148.
[137] 4 G. W., 128. The number present for duty, fit, Nov. 18, 1775, had been 12,741. See 3 Force (4) p. 1611.
[138] 4 G. W., 128–29; R. H. Harrison to Artemas Ward, Nov. 29, 1775; Artemas Ward Papers, 49, MHS.

At the council, the grim-faced seniors could give no encouragement: the Connecticut troops stood fast in their resolution; pleas and argument alike were vain; patriotism no longer stirred them.[139] They must be replaced at continental expense with minutemen from other Colonies until Jan. 15, 1776, by which date the new army would be organized or the American cause hopeless. Massachusetts must be asked for 3000. As John Sullivan reported that New Hampshire had many men ready to move on short notice,[140] he was asked to find 2000 minutemen and militia and to have them on the lines within ten days. Being optimistic and self confident as well as ambitious, Sullivan responded as if he believed it could be done.[141] The Massachusetts representatives doubtless gave assurance that they would do their utmost, though there were suggestions that it might be necessary to assign quotas to the townships.[142]

Even if the men from the Bay Colony and from New Hampshire could be brought to the lines within ten days—and Washington's own unhappy experience in Virginia made him doubt it—the absence of the troops on furlough and the departure of the Connecticut Regiments would weaken the defence critically, perhaps hopelessly, for a week and more. Something *must* be done to keep the Connecticut soldiers at their posts till the minutemen arrived. To this end, it probably was argued that the different Connecticut Regiments had been enlisted for five months to seven months and that they were not entitled to leave until the expiration of the full number of months from the time the men actually had entered the service of their Colony. This would make the latest defensible date of muster-out December 10, for most of them, though officers of two Regiments were free to leave December 6. Private soldiers must be so notified and must be required to remain at their posts till the 10th.[143]

---

139 Cf. *Thacher*, 34: "The spirit of patriotism appears in some degree to have subsided . . ."
140 4 *G. W.*, 143.
141 See *ibid.*, 137, and John Sullivan to John Adams, Dec. 21, 1775, in 1 *Sullivan Papers*, 151–52.   142 4 *G. W.*, 142–43.
143 Sullivan to New Hampshire Comm. of Safety, Nov. 30, Dec. 2, 1775; 1 *Sullivan Papers*, 129–33, 134–35; 4 *G. W.*, 137. The law passed at the session of the Connecticut General Assembly in April, 1775, as printed in 2 *Force* (4) p. 411, provided for the enlistment of six Regiments to serve for not more than seven months. A supplementary act of July, 1775, (*ibid.*, 1580–81), added two Regiments, "to serve during the pleasure of this Assembly, not exceeding five months." Officers' commissions of these two Regiments were to "bear date the sixth day of July instant" (*ibid.*, 1582). In commenting to Washington on the behavior of the Connecticut soldiers, Governor Trumbull explained, Dec. 7, 1775: ". . . the treatment they met, and the order and request made to them was so reasonable, and apparently necessary for the defence of our common cause and safety of our rights and privileges for which they freely engaged; the term they voluntarily enlisted to serve not expired, and probably would not end before the time when they would be relieved, provided their circumstances and inclination forbid their undertaking further" (4 *Force* (4) p. 213).

Again, then, on the 1st of December, the Connecticut Companies were addressed by their officers [144] and were asked to keep their faces toward the enemy until other soldiers took their places. The report was the same: Unless they were given extra pay, most of the men resolved to go home, regardless of what happened. When some actually started, that was more than Washington could or would endure. He sent after the men,[145] precisely as he had pursued deserters in Virginia during the seventeen-fifties; he apprehended most of them,[146] brought them back, and sternly warned them not to leave until December 10 and not then until they received their formal, written discharges.[147] At the same time, he put all the troops on the alert and he undertook to make the camps as secure as possible.

These arrangements rendered it reasonably certain the men would not leave their stations without passes, and made it less likely, too, that a British attack would be successful; but, of course, in the see-saw of Washington's mind between hope and dismay, offensive and defensive, the certain loss of the Connecticut Regiments within ten days put an attack on the British so far beyond the reach of immediate practicality that Washington scarcely need spend thought on it.[148] All the while, too, he had in candor to tell himself there was no reason for expecting the troops from the other Colonies to do any better, when their enlistment ended, than the Connecticut soldiers had done. He could not believe that voluntary enlistment would bring the Army to the accepted maximum—18,928 "battalion men" and 1444 riflemen and artillerists, a total of 20,372.[149] Some of his subordinates, on the other hand, found in the behavior of the Connecticut men an argument they thought they might use effectively in arousing a fighting spirit among their own people. John Sullivan fairly shouted in writing to the New Hampshire Committee of Safety: "[The Connecticut troops] have deceived us and their officers by pretending there would be no difficulty with them till they have got so near the close of their term and now to their eternal infamy demand a bounty to induce them to tarry only three weeks. This is such an insult to every American that we are determined to release them at the expiration of their term at all hazards and find our-

144 Ezekiel Price quoted, though he had not authenticated, a report that Washington himself pleaded with the men and prevailed on some of them to remain (*MHSP*, 1863–64, p. 217).
145 Cf. 4 *G. W.*, 137.
146 Eighty still were missing on December 4. See 4 *G. W.*, 142.
147 4 *G. W.*, 137, 138.   148 4 *G. W.*, 135–36, 316.
149 These figures are written in the margin of the copy of the council minutes of Oct., 8, 1775, in 19 *Papers of G. W.*, 14, LC.

selves obliged immediately to supply their place with troops from New Hampshire and Massachusetts Bay."[150] Again he roared: ". . . We can have no hope of [the] tarrying [of the Connecticut men] after the 6th—half General Putnam's Regiment is now under guard—the people who have escaped from Boston inform us that the enemy are fully acquainted with our situation and will probably take advantage of it. For Heaven's sake dispatch your forces as soon as possible . . ."[151]

Appeals of this sort, seconding Washington's own, might succeed. It was impossible to say more than that where three contingencies pulled one against another—the continued refusal of the Connecticut troops to remain beyond the 10th and to that date under compulsion only, the success of Massachusetts and New Hampshire in getting their minutemen to Cambridge by that time, and the decision of Howe to attack or to remain quiescent. There were, in short, a y and a z, as well as an x in the equation. After the departing Connecticut troops were brought back, they did their duty for several days without complaint. No mutiny swept the camps; the sentinels on Bunker Hill gave not one indication of uneasiness or of any preparation for an assault; the 3rd passed without alarm, a movement of troops to Charlestown on the 4th amounted to nothing.[152] The 5th was quiet. Routine was restored in the Army even though everyone knew it could be pursued a few days only. In place of the question, "What are the Connecticut troops going to do?" every man now could ask his neighbor, "What do you think of the Enos case?" The courtmartial acquitted the Colonel "with honor" on the ground that he was compelled by the scarcity of provisions to return, a verdict that Washington accompanied, on publication, with an order for Enos's immediate release from arrest[153] and with no other comment.[154]

---

150 Letter of Nov. 30, 1775; 1 *Sullivan Papers*, 129–30.
151 Letter of Dec. 2, 1775; *ibid.*, 134–35.
152 Gates to Ward, Dec. 4, 1775; *Artemas Ward Papers*, 51, MHS.
153 4 *G. W.*, 139.
154 Cf. *ibid.*, 149, 157–58. The testimony was that Enos reduced his provisions to three days' supply in order to feed the men nearer the front. He wished to go on, even if his men had to return, but some of his officers prevailed on him to lead the way back to the settlements because 150 men of other "divisions" were with him, under the command of a subaltern. It would be impossible to manage these stragglers, the officers said, unless Enos was present. See the testimony in 3 *Force* (4) p. 1709–10. General Sullivan made a supplementary statement, Apr. 28, 1776, to the effect that "so much provision had been sent forward to support the other divisions as left them so small a quantity that their men were almost famished with hunger on their return; and some would undoubtedly have starved had they not, by accident, come across and killed a large moose." Sullivan added that, in his opinion, if Enos had carried his men forward, "it would have been the means of causing the whole to have perished in the woods, for want of sustenance" (3 *Force* (4) p. 1710). Twenty-five officers, including Brig. Gen. William Heath, joined in a testimonial that Enos deserved "applause rather than censure" (*ibid.*, 1710–11).

The day Enos was acquitted, Dec. 4, 1775, Washington received a dispatch from Schuyler, dated November 22, that contained letters of Montgomery and of Arnold.[155] In brief terms, Montgomery reported that American artillery fire had kept Carleton and his men from moving on their ships down the St. Lawrence, and past the mouth of the Richelieu[156] to Quebec. Arnold, for his part, wrote at St. Mary's, "four leagues"[157] from Point Levi, on the St. Lawrence opposite Quebec. He told of his purpose to cross the river in a few days and to attack the city, though he feared it might have been reenforced. If it was too strong for him, he would march to join Montgomery at Montreal. Nothing was said of shortage of rations. On the contrary, the natives seemed friendly and willing to supply provisions.

This was encouraging and it led Washington to hope that Montgomery's early juncture with Arnold not only would assure the capture of Quebec but also would complete the conquest of Canada;[158] but these were the possible achievements of "a brother far off." It was the "neighbor that is near" over whom Washington was concerned. "I conceive our affairs are in a very critical situation," he said on the 6th[159] and he found new danger in a report that Massachusetts intended to pay her militia on the basis of a lunar month instead of the calendar month of continental allowance to the troops. Fortunately this was settled almost immediately through the ready acceptance by the Colony of the pay-month Congress had voted.[160]

Another immediate perplexity involved small arms. In accordance with the principles of the militia laws of the Colony, every man who entered the ranks was supposed to provide his own musket or firelock. This requirement meant, of course, that the small arms of the men were of many sorts, good and bad, and that some men had come without any arms. As far as practicable, these empty-handed soldiers had been supplied, until private and public arms had become so confused that head-

[155] Schuyler's letter is in the *Papers of G. W.*, LC; Schuyler to the President of Congress, Nov. 18, Nov. 22, 1775, are in 3 *Force* (4) 1593 and 1633. Arnold's letter of Nov. 7, 1775, and Montgomery's of Nov. 17, 1775 appear in *ibid.*, 1633–34.

[156] The Americans in nearly all instances called this the Sorel River.

[157] This is an interesting example of the misconceptions that arose from the careless use of the word "league," which apparently never was a standard of English linear measure on land. A French league of the eighteenth century was usually computed at 3000 yards, though in some parts of the Kingdom it was 3500. The distance from Ste. Marie to Point Levi, the modern Levis, is about twenty-two miles on a straight line, or nearly twice as far as Arnold's "four leagues" probably would have been taken by Washington to indicate.

[158] 4 *G. W.*, 147.   [159] 4 *G. W.*, 149.

[160] *Ibid.*; *Boardman's Diary*, Nov. 1, 1775 in *MHSP*, 1871–72, p. 412; Mass. Council Proceedings in 4 *Force* (4) p. 1221 ff. Cf. *ibid.*, 194.

quarters did not know what percentage of the total stock of muskets would be retained and what would be returned to the store when the enlistment of the users ended.[161] From the time he assumed command, Washington had been alarmed over the scarcity of arms and over the laborious care required to provide balls and cartridges for muskets of different bore,[162] and at this crisis he reasoned that if Connecticut troops were allowed to take any good arms away with them, it would be almost impossible to find muskets for the soldiers who replaced them. A brief, inclusive order had been issued on the 20th of November to this effect: "No soldier, whenever dismissed, is to carry away any arms with him that are good and fit for service. If the arms are his own private property, they will be appraised, and he will receive the full value thereof. Proper persons will be appointed to inspect and value the arms so detained." [163]

Washington had now to see that this order was enforced among those of his men who might wish to steal public muskets or to take with them cherished arms of their own. He concluded, after discussion, that the easiest and perhaps the surest way of stopping this manifestly was to hold a review of the men who were about to leave camp, to see that all of them had their arms, and then, without further ceremony, to take those that were worth having. So, on the 7th, the order went out for the Connecticut troops to be ready at 11 o'clock on Saturday, December 9, for a review. "They are," the order ran, "to have their arms in good order; the rolls to be called over, and no man to be absent. Every one that is able must appear. For this purpose they are to be exempt from all other duty upon that day." [164] General Sullivan was notified that the real purpose of the review was to procure the arms, and he was admonished to say nothing of the plan till his troops were paraded. Thereupon, with his field officers, he was to inspect the arms, appropriate the good muskets, and note the names of owners so that they could be paid.[165]

---

[161] In the open country and in the villages, the ownership of arms was general, though doubtless many persons possessed worthless firelocks that had been passed from father to son. The surprise to the student is in the large number of arms held by city dwellers. John Rowe noted (*Letters and Diary*, 293, April 24, 1775), that on order of General Gage, the people of Boston turned in 2674 small arms. As the population of Boston was then 15,000 or approximately that, one small arm was delivered for every 5.6 inhabitants. Doubtless many other arms were concealed.

[162] 4 *G. W.*, 26.   [163] *Ibid.*, 103, drastically repunctuated.

[164] *Ibid.*, 150–51, with some punctuation modernized.

[165] *Ibid.*, 152–53.

It was done accordingly, but with disappointing result because so large a part of the small arms were not worth purchasing and storing.[166] This was a shock and surprise to field officers. They did not realize— if indeed the company officers understood—how poor the arms of many of the men were, until the muskets were examined one by one. When the facts were known, Washington proceeded immediately to improve the firepower of the troops as far as he could by directing the issue of twenty-five stand of the recently captured, standard British arms from *Nancy* to the most reliable men of each Regiment.[167]

The day of the review that disclosed the badness of the Army's small arms was the last on which the Connecticut troops could be held. Final appeals to their patriotism were as futile as early exhortation had been. Doubtless in their hearts, many of the Connecticut soldiers planned to reenlist later, but they had been among the first volunteers to come to aid the people of Massachusetts Bay and they felt themselves entitled to be the first to have relief. It was entirely human. They had enlisted to December only; they had been looking forward to going home in time for Christmas; they were cold; many of them had not procured their winter clothing; some who had brought blankets with them had rubbed away most of the wool. Theirs was not the mood in which to receive preachment, even when Washington in his general orders of December 10 formally praised the men of Col. Ebenezer Bridge's Regiment, the Twenty-seventh, who had agreed to remain in service until the new Army was organized. "Such a conduct at this important crisis," said Washington, "cannot fail of giving pleasure to every well-wisher to his country, and next to engaging for another year is the highest proof they can give of their attachment to the noble cause of liberty." The General added solemnly: "At the same time that it reflects honor upon themselves, it may under Providence give Posterity [168] reason to bless them as the happy instruments of their delivery from those chains which were actually forging for them." [169]

If impatient or ignorant soldiers in the Connecticut force disregarded this language, many other New Englanders reflected in dismay on the behavior of men who were not fighting for a master but for themselves.

---

[166] This was not stated flatly, as of December 9 specifically, but it was mentioned as of Jan. 13, 1776 by Washington in reviewing the shortage of arms after the muster-out of Dec. 31, 1775. There is no reason to assume conditions then were different from those prevailing at the discharge of the Connecticut troops, Dec. 10, 1775.

[167] 4 G. W., 159.   [168] Washington capitalized both these nouns.

[169] 4 G. W., 153-54.

James Winthrop reported to Mercy Warren a rumor that the trouble in
the Connecticut Regiments was "occasioned by some officers who disliked the new modeling the Army and were willing to risk the public
safety through private resentment." [170] He mentioned the wish of some
to get a bounty for remaining with the colors, and then he added
reflectively: "It is a little surprising that in a cause which has (or ought
to have) public virtue for its bases, men must be hired to be virtuous.
I wish it was possible to get an army of volunteers who would fight
without pay . . ." [171] In Philadelphia, when it was plain that the Connecticut troops were going home, Delegates blanched. Thomas Lynch,
one of the members to visit the camp in October, was particularly
alarmed. When he recalled on the 8th that the extended time of the
Connecticut men was expiring, he wrote Washington: "I shall not take
upon me to advise; it is as improper as it is needless. Your riflemen,
negroes and deserters may, in proper passes, defend your artillery,
ammunition and stores." [172]

Would it, could it come to that? Some of the Connecticut troops
refused on the 10th to perform any military duty and at least passively
demanded that they be allowed to start home at once. Washington
again had to refuse [173] but this time he had an encouraging reason.
Militia from other New England Colonies were beginning to arrive
in noticeable numbers. If they continued to move into the camps, the
Connecticut Regiments might leave, but not until then. The safety of
the lines had to prevail over the letter of old enlistment resolutions.
On the 11th, it looked as if a new necessity was developing. Fretful
activity was observed around Bunker Hill; large numbers of men
moved from their encampments and crossed to Boston by the ferry.
Washington observed, questioned, weighed possibilities, and concluded
that the British either were reconcentrating in the city for an attack at
some undisclosed point, or else were transferring the men to less exposed winter quarters.[174] The more formidable of these alternatives was
enough to make Washington ask once again whether Howe might not
have spies who were keeping the British informed of what had occurred
in the American camps. Howe might be withholding his attack until
the day some secret agent would hurry to British headquarters and say,
in effect, "The rebels are at their weakest now!"

[170] Cf. 1 *Lee Papers*, 219.

[171] Letter of Dec. 1, 1775; 2 *Mercy Warren Letters*, 108; MHS.

[172] 4 *Force* (4) p. 218. Lynch added: "Should your lines be deserted, and the glorious,
golden opportunity of ending the war be lost, let not hope be lost also."

[173] *E. Clarke's Journal*, 28.   [174] *Martyn's Ward*, 185, n 40.

Keep the Connecticut Regiments, then—will they, nil they—till a corresponding number of militia filed into the tents and barracks. That, in substance, was the order. It might have provoked mutiny that would have saved Howe the lead he would have had to expend in killing disobedient subjects of the King; but, mercifully, the worst of the danger appeared to be over almost before the Connecticut men had time to get angry. The British made no further movement at Bunker Hill or from Boston;[175] militia Companies reported with a briskness that surprised a General who had laid it down as a maxim in Virginia never to expect militia within days of the time they were ordered to report. Now he could say: "I am much pleased with the alacrity which the good people of this province [of Massachusetts] as well as those of New Hampshire have shown upon this occasion; I expect the whole will be in this day and tomorrow, when what remains of the Connecticut Gentry who have not enlisted will have liberty to go to their firesides."[176]

Veterans dubbed the militiamen the "Long-Faced People"; but if that derisive term was familiar at headquarters it was, at least this time, a tribute and not a reproach.[177] The militia came the more readily because they were outraged by the news that the Connecticut troops were going to leave, regardless of what happened to Boston.[178] Within a few days it was to be manifest, also, that the leaders of Connecticut and many of the humble folk were humiliated and outraged by the virtual defection of so many of their troops in an hour of manifest peril.[179] At the moment, hot resentment against the departing Connecticut contingents warmed the welcome of the "Long Faces" from Massachusetts and New Hampshire, and gave violence, almost hate, to the farewell accorded the Connecticut men. "They . . . marched off

[175] The transfer was, in reality, from tents to winter quarters. See *Carter, Letters to a Friend*, 18.

[176] Letter of Dec. 11, 1775, to the President of Congress; 4 *G. W.*, 156–57. See *ibid.*, 185, for his statement as of December 25 that the militia "behave much better than I expected under our want of wood, barracks (for they are not yet done) and blankets, etc."

[177] *Samuel Haws's Diary*, 80, 84. In February, 1776, Samuel, who scarcely could have qualified as an American authority on spelling, referred to these temporary soldiers as the "melitious men."

[178] James Warren in 1 *Warren-Adams Letters*, 193–94.

[179] 4 *G. W.*, 163; Jonathan Trumbull to Washington, Dec. 7, Dec. 9, 1775, Jan. 1, 1776; 4 *Force* (4) p. 213, 227, 531–32; Connecticut Act, December, 1775, "for raising and equipping," etc., *ibid.*, 267. Cf. Silas Deane to Mrs. Deane, Dec. 15, 1775: "The behavior of our soldiers has made me sick; but little better could be expected from men trained up with notions of their right of saying how, and when, and under whom, they will serve; and who have, for certain dirty political purposes, been tampered with by their officers, among whom no less than a General has been busy" (1 *Deane Papers*, 95). See also Nathanael Greene to Samuel Ward, Dec. 31, 1775; 4 *Force* (4) p. 484.

bag and baggage," wrote Charles Lee, "but in passing through the lines of other Regiments they were so horribly hissed, groaned at and pelted that I believe they wished their aunts, grandmothers and even sweethearts to whom the day before they were so much attached at the Devil's own palace." Lee was glad to add: "It is said they have been scurvily treated on the road, and worse by the very connections from whom they could not bear to be separated." [180]

If the uncertainty created by the departure and arrival of these desperately needed troops had not absorbed Washington's thought on the 11th of December, he might have indulged a different and sentimental resentment. It would have been this: After much exchange of correspondence, long preparation and the muster of a considerable entourage, Martha had started for Cambridge from Virginia and she arrived that day. There were, of course, affectionate greetings for her and for her fellow-travelers from Virginia, and there was as much of comfort at headquarters as could be provided by fumbling males; but a man of other temperament might have complained that of all days on which a chivalrous foe and a considerate Army should have left a Commander-in-Chief alone, it would have been when he wished to receive a wife whom he had not seen for seven months. Washington had written her prior to October 13 to come to Cambridge if she cared to make the journey and he had erred in thinking she would not do so because of the lateness of the season. [181] There had been much chatter in Alexandria of the risk she was thought to be running at Mount Vernon, and in Loudoun some had talked of sending a company of gentlemen to escort her into Berkeley County; but she, Lund Washington and Burwell Bassett believed her safe in her home. Lund said he did not see how she could be caught, save by a secret expedition at night, because ten minutes' warning in daylight hours would suffice for her to get safely away. [182] She had visited on the York and the Rappahannock in October [183] and was at Colonel Daingerfield's the 23rd of that month. [184] About the middle of November, attended by several friends, she had proceeded in her chariot to Philadelphia,

[180] Letter of Dec. 12, 1775, to Benjamin Rush; 1 *Lee Papers*, 226.

[181] 4 *G. W.*, 28.

[182] Lund Washington to Washington, Oct. 5, 1775; *Thom MSS*, Mount Vernon. Cf. 3 *G. W.*, 432.

[183] Lund Washington's letter, as *supra*.

[184] *Harrower's Diary* in 6 *A. H. R.*, 103. She was at Eltham, November 2. See her letter of that date to Davenport, concerning provisions to be given "Mrs. Bayley that lives at West Point" (MS., *PHS*).

where she had arrived on the 21st. With Joseph Reed's assistance and with prudent counsel from other quarters, she had seen those persons she should have received, and had avoided those she should have shunned.[185] Then on the 28th, she had left the Quaker Town [186] ceremoniously. "I don't know," she excitedly wrote a friend later, "but you have seen the figure our arrival made in . . . Philadelphia proper and I left it in as great pomp as if I had been a very great somebody." [187] On the last stages of her journey she had welcomed George Baylor of Washington's staff as her escort.[188] Now her vehicle poured out Virginians as if they had been apples from a barrel—herself, Mrs. Horatio Gates, "Jack" Custis, his wife and George Lewis.[189] As Washington and his aides helped these well-clad and rosy ladies from their vehicle in the December chill of Cambridge, some of the welcoming smiles may have been broadened by the recollection of a remark in one of Joseph Reed's letters from Philadelphia—that such lovely persons were "not a bad supply, I think, in a country where wood is scarce." [190] Martha had never seen previously any of the cities through which she passed but, being a lady innately discreet, she expressed more of pleasure than of surprise at the unfamiliar scenes she observed.[191]

It was to Washington's comfort that she was with him in Cambridge when almost every hour of those frosty December days brought some new problem to the man who had hoped that a single campaign, ended ere this, would have decided the dispute with the Mother Country and would have permitted his untroubled return to the private joy of his own estate. Acute human woe was added to all the perplexities of

[185] *Marshall's Diary*, 51, 52; 4 *G. W.*, 106, 165, 184. George Lux was an escort as far as Philadelphia, but, gossip though he was, he left no story of the pilgrimage. Cf. Lux to Edward Shippen Burd, Nov. 23, 1775; Burd Papers, PHS.

[186] 1 *Ballagh, Lee Letters*, 159; *Penn. Gazette*, Nov. 29, 1775; *Marshall's Diary*, 53.

[187] Letter of Dec. 30, 1775, to Miss Ramsay; *J. P. Morgan Lib.* The gap in the quotation represents a break in the MS.

[188] 4 *G. W.*, 123.   [189] 4 *Force* (4) p. 283 n.

[190] Letter of Nov. 26, 1775, to S. B. Webb; 1 *Webb*, 121.

[191] Mrs. Washington established herself at Cambridge headquarters and there entertained her husband's guests and the fashionables of her own sex who came to call. Her hospitality always was tasteful but never ostentatious. For example, when Samuel Cooper and his wife called on the Washingtons, Mrs. Gates and Nelly, Dec. 19, 1775, they were "treated," as Cooper wrote, with oranges and a glass of wine, and were invited to dinner, which they declined (6 *A. H. R.*, 328). When Mrs. Washington and the General had guests at table, it usually was for the principal meal of the day at 2 o'clock (Cf. the invitation to "Colonel Knox and Lady," Feb. 1, 1776, in 2 *Knox Papers*, 29; MHS). She and the wives of some of Washington's officers—specifically Mrs. Gates and Mrs. Thomas Mifflin—returned the calls of ladies (6 *A. H. R.*, 333). Mrs. Washington was accepted in every way as she should have been. If she perplexed or disappointed any of the wise women of the Bay Colony, it was by the vagaries of her spelling. See her letter of Jan. 8, 1776, to Mercy Warren in 1 *Warren-Adams Letters*, 200.

command.[192] The poor of Boston who had been authorized to leave the city in November had done so to the number of about 300.[193] Some healthy persons who still clung to small belongings had left in the belief that life could not be harder or food and fuel higher and scarcer than in a town occupied and dominated by the British.[194] For these refugees, Washington had made such provision as he could, but because of the suspicion that some of them might develop smallpox, he had forbidden them to enter the camps.[195] Now, an additional 150 of the Boston poor appealed for permission to pass the American lines [196] at a time when Washington discovered that some of those who previously had left Boston had slipped into Cambridge in spite of guards and instructions. It was an obnoxious task to have to send out new orders to bar these refugees from the town and to give warning that violators would be punished.[197]

This was a temporary if heavy strain. A larger and a daily burden was the almost unsupportable one of finishing the required barracks and of getting firewood from snow-bound forests and over ice-covered roads.[198] As the need of this fuel was beyond the resources of the

192 4 G. W., 118.

193 Washington apparently thought they had been compelled to leave (4 G. W., 118).

194 In *Cheever's Diary*, 95, entry of Nov. 30, 1775, is an informative list of some of the high prices prevailing in Boston. British officers complained of their food and insisted that fresh meat, brought from Florida, was so frozen that it broke like glass and was, besides, too tough to eat. See *Carter, Letters to a Friend*, 20. As long previously as Sept. 5, 1775, Rev. Andrew Eliot, who was held in Boston, wrote that he would be willing to preach if he were allowed nothing more than his firewood, "which," he said, "would cost me more than I am like to receive if it is to be got at all" (*MHSP*, 1878, p. 298). The *Journal of Mrs. John Amory* (76 ff) includes letters from her father, Rufus Greene, with numerous references to the shortage and high price of wood and of sea coal in Boston. Sometimes, even well-to-do persons were compelled to use horse dung, when they could get it, as fuel. See *Letters of John Andrews* in *MHSP*, 1864–65, p. 411.

195 Harrison to Loammi Baldwin, Nov. 26, 1775; *Baldwin Papers*, Harvard Coll. Lib. It is pleasing to note that Colonel Baldwin anticipated the part of his instructions that authorized him to feed these needy persons.

196 4 G. W., 162.

197 Harrison to Baldwin, Dec. 13, 1775, *loc. cit.*

198 The original estimate of the cost of 120 shingled, wooden barracks, ninety-six by six-teen feet, to accommodate 100 men each, was filed by Quartermaster General Mifflin Oct. 5, 1775. His figure was £96, 8s each or, in round numbers £12,000 for the whole (152 *Papers of Continental Congress*, pt. 1, p. 229). Final housing arrangements on the Cambridge Common and on Harvard property are described briefly in S. F. Batchelder, *Bits of Harvard History*, 244 ff. In 4 *Force* (4) p. 844 ff is an "Account of the Barracks Improved by the Continental Troops." This document, the original of which is in 23 *Papers of G. W.*, LC, 11–12, contains a list of the quarters of different Regiments, etc., in the various camps. Completion of these barracks was a long, long labor. By November 22, some men were moving in (4 G. W., 109), but certain commands, crowded into private houses, did not have barracks until February. For some guiding references, see 4 G. W., 185, 275; *Diary of Samuel Richards*, 21; *Diary of Isaac Bangs*, 8. Mifflin's original estimate of firewood (*loc. cit.*) was made on the basis of one and a half cords per week for each 100 men, or 8000 cords for the entire army during a period of six months. Large military detachments, as noted *supra*, were made for woodcutting October

Army itself, the Massachusetts House of Representatives undertook, December 2, to keep the soldiers from freezing by calling on the various nearby townships to furnish eighty-eight and a half cords daily of the 117 cords required for all the forces.[199] Formal resolves did not fell trees. In a short time, committees were to be sent out to urge on the townships an increase of half as much again as had been asked of them.[200] Another difficulty concerned alleged shortcomings of the sick and absent Commissary General Joseph Trumbull, whom Washington decided to bring before a court of inquiry.[201] Still another delicate labor was that of preparing a formal protest to General Howe against the mistreatment of Col. Ethan Allen who had been captured near Montreal the previous September.[202]

Behind these and all the other burdens of command was gnawing concern over Arnold's Canadian expedition and over the course of the reenlistment, a double dread—to darken a Christmas that Nature did her best to drape and to brighten. The night of December 21–22 and the day of the 22nd were exceedingly cold; the 23rd was scarcely more tolerable; Christmas Eve brought a heavy snow, but Christmas Day itself was full of sunshine and, if not benevolently moderate, at least was not maliciously severe.[203] Some of the officers came, of course, to call on the General and his lady during the day,[204] though Charles Lee was absent in Rhode Island.[205] In the unfinished barracks and in the crowded houses of the towns the soldiers made such mirth as they might. A few who had money and the courage with which to face untrodden snow went out into the country and bought themselves such fruit and fowl as the farmers had.[206] The enemy, too, kept the peace of the Prince of Peace.

It was altogether a quiet day, but on the roads to Cambridge, two

---

15 (4 *G. W.*, 30), and were at work thereafter, apparently, whenever the weather permitted. (Cf. *Jabez Fitch's Diary* in *MHSP*, 1894–95, p. 87). Estimated army requirements were raised November 2 to 10,000 cords (4 *G. W.*, 60. Cf. *ibid.*, 101, 102).

199 4 *Force* (4) p. 1316–18.

200 *Ibid.*, 1356–57. Some useful references on wood-cutting and supply will be found in *Ezekiel Price's Diary*, Nov. 29, 1775 in *MHSP*, 1863–64, p. 216 and in *Samuel Cooper's Diary* in 6 *A. H. R.*, 330 ff. The most dramatic picture—that of soldiers compelled to eat provisions raw for lack of wood to cook them—is in Nathanael Greene to Samuel Ward, Dec. 31, 1775; 4 *Force* (4) p. 484.

201 4 *G. W.*, 176, 187.

202 4 *G. W.*, 170–71, 173, 175. For Allen's capture, see 3 *Force* (4) p. 799 n ff.

203 *Ezekiel Price's Diary* in *MHSP*, 1863–64, 222–23; *S. Cooper's Diary* in 6 *A. H. R.*, 329; *McCurtin's Journal*, 29.

204 Jeduthan Baldwin, for example in his *Journal*, 19.

205 Cf. Ezra Stiles's *Literary Diary*, v. 1, p. 646.

206 *McCurtin's Journal*, 30.

expresses were fighting their way through the snow. One of them came from Fort George with a dispatch from young Henry Knox, whom Washington in November had sent to New York and thence to Ticonderoga to get additional cannon and ammunition.[207] While Knox was at work on this, command of all the guns of the Army was transferred from Colonel Gridley to him, and he was made Colonel of Artillery in the new establishment.[208] On Christmas Eve, Washington had expressed the hope of hearing from Knox;[209] but he was not to relish one part of the dispatch now being brought to him.[210] Knox, writing December 17, reported excellent progress on his own account, but he said near the end of his letter: "There is no other news here of Colonel Arnold than that, from Colonel McLean's having burnt the houses round Quebec, Colonel Arnold was obliged to go to Point-aux-Trembles, about six miles from the city and that General Montgomery had gone to join him with a considerable body of men, and a good train of artillery, mortars, &c. There are some timid, and some malevolent spirits, who make this matter much worse; but from the different accounts which I have been able to collect, I have very little doubt that General Montgomery has Quebec now in his possession." [211] That had been Washington's hope, but his confidence could not be fixed until he learned that Montgomery was with Arnold.[212] If those "timid" and those "malevolent spirits" had information not known generally; and if Arnold had met with a serious reverse in front of Quebec, then . . . then there would be nothing to do except to make a new and larger effort. Canada must not be lost!

Yes, there must be another effort in Canada, if this one failed; but would there be a second opportunity at Boston? The Massachusetts committee for the supply of wood was hinting to the townships of the "great danger the country is exposed to from a dispersion of the Army, which must take place if it is not supplied with wood"; [213] Wash-

[207] The decision to send surplus ordnance to the Boston lines had been reached during the conference with the Committee from Congress (4 *G. W.*, 91, 92), and had been communicated, November 16, to the New York Legislature and to General Schuyler (*ibid.*). For Knox's instructions, see *ibid.*, 93. Cf. Knox to his wife, Nov. 16, 1775, and Stephen Moylan to Gouverneur Morris, same date, 1 *Knox Papers*, 172, 173; MHS. A general statement of Knox's ambitions and of his attitude toward Col. Richard Gridley, artillery commander, will be found in his letter of Oct. 26, 1775, to John Adams, *AASP*, Oct., 1946, p. 208.

[208] 4 *G. W.*, 74, 158.   [209] *Ibid.*, 179.

[210] This indirect approach has to be employed because the date of the reecipt of Knox's dispatch is not known. In favorable weather it would have reached Washington December 24 or 25.

[211] 1 *LTW.*, 95.   [212] 4 *G. W.*, 174.   [213] 4 *Force* (4) p. 1356.

ington's concern was whether reenlistment would yield a sufficient force to hold the line at the Year's End, when those men from the other New England Colonies who would not reenlist for 1776 would leave the Army and go home. By the last returns prior to December 15, not more than 5917, including Connecticut volunteers, had agreed to sign for another year, though Charles Lee was optimistic and other officers gave assurance that more of their troops would do so.[214] On December 18, total reenlistments were computed at 7140. "It is really discouraging," said Nathanael Greene, who had begun to doubt, as had Washington, whether an Army of the size authorized by Congress could be enlisted in time to assure the Colonies the numerical superiority of force they had resolved to have.[215] Even with the reduction in the number of Regiments from thirty-four to twenty-seven,[216] the task seemed an impossible one. As the Year's End came within a bare hundred hours or so, Washington received from the second express who had been on the road at Christmas time the answer of Congress to the question the General and later the committee of Franklin, Lynch and Harrison had submitted to Philadelphia. The reply was, "Resolved, that if General Washington and his council of war should be of opinion that a successful attack may be made on the troops in Boston, he do it in any manner he may think expedient, notwithstanding the town and property in it may thereby be destroyed." [217] In dispatching the measure John Hancock wrote: "This passed, after a most serious debate, in a Committee of the Whole House, and the execution was referred to you; and may God crown your attempt with success. I most heartily wish it, though individually I may be the greatest sufferer." [218] Here, then was the authorization: would there be an opening and the men to make the most of it? Insofar as the opportunity depended on the enemy's lack of initiative, it might be forthcoming, because Howe remained passive, perhaps suspiciously passive. The start of work on the fort at Lechmere Point had been followed by no counter-action after the British cannonade had failed to drive off the Americans who wielded their defiant picks within sight of the enemy.[219] On the 28th, General Sullivan undertook to seize the outguard and then to burn the barracks

---

[214] 4 *G. W.*, 166; 1 *Lee Papers*, 226: "enlisting goes on most swimmingly . . ."
[215] Letter of Dec. 20, 1775, to Jacob Greene, 4 *Force* (4) p. 368.
[216] 4 *G. W.*, 183. [217] 3 *JCC.*, 444–45.
[218] Letter of Dec. 22, 1775; 1 *LTW.*, 98–100. The final vote was seven Colonies to two. For the circumstances, see *Richard Smith's Diary*, Dec. 21, 22, 1775, in 1 *Burnett*, 283, 284.
[219] 4 *G. W.*, 184; *Heath*, 41–42; *Barker's Diary*, 69.

at Bunker Hill, but the fall of a soldier on the ice in the darkness and the accidental discharge of his piece alarmed the sentinels.[220] The British seemed quite content to let the American failure be just that, a failure. They did not attempt to exploit it.

So much for a passive foe. He might nod or lower his guard and give Washington a chance if, when powder was adequate and artillery was strong enough, the troops were there to secure the line. If again, Howe deliberately was pretending to be cautious or timid, in order to deceive the Americans, would there be men to repulse him, or could he sweep aside a thin and shivering line? It was the old baffling contingency of war, the mocking, recurring if, if, if!

As with strategy, so with men—if, if, if. At the very last Washington appealed to the troops to stay, even *if* their officers went home because many commissions had expired when Regiments had been reduced. The same effort as in the case of the departing Connecticut troops was made to retain the good arms.[221] In reversal of policy concerning recruitment of Negroes, free men of color were invited to enlist.[222] Every soldier who could be kept ready for attack or defence was held with his Regiment.[223] All this and all else seemed in vain. Patriotism did not stifle muttering over the fact that one month's pay only was at hand for the men who were about to leave.[224] The selfish sought the shilling; the ignorant heard and did not heed; as always, the burden was borne by the few. Amid desperate attempts to prevail on more men to stay and fight for their country, the final day of the year came. Present, fit for duty, were 11,752 rank and file.[225] Enlistments of every sort for the new establishment were 9650.[226] Nathanael Greene heard the figures and spoke for his chief and for all his patriotic brother-officers when he wrote: "Nothing but confusion and disorder reign . . . We never have been so weak as we shall be tomorrow . . ."[227]

220 The thinness of the ice likewise discouraged the attacking party (*Heath,* 43). See also 1 *Sullivan Papers,* 154; Joseph Reed to S. B. Webb, Jan. 16, 1776 (1 *Webb,* 127); Stephen Moylan to Joseph Reed, Jan. 2, 1776 (1 *Reed,* 139). Charles Lee's friends thought Sullivan undertook this affair in the hope of winning fame in the absence of his superior officer. On returning from Rhode Island, where he was arresting Tories and advising as to defensive measures, Lee was much incensed because, he said, the enemy had been put on the alert where he was planning to thrust.

221 4 *G. W.,* 189–90. 222 4 *G. W.,* 194.

223 Cf. Washington's refusal of December 20 to send even a single Regiment to Rhode Island unless the enemy manifestly intended to land there (4 *G. W.,* 176–77).

224 4 *G. W.,* 194–95. Rations for use on the road home were issued (4 *G. W.,* 193).

225 As of Dec. 30, 1775; 4 *Force* (4) p. 491–92.

226 4 *G. W.,* 198.

227 Letter of Dec. 31, 1775 to Samuel Ward; 4 *Force* (4) p. 484.

APPENDIX III–1

THE MOUNT VERNON COMMUNITY IN 1759

AMONG WASHINGTON's neighbors in the general vicinity of Belvoir was a gentleman Washington had recently seen often in Williamsburg, Burgess George Johnston of Belvale. Although associated more closely with Alexandria than with his estate below the town, Johnston was a respected neighbor, a courageous man and as good a Scot as he was a wise legal counsellor.[1] Adjoining Gunston Hall was Springfield, home of the Martin Cockburns, who were to be credited, in time, with fifty years of married life not scarred by a single disagreement. Mrs. Cockburn was George Mason's cousin, Ann Bronaugh, whose kinship meant constant friendship.[2] Northwest of Gunston Hall and directly West of Daniel McCarty's Cedar Grove was Rovers' Delight, the home of Capt. John Posey.[3]

Down the bounteous Potomac below Gunston Hall were bays and promontories, small farms and sprawling plantations [4]—past Marlborough Point and Aquia Creek and Potomac Creek and quiet Chotank,[5] and on to the shores of Washington's native County, Westmoreland. The old estates of that region were seventy miles or more by road from Washington's seat— almost as far as Winchester—but sentimentally they were closer because George's half-brother, "Austin," resided in Westmoreland. The great name in that County still was Lee. During the eight years that had elapsed since the death of Thomas Lee,[6] most of his six surviving sons had reached manhood. The eldest of them, Philip Ludwell Lee, already was a member of

---

[1] Stetson, *Four Mile Grants*, 22 n; 2 *W* (2), 75; 8 *W* (2), 141; *Hayden*, 87; Hill, *Mason*, 48; *Proceedings of Trustees Alexandria*, 19. The inventory of his estate shows that he or some member of his family had excellent taste and the means of gratifying it.

[2] Numerous details of far more than the usual genealogical interest will be found in *Rowland, Mason*, v. 1, p. 110, which is part of a valuable chapter on the neighborhood of Gunston Hall. See also Ewell, *Virginia Scenes*, 159. Sir George Cockburn, Admiral of the Fleet and commander of the British naval forces in the Chesapeake and Potomac during the War of 1812, is said to have been a nephew of Martin Cockburn's. The location of Springfield is given on Plate 32 of the *George Washington Atlas*.

[3] See Plate 32 of the *George Washington Atlas*. That plate is the basis of the sketch map in this volume, p. 589.

[4] When J. F. D. Smyth made his tour (*op. cit.*, v. 2, p. 146), he listed numerous homes on the Virginia side of the Potomac below Alexandria and diplomatically stated that all of them were so beautiful none could claim preeminence.

[5] The "neighborhood" on the road from Mount Vernon to Potomac Creek is described in Vol. I, p. 203 ff. A brief account of Chotank will be found in *ibid.*, 224 ff.

[6] Nov. 30, 1750. See *Lee of Virginia*, 124, and *supra*, Vol. I, p. 244.

the Council of Virginia;[7] the next son to outlive infancy, Thomas Ludwell Lee, was a young man quick to make friends and sure to hold them. After Thomas Ludwell came the two with whom Washington had served in the House of Burgesses—Richard Henry Lee and Francis Lightfoot Lee. The fifth living male heir of Thomas Lee was William, not yet 20. His younger brother Arthur was in his nineteenth year and probably was at Eton.[8]

Washington had not found time during his five years of military service to visit often his brother at Wakefield in the land of the Lees. Those of his journeys that went beyond the neighborhood of Mount Vernon usually were inland, down the main road of the region, or northward to Alexandria. In that upstream area, nearer the Falls of the Potomac, countryside and town alike had developed greatly since the days when Washington first had resided at Epsewasson, before it received the more distinguished name, Mount Vernon. Daniel French now had an excellent plantation close by at Rose Hill; the Alexanders of Preston, Mount Idah and Summer Hill[9] were conspicuous still but were not of an age to supply young men for the public service.[10] This was true also, of the Colvilles of Clich. John of that name, a heavy speculator in Catoctin lands,[11] had died in January, 1756, and had scandalized half the neighborhood by avowing the paternity of a daughter born out of wedlock.[12] As he had no son, his brother Thomas moved from Cecil County, Maryland, to administer the estate.[13]

At Alexandria, the man most active in transforming a cluster of warehouses into a prosperous town was Washington's friend, John Carlyle. When the need of a new and better landing became apparent, John Carlyle, with the assent of his partner, had offered to construct it and, in return for the privilege, to give the public the use of half of it. Almost every local enterprise commanded his aid. If his fine mansion continued to dominate the panorama,

[7] He did a splendid part in guiding his younger brothers but personally he appears to have been overbearing and pompous. See the "Narrative of George Fisher" in 17 W (1) p. 135–38, reprinted in Armes, Stratford Hall, 97 ff.

[8] Nearly all important known facts concerning these remarkable brothers are given in Lee of Virginia. As that genealogy is detailed, the following page references may be useful: Thomas Lee, 103; his issue, 125; Philip Ludwell Lee, 165; Thomas Ludwell Lee, 168; Richard Henry Lee, 172; Francis Lightfoot Lee, 215; William Lee, 235; Arthur Lee, 254.

[9] Mrs. Powell, 62.

[10] For their estates and their connection with the birth of Alexandria, see Vol. I, p. 232 and n; Mrs. Powell, 26; Landmarks, 406, 415; 7 W (1), 119; 9 W (1), 253; Journ. H.B., 1752–58, p. 112; 6 H 399; Fairfax Records, B, 327; Stafford Deeds, O, 252, 282; Stafford Wills, 1729–48, p. 279–284, 303, 318.

[11] Landmarks, 273; Land Office Records, N.N., E, 45, 47, 49, 127, 128, 131, 182, 183, 210, 512.

[12] See Vol. I, p. 100. For Colville, see 5 E. J., 100, 109; Prince William Deeds, B, 444, 463, 488; ibid., D, 203, 207; ibid., E, 191, 199, 207, 219. His last testament is in Fairfax Wills, B, 1, p. 97; his inventory appears in ibid., 135. See, also, Mrs. Powell, 24.

[13] 1 Diaries, 214 n, with citation of Archaeologica Æliana, ser. 2, v. 2, 120, and v. 19, p. 115. Washington, in time, became one of the executors of the estate. See supra, p. 206, 245, and 3 W (1), 252–54.

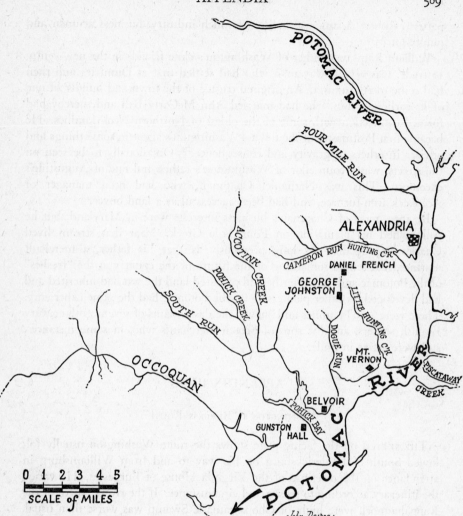

The Mount Vernon Neighborhood in 1759

his work entitled him to that distinction.[14] His failures as a commissary during the campaigns against the French fort on the Ohio had not impaired his reputation. He was primus inter pares in the town, as citizen, as merchant, as importer, and as buyer not only of tobacco but also of wheat, the production of which was beginning to increase in Northern Virginia.[15] Carlyle's

[14] Cf. 18 W (1) 2; Mrs. Powell, 67.

[15] As stated in Vol. I, p. 142, it is almost impossible to say when this shift from tobacco to wheat became commercially important. For some references, principally to the period after 1760, see Landmarks, 416, n. 46.

partner, Robert Adam, was a Scot of much industry, business acumen and public spirit.[16]

William Ramsay, another of Washington's close friends in the new centre of trade, was a Galloway man who had settled first at Dumfries and then had come to Alexandria. An original trustee of the town and builder of one of its earliest houses,[17] he had married Ann McCarty Ball and thereby had formed connection with some of the oldest of Northern Neck families. He became first Postmaster of the town—Washington's agent in some things and adviser in others of gravity and consequence.[18] Occasionally to be seen on the streets, was a counsellor of Washington's father and one of Augustine's executors. This was Nathaniel Chapman, who had been manager of Accokeek iron-furnace, and had been successful as a land buyer.[19]

By 1759, most of Chapman's business interests were in Maryland, but he still owned his plantation on Four Mile Creek. Near that stream lived Charles Broadwater. As long previously as 1722 his father, a merchant mariner, had sensed something of the future of the country at the "freshes" of the Potomac and thereafter he had patented land the son had inherited and had developed.[20] Other planters along the Potomac had the same experience. There were "old" families and "new," the descendants of seventeenth-century English settlers, and the sons of Scotch merchants who, in some instances, still were active in trade.

APPENDIX III–2

Washington's "Burgess Route"

The sketch on the facing page shows the route Washington usually followed South of Fredericksburg on his way to and from Williamsburg in attendance on the meetings of the Virginia House of Burgesses. He varied the itinerary according to season and circumstance. If the rivers North of the Rappahannock were high, or Chopawamasic Swamp was worse than usual, Washington on occasion would cross the Potomac at one of the ferries above Mount Vernon, would proceed down the left bank of the river, recross the Potomac at Hooe's Ferry, and ride or drive over the Northern Neck. This

16 *Mrs. Powell,* 168, 208.

17 At the northeast corner of King and Fairfax Streets.

18 *Mrs. Powell,* 65; *Landmarks,* 407; *Hayden,* 88.

19 He was operating the Accokeek Furnace as late as November, 1752 (*Va. Gazette,* Nov. 3, 1752). One of his purchases of 669 acres is recorded in *Land Books, N.N.* G, 151. His inventory is recorded in *Fairfax Wills,* B, 1, p. 325; the will of his wife will be found in Culbertson, *Hunter Family,* 177. Cf. *ibid.,* 170–71.

20 *Land Office Records, N.N.,* A, 40, 112; *ibid.,* B, 42. Virtually nothing is known of the early life of Charles Broadwater. His later public service is sketched in 47 *V* 234–38.

FREDERICKSBURG · FERRY FARM

POTOMAC RIVER

RAPPAHANNOCK

BOWLING · GREEN

HOBBS HOLE

PAMUNKEY RIVER

MATTAPONY

RIVER

TODD'S BRIDGE

RIVER

JAMES

CHICKAHOMINY RIVER

WHITE HOUSE

B. MOORE

CLAIBORNE'S · ELTHAM

RICHMOND

RIVER

DONCASTLE'S

APPOMATTOX RIVER

CHISWELL'S

WILLIAMSBURG

PETERSBURG

YORKTOWN

HAMPTON

0 5 10 20 30

SCALE of MILES

John Draper

route might take him to Hobbs Hole and thence to Todd's Bridge and the
highway to Williamsburg. Similarly, too, the southern part of the journey
might be modified if Washington had business that carried him southeastward down the "Middle Neck," the region between the Rappahannock and
the York.

APPENDIX III–3

The Original Form of Henry's Resolutions on the Stamp Act

Among private papers left by Patrick Henry at his death in 1799 was a sheet on which five resolutions appeared. Accompanying this was a memorandum in Henry's autograph that began: "The within resolutions passed the House of Burgesses in May, 1765." He went on to describe the circumstances and wrote: ". . . I determined to venture, and alone, unadvised, and unassisted, wrote the within."[1] It is a matter of interpretation whether he meant to say that the copy preserved by him was the original manuscript of the historic "Stamp Act resolutions." As reproduced in *Journ. H.B.,* 1761–65, frontispiece, the document looks as if it might be a "clean copy" of an original rough draft. One hasty correction appears on it. The resolutions end at the bottom of the sheet. Nothing indicates that there were others. Had there been additional declarations of the nature presently to be described, it is not likely that Henry would have forgotten them or would have failed to claim the authorship. His fifth resolution begins, moreover, with the finality of a "Resolved therefore." The preceding four do not include any "therefore."

In the *Journal of the House of Burgesses,* they number four. The fifth is missing altogether; the others are in a form that suggests amendment in Committee of the Whole and on the floor of the House, but there is no mistaking the fact that the four are Henry's in spirit and in argument. Contemporary authorities explained how the fifth was expunged. Gov. Francis Fauquier's letter of June 5, 1765, to the Lords of Trade,[2] recorded in detail the legislative course of the resolutions.

The unidentified French visitor wrote in his Diary: "The whole House was for entering resolves on the records but they differed much with regard the contents or purport thereof. Some were for showing their resentment to the highest. One of the resolves that these proposed was that any person that would offer to sustain that the Parliament of England had a right to impose or levy any tax or duties whatsoever on the American Colonies, without the consent of the inhabitants thereof, should be looked upon as a traitor and deemed an enemy to his country. There were some others to the same purpose, and the majority was for entering these resolves, upon which the Governor dissolved the Assembly, which hindered their proceeding."[3]

Rev. William Robinson, Commissary for Virginia, wrote his principal, the Bishop of London, Aug. 12, 1765 that Henry "made a motion for several

[1] *W. W. Henry,* v. 1, p. 81.
[2] *Journ. H.B.,* 1761–65, p. lxvii–lxviii.
[3] French Visitor's Diary, 26 *A. H. R.,* 746, with the spelling and punctuation revised for clarity.

outrageous resolves some of which passed, and were again erased as soon as his back was turned." Robinson told, also, of the dissolution of the General Assembly and he thus described one of the resolutions he understood the House had defeated: "The concluding resolution . . . was that any person who should write or speak in favor of the act of Parliament for laying stamp duties should be deemed an enemy to the Colony of Virginia." [4]

The natural place for the publication of any rejected or expunged resolutions would be the *Virginia Gazette*. Writing about 1859, Charles Campbell stated unequivocally in his *History of Virginia,* p. 543, that "the four resolutions remaining on the Journal, and the two additional ones offered in committee, but not reported, were published in the *Gazette*." He said of the supplementary resolutions: "Two others . . . were offered but not by Henry, to the effect that the people of Virginia were under no obligation to obey laws not enacted by their own assembly, and that any one who should maintain the contrary, should be deemed an enemy to the Colony. These two did not pass." [5] Apparently Campbell, a careful writer, had access to the newspaper, but no copy of that particular issue is believed to be in existence now. Only one edition, in fact, for the entire year 1765 has been found.

In this situation, where no copy of a needed *Virginia Gazette* is at hand, recourse is had, as usual, to the corresponding *Maryland Gazette* of Annapolis which reprinted many articles from the Williamsburg paper and published much news from the Old Dominion on its own account. In the *Maryland Gazette* of July 4, 1765, is this note: "We have had several manuscript copies of some resolves of the House of Burgesses in Virginia just before their dissolution, desiring a place for them in this paper. The following are received from a gentleman in that Colony and if any error the fault lies not here." The text is without the "resolved" at the beginning of each declaration, but it conforms to the first four resolutions as printed in the *Journal of the House of Burgesses*. When the fifth resolution is reached, the text in the Maryland paper is substantially that of Henry's original version. There follow the sixth and a seventh, which read thus:

"That his Majesty's Liege People Inhabitants of this Colony are not bound to yield obedience to any Law or Ordinance whatsoever designed to impose any taxation upon them other than the Laws or Ordinances of the General Assembly as aforesaid.

"That any person who shall be Speaking or Writing assert or maintain that any Person or Persons other than the General Assembly of this Colony with such consent as aforesaid, have any right or authority to lay or impose any tax whatever on the inhabitants thereof, shall be deemed an enemy to this his Majesty's Colony."

[4] Letter in Perry, *op. cit.,* 514, quoted in *W. W. Henry,* v. 1, p. 90.
[5] Campbell, *op. cit.,* 541 n.

In two other more familiar versions of these Virginia resolutions, printed in Newport, Rhode Island, and in Boston, Henry's original third resolution was omitted, with the result that the fourth became the third, the fifth the fourth, etc.[6]

Such is the contemporary evidence. It is supplemented by no later testimony of any value other than that of Thomas Jefferson, who retained a vivid memory of Henry's speech and of an effort to expunge part of the resolutions, he was not sure which part.[7] At the time Jefferson wrote in 1814, he expressed some curiosity [8] concerning the text of the resolutions printed by John Marshall in his *Life of George Washington*,[9] but that version proves to be substantially the one printed in the *Maryland Gazette,* etc.

In appraising this evidence, the first question concerns the "sixth" and "seventh" resolutions, those quoted from the Annapolis paper. Henry's memorandum and the evidence presented by his copy of the original resolutions do not exclude completely the possibility of additional resolutions from his hand, though the weight of inference is strongly against the probability of this.

Both Fauquier and Robinson agree that there were other resolutions. All the contemporary printed copies include them without any indication that they were not parts of the original paper. Campbell's account of the incident suggests that he saw in the *Virginia Gazette* or elsewhere what undoubtedly were the sixth and the seventh resolutions in the Maryland version. Were those two resolutions, then, submitted and defeated, or were they withheld? On this, unfortunately, the evidence is contradictory. Unless it had been read on the floor the French visitor manifestly would not have known of the resolution that denounced supporters of direct taxation as enemies of their country. Governor Fauquier, on the other hand, writing five days after the expunging of the fifth resolution, described correctly the proceedings as far as these can be checked from the records, and then he said: "I am informed the gentlemen had two more resolutions in their pockets, but finding the difficulty they had in passing the fifth, which was by a single voice, and knowing them to be more virulent and inflammatory, they did not produce them." [10]

It will be observed that Fauquier did not say Henry had more resolutions. The Governor's reference was plural—"the gentlemen" had two other reso-

[6] Publication of the resolutions in the *Newport,* Rhode Island, *Gazette* of June 24 was preceded by an "extract from a letter of a gentleman in Philadelphia enclosing the resolves of the Virginia Assembly on debating the Stamp Act." The "extract" contains nothing more than a brief account of the dissolution. For William Gordon's doubtful account of the transmission of the resolutions, et cetera, see *W. W. Henry,* v. 1, p. 90 ff.

[7] See his letters to William Wirt, Aug. 14, 1814 and Aug. 5, 1815; 14 *Jefferson,* 162, 335.

[8] *Ibid.,* 167.

[9] 2 *Marshall,* Appendix, p. 25–27, Note 4.

[10] *Journ. H.B.,* 1761–65, p. lxvii–lxviii.

lutions. These were "more virulent and inflammatory," which numbers six and seven assuredly were. The question consequently becomes essentially this: Were these vehement resolutions adopted and expunged, or rejected when offered? Rev. William Robinson's report stated that the concluding resolution was among those rejected; but in the same sentence the clergyman inferentially identified this as the "seventh" of those printed in the *Maryland Gazette*. Robinson, it should be noted, was not present at the time, though his second-hand information may have been from his cousin, the Speaker. Charles Campbell's testimony has been given already—that the supplementary resolutions "were offered but not by Henry."

The puzzle cannot be solved on the basis of the evidence submitted. Undoubtedly, Henry wrote five resolutions and showed them to men whose views were similar to his own. Other Burgesses of his following drafted two others that carried further and applied the broad principles Henry laid down. These two resolutions doubtless were acceptable to Henry, and afterwards they were regarded as part of the original series; but at the beginning of the debate they probably were held in reserve because it was thought that so strong a declaration as was included in these two might prejudice the House against the others. The decision of the advocates of the resolutions was to test the House on the first five. When the vote on the fifth showed a majority of one only, the sixth and the seventh may or may not have been offered in Committee of the Whole but they more probably were presented on the 31st from the floor and may then have been rejected. The men who drafted those two resolutions still believed they were "not bound to yield obedience to any law or ordinance designed to impose any taxation upon them other than the laws or ordinances of the General Assembly . . ." They were willing to maintain, too, that any man who held the contrary view was "an enemy to this his Majesty's Colony."

APPENDIX III–4

Mary Washington's Move to Fredericksburg

THE TIME and the circumstances of Mary Ball Washington's removal from Ferry Farm to Fredericksburg have been given variously but never with any citation of authority. Chief reliance has been on tradition. The known facts are as follows:

1. On May 11, 1771, Washington made an initial payment of £75 on two lots he had agreed to purchase in Fredericksburg from Michael Robinson.

These were the lots on which the house occupied later by his mother then was located or soon was built.[1]

2. In September, 1771, Washington visited Ferry Farm, surveyed it, conferred with Charles Washington and Fielding Lewis, and made contracts with overseers of that farm and of his mother's quarter farther down the Rappahannock. His brother and his brother-in-law on September 15 appraised his mother's personal effects.[2]

3. On Nov. 7, 1771, Washington paid the remaining £200 on the lots bought of Michael Robinson.[3]

4. Beginning September, 1772, Washington's payments to his mother were larger and more frequent than they previously had been.[4] He described as an "advance" a sum of £5 he placed in her hands Feb. 25, 1772.[5]

5. On Sept. 14, 1772 Washington went from Mount Vernon to Fredericksburg, arrived there "about dusk" and, as he wrote in his diary "lodged at my mother's."[6]

6. The next day the entry reads in part "Rid to my two plantations on the river and returned to Mr. Lewis's to dinner."[7]

7. During this visit, Washington revised his contract with the overseer of the lower plantation and noted that the man's share of the crops was to be changed "if I should add a hand or two more and let him . . . choose five of the best horses at that quarter and the upper one."[8]

8. At this time[9] Michael Robinson transferred to George Washington the two lots on which were the house and garden used by Mrs. Mary Washington in later years.[10]

9. On Dec. 7, 1772, Edward Jones, in answer to a letter from Washington, wrote an account of what had occurred "since I have been your overseer." In this statement Jones wrote "I paid your mother £5, 10s last fall." He then described the shoats and lambs he had delivered Mrs. Washington in the summer and autumn of 1772 and he added: "I had four barrels of corn of her and when it came to be measured, it was but seventeen bushels . . ."[11]

10. In *Rind's Gazette* of Nov. 5 and 19, 1772, Washington advertised 600 acres "on the north side of the Rappahannock, opposite the lower end of Fredericksburg." This was Ferry Farm and the "lower quarter" which he

[1] *Ledger A*, folio 327, 336.
[2] 2 *Diaries*, 33–34, 36, and *supra*, p. 281. Included in the appraisal were "four wenches" at £8 each.
[3] *Ledger A*, folio 345.
[4] *Ledger B*, folio 45.
[5] *Ledger B*, folio 3.
[6] 2 *Diaries*, 79.
[7] *Ibid*.
[8] *Ibid.*, 81.
[9] Sept. 18, 1772.
[10] *Spotsylvania Deeds*, Book H, 224.
[11] 4 *Hamilton*, 164–65.

sold for £2000, probably in April, 1774, to Dr. Hugh Mercer, though no recordation of the deed has been found.[12]

11. On Jan. 13, 1775, Washington remarked that his mother's affairs were entirely in his hands, but he had no title to her Deep Run tract.[13]

12. He noted, Mch. 21, 1781, that he paid her "a certain yearly rent."[14]

13. Washington never wrote in more detail of financial relations with his mother until after her death in 1789. He then said: "She has had a great deal of money from me at times . . . and over and above this has not only had all that ever was made from the plantation but got her provisions and everything else she thought proper from thence. In short, to the best of my recollection I have never in my life received a copper from the estate, and have paid many hundred pounds (first and last) to her in cash. However, I want no retribution. I conceived it to be a duty whenever she asked for money, and I had it, to furnish her notwithstanding she got all the crops or the amount of them, and took everything she wanted from the plantation for the support of her family, horses, &c besides."[15]

The items of September, 1771, indicate that Washington was paying for the house she later occupied and that he was preparing to take over the management of the Ferry Farm and of his mother's "quarter." A year later, he was referring to the lower plantation as his own. The Ferry Farm had been his, at law, if not in occupancy, from the time he came of age in 1753; the lower plantation always had belonged to his mother, who usually held on to her possessions. If it had passed from her hands at an undetermined date between September, 1771, and September, 1772, the chances are strong that her folios in George's Ledger would include some large item or a note of the yield of the property after its transfer to her oldest son. No record has been found in any of his accounts of any credit or payment to her of a capital sum that could be regarded as equivalent to the value of the farm. On the other hand, Washington subsequently paid her as if he were receiving and selling the crops of the two farms and were remitting the proceeds or "income" to her. In his Ledger, opposite two entries of September and November, 1772, Washington noted in whose presence he handed his money, £30 on one occasion and £15 on another, as if to make sure that these were formal business payments and not gifts.[16] Again, in March, 1775, when he turned over £30 to his mother as "part of her income," his ledger showed no corresponding credit entries on her account.

Mrs. Washington, then, was certainly at Ferry Farm in September, 1771

[12] 4 *Hamilton*, 366. See Fredericksburg *Virginia Herald*, Sept. 13, 1826, for offer of this property which, said Col. Hugh Mercer, "was purchased by my father from General Washington." The circumstances are described *supra*, Chap. XV.

[13] 3 *G. W.*, 261–62; 12 *ibid.*, 63, and *supra*, p. 302.   [14] 21 *G. W.*, 341.

[15] Letter of Sept. 13, 1789, to Elizabeth Washington Lewis; 30 *G. W.*, 401.

[16] *Ledger B*, folio 45.

and she was not there a year later. On this second point, the evidence of Washington's Diary, Sept. 14, 1772, would seem to be conclusive. Washington, arriving at Fredericksburg by his usual route, lodged at his mother's. Had she then been at the old farm he certainly would not have crossed the river to the town at that late hour "about dusk" and then have recrossed. He would have ridden straight down the left bank from the turnout on the Dumfries-Fredericksburg road.

How long before September 14, 1772, Mrs. Washington left the farm to reside in the town, the evidence does not show. Mention on Feb. 25, 1772, of an "advance" to her shows that the new financial arrangement with her then was in effect. She may by that time have been in her Fredericksburg home, but there is no proof of this. Again, the overseer's references to the lambs and shoats delivered Mrs. Washington in the summer and fall of 1772 suggest that she may have been residing in Fredericksburg during the summer. Mention in December, 1772, of the fact that she had not delivered all the corn she was supposed to have turned over to the overseer might be interpreted to mean that the transaction occurred at the end of Mrs. Washington's tenancy.

Taken together, this evidence justifies only the broad conclusions that Washington took over Ferry Farm and the "lower quarter" in September, 1771, that his mother vacated her place between that date and September, 1772, that Washington bought her a house in Fredericksburg, that he sold the two farms across the river in 1774, and that from September, 1772, onward he made her irregular payments of considerable amount, which on the aggregate must have constituted fixed rent. She was free to get provisions from Ferry Farm and the "lower quarter" until Washington sold those properties. She also drew some requirements from the "Falls Quarter" or "upper quarter," the Deep Run property, which had by that time become a plantation.[17] These are the facts and the only facts that have been brought to light. If one wishes to theorize beyond the determinable verities, it seems probable that the burden of farm management had become too much for Mrs. Washington by 1771 and that under the lease of the two quarters to George, she received (1) supplies and provisions and (2) good rent for her property, which later was operated jointly with Ferry Farm as one plantation. She probably moved to Fredericksburg soon after she made this arrangement in September, 1771. Washington himself is authority for saying she thereafter consumed virtually all that both places produced.

[17] Reference to her receipt of more than 1100 pounds of pork from the "Falls Qr" appears in *Ledger B*, folio 45, as early as 1773.

APPENDIX III-5

Maps and Elevations of the Boston Area (1775-76)

THE TWO "base" maps of Boston and the adjacent country for the period of the siege are those of Pelham and Page. The one made by Henry Pelham was undertaken with General Gage's permission, given August 28, 1775, and is entitled "A Plan of Boston in New England with Its Environs." The dedication is to Lord George Germaine; publication was in 1777. For the area open to him when he made the map, Pelham appears to have been accurate in detail. Outside that area he usually was almost correct as to distances but quite frequently was in error as to compass bearings. The second "base" map is styled "Boston Its Environs and Harbor with the Rebel Works Raised against the Town in 1775 from the Observations of Lieut. Page of His Majesty's Corps of Engineers and from those of other Gentlemen." No date of publication appears on the original printing. Evidently this map was begun before the British withdrawal and was amended afterwards with little knowledge of the terrain within the American lines. For example, "Leachmore Point" is marked on Dorchester Peninsula, almost directly North of Nook's Hill. In most other respects, Page's map is substantially accurate, but both this map and Pelham's err in the precise location of Plowed Hill, Cobble Hill and the works on Lechmere Point. Both are slightly defective, also regarding Bush Tree Hill. Nearly all these positions are placed somewhat farther from Beacon Hill than the contours justify.

Pelham and Page evidently were used by the cartographers of the excellent map, styled "Boston with its Environs," that appeared in Vol. II of Gordon's familiar *History of the Rise, Progress and Establishment of the Independence of the United States of America . . .*" Gordon himself must have corrected some of the errors of the two "base" maps, but he did not make the necessary changes in distances. In the present work, the effort has been to check Pelham, Page and Gordon one against the other and all of them against the modern contour maps and then against an interesting document in the Washington Papers, LC. This is styled "A Chart of some of the Most Important Posts and Rising Ground Either occupied by or in the Possession of the American and Ministerial Armies, near and in Boston." It is undated but evidently was prepared or revised after the construction of the works on Lechmere Point and when it had become important to know the ranges from Nook's Hill. This paper shows that the three positions on Dorchester Neck then regarded of the largest value for artillery were Nook's Hill, Forster's Hill and the ground where the three-gun battery, overlooking the harbor, was

599

located. The chart is for ranges in terms of rods and it is in error to the extent of a few yards only. American engineers, for example, put Fort Hill in Boston 520 rods (2860 yards) from Dorchester Heights (Forster's Hill), the "Twin Hills" on Pelham's map. Pelham gives substantially the same range. From Nook's Hill, according to Washington's chart, the range of the same target is 1842 yards. Pelham made it about 1700. From the three-gun battery to Fort Hill, Washington's surveyors computed the range at 2640 yards, compared with 2530 by Pelham's calculation. In the case of Lechmere Point, the difference in the reckonings was 145 yards, and so for other positions. A student, therefore, is not apt to be far wrong in following either Washington's chart or Pelham's map but he has to be careful to check Pelham's compass bearings.

Warning must be given against an early map that bears the legend "A Plan of the Town of Boston and Its Environs, with the Lines, Batteries and Incampments of the British and American Armies." This is grossly at fault as respects the topography and size of Dorchester Peninsula and is not to be trusted for many other details, though it is useful for the approximate determination of some American positions that do not appear on other maps. The sketch reproduced in 3 *Force* (4) p. 33 evidently was based on one that dealt with the first works thrown up by the Americans. It should not be used for the later operations. See the note, Chap. XX, p. 485, concerning the condition of the defences at a particular time. An extensive bibliography of the early maps was prepared by Justin Winsor and was published in Vol. III of *The Memorial History of Boston*.

Elevations are even more difficult to determine than are the precise location of the different batteries. G. G. Wolkins of Newton Highlands, Massachusetts, most generously responded to the request made of members of the Massachusetts Historical Society for information on this subject. His researches show that most of the lesser hills around Boston have been cut down so much, through the centuries, that only such high ground as that of Forster's (Telegraph) Hill in South Boston, of the "upper fort" in Roxbury, and of Winter Hill in Somerville can be assigned a specific elevation with the assurance that it is not now materially lower than it was in 1775–76. For purposes of study it is safe to assume that the maximum elevation of these sites was 150 to 160 feet above sea level.